Ivy Global

Ultimate
SAT Guide

For automatic scoring and scaling, please visit **cloud.ivyglobal.com**.

Ultimate SAT Guide, Edition 3.1

This publication was written and edited by the team at Ivy Global.

Editor-in-Chief: Sarah Pike
Producers: Lloyd Min and Junho Suh

Editors: Sacha Azor, Corwin Henville, Nathan Létourneau, and Kristin Rose

Contributors: Sarah Atkins, Amanda Bakowski, Sabrina Bartlett, Spencer Bass, Stephanie Bucklin, Alexandra Candib, Ho-Jae Cha, Shavumiyaa Chandrabalan, Beini Chen, Natalia Cole, Elizabeth Cox, Shayna Darling, Lisa Faieta, Howard Fung, Aleah Gornbein, Yvonne Greenen, Keven Gungor, Elizabeth Hilts, Helen Huang, Lei Huang, Caroline Incledon, Keven Ji, Caroline Jo, Lana Lam, Somin Lee, James Levine, Lucy Liu, Amelia McLeod, Mark Mendola, Casey O'Leary, Laurel Perkins, Michael Protacio, Julia Romanski, Martha Schabas, Meena Sundararaj, Yolanda Song, Nathan Tebokkel, and Kalden Tsung

About the Publisher

Ivy Global is a pioneering education company that delivers a wide range of educational services.

E-mail: publishing@ivyglobal.com
Website: http://www.ivyglobal.com

Contents

Chapter 5: Math

Chapter 6: Practice Tests

Chapter 7: Answers

Introduction

Chapter 1

Section 1
About This Book

Welcome, students and parents! This book is intended to help students prepare for the SAT, a test created and administered by the College Board.

Many colleges and universities in the United States require the SAT as part of the application process. It is our goal to demystify the SAT by offering you tips, tricks, and plenty of practice to help you do your best. This book will help you turn this challenging admissions requirement into an opportunity to demonstrate your skills and preparation to colleges.

We'll provide you with you with a comprehensive breakdown of the SAT and proven test-taking strategies for the different sections and question types. There are chapters about the SAT's Reading Test, Writing and Language Test, Essay, and Math Test, as well as multiple practice tests. Here is what's inside:

- Key test-taking strategies
- A breakdown and detailed review of the content of each section
- Lists of SAT word roots to build vocabulary
- 3 full-length practice tests and more than 450 practice problems and drills
- Answer keys at the back of this book, and full answer explanations and scoring online

The first key to succeeding on the SAT is knowing the test, so the rest of this chapter provides details about its structure, format, and timing along with key strategies to use in all sections. Chapters 2-5 delve into the question types and content you will encounter in each section. We recommend working through these chapters, taking the practice exams in Chapter 6, and then reviewing any challenging material.

Check out our website for additional resources, including review of foundational concepts, extra practice, answer explanations, and online scoring sheets. You'll also find information about upcoming tests, tutoring services and prep classes, and other tips to help you do your best. Good luck studying!

 For additional resources, please visit **ivyglobal.com/study**.

What is the SAT?
Part 1

Introduction

The SAT is a standardized examination designed to measure students' abilities in three areas: reading, writing, and mathematical reasoning. The SAT is written and administered by the College Board. Many American colleges and universities require SAT scores for admission and consider these scores an important factor in assessing applications.

Why do colleges care about the SAT? Since grading standards vary from one high school to another, it can be hard for colleges to know whether two applicants with the same grades are performing at the same level. Therefore, having everyone take the same standardized test gives colleges another metric for comparing students' abilities.

Of course, SAT scores aren't the only things that colleges consider when assessing applicants. Your high school grades, course selection, extracurricular activities, recommendation letters, and application essays are all factors that colleges will use to decide whether you are a good fit for their school. However, in today's highly competitive admissions process, a solid SAT score may provide you with the extra edge needed to be successful.

What's on the Test?

If you're already familiar with the SAT, and just want to confirm some details, you should review the following breakdown of the exam. If this is your first time learning about the SAT, skip ahead to The SAT in Detail.

SAT Breakdown	
Timing	• 3 hours 50 minutes (including the optional 50-minute Essay)
Sections	• Evidence-Based Reading and Writing • Math • Essay (optional and separate from the Writing Test)
Areas of Emphasis	• Applying reasoning and knowledge to real-world situations • Using reading, writing, and math skills to analyze evidence • Understanding vocabulary and word choice in a greater range of contexts • Demonstrating core applied reasoning skills in algebra and data analysis
Question Types	• 141 multiple choice • 13 grid-in
Answer Choices	• 4 answer choices (A to D) for multiple choice questions
Penalty	• No penalty for wrong answers
Scoring	• Total scaled score from 400 to 1600, comprised of area scores from 200-800 in Math and in Evidence-Based Reading and Writing • Essay score reported separately • Subscores and cross-test scores based on demonstration of skills in more specific areas

The SAT in Detail
Part 2

Understanding the format and scoring of the SAT will help you pick appropriate strategies and know what to expect on test day.

The Format

The SAT is 3 hours long (plus 50 minutes for the optional Essay). It is composed of the following sections:

- 100-minute Evidence-based Reading and Writing section
  - Reading Test (65 minutes, 52 questions)
  - Writing and Language Test (35 minutes, 44 questions)
- 80-minute Math section
  - Calculator allowed section (55 minutes, 38 questions)
  - No-calculator allowed section (25 minutes, 20 questions)
- Optional Essay-writing section (50 minutes)

The Scoring System

The SAT has **test scores** on a scale from 10 to 40. There is one test score for each test: the Reading Test, the Writing Test, and the Math Test. The Reading Test score and the Writing and Language Test score are added together and converted to a single **area score** in Evidence-Based Reading and Writing; there is also an area score in Math based on the Math Test Score.

The area scores are on a scale from 200 to 800. Added together, they form the **composite score** for the whole test, on a scale from 400 to 1600. The Essay is scored separately and will not affect your scores in other areas.

SAT Scoring	
Test Scores (10 to 40)	• Reading Test • Writing Test • Math Test
Area Scores (200 to 800)	• Evidence-Based Reading and Writing • Math
Composite Score (400 to 1600)	• Math (Area Score) + Evidence-Based Reading and Writing (Area Score)
Essay Scores (1 to 4)	• Reading • Analysis • Writing
Cross-test Scores (10 to 40)	• Analysis in Science • Analysis in History/Social Studies
Subscores (1 to 15)	• Words in Context • Command of Evidence • Expression of Ideas • Standard English Conventions • Heart of Algebra • Problem Solving and Data Analysis • Passport to Advanced Math

Cross-test scores for **Analysis in Science** and **Analysis in History/Social Studies** are based on performance on specific questions across different tests relating to specific types of content. For example, your cross-test score in Analysis in Science is based on your performance on questions relating to science passages on the Reading Test as well as questions using scientific data on the Math Test. These scores are on a scale from 10 to 40.

There are also seven **subscores** based on particular question types within each test section. Subscores are reported on a scale from 1 to 15. Four are related to particular questions in the Reading and Writing Test: Words in Context, Command of Evidence, Expression of Ideas, and Standard English Conventions. The other three relate to specific types of questions on the Math Test: Heart of Algebra, Problem Solving and Data Analysis, and Passport to Advanced Math. You'll learn more about what these subscores are measuring in the chapters explaining what these questions are like.

Taking the SAT
Part 3

Now that we've covered the format and content of the SAT, let's talk about how you go about taking the exam. The SAT is administered at standard testing dates and locations worldwide throughout the academic year. These standard dates fall in March, May, June, August, October, November, and December, but the June and August test dates are only available in the United States. You can see the upcoming dates in your location on the College Board website: sat.collegeboard.org.

How Do I Register?

The easiest way to sign up for the exam is on the College Board website: sat.collegeboard.org. You'll need to fill out a personal profile form and upload a recognizable photo, which will be included on your admission ticket.

You can also register by mail. To do this, ask your school counselor for *The Student Registration Guide for the SAT and SAT Subject Tests*, which includes a registration form and a return envelope. You'll need to enclose a photo with this paper registration form.

When you register, you can sign up for your preferred date and location. However, testing centers often run out of room, so make sure you sign up early in order to reserve your place! There is also a cut-off for registrations a month before the test date, after which you'll need to contact the College Board to see if late registration or standby testing is an option.

When Should I Take the SAT?

Typically, students take the SAT during 11th grade or the beginning of 12th grade. However, you should plan to take the exam when you feel most prepared, keeping in mind when colleges will need your scores.

Almost all schools will accept scores through December of your 12th grade year. After December, it really depends on the school to which you are applying. If you are planning to apply for Early Admission to any school, you'll need to take the test by November of 12th grade at the very latest.

Can I Re-Take the SAT?

Yes! The College Board has no limits on how many times you can take the SAT. Many students take the exam two or three times to ensure their scores represent the best they can do. However, we don't recommend taking the exam more than two or three times, because you'll get fatigued and your score will start to plateau. Prepare to do your best each time you take the test, and you shouldn't have to re-take it too many times.

In order to give yourself the option to re-take the test, it is always wise to choose a first testing date that is earlier than you need. That way, if you decide you'd like to re-take the test you won't miss any deadlines.

How Do I Send My Scores to Colleges?

When you sign up for the SAT, you can select which schools you'd like to receive your scores. You can also do this after taking the SAT by logging onto your account on the College Board website. If you have taken the SAT more than once, the College Board's "Score Choice" program allows you to choose which test results you would like to report to schools. You can't "divide up" the scores of different tests—all sections of the SAT from a single test date must be sent together.

However, certain schools don't participate in the "Score Choice" program. These schools request that applicants send the results of every SAT test they have taken. Even so, most schools have a policy of only considering your highest scores. Some schools will take your best overall score from a single administration while others will mix and match your best scores for your entire test history, called a "Superscore." You can see how your prospective schools consider your scores by visiting their admissions websites.

What's the "Disadvantage Score" on the SAT?

The College Board includes an "Environmental Context Panel" in the information that it sends to schools, which includes a score that you may have read described as a "disadvantage score." This score is not included in the calculation of your overall scores. It is a form of supplementary information presented alongside your scores.

The Environmental Context Panel includes information about your high school and the area in which you live. It's not a direct measure of your achievements; rather, it's intended to help place your achievements in context. The score considers factors like average education levels, household incomes, housing and family stability, and college attendance rates in your area.

Many of the factors considered are correlated with test scores, so students with high disadvantage scores will likely have had to cope with circumstances that make it more difficult to do well on the SAT.

Can I Do Anything to Influence My Disadvantage Score?

No, not really. You should try not to worry about your disadvantage score. Short of making major life changes, like moving to a new school or neighborhood, you can't do much to influence it. It's also not entirely new information. Social context has always factored into admissions processes. Schools have always considered the schools students attend, and personal essays often explore a student's social context. The Environmental Context Panel just provides an organized, standardized panel of information from objective sources.

How Do I Improve My Score?

The key to raising your SAT score is to adopt a long-term strategy. Score improvement on the SAT occurs only after consistently practicing and learning concepts over a long period of time. Early on in your high school career, focus on building vocabulary and improving essay-writing skills. Read as much as you can beyond your school curriculum—materials like novels, biographies, and current-event magazines. Keep up with the math taught in your classes and ask questions if you need help.

In addition to keeping up with the fundamental concepts and skills tested on the SAT, you'll need to learn how to approach the specific types of questions included on the exam. In the next section, we'll talk about some general test-taking strategies that will help you tackle the format of the SAT as a whole. Then, you can work through Chapters 2-5 to learn specific strategies for the SAT Reading, Writing, Essay, and Math Tests. In Chapter 6, you'll be able to apply these strategies to 3 full-length practice tests.

With enough practice, you'll be prepared to score your personal best on test day! Let's get started.

Section 2
Approaching the SAT

In this section, we will help you prepare for the SAT with effective ways to approach studying and test taking. We will cover some tips to keep in mind before test day, essential strategies to tackle the test, and what to keep on your radar after you walk out of that test center.

Test-Taking Basics
Part 1

Now that you're familiar with the SAT, there are a few more things you need to know about how to take the test. These strategies include knowing what you're going to see on the test, managing your time, guessing effectively, and entering your answers.

Know the Test

The first step to tackling the SAT is to know the test. Because it is a standardized exam, the format of the SAT is the same every time it's administered. By knowing the time limit, number of questions, and directions for each section, you will be ahead of the game. Review these key details for each portion of the test until you know them inside out. On test day, you'll save time by skipping over the directions, and can relax knowing there won't be any surprises!

It is also important to know that the SAT is not like certain tests that require you to show your work or explain your answers. Except for the optional essay, you will enter all of your answers on an answer sheet that will be graded by a machine. Thus, it is important to correctly enter your answer choices on your answer sheet; otherwise, you will not receive credit for them.

Also remember that there is a set time limit. Even though the test is broken up into multiple parts, you do not have control over how to divide the total time among the individual sections. Once time is up for a certain section, you have to move on and can't work on previous sections.

Manage Your Time

Similarly, to do well on the SAT, you need to know the length of the test, the time allowed for each section, and the time allotted for snack/bathroom breaks so you can work strategically and be prepared for test day.

Unlike a normal hour-long high school test, the SAT runs between three and four hours long—so you'll want to practice building your stamina! Doing timed practice tests or timed sections will help you learn to stay focused for the duration of the test.

Remember that time between sections isn't transferable; you're given a set amount of time for each section and you can't proceed to the next section or look at previous sections if you finish early. Time yourself while practicing in order to develop a sense of what "a quarter-of-the-way through" and "halfway through" feels like in each section. Finished early? Use that leftover time to go over your answers and make sure you entered them correctly.

To maximize your time, it's important not to get too stuck on any single question and to move through the test at a steady pace. Don't waste 10 minutes on a question that stumps you, only to find that you do not have enough time to answer the things you know inside out. Each question is only worth one point, regardless of its difficulty. If you are stuck on a problem, you should make your best guess and move on quickly. Circle the problem in your question booklet so you can look at it again if you have time. You don't want to leave any question unanswered, as there's no penalty for guessing!

You should try to answer every question because you have nothing to lose—just more points to gain! At the same time, you should strike a balance between quality and quantity. Budget your time so you can get to every or almost every question, but you also have the opportunity to read each question carefully and consider each answer choice.

Guess Effectively

The SAT does not deduct any points for choosing the wrong answer. That means that there is no downside to guessing! You should always guess on any questions you cannot answer with certainty.

But how can you guess to maximize your chances of gaining a few extra points? First, attempt each question using the processes discussed below and in the chapters that follow. Even if a question is difficult, eliminating any wrong answers will improve your odds of guessing correctly.

If you aren't sure of the answer, bubble in a guess on your answer sheet, circle the question in your test booklet, and return to it later. Once you have attempted all the other questions in the section, come back to any circled questions and re-read them carefully. Then, try again to answer them. Eliminate any wrong answers, and see if you want to change the answer you originally guessed.

It is possible you will not have time to attempt every question in a section. Because of this, it is a good idea to choose a letter beforehand that you will always use when guessing. This will save you from spending time deciding what answer choice to pick, and makes it easier to bubble in guesses. For any questions you do not have time to answer, simply fill in your bubble sheet using your chosen answer choice. Make sure you have time to enter a guess for every question you do not attempt before time is up for that section.

Write and Bubble Clearly

As noted above, except for the Essay, all of your work on the SAT will be graded by a machine. What you write in your answer sheet determines whether you'll get a point or not, so you don't want to make a mistake when it comes to bubbling your answers!

Always mark your answer in your answer sheet. Your exam booklet will not be graded, but this will provide you with a reference so you can correctly and confidently transfer your responses to your answer sheet. Make sure to fill in each bubble completely using only a No. 2 pencil. Also, always make sure you are filling in the correct section of the answer sheet. Before beginning each section, double check that you are working on the corresponding section of the answer sheet.

You can either bubble your answers in after every question, or bubble them in in groups. If you bubble your answers in groups, you may disrupt your concentration less and be more efficient. Fill in your answers after completing a specific portion of the test, such as all of the questions on one or two pages, or after finishing all the questions for a Reading passage. If you are feeling frustrated during the test, you can also take a quick 'break' to fill in your answers and clear your head, and then return to the questions feeling refreshed.

When you write your essay, write as legibly as you can. Even though you're trying to write quickly, your readers need to be able to read your handwriting in order to give you points. Remember to write your essay only in the lines of the lined pages provided in your answer sheet—your readers won't be able to see anything you write outside of these margins! Don't write any part of your essay in your test booklet, though you can use this space for jotting down notes or an outline for your essay.

While you are not given credit for anything written in your test booklet, you are not penalized either. The test booklet is yours to use how you choose, so mark it up however will help you do your best. Cross out answer choices you know are wrong. Use margins and blank space in the test booklet to work out math problems and outline your essay. Underline key words, phrases, or sections of reading passages.

Key Strategies
Part 2

In addition to learning the material tested on the SAT, to perform your best you must also use the best strategies for tackling the questions. Below we outline four key techniques that we call the **4 Ps**. They can be used across the test to help you choose answers confidently and improve your score. The strategies are:

- Plugging in Options
- Pencil on Paper
- Process of Elimination
- Pick and Skip

Plugging in Options

Even if you're not sure how to approach a multiple choice question, because you are given 4 answer options you will always have somewhere to start—you can plug in the answer choices to see which might work.

This can be especially helpful in the Math Test, where plugging in answer choices can often help you avoid completing long calculations. When you use this strategy, it is best to start with choice (B) or (C), as most answer choices are listed in increasing or decreasing numerical order. If you start with (B) or (C), you may be able to eliminate multiple answers based on the result. For example, if the answers increase in value from (A) to (D) and you determine that choice (C) is too small, you can eliminate choices (A), (B), and (C).

You can see the value of this approach with an example math problem:

Example

$$\frac{9}{4x} = \frac{3}{8}$$

What is the value of x?

A) 2 B) 4 C) 6 D) 8

To solve by testing answer choices, start with (B) or (C). If you start with (B), then substitute 4 for x:

$$\frac{9}{4 \times 6} = \frac{9}{16}$$

Next, check your answer with the question:

$$\frac{9}{16} \neq \frac{3}{8}$$

Your answer $\frac{9}{16}$ does not reduce to $\frac{3}{8}$, so (B) is not the right answer. However, you can use this to eliminate more than one answer choice. $\frac{9}{16}$ is greater than $\frac{3}{8}$, so you know that 4 is too small a value of x. Therefore, you can also eliminate any other values smaller than 4, such as answer choice (A).

Next, try (C), substituting 6 for x:

$$\frac{9}{4 \times 6} = \frac{9}{24}$$

This fraction can be simplified by dividing both the numerator and denominator by three. Checking this with the original answer:

$$\frac{9}{24} = \frac{3}{8}$$

Since $\frac{9}{24}$ can be reduced to $\frac{3}{8}$, (C) is the correct answer.

On the Writing Test, you can also apply this strategy by plugging each answer choice in to the original passage, and reading the resulting sentence in your head. Even if you can't say exactly what the error is, your everyday English skills can help you to eliminate choices that clearly sound wrong. Consider the following example:

Example
Yesterday, John ran the store until 5:00, then Lisa <u>will take</u> over.
A) NO CHANGE
B) took
C) is taking
D) DELETE the underlined portion

This type of error is called an "inappropriate shift in verb tense." "John ran the store" is in the past tense, and since Lisa took over at 5:00 yesterday, that should also be in the past tense. But even if you can't quite articulate all of that using your explicit knowledge of the rules of English, you can probably guess that (D) is wrong by imagining the sentence with that option plugged in: "John ran the store until 5:00, then Lisa over." The phrase "then Lisa over" doesn't really make any sense, because there's no verb.

You might also be able to eliminate (A) and (C) by noticing that they just don't sound right. (B) solves the error, sounds right, and is the correct answer. This is a fast and easy way of handling many Writing Test problems, but be careful: if you only go by what sounds right, and you're never sure exactly what sort of errors you're looking at, then it's possible that you'll make a careless mistake by picking something that sounds okay but is technically wrong, or vice versa. You'll have a chance to learn about specific grammar errors in Chapter 3, Section 3.

This same technique can be used on the Reading Test for questions that ask you about the meaning of words in the passage. These questions are called Words in Context questions, and are discussed further in Chapter 2, Section 4. To answer these questions, you can sub the answer choices back in to the original sentence to see what choice works best in context. Consider the following example, taken from Charles Dickens's *Great Expectations*:

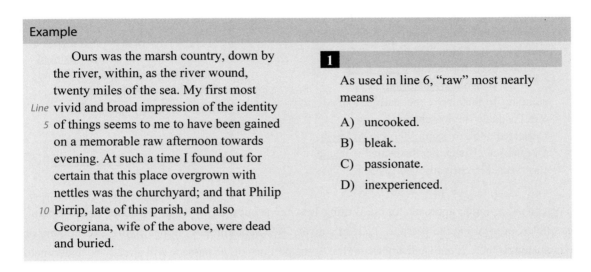

Example

Ours was the marsh country, down by the river, within, as the river wound, twenty miles of the sea. My first most
Line vivid and broad impression of the identity
5 of things seems to me to have been gained on a memorable raw afternoon towards evening. At such a time I found out for certain that this place overgrown with nettles was the churchyard; and that Philip
10 Pirrip, late of this parish, and also Georgiana, wife of the above, were dead and buried.

1

As used in line 6, "raw" most nearly means

A) uncooked.

B) bleak.

C) passionate.

D) inexperienced.

Though all four choices could be synonyms of raw, only answer choice (B) makes sense when we plug it into the original sentence. An afternoon cannot be "uncooked," or "inexperienced," so (A) and (D) are incorrect. While an afternoon could be "passionate" this word does not match with the tone of the surrounding lines, which are describing a graveyard. Thus, (C) is also incorrect.

Pencil on Paper

When you take the SAT, you don't want to passively read the information presented to you, but rather you want to engage with and understand it. The best way to do this is to be an **active reader** and interact with the passages and questions to find and understand the information you will be tested on. You can use your pencil to mark up or add information in your test booklet.

In the Reading Test, you can be an active reader by using your pencil to **mark up** passages as you read them by underlining important parts of the text and adding your own notes to emphasize key information. This will help you stay focused, understand what you read, and make it easy to find ideas in the passage when you refer back to it. Active reading will be discussed further in Chapter 2, Section 2.

Here's how a reading passage may look once it has been marked up. Aim to circle or underline two to three **main ideas** per paragraph that relate to the **5 w's:** "who," "what," "where," "when," and "why."

This passage is adapted from Daniel Zalewski, "Under a Shroud of Kitsch May Lie a Master's Art." ©2001 by The New York Times Company.

Tommaso Strinati clambers to the top of the rickety scaffold and laughs. "It's a good thing that all this Baroque work is so
Line unimpressive," he says, pointing at the
5 clumsy trompe l'oeil painting covering the wall in front of him. "Otherwise, we might not have been allowed to scrape it off!"

A 28-year-old art historian, he is standing 16 feet above the marble floor of
10 San Pasquale Baylon chapel, a long-neglected nook of Santa Maria in Aracoeli, a Franciscan basilica in the center of Rome. Last year, Mr. Strinati, who is still a graduate student, began studying the church's history.
15 Records suggested that the Roman artist Pietro Cavallini—a painter and mosaicist whose greatest works have been destroyed—spent years decorating Aracoeli toward the end of the
20 13th century. Yet only one small Cavallini fresco, in the church's left transept, remained visible. Mr. Strinati wondered: had other Cavallini frescoes been painted over with inferior work? And if so, could
25 modern restorers uncover them?

"The answer to both questions was yes," Mr. Strinati says. A close-up examination of the chapel's walls last summer revealed ghostly images lying

You can use a similar approach for the Writing Test. Some questions will ask you about the main point, examples, or errors in the passage. To read actively, you should focus on identifying a main point or conclusion (if there is one) and any examples. Some portions of the passage will already be underlined. You will be asked to replace the underlined portion if it contains an error or can be improved, or leave it as-is if it does not need to be changed. It can therefore help to circle or underline the parts of a sentence that seem related to an error, as in the following example.

Example

While he claimed to have a wealth of relevant experience, he had neither served in an elected office nor business management.

A) NO CHANGE
B) even business management
C) even managed a business
D) even the management of a business

The error in this problem is related to "parallel structure." "Neither" and "nor" are a common word pair. These sorts of word pairs are called "correlative conjunctions," but even if you haven't memorized this term, you might still know that they are frequently paired. Underlining important features can help you work out this subtle error; we've circled "neither" and "nor" because they're a common word pair and "nor" comes right before the underlined portion. We've also underlined "served in elected office," because that comes right after "neither." As you read through the answer options, notice that only (C) has the same structure as the part of the sentence following "neither:" a verb and its object.

Some passages will be missing information or have sentences that are in the wrong place in the paragraph. These parts of the passage might sound a little funny to you, so don't be surprised if this happens. If you can identify these types of errors while you're reading, selecting the correct answer choice will be much easier!

In the Math Test, you can use active reading techniques by underlining what the question is asking you to find. This will help you focus on solving the problem rather than being distracted by details.

You can also actively use your pencil by drawing a diagram for questions where no diagram is provided, or where it is labeled as not to scale. Here's an example:

Example

A square and a rectangle have the same perimeter. The square has a length and width of 4 and the rectangle has a length of 5. What is the area of the rectangle?

A) 3   B) 6   C) 15   D) 30

First, draw a diagram of the square and rectangle:

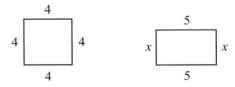

Since the perimeter of the square is $4 \times 4 = 16$, the perimeter of the rectangle is also 16. The perimeter is $2 \times 5 + 2x$, so you can set this expression equal to 16 and solve for x:

$$2 \times 5 + 2x = 16$$

$$10 + 2x = 16$$

$$2x = 6$$

$$x = 3$$

Remember that you are solving for the area, not x! From the diagram, you can calculate the area as $3 \times 5 = 15$, so (C) is the correct answer.

To check this answer, you can use the figures you drew. The area of the rectangle is close to the area of the square. None of the other answer choices are close to 15.

This technique can even be helpful on the Essay. You can use your pencil to mark up ideas or information in the prompt that you wish to analyze in your essay. You'll learn more about this in Chapter 4, Section 3.

Process of Elimination

Sometimes the easiest way to answer a question is by finding the wrong answers. You may have used the Process of Elimination before; it's a great technique to narrow down your possible answer choices.

As you read through the answer choices, don't select an answer on your first read-through. Assess each answer choice one by one. If you know an option is incorrect, knock it out of consideration and strike it through or mark it with an X in your test booklet. If an answer choice seems possible, leave it open to reconsider. Once you have assessed all of the answer choices, compare any that you left open and select the best one. In some cases you may even be able to knock out every answer except for one. In this case, you will have found the correct answer!

Let's look at how this works with an example math problem:

Example
If $y = x^2$ and $-1 < x < 1$, which of the following could be a possible value for y?   A) $-\dfrac{5}{4}$ B) $-\dfrac{1}{4}$ C) $\dfrac{1}{4}$ D) $\dfrac{5}{4}$

If you think about this equation a bit, you'll see that there are some choices you can eliminate immediately. The equation says that y is the square of x. Think about what happens when you square a positive or negative number—the result is always positive! Therefore, choices (A) and (B) are impossible—if x is a real number, then x^2 can't be a negative number. You can knock out (A) and (B) right away.

A) $\cancel{-\dfrac{5}{4}}$ B) $\cancel{-\dfrac{1}{4}}$ C) $\dfrac{1}{4}$ D) $\dfrac{5}{4}$

Now you're left with (C) and (D). If you're short on time, you could guess and you'd have a 50-50 chance of gaining a point. Or, you could look at the given information again and reason that because x is a fraction greater than -1 and less than 1, x^2 can't be greater than 1. This means that you can eliminate choice (D) as well, leaving you with the correct answer: (C).

You can use this same approach in the Reading and Writing Tests as well. In the Reading Test, you can immediately knock out any answers that contradict information given in the passage. Next, you can knock out any answers that could generally be true, but aren't supported by information in the passage.

On the Writing Test, you can use the Process of Elimination in two ways. First, you should eliminate answer choices that don't correct the error in the underlined section. Then, you should eliminate answer choices that correct the error but introduce new errors. Because the correct answer has to be the *best* version of the underlined portion, any answers that have grammatical or stylistic errors cannot be the correct choice and should be eliminated.

Let's see how the process of elimination can lead to the correct answer in the Writing question below:

Example

The Iron Age and the Middle Ages bookend the classical cultures of Greece and Rome. For over a thousand years, Greek and Roman societies were the center of achievement in the **2** Mediterranean, in fact, the political, philosophical, and scientific roots of our own modern society were formed from Greek and Roman culture.

2

A) NO CHANGE

B) Mediterranean. In fact, the political philosophical and scientific

C) Mediterranean, in fact, the political philosophical and scientific

D) Mediterranean. In fact, the political, philosophical, and scientific

In this example, the original sentence is a run-on sentence, which needs to be divided into two separate sentences (you can read more about run-on sentences in Chapter 3, Section 3). First, eliminate any choices that don't correct this error. You can eliminate choices (A) and (C) because neither of those choices correct the run-on sentence. Only choices (B) and (D) split it into two separate sentences.

You're left with two possible choices that correct the run-on sentence: choices (B) and (D). Now, check to see whether one of these choices introduces new errors. Choice (B) corrects the run-on sentence by adding a period to separate the underlined portion into two sentences. However, choice (B) also takes away the commas between "political, philosophical, and scientific," which the sentences need. Therefore, you can eliminate choice (B) because it introduces a new error. You are now only left with choice (D), which is the correct answer! Choice (D) corrects the original error by separating the sentences without adding any new errors.

Next, take a look at the following Reading example, taken from Teddy Roosevelt's speech "Citizenship in a Republic."

Example

Strange and impressive associations rise in the mind of a man from the New World who speaks before this august body in this
Line ancient institution of learning. Before his
5 eyes pass the shadows of mighty kings and war-like nobles, of great masters of law and theology; through the shining dust of the dead centuries he sees crowded figures that tell of the power and learning and splendor
10 of times gone by; and he sees also the innumerable host of humble students to whom clerkship meant emancipation, to whom it was well-nigh the only outlet from the dark thraldom of the Middle Ages.

3

Roosevelt uses language like "kings," "nobles," and "dead centuries" in order to

A) emphasize the high class of men who make up the institution.

B) call to mind the age and venerability of the university.

C) equate the institution of learning with a medieval castle.

D) flatter the professors and administrators he is addressing.

Here, read the full paragraph in order to understand the context. Based on clues in the text, such as "ancient institution of learning," "masters of law and theology," and "host of humble students," you can conclude that Roosevelt is discussing a school or university. From there, consider why Roosevelt would use language like "kings," "nobles," and "splendor." These references and adjectives are creating a positive description.

Answer choices (A) and (D) can be eliminated, since nowhere does the paragraph indicate that Roosevelt is trying to focus on or flatter the men he is addressing; instead, he is describing the history of the school itself. Choice (C) can also be eliminated as too literal. We are then left with choice (B), which gets to Roosevelt's purpose in including this language—specifically, bringing to mind the long and impressive history of the institution.

Pick and Skip

Working strategically doesn't only apply to individual questions; you should be clever in your approach to each section as a whole. Remember that every question on the SAT is worth one point, no matter how easy or difficult it is. That means it can be to your advantage to work on questions that are easier for you first, and leave more challenging or time-consuming questions for later. If after doing some timed practice you sense you need to improve your speed, you can apply this strategy. However, be sure to use it with caution, as it can increase your chances of making errors when bubbling in your answers.

On the Reading and Writing Tests, you might apply this strategy by first reading passages on topics that are the most interesting or familiar to you. If the first passage to appear doesn't fit this description, move on to other passages and come back later.

You can also attempt the questions for each passage out of order. On the Reading Test, you may answer more specific questions first, especially those that provide line references. As you learn more about the passage by answering these questions, you may feel more confident in answering the general questions about the passage. Citing Textual Evidence questions (discussed further in Chapter 2, Section 4) ask you to provide support for your answer to a previous question, and should thus always be answered after the preceding question.

On the Writing Test, most questions about parts of speech, punctuation, and sentence combination can be answered right after you read the appropriate sentence. When a word or short phrase is underlined in a sentence, you may be able to correct it as you read it. Try to anticipate the correct answer and then compare it to the available revisions.

However, for other questions you'll need to read other sentences in the paragraph to make your answer choice. For example, you may be asked to select the best version of a word to match the author's tone.

You may also be asked to add, delete, or move sentences within a paragraph. Wait to answer these questions until after you have read the whole paragraph.

Finally, some questions are related to the passage as a whole. For example, a question may ask you to insert new information to support the passage's main idea or additional evidence to support a conclusion. Wait to answer these questions until after you have read the whole passage.

On the Math Test, you can also do the questions out of order by skipping over those that are the most challenging or time-consuming to complete. If you attempt questions out of order, be sure to circle those you are skipping in your test booklet, so you know to come back to them after. Also remember to guess on every question, in case you don't have time to attempt it later.

As you practice for the SAT, you are bound to figure out the kinds of questions you can answer quickly versus those that take some time, so it will become easier to apply this strategy. If you wish, you can skim through each section and answer the questions you can handle easily first, then move on to the types of questions that you tend to find more difficult or time-consuming. Remember to make a guess and circle any questions that you skip.

Create a Study Schedule
Part 3

To prepare to do your best on test day, you'll need to organize your time leading up to the exam. First, you'll need to assess your strengths and weaknesses in order to figure out *what* to study. Then, you'll need to organize *how* you will study in order to make the best use of your time before your test date.

Identify Your Strengths and Weaknesses

To determine your areas of strength and weakness and to get an idea of which concepts you need to review, work through some practice questions. You can try out the questions for the Reading, Writing, Essay, and Math tests in Chapters 2-5 of this book, or you can take one of the full-length practice tests in Chapter 6.

Then, check your answers against the correct answers. Write down how many questions you missed, and note the topics or types of questions you found most difficult. What was challenging for you? What did you feel good about? Did you get questions wrong because you made an avoidable error, or did you get questions wrong because you did not know how to solve them? Reflecting on these questions will help you determine your individual strengths and weaknesses, and will help you decide what to focus on before your test date.

Plan Your Study Time

After determining your areas of strength and weakness, create a study plan and schedule for your SAT preparation. Work backward from your test date until you arrive at your starting point for studying. The number of weeks you have until your exam will determine how much time you can (and should) devote to your preparation. Make sure you leave enough time to review and practice each concept you'd like to improve—remember, practice is the most important!

To begin, try using this sample study plan as a model for your own personalized study schedule.

My test date is: _____.

I have _____ weeks to study. I will make an effort to study _____ minutes/hours every day/week, and I will set aside extra time on _____ to take timed sections.

I plan to take _____ full-length tests between now and my test date. I will study for _____ weeks and then take a practice test. My goal for this test is to improve my score in the following specific areas:

_____

_____

_____

_____

_____

If I do not make this goal, then I will spend more time studying.

Study Schedule				
Date	Plan of Study	Time Allotted	Goal Reached?	Further Action
Jan 1	Review 10 vocabulary words and quadratic equations	1 hr	Yes, I know these 10 words and feel comfortable with quadratic equations.	
Jan 3	Review the next 10 vocabulary words and parts of speech	1 hr	I know these 10 words, but I'm still a bit shaky on parts of speech.	I'll review this again tomorrow and ask my English teacher for advice.

_____

_____

Test Day
Part 4

After you've prepared by reviewing and practicing each area you need to improve, you're ready for test day! Here are some tips to make sure you can do your best.

Before the Test

On the night before the test, review only lightly, if at all. You can review a few concepts you find challenging, but don't try to learn anything new. Pick out what you are going to wear to the test—try wearing layers in case the exam room is hotter or colder than you expect. Organize everything you need to bring. Know where the test center is located and how long it will take to get there. Have a nutritious meal and get plenty of sleep!

On the morning of the exam, let your adrenaline kick in naturally. Eat a good breakfast and stay hydrated; your body needs fuel to help you perform. Allow enough time for traveling to the test center, and be sure to follow your admissions ticket for directions on how early you should arrive. Remember to bring the following items with you:

Test Day Checklist

- Admission ticket
- Approved photo ID
- No. 2 pencils and erasers
- Calculator with new batteries and back-up batteries
- Non-beeping watch
- Snack and water bottle
- Directions to the test center and instructions for finding the entrance

Make sure you set your alarm and plan a time to leave that allows for delays. You need to be on time, or you can't take the test!

During the Test

During the test, you cannot overestimate the importance of a positive outlook. You have spent months preparing for the SAT—now it is time to be confident in the work you have done and in the knowledge you have acquired. Stay confident. Trust yourself, your abilities, and all of your preparation. Walk into the test room with every expectation that you will do well.

Stay focused. This is your time to show colleges what you are capable of. Keep your mind on the task at hand, which should be nothing but the question in front of you. If you find your mind wandering, pull your focus back to the test. Don't look around the room to compare your progress to that of your neighbors. Everyone works at their own pace, and you have no idea which particular part of the section your neighbors are working on.

Remember the test-taking strategies that you've practiced. Read and think carefully. Be sure to read each question in its entirety, and consider each answer choice. Work at a good, even pace, and keep moving. Keep an eye on your time throughout each section (and make sure your watch's time matches the proctor's clock). Frequently double check that you are bubbling answers in the correct section of your answer sheet.

Make educated guesses and remember to utilize the 4 Ps and other relevant strategies. Use your test booklet to cross out answers that you know are wrong, work out math problems, and annotate reading passages. Answer the easy questions first, and make a guess for those you're not sure of. Be sure to mark questions where you guessed so that you can quickly turn back to them after you finish all the other questions in the section.

Take a deep breath and remember: you are smart and accomplished! Believe in yourself and you will do well.

After the Test

First things first: give yourself a pat on the back! You have just completed a huge step in your educational career. Take some time to relax and unwind with friends or family.

Your score report should become available to you about two to four weeks after you take the test. This score report will contain your composite score, area scores, test scores, subscores, and cross-test scores. While these scores are important, remember to keep things in perspective. College applications will also entail submitting essays, letters of recommendation, high school grades, an activities list, and more. Even if you feel that your SAT scores are not an accurate reflection of your capabilities, you have many opportunities to shine in the other areas of your applications.

Remember that you can also retake the SAT. After you take the SAT the first time, you can pinpoint which areas you need to practice more. Students often improve their scores after taking the test a second time.

Either way, congratulate yourself on completing this challenge!

Reading
Chapter 2

Section 1
Introduction to the Reading Test

The SAT Reading Test is a test of advanced reading comprehension. You will be given a variety of reading passages, and asked questions about each one. While the passages and questions will be new every time, the structure of the SAT Reading test will always be the same. By learning about it now, you can make sure you will not encounter any surprises on test day!

The Basics

You will have 65 minutes to complete the SAT Reading Test, which is composed of four individual passages and one pair of passages. You will learn more about passage pairs in Section 6. Each passage or pair will be between 500 and 750 words, or about one to one and a half pages.

Each passage or pair will have 10 or 11 questions, for a total of 52 questions. There will also be two passages with accompanying graphics in every SAT Reading Test. You will be asked questions about these graphics and how they relate to the passage.

SAT Reading Test by the Numbers

- 65 minutes to complete section
- 4 single passages and 1 passage pair
- 500-750 words per passage or pair for a total of 3250 words
- 10-11 questions per passage or pair for a total of 52 questions
- 2 passages with 1 or more accompanying graphics

Scoring

You will receive several different scores based on your answers on the Reading Test.

You will receive an individual **test score** for Reading, from 10-40. You will also receive an **area score** for Evidence-Based Reading and Writing, which combines your scores from the Reading and Writing Tests. You will receive an Evidence-Based Reading and Writing score from 200-800, making up half of your total **composite score** on the SAT.

Questions from the Reading Test will contribute to two **cross-test scores**, which evaluate your skills in Analysis in History/Social Studies and Analysis in Science by looking at your performance on questions across different sections of the SAT. Your answers on the Reading Test will also contribute to two of your **subscores** on the SAT: Command of Evidence and Words in Context.

Passages

All passages in the SAT Reading Test will come from previously published sources, and may represent a variety of tones and styles. The passages will contain all the information you need to answer the questions on the test; you will never need to rely on any prior knowledge about the material to answer questions. The chart below shows the specific passage types that you will see in each Reading Test.

Passage Breakdown

Passage Type	Topics	Number of Passages
Literature	Classic and contemporary literature from the United States and around the world	1
History and Social Studies	Topics from history and social studies, including anthropology, communication studies, economics, education, geography, law, linguistics, political science, psychology, and sociology	1
Founding Document or Great Global Conversation	Historically important, foundational texts from the United States (Founding Documents); other historically and culturally important works dealing with issues at the heart of civic and political life (Great Global Conversation)	1
Science	Both basic concepts and recent developments in the natural sciences, including Earth science, biology, chemistry, and physics	2

The passages will not be presented in order of difficulty. As you learned in Chapter 1, you can choose to read them out of order, such as by tackling passages with familiar subjects first.

Questions

The questions associated with the passages will assess whether or not you understand the information and ideas in the text, and also ask you to analyze the author's use of persuasive language and argument. You will also be tested on combining information from the two passages of the passage pair, as well as from passages and their accompanying graphics.

The questions will be presented in a consistent order. However, they are not presented in order of difficulty. You will first be asked more general questions about central ideas, themes, points of view, and the overall text structure. These will be followed by more specific questions about the meaning of a particular word or phrase, or specific evidence that supports a claim. Many of these questions will have line references, which will point you to the material being discussed in the question.

Although you'll see a variety of questions on the Reading Test, two question types will appear with every passage or pair: Words in Context and Command of Evidence questions. Both of these question types will be discussed further in Section 4 of this chapter.

The rest of this chapter will introduce you to all of these concepts in more detail, and will teach you strategies for approaching the passages and correctly answering questions. Reading comprehension is something you can improve with practice, so take your time to work through all of the lessons and exercises in this chapter. You can also improve your reading speed and comprehension by reading every day. You can find a reading list organized by grade and subject matter in the supplementary materials online.

 For additional resources, please visit **ivyglobal.com/study**.

Section 2
Approaching the Reading Test

In this section, you'll first learn what to look for in a passage, how to be an active reader, and how to summarize paragraphs to better understand what you read. Then, you'll learn how to read the questions and answer them efficiently and accurately. You'll practice with individual questions, and then have a chance to put everything you've learned into action with full-length practice passages at the end of the section.

Reading a Passage
Part 1

You will encounter different types of passages on the SAT Reading Test, just as you encounter various types of content in your everyday reading. While the different kinds of passages will be explored further in Section 3, the basic strategy for reading a passage will remain the same regardless of its content.

What Makes the SAT Different?

The SAT requires a different kind of reading than what you may do in your everyday life. Normally when you read, you are probably focused on the content of the text, rather than on how an author has organized her writing, or why she chooses certain words.

However, the techniques, evidence, and structure an author uses are all things you are likely to be asked about on the SAT Reading Test. Thus, when you read SAT passages you will need to understand their content and also *how* and *why* the author organized that content in a certain way.

Questions on the SAT Reading Test will go beyond basic comprehension to test how different parts of the passage relate to each other, how the author makes her point or persuades the reader, and the opinions of the author and other people discussed in the passage. If you are already looking for these things as you read, answering the questions will be faster and easier.

Plan Your Approach

1. **Read one at a time.** Read only one passage or pair at a time, and try to answer all the related questions before moving on to the next passage. Switching between passages will make it harder to recall what you have read.

2. **Read the passage introductions.** Read any bolded information at the beginning of a passage. This can include details about the passage such as its author, intended audience, date, topic, and other important information to help you understand the passage.

3. **Pick and Skip.** As you learned in Chapter 1, you are free to answer questions in the order that works best for you. The reading passages are not presented in order of difficulty, so you may choose to read passages that seem easier or more familiar to you first. If you do this, be sure to bubble in your answers on the correct part of your answer sheet!

4. **Read the whole passage**. You may have heard you can avoid reading the full passage by reading just the lines each question asks about. However, not all questions will have line references, and some questions will require you to understand the passage as a whole. You

will answer questions more accurately when you read the entire passage. One exception to this rule is if the five-minute warning has been called or you do not have time to read another passage. In that case, you may look for a question that gives you a line reference, read that portion of the passage, and attempt the question.

It's very important to read the whole passages and not just skim them! You'll answer the questions more accurately if you've read the passages. The passages on the Reading Test average a little more than 600 words in length, and most of us can comfortably read at a speed of about 200 words-per-minute, so it only takes about 3 minutes to read a full passage at a comfortable pace. If you're reading carefully and marking things up, you might read a little bit more slowly than that. You'll probably also be able to spend less time re-reading when you're answering questions, though. The chart below offers some suggestions about how you might pace yourself. You have 65 minutes for the whole Reading Test.

Pacing Yourself			
Reading Pace	Minutes Spent Reading Passage	Minutes Spent Answering Questions	Total Minutes Per Passage
Comfortable	3	10	13
Careful	5	8	13

Mark Up the Passage

On the SAT, you know you will be tested about the content you read, so you want to make an effort to understand as you go. Don't wait until you reach the questions to try to make sense of what you read. As you learned in Chapter 1, you can achieve this by using the Pencil on Paper strategy. This will help you to be an **active reader**, by encouraging you to interact with the passages to find and understand the information you will be tested on.

Specifically, the best way to be an active reader is to use your pencil to **mark up** the passage as you read by underlining text, and adding your own notes and symbols to highlight what is important. The goals of marking up the passage are to help you stay focused, understand what you read, and make it easier to find key ideas in the passage when you refer back to it.

Use your pencil to circle or underline two to three **main ideas** per paragraph. Main ideas are those that relate to the **5 w's:** "who," "what," "where," "when," and "why." Stay focused on the bigger picture by making sure the main points you identify help answer the following questions:

1. **Who** is involved in this passage? Look for the people being discussed (artists, scholars, scientists, politicians) or the characters in a literature passage, and think about who might be writing the passage.

2. **What** is being discussed in this passage? Are specific events, theories, or ideas discussed? Look for the major concepts in each section of the passage.

3. **Where** are the events in the passage taking place? This can mean a specific location (one science laboratory) or a general setting (schools in North America).

4. **When** are the events in the passage taking place? It is usually more important to know the order in which things occur than to know specific dates.

5. **Why** is the information in this passage important? How are the ideas in the passage connected, and what is the author's purpose for writing the passage?

Let's look at the first few paragraphs from a reading passage and see how it might look if we mark it up using these ideas.

Example

This passage is adapted from Daniel Zalewski, "Under a Shroud of Kitsch May Lie a Master's Art." ©2001 by The New York Times Company.

Tommaso Strinati clambers to the top of the rickety scaffold and laughs. "It's a good thing that all this <u>Baroque work</u> is so
Line <u>unimpressive</u>," he says, pointing at the
5 clumsy trompe l'oeil painting covering the wall in front of him. "Otherwise, we might not have been allowed to <u>scrape it off!</u>"
A 28-year-old <u>art historian</u>, he is standing 16 feet above the marble floor of
10 San Pasquale Baylon chapel, a long-neglected nook of <u>Santa Maria in Aracoeli</u>, a Franciscan basilica in the center of <u>Rome</u>. Last year, Mr. Strinati, who is still a graduate student, began
15 studying the church's history. <u>Records suggested</u> that the <u>Roman artist Pietro</u>

<u>Cavallini</u>—a painter and mosaicist whose greatest works have been destroyed—spent <u>years decorating Aracoeli</u> toward
20 the <u>end of the 13th century. Yet only</u> one small Cavallini <u>fresco</u>, in the church's left transept, remained visible. Mr. Strinati wondered: had other Cavallini frescoes been <u>painted over</u> with inferior work?
25 And if so, could modern restorers uncover them?
"The answer to both questions was yes," Mr. Strinati says. A close-up examination of the chapel's walls last
30 summer revealed ghostly <u>images lying beneath the surface.</u> The entire chapel, it seemed, was a painted palimpsest. And when a heavy altarpiece was removed from one wall, a remarkably <u>tender</u>
35 <u>portrait</u> of the Madonna and Child was <u>found hidden</u> behind it.

Let's see how these key words helped us locate the 5 w's for this passage:

1. **Who** is involved in this passage?
   - The art historian Tommaso Strinati
   - The Roman artist Pietro Cavallini

2. **What** is being discussed in this passage?
   - How Strinati discovered Cavallini frescos that had been painted over

3. **Where** are the events in the passage taking place?
   - Santa Maria in Aracoeli, the basilica in Rome where Cavallini's art was found

4. **When** are the events in the passage taking place?
   - Cavallini painted the frescos at the end of the 13th century
   - The passage is written in the present tense and modern English, so we can assume the discovery of the frescos was fairly recent.

5. **Why** is the information in this passage important?
   - The information we underlined in the second paragraph shows a surprising contrast between ideas. If Cavallini spent years painting the basilica, why is there only one fresco? This sets up a bit of a mystery, which Strinati begins to solve in the third paragraph.

Though it can be tempting, don't go overboard with your active reading! If you mark up your entire passage, nothing will stand out as important, and you won't be able to find anything.

Exercise on Marking Up a Passage

Now that you've seen how to mark up a text, practice marking up the rest of the Cavallini passage below. This passage contains a lot of information, but not all of it contributes to the main ideas of the paragraph. Remember to stay focused on the 5 w's! When you are finished, compare your work with the fully marked-up version of this passage in the answer key at the end of the book.

This passage is adapted from Daniel Zalewski, "Under a Shroud of Kitsch May Lie a Master's Art." ©2001 by The New York Times Company.

Tommaso Strinati clambers to the top of the rickety scaffold and laughs. "It's a good thing that all this Baroque work is so
Line unimpressive," he says, pointing at the
5 clumsy trompe l'oeil painting covering the wall in front of him. "Otherwise, we might not have been allowed to scrape it off!"

A 28-year-old art historian, he is standing 16 feet above the marble floor of
10 San Pasquale Baylon chapel, a long-neglected nook of Santa Maria in Aracoeli, a Franciscan basilica in the center of Rome. Last year, Mr. Strinati, who is still a graduate student, began
15 studying the church's history. Records suggested that the Roman artist Pietro Cavallini—a painter and mosaicist whose greatest works have been destroyed—spent years decorating Aracoeli toward
20 the end of the 13th century. Yet only one small Cavallini fresco, in the church's left transept, remained visible. Mr. Strinati wondered: had other Cavallini frescoes been painted over with inferior work? And
25 if so, could modern restorers uncover them?

"The answer to both questions was yes," Mr. Strinati says. A close-up examination of the chapel's walls last
30 summer revealed ghostly images lying beneath the surface. The entire chapel, it seemed, was a painted palimpsest. And when a heavy altarpiece was removed from one wall, a remarkably tender
35 portrait of the Madonna and Child was found hidden behind it.

After months of careful paint-peeling, what has been uncovered are dazzling fragments of a late-medieval masterpiece
40 completed shortly after 1285. Although the Aracoeli fresco is not signed, the figures strongly resemble those in a surviving Cavallini work, the resplendent "Last Judgment" fresco at nearby Santa
45 Cecilia.

Mr. Strinati has grand ambitions for his discovery. He hopes that in a few years the fully restored fresco will not only rescue Cavallini's name from
50 obscurity, but also upend the widespread notion that the first flowers of the Renaissance budded in Florence, not Rome. For the fresco's lifelike figures—in particular, an impish Christ child with
55 charmingly flushed cheeks—suggest to Strinati that Cavallini may have anticipated some of the extraordinary naturalistic innovations that have long been credited to the Florentine artist
60 Giotto.

Moreover, the Aracoeli fragments may provide a critical new clue in a decades-old battle concerning the "St. Francis Legend," the 1296 fresco cycle at Assisi,
65 universally recognized as one of the foundations of the Renaissance. For centuries, the 28-scene cycle—which recounts the life of the saint with a narrative zest and compositional depth
70 that leave the flat tableaus of the Byzantine era far behind—was attributed to Giotto. But since the 1930's, various scholars have questioned this judgment, claiming that the Assisi cycle doesn't
75 resemble Giotto's other work. Now, the Aracoeli discovery is ammunition for Italian art historians who believe that Cavallini might actually be the primary creative force behind the "St. Francis
80 Legend."

The growing debate about Cavallini's importance was the occasion for a symposium in Rome in November. *La Republicca*, an Italian daily, has cast the
85 debate as "War Between Rome and Florence." Mr. Strinati is enjoying the ruckus. "I had a hunch that there was more Cavallini lurking around here," he says of the Aracoeli basilica. "But I
90 didn't expect to find an exquisite work that could shake up the history of art."

Summarize

Another good way to be an active reader is to summarize as you read the passage. Summarizing helps ensure that you understand what you read, and that you stay focused throughout the passage rather than "zoning out." This way you can avoid the dreaded feeling of finishing a passage and wondering what you just read!

Summarizing also makes long passages easier to manage. Breaking passages up into smaller pieces to analyze is easier than trying to make sense of the entire passage all at the end.

As you read, make a summary after each paragraph. Use the words you have underlined to help you. Your summaries should be short and snappy and cover only main ideas, not details or specific examples. Try to keep your summaries three to six words long, like a newspaper headline. Summarize in your own words. That helps you to understand the paragraph, and remember key information.

Let's refer back to our passage about Cavallini, and see how we could summarize the main ideas in the second paragraph.

> Tommaso Strinati clambers to the top of the rickety scaffold and laughs. "It's a good thing that all this Baroque work is so
> Line unimpressive," he says, pointing at the
> 5 clumsy trompe l'oeil painting covering the wall in front of him. "Otherwise, we might not have been allowed to scrape it off!"
>
> A 28-year-old art historian, he is standing 16 feet above the marble floor of
> 10 San Pasquale Baylon chapel, a long-neglected nook of Santa Maria in Aracoeli, a Franciscan basilica in the center of Rome. Last year, Mr. Strinati,
>
> who is still a graduate student, began
> 15 studying the church's history. Records suggested that the Roman artist Pietro Cavallini—a painter and mosaicist whose greatest works have been destroyed—spent years decorating Aracoeli toward
> 30 the end of the 13th century. Yet only one small Cavallini fresco, in the church's left transept, remained visible. Mr. Strinati wondered: had other Cavallini frescoes been painted over with inferior work?
> 35 And if so, could modern restorers uncover them?

While there is a lot of information in this paragraph, the most important idea is about Cavallini's "missing" art. He reportedly spent a lot of time painting the basilica, so Strinati wonders why there is only one Cavallini fresco. To capture this we might write something as simple as "Seems could be more Cavallini." You might also choose to abbreviate the names of people mentioned in a passage using their initials or something else. So another summary for this paragraph might read "T.S. thinks hidden P.C. frescos."

Exercise on Summarizing

Now that you've seen how to make a good summary, you can practice with the rest of the Cavallini passage. Remember to keep your summaries short! The first three paragraphs have summaries. Write your own summaries for paragraphs four through seven, and compare them to the answer key at the end of this book.

This passage is adapted from Daniel Zalewski, "Under a Shroud of Kitsch May Lie a Master's Art." ©2001 by The New York Times Company.

#1 T.S. glad remove Baroque

#2 Continued on next column…

> Tommaso Strinati clambers to the top of the rickety scaffold and laughs. "It's a good thing that all this Baroque work is so
> Line unimpressive," he says, pointing at the
> 5 clumsy trompe l'oeil painting covering the wall in front of him. "Otherwise, we might not have been allowed to scrape it off!"
>
> A 28-year-old art historian, he is standing 16 feet above the marble floor of
> 10 San Pasquale Baylon chapel, a long-

neglected nook of Santa Maria in Aracoeli, a Franciscan basilica in the center of Rome. Last year, Mr. Strinati, who is still a graduate student, began
15 studying the church's history. Records suggested that the Roman artist Pietro Cavallini—a painter and mosaicist whose greatest works have been destroyed—spent years decorating Aracoeli toward
20 the end of the 13th century. Yet only one small Cavallini fresco, in the church's left transept, remained visible. Mr. Strinati wondered: had other Cavallini frescoes been painted over with inferior work? And

#2 T.S. thinks hidden P.C. frescos

25 if so, could modern restorers uncover
them?

#3. Found P.C. frescoes

"The answer to both questions was
yes," Mr. Strinati says. A close-up
examination of the chapel's walls last
30 summer revealed ghostly images lying
beneath the surface. The entire chapel, it
seemed, was a painted palimpsest. And
when a heavy altarpiece was removed
from one wall, a remarkably tender
35 portrait of the Madonna and Child was
found hidden behind it.

#4.

After months of careful paint-peeling,
what has been uncovered are dazzling
fragments of a late-medieval masterpiece
40 completed shortly after 1285. Although
the Aracoeli fresco is not signed, the
figures strongly resemble those in a
surviving Cavallini work, the resplendent
"Last Judgment" fresco at nearby Santa
45 Cecilia.

#5.

Mr. Strinati has grand ambitions for
his discovery. He hopes that in a few
years the fully restored fresco will not
only rescue Cavallini's name from
50 obscurity, but also upend the widespread
notion that the first flowers of the
Renaissance budded in Florence, not
Rome. For the fresco's lifelike figures—in
particular, an impish Christ child with
55 charmingly flushed cheeks—suggest to
Strinati that Cavallini may have
anticipated some of the extraordinary
naturalistic innovations that have long

been credited to the Florentine artist
60 Giotto.

#6. ... continued

Moreover, the Aracoeli fragments
may provide a critical new clue in a
decades-old battle concerning the "St.
Francis Legend," the 1296 fresco cycle at
65 Assisi, universally recognized as one of
the foundations of the Renaissance. For
centuries, the 28-scene cycle—which
recounts the life of the saint with a
narrative zest and compositional depth
70 that leave the flat tableaus of the
Byzantine era far behind—was attributed
to Giotto. But since the 1930's, various
scholars have questioned this judgment,
claiming that the Assisi cycle doesn't
75 resemble Giotto's other work. Now, the
Aracoeli discovery is ammunition for
Italian art historians who believe that
Cavallini might actually be the primary
creative force behind the "St. Francis
80 Legend."

#7.

The growing debate about Cavallini's
importance was the occasion for a
symposium in Rome in November. *La
Republicca*, an Italian daily, has cast the
85 debate as "War Between Rome and
Florence." Mr. Strinati is enjoying the
ruckus. "I had a hunch that there was
more Cavallini lurking around here," he
says of the Aracoeli basilica. "But I
90 didn't expect to find an exquisite work
that could shake up the history of art."

Part 1 Practice: Reading a Passage

Use your active reading techniques to read and mark up the following passage. Also write a short summary for every paragraph as you read. Use the answer key at the end of this book to check your work.

This passage is adapted from Glenn Hubbard, "The Unemployment Puzzle: Where Have All the Workers Gone?" ©2014 by Dow Jones & Company.

The unemployment rate, the figure that dominates reporting on the economy, is the fraction of the labor force (those
Line working or seeking work) that is
5 unemployed. This rate has declined slowly since the end of the Great Recession. What hasn't recovered over that same period is the labor force participation rate, which today stands roughly where it did in 1977.

10 Labor force participation rates increased from the mid-1960s through the 1990s, driven by more women entering the workforce, baby boomers entering prime working years in the 1970s and
15 1980s, and increasing pay for skilled laborers. But over the past decade, these trends have leveled off. At the same time, the participation rate has fallen, particularly in the aftermath of the
20 recession.

In one view, this decline is just a temporary, cyclical result of the Great Recession. If so, we should expect workers to come back as the economy
25 continues to expand. Some research supports this view. A 2013 study by economists at the Federal Reserve Bank of San Francisco found that states with bigger declines in employment saw
30 bigger declines in labor-force participation. It also found a positive relationship between these variables in past recessions and recoveries.

But structural changes are plainly at
35 work too, based in part on slower-moving demographic factors. A 2012 study by economists at the Federal Reserve Bank of Chicago estimated that about one-quarter of the decline in labor-force
40 participation since the start of the Great Recession can be traced to retirements. Other economists have attributed about half of the drop to the aging of baby boomers.

Reading the Questions
Part 2

You can answer every question on the SAT Reading Test with information from the passage. Don't answer the questions using outside knowledge or opinions. Applying all the strategies you learned for understanding passages is the first step to answering questions quickly and correctly. Keep reading for more strategies to help you conquer reading questions!

Refer Back to the Passage

For every question, the correct answer will be based on something stated explicitly in the passage, or that can be inferred by reading between the lines of the text. Take advantage of the fact that in the SAT Reading Test, you can refer back to the material you are being asked about.

Don't answer the questions by memory alone, and don't rely on your own knowledge or opinion of the subject, which might lead you to the wrong answer. You should always be able to support your answer choice with specific lines or words in the text, even if none are specified in the question.

Some questions use **line references** to indicate which part of the passage they are asking you about. When you are given a line reference, always return to the passage to review that line, as well as two to three lines before and after the one you are asked about. This helps you understand the context of the line in question, and there are often clues there that will help you find the correct answer.

Let's see how this works with a line reference question from the Cavallini passage.

Example
The author mentions "an impish Christ child with charmingly flushed cheeks" (lines 54-55) in order to
A) provide an example of the fresco's lifelike figures.
B) describe Giotto's naturalistic style.
C) rescue Cavallini's name from obscurity.
D) suggest that it could help solve the "St. Francis Legend."

You may not remember this line from the passage, but if you refer back to the text, you can easily answer this question. Here is the paragraph:

> Mr. Strinati has grand ambitions for his discovery. He hopes that in a few years the fully restored fresco will not
> Line only rescue Cavallini's name from
> 50 obscurity, but also upend the widespread notion that the first flowers of the Renaissance budded in Florence, not Rome. For the fresco's lifelike figures—in particular, an impish Christ child with
> 55 charmingly flushed cheeks—suggest to Strinati that Cavallini may have anticipated some of the extraordinary naturalistic innovations that have long been credited to the Florentine artist
> 60 Giotto.

If you read the lines referenced and skim the two lines above and below it, you learn that this fresco has particularly lifelike figures and is a good indicator of the naturalistic innovations in Cavallini's work. Thus, only answer choice (A) matches the passage.

The other answer choices are all ideas mentioned at different points of the passage, but not in reference to the painting of the child or in the lines you were asked about. Therefore, you know they do not match and you can eliminate them.

When you answer questions that do not provide line references, you should still refer back to the passage. Because you will have marked up your passage, you will likely know where to find the evidence you need. If a question asks you something general about the passage, you can refer back to the summaries you made while reading, and any notes you made in the margins.

Pick & Skip

Generally, the question set will begin with more general questions on central ideas, tone, and structure, and then move onto more detailed questions that follow the order of the passage. However, just like the passages themselves, the questions will not necessarily be presented in order of difficulty. As you learned in Chapter 1, if you are unsure of the answer to any one question, you can mark it in your test booklet, bubble in your best guess, and come back to it later if you have time.

Part 2 Practice: Reading the Questions

Consider how you will approach the passage and questions below. Think about what strategies you might use if you cannot answer a question. Practice marking up this passage and making paragraph summaries the way you learned to earlier in this section.

This passage is adapted from Robert Lee Hotz, "A Wandering Mind Heads Straight Toward Insight." ©2009 by Dow Jones & Company.

In our fables of science and discovery, the crucial role of insight is a cherished theme. To these epiphanies, we owe the
Line concept of alternating electrical current,
5 the discovery of penicillin, and on a less lofty note, the invention of Post-its, ice-cream cones, and Velcro. The burst of mental clarity can be so powerful that, as legend would have it, Archimedes jumped
10 out of his tub and ran naked through the streets, shouting to his startled neighbors: "Eureka! I've got it."

In today's innovation economy, engineers, economists, and policy makers
15 are eager to foster creative thinking among knowledge workers. Until recently, these sorts of revelations were too elusive for serious scientific study. Scholars suspect the story of Archimedes isn't even entirely
20 true. Lately, though, researchers have been able to document the brain's behavior during Eureka moments by recording brain-wave patterns and imaging the neural circuits that become active as
25 volunteers struggle to solve anagrams, riddles, and other brain teasers.

Following the brain as it rises to a mental challenge, scientists are seeking their own insights into these light-bulb
30 flashes of understanding, but they are as hard to define clinically as they are to study in a lab.

To be sure, we've all had our "aha" moments. They materialize without
35 warning, often through an unconscious shift in mental perspective that can abruptly alter how we perceive a problem. "An 'aha' moment is any sudden comprehension that allows you to
40 see something in a different light," says psychologist John Kounios at Drexel University in Philadelphia. "It could be the solution to a problem; it could be getting a joke; or suddenly recognizing a
45 face. It could be realizing that a friend of yours is not really a friend."

These sudden insights, they found, are the culmination of an intense and complex series of brain states that require
50 more neural resources than methodical reasoning. People who solve problems through insight generate different patterns of brain waves than those who solve problems analytically. "Your brain is
55 really working quite hard before this moment of insight," says psychologist Mark Wheeler at the University of Pittsburgh. "There is a lot going on behind the scenes."

1

Which of the following can be inferred from the passage about anagrams, riddles, and other brain teasers?

A) It is possible to experience insight while solving them.

B) They can only be solved through insight.

C) They are best solved by thinking analytically.

D) They are best solved in a lab setting.

2

The main purpose of the first paragraph (lines 1-12) is to

A) list several inventions created through insight.

B) introduce the general concept of insight.

C) describe the story of Archimedes.

D) explain the origin of the phrase "Eureka!"

3

As used in line 50, "resources" most nearly means

A) capital.

B) energy.

C) resort.

D) finances.

4

The author quotes John Kounios in order to

A) prove that numerous scientists are studying insight.

B) suggest that research on insight is very basic.

C) offer a definition and examples of insight.

D) demonstrate that people often do not recognize insight.

Selecting Your Answers
Part 3

Now that you have learned how to effectively read passages, you are ready to tackle some different techniques for answering questions. Make sure to always refer back to the passage when selecting your answer choices!

Think for Yourself

One of the best ways to answer reading questions is by **thinking for yourself** rather than relying on the answer choices. Three of the four answer choices will be incorrect, and may be designed to trick you; simply reading them without knowing what you are looking for is not the best strategy. Because you have already done a lot of work to understand the passage, you will likely already be able to figure out how to answer a question without even looking at the answer choices.

Once you read a question, try to come up with your own answer based on the knowledge you gathered when you read the passage. You can refer back to your paragraph summaries, and to the words and ideas you circled and underlined. Then, imagine an answer in your own words. Practice covering up the answer choices to be sure you are coming up with your own answer rather than using the given choices as a crutch.

Let's practice using this technique with a question about the Cavallini passage, which you can refer back to in Part 1 of this Section:

Example
The primary purpose of the passage is to

Based on your summaries and marking of the passage, what do you think it was trying to do? The passage explained how Strinati correctly guessed that Cavallini's work was covered over in the basilica. It then discussed the lost frescos Strinati was able to reveal, and the potentially major implications of Cavallini's work for art history.

We might summarize that as "explaining big artistic finding." Now let's look for an answer choice that matches our prediction.

The primary purpose of the passage is to

A) explain an exciting discovery.

B) describe Cavallini's artistic style.

C) emphasize the importance of art history.

D) discuss Giotto's role in the Renaissance.

Does one answer choice jump out at you right away? Answer choice (A) is almost an exact match with what you predicted! The other options are not focused on the main ideas and purpose of the passage, so you can be confident in ruling them out. Doing the mental work of answering the question in your own words pays off when you can make your choice and gain a point so quickly.

Process of Elimination

If you are unsure of an answer, you may want to use the **Process of Elimination,** which you learned about in Chapter 1. Feel free to review that information to refresh your memory. Because there is only one correct answer for each question, it can be helpful to eliminate the choices you know are wrong.

Make sure you only eliminate answer choices you are certain are wrong, either because they are directly contradicted by the passage, or because there is no information in the passage to support them. You can eliminate answers by crossing them out in your test booklet.

Let's put this to use with a question from the Cavallini passage:

Example

Based on the passage, which choice best describes the relationship between the fresco cycle titled the "St. Francis Legend" and the artist Giotto?

A) The fresco cycle established Giotto as the founder of the Renaissance.

B) Cavallini was originally thought to be the fresco cycle's artist, but many art historians now believe it was Giotto.

C) Giotto was originally thought to be the fresco cycle's artist, but some art historians now believe it was Cavallini.

D) Giotto painted the fresco cycle to capture the story of his life with narrative zest.

Refer back to the sixth paragraph, which discusses the "St. Francis Legend," and compare it to the answer choices to see if they are supported. Here is the sixth paragraph:

Moreover, the Aracoeli fragments may provide a critical new clue in a decades-old battle concerning the "St. Francis
Line Legend," the 1296 fresco cycle at Assisi,
65 universally recognized as one of the foundations of the Renaissance. For centuries, the 28-scene cycle—which recounts the life of the saint with a narrative zest and compositional depth
70 that leave the flat tableaus of the Byzantine era far behind—was attributed to Giotto. But since the 1930's, various scholars have questioned this judgment, claiming that the Assisi cycle doesn't
75 resemble Giotto's other work. Now, the Aracoeli discovery is ammunition for Italian art historians who believe that Cavallini might actually be the primary creative force behind the "St. Francis
80 Legend."

Answer choice (A) goes too far, as the passage never states that Giotto was the founder of the Renaissance. It only states that the "St. Francis Legend" is a foundational piece of art in the Renaissance, which is not the same. You can knock it out. Answer choice (B) contradicts the passage, which says, "For centuries, the 28-scene cycle … was attributed to Giotto." You can knock it out.

Answer choice (C) matches the passage, so we can keep it open for now. Answer choice (D) contradicts the passage, as the paintings depict the life of St. Francis, not the life of Giotto. You can knock it out, and choose answer choice (C) as your correct response.

The Process of Elimination cannot always help you knock out all the wrong answers, but it is always helpful to have fewer answer choices to consider. Be sure to use it whenever you get stuck!

Best Choices

Remember that every question has only one correct answer. For many questions it will be clear that only one answer relates to the passage, as the others contain information not mentioned in the passage, or contradict information given in the passage.

However, other questions may have more than one answer option that could potentially be true. Remember you are looking for the **best choice**, which means the answer that most directly and completely answers the question, and is most supported by the passage. The best way to ensure that you select the best answer choice is to make sure you can find a word, line, or selection of lines in the text that support your answer.

Here is another example question from the Cavallini passage:

Example

The passage most strongly suggests that the Renaissance

A) began in the 1930s.
B) had roots in neither Rome nor Florence.
C) began in numerous Italian cities simultaneously.
D) featured naturalistic styles of painting.

First, use the Process of Elimination to knock out any answer choices you know are wrong. Both answer choice (A) and answer choice (B) contradict the passage, so you can eliminate them.

Answer choices (C) and (D) do not contradict the passage, so you can now consider each one more closely. Which answer choice has more support from the passage?

While answer choice (C) doesn't contradict the passage, there is nothing in the text to indicate that the Renaissance started in multiple places simultaneously. Remember you cannot use outside information to answer questions, or make assumptions. You must find support for your answers in the passage itself.

On the other hand, you can find specific evidence to support answer choice (D). Lines 56-57 talk about how Cavallini's lifelike figures are evidence that he "may have anticipated some of the extraordinary naturalistic innovations" of the Renaissance. Line 34 also describes a Cavallini portrait as "remarkably tender." While answer choice (C) could potentially be true, answer choice (D) can be proven true by the passage, and is therefore the best choice for this question.

What should you do if it seems that you can support two separate answer choices with information from the passage? First, make sure that the evidence supports the answer choice in the way you think it does. For example, some answer choices may use the same words as the passage, but in a way that means something different than the original text.

Second, for questions that ask what you can infer about the passage by reading between the lines, be sure to look for the most likely, or plausible, conclusion you can reach. Try to make as few leaps between ideas as possible. If your answer choice feels like a stretch, requires making a lot of assumptions, or relies on information or ideas not found in the text, it is likely incorrect. Avoid using your outside knowledge and stick to what is on the page.

Finally, if you really can't decide between options, it's okay to make your best guess and move on.

Part 3 Practice: Selecting Your Answers

Practice marking up this passage and making paragraph summaries the way you learned earlier in this section.

This passage is adapted from Nina Teicholz, "The Questionable Link Between Saturated Fat and Heart Disease." ©2014 by Dow Jones & Company.

After the AHA[1] advised the public to eat less saturated fat and switch to vegetable oils for a "healthy heart" in
Line 1961, Americans changed their diets. Now
5 these oils represent 7% to 8% of all calories in our diet, up from nearly zero in 1900, the biggest increase in consumption of any type of food over the past century.

This shift seemed like a good idea at
10 the time, but it brought many potential health problems in its wake. In those early clinical trials, people on diets high in vegetable oil were found to suffer higher rates not only of cancer but also of
15 gallstones. And, strikingly, they were more likely to die from violent accidents and suicides. Alarmed by these findings, the National Institutes of Health convened researchers several times in the early
20 1980s to try to explain these "side effects," but they couldn't. (Experts now speculate that certain psychological problems might be related to changes in brain chemistry caused by diet, such as fatty-acid
25 imbalances or the depletion of cholesterol.)

We've also known since the 1940s that when heated, vegetable oils create oxidation products that, in experiments
30 on animals, lead to cirrhosis of the liver and early death. For these reasons, some midcentury chemists warned against the consumption of these oils, but their concerns were allayed by a chemical fix:
35 oils could be rendered more stable through a process called hydrogenation, which used a catalyst to turn them from oils into solids.

From the 1950s on, these hardened
40 oils became the backbone of the entire food industry, used in cakes, cookies, chips, breads, frostings, fillings, and frozen and fried food. Unfortunately, hydrogenation also produced trans fats,
45 which since the 1970s have been suspected of interfering with basic cellular functioning and were recently condemned by the Food and Drug Administration for their ability to raise our levels of "bad" LDL
50 cholesterol.

Yet paradoxically, the drive to get rid of trans fats has led some restaurants and food manufacturers to return to using regular liquid oils—with the same long-
55 standing oxidation problems. These dangers are especially acute in restaurant fryers, where the oils are heated to high temperatures over long periods.

[1]The American Heart Association

Think about the primary purpose of this passage, and try to put it in your own words. Consider the author's tone. If you can, analyze the individual parts of the passage and try to figure out why the author included certain bits of information. For example, in lines 41-43, the author lists the types of foods that use hydrogenated oils in order to demonstrate how widespread the use of hardened hydrogenated oils has become.

For the following questions:

- Note which answers you can eliminate using the Process of Elimination, and why you know they are wrong.
- Note why the answer you selected is the best one, using words and lines from the passage to support your answer choice.

1

The author of the passage would probably agree with which of the following statements?

A) While trans fats are unhealthy, they are preferable to saturated fats.

B) Using large amounts of vegetable oil is safe as long as the oil is not hydrogenated.

C) Americans' attempt to avoid saturated fats has had unhealthy consequences.

D) The process of hydrogenation eliminates the only problem with vegetable oils.

2

It can reasonably be inferred from the passage that it is best to consume vegetable oils

A) in regular liquid form, in large quantities.

B) in regular liquid form, lightly heated.

C) in solid form after hydrogenation.

D) in small amounts or not at all.

3

Which of the following situations is most analogous to the problem presented in the passage?

A) Drivers are advised to avoid a certain highway because it has a lot of traffic, but the other road they take is backed up because of an accident.

B) Doctors prescribe an effective medicine for an illness, although it causes side effects for a small percentage of patients.

C) Shoppers frequent a local grocer, but when it closes they are forced to buy food at a more expensive market.

D) Farmers have a problem with frequent pests, but when they use a new harvesting technique fewer crops are eaten by insects.

Practice Set
Part 4

This passage is adapted from Richard Halloran, "Tapping Ocean's Cold For Crops." ©1990 by The New York Times Company.

On a wind-swept point of black lava jutting into the Pacific Ocean, a small band of scientists and entrepreneurs is
Line generating electricity, raising lobsters, and
5 growing strawberries using cold water from the depths of the sea. Eventually, they say, they hope the techniques they are devising here may increase food supplies and produce energy without pollution and without the
10 use of fossil fuels. For now, however, "cold water is the resource we're selling," said Thomas H. Daniel, technical director of the Natural Energy Laboratory of Hawaii, where the projects are under way.
15 That water, pumped from a depth of 2,000 feet, comes up at a nearly constant temperature of 6 degrees Celsius, or 43 degrees Fahrenheit. It has a high concentration of nutrients like nitrates,
20 phosphates, and silicates that foster the growth of plants and algae. And it is pure, having been out of contact with the surface for centuries as it drifted slowly along the bottom, and thus is free of the pathogens
25 that carry diseases.

When the laboratory began the project about 10 years ago, scientists here were confident it would be possible to put the water to profitable use. While profits have
30 so far been elusive, the researchers have demonstrated the feasibility of several ideas, solved formidable engineering problems, and produced a wealth of data.

The lab, which operates on a budget of
35 $1.5 million a year and has a staff of 20, began by seeking to use the differences in temperature between surface and deep sea water to produce electricity in a process

called ocean thermal energy conversion.
40 But it is the other projects developed on this 322-acre site that seem more promising today: growing lobsters in half the time it takes in their natural habitat along the coast of Maine; raising
45 flounder, sea urchins, and salmon; distilling fresh water and cooling buildings and industrial plants.

Next to the energy lab is the Hawaii Ocean Science and Technology park, a
50 547-acre site set aside by the state for commercial development of the laboratory's findings. Once a project developed at the lab becomes profitable, it must move out, either to the park or
55 elsewhere. Aquaculture Enterprises has already moved to the park. The company has been experimenting since 1987 with lobsters and has begun test sales locally. The lobsters are raised in shallow tanks
60 under green tents that block the heat of the sun. They are kept in separate pans so they will not eat each other.

Joseph Wilson, a partner in the enterprise, said that by mixing cold and
65 warm sea water to maintain a steady temperature of 22 degrees Celsius, researchers have eliminated the near-hibernation of the lobsters in winter. That has cut growing time to less than four
70 years from the seven and a half years it takes in nature. As they learn more about the lobsters' environment, nutrition, and genetics, he said, "we think that could be cut again to 30 months." But the cold
75 water also finds uses on land. Run through pipes the energy laboratory has laid in strawberry, lettuce, and flower beds, the cold water keeps the plants at the cool temperature they like and causes

80 fresh water to condense on the pipes. The
fresh water drips from the pipes to water
the plants. "When we want the
strawberries to think it's winter," Mr.
Daniel said, standing under a tropical sun,
85 "we just run the cold water faster."
Strawberries with five times more sugar
than those in nature have been produced.

1

This passage is primarily concerned with

A) describing a new alternative source of
energy.

B) advocating alternatives to fossil fuels.

C) discussing new applications of a natural
resource.

D) explaining the challenges of food
production.

2

The purpose of the second paragraph (lines
15-25) is to

A) describe the beneficial properties of
cold ocean water.

B) explain how nitrates, phosphates, and
silicates foster plant and algae growth.

C) convey the author's interest in the
numerous uses of cold ocean water.

D) explore the process used to move cold
water up to the ocean surface.

3

Based on the passage, which choice best
describes the relationship between the
electricity and food production projects
involving cold ocean water?

A) The food production projects are more
successful than the electricity project.

B) The food production projects are less
profitable than the electricity project.

C) The food production projects depend on
the electricity projects.

D) The food production projects
undermine the electricity projects.

4

Which choice provides the best evidence for
the answer to the previous question?

A) Lines 6-10 ("Eventually … fossil
fuels")

B) Lines 26-29 ("When … profitable
use")

C) Lines 40-42 ("But it … today")

D) Lines 59-61 ("The lobsters … sun")

5

As used in line 33, "wealth" most nearly
means

A) investment.

B) fortune.

C) means.

D) abundance.

6

As used in line 80, "condense" most nearly
means

A) compress.

B) squeeze.

C) form.

D) consolidate.

7

Based on the passage, the interviewed
scientists' attitude toward their current
agriculture projects could best be described
as

A) optimistic.

B) contemptuous.

C) skeptical.

D) disappointed.

Which choice provides the best evidence for the answer to the previous question?

A) Lines 29-33 ("While profits … data")

B) Lines 56-58 ("The company … locally")

C) Lines 60-64 ("Joseph Wilson … winter")

D) Lines 67-70 ("As they … months")

According to the passage, the growing time for lobsters can be reduced by

A) eliminating cold temperatures to prevent their near-hibernation.

B) preventing them from eating one another.

C) running cool water over them at a faster rate.

D) providing them with a high concentration of nutrients like nitrates.

10

What is the most likely reason the author describes Mr. Daniel as "standing under a tropical sun" (line 84)?

A) To contrast the local weather with the cold conditions created for the strawberries

B) To give the reader a sense of place through vivid description

C) To indicate that tropical locations are the usual growing region for strawberries

D) To suggest that the local weather could pose a threat to the success of the strawberry crop

This passage is adapted from Sir Arthur Conan Doyle, *A Study in Scarlet*, originally published in 1887. Here, the narrator, Dr. John Watson, describes the detective Sherlock Holmes.

His very person and appearance were such as to strike the attention of the most casual observer. In height he was rather
Line over six feet, and so excessively lean that
5 he seemed to be considerably taller. His eyes were sharp and piercing, save during those intervals of torpor to which I have alluded; and his thin, hawk-like nose gave his whole expression an air of alertness
10 and decision. His chin, too, had the prominence and squareness which mark the man of determination. His hands were invariably blotted with ink and stained with chemicals, yet he was possessed of
15 extraordinary delicacy of touch, as I frequently had occasion to observe when I watched him manipulating his fragile philosophical instruments.

The reader may set me down as a
20 hopeless busybody, when I confess how much this man stimulated my curiosity, and how often I endeavoured to break through the reticence which he showed on all that concerned himself. Before
25 pronouncing judgment, however, be it remembered, how objectless was my life, and how little there was to engage my attention. My health forbade me from venturing out unless the weather was
30 exceptionally genial, and I had no friends who would call upon me and break the monotony of my daily existence. Under these circumstances, I eagerly hailed the little mystery which hung around my
35 companion, and spent much of my time in endeavouring to unravel it.

He was not studying medicine. He had himself, in reply to a question, confirmed Stamford's opinion upon that world. Yet
40 his zeal for certain studies was remarkable, and within eccentric limits his knowledge was so extraordinarily ample and minute that his observations have fairly

astounded me. Surely no man would work
so hard or attain such precise information
unless he had some definite end in view.
Casual readers are seldom remarkable for
the exactness of their learning. No man
burdens his mind with small matters
unless he has some very good reason for
doing so.

His ignorance was as remarkable as his
knowledge. Of contemporary literature,
philosophy and politics he appeared to
know next to nothing. Upon my quoting
Thomas Carlyle, he inquired in the naivest
way who he might be and what he had
done. My surprise reached a climax,
however, when I found incidentally that
he was ignorant of the Copernican Theory
and of the composition of the Solar System.
That any civilized human being in this
nineteenth century should not be aware
that the earth travelled round the sun
appeared to be to me such an extraordinary
fact that I could hardly realize it.

"You appear to be astonished," he
said, smiling at my expression of surprise.
"Now that I do know it I shall do my best
to forget it."

"To forget it!"

"You see," he explained, "I consider
that a man's brain originally is like a little
empty attic, and you have to stock it with
such furniture as you choose. A fool takes
in all the lumber of every sort that he
comes across, so that the knowledge which
might be useful to him gets crowded out,
or at best is jumbled up with a lot of other
things so that he has a difficulty in laying
his hands upon it. Now the skillful
workman is very careful indeed as to what
he takes into his brain-attic. He will have
nothing but the tools which may help him
in doing his work, all in the most perfect
order. It is a mistake to think that that little
room has elastic walls and can distend to

any extent. There comes a time when for
every addition of knowledge you forget
something that you knew before. It is of
the highest importance, therefore, not to
have useless facts elbowing out the useful
ones."

"But the Solar System!" I protested.

"What the deuce is it to me?" he
interrupted impatiently; "you say that we
go round the sun. If we went round the
moon it would not make a pennyworth of
difference to me or to my work."

11

Watson's attitude toward Sherlock in the
passage is best described as

A) impatient.

B) disdainful.

C) adoring.

D) fascinated.

12

Which choice provides the best evidence
for the answer to the previous question?

A) Lines 19-24 ("The reader … himself")

B) Lines 36-39 ("He had … world")

C) Lines 44-46 ("Surely … in view")

D) Lines 62-66 ("That any … it")

13

The primary purpose of the first paragraph
(lines 1-18) is to

A) provide a description of Sherlock.

B) explain why Watson is interested in
Sherlock's strange mannerisms.

C) describe Sherlock's delicacy in using
his instruments.

D) introduce the tools Sherlock uses to
solve mysteries.

Watson sees a surprising contrast between

A) Sherlock's expertise in some subjects and unfamiliarity with others.

B) his impression of Sherlock and Sherlock's attitude toward him.

C) Sherlock's motivations and enthusiasm for learning.

D) his own intellect and that of Sherlock.

Which choice provides the best evidence for the answer to the previous question?

A) Lines 1-3 ("His ... casual observer")

B) Lines 48-51 ("No ... doing so")

C) Lines 52-53 ("His ignorance ... knowledge")

D) Lines 55-58 ("Upon my ... done")

As used in line 17, "manipulating" most nearly means

A) exploiting.

B) tricking.

C) tampering.

D) handling.

The second paragraph (lines 19-36) suggests that Watson feels his interest in Sherlock is

A) understandable, but something for which he may be judged.

B) routine, but something that he indulges too frequently.

C) embarrassing, as it fails to break the monotony of his existence.

D) acceptable, as it allows him to unravel the mystery surrounding the detective.

As used in line 25, "pronouncing" most nearly means

A) uttering.

B) declaring.

C) reciting.

D) articulating.

Once Watson learns Sherlock is unfamiliar with the Solar System, he

A) mocks him for his lack of education.

B) explains the concept to him.

C) asks Sherlock about his opinion on human memory.

D) decides it is not as important as he originally thought.

Which hypothetical situation involves the same form of expertise demonstrated by Sherlock?

A) A librarian is familiar with all types of media, both modern and antiquated.

B) A highly accomplished classical musician can play few other types of music.

C) A carpenter works with numerous types of wood but prefers one.

D) A new art student has been studying theory but has not yet created anything.

21

According to the passage, Sherlock believes the brain is like an attic because

A) a room can only hold so many items, similar to how human memory is not unlimited.

B) the human brain cannot grow, similar to how the walls of a room cannot be extended.

C) a person cannot store endless memories, similar to how a skillful workman carefully chooses his projects.

D) a cluttered mind makes it difficult to recall important information, similar to how a crowded room can become dangerous.

Section 3
SAT Passage Types

Now that we've outlined the basic strategies that you'll use to approach the Reading section, let's get specific. In this section, we'll explain the different types of passage that show up on the SAT, what kind of content to expect in each one, and how to apply the skills we've already reviewed to different types of passage.

As you saw in Section 1 of this chapter, there are five passages in the Reading section. These passages fall into three domains: one passage will be in the Literature domain, two will be in the Science domain, and two will be in the History/Social Studies domain.

There are also a couple of special passage types: passages with graphics (like charts, graphs, or diagrams), and passage pairs. One of the two Science passages will include a graphic, and one of the two History/Social Studies passages will include a graphic. One passage will actually be a set of two shorter, paired passages.

In this section, we'll discuss the important elements of each of the following passage types, and give you the chance to practice with each type:

- Literature Passages
- Science Passages
- Social Studies and History Passages

Literature Passages
Part 1

There is one Literature passage in the Reading section of the SAT. It will usually be an excerpt from a novel or short story. Sometimes it will be taken from a recently published source, and other times it may be taken from an older source. Passages from older sources might contain some phrases that you're not familiar with, but most of the language will be understandable to modern readers. Literature passages will never include graphics, and will not be presented as passage pairs.

Literature passages will usually tell a story, or describe a scene, object, or character—often with an underlying message that is implied rather than stated directly. With Literature passages, your goals are to follow the details of what is actually being described, to try to understand any underlying message of the passage, and to pay attention to how the author uses language and literary techniques to convey that message. The tips that follow will help you put Pencil on Paper and use your active reading skills to accomplish those goals.

You won't be tested on your knowledge about specific works, but you will need to be comfortable reading various types of literature. The best way to increase your familiarity with literature is to read it; once you've finished the practice exercises in this book, go online to see our reading list with recommended literature passages listed by grade.

 For additional resources, please visit **ivyglobal.com/study**.

Important Details in Literature Passages

As we mentioned in Section 2, you should pay special attention to important details in a passage as you're reading it. Which details are the most important will depend largely on what type of passage you're reading. The following are important elements to keep in mind when reading Literature passages.

Figurative Language

Literature passages often contain **figurative language**, which is language that's used in some creative or unusual way. Figurative language often doesn't mean exactly what it says, but instead has a second meaning. The SAT will often ask you to interpret specific pieces of figurative language, or to analyze how they affect the passage or why the author chose to use them.

There are five basic kinds of figurative language:

Types of Figurative Language		
Hyperbole	Hyperbole is language that involves major exaggeration.	I ate about ten tons of candy last Halloween.
Idioms	An idiom is a phrase that has meaning beyond what the words themselves mean (although it might also be literally true).	That's not exactly brain surgery.
Personification	Personification is language that ascribes human characteristics, like personality traits, intentions, or human-like actions, to non-human things.	As we approached the mouth of the cavern, it belched out a noxious breath, and its foul exhalation warned of a deadly distaste for intruders.
Metaphor	Metaphor is language that uses one thing to represent another thing or an idea, especially when they aren't very much alike.	Luke was adrift on a sea of opportunities, with no current to direct his course.
Simile	A simile is language that compares two things of different kinds, using the words "like" or "as."	With the children finally all away at school, Sally's home was as vast and empty as a starless sky.

Correctly identifying figurative language can give you a lot of insight into the meaning of a story. You won't need to categorize these elements in order to understand the story, but you will need to analyze how they're being used in the passage—so pay attention to them, and to the effect that they have in the passage.

Take a look at the following example:

Example

This passage is adapted from Tom Gallon, *Tinman*, originally published in 1907.

In all that I shall set down here, in telling the strange story of my poor life, I shall write nothing but the truth. It has
Line been written in many odd times and in
5 many odd places: in a prison cell, on paper stamped with the prison mark; on odd scraps of paper in a lonely garret under the stars, with a candle-end for light—and I, poor and old and shivering—scrawling
10 hastily because the time was so short. I have been at once the meanest and the greatest of all men; the meanest—because all men shuddered at the mere mention of my name, and at the thought of what I had

done; the greatest—because one woman
15 loved me, and taught me that beyond that nothing else mattered. I have lived in God's sunlight, and in the sunlight of her eyes; I have gone down into the Valley of the Shadow of Death, and have not been
20 afraid; I have been caged like a wild beast, until I forgot the world, just as the world forgot me. In a mere matter of the counting of years I am but little past forty years of age; yet I am an old man, and I
25 have lived two lives—just as, when my time comes, I shall have died two deaths. I have touched the warm lips of Love; I have clasped the gaunt hands of Misery. I have warmed both hands at the fire of

The author uses metaphors here to represent a state of being.

Here, the author uses a simile, which can be spotted with the clue word like.

The author here uses personification to attribute human characteristics, such as lips and hands, to Love and Misery.

Life; but now the fire has gone out, and only the cold grey ashes remain. But of all that you may read, just as I have written it, and as the memory of it has come back to me. Roll up the curtain—and see me as I was—and judge me lightly.

Here, the author includes an idiom as the narrator invites readers to look more deeply into his life.

What sorts of figurative language does the author use in this passage? You might note that he uses similes such as "I have been caged like a wild beast" and personification such as "the warm lips of Love" and "the gaunt hands of Misery." Consider the author's purpose in using this language. How does it set the scene or provide insight into the narrator's character? Here, you will notice that the narrator is using such description to set the scene and convey the highs and lows of his own life.

Characterization

The people in stories, plays, and novels are characters. **Characterization** is the process where the author gives the reader new information about the characters.

Writers can use a number of techniques for characterization. Here are some of the main ones:

Techniques for Characterization		
Type	Definition	Example
Description	An author might use physical details to suggest something about the character's life or personality.	She wore an expensive business suit, diamond earrings, and an elegant gold watch.
Dialogue	The style or content of a character's speech can reveal what the character believes or how he feels.	He stammered, "W-would you, um, I mean, would you like to maybe, uh, go out with me sometime?"
Action	The way an author describes a character's actions can tell you more than just what the character is doing.	As the time drew closer to her audition, she reviewed her script over and over, biting her nails.
Internal Speech	An author might state or paraphrase a character's inner monologue to let the reader know what the character is thinking.	She smiled and thanked her boss, privately thinking that she was looking forward to the day she never had to see his smug face again.
Responses	The way other characters respond to someone can give you clues about that character's situation.	When he walked into the guidance counselor's office, the secretary raised an eyebrow and said, "Again?"

Paying attention to how the author uses these techniques will help you to answer questions about characters and their relationships, and about the author's purpose. Keep an eye out for characterization, and pay attention to how it shapes individual characters, their relationships to one another, and their role in the story.

Let's look at another excerpt from the story *Tinman*. Take a look at the following portion, when the narrator goes to meet his guardian.

Example

This passage is adapted from Tom Gallon, *Tinman*, originally published in 1907.

I was beginning to feel uncomfortable when at last he dropped the paper-knife, and stood up to shake hands with me. "So
Line you are Charles Avaline?" he said. "I'm
5 glad to see you. How old are you? I forget times and dates."

"I shall be twenty in a month," I replied, "but I feel much older."

"Most people do at your age," he
10 retorted. "Well—there are certain arrangements to be made about your future—your income, and so on"—he was looking down at the desk, and shifting some papers about uneasily
15 there—"and perhaps it would be better if you came round to my rooms to-night to see me. I've got an old-fashioned place in Bloomsbury; perhaps you'll dine with me there. I'll write the
20 address down for you; seven sharp, please."

Now, take a look at the following question:

Example

Based on the passage, it can best be concluded that the narrator's guardian is

A) thrilled to finally meet his charge.

B) disappointed by the narrator's greed.

C) surprised by the narrator's young age.

D) apprehensive about news he has to deliver.

How would you go about answering this question? The passage does not directly state that the guardian is thrilled, disappointed, surprised, or apprehensive. Instead, it is important to pay attention to the different techniques for characterization employed by the author in order to draw a conclusion. Here, the guardian's dialogue and responses provide insight into his attitude. He mentions "certain arrangements to be made" about the narrator's future before "shifting some papers about uneasily," suggesting that he needs to have an uncomfortable conversation with the narrator. Thus, answer choice (D) is best supported by the passage.

As you continue to read and practice with a variety of sources, you'll become an expert at recognizing these techniques.

The Structure of a Literature Passage

As you read the passage, you should pay attention to how it's structured, meaning the focus of different parts of the passage and how they fit together.

Some Literature passages will be mostly narrative, which means that they focus on telling a story. A narrative passage describes events that happen in a certain order. Others will be mostly **descriptive**, which means that they focus on describing an important person, place, or thing in detail. For example, the excerpt of *Tinman* above, showing the meeting between the narrator and his guardian, is mostly narrative, while the first excerpt of *Tinman*, a broader paragraph about the narrator's life, is mostly descriptive.

Many of the passages you encounter will mix some narrative and descriptive elements. In these passages, the two kinds of elements are usually intended to support one another. Descriptive elements in a narrative passage often provide additional details about an important figure in the story, while narrative elements in a descriptive passage often help characterize the subject that the passage is describing.

Part 1 Practice: Literature Passages

Below is an example passage. Read the passage, paying special attention to the elements we have discussed, and then answer the accompanying practice questions.

This passage is adapted from Jerome K. Jerome, *Three Men in a Boat (to Say Nothing of the Dog)*. Originally published in 1889.

We were planning supplies for our trip. George said:

"Begin with breakfast." (George is so
Line practical.) "Now for breakfast we shall
5 want a frying-pan"—(Harris said it was
indigestible; but we merely urged him not
to be a fool, and George went on)—"a
tea-pot and a kettle, and an ethanol stove.

"No oil," said George, with a
10 significant look; and Harris and I agreed.
We had taken an oil-stove on a boat trip
once, but "never again."

It had been like living in an oil-shop
that week. It oozed. I never saw another
15 thing ooze like kerosene oil. We kept it in
the nose of the boat, and, from there, it
oozed down to the rudder, impregnating
the whole boat and everything in it on its
way, and it oozed over the river, and
20 saturated the scenery and spoilt the

atmosphere. Sometimes a westerly oily
wind blew, and at other times an easterly
oily wind, and sometimes it blew a
northerly oily wind, and maybe a
25 southerly oily wind; but whether it came
for the Arctic snows, or was raised in the
waste of the desert sands, it came alike to
us laden with the fragrance of kerosene
oil. And that oil oozed up and ruined the
30 sunset; and as for the moonbeams, they
positively reeked of kerosene.

We tried to get away from it at
Marlow. We left the boat by the bridge,
and took a walk through the town to
35 escape it, but it followed us. The whole
town was full of oil. We passed through
the church-yard, and it seemed as if the
people had been buried in oil. The High
Street stunk of oil; we wondered how
40 people could live in it. And we walked
miles upon miles out Birmingham way;
but it was no use, the country was steeped
in oil.

At the end of that trip we met together
45 at midnight in a lonely field, under a
    blasted oak, and took an awful oath (we
    had been swearing for a whole week
    about the thing in an ordinary, middle-
    class way, but this was a swell affair)—an
50 awful oath never to take kerosene oil with
    us in a boat again.

    And so for this trip, we confined
    ourselves to an ethanol stove. Even that is
    bad enough. You get ethanol pie and
55 ethanol cake. But ethanol is more
    wholesome than kerosene, and much less
    persistent.

1

The main purpose of this passage can best
be described as

A) suggesting that planning an adventure
   might be more fun than going on one.

B) telling the story of how a group of
   friends learned from a past mistake.

C) describing the process of planning and
   preparing to go on a trip.

D) explaining why it is important to avoid
   using certain types of fuel in enclosed
   spaces.

2

Based on the passage, we can most
reasonably infer that Harris, George, and
the narrator are

A) recent acquaintances planning a trip to
   get to know one another.

B) traveling companions who first met
   during an unfortunate journey by boat.

C) seasoned adventurers who regularly
   travel great distances.

D) old friends planning a trip similar to
   one they had taken before.

3

The author's purpose in describing how the
oil affected the sunset and moonbeams
(lines 29-31) is mainly to

A) describe the widespread pollution that
   the men encountered as they travelled
   down the river.

B) contrast the environment of the boat
   with the lonely field the men would
   visit later.

C) suggest that the smell of kerosene was
   so overwhelming that it tainted every
   other experience.

D) relate the specific event that finally
   persuaded the friends never to bring
   kerosene again.

Science Passages
Part 2

There are two Science passages in the SAT Reading Test. The Science passages you encounter on the SAT will usually come from magazines, newspapers, or non-fiction books on popular science. Science passages will almost always be from contemporary sources, which means they're current science. Science passages will be about natural or physical sciences—physics, biology, astronomy, chemistry, or similar fields.

You won't be tested on your knowledge of science, but you will have to be comfortable reading passages that use scientific language. Check out our reading list online for some recommended reading in science, including sources that will help familiarize you with this type of writing.

 For additional resources, please visit **ivyglobal.com/study**.

One of the Science passages will include one or two graphics, which we cover in Part 4 of this chapter. One of the Science passages might actually be a passage pair, which we cover in Part 5.

With Science passages, your goal is to identify the main topic or argument, and understand how the additional information and evidence provided explains the topic or supports the argument. The tips that follow will help you to accomplish that goal.

Important Details in Science Passages

Science passages will focus on communicating specific facts, either to help the reader understand a broader topic or to build an argument in support of the author's opinion on a scientific issue. You need to pay special attention to data and experimental evidence, and to the elements of the argument presented in a passage.

Elements of an Argument

Often, Science passages build an argument that shows, using evidence and logic, why the author believes that some basic idea is true.

Keep an eye out for all of the following elements of an argument in Science passages:

Elements of an Argument	
Category	Definition
Thesis	The main idea that the author is defending with her argument. There may be a sentence near the beginning that clearly states the thesis. However, there may not be one; be careful not to assume that whatever idea is mentioned earliest is the thesis. Look instead for the idea that the passage as a whole supports.
Claims	Claims are statements that the author says are true, or that we know she wants us to believe are true based on the surrounding context.
Supporting Evidence	Supporting evidence is the information that an author provides to back up her claims. It can take the form of data from studies, quotes from experts, historical examples, or other claims or facts that you might already agree with.
Counterclaims and Refutations	Counterclaims are claims that disagree with or contradict claims made elsewhere in the passage, and refutations are statements intended to disprove other statements. Authors may include them to argue against a specific claim already made, analyze a general alternative position in an argument, or anticipate a reader's possible objections.
Conclusion	Persuasive passages often end with a concluding statement that restates the thesis. This is more than just repetition; the concluding statement is usually stronger than the thesis statement, and often includes a summary of the evidence presented in the text.

Below is an example. Read the passage, paying special attention to the elements we have discussed:

Example

Europa, a moon of Jupiter, is the place where we are most likely to find extraterrestrial life in our own solar
Line system. Liquid water is widely considered
5 to be one of the most important preconditions for life, and there are likely vast oceans of liquid water beneath Europa's surface. Certain organic chemicals are also considered necessary
10 precursors for life, and we have reason to believe that natural processes on Europa's surface create them in abundance.

Given that sunlight is the main source of energy for life on Earth, it may seem
15 that Europa's thick icy crust, which prevents any sunlight from reaching the ocean, would make life on the moon impossible. But there is an alternative source of energy on Europa: tidal
20 flexing, a process in which gravitational tugs cause Europa's oceans to slosh about, generating heat and energy.

With its suitable environment, and sources of the chemicals and energy
25 necessary for life, it would be more surprising to find that Europa was barren than to discover life beneath its crust.

The first paragraph begins with a clear statement of the thesis. It proceeds to offer a couple of pieces of supporting evidence. The second paragraph then raises a counterclaim, but only for the purpose of refuting it. Finally, the third paragraph concludes with a summary of the evidence and a restatement of the thesis.

Reading about Experiments

Science passages will often discuss specific experiments. Sometimes details about an experiment may be offered as supporting evidence, and other times an experiment may be the main subject of the passage. To be sure that you understand Science passages, you should make sure that you're familiar with some basic facts about how experiments are conducted and what they mean.

The Basic Idea

Experiments measure one thing: the interaction between cause and effect. Experiments measure whether a change in one thing causes a change in another, and what kind of change occurs.

To start, scientists identify the **variables**—things or circumstances which might change or can be changed—that might have some influence on the relationship they want to test. You can get a good idea of what any experiment is about by paying attention to just two pieces of information: which variables the scientists *change* (independent variables), and which they *measure* (dependent variables).

There may also be a **control variable**. This is a variable that will be left unchanged, so that scientists can be sure it is not affecting their results, or so they can compare it to a variable that has been manipulated.

Experiments are designed to measure the effect of the variable that scientists change on the variable that they measure. Let's look at an example:

Example
Using timed growth lights, scientists provided 12 hours of light to plants in Group 1 and 4 hours of light to plants in Line Group 2. Scientists controlled for the   5 effects of nutrition and hydration by using identical soil sources and equal amounts of water and fertilizer to all plants. Growth was measured by periodically recording the height and leaf size of   10 plants, and weighing the pots.

We can see that the variable that changed (independent variable) was the amount of light plants received, and the variable that was measured (dependent variable) was growth. By looking at which variable scientists changed and which they measured, we can conclude that the experiment was designed to measure the effect of light exposure on plant growth. We can also tell that scientists were *not* interested in measuring the effects of hydration or nutrition; the use of "controlled" indicates that soil type, water, and fertilizer are all control variables.

Drawing Conclusions

Whether a passage describes an experiment in detail or only talks about the results of an experiment, there are some important things to keep in mind when drawing conclusions from experimental evidence.

Experiments only demonstrate very specific relationships. You can make some inferences about what else an experiment *suggests*, and what other ideas an experiment *supports*, but not what is *demonstrated* beyond the very specific relationship tested. This relationship will be between the independent variable—what is changed or manipulated—and the dependent variable, or what is measured.

Summarizing a Science Passage

Just as Literature passages could be divided into two basic categories, narrative or descriptive, we can generally split Science passages into two broad categories as well. Being able to identify which type of passage you're reading will help you to answer questions about the main idea and about the author's purpose.

Explanatory passages will provide information about a topic. Their purpose is simply to inform the reader. These passages will not support any particular side of an issue, although they might describe the positions taken about the issue.

Persuasive passages will take a certain position on an issue, and provide additional information as evidence to support that position. The purpose of a persuasive passage is to build support for the author's position using specific evidence and logical arguments.

Pay attention to the author's position and to the balance of evidence to help you decide what type of passage you're reading. Knowing whether a passage is explanatory or persuasive will help you answer questions about the author's purpose, or the main purpose of the passage. Be sure to also pay attention to the elements of specific paragraphs and to identify their purpose, as you might be asked about the purpose of only a part of the passage.

Part 2 Practice: Science Passages

Below is an example passage. Read the passage, paying special attention to the elements we have discussed, and then answer the accompanying practice questions.

This passage is adapted from Joseph Heremans, "Magnetic Fields Can Control Heat and Sound." ©2015 by Joseph Heremans.

Sound is carried by periodic vibrations of atoms in gases, liquids, and solids. When we talk to each other, the vocal
Line chords of the speaker vibrate, causing the
5 air coming from his lungs to vibrate as well. This creates sound waves, which then propagate through the air until they hit a listener's eardrums and make them vibrate as well. From these vibrations, the
10 listener can then reconstruct the speaker's words.

Sound is affected by the surroundings in which it travels and by the frequency of the sound waves. We design musical
15 instruments to manipulate the sound waves they produce. Further, we know that there are sound waves that are outside the range of human hearing, such as those produced by a dog whistle. As physicists have
20 researched sound both inside and outside the range of human hearing, interesting properties have been discovered.

More than a hundred years ago, physicists understood that heat is simply the
25 energy stored in the vibrations of atoms, and therefore realized that heat and sound are related. Now my lab has shown for the first time that these atomic vibrations have magnetic properties too.

30 Physicists called the sound wave particles "phonons," derived from the Greek word for sound. In the March 23 issue of *Nature Materials*, we offer experimental proof that sound waves interact with
35 external magnetic fields.

The experiment was carried out on a large, single crystal of a very pure semiconductor, indium antimonide, which had been cut into two unequal sections and

40 then cooled to about −445°F (−265°C). A controlled amount of heat was made to flow in each section separately.

At these temperatures, the phonons can be thought of as individual particles, like
45 runners on a racetrack each carrying a little bucket of heat.

In the small section, the phonons often run into the walls, which slows them down. The small section is used as a reference, to
50 make the experiment independent of the other properties of the solid that might interfere. In the large section, the phonons can go faster, and they don't run into the walls as much as into each other. When we
55 apply a magnetic field, they tend to run into each other more frequently. Because the magnetic field increases the number of collisions, it also slows the phonons down and lowers the amount of heat they carry by
60 12%.

We think this is due to the electrons that rotate in orbits around each atom in the solid. The orbital motion of these electrons emits a very small intrinsic magnetic field
65 that interacts with the externally applied field—an effect called "diamagnetism." This property exists even in substances we don't traditionally think of as magnetic, such as glass, stone, or plastic. When the
70 atoms vibrate due to the passing of the phonons, this interaction creates a force on the atoms that makes the phonons collide with each other more often.

At this point, we've just described a new
75 concept, something that had never been thought of before. Engineers can perhaps use this concept to control heat and sound waves magnetically. Sound waves can be effectively steered already by using multiple
80 sources of sound, as is done in ultrasound imaging systems, but controlling heat conduction is much harder.

Conversion of heat into electrical or
mechanical power, as is done in engines
85 and in power stations, supplies over 90%
of the energy humanity uses. Therefore,
being able to control heat conduction
could have an enormous impact on energy
production, though, obviously,
90 applications of this emergent concept are
still quite a way in the future.

1

The main purpose of this passage is to

A) suggest new technologies that could
be developed from recent
breakthroughs.

B) describe a new discovery by the
author's lab and its implications for
the field.

C) compare the magnetic and
thermodynamic properties of sound.

D) educate readers about the different
way sound waves are measured.

2

The author includes the paragraph on
diamagnetism (lines 61-73) to

A) establish his authority as a specialist in
diagmagnetic properties of sound
waves.

B) suggest a new area for research on
magnetic waves and phonons.

C) provide background on the structure
and function of magnetic fields.

D) propose a theory to explain some of
his research team's results on
phonons.

3

Based on information in the passage, it can
be inferred that the author believes that the
evidence about the magnetic properties of
sound waves

A) is a fascinating but unsupported
theoretical claim.

B) requires additional research to prove
results were not an anomaly.

C) is a groundbreaking result ripe for
further exploration.

D) ignores other essential properties of
waves that should be investigated.

Social Studies and History Passages
Part 3

There are two Social Studies/History passages on the SAT. One of these two passages will resemble a Science passage, as it will have a similar structure and focus, and will ask similar types of questions. It will probably come from a magazine, newspaper, or non-fiction book, and it will be from a contemporary source. However, it will be from a field in the social sciences rather than the natural or physical sciences. The social sciences include fields like economics, psychology, linguistics, and history. This passage will likely include a graphic. You can approach a Social Studies passage on one of these subjects much like you would approach a Science passage.

The other Social Studies/History passage will be very different, and will be the focus of this part of this section. On each SAT, there will be one historical document that fits into one of two categories: either the Founding Documents of the United States or the Great Global Conversation.

Founding Documents are those documents that shaped the history of the United States. This category includes documents like the Declaration of Independence, the U.S. Constitution, and the Bill of Rights. The Great Global Conversation refers to the ongoing global conversation about civic life. This category could include a Winston Churchill speech, a passage from a work written by Nelson Mandela, a letter from Gandhi, or a wide variety of other historically important documents and speeches. This category could also include passage pairs, where one author responds directly to another, or two authors write on similar themes.

Founding Documents or Great Global Conversation passages are most often **persuasive**: the author or speaker attempts to persuade the reader or listener to agree with their position using techniques besides evidence and logical arguments. Persuasive passages might also use **appeals to emotion**, in which the author makes statements designed to make you *feel* that they are right, rather than providing evidence on which to build their argument.

In such passages, you should aim to identify the thesis, and how each portion of the passage works to support that thesis—either by providing evidence, or by using rhetorical techniques that have a compelling emotional effect on the reader. Examine how the author or speaker uses language, evidence, and arguments to emphasize certain points.

Historical documents frequently use dated language that might not be very familiar. They also address complex topics: the nature of liberty, the role of government, the relationship between individuals and society, and so on. Check out our reading list online for some recommended material to help you practice.

 For additional resources, please visit **ivyglobal.com/study**.

They're not exactly light reading, but don't worry! With practice, you can develop all the skills that you need to tackle these challenging passages.

Active Reading with Historical Passages

As with literature and science passages, you want to pay attention to claims and facts in the passage, as the author or speaker of the passage may be building an argument. But in historical passages, you are going to want to pay special attention to the way that the speaker or author uses **rhetoric**, or language which is designed to have a persuasive effect on a listener or reader. The techniques employed will vary and will depend upon the author's overall purpose. Analyzing these techniques will help you pinpoint the author's main argument and supporting points.

In historical passages, you should keep an eye out for all of the following elements:

Common Rhetorical Techniques		
Type	Description	Example
Rhetorical Emphasis	There are several techniques that speakers and authors might use to add emphasis to a point. They might repeat an important phrase or word several times, use several words in a row that all mean roughly the same thing, ask questions which they themselves answer, or use unusual or repetitive sentence structures to emphasize important points.	Were the original documents provided? No. Were uncensored copies provided? No. Was any reasonable effort made to share key information about the contents of the documents? No. Each and every request for additional information was totally and completely ignored.
Juxtaposition	Juxtaposition is used in order to highlight the contrast between the things being compared. A speaker or writer might place two very different things close together in a passage or speech, or provide a real-world example where two very different things meet.	In the shadow of scrap-heaps piled high with the discarded luxuries of the world's richest economies, there live and work some of the poorest people in the developing world.

	In addition to using devices like metaphors and similes, the speaker or author in a Historical passage might employ analogies to compare the relationships between different sorts of things. Unlike metaphors and similes, however, analogies are often used to imply that if the things being compared are alike in some ways, they may also be alike in other ways. Analogies can also be used to make complex ideas easier to understand.	The government is like a pair of work boots: it protects us from injury and discomfort, but only if it is properly fitted. A pair of work boots which is too large or too small may do more harm than good, and had better be replaced.
Analogies		

Part 3 Practice: Social Studies and History Passages

Below is an example passage. Read the passage, paying special attention to the elements we have discussed, and then answer the accompanying practice questions.

This passage is adapted from John F. Kennedy, "Speech on His Religion," originally delivered to the Greater Houston Ministerial Association on September 12, 1960. President John F. Kennedy was the first Catholic to be elected president of the United States. During the campaign for the presidency, Kennedy faced attacks over the positions of the Catholic Church, and charges that as president he would "take orders from the Pope." In this speech, Kennedy addresses the "religious issue."

While the so-called "religious issue"
is necessarily and properly the chief topic
here tonight, I want to emphasize from
Line the outset that I believe that we have far
5 more critical issues to face in the 1960
election: the spread of Communist
influence, until it now festers 90 miles off
the coast of Florida; the humiliating
treatment of our president and vice
10 president by those who no longer respect
our power; the hungry children I saw in
West Virginia; the old people who cannot
pay their doctors' bills; the families forced
to give up their farms; an America with
15 too many slums, with too few schools,
and too late to the moon and outer space.
These are the real issues which should
decide this campaign. And they are not
religious issues—for war and hunger and
20 ignorance and despair know no religious

religious barriers. But because I am a
Catholic, and no Catholic has ever been
elected president, the real issues in this
campaign have been obscured—perhaps
25 deliberately, in some quarters less
responsible than this.
So it is apparently necessary for me to
state once again not what kind of church I
believe in—for that should be important
30 only to me—but what kind of America I
believe in. I believe in an America where
the separation of church and barriers. But
because I am a Catholic, and state is
absolute, where no Catholic prelate would
35 tell the president (should he be Catholic)
how to act, and no Protestant minister
would tell his parishioners for whom to
vote; where no church or church school is
granted any public funds or political
40 preference; and where no man is denied
public office merely because his religion
differs from the president who might
appoint him or the people who might
elect him.
45 I believe in an America that is
officially neither Catholic, Protestant, nor
Jewish; where no public official either
requests or accepts instructions on public
policy from the Pope, the National Council
50 of Churches, or any other ecclesiastical
source; where no religious body seeks to

impose its will directly or indirectly upon the general populace or the public acts of its officials; and where religious liberty is
55 so indivisible that an act against one church is treated as an act against all.

For while this year it may be a Catholic against whom the finger of suspicion is pointed, in other years it has
60 been, and may someday be again, a Jew, or a Quaker, or a Unitarian, or a Baptist. It was Virginia's harassment of Baptist preachers, for example, that helped lead to Jefferson's statute of religious
65 freedom. Today I may be the victim, but tomorrow it may be you—until the whole fabric of our harmonious society is ripped at a time of great national peril.

Finally, I believe in an America where
70 religious intolerance will someday end; where all men and all churches are treated as equal; where every man has the same right to attend or not to attend the church of his choice; where there is no Catholic
75 vote, no anti-Catholic vote, no bloc voting of any kind; and where Catholics, Protestants, and Jews, at both the lay and the pastoral level, will refrain from those attitudes of disdain and division which
80 have so often marred their works in the past, and promote instead the American ideal of brotherhood.

That is the kind of America in which I believe. And it represents the kind of
85 presidency in which I believe: a great office that must neither be humbled by making it the instrument of any one religious group, nor tarnished by arbitrarily withholding its occupancy
90 from the members of any one religious group.

I believe in a president whose views on religion are his own private affair, neither imposed by him upon the nation, nor imposed by the nation upon him as a condition to holding that office.

1

Kennedy's main purpose in this passage is to

A) urge Americans to reconsider their religious views, in light of the many issues facing society.

B) argue against providing government funds to religious organizations.

C) express his view that religion and politics should be strictly separated.

D) suggest that since all churches are equal they deserve equal representation in government.

2

Kennedy's tone in lines 6-8 ("the spread … Florida") suggests that he feels that "Communist influence" is

A) slowly decaying until it finally disappears.

B) an offensive problem about which too little has been done.

C) an unpleasant but mostly harmless irritation.

D) the cause of most of the other problems in the United States.

3

Lines 65-68 ("Today I … peril") are most likely intended to suggest that

A) when one religious group is treated unfairly, others are more likely to be treated unfairly in the future.

B) people are most likely to discriminate on the basis of religion during times of crisis.

C) religious diversity and political harmony cannot exist in the same society.

D) religious discrimination could lead to divisions which harm all Americans.

Section 4
Understanding the Facts

In this section, you will learn about some common question types associated with every passage. These question types fall under the category of **Information and Ideas**, which means that they require you to understand the facts of the passage. This includes understanding specific lines from a passage, identifying main ideas, and analyzing how parts of the text relate to one another. In this section, we will cover questions on:

- Words and Phrases in Context
- Explicit and Implicit Meaning
- Summarizing, Central Ideas, and Relationships
- Command of Evidence
- Analogical Reasoning

We'll describe each question type and the strategies for answering it, followed by practice exercises so you can try questions on your own. At the end of this section you will have a chance to apply what you've learned to full-length practice passages.

Words in Context
Part 1

Every passage or pair of passages will be accompanied by one or two **Words in Context** questions. These questions will give you a word or phrase from the passage and ask you to select the answer choice that could best replace it. Some answer choices will be valid synonyms of the word or phrase you are asked about, but only one will make sense in the original sentence. Other words may work in the context of the sentence, but don't convey the exact same meaning or have the same connotation.

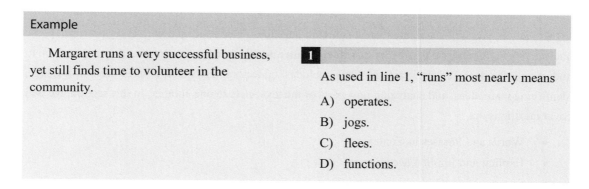

Example

    Margaret runs a very successful business, yet still finds time to volunteer in the community.

1

As used in line 1, "runs" most nearly means

A) operates.

B) jogs.

C) flees.

D) functions.

This question is asking you to identify the word that could best replace "runs" in the original sentence. Notice that all of the answer choices are possible meanings of "runs"—your job is to find the meaning that is closest to what the author of the passage intended. Here are some strategies to help you identify this meaning.

Think for Yourself

As you learned in Section 2, it is helpful to think for yourself when answering questions. You should use this approach for Words in Context questions. Refer back to the passage, and try thinking of a suitable word or phrase to replace the one you are asked about. Be sure to read the full sentence in which the word or phrase appears. You can also read a few lines above and below to help you understand the context in which the word or phrase is being used.

    Margaret runs a very successful business, yet still finds time to volunteer in the community.

1

As used in line 1, "runs" most nearly means

A) operates.

B) jogs.

C) flees.

D) functions.

What is a word you can think of to define "runs" in this sentence? Perhaps something like "manages," as the sentence refers to a business that Margaret is in charge of. Now you can compare this idea to the answer choices. The word "operates" is closest to your word "manages," and is the only answer that captures the right meaning for the sentence.

(B) and (C) refer to the physical act of running. (D) refers to the way something works, as in "The car only runs/functions if it is filled with premium gas." Notice that these are all valid ways you can use the word "runs," but only the first answer would make sense in the original sentence.

Plugging In Options

As you learned in Chapter 1, you can test each answer choice by plugging it back into the original sentence to see what choice works best in context. Remember that the correct answer must provide nearly the same meaning as the original word. Compare your choice to the original sentence and ensure it matches the context of the lines above and below in order to be sure of your answer.

If you weren't sure of your answer for the example question above, you could try plugging each answer choice into the original sentence to see which one makes sense:

- ✓ Margaret operates a very successful business …
- X Margaret jogs a very successful business …
- X Margaret flees a very successful business …
- X Margaret functions a very successful business …

Only answer choice (A) makes sense when you plug it into the original sentence, so you know (A) must be the correct answer.

Part 1 Practice: Words in Context

For each question below, choose the answer choice that most nearly means the same thing as the word or phrase specified in each question.

The safety of the nation has been threatened, and it is imperative that we respond. Though we do not go lightly into
Line this conflict, we go with the certainty that
5 to act is to protect our great country. We will call upon our citizens to act bravely in this time of need. Sacrifices will need to be made, but we are confident that our citizens are ready and able to take on these
10 challenges.

1

As used in line 6, "call upon" most nearly means

A) shout at.
B) visit briefly.
C) appeal to.
D) cry for.

Before they set out, Charu provided her companions with some practical advice about hiking in Death Valley. She warned
Line them not to bring overly heavy packs, and
5 to make sure that they wore shoes that were comfortable and broken in. A few of her companions asked her about food and water, and Charu explained that, on the route they were taking, they would only be
10 gone for a maximum of five hours and should pack accordingly.

The lab has produced some groundbreaking research in recent years. A significant amount of press has been
Line devoted to their results, leading to a
5 significant influx of donors. But the most intriguing aspect of this new scholarship is its synthesis of modern and traditional techniques.

Hank arrived at the party a little late, and hurried to hang up his coat and hat and join the rest of the guests. He found, to his
Line embarrassment, that he was underdressed,
5 and spent the first hour pressed against the back wall sipping his drink. The hostess, his cousin's college friend, eventually pulled him into a conversation with a viscount and an earl. Hank was not used to
10 being in the company of such refined individuals, and strove to choose his words and references carefully.

The doctor suggested an aggressive treatment plan upon learning of her patient's rare diagnosis. She explained the
Line various options open to him, and provided
5 an analysis of the drawbacks and benefits of each one. After, she encouraged her patient to follow up with her if he had any other questions.

As used in line 2, "practical" most nearly means

A) functional.

B) applied.

C) useful.

D) grounded.

As used in line 7, "synthesis" most nearly means

A) fusion.

B) alloy.

C) conflation.

D) overlap.

As used in line 11, "refined" most nearly means

A) developed.

B) unadulterated.

C) cultured.

D) delicate.

As used in line 1, "aggressive" most nearly means

A) intensive.

B) violent.

C) militant.

D) enterprising.

Today's economists are quick to point out that constant spending on consumer goods could leave you saddled with debt.
Line Even with salaries increasing in numerous
5 fields, consumer spending is vastly outpacing income. Worse is when you use credit cards to pay for new goods, and then delay paying off the debts for these new items; interest quickly accrues and you end
10 up spending nearly double the cost of the original item.

6

As used in lines 3-4, "saddled with" most nearly means

A) burdened by.

B) packed with.

C) freighted by.

D) strained with.

Explicit and Implicit Meaning
Part 2

All passages will usually have questions that ask you about specific ideas discussed in the text. These questions can come in two forms: Explicit Meaning and Implicit Meaning questions.

Explicit Meaning

Explicit Meaning questions ask you about something stated more or less directly in the passage. "Explicit" means direct or fully expressed. To answer these questions, you will need to refer back to the text and read closely to understand what the author wrote. Use the Process of Elimination to knock out any answers that contradict what the author wrote, or any answers that are not directly stated in the passage. You are looking for ideas the author has stated directly.

Here are some ways that Explicit Meaning questions might be phrased:

- According to the passage, which choice best describes …
- The author suggests that …
- The narrator indicates that …

Remember the passage about the artist Cavallini from Section 2? Let's have a look at it again and see how an Explicit Meaning question about that passage would work.

Example

This passage is adapted from Daniel Zalewski, "Under a Shroud of Kitsch May Lie a Master's Art." ©2001 by The New York Times Company.

Tommaso Strinati clambers to the top of the rickety scaffold and laughs. "It's a good thing that all this Baroque work is so
Line unimpressive," he says, pointing at the
5 clumsy trompe l'oeil painting covering the wall in front of him. "Otherwise, we might not have been allowed to scrape it off!"

A 28-year-old art historian, he is standing 16 feet above the marble floor of
10 San Pasquale Baylon chapel, a long-neglected nook of Santa Maria in Aracoeli, a Franciscan basilica in the center of Rome. Last year, Mr. Strinati, who is still a graduate student, began
15 studying the church's history. Records suggested that the Roman artist Pietro Cavallini—a painter and mosaicist whose greatest works have been destroyed—spent years decorating Aracoeli toward
20 the end of the 13th century. Yet only one small Cavallini fresco, in the church's left transept, remained visible. Mr. Strinati wondered: had other Cavallini frescoes been painted over with inferior work? And
25 if so, could modern restorers uncover them?

"The answer to both questions was yes," Mr. Strinati says. A close-up examination of the chapel's walls last summer revealed ghostly images lying beneath the surface. The entire chapel, it seemed, was a painted palimpsest. And when a heavy altarpiece was removed from one wall, a remarkably tender portrait of the Madonna and Child was found hidden behind it.

After months of careful paint-peeling, what has been uncovered are dazzling fragments of a late-medieval masterpiece completed shortly after 1285. Although the Aracoeli fresco is not signed, the figures strongly resemble those in a surviving Cavallini work, the resplendent "Last Judgment" fresco at nearby Santa Cecilia.

Mr. Strinati has grand ambitions for his discovery. He hopes that in a few years the fully restored fresco will not only rescue Cavallini's name from obscurity, but also upend the widespread notion that the first flowers of the Renaissance budded in Florence, not Rome. For the fresco's lifelike figures—in particular, an impish Christ child with charmingly flushed cheeks—suggest to Strinati that Cavallini may have anticipated some of the extraordinary naturalistic innovations that have long been credited to the Florentine artist Giotto.

Moreover, the Aracoeli fragments may provide a critical new clue in a decades-old battle concerning the "St. Francis Legend," the 1296 fresco cycle at Assisi, universally recognized as one of the foundations of the Renaissance. For centuries, the 28-scene cycle—which recounts the life of the saint with a narrative zest and compositional depth that leave the flat tableaus of the Byzantine era far behind—was attributed to Giotto. But since the 1930's, various scholars have questioned this judgment, claiming that the Assisi cycle doesn't resemble Giotto's other work. Now, the Aracoeli discovery is ammunition for Italian art historians who believe that Cavallini might actually be the primary creative force behind the "St. Francis Legend."

The growing debate about Cavallini's importance was the occasion for a symposium in Rome in November. *La Republicca*, an Italian daily, has cast the debate as "War Between Rome and Florence." Mr. Strinati is enjoying the ruckus. "I had a hunch that there was more Cavallini lurking around here," he says of the Aracoeli basilica. "But I didn't expect to find an exquisite work that could shake up the history of art."

2

According to the passage, Cavallini

A) was widely known before the recent discovery of his frescos.

B) was the undisputed creator of the "St. Francis Legend."

C) painted frescos exclusively in Roman churches.

D) had some of his work painted over by later artists.

To answer this question, see which choice is supported by information clearly stated in the text. Answer choice (A) directly contradicts the passage, as we're told that Mr. Strinati wants to "rescue Cavallini's name from obscurity" (line 49). Answer choice (B) also contradicts the passage, as lines 71-79 state that "since the 1930's, various scholars have questioned" whether Giotto painted the "St. Francis Legend." Therefore, you can eliminate both (A) and (B).

Answer choice (C) is simply not supported by the passage. While the passage lists two churches in which Cavallini frescoes have been found, you are not given any other information about where else he may have painted. Remember that explicit meaning questions are asking about what is presented in the passage, so avoid making assumptions. You can eliminate answer choice (C).

You are left with answer choice (D), which matches exactly the information from the passage. In the first paragraph, Strinati points to a "clumsy trompe l'oeil painting" in front of him while discussing unimpressive Baroque art. This is the type of art he was removing to reveal Cavallini's frescoes, so it must have been painted later. Because (D) is the only answer stated directly in the passage, it is the correct answer.

Implicit Meaning

Implicit Meaning questions ask you about ideas that are presented more subtly in the text. "Implicit" means implied rather than stated directly. For these questions you will need to read between the lines or combine clues from different parts of the text to understand what the author is suggesting. In some passages this may mean understanding literary devices such as metaphor. These concepts will be discussed further in Section 5.

Here are some ways that Implicit Meaning questions might be phrased:

- It can reasonably be inferred from the passage that …
- The passage most strongly suggests that …
- In lines 30-31 the phrase "better late than never" implies that …

Be careful not to take everything the author says too literally when answering Implicit Meaning questions. In real life, you are probably good at picking up on implied meanings. For example, if your friend says she is "thrilled" to take out the trash but rolls her eyes as she says it, you know she is being sarcastic. Similarly, things like the tone and structure of a passage can help indicate what an author really means.

Let's look at another question about the Cavallini passage to see how Implicit Meaning questions work.

Example
The passage most strongly suggests that
A) Strinati believes Cavallini to be a superior artist to Giotto.
B) similarities between paintings can be used to determine who painted them.
C) Baroque artwork is considered less impressive than Renaissance pieces.
D) Renaissance frescoes were frequently painted over in Italian churches.

Which of these ideas are suggested by the passage? While answer choice (A) may be true, there is no information in the passage to support this idea. We know that Strinati thinks highly of Cavallini's work because of the adjectives he uses, like when he calls it "exquisite" at the end of the passage. However, he never compares Cavallini to Giotto.

Answer choices (C) and (D) are similarly not things that you could reasonably conclude on the basis of the passage. You are not given wider information about the Renaissance or about Baroque artwork in general; the passage only discusses the artwork at the Aracoeli basilica. While implied meaning questions require you to extrapolate slightly from the passage, you must still have evidence in the text to support your answer! Be careful of answers like these that are too broad.

Answer choice (B) can be supported by two different portions of the text. First, lines 71-79 indicate some historians believed Giotto had painted the "St. Francis Legend," but they began to question this because it does not resemble his other work. Lines 40-45 suggest that the Aracoeli frescoes are likely Cavallini's because they do resemble his other work. These both indicate that historians look at similarities between paintings to help determine if the same person painted them. Therefore, (B) is the correct answer.

Part 2 Practice: Explicit and Implicit Meaning

Review the techniques we discussed in Section 2, and mark up and summarize this passage excerpt. Then, answer the Explicit and Implicit Meaning questions using the strategies you just learned.

This passage is adapted from Steve Lohr, "The Vaccination Effect: 100 Million Cases of Contagious Disease Prevented." ©2013 by The New York Times Company.

Vaccination programs for children have prevented more than 100 million cases of serious contagious disease in the
Line United States since 1924, according to a
5 new study published in *The New England Journal of Medicine*. The research, led by scientists at the University of Pittsburgh's Graduate School of Public Health, analyzed public health reports going back
10 to the 19th century. The reports covered 56 diseases, but the article in the journal focused on seven: polio, measles, rubella, mumps, hepatitis A, diphtheria and pertussis, and whooping cough.
15 Researchers analyzed disease reports before and after the times when vaccines became commercially available. Put simply, the estimates for prevented cases came from the falloff in disease reports
20 after vaccines were licensed and widely available. The researchers projected the number of cases that would have occurred had the pre-vaccination patterns continued as the nation's population increased.
25 The University of Pittsburgh researchers also looked at death rates, but decided against including an estimate in the journal article, largely because death certificate data became more reliable and
30 consistent only in the 1960s, the researchers said. But Dr. Donald S. Burke, the dean of Pittsburgh's Graduate School of Public Health and an author of the medical journal article, said that a reasonable
35 projection of prevented deaths based on known mortality rates in the disease categories would be three million to four million.

1

All of the following are directly addressed in the passage EXCEPT

A) how researchers estimated the preventative impact of vaccinations.

B) why the researchers did not include death rate estimates in the journal article.

C) some diseases for which vaccines became commercially available.

D) why death certificate data only become reliable in the 1960s.

2

Which of the following statements is supported by the passage?

A) Childhood vaccination programs can be effective at preventing certain contagious diseases.

B) Without the effect of successful vaccinations, the American population would have soared.

C) It is difficult for researchers to obtain reliable death certificate data.

D) Vaccinations for certain diseases are much more effective than vaccinations for other diseases.

3

It can reasonably be inferred from the passage that

A) most vaccines were very expensive when first introduced.

B) some vaccines became commercially available around the 1920s.

C) American public health reports only date back to the 19th century.

D) it is impossible to accurately predict the effect of disease on population growth.

4

The passage most strongly suggests that

A) the mortality rates for all diseases are well-known today.

B) scientists may choose not to publish all data estimates they make.

C) researchers always struggle to create accurate predictions when working with historical data.

D) the diseases the scientists focused on in their publication were those with the highest mortality rates.

Summarizing, Central Ideas, and Relationships

Part 3

There are several types of questions on the SAT Reading Test that require you to summarize ideas in the text, identify central ideas of the whole text, and examine relationships among these ideas. Be sure you are using the active reading and summarizing strategies discussed in Section 2 as you read each passage. Referring to the summaries you have already made will make these questions much easier!

Summarizing

Summarizing questions ask you to identify a reasonable summary of specific parts of the passage. This will require you to paraphrase certain lines from the text, which means to provide a short, clear restatement of what you have read. The techniques you learned about summarizing in Section 2 will help you to paraphrase concisely and accurately, so review that section for guidance.

If you are asked for a summary of a paragraph you can also refer to your notes and paragraph summaries. Then, compare your summary to the answer choices. Be sure you select an answer that is focused on the most important ideas of the paragraph. Make sure your answer contains ideas discussed within the paragraph in question rather than elsewhere in the passage, and make sure it is truly the focus of the paragraph and not merely a detail.

Here are some ways that Summarizing questions might be phrased:

- Which best summarizes lines 63-82?
- Which choice best summarizes the first paragraph of the passage?
- Which choice best summarizes the passage?

Moreover, the Aracoeli fragments may provide a critical new clue in a decades-old battle concerning the "St. Francis

Line Legend," the 1296 fresco cycle at Assisi,
65 universally recognized as one of the foundations of the Renaissance. For centuries, the 28-scene cycle— which recounts the life of the saint with a narrative zest and compositional depth
70 that leave the flat tableaus of the Byzantine era far behind—was attributed to Giotto. But since the 1930's, various scholars have questioned this judgment, claiming that the Assisi cycle doesn't
75 resemble Giotto's other work. Now, the Aracoeli discovery is ammunition for Italian art historians who believe that Cavallini might actually be the primary creative force behind the "St. Francis
80 Legend."

 1

Which best summarizes lines 60-79?

A) The Aracoeli discovery has contributed to the debate about who painted the "St. Francis Legend."

B) The "St. Francis Legend" is important as an example of early Renaissance work.

C) Many scholars doubt that Giotto was the artist responsible for the "St. Francis Legend."

D) Cavallini was almost certainly the artist who painted the "St. Francis Legend."

Here, only answer choice (A) provides an overall summary of the paragraph. Answer choices (B) and (C) are too narrowly focused, and answer choice (D) makes a judgment that goes beyond what can be supported by the passage.

Central Ideas

Determining Central Ideas and Themes questions ask you about the central ideas that are the focus of the text. We'll call these "Central Ideas" questions. To answer them, review the paragraph summaries you created to come up with an overall summary or to spot recurring themes in the passage. Then look for the answer choice that best matches your prediction.

You can also use Process of Elimination to knock out incorrect answer choices. Check each option to be sure it meets the following two criteria: it is true according to the passage and it deals with most of the passage.

Making sure your answer is true according to the passage helps you knock out answer choices that mention new information or go beyond the passage. For example, just because a passage suggests that a new technology is a good idea does not mean that the author believes it is the best solution to a problem, unless that is stated in the text. Be wary of answer choices that include stronger opinions than the passage itself.

Ensuring your answer to a Central Ideas question deals with most of the passage helps you stay focused on the big picture of the passage, rather than details. Just because something is mentioned in the passage does not necessarily mean it is a main idea! Look for ideas that are mentioned multiple times or are discussed in-depth across multiple lines and paragraphs.

Here are some ways that Central Ideas questions might be phrased:

- The passage primarily focuses on …
- What is the author's main point about …
- The central claim of the passage is that …

With these ideas in mind, let's look at a Central Ideas question about the Cavallini passage. You can find it in Part 2 of this chapter if you need to refresh your memory.

Example

The events presented in the passage are best described as

A) a potential solution to the mystery of who painted a specific work of art.
B) one researcher's quest which is of little interest to other historians.
C) the painstaking removal of certain artwork to reveal more valuable pieces.
D) a new discovery with potentially major implications for art history.

Answer choice (A) demonstrates the second type of wrong answer discussed above, as it does not deal with the entire passage. While the mystery of who painted the "St. Francis Legend" is important, it is too specific to be considered the main idea of the passage as a whole. Rather, it serves as one example of how the discovery of Cavallini's work might impact art history in Italy. Answer choice (C) is also too narrow, because it only discusses events in the first few paragraphs of the passage.

Answer choice (B) does not meet our first criterion, as it is not true according to the passage. Strinati's discovery and attempts to rescue Cavallini's work are described as having a big impact on other art historians and leading to many important debates. Therefore, they *are* of interest to other historians.

Answer choice (D) captures all of the main ideas of the passage. It first mentions discovery, which relates to the first half of the passage about Cavallini's hidden frescoes. It also notes how this will impact the art world, which is what the author discusses in the final three paragraphs. You've found your answer!

Relationships

Some questions will ask you to describe the ways parts of the passage relate to one another. **Understanding Relationships** questions will ask you to identify relationships between individuals, events, or ideas in a passage. We'll refer to these as "Relationship" questions. These relationships may be explicitly stated, or may be implied and require you to read between the lines.

To answer these questions, consider what elements you are asked about and put the relationship between them into your own words. As always, this ensures that you know what you are looking for and will be precise when selecting your answer.

To figure out the relationship between elements, look back to the passage. Where are the people or ideas mentioned, and what is said about them? You can also refer back to any important parts of the passage you marked up, or the summaries you made for each paragraph.

Here are some ways that Relationships questions might be phrased:

- Based on the passage, which choice best describes the relationship between …
- The author's statement in lines 29-31 implies that purines and pyrimidines …
- The author indicates that, in comparison to individuals, traditional organizations have tended to be …

Let's look at a Relationship question about the Cavallini passage to practice these strategies.

Example
Based on the passage, which choice best describes the relationship between Cavallini and Giotto?

A) Giotto may have anticipated Cavallini's work.

B) Cavallini may have anticipated Giotto's work.

C) Giotto is a more contemporary artist than Cavallini.

D) Giotto is a less contemporary artist than Cavallini.

First, try to think of what you know about these two artists from the passage. You know that they worked around the same time period and have both been credited with the same work of art. New discoveries about Cavallini suggest he may have anticipated some of Giotto's techniques. Now see which answer choice best matches what you know.

You can use the Process of Elimination to knock out choices (C) and (D) because you know the artists painted around the same time. There is nothing in the passage to support answer (A). However, answer choice (B) matches what you know about the artists, and is the correct response!

Try another Relationship question from this passage:

Here, only answer choice (B) is supported by the passage. Remember that Strinati is trying to "upend the widespread notion that the first flowers of the Renaissance budded in Florence" (lines 50-52). Therefore, you can infer that it is generally believed that Florence started the Renaissance and other cities followed. Choices (A) and (C) directly contradict the idea that Florence started the Renaissance, while choice (D) talks about the abandonment instead of the adoption of Renaissance styles, which is unsupported by the passage.

Part 3 Practice: Summarizing, Central Ideas, and Relationships

Review the techniques we discussed in Section 2, and mark up and make summaries for this passage excerpt. Then, answer the Summarizing, Central Ideas, and Relationships questions using the strategies you just learned.

This passage is adapted from Robert Lee Hotz, "A Neuron's Obsession Hints at Biology of Thought." ©2009 by Dow Jones & Company.

Neurons process and transmit information through electrical and chemical signals, and researchers have
Line discovered neurons that respond only to
5 certain famous figures.

Probing deep into human brains, a team of scientists discovered a neuron roused only by Ronald Reagan, another cell smitten by the actress Halle Berry,
10 and a third devoted solely to Mother Teresa. Testing other single human neurons, they located a brain cell that would rather watch an episode of "The Simpsons" than Madonna.
15 In one sense, these findings are merely noise. They arise from rare recordings of electrical activity in brain cells, collected by neuroscientists at the University of California, Los Angeles, during a decade
20 of experiments with patients awaiting brain surgery for severe epilepsy. These tingles of electricity, however, gave the researchers the opportunity to locate neurons that help link our perceptions,
25 memories and self-awareness.

In their most recent work this year, the research team reported that a single human neuron could recognize a personality through pictures, text, or the sound of a
30 name—no matter how that person was presented. In tests, one brain cell reacted only to Oprah Winfrey; another just to Luke Skywalker; a third singled out Argentine soccer star Diego Maradona.
35 Each neuron appeared to join together pieces of sensory information into a single mental impression. The researchers

believe these cells are evidence that it only takes a simple circuit of neurons to
40 encode an idea, perception, or memory.

"These neurons will fire to the person no matter how you present them," says bioengineer Rodrigo Quian Quiroga at the U.K.'s University of Leicester who
45 studied the neurons with colleagues at UCLA and the California Institute of Technology. "All that we do, all that we think, all that we see is encoded by neurons. How do the neurons in our brain
50 create all our perceptions of the world, all our emotions, all our thinking?"

1

Which of the following best summarizes lines 26-34?

A) Individual neurons can identify personalities presented in different forms.

B) Individual neurons combine different pieces of information using a simple circuit.

C) Every neuron in the human brain is capable of identifying different celebrities.

D) Famous personalities can be presented in a variety of ways and still be recognizable.

2

The passage primarily focuses on which of the following characteristics of neurons?

A) Their ability to recognize people and personalities

B) Their involvement in conditions like epilepsy

C) Their ability to be recorded during rare forms of research

D) Their profound effect on all human perceptions

3

Based on the passage, which choice best describes the relationship between neurons and celebrities?

A) Every neuron can recognize all celebrities.

B) Every neuron can recognize one celebrity.

C) A single neuron can recognize a single celebrity.

D) All celebrities are recognized by all neurons.

Command of Evidence
Part 4

As we discussed in Section 2, you should always be able to support any answer you choose by referring to words or lines in the passage. On the redesigned SAT Reading Test, there are also questions in each passage that explicitly test this skill—two **Command of Evidence** questions that ask you to identify the support for your answer to another question. We'll refer to these as "Evidence" questions.

Evidence questions will list four different selections from the passage, and ask which one provides the best evidence to support your answer to the previous question. You should be sure you have answered the previous question before you attempt an Evidence question. Evidence questions are always worded as follows:

- Which choice provides the best evidence for the answer to the previous question?

Refer Back

Once you see that you are being asked an Evidence question, refer back to your answer to the previous question and consider why you selected it. Find the paragraph or lines that supported your choice. Then, look at each answer choice for the Evidence question. Look for the choice that is a match for the paragraph or lines you identified, or for a choice that could be another piece of evidence for your answer to the previous question. Be sure to read each line reference you are given in its original context in the passage.

Example

This passage is adapted from Daniel Zalewski, "Under a Shroud of Kitsch May Lie a Master's Art." ©2001 by The New York Times Company.

Tommaso Strinati clambers to the top of the rickety scaffold and laughs. "It's a good thing that all this Baroque work is so
Line unimpressive," he says, pointing at the
5 clumsy trompe l'oeil painting covering the wall in front of him. "Otherwise, we might not have been allowed to scrape it off!"
  A 28-year-old art historian, he is standing 16 feet above the marble floor of
10 San Pasquale Baylon chapel, a long-neglected nook of Santa Maria in Aracoeli, a Franciscan basilica in the center of Rome. Last year, Mr. Strinati, who is still a graduate student, began
15 studying the church's history. Records suggested that the Roman artist Pietro Cavallini—a painter and mosaicist whose greatest works have been destroyed—spent years decorating Aracoeli toward
20 the end of the 13th century. Yet only one small Cavallini fresco, in the church's left transept, remained visible. Mr. Strinati wondered: had other Cavallini frescoes been painted over with inferior work? And
25 if so, could modern restorers uncover them?

"The answer to both questions was yes," Mr. Strinati says. A close-up examination of the chapel's walls last
30 summer revealed ghostly images lying beneath the surface. The entire chapel, it seemed, was a painted palimpsest. And when a heavy altarpiece was removed from one wall, a remarkably tender
35 portrait of the Madonna and Child was found hidden behind it.

After months of careful paint-peeling, what has been uncovered are dazzling fragments of a late-medieval masterpiece
40 completed shortly after 1285. Although the Aracoeli fresco is not signed, the figures strongly resemble those in a surviving Cavallini work, the resplendent "Last Judgment" fresco at nearby Santa
45 Cecilia.

Mr. Strinati has grand ambitions for his discovery. He hopes that in a few years the fully restored fresco will not only rescue Cavallini's name from
50 obscurity, but also upend the widespread notion that the first flowers of the Renaissance budded in Florence, not Rome. For the fresco's lifelike figures—in particular, an impish Christ child with
55 charmingly flushed cheeks—suggest to Strinati that Cavallini may have anticipated some of the extraordinary naturalistic innovations that have long been credited to the Florentine artist
60 Giotto.

Moreover, the Aracoeli fragments may provide a critical new clue in a decades-old battle concerning the "St. Francis Legend," the 1296 fresco cycle at Assisi,
65 universally recognized as one of the foundations of the Renaissance. For centuries, the 28-scene cycle—which recounts the life of the saint with a narrative zest and compositional depth
70 that leave the flat tableaus of the

Byzantine era far behind—was attributed to Giotto. But since the 1930's, various scholars have questioned this judgment, claiming that the Assisi cycle doesn't
75 resemble Giotto's other work. Now, the Aracoeli discovery is ammunition for Italian art historians who believe that Cavallini might actually be the primary creative force behind the "St. Francis
80 Legend."

The growing debate about Cavallini's importance was the occasion for a symposium in Rome in November. *La Republicca*, an Italian daily, has cast the
85 debate as "War Between Rome and Florence." Mr. Strinati is enjoying the ruckus. "I had a hunch that there was more Cavallini lurking around here," he says of the Aracoeli basilica. "But I
90 didn't expect to find an exquisite work that could shake up the history of art."

4

The passage most strongly suggests that the discovery of Cavallini's work

A) was a fortuitous accident.

B) will impact art history broadly.

C) is one of many discoveries in the Aracoeli basilica.

D) was a shocking surprise for Tommasso Strinati.

5

Which choice provides the best evidence for the answer to the previous question?

A) Lines 28-31 ("A close-up … surface")

B) Lines 37-40 ("After months … 1285")

C) Lines 65-71 ("For centuries … Giotto")

D) Lines 80-82 ("The growing … November")

First select your answer to the implicit meaning question. Which one can you support with information from the passage? Answer choices (A) and (D) contradict the passage, as you are told that Strinati had a hunch that he would find more work by Cavallini, and worked purposively to uncover this work. Answer choice (C) could be true, but the passage never discusses other discoveries in the Aracoeli basilica, so you cannot support this answer.

Answer choice (B) is supported in the passage by several ideas, such as the reconsideration of the "St. Francis Legend," Mr. Strinati's "grand ambitions," and other lines in the final three paragraphs. Therefore, (B) is the correct answer.

With this answer in mind, look at the options for the Evidence question. Remember that you are looking for the lines that most strongly suggest that Cavallini's work will have an impact on art history. Here is the question again:

> Which choice provides the best evidence for the answer to the previous question?
>
> A) Lines 28-31 ("A close-up … surface")
> B) Lines 37-40 ("After months … 1285")
> C) Lines 65-71 ("For centuries … Giotto")
> D) Lines 80-82 ("The growing … November")

Here, none of the answers mention the "St. Francis Legend," or quote Strinati. But remember that there can be lots of ways to support an answer choice! Answer choice (D) also suggests that the Cavallini discovery is making waves, as a symposium (a meeting to discuss a topic) was held to discuss how important this discovery might be. (D) is the correct response.

The other answer choices do not relate to the impact of the Cavallini discovery. Answer choice (C) is about Giotto, not Cavallini, so you can eliminate it. Answer choices (A) and (B) relate to characteristics of the Cavallini discovery but don't address the impact or importance the discovery may have for art history. You can knock them out as well.

Using the Evidence Question to Answer the Previous Question

If you're having trouble with an Evidence question, keep in mind that the lines that best support a given answer choice could be anywhere in the passage. An argument made in the second paragraph may be backed up by data or reasoning in the third or fourth paragraph, rather than appearing immediately after the argument.

If none of the answer choices seem to support your previous answer, take another look at each option and see if they might work in a creative or unexpected way. If they still don't seem to work, review the previous question. It is possible your original answer choice was incorrect and therefore does not match with the lines given in the Evidence question! If you ever change your answer to a question that precedes an Evidence question, be sure to redo the accompanying Evidence question as well. On the other hand, if you are stumped on a question that precedes an Evidence question, you may be able to look ahead to the line references for clues as to which answer will make sense.

Part 4 Practice: Evidence in a Passage

Review the techniques we discussed in Section 2, and mark up and make summaries for this passage excerpt. Then, answer the questions using the evidence strategies you just learned.

This passage is adapted from Kelly Crow, "Colombia's Art Scene Heats Up." ©2014 by Dow Jones & Company.

Across Colombia—from the walled coastal city of Cartagena to the sugar-cane fields outside Cali—there's a
Line palpable feeling of flux, of a society
5 shaking off its solitude and stretching out. Crime and poverty persist, but a measure of peace is making it safer to travel and do business across the region. This calm is also allowing Colombia to
10 export greater supplies of oil, gas, sugar, and cut flowers, boosting the pace of its economic growth. Last year alone, the country attracted nearly $16 billion in foreign investments. Luxury malls and
15 beach resorts are sprouting up to cater to the country's 36,000 high-net-worth individuals. Tourism campaigns cheekily play down Colombia's war-torn reputation with slogans such as "The only risk is
20 wanting to stay."

Similar wealth booms have recently helped transform China and Brazil into global art hubs, so it makes sense to see international curators and dealers booking
25 trips to Colombia now. New York's Museum of Modern Art, Houston's Museum of Fine Arts, and London's Serpentine Galleries, among others, have all recently sent delegations of curators
30 and patrons to scout art in Colombia.

Pablo León de la Barra, a curator for New York's Solomon R. Guggenheim Museum, was among the early explorers, and the art he's uncovered since is impressive, he
35 says. "For some, art has become a way of working through the communal trauma, but the younger ones are trying to use art as an instrument of usefulness for something else. There are many things at
40 play, but one of them is a desire for normalization."

Whenever curators and collectors start sniffing around a new region, dealers and auctioneers invariably follow, eager to
45 pounce on whatever the tastemakers discover. (A similar phenomenon has lately pushed up prices for China's Zeng Fanzhi and Brazil's Beatriz Milhazes.) In the past year, these market movers have
50 begun championing a potential poster boy for Colombia's rise in Oscar Murillo, the 28-year-old son of Cali sugar-cane farmers who now lives in London. Three years ago, Murillo's frenetic paintings—often
55 made with the help of relatives using dust and debris from his studio floor—were selling for as little as $10,000 apiece.

But last fall, Phillips in New York auctioned off one of the artist's 2011
60 canvases, Untitled (Drawings Off the Wall), for $401,000, or 10 times its highest estimate.

The passage most strongly suggests that

A) most Colombian artists now earn high prices for their work.

B) Colombia was not always as stable a country as it is now.

C) Colombian art has a long history of engaging dangerous themes.

D) Colombian art will become less popular as the initial interest subsides.

Which choice provides the best evidence for the answer to the previous question?

A) Lines 6-8 ("Crime … the region")

B) Lines 12-14 ("Last … investments")

C) Lines 31-35 ("Pablo … he says")

D) Lines 43-47 ("Whenever … tastemakers discover")

Based on the passage, which choice best describes the relationship between national prosperity and art?

A) Increased wealth in a nation leads to higher prices on the work of its oldest artists.

B) When a nation becomes less prosperous, it uses art to work through the trauma.

C) Economic prosperity can attract art buyers and collectors to a previously overlooked country.

D) As a country grows wealthier, its artists feel more encouraged to create.

Which choice provides the best evidence for the answer to the previous question?

A) Lines 9-12 ("This calm … growth")

B) Lines 14-17 ("Luxury malls … individuals")

C) Lines 21-25 ("Similar wealth … now")

D) Lines 60-64 ("But last … estimate")

Analogical Reasoning
Part 5

Analogical Reasoning questions ask you to find an answer choice that is analogous to (the same as) an idea or relationship presented in the passage. An **analogy** is an extended comparison between two things or situations. For example, if a character in a literature passage lies to a friend about a surprise party for them, you would look for an answer choice that presents an analogy for that situation—such as another situation where someone is harmlessly deceived for their own benefit.

These questions can be phrased in a variety of ways:

- Which of the following situations is most analogous to the problem presented in the passage?
- Which hypothetical situation involves the same paradox discussed by the author?
- The principle illustrated in lines 16-19 ("By … life") is best conveyed by which additional example?

Your job is to identify the situation that follows a similar pattern as an idea or relationship from the passage. The content or topics of the answer choices do not matter. Just because a passage is about cancer research does not mean the right answer will also be about cancer research, or scientific research at all. It might be about music, or politics, or any other subject, as long as it illustrates the same idea or reasoning as the original passage.

Use Your Own Words

To answer these questions, refer back to the passage and restate the idea, principle, or relationship you are asked about in your own words. Then look for an answer choice that matches your description.

A 28-year-old art historian, he is
Line standing 16 feet above the marble floor of
10 San Pasquale Baylon chapel, a long-
neglected nook of Santa Maria in
Aracoeli, a Franciscan basilica in the
center of Rome. Last year, Mr. Strinati,
who is still a graduate student, began
15 studying the church's history. Records
suggested that the Roman artist Pietro
Cavallini—a painter and mosaicist whose
greatest works have been destroyed—
spent years decorating Aracoeli toward the
20 end of the 13th century. Yet only one
small Cavallini fresco, in the church's left
transept, remained visible. Mr. Strinati
wondered: had other Cavallini frescoes
been painted over with inferior work? And
25 if so, could modern restorers uncover
them?

6

Which of the following situations is most analogous to the mystery presented in lines 15-22?

A) A muralist spent weeks sketching and eventually completed a beautiful design.

B) A lawmaker took less time than originally expected to draft a bill.

C) Dancers took a few minutes to practice but did not master new choreography.

D) A chef developed recipes for years but few survive today.

To answer this question, first put the "mystery" from the referenced lines into your own words. Cavallini spent years decorating Aracoeli, and yet there is very little art by him in the basilica. We would expect there to be a lot of Cavallini paintings in Aracoeli. You might phrase this "mystery" more generally as "spent lots of time but little to show for it" or "less work than expected."

Which answer choice best matches your description of these lines? Only answer choice (D) shows another scenario where someone produced "less work than expected." Notice that this answer choice does not need to be about art to be analogous to the idea from the passage. However, it closely mirrors the situation in lines 15-22, and even hints that there was more work at some point that was destroyed or lost, just as with Cavallini's art in the passage.

Answer choice (A) is about art but does not match the passage, because here the amount of effort seems to match the output. Answer choice (C) also doesn't match the passage—it is not surprising that dancers did not improve during only a few minutes. Choice (B) is almost the opposite of the passage, as more work was accomplished than expected. Therefore, none of these situations would be a good analogy for the mystery in the passage.

Part 5 Practice: Analogical Reasoning

Answer the following analogical reasoning questions using the approach you have just learned.

According to scientists, the relationship between sugar and adult-onset diabetes is different from what the population
Line generally believes it to be. Most people
5 believe that a high sugar diet leads directly to adult-onset diabetes. In reality, eating a diet high in refined sugar can lead to excess weight, and being overweight can predispose individuals to adult-onset
10 diabetes.

1

Which of the following situations is most analogous to the relationship between sugar and adult-onset diabetes?

A) Increased exercise can lead to both improved mood and lower cholesterol over time.

B) Studying leads to increased comprehension, and increased comprehension always ensures a higher grade.

C) Advertising can cause companies to grow rapidly, and expanding companies are more prone to mistakes.

D) Having a father who is colorblind can predispose a child to colorblindness.

As a new yoga instructor, Juri faced a challenge: guiding her students into the right alignment in their poses. As creative
Line as she was in her descriptions of each
5 position, it seemed they did not help her students recreate them. One day she began adopting the poses herself at the front of the class, hoping she could better describe them by focusing on her own muscle
10 movements. Instead, she looked up and saw her students perfectly copying her form on their own mats.

2

Which hypothetical situation involves the same approach ultimately used by the yoga instructor?

A) A rugby coach uses a video of professional games to explain a new strategy.

B) An electrician demonstrates to an assistant the process of rewiring.

C) Violin teachers have their students sing a melody before they attempt to play it.

D) A public speaker suggests a list of books to read for inspiration.

When the scandal came to light I must admit I was hardly surprised; the mayor did, after all, have a reputation for
Line deception and bending the truth. In a way,
5 then, I felt the journalists were nearly equally to blame. After all, was it not their job to investigate the credibility of claims, especially those coming from such an
10 untrustworthy figure? Instead of uncovering his secrets they had been busy propagating the mayor's lies.

3

The narrator's attitude towards the journalists is most similar to which example?

A) The advertisers who overlooked a key defect in a car they are promoting are nearly as responsible as the engineers who built it incorrectly.

B) Police officers who arrest criminals on the wrong charges should be reprimanded for their mistake.

C) It is not a driver's fault if she gets lost because the map she is using is outdated.

D) A mail officer who delivers a package to the wrong address is more responsible than the sender who miswrote the address.

Practice Set
Part 6

The following passages have been designed to test the question types you learned about in this section. Review the techniques we discussed in Section 2, and mark up and make summaries for this passage. Then, answer the questions using the strategies you just learned.

This passage is adapted from Gretchen Reynolds, "This Is Your Brain on Coffee." ©2013 by The New York Times Company.

For hundreds of years, coffee has been one of the two or three most popular beverages on earth. But it's only recently
Line that scientists are figuring out that the
5 drink has notable health benefits. In one large-scale epidemiological study from last year, researchers primarily at the National Cancer Institute parsed health information from more than 400,000
10 volunteers, ages 50 to 71, who were free of major diseases at the study's start in 1995. By 2008, more than 50,000 of the participants had died. But men who reported drinking two or three cups of
15 coffee a day were 10 percent less likely to have died than those who didn't drink coffee, while women drinking the same amount had 13 percent less risk of dying during the study. It's not clear exactly
20 what coffee had to do with their longevity, but the correlation is striking.
  Perhaps most consequential, animal experiments show that caffeine may reshape the biochemical environment
25 inside our brains in ways that could stave off dementia. In a 2012 experiment at the University of Illinois at Urbana-Champaign, mice were briefly starved of oxygen, causing them to lose the ability
30 to form memories. Half of the mice received a dose of caffeine that was the equivalent of several cups of coffee.
  After they were reoxygenated, the caffeinated mice regained their ability to

35 form new memories 33 percent faster than the uncaffeinated. Close examination of the animals' brain tissue showed that the caffeine disrupted the action of adenosine, a substance inside cells that usually
40 provides energy, but can become destructive if it leaks out when the cells are injured or under stress. The escaped adenosine can jump-start a biochemical cascade leading to inflammation, which
45 can disrupt the function of neurons, and potentially contribute to neurodegeneration or, in other words, dementia.
  In a 2012 study of humans, researchers from the University of South Florida and
50 the University of Miami tested the blood levels of caffeine in older adults with mild cognitive impairment, or the first glimmer of serious forgetfulness, a common precursor of Alzheimer's disease, and
55 then re-evaluated them two to four years later. Participants with little or no caffeine circulating in their bloodstreams were far more likely to have progressed to full-blown Alzheimer's than those whose
60 blood indicated they'd had about three cups' worth of caffeine.
  There's still much to be learned about the effects of coffee. "We don't know whether blocking the action of adenosine
65 is sufficient to prevent or lessen the effects of dementia," says Dr. Gregory G. Freund, a professor of pathology at the University of Illinois who led the 2012 study of mice. It is also unclear whether
70 caffeine by itself provides the benefits associated with coffee drinking or if

coffee contains other valuable ingredients. In a 2011 study by the same researchers at the University of South Florida, for
75 instance, mice genetically bred to develop Alzheimer's and then given caffeine alone did not fare as well on memory tests as those provided with actual coffee. Nor is there any evidence that mixing
80 caffeine with large amounts of sugar, as in energy drinks, is healthful. But a cup or three of coffee "has been popular for a long, long time," Dr. Freund says, "and there's probably good reasons for that."

1

The passage suggests the author would most likely agree with which of the following?

A) Current research does not yet show convincing health benefits of coffee.

B) The historical popularity of coffee is enough to demonstrate that its health benefits are significant.

C) It would be beneficial to conduct further research on the health benefits of coffee.

D) Doctors must begin advising patients at risk for dementia to increase their coffee intake.

2

Which choice provides the best evidence for the answer to the previous question?

A) Lines 22-26 ("Perhaps most … dementia")

B) Lines 62-63 ("There's still … coffee")

C) Lines 79-81 ("Nor … is healthful")

D) Lines 81-84 ("But … for that")

3

It can reasonably be inferred from the passage that

A) caffeine consumption is a major cause of Alzheimer's disease.

B) caffeine may stimulate memory formation under certain conditions.

C) once it is better understood, coffee will provide a cure for Alzheimer's disease.

D) coffee consumption will increase once its health benefits are publicized.

4

Based on the passage, which choice best describes the relationship between caffeine and coffee?

A) Coffee is only healthful when it contains caffeine.

B) Coffee may be healthier than isolated caffeine.

C) Coffee may be less healthy than isolated caffeine.

D) Coffee is most healthful when supplemented with additional caffeine.

5

Which choice provides the best evidence for the answer to the previous question?

A) Lines 30-32 ("Half of … coffee")

B) Lines56-61 ("Participants with … caffeine")

C) Lines 63-69 ("We don't … mice")

D) Lines 73-78 ("In … actual coffee")

6

According to the "large-scale epidemiological study" (line 6) cited in the passage, women participants who were coffee drinkers

A) were more likely to drink two to three cups of coffee a day than men.

B) were less likely to drink two to three cups of coffee a day than men.

C) were less likely to die than women who did not drink coffee.

D) were more likely to die than men who drank coffee.

7

Which of the following is most analogous to the description in lines 38-42 ("adenosine … under stress")?

A) Antibiotics are often helpful in fighting infections, but only if they are used consistently.

B) Even a small amount of arsenic can be dangerous, but consuming large amounts is deadly.

C) Humor gives an essay character, but can detract from the argument if used in the wrong context.

D) Operating power tools is very risky, except when done by trained professionals.

8

As used in line 54, "precursor" most nearly means

A) model.

B) prototype.

C) predecessor.

D) harbinger.

9

As used in line 77, "fare" most nearly means

A) travel.

B) survive.

C) perform.

D) happen.

This passage is adapted from Matt Ritchel, "The Search for Our Inner Lie Detectors." ©2014 by The New York Times Company.

Is a job applicant lying to you? What about your boss, or an entrepreneur who is promising to double your investment? Most of us are bad at spotting a lie, at least consciously. New research, published last month in *Psychological Science*, suggests that we have good instincts for judging liars, but that they are so deeply buried that we can't get at them.

This finding is the work of Leanne ten Brinke, a forensic psychologist. "Perhaps our own bodies know better than our conscious minds who is lying," explained Dr. ten Brinke, now at the Haas School of Business at the University of California, Berkeley.

It's well accepted that most of us are no better than a flip of the coin at seeing a lie. A classic experiment involves showing study subjects videotapes of people, some of whom are lying, who say they did not steal $100; the subjects correctly guess the liars about half the time. Dr. ten Brinke and her collaborators at Haas built on that experiment, with a twist: after the subjects watched the video and made their conscious assessments of who was lying, the researchers tried to measure the subjects' unconscious reactions.

To do so, the researchers flashed images of someone already seen in the videotape—but this time in milliseconds, indiscernible consciously. The subjects then completed a word task that involved placing "truth" words (like truthful, honest, valid) and "lie" words (dishonest, invalid, deceitful) into their proper categories. When study subjects were flashed a picture of a liar, they were significantly slower to lump words like truthful or honest into the "truth" category, but faster to lump words like deceitful into the "lie" category. The opposite was true when the subjects saw a truthful person. So, in general, the same people seemed better at detecting lies unconsciously than consciously. By scientific measures, the size of the effect was decidedly non-trivial, but not overwhelming.

There are many theories about why the ability to pick out liars gets lost in translation to consciousness. Dr. ten Brinke speculated that we tell one another little lies all the time—for survival, reproductive strategy, and so on—and that part of getting along socially is being able to let those harmless lies escape notice.

Is it possible to tap into the unconscious ability? "It's the million-dollar question," she said. The study fits into a rich history of lie-detection research, with some researchers saying they can read lies in facial expressions, and others arguing that liars just don't give off enough clear signals to allow detection. "The cues are so faint," said Dr. Bella DePaulo, a visiting professor of psychology at University of California, Santa Barbara and an expert in the science of lie detection. She said that there was some evidence, including her own research, that supported the idea of unconscious or indirect lie detecting, but she doubted that it would ever become a truly effective system. Dr. ten Brinke has started a new experiment, one that she hopes will offer concrete tactics to help us identify liars. It entails measuring physiological symptoms like blood flow and perspiration in study subjects who are listening to a liar. That, too, is a twist. The traditional lie-detector test makes similar measures of a person suspected of lying. Maybe the better detector will be the person listening, at least if the conscious mind can be left out of it.

10

The passage serves mainly to

A) discuss ongoing scientific research.

B) resolve a longstanding debate.

C) suggest a definitive solution to a problem.

D) describe breakthroughs in treating a disease.

11

Based on the passage, which choice best describes the relationship between lying and detection?

A) It is easiest to detect lies using the unconscious mind.

B) We unconsciously detect lies more accurately than we're aware of.

C) We can most accurately detect lies using the conscious mind.

D) We can most accurately detect lies when the liar is unconscious of their lie.

12

The passage most strongly suggests that

A) there is still no consensus on the best way to catch liars.

B) in the future there will be methods to detect lies with very high accuracy.

C) humans' accuracy in distinguishing lies from truth is improving.

D) there are fewer studies about lying conducted now than in the past.

13

Which choice provides the best evidence for the answer to the previous question?

A) Lines 46-48 ("So ... than consciously")

B) Lines 63-69 ("The study ... detection")

C) Lines 81-84 ("It entails ... a liar")

D) Lines 87-89 ("Maybe ... of it")

14

The results of the "classic experiment" (lines 19) most strongly suggest that

A) people are more successful in guessing if someone is lying to them than in actively trying to figure it out.

B) making a random guess would be about as accurate as consciously trying to figure out if someone is lying.

C) people are such poor judges of lying they are better off guessing if they are being deceived.

D) most of the time people assume that they are not being lied to.

15

Which of the following experiments would be most similar to the experiment described in lines 31-39?

A) An image of a clean or messy place is flashed for a few milliseconds and subjects are asked to complete word sets with clean or messy sounding words.

B) An image of a person is flashed for a few milliseconds and subjects are asked to say whether they've met that person before.

C) Subjects are allowed to examine the face of a person and then guess whether they will be likely to lie in the future.

D) Subjects are asked to examine an image of a house and then match the image with the most accurate descriptive words.

16

According to Dr. ten Brinke, humans' inability to spot lies may

A) be remedied with her current techniques.

B) help us study the brain.

C) serve a social purpose.

D) be overcome through concentration.

17

Which choice provides the best evidence for the answer to the previous question?

A) Lines 5-9 ("New research … them")

B) Lines 19-24 ("A classic … time")

C) Lines 54-60 ("Dr. ten Brinke … escape notice")

D) Lines 78-81 ("Dr. ten Brinke … identify liars")

18

As used in line 41, "lump" most nearly means

A) group.

B) congregate.

C) accumulate.

D) trudge.

19

As used in line 80, "concrete" most nearly means

A) specific.

B) established.

C) physical.

D) realistic.

Section 5
Persuasive Language

Passages on the SAT Reading Test will use a variety of techniques, devices, and language to communicate ideas to the reader. The questions that test these techniques fall under a category that the College Board calls **Rhetoric**. This section will cover the types of questions you will be asked about these types of persuasive language and how to answer them.

First, you'll learn how to analyze word choice as well as the overall structure of a text. Next, you'll learn how to decipher the point of view and purpose of a passage. Finally, you'll learn how to assess arguments made by the author. There will be practice exercises for you to try along the way, and two passages at the end of the section where you will put together everything you've learned.

In this section, we'll cover all of the following topics:

- Analyzing Word Choice
- Analyzing Text Structure
- Point of View and Analyzing Purpose
- Analyzing Arguments

We'll explain each topic in detail, and provide some practice questions in each one of those parts. After that, we provide a mixed practice set that includes questions related to all of those topics.

Analyzing Word Choice
Part 1

Analyzing Word Choice questions ask you how specific words, phrases, or patterns shape the meaning and tone of the text. They will often require you to read between the lines and decipher the passage beyond a literal understanding of what is being said.

Here are some ways that Word Choice questions might be phrased:

- The author uses the phrase "is written in" (line 6) most likely to ...
- The analogy in the final sentence of Passage 2 has primarily which effect?
- What main effect do the quotations by Andrews in lines 10-18 have on the tone of the passage?

Rhetorical Devices

You may be asked what certain rhetorical devices are achieving in the text. Remember that **rhetorical devices** are tools that the author uses to convey her argument, such as repetition, metaphor, or simile. You can refer back to Section 3 for a review of these devices. However, you don't need to know the definitions of rhetorical devices in order to answer these questions. Instead, you'll need to know how rhetorical devices shape the text.

For example, repetition is often used to make or emphasize a point. Metaphors and similes are often used to describe or explain an interesting concept. To understand specific metaphors and similes, think about what is being used as a comparison. For example, birds are free to fly wherever they like, so comparing something to a bird is often meant to indicate freedom. Referring to a caged animal might suggest the opposite. Be careful of choosing an answer that is too literal when answering questions about these devices.

Let's see what a Word Choice question might look like for the following paragraph, taken from John F. Kennedy's inaugural address.

Be wary of interpreting the images of light and fire literally. Here, Kennedy is using a metaphor to make a point about the power of citizen action. This is clearer when you read the entire paragraph, so always be sure to read the lines surrounding a Word Choice question. Also consider the author's main purpose, or the structure of the overall passage, to help you determine how the figurative language functions within it. Answer choice (B) demonstrates that the light represents how the actions of the listeners will benefit the United States and the rest of the world. Therefore, (B) is the correct answer.

You can use Process of Elimination to rule out the other answer options. Answer choices (A) and (C) interpret the imagery too literally, so they can be knocked out. Answer choice (D) talks about action being taken, but the paragraph refers to the energy and faith of those listening, not of a previous generation.

Tone

Word Choice questions may also ask you to analyze how certain words or lines shape the tone of a text, or to describe the tone of a passage overall. **Tone** refers to the feeling or attitude the author demonstrates in his writing. You can determine the tone of a passage by paying attention to the words the author uses, and to how you feel as you read the passage. Adjectives in particular help shape the tone of a text, so look out for them as you read. Refer back to the notes you made when marking up the passage, as discussed in Chapter 1 and Section 2 of this chapter as part of the Pencil on Paper strategy.

The following words may be used by the SAT to describe the tone of the passage, or the attitude of someone mentioned in the text. This is only a partial list—the SAT may use a number of different words to describe an author's tone.

Tone Words	
Positive	Captivated, Effusive, Enthusiastic, Engaged, Excited, Humorous, Intrigued, Laudatory, Reverent , Whimsical
Neutral	Academic, Candid, Contemplative, Detached, Dispassionate, Impartial, Judicious, Pragmatic, Scholarly
Negative	Apathetic, Caustic, Condescending, Contemptuous, Cynical, Derisive, Disparaging, Flippant, Grudging, Skeptical, Vindictive

When you answer a tone question, think back to your impression of the passage, or the section you are asked about. How did it make you feel? Think of your own word to describe the tone of the text. If you cannot think of a specific word, try to think more generally about the tone. Was it strong or neutral? Positive or negative? Happy or sad? Then, compare your prediction to the answer choices.

Let's look at a tone question about a paragraph from the John F. Kennedy speech excerpt we looked at earlier.

Example

In the long history of the world, only a few generations have been granted the role of defending freedom in its hour of
Line maximum danger. I do not shrink from
5 this responsibility—I welcome it. I do not believe that any of us would exchange places with any other people or any other generation. The energy, the faith, the devotion which we bring to this endeavor
10 will light our country and all who serve it—and the glow from that fire can truly light the world.

2

The tone of the paragraph is best described as

A) uncertain.

B) confident.

C) biting.

D) delicate.

How would you describe the tone of these lines? The word "devotion" demonstrates Kennedy's strong commitment, and stating, "the glow from that fire can truly light the world" suggests he's convinced that things will move forward in a positive way. You might choose a word like "encouraging" or "optimistic" to describe this tone. Once you compare this word to the answer choices, (B) is the only option that is close to your prediction.

Answer choice (A) is nearly the opposite of what you are looking for, as the declarative language in the paragraph reflects Kennedy's sure attitude ("I do not shrink…I welcome…I do not believe"). (C) is too negative to describe the lines in question, since Kennedy talks here about faith, devotion, light, and freedom. (D) is a poor fit as Kennedy's words are decisive and bold.

Part 1 Practice: Analyzing Word Choice

Review the techniques we discussed in Section 2, and mark up and make summaries for this passage excerpt. Then, answer the Analyzing Word Choice questions using the strategies you just learned.

This passage is adapted from Kate Chopin, *The Awakening and Selected Short Stories*, first published in 1899.

Edna often wondered at one propensity which sometimes had inwardly disturbed her without causing any outward show or
Line manifestation on her part. At a very early
5 age—perhaps it was when she traversed the ocean of waving grass—she remembered that she had been passionately enamored of a dignified and sad-eyed cavalry officer who visited her father in Kentucky. She
10 could not leave his presence when he was there, nor remove her eyes from his face, which was something like Napoleon's, with a lock of black hair falling across the forehead. But the cavalry officer melted
15 imperceptibly out of her existence.
At another time her affections were deeply engaged by a young gentleman who visited a lady on a neighboring plantation. It was after they went to
20 Mississippi to live. The young man was engaged to be married to the young lady, and they sometimes called upon Margaret, driving over some afternoons in a buggy. Edna was a little miss, just merging into
25 her teens; and the realization that she

herself was nothing, nothing, nothing to the engaged young man was a bitter affliction to her. But he, too, went the way of dreams.

1

The main rhetorical effect of the repeated word in lines 28-29 is to

A) underscore how frequently Edna had felt ignored in her teens.

B) suggest that Edna often had to remind herself of her proper place.

C) emphasize how little Edna mattered to the young man.

D) imply that Edna lacked self-confidence around the young man and Margaret.

2

The author's tone is best described as

A) apologetic.

B) disturbed.

C) invigorated.

D) reflective.

Analyzing Text Structure
Part 2

Analyzing Text Structure questions ask you about the structure of the text as a whole, or about the relationship between the whole text and a specific part of the text, such as one sentence or paragraph.

Analyzing Text Structure questions might be phrased as follows:

- Which choice best reflects the overall sequence of events in the passage?
- Which choice best describes the structure of the first paragraph?
- Over the course of the passage, the focus shifts from …

Use Your Summaries

Referring back to the summaries you made while reading the passage can help you answer Analyzing Text Structure questions. Reading these summaries will help you understand how the paragraphs relate to one another, and can help you figure out the relationship between a specific part of the text and the text as a whole. Look for points where certain ideas were introduced or where the focus of the passage changed. You can then describe the structure of the passage in your own words and compare it to the answer choices.

Let's see how this works with a question about the overall structure of a passage. Remember the summaries you wrote for the Cavallini passage in Section 2? Here is the passage and the paragraph summaries again:

Example

This passage is adapted from Daniel Zalewski, "Under a Shroud of Kitsch May Lie a Master's Art." ©2001 by The New York Times Company.

#1 T.S. glad remove Baroque

Tommaso Strinati clambers to the top of the rickety scaffold and laughs. "It's a good thing that all this Baroque work is so
Line unimpressive," he says, pointing at the
5 clumsy trompe l'oeil painting covering the wall in front of him. "Otherwise, we might not have been allowed to scrape it off!"

A 28-year-old art historian, he is standing 16 feet above the marble floor of
10 San Pasquale Baylon chapel, a long-neglected nook of Santa Maria in Aracoeli, a Franciscan basilica in the center of Rome. Last year, Mr. Strinati, who is still a graduate student, began
15 studying the church's history. Records suggested that the Roman artist Pietro Cavallini—a painter and mosaicist whose greatest works have been destroyed—

#2 Continued on next column…

#2. T.S. thinks hidden P.C. frescos

spent years decorating Aracoeli toward
20 the end of the 13th century. Yet only one
small Cavallini fresco, in the church's left
transept, remained visible. Mr. Strinati
wondered: had other Cavallini frescoes
been painted over with inferior work? And
25 if so, could modern restorers uncover
them?

#3. Found P.C. frescoes

  "The answer to both questions was
yes," Mr. Strinati says. A close-up
examination of the chapel's walls last
30 summer revealed ghostly images lying
beneath the surface. The entire chapel, it
seemed, was a painted palimpsest. And
when a heavy altarpiece was removed
from one wall, a remarkably tender
35 portrait of the Madonna and Child was
found hidden behind it.

#4. Resemble other P.C. work

  After months of careful paint-peeling,
what has been uncovered are dazzling
fragments of a late-medieval masterpiece
40 completed shortly after 1285. Although
the Aracoeli fresco is not signed, the
figures strongly resemble those in a
surviving Cavallini work, the resplendent
"Last Judgment" fresco at nearby Santa
45 Cecilia.

#5. P.C. maybe anticipated Giotto/ Renaissance

  Mr. Strinati has grand ambitions for
his discovery. He hopes that in a few
years the fully restored fresco will not
only rescue Cavallini's name from
50 obscurity, but also upend the widespread
notion that the first flowers of the
Renaissance budded in Florence, not
Rome. For the fresco's lifelike figures—in
particular, an impish Christ child with
55 charmingly flushed cheeks—suggest to
Strinati that Cavallini may have
anticipated some of the extraordinary
naturalistic innovations that have long
been credited to the Florentine artist
60 Giotto.

#6. Cont. on next column...

  Moreover, the Aracoeli fragments may
provide a critical new clue in a decades-
old battle concerning the "St. Francis

Legend," the 1296 fresco cycle at Assisi,
65 universally recognized as one of the
foundations of the Renaissance. For
centuries, the 28-scene cycle—which
recounts the life of the saint with a
narrative zest and compositional depth
70 that leave the flat tableaus of the
Byzantine era far behind—was attributed
to Giotto. But since the 1930's, various
scholars have questioned this judgment,
claiming that the Assisi cycle doesn't
75 resemble Giotto's other work. Now, the
Aracoeli discovery is ammunition for
Italian art historians who believe that
Cavallini might actually be the primary
creative force behind the "St. Francis
80 Legend."

#6. P.C. maybe painted "St. F"

  The growing debate about Cavallini's
importance was the occasion for a
symposium in Rome in November. *La
Republicca*, an Italian daily, has cast the
85 debate as "War Between Rome and
Florence." Mr. Strinati is enjoying the
ruckus. "I had a hunch that there was
more Cavallini lurking around here," he
says of the Aracoeli basilica. "But I
90 didn't expect to find an exquisite work
that could shake up the history of art."

#7. P.C. causing art history debates

3

Which of the following best describes
the structure of the passage as a whole?

A) The passage introduces a scholar,
and then focuses on a discovery he
has made.

B) The passage introduces an artist,
and details a new discovery of his
art.

C) The passage makes an argument
about an artist, then supports it with
historical evidence.

D) The passage considers both sides of
an issue, yet reaches no conclusion.

The summaries for the Cavallini passage show that the first paragraph is about Strinati, and the second and third paragraphs introduce the Cavallini frescoes Strinati discovered. The rest of the passage is focused on Cavallini's work and the impact it might have on theories of art history. Answer choice (A) matches this progression, as Strinati is an art historian, and the remainder of the passage discusses the Cavallini discovery. Therefore, answer (A) is correct.

Answer choice (B) is close, but the passage does not begin by introducing the reader to the artist Cavallini. It introduces Strinati, who is an academic and not an artist; this answer is therefore incorrect. Answer choice (C) is incorrect because the passage as a whole isn't focused on one argument about Cavallini. Instead, there are several smaller arguments supported with historical evidence in individual paragraphs, such as the "St. Francis Legend" in the sixth paragraph. Thus, (C) does not represent the structure of the passage as a whole. Answer choice (D) is also incorrect, as the passage does not debate two sides of an issue throughout.

Mark Up the Structure

To help you get a better sense of the structure of a passage, you can also build upon the techniques you learned in Section 2 and mark up additional items in your passage. You can look for transition words, evidence, and examples in the passage.

Marking up Passage Structure		
Concept	Importance	How to mark it in the passage
Transition words	Indicate a change in direction of author's reasoning or argument	Circle the word
Examples or evidence	Clarify concepts discussed by the author; can reveal how an author has supported his or her argument	Note "e.g." for examples or "e.v." for evidence in the margin

Here are a few paragraphs from the Cavallini passage. We've marked up transition words, evidence, and examples to show you how this works.

Example

Moreover, the Aracoeli fragments may provide a critical new clue in a decades-old battle concerning the "St. Francis

Line Legend," the 1296 fresco cycle at Assisi,
65 universally recognized as one of the foundations of the Renaissance. For centuries, the 28-scene cycle—which recounts the life of the saint with a narrative zest and compositional depth
70 that leave the flat tableaus of the

Byzantine era far behind—was attributed to Giotto. But since the 1930's, various scholars have questioned this judgment, claiming that the Assisi cycle doesn't
75 resemble Giotto's other work. Now, the Aracoeli discovery is ammunition for Italian art historians who believe that Cavallini might actually be the primary creative force behind the "St. Francis
80 Legend."

The growing debate about Cavallini's importance was the occasion for a symposium in Rome in November. *La Republicca*, an Italian daily, has cast the debate as "War Between Rome and Florence." Mr. Strinati is enjoying the ruckus. "I had a hunch that there was more Cavallini lurking around here," he says of the Aracoeli basilica. "But I didn't expect to find an exquisite work that could shake up the history of art."

By noting the transition words, you can see how parts of the paragraph relate to one another, and also how assertions are supported with evidence and examples. For example, lines 71 to 79 provide evidence against the previous assertion about Giotto. It also provides the reason for questioning whether he was the original artist of the "St. Francis Legend."

Part 2 Practice: Analyzing Text Structure

Review the techniques we discussed in Section 2, and mark up and make summaries for this passage excerpt. Then, answer the Analyzing Text Structure questions using the strategies you just learned.

This passage is adapted from Matt Ridley, "The World's Resources Aren't Running Out." ©2014 by *Dow Jones & Company*.

How many times have you heard that we humans are "using up" the world's resources, "running out" of oil, "reaching
Line the limits" of the atmosphere's capacity to
5 cope with pollution or "approaching the carrying capacity" of the land's ability to support a greater population? The assumption behind all such statements is that there is a fixed amount of stuff—
10 metals, oil, clean air, land—and that we risk exhausting it through our consumption. "We are using 50% more resources than the Earth can sustainably produce, and unless we change course,
15 that number will grow fast—by 2030, even two planets will not be enough," says Jim Leape, director general of the World Wide Fund for Nature International (formerly the World Wildlife Fund). But
20 here's a peculiar feature of human history: we burst through such limits again and again. After all, as a Saudi oil minister once said, the Stone Age didn't end for lack of stone. Ecologists call this
25 "niche construction"—that people (and indeed some other animals) can create new opportunities for themselves by making their habitats more productive in some way. Agriculture is the classic
30 example of niche construction: we stopped relying on nature's bounty and substituted an artificial and much larger bounty.

1

Which of the following best describes the general organization of the passage?

A) A problem is introduced, the evidence supporting it is questioned, and then the author concludes the problem is solvable.

B) A problem is introduced with evidence to support it, and then the author introduces a competing argument.

C) Evidence is introduced, a problem is identified, and then the author offers additional information.

D) A problem is introduced, a solution is proposed, and then the author offers an alternative solution.

2

The author's statement in lines 20-21 ("we … and again) serves primarily to

A) introduce new evidence for his conclusion.

B) provide support for an earlier argument.

C) summarize the passage.

D) introduce his main argument.

3

The author discusses "niche construction" (line 24) in order to

A) help explain his claim that humans can overcome the limits of existing resources.

B) counter the argument that humans are rapidly consuming resources.

C) provide an example of how humans can reduce their usage of limited resources.

D) suggest that the earlier claim that certain resources are limited is false.

Point of View and Analyzing Purpose
Part 3

Just like all texts you read, the passages on the SAT Reading Test were written from a specific point of view and for a specific reason. You may be asked two different kinds of questions about this: **Point of View** questions and **Analyzing Purpose** questions.

Here are some ways Point of View questions might be phrased:

- The passage is written from the perspective of someone who is …
- Over the course of the passage, the narrator's attitude shifts from …
- The author's attitude toward Dr. Brown's discovery is best described as …

Here are some ways Analyzing Purpose questions might be phrased:

- The passage serves primarily to …
- The most likely purpose of the parenthetical information in lines 63-64 is to …
- The author of Passage 2 refers to the novel *War and Peace* primarily to suggest that …

Point of View

Point of View questions ask you to determine the point of view or attitude of the author. This may involve determining what the author's attitude is towards a specific subject, or describing how the author approached writing the text overall. These questions can sometimes be similar to Word Choice questions about tone, which you learned about earlier in this section.

One good place to find the author's point of view or opinion is through certain adjectives she may use. Adjectives can be simple and descriptive, such as "the sky is blue," or can demonstrate how we feel about something, such as "Brussels sprouts are delicious." When you see adjectives that convey an opinion in the text, and they are not attributed to another person or character in the passage, you can assume they represent the point of view of the author.

There may be passages with very few strong adjectives or statements by the author that indicate her opinion. In that case, do not make assumptions that go beyond what is stated in the passage. Be wary of answer choices that state the author's opinion too strongly, or use absolute language like "best" or "worst" that doesn't fit with the passage.

Let's look at a Point of View question to see how this works:

Example

Dr. Chabra has found a way to help serious athletes recover more quickly from the stiffness caused by heavy training.
Line Like any new medical intervention, Dr.
5 Chabra's novel approach to treating muscle soreness has been met with some skepticism and a lot of questions. Still, many of her colleagues praised the innovative treatment; they rightly
10 recognized the valuable impact it could have on athletic performance.

4

The author's attitude toward Dr. Chabra's new treatment is best described as

A) uncertain.

B) relieved.

C) disparaging.

D) approving.

While the second sentence of this paragraph indicates that there has been some skepticism about Dr. Chabra's treatment, it does not appear to be the author's attitude. Instead, the author aligns herself with Dr. Chabra's colleagues who have "rightly" praised the treatment, which indicates a positive attitude. The adjectives "innovative" and "valuable" are also very complimentary and suggest the author thinks highly of Dr. Chabra's discovery. Answer (D) is therefore the correct response.

Answer choice (A) does not work, as the author is not hesitant about Dr. Chabra's work. Neither is the author disparaging; while some "skeptics" are mentioned the author does not count himself among them, and does not make any negative or derogatory statements about Dr. Chabra's research. Thus, answer choice (C) can also be eliminated. Answer choice (B) does not make sense in the context of the passage, as nothing indicates that the author was previously worried and then consoled once she learned of Dr. Chabra's discovery.

Analyzing Purpose

Analyzing Purpose questions ask you about the purpose of either an entire passage or specific lines or paragraphs. To answer these questions you need to analyze what the author was trying to achieve with his writing.

For questions that ask you about the purpose of the passage as a whole, you will want to choose a "big-picture" answer. Ask yourself why the passage was written. Was it to persuade the reader of something, to argue against a previously held idea, or just to introduce a new concept? Describe the goal of the passage in your own words before looking at the answer choices.

Here's an example of an Analyzing Purpose question from the Cavallini passage that you already tackled in Section 2:

<table>
<tr><td>Example</td></tr>
</table>

The primary purpose of the passage is to

A) explain an exciting discovery.

B) describe Cavallini's artistic style.

C) emphasize the importance of art history.

D) discuss Giotto's role in the Renaissance.

Here, answers (B) and (D) are too narrow, and answer choice (C) is not discussed at all in the passage. Therefore, (A) is the correct answer as the passage discusses the discovery of the hidden frescoes.

You may also be asked about the purpose of individual lines or paragraphs. Again, try to think of what the author is trying to achieve with the portions of text you are asked about. Is she introducing or summarizing concepts? Providing arguments or counterarguments? Presenting a contrast for emphasis? Review your summaries and notes on the passage to see how the section you are analyzing relates to other parts of the text.

Remember that you are being asked about the role of a certain part of the passage, and not just what it says. You may need to read critically to understand the author's intent or goal! Be sure to carefully analyze persuasive language, and look at the lines before and after the ones you are asked about for clues as to the author's intent.

Part 3 Practice: Point of View and Analyzing Purpose

Review the techniques we discussed in Section 2, and mark up and make summaries for this passage excerpt. Then, answer the Point of View and Purpose questions using the strategies you just learned.

This passage is adapted from Charles Dickens, *Great Expectations*, first published in 1861.

Dinner done, we sat with our feet upon the fender. I said to Herbert, "My dear Herbert, I have something very particular
Line to tell you."
5   "My dear Handel," he returned, "I shall esteem and respect your confidence."
"It concerns myself, Herbert," said I, "and one other person."
Herbert crossed his feet, looked at the
10 fire with his head on one side, and having looked at it in vain for some time, looked at me because I didn't go on.
"Herbert," said I, laying my hand upon his knee, "I love—I adore—Estella."
15   Instead of being transfixed, Herbert replied in an easy matter-of-course way, "Exactly. Well?"
"Well, Herbert? Is that all you say? Well?"
20   "What next, I mean?" said Herbert. "Of course I know that."
"How do you know it?" said I.
"How do I know it, Handel? Why, from you."
25   "I never told you."
"Told me! You have never told me when you have got your hair cut, but I have had senses to perceive it. You have always adored her, ever since I have

30 known you. You brought your adoration and your portmanteau here together. Told me! Why, you have always told me all day long. When you told me your own story, you told me plainly that you began
35 adoring her the first time you saw her, when you were very young indeed."

1

The primary purpose of lines 26-31 is to

A) explain how Herbert knows that Handel loves Estella.

B) introduce the fact that Handel has loved Estella for a long time.

C) highlight Herbert's keen powers of perception.

D) suggest that many people must be aware of Handel's love for Estella.

2

The passage serves mainly to

A) describe the relationship between one friend and another.

B) recount a conversation between two friends.

C) reveal a mysterious character's secret motives.

D) foreshadow an upcoming action in a story.

Analyzing Arguments
Part 4

Analyzing Arguments questions ask you to analyze the way the author of the passage makes and supports her arguments. You may be asked to identify claims or counterclaims in a passage, whether explicit or implicit. You may also be asked to assess an author's reasoning and evidence.

Here are some ways Analyzing Arguments questions might be phrased:

- In lines 6-10 the author argues that …
- In Passage 2, the author claims that …
- The authors most likely use the examples in lines 1-9 of the passage to …
- An unstated assumption made by the author is that …
- In the passage, the author anticipates which of the following objections to her argument?

Analyzing Claims and Counterclaims

Analyzing Claims and Counterclaims questions, or "Claims" questions, ask you to locate the claims that an author makes to support an argument or the counterclaims an author uses to attack an argument.

An **argument** is the logical reasoning an author uses to persuade you that something is true. **Claims** are the specific facts or ideas that support their reasoning. Here's an argument for studying more: "reading helps you learn, so if you want to learn more you should read more." It includes the claim that studying contributes to learning to make the argument that you should study more to learn more.

A **counterargument** is the logical reasoning an author uses to persuade you that some opposing argument is wrong. **Counterclaims** are are the facts or ideas they use to attack the claims supporting an opposing argument. Here's a counterargument to our previous argument: "reading is not the only thing required for learning; you also need to get a healthy amount of sleep, and try to apply what you learn in stimulating ways. If you want to learn more, you should try to lead a healthy, stimulating life that is conducive to learning." It uses a counterclaim to directly attack the previous argument, and it also introduces its own claims to develop a new argument.

Take a look at the following example.

This passage is adapted from Diane Lewis, "The Toxic Brew in Our Yards." ©2014 by The New York Times Company.

A study by the United States Geological Survey released in 1999 found at least one pesticide, and often more than one, in
Line almost every stream and fish sample
5 tested, and in about half of the samples drawn from wells throughout the country. These pesticides are going from our lawns and gardens into our drinking water and into our bodies.

10 The amounts of these chemicals are small and often considered "acceptable," but scientists now know that they have a cumulative effect. Many chemicals that we use very casually on our lawns cause long-
15 term health problems in ways that have only recently been understood. They "disrupt," or throw out of whack, the endocrine system, made up of glands and hormones that control almost every aspect
20 of our bodies' functions.

Can you spot the counterargument in this excerpt? Consider the author's main point and arguments, and how she structures her evidence. You should notice that, in the second paragraph, the author mentions that "the amount of these chemicals are small and often considered 'acceptable,'" before explaining why this fact is actually not enough to discredit her larger claim. Even though the chemical amounts are small, the author explains, they still cause long-term health problems.

If you have trouble identifying arguments, ask yourself what the author seems sure about, or what he is trying to persuade you to believe.

Now let's practice by answering a Claims question about the paragraph below, from a speech by Anna Howard Shaw. Focus on identifying her argument as you read.

This passage is adapted from a speech by Anna Howard Shaw, "The Fundamental Principle of a Republic." Delivered during the New York State equal suffrage campaign on June 21, 1915.

Now if we should take a vote and the men had to read their ballot in order to vote it, more women could vote than men. But
Line when the government says not only that you
5 must be twenty-one years of age, a resident of the community, and native born or naturalized, those are qualifications, but when it says that an elector must be a male, that is not a qualification for citizenship;

10 that is an insurmountable barrier between one half of the people and the other half of the citizens and their rights as citizens. No such nation can call itself a Republic. It is only an aristocracy. That barrier must be
15 removed before the government can become a Republic, and that is exactly what we are asking right now, that this great state of New York shall become in fact as it is in theory, a part of a
20 government of the people, by the people, and for the people.

5

In lines 13-17 the author argues that

A) a Republic is the only acceptable form of government.

B) only those who can read should be allowed to vote in a Republic.

C) a true Republic must allow both women and men to vote.

D) a Republic is necessary to allow women to vote.

In this paragraph, Shaw is speaking about republics in order to make a point about women's right to vote. Her comments about women and men in the earlier lines of the paragraph help make this clear, even though the heart of the argument is in lines 13-17. When Shaw says "that barrier must be removed," she is referring to women's inability to vote, as stated in lines 8-13. Only answer choice (C) sums up this argument.

You can knock out answer choice (A) since it is too strong; you only know that Shaw is in favor of a true republic. As she doesn't discuss other forms of government, we can't be sure that she thinks republics are the best possible form. (B) refers to something mentioned in the first line, which is also not an argument but an observation. Answer choice (D) is almost the inverse of Shaw's argument—she never says that having a republic is the only way to grant women the right to vote.

Assessing Reasoning

Assessing Reasoning questions ask you to follow an author's line of reasoning, analyze whether an author's reasoning makes sense, or determine why an author used a certain type of reasoning. If you are asked why an author used a certain type of reasoning, you can use a similar approach as you learned for Purpose questions earlier in this section. Focus on what the author's overall goal or purpose is for the lines you are asked about, so you can determine how the reasoning the author uses lines up with what she is trying to prove.

To assess if an author's reasoning makes sense, look at whether the evidence she has given truly supports or matches up with the argument she is trying to make. This may require looking at evidence over more than one paragraph, and combining it in ways that allow you to draw new conclusions.

Let's look again at an excerpt from the Cavallini passage.

Mr. Strinati has grand ambitions for his discovery. He hopes that in a few years the fully restored fresco will not
Line only rescue Cavallini's name from
50 obscurity, but also upend the widespread notion that the first flowers of the Renaissance budded in Florence, not Rome. For the fresco's lifelike figures—in particular, an impish Christ child with
55 charmingly flushed cheeks—suggest to Strinati that Cavallini may have anticipated some of the extraordinary naturalistic innovations that have long been credited to the Florentine artist
60 Giotto.

Moreover, the Aracoeli fragments may provide a critical new clue in a decades-old battle concerning the "St. Francis Legend," the 1296 fresco cycle at Assisi,
65 universally recognized as one of the foundations of the Renaissance. For centuries, the 28-scene cycle—which recounts the life of the saint with a narrative zest and compositional depth
70 that leave the flat tableaus of the Byzantine era far behind—was attributed to Giotto. But since the 1930's, various scholars have questioned this judgment, claiming that the Assisi cycle doesn't
75 resemble Giotto's other work. Now, the Aracoeli discovery is ammunition for Italian art historians who believe that Cavallini might actually be the primary creative force behind the "St. Francis
80 Legend."

Consider the author's statement that the Aracoeli discovery may suggest Cavallini painted the "St. Francis Legend." Does this argument make sense?

It does if we consider information the author has introduced over the previous two paragraphs. The author states that Cavallini's work may have been done before some of Giotto's, and thus may have been important to the start of the Renaissance. The "St. Francis Legend" is also described as a foundation of the Renaissance, but doesn't look like Giotto's other work. It would therefore make sense that Cavallini, who was painting during the early Renaissance before Giotto and may have been one of its leaders, could be the artist behind the painting.

When answering Assessing Reasoning questions, think critically about whether the author has supported his point, and whether you are convinced by the type of evidence he has used.

Some questions will ask you about what kinds of evidence the author uses to support her arguments, or whether she fails to use any. These are called **Analyzing Evidence** questions. Some kinds of evidence are more common in certain contexts. For example, an argument about the increasing infection rates for a certain disease would be better proven by data than by a personal anecdote. To answer these questions, first locate the author's argument, and then ask yourself what he did to prove it. Keep in mind that an author may use multiple types of evidence, which may appear either before or after the argument itself.

Part 4 Practice: Analyzing Arguments

Review the techniques we discussed in Section 2, and mark up and make summaries for this passage excerpt. Then, answer the Analyzing Arguments questions using the strategies you just learned.

This passage is adapted from Dayo Olopade, "Africa's Tech Edge." ©2014 by *The Atlantic Monthly Group*.

It's a painfully First World problem: splitting dinner with friends, we do the dance of the seven credit cards. No one, it
Line seems, carries cash anymore, so we blunder
5 through the inconvenience that comes with our dependence on plastic. Just as often, I encounter a street vendor or taxi driver who can't handle my proffered card and am left shaking out my pockets and purse.
10 When I returned to the United States after living in Nairobi on and off for two years, these antiquated payment ordeals were especially frustrating. As I never tire of explaining to friends, in Kenya I could
15 pay for nearly everything with a few taps on my cellphone.

Every few weeks, I'd pull cash out of my American bank account and hand it to a contemplative young man stationed
20 outside my local greengrocer. I'd show him my ID and type in a PIN, and he'd credit my phone number with an equivalent amount of digital currency.

Through a service called M-Pesa, I
25 could store my mobile money and then, for a small fee, send it to any other phone number in the network, be it my cable company's, a taxi driver's, or a friend's. Payments from other M-Pesa users would
30 be added to my digital balance, which I could later withdraw in cash from my local agent.

For me, M-Pesa was convenient, often simpler than reaching for my credit card or
35 counting out paper bills. But for most

Kenyans, the service has been life-changing. Kenya has one ATM for every 18,000 people—the U.S., by contrast, has one for every 740—and across sub-
40 Saharan Africa, more than 75 percent of the adult population had no bank account as of 2011. When Safaricom, the major Kenyan telecommunications firm, launched M-Pesa in 2007, pesa—Swahili
45 for "money"—moved from mattresses to mobile accounts virtually overnight. Suddenly, payment and collection of debts did not require face-to-face interactions. Daylong queues to pay electric- or water-
50 utility bills disappeared. By 2012, 86 percent of Kenyan cellphone subscribers used mobile money, and by 2013, M-Pesa's transactions amounted to some $35 million daily. Annualized, that's more
55 than a quarter of Kenya's GDP.

M-Pesa isn't the first mobile-money service. The Philippines has had at least rudimentary mobile money-transfer systems since 2001, but nine years later,
60 fewer than 10 percent of Filipino mobile users without bank accounts actively used them, while the long tail of mobile-payment systems has already transformed Africa. Parrot programs like Paga,
65 EcoCash, Splash Mobile Money, Tigo Cash, Airtel Money, Orange Money, and MTN Mobile Money have sprung up in several African countries. Even government has elbowed its way in: the
70 Rwanda Revenue Authority has introduced a service that allows citizens to declare and pay taxes right from their cellphones.

1

The author makes which of the following arguments?

A) Americans should begin implementing and using M-Pesa.

B) M-Pesa is more convenient than most forms of payment in the United States.

C) Making easy payments is now only a problem in the United States.

D) Mobile money was difficult to introduce in Kenya.

2

The author supports the claim that M-Pesa "has been life-changing" (lines 36-37) by

A) explaining how M-Pesa works.

B) describing some common financial transactions in Kenya.

C) offering statistics about the use of mobile money services in the United States.

D) citing statistics about the use of M-Pesa in Kenya.

3

In lines 57-64, the author uses the example of the Filipino mobile money services to

A) suggest mobile money services do not work well in all types of economies

B) contrast the limited success of mobile money services in the Philippines with the huge impact of mobile money systems in African countries

C) provide evidence that M-Pesa was not the first mobile money service to be widely used

D) imply that mobile payment services will continue to spread to new places in the coming years

Practice Set
Part 5

The following passages have been designed to test the question types you learned about in this section. Review the techniques we discussed in Section 2, and mark up and make summaries for this passage. Then, answer the questions using the strategies you just learned.

This passage is adapted from a speech delivered to the United States Senate by Senator Robert La Follette on October 6th, 1917, shortly after the US entered the First World War.

I think all men recognize that in time of war the citizen must surrender some rights for the common good that he is entitled to
Line enjoy in time of peace. But the right to
5 control their own Government according to constitutional forms is not one of the rights that the citizens of this country are called upon to surrender in time of war.
Rather in time of war the citizen must
10 be more alert to the preservation of his right to control his Government. He must be most watchful of the encroachment of the military upon the civil power. He must beware of those precedents in support of
15 arbitrary action by administrative officials, which excused on the plea of necessity in war time, become the fixed rule when the necessity has passed and normal conditions have been restored.
20 More than all, the citizen and his representative in Congress in time of war must maintain his right of free speech. More than in times of peace, it is necessary that the channels for free public discussion
25 of governmental policies shall be open and unclogged. I believe that I am now touching upon the most important question in this country today—and that is the right of the citizens of this country and their
30 representatives in Congress to discuss in an orderly way frankly and publicly and

without fear, from the platform and through the press, every important phase of this war: its causes, the manner in
35 which it should be conducted, and the terms upon which peace should be made. The widespread belief that this most fundamental right is being denied to the citizens of this country is a fact the
40 tremendous significance of which those in authority have not yet begun to appreciate. I am contending for the great fundamental right of the sovereign people of this country to make their voice heard
45 and have that voice heeded upon the great questions arising out of this war, including not only how the war shall be prosecuted but the conditions upon which it may be terminated with a due regard
50 for the rights and the honor of this nation and the interests of humanity.
I am contending for this right because the exercise of it is necessary to the welfare of this Government, to the
55 successful conduct of this war, and to a peace that shall be enduring and for the best interest of this country.
Suppose success attends the attempt to stifle all discussion of the issues of this
60 war, all discussion of the terms upon which it should be concluded, and all discussion of the objects and purposes to be accomplished by it. If we then concede to the demand of the war-mad
65 press and war extremists, who monopolize the right of public utterance upon these questions unchallenged, what

would be the consequences to this country, not only during the war but after the war?

70 Our Government, above all others, is founded on the right of the people freely to discuss all matters pertaining to their Government, in war not less than in peace, for in this Government the people are the 75 rulers in war no less than in peace. Though the right of the people to express their will by ballot is suspended during the term of office of the elected official, nevertheless the duty of the official to obey the popular 80 will continues throughout this entire term of office. How can that popular will express itself between elections except by meetings, by speeches, by publications, by petitions, and by addresses to the 85 representatives of the people? Any man who seeks to set a limit upon those rights, whether in war or peace, aims a blow at the most vital part of our Government. And then as the time for election 90 approaches and the official is called to account for his stewardship the people must have the right to the freest possible discussion of every question upon which their representative has acted, of the merits 95 of every measure he has supported or opposed, of every vote he has cast and every speech that he has made. And before this great fundamental right every other must, if necessary, give way, for in no 100 other manner can representative government be preserved.

1

The main purpose of the passage is to

A) explain the responsibilities of citizens.

B) suggest that people should be allowed to have new rights.

C) advocate for the protection of traditional freedoms.

D) seek the middle ground between two extreme positions.

2

Which of the following best characterizes the overall structure of the passage?

A) An idea is introduced and then supported with arguments.

B) Competing claims are described, the first is criticized, and the second is praised.

C) A claim is presented and its supporting evidence is refuted.

D) A proposal is outlined, its impact is analyzed, and an alternative is proposed.

3

La Follette's tone throughout the passage can best be described as that of a

A) neutral observer.

B) reluctant supporter.

C) determined advocate.

D) unrelenting critic.

4

In this passage, La Follette argues that the public must be more protective of its right to free speech during wartime because

A) free public discussion is necessary to ensure that the war is conducted properly.

B) the military is more likely than the government to violate citizens' rights.

C) people's right to express their will through their vote is suspended during wartime.

D) government officials have not yet recognized the growing belief that certain rights are being ignored.

5

The first sentence of the passage (lines 1-4) serves to

A) establish the position that La Follette will proceed to argue against.

B) define a concept that will be crucial to La Follette's claim.

C) express a general idea that La Follette will describe in greater detail.

D) state a general principle to which La Follette will discuss an exception.

6

La Follette claims that the right to free speech

A) should only be maintained as long as a number of other rights are guaranteed as well.

B) is the most important right for the proper functioning of democratic government.

C) must sometimes be limited in order for other rights to be upheld.

D) is the only protection necessary in a free society.

7

Which choice provides the best evidence for the answer to the previous question?

A) Lines 9-11 ("Rather … Government")

B) Lines 23-26 ("More than … unclogged")

C) Lines 81-85 ("How can … people")

D) Lines 97-101 ("And before … preserved")

8

The list of activities included in lines 93-97 ("every question…made") is most likely included to

A) describe the important public work that is done by La Follete and other representatives.

B) imply that La Follette's colleagues fear public discussion because they have acted   improperly.

C) emphasize the broad scope of the public's right to speak about their representatives.

D) explain the limits of the public's right to speak about the government during wartime.

This passage is adapted from Patricia Hampl, *I Could Tell You Stories: Sojourns in the Land of Memory.* ©1999 by W.W. Norton.

When I was seven, my father, who played the violin on Sundays with a nicely tortured flair which we considered artistic,
Line led me by the hand down a long, unlit
5 corridor in St. Luke's School basement, a sort of tunnel that ended in a room full of pianos. There many little girls and a single sad boy were playing truly tortured scales and arpeggios in a mash of troubled sound.
10 My father gave me over to Sister Olive Marie, who did look remarkably like an olive.

Her oily face gleamed as if it had just been rolled out of a can and laid on the
15 white plate of her broad, spotless wimple. She was a small, plump woman; her body and the small window of her face seemed to interpret the entire alphabet of olive: her face was a sallow green olive placed upon
20 the jumbo ripe olive of her black habit. I trusted her instantly and smiled, glad to have my hand placed in the hand of a woman who made sense, who provided the satisfaction of being what she was: an
25 Olive who looked like an olive.

My father left me to discover the piano with Sister Olive Marie so that one day I would join him in mutually tortured piano-violin duets for the edification of my
30 mother and brother who sat at the table meditatively spooning in the last of their pineapple sherbet until their part was called for: they put down their spoons and clapped while we bowed, while the sweet
35 ice in their bowls melted, while the music melted, and we all melted a little into each other for a moment. But first Sister Olive must do her work. I was shown middle C, which Sister seemed to think terribly
40 important. I stared at middle C and then glanced away for a second. When my eye returned, middle C was gone, its slim finger lost in the complicated grasp of the keyboard. Sister Olive struck it again,
45 finding it with laughable ease. She

emphasized the importance of middle C, its central position, a sort of North Star of sound. I remember thinking, "Middle C is the belly button of the piano," an insight
50 whose originality and accuracy stunned me with pride. For the first time in my life I was astonished by metaphor. I hesitated to tell the kindly Olive for some reason; apparently I understood a true
55 metaphor is a risky business, revealing of the self. In fact, I have never, until this moment of writing it down, told my first metaphor to anyone.

Sunlight flooded the room; the pianos,
60 all black, gleamed. Sister Olive, dressed in the colors of the keyboard, gleamed; middle C shimmered with meaning and I resolved never—never—to forget its location: it was the center of the world.
65 Then Sister Olive, who had had to show me middle C twice but who seemed to have drawn no bad conclusions about me anyway, got up and went to the windows on the opposite wall. She pulled
70 the shades down, one after the other. The sun was too bright, she said. She sneezed as she stood at the windows with the sun shedding its glare over her. She sneezed and sneezed, crazy little convulsive
75 sneezes, one after another, as helpless as if she had the hiccups.

"The sun makes me sneeze," she said when the fit was over and she was back at the piano. This was odd, too odd to grasp
80 in the mind. I associated sneezing with colds, and colds with rain, fog, snow, and bad weather. The sun, however, had caused Sister Olive to sneeze in this wild way, Sister Olive who gleamed benignly and
85 who was so certain of the location of the center of the world. The universe wobbled a bit and became unreliable. Things were not, after all, necessarily what they seemed. Appearance deceived: here was the sun
90 acting totally out of character, hurling this woman into sneezes, a woman so mild that she was named, so it seemed, for a bland object on a relish tray.

9

The main purpose of the passage is to

A) explain the narrator's love for a particular instrument.

B) provide a description of the narrator's family.

C) argue that the world is not always as it appears.

D) share a certain memory from the narrator's childhood.

10

Which of the following best characterizes the overall structure of the passage?

A) A story is told, using vivid descriptions of the setting and characters to illustrate the thoughts and memories of the narrator.

B) A mysterious character's past is explored by recounting the events from the point of view of a child.

C) A story is told as a series of initially separate events that are tied together in the end.

D) A location is described and a story is told about the location to explain its importance in the life of the narrator.

11

Which of the following best describes the narrator's first impression of Sister Olive?

A) She did not seem interesting because she resembled a dull food.

B) She seemed trustworthy because her appearance matched her name.

C) She seemed competent because she could quickly and easily identify middle C.

D) She seemed reliable because the narrator's father left the narrator in her care.

12

The third paragraph serves primarily to

A) emphasize the musical skill of the narrator's father.

B) introduce a new character.

C) describe one goal of the narrator's new lessons.

D) speculate about the most likely outcome of current events.

13

The effect of the phrase "we all melted a little into each other" (lines 36-37) is mainly to

A) suggest that when they performed music together her family members were equal in talent.

B) show how the family was as sweet as the pineapple sherbet that was melting in their bowls.

C) express that the musical performance brought the family closer together.

D) provide a vivid description of the melting sound of the performance.

14

The narrator had been reluctant to tell anyone about her first metaphor because

A) she only realized that it was a metaphor once she was older.

B) she understood that a metaphor can expose a person's private thoughts and feelings.

C) she had used the metaphor to remember the place of middle C, and did not want to reveal her trick.

D) she has always preferred to express herself through her music.

Which choice provides the best evidence for the answer to the previous question?

A) Lines 1-7 ("When I … pianos")

B) Lines 20-25 ("I trusted … olive")

C) Lines 52-56 ("I hesitated … self")

D) Lines 65-69 ("Then Sister … wall")

What is the main rhetorical effect of the repetition of the word "sneezed" in lines 71-74?

A) To denote the exact number of occurrences of a particular action

B) To subtly shift the meaning of the word in each iteration

C) To imply that there was no discernible difference between a set of incidents

D) To emphasize the frequency and extent of an action

17

The narrator comes to believe that "Things were not, after all, necessarily what they seemed" (lines 87-88) because

A) Sister Olive looked like an olive but was actually a regular person.

B) although Sister Olive was mild-mannered, she had a wild sneezing fit.

C) middle C seemed to disappear when she briefly looked away.

D) sunshine was the opposite of bad weather, yet still made Sister Olive sneeze.

Section 6
Combining Ideas

This section on Combining Ideas covers **Synthesis** questions, which you will encounter in certain passage sets. To **synthesize** means to combine, and Synthesis questions ask you to integrate information from more than one source to discover new insights and arrive at an answer. These question types appear only when you are dealing with passage pairs or passages with graphics.

In this section, we'll cover the following topics:

- Paired Passages
- Passages with Graphics

We'll explain how to approach the two main kinds of Synthesis questions, and provide practice for each. After that, we provide a mixed practice set that includes both types of Synthesis questions.

Paired Passages
Part 1

One of the five sets of questions on the Reading section of the SAT will be about a set of two short passages, rather than one long one.

In many ways, these paired passages can be treated as a single passage of a special type. Combined, the two passages in the pair are the same length as a single regular passage, have the same number of questions as a single regular passage, and—most importantly—are worth *the same number of points* as a single regular passage. Approach them as though they are just a special passage type that presents two points of view.

Each passage pair will always be of the same type—either Science or Social Studies—and about the same general subject. The passages might agree with one another, or they might disagree. They might just explore different aspects of the same subject, without directly agreeing or disagreeing with one another at all.

You should treat each of the two short passages the same way that you treat other passages of that type. But remember to also pay attention to the relationship between the two passages.

Look for Similarities and Differences

Paired passages always have some similarities. There will also always be some differences between them. Look for similarities and differences in:

- **Main Ideas:** Pay attention to the main ideas in each passage, and consider how they compare. Do they agree? Disagree? Are they talking about *exactly* the same thing, or only related things?
- **Purpose:** Look for differences in the purpose of the passages. Is one author trying only to provide information about the subject, while the other is expressing an opinion?
- **Claims:** Pay attention to what the authors claim is true. See which claims the authors seem to agree about, which ones they disagree about, and which ones are addressed by only one author.
- **Style and Tone:** Pay attention to how the passages are alike or different in style and tone. Do they both contain dry, slightly boring exposition? Is one an exciting story about football, while the other is an impassioned argument against allowing high-school students to play such a dangerous sport?
- **Focus:** Even if the passages are about the same main topic, they might focus on slightly different aspects of that topic. It might be that both passages are about tax policy, but one focuses on the effects of tax policy on the government's ability to raise revenues while the other focuses on the effects of tax policy on individuals and businesses.

Summarizing Paired Passages

When summarizing paired passages, start by jotting down summaries of each passage in the pair as you read them—just as you would with regular passages. Then, consider the relationship between the two passages, and think of a quick summary about how they relate to one another.

This summary won't usually be as simple as "Authors 1 and 2 agree" or "Authors 1 and 2 disagree." If that's all that comes to mind, you might want to think for just a moment longer; there's usually something subtler going on. Consider the elements that are most different and most similar between the two passages, and make a note about them.

Finding Repeated Ideas

To figure out the relationship between two passages, pay attention to information that appears in both. Remember the Pencil on Paper strategy mentioned in Chapter 1 and earlier in this chapter—you want to make sure you engage with and interact with the text. Mark up the passage and add your own notes to emphasize key information.

In addition to your usual notes and markings on passages, you can note ideas or important words in the second passage that are repeated from the first passage. You can also note any contrasts or opposites that you find as you read the second passage. This will help you easily find these lines if you are asked about any of these concepts.

Let's see how this works with an example of two short passage excerpts:

Example

Passages 1 and 2 are adapted from Daniela Dimitrova Russo, Todd Myers, "Should Cities Ban Plastic Bags?" ©2012 by Dow Jones & Company.

Passage 1

Plastic pollution is the nexus of some of the <u>major environmental challenges</u> facing us today. <u>Discarded plastic bags</u>
Line float in the ocean, they tumble in the
5 desert, they are found in riverbeds and dams. <u>They kill off marine animals</u> that confuse the bags with plankton and jellyfish; they end up calcified in the <u>stomachs of animals on land</u>.
10 But the <u>greatest damage is economic</u>— the cost of cleaning up all that waste. That's why <u>dozens of countries and cities</u>

Bags env. problem

around the world, including 47 municipalities in California alone, have
15 adopted ordinances <u>banning plastic bags</u>.

Bags banned

Passage 2

Across the world, cities are joining the latest <u>environmental fad—banning plastic grocery bags</u>. Activists think banning the bags is a simple and environmentally
20 responsible approach. Some ban supporters <u>claim plastics harm human health</u>, even when studies from organizations like the Environmental Protection Agency, the Centers for
25 Disease Control and Prevention, and Pacific Northwest National Labs show these <u>claims are false or exaggerated</u>.

Bags fad, harm exaggerated

Passage 1 shows the main ideas marked up using the 5 w's you learned about in Section 2. Passage 2 also has main ideas underlined in its second paragraph, as these are new ideas that are not related to Passage 1.

However, some ideas in the first paragraph of Passage 2 overlap with ideas from Passage 1, and we've underlined these overlapping ideas with a wavy line. The idea of "banning plastic grocery bags" is underlined because it is repeated from lines 15-16 in Passage 1. The term "environmental fad" is underlined because it suggests the issue is not serious, which is the opposite of the idea of "major environmental challenges" (line 2) in Passage 1.

By noting how the passages overlap, you can see how they fit together. You can tell that the author of Passage 2 disagrees with the author of Passage 1 over whether plastic bags are a major environmental issue. Passage 2 also discusses other topics like human health that Passage 1 does not address.

Approaching the Questions

Analyzing Multiple Texts questions ask you about both passages in a pair. We will refer to these as "Multiple Texts" questions. These questions will require you to consider elements from both passages at once. This can mean comparing the information from the passages, as well as their structure, tone, or way of making an argument.

To answer these questions, look for the element you are asked about in each individual passage first. For example, if you are asked about bird flight patterns, identify what each passage says about that topic. If you are asked about something more general, like tone, use your notes and summaries to determine the tone of each passage first. Then you can combine or compare these ideas to find your answer.

Let's see how this works with a question about the plastic bag passage excerpts from above. Read the longer excerpts of the passages below and mark up the repeated and contrasting ideas. Then attempt the question that follows.

Example

Passages 1 and 2 are adapted from Daniela Dimitrova Russo, Todd Myers, "Should Cities Ban Plastic Bags?" ©2012 by Dow Jones & Company.

Passage 1

Plastic pollution is the nexus of some of the major environmental challenges facing us today. Discarded plastic bags
Line float in the ocean, they tumble in the
5   desert, they are found in riverbeds and dams. They kill off marine animals that confuse the bags with plankton and jellyfish; they end up calcified in the stomachs of animals on land.
10   But the greatest damage is economic—the cost of cleaning up all that waste. That's why dozens of countries and cities around the world, including 47 municipalities in California
15   alone, have adopted ordinances banning plastic bags.

Communities don't have much of a choice if they leave things as they are: They either drown in plastic bags or spend 20 millions of dollars to clean up the mess—tax dollars that should go toward infrastructure, education and libraries.

San Jose, Calif., reports that it costs about $1 million a year to repair recycling 25 equipment jammed with plastic bags. San Francisco estimates that to clean up, recycle and landfill plastic bags costs as much as 17 cents a bag, or approximately $8.5 million a year.

30 Elsewhere in the world, Bangladesh banned plastic bags because they clog storm-drain systems and cause major flooding, which in turn has significant economic cost. Ireland's PlasTax was 35 prompted by the cost of litter. The United Arab Emirates plans to eliminate the use of conventional plastic bags by 2013.

Passage 2

Across the world, cities are joining the latest environmental fad—banning plastic 40 grocery bags. Activists think banning the bags is a simple and environmentally responsible approach.

Some ban supporters claim plastics harm human health, even when studies 45 from organizations like the Environmental Protection Agency, the Centers for Disease Control and Prevention, and Pacific Northwest National Labs show these claims are false or exaggerated. 50 Consider a study from the U.K. Environment Agency that found plastic grocery bags have the lowest environmental impact in "human toxicity" and "marine aquatic toxicity" as well as "global-55 warming potential" even after paper bags are used four times and reusable cotton

bags are used 173 times. Why? Largely because paper and cotton bags come from crops that require fertilizer, pesticides, 60 herbicides and the like.

Critics also say that ban opponents ignore the environmental impact of bags over the course of their lifetime. But many studies do just that. The U.K. Environment 65 Agency's study, for instance, compared the energy expended in creating, using and disposing of plastic, paper and reusable bags to arrive at its figures. Consumers would have to use a cotton bag 173 times 70 before they match the energy savings of one plastic bag, assuming 40% of bags are reused—a percentage that's actually lower than the rate in some cities.

Some critics say we need to ban bags 75 because voluntary take-back programs don't work. But the point of the programs is simply to reuse bags, and consumers already reuse bags to hold garbage or pick up after pets. As for the idea that plastic 80 bags cost consumers more, the reason grocery stores use plastic instead of paper or other bags is that they cost less and hold more. Reusable bags are even more expensive.

1

Passage 2 differs from Passage 1 in that only Passage 2

A) discusses the impact of alternative types of bags.

B) mentions types of costs associated with plastic bags.

C) uses quantitative information to support its claims.

D) provides examples of places that have banned plastic bags.

To answer this question, you can refer back to the things you underlined and noted in the passages. Pay particular attention to ideas that overlap between the two passages. This can help you select the correct answer choice, (A), as lines 73-78 describe a concept that is not repeated from Passage 1.

You can use Process of Elimination to knock out incorrect answer choices. For this question, answers are incorrect if they mention something not covered in Passage 2, or something that is mentioned in Passage 1.

You can therefore eliminate answer choice (B), as cost appears in both passages, though in different ways. Passage 1 discusses the cost of cleaning up bags, and Passage 2 discusses the cost to the consumer. Answer choice (C) is incorrect, as both passages use numbers to bolster their arguments; you may have noted this in lines 23-30 and 73-78. You can knock out choice (D) because only Passage 1 lists places that have banned plastic bags, and the question is asking about an idea only present in Passage 2.

Part 1 Practice: Paired Passages

Below is an example passage. Read the passage, paying special attention to the elements we have discussed, and then answer the accompanying practice questions.

Passages 1 and 2 are adapted from Steven W. Lockley, Jane Orient, "Should Medical Residents Be Required to Work Shorter Shifts?" ©2012 by Dow Jones & Company.

Resident physicians are physicians who have graduated from a medical school and are continuing their professional training by performing supervised work in a medical care facility.

Passage 1

At Brigham and Women's Hospital, we quantified the effects of work hours on medical error rates in a group of first-year
Line residents who worked in intensive-care
5 units under two sets of conditions: a traditional schedule with 24- to 30-hour shifts every other shift, and a schedule with 16-hour limits. On the former schedule, the residents made 36% more
10 serious medical errors than on the latter, and inadvertently fell asleep on duty twice as often on overnight duty. Longer shifts affect not just the safety and health of patients but that of physicians as well. In
15 surveys conducted by our group, residents working 24 or more hours in a row reported sticking themselves with needles 60% more often, and had more than double the odds of having a car crash on
20 the drive home from work as compared with shorter shifts. In a 2010 review of

23 studies on the effects of reducing resident work hours, all but one showed an improvement or no change in patient
25 care or resident sleep or quality of life. There were no objective data showing that shorter work hours were worse for patients or physicians.

Despite the increasing emphasis on
30 evidence-based decision-making in medicine, these data have often been met with a negative response. Those who oppose stricter work-hour limits say continuity of care demands long shifts.
35 But even with 30-hour shifts, care of a patient eventually has to be handed over to another team.

Medicine is also increasingly filled with specialists, a development requiring
40 a team approach to deliver the best care. So we need to find better ways for teams to communicate and to transfer information, rather than insist that doctors risk their own and their patients' health by working
45 beyond their biological limits.

Doctors are not immune to biology. While we appreciate their dedication and sacrifice, we cannot allow them to harm others or themselves with the outdated
50 and unnecessary "rite of passage" of 24-hour shifts.

Passage 2

For a half-dozen years, the Accreditation
Council for Graduate Medical Education
has experimented with reduced work hours
55 for physicians-in-training. The current
limit is no more than 80 hours per week.
Now some want to reduce this even further.

I think we should challenge the whole
idea of having a central committee dictate
60 work limitations for all residency programs.

Treating new physicians like shift
workers is destroying the individual
patient-physician relationship. Having
shorter shifts means more frequent
65 "handoffs," which disrupts both education
and patient care. Those who favor shorter
shifts, and thus more handoffs, may argue
that quality of handoffs matters more than
quantity. But quantity matters too. The
70 shift-work culture means working until
time is up, rather than until work is done.
The incentive is to leave problems for the
next shift rather than to find and address
them as early as possible.
75 Patients are now the collective
responsibility of the team, rather than
primarily the responsibility of "their
doctor." In the old system, the patient's
doctor was expected to take care of
80 anticipated problems as well as possible
before signing out. It is also more efficient
for the doctor who already knows the
patient to order the fever work-up, talk to
the family, or assess progress and the
85 potential need for a change in the treatment.

In the old days, it was understood that
residency would be grueling. A surgical
residency was specifically compared with
becoming a Marine.
90 The enemy was disease or death or
human suffering, and the schedule of
fighting was determined by the enemy, not
by a central committee.

1

Both passages suggest which of the
following is a main reason to be concerned
about shift-length during residency?

A) Freedom of choice for doctors

B) The quality of medical care

C) The safety of doctors

D) Preserving traditional training methods

2

Which of the following types of evidence is
used in Passage 1, but NOT in Passage 2?

A) An appeal to emotions with the
illustration of a specific case

B) Quotations from sleep experts about
the requirements of proper rest

C) Personal anecdotes about the author's
own experience as a resident

D) Data from studies on the effects of
resident working hours on performance

3

The author of Passage 2 would most likely
respond to the argument in lines 32-37
("Those who … team") by

A) arguing that fewer hand-overs are still
preferable, even if some are
unavoidable.

B) suggesting that doctors should continue
to work until patients recover.

C) pointing out that specialist training
would not be possible with shorter
shifts.

D) proposing that we should develop a
better system for hand-overs.

Passages with Graphics
Part 2

Two reading passages on the SAT will include graphics. One of the passages will be a Science passage, and the other will be a Social Studies passage. There will be one or two graphics accompanying each passage. The graphics will contain additional information that supplements the passage, and will always be related to the main topic of the passage. Most often, the graphics will be representations of statistical data—including bar graphs, tables, and pie charts.

Graphics may provide supporting evidence for the passage, with accompanying questions that require you to correctly interpret the graphic in relation to the passage. You may also be asked questions that will require you to interpret information presented *only* in the graphic.

Reading the Graphics

Graphs can contain a lot of information. Here are some of the key elements to look for.

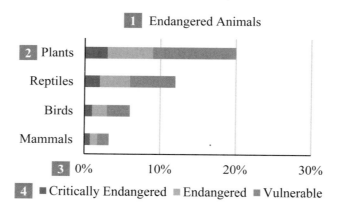

5 This chart shows the percentage of various species, by group, on the IUNC Red List as of 2007. The Red List is an online listing of endangered species categorized by taxonomy, type of threat and other criteria.

1 **Title.** The title of a graphic usually tells you what the graphic is intended to show.

2 **Labels.** Be sure to read all of the labels in a graphic, and make sure that you understand which elements they refer to and what they say about them.

3 **Units.** Be sure you know what units a graphic is using for data. The number ten will mean something very different on a chart showing distances in feet than on one showing distance in *thousands* of feet.

4 **Legend.** A legend is a guide to the graphic that shows you what different shades, images, or patterns mean in the image. Always read legends carefully when they're available.

5 **Caption.** If there's a caption below the graphic, read it carefully. The captions often provide directions for how to properly read the graphic, and extra details about the information provided in the graphic.

6 **References in the Passage.** If the passage refers to the graphic, or to information in the graphic, pay attention to which information the passage is referring to and how the author is using the information from the graphic in the passage.

Sometimes, a graphic might contain a lot of information. You don't need to scrutinize every detail: just try to understand the graphic's relationship to the passage, and look for the essential elements described above so that when you need to check the graphic to get a specific piece of information, you'll be able to find it quickly.

Analyzing Quantitative Info

Be careful not to make any assumptions about information that you are not given, or to assume that trends presented in the graphic will remain true for other scenarios.

Let's look at an example to see how this works.

Example

Temperatures in Singapore		
Month	Record High °F	Average High °F
Jan	93.7	86.2
Feb	95.4	88.2
Mar	96.8	88.9
Apr	96.4	89.1
May	95.7	88.9
Year	96.8	86.2

This chart shows temperatures in Singapore for the years 1929–1941 and 1948–2011.

1

Which claim about Singapore's weather is supported by the graphic?

A) January is on average the coldest month of the year in Singapore.

B) There have been higher record temperatures in April than in March.

C) The average high in March is lower than the yearly average.

D) The average high in March is higher than the yearly average.

Here only answer choice (D) is actually supported by the chart. You can easily compare the average temperatures for given for March and fir the year overall, and see that 88.9 is higher than 86.2. Answer choice (C) gives the opposite answer, so you know it is incorrect.

You can also use the Process of Elimination to knock out answer choice (A) because even though January is the coldest month according to the chart, the chart does not include data for the entire year. Answer choice (B) can be eliminated as it confuses average temperature for the record temperature; the record high for March is higher than that for April.

Relating Graphics to Passages

To relate a graphic back to information in the passage, look for lines in the passage that discuss the same subjects being measured and presented in the graphic. You may have marked up these lines as you first read the passage. Then, compare the information from the passage to what is presented in the graphic. You can underline or circle the items on the graphic that you are asked about or that are repeated from the passage.

The graphic may present slightly different information than the passage, and you may need to combine these two sources of information in order to reach a broader conclusion than what you could support from just one source.

Let's look at an example of a passage excerpt and graphic to see how this works.

Example

Gross domestic product (GDP) is the market value of all goods and services produced within a country in a year. GDP
Line is an aggregate figure, which does not
5 consider the differing sizes of nations. Therefore, GDP can be stated as GDP per capita, in which the total GDP is divided by the resident population on a given date. GDP per capita is not a measure of
10 personal income, as it is measured by dividing the total amount of GDP equally among all citizens. However, a high GDP per capita is generally considered an indicator of the economic health of a
15 nation and the living standards of its citizens generally.

3

It can reasonably be inferred from the passage and graphic that

A) the United States produced more goods and services than the United Kingdom for all years measured.

B) the United Kingdom produced more goods and services than the United States for all years measured.

C) the United States likely experienced better economic health than the United Kingdom for all years measured.

D) the United Kingdom had a lower GDP than the United States in 2008.

GDP per Capita in US Dollars		
Year	United States	United Kingdom
2008	46,760	43,147
2009	45,305	35,331
2010	46,612	36,238
2011	48,112	38,974
2012	49,641	39,090

To answer this question, you need to combine information given in the chart with information stated in the text of the passage. Only answer choice (C) is supported by information from both sources. The chart shows you that the United States had a higher GDP per capita, and the passage tells you this is usually "considered an indicator of the economic health of a nation" (lines 14-15). By combining these pieces of information, you can select this answer.

Answer choice (A) is contradicted by information in the passage, which clarifies that GDP per capita does not measure total goods and services, but divides that number by the number of total citizens. Without knowing the population of the two countries for the years measured, it is not possible to determine which country produced more goods and services. There is a similar issue with answer choice (B). Answer choice (D) is incorrect as the chart only indicates GDP per capita, which is different from regular GDP as defined by the passage.

Part 2 Practice: Passages with Graphics

Below are two example passages. Read the passages, paying special attention to the elements we have discussed, and then answer the accompanying practice questions.

This passage is adapted from Justin Gillis, "Heat-Trapping Gas Passes Milestone, Raising Fears." ©2013 by The New York Times Company.

The level of the most important heat-trapping gas in the atmosphere, carbon dioxide, passed a long-feared milestone,
Line scientists reported in May 2013, reaching
5 a concentration not seen on the earth for millions of years.

Scientific instruments showed that the gas had reached an average daily level above 400 parts per million—just an
10 odometer moment in one sense, but also a sobering reminder that decades of efforts to bring human-produced emissions under control are faltering.

"It symbolizes that so far we have
15 failed miserably in tackling this problem," said Pieter P. Tans, who runs the monitoring program at the National Oceanic and Atmospheric Administration (NOAA) that reported the new reading.
20 Ralph Keeling, who runs another monitoring program at the Scripps Institution of Oceanography in San Diego, said a continuing rise could be catastrophic. "It means we are quickly losing the
25 possibility of keeping the climate below what people thought were possibly tolerable thresholds," he said.

China is now the largest emitter, but Americans have been consuming fossil
30 fuels extensively for far longer, and experts say the United States is more responsible than any other nation for the high level.

The new measurement came from
35 analyzers atop Mauna Loa, the volcano on the big island of Hawaii that has long been ground zero for monitoring the worldwide trend on carbon dioxide, or CO_2. Devices there sample clean, crisp
40 air that has blown thousands of miles across the Pacific Ocean, producing a record of rising carbon dioxide levels that has been closely tracked for half a century.

45 Carbon dioxide above 400 parts per million was first seen in the Arctic last year, and had also spiked above that level in hourly readings at Mauna Loa.

But the average reading for an entire
50 day surpassed that level at Mauna Loa for the first time in the 24 hours that ended at 8 p.m. Eastern Daylight Time on Thursday, May 9, 2013. The two monitoring programs use slightly
55 different protocols; NOAA reported an average for the period of 400.03 parts per million, while Scripps reported 400.08.

Carbon dioxide rises and falls on a seasonal cycle, and the level will dip below 400 this summer as leaf growth in the Northern Hemisphere pulls about 10 billion tons of carbon out of the air. But experts say that will be a brief reprieve—the moment is approaching when no measurement of the ambient air anywhere on earth, in any season, will produce a reading below 400.

From studying air bubbles trapped in Antarctic ice, scientists know that going back 800,000 years, the carbon dioxide level oscillated in a tight band, from about 180 parts per million in the depths of ice ages to about 280 during the warm periods between. The evidence shows that global temperatures and CO_2 levels are tightly linked.

For the entire period of human civilization, roughly 8,000 years, the carbon dioxide level was relatively stable near that upper bound. But the burning of fossil fuels has caused a 41 percent increase in the heat-trapping gas since the Industrial Revolution, a mere geological instant, and scientists say the climate is beginning to react, though they expect far larger changes in the future.

Indirect measurements suggest that the last time the carbon dioxide level was this high was at least three million years ago, during an epoch called the Pliocene.

Geological research shows that the climate then was far warmer than today, the world's ice caps were smaller, and the sea level might have been as much as 60 or 80 feet higher.

Countries have adopted an official target to limit the damage from global warming, with 450 parts per million seen as the maximum level compatible with that goal. "Unless things slow down, we'll probably get there in well under 25 years," Ralph Keeling said.

Yet many countries, including China and the United States, have refused to adopt binding national targets. Scientists say that unless far greater efforts are made soon, the goal of limiting the warming will become impossible without severe economic disruption.

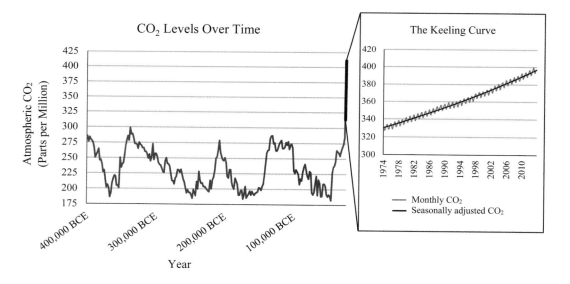

1

The passage indicates that, during the winter, which of the following is true?

A) Dropping temperatures will also cause a drop in carbon dioxide levels.

B) Atmospheric sampling is less likely to produce accurate results.

C) Atmospheric carbon dioxide levels are higher than at other times in the year.

D) Scientists are able to sample air bubbles trapped in ice.

2

Based on information from the passage and graph, carbon dioxide levels

A) never reached 400 parts per million before the Industrial Revolution.

B) never reached levels as high as today in the preceding 400,000 years.

C) have been as high as 400,000 parts per million in the past.

D) are usually around 200 parts per million.

3

Information from the graph best supports which of the following statements?

A) From 1974 to 2010, carbon dioxide levels rose more slowly but to a higher point than at any other time in the past 400,000 years.

B) Seasonally adjusted carbon dioxide levels have been above 300 parts-per-million for more than 200,000 years.

C) Due to increasing carbon dioxide, sea levels in 2010 most likely rose to levels similar to those in the Pliocene.

D) Between 1974 and 2010, carbon dioxide levels sometimes dropped from month-to-month, but seasonally adjusted levels rose steadily.

This passage is adapted from "Age Invaders." ©2014 by The Economist.

According to the UN's population projections, the standard source for demographic estimates, there are around
Line 600 million people aged 65 or older alive
5 today. That is in itself remarkable; the author Fred Pearce claims it is possible that half of all the humans who have ever been over 65 are alive today. But as a share of the total population, at 8%, it is
10 not that different to what it was a few decades ago.

By 2035, however, more than 1.1 billion people—13% of the population— will be above the age of 65. This is a
15 natural corollary of the dropping birth rates that are slowing overall population growth; they mean there are proportionally fewer young people around. The "old-age dependency ratio"—the ratio of old
20 people to those of working age—will grow even faster. In 2010 the world had 16 people aged 65 and over for every 100 adults between the ages of 25 and 64, almost the same ratio it had in 1980. By
25 2035 the UN expects that number to have risen to 26.

In rich countries it will be much higher. Japan will have 69 old people for every 100 of working age by 2035 (up
30 from 43 in 2010), Germany 66 (from 38). Even America, which has a relatively high fertility rate, will see its old-age dependency rate rise by more than 70%, to 44. Developing countries, where
35 today's ratio is much lower, will not see absolute levels rise that high, but the proportional growth will be higher. Over the same time period, the old-age dependency rate in China will more than
40 double from 15 to 36. Latin America will see a shift from 14 to 27.

The Big Shift; Old-age dependency,
population aged 65 and over per 100 people aged 25-64

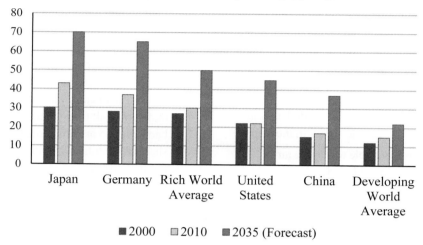

Adapted from "Age Invaders." ©2014 by The Economist

4

It can reasonably be inferred from the passage and graphic that

A) Latin America will have a lower old-age dependency ratio than the rich world average in 2035.

B) Latin America had a lower old-age dependency ratio than the developing world average in 2000.

C) Japan will have 70 old people for every 100 of working age by 2040.

D) the United States will never have as high an old-age dependency ratio as Germany.

5

Which claim about old-age dependency is supported by the graphic?

A) Japan has historically had a lower old-age dependency ratio than the United States.

B) The developing world will have a lower old-age dependency ratio than China in 2035.

C) The developing world had a higher old-age dependency ratio than China in 2010.

D) Germany's growing old-age dependency ratio is representative of rich countries overall.

Practice Set
Part 3

The following passages have been designed to test the question types you learned about in this section. Review the techniques we discussed in Section 2, and mark up and make summaries for these passages. Then, answer the questions using the strategies you just learned.

Passages 1 and 2 are adapted from Richard G. Little, Wenonah Hauter, "Are We Better Off Privatizing Water?" ©2012 by Dow Jones & Company.

Passage 1

Our nation's aging drinking-water systems will require staggering amounts of investment in the coming decades—as
Line much as $1 trillion over the next 25 years,
5 the American Water Works Association estimates. As things stand now, this burden will fall mostly on the public water utilities that serve about 80% of the U.S. population.

10 But these bodies don't have the money to pay such bills. Many of them already have put off necessary improvements for years due to insufficient public funding. And there is little chance of meaningful
15 federal aid, given the national focus on debt reduction. The root of the problem is the artificially low rates the public utilities have charged for years. These rates, kept low for political purposes, don't come
20 close to supporting the long-range capital investment we would expect of any well-run business.

Is privatization the solution in every case? Of course not. We must strive to
25 find what works best for the customers in a specific situation. Mismanagement is not a problem limited to private operators, just as good management is not intrinsic to public systems. But private management
30 can be successful much more often than its critics would like to believe. Private

-sector managers focus on the cost of service and return on capital. The new and innovative technologies in which
35 they invest may have a higher initial cost, but they offer savings, too, which can be shared with customers while improving service and quality.

Ultimately, the best water provider is
40 the one that is best able to deliver safe, reliable, and accessible service. If the provider can also make a profit, that should be of less concern than its ability to deliver safe and affordable drinking
45 water.

Passage 2

Privatization is not the solution for deteriorating public water systems already feeling the double-pinch of dwindling local and federal funds. Private
50 companies that operate water systems have appalling track records of rate increases, poor system maintenance, faulty billing practices and other failures, sometimes even jeopardizing the health
55 and safety of local residents.

Some municipalities have taken their water systems back from private water providers. Indeed, some are realizing what cities like New York, Baltimore,
60 and Boston realized a century ago—that water is best controlled by an entity that is accountable to the public, not outside shareholders.

Water service isn't a business
65 enterprise; it's a basic human right, and

what privatization proponents refer to as "political pressure" is actually our democratic processes at work. Our elected leaders should absolutely respond to
70 public concern about the affordability of their water service. The provision of water service is a natural monopoly, and the public can exercise choice only at the ballot box through the election of the
75 officials who oversee the service. How government-run utilities decide to allocate costs among different users is a local decision that should be made in an open and democratic manner.

80 　　Rather than privatizing water systems or asking household users to pay more, why not ask commercial and industrial water users to pay more for the services they profit from? We should also ask the
85 federal government to establish a dedicated source of federal funding in the form of a clean-water trust fund, similar to the program that provides funding for highways. This would provide a
90 guaranteed source of funding for replacing and maintaining public infrastructure systems, thereby alleviating communities of the burden of having to finance improvement projects on their own. When
95 it comes to efficiently and affordably providing water to our communities, public control trumps private profits.

1

Both passages are primarily concerned with

A) how to charge individuals for drinking water.

B) investing in new infrastructure for public water systems.

C) privatizing public water systems.

D) regulating American's drinking-water system.

2

Which of the following best describes the relationship between the two passages?

A) Passage 2 advocates a different solution to the same problem discussed in Passage 1.

B) Passage 2 provides a more detailed explanation for the situation described in Passage 1.

C) Passage 2 offers alternative evidence in support of the argument made in Passage 1.

D) Passage 2 focuses on a narrow aspect of the problem defined in Passage 1.

3

The authors of both passages agree that water service should be

A) priced to discourage excessive use.

B) financially profitable for public operators.

C) priced differently for industrial use than for common use.

D) affordable for all water consumers.

4

Unlike the author of Passage 2, the author of Passage 1

A) appeals to emotion by invoking the idea of human rights.

B) refers to the argument of the opposing side in order to refute it.

C) uses specific data to demonstrate the seriousness of the problem.

D) provides evidence to show that privatization of water services has been successful in the past.

5

The author of Passage 1 would most likely respond to Passage 2's claim that private water systems "have appalling track records of rate increases" (lines 51-52) by

A) demonstrating that rate increases best allow water providers to invest in future projects and other industries.

B) stating that public utility rates are too low and that raising them is necessary to ensure long-term sustainability.

C) explaining that high prices are, unfortunately, necessary due to dwindling federal aid for public works.

D) countering that political pressure will prevent prices from rising even if water companies are privatized.

6

What would the author of Passage 1 most likely think about the "clean-water trust fund" (line 87) proposed by the author of Passage 2?

A) That it is unlikely to be established while the federal government is trying to reduce its debt

B) That it would likely prohibit spending on vital technological development

C) That it is a good first step towards revitalizing struggling water systems and helping them to remain public

D) That it would be a risky investment because no similar fund has ever existed

7

Which best describes the difference between the main focus of Passage 1 and the main focus of Passage 2?

A) Passage 1 is focused on how water utilities might turn a profit, while Passage 2 is focused on how citizens can campaign for better water use rates.

B) Passage 1 is focused on political problems that can be solved through privatization, while Passage 2 is focused on economic problems that can be solved through public policy.

C) Passage 1 is focused on the danger posed to water utilities by political corruption, while Passage 2 is focused on the maintenance of a free public debate over water use.

D) Passage 1 is focused on the difficulties water utilities will face in the future, while Passage 2 is focused on the causes of these problems.

8

How would the author of Passage 2 most likely respond to the assertion in Passage 1 that current rates for water service are too low to support necessary investments (lines 16-22)?

A) By arguing that it is not necessary to invest additional funds in water services

B) By suggesting that price increases should be avoided because they are undemocratic

C) By observing that public utilities are able to invest in water services without raising rates

D) By conceding that some price increases may be necessary, but should fall on commercial water users

This passage is adapted from Olga Khazan, "How We Get Tall." ©2014 by The Atlantic.

Last year, Tim Hatton, an economist at the University of Essex in the U.K., rounded up data on the heights of European 21-year-olds dating from 1860 to about 1980. The results, published in the Oxford Economic Papers, were impressive: The average European man became about 11 centimeters taller between 1870 and 1970, gaining about a centimeter per decade. A mid-19th century British man stood just five feet, four inches tall, but he was five-foot-ten by 1980.

While about 80 percent of height is determined by genes, auxologists (those are height scientists) now believe that nutrition and sanitation determine much of the rest. As the New Yorker's Burkhard Bilger put it in 2004: "Height variations within a population are largely genetic, but height variations between populations are mostly environmental, anthropometric history suggests. If Joe is taller than Jack, it's probably because his parents are taller. But if the average Norwegian is taller than the average Nigerian it's because Norwegians live healthier lives."

Hatton and his colleagues, Roy E. Bailey from the University of Essex and Kris Inwood from the University of Guelph, created a database of 2,236 British soldiers who served in World War I, and then they looked up their birth records. The soldiers were relatively representative of the male population as a whole—about two-thirds of the 1890 British male birth cohort* enlisted. It turns out that subtle differences in their heights hinted at their origins.

The more kids there were in a household, the shorter they were. Not only because there was less food to go around, but also because it made it more likely that there were more people in each bedroom. "Crowding can help spread respiratory and gastrointestinal infections,"

Hatton said. "People sneezing on each other, that sort of thing."

People from industrial districts were shorter than those from agricultural areas. Regardless of income, the Dickensian living conditions of 19th century British cities suppressed height by about nine-tenths of an inch. On top of being hit with factory pollution, urban dwellers were packed into filthy, disease-ridden slums. As Kellow Chesney described in *The Victorian Underworld*, "Hideous slums, some of them acres wide, some no more than crannies of obscure misery, make up a substantial part of the metropolis … In big, once handsome houses, thirty or more people of all ages may inhabit a single room."

But as the 20th century wore on, that description became less and less apt. Tenements and slums were replaced with better housing; sewage systems and running water became standard. Women attended school in greater numbers and went from having five children, on average, to two. The 20th century was when Europeans achieved modernity, and as a result, it seems, they had to buy longer pants. "Together these developments help to explain the apparent puzzle of rapid improvement in average health status during a period of war and depression that predates the advent of universal health services," Hatton and his colleagues wrote.

For centuries, Americans were the NBA players of the world. We were two inches taller than the Red Coats we squared off against in the American Revolution. In 1850, Americans had about two and a half inches on people from every European country. But our stature plateaued after World War II, and since then, other countries shot past us. Now, the Dutch are the tallest, at an average of six feet for men and five-foot-seven for women. They've come a long way: In 1848, a quarter of Dutch men

were rejected from military service
95 because they didn't meet the five-foot-two height limit. "Today, fewer than one in 1,000 is that short," the Associated Press noted in 2006.

The Danes, Norwegians, and Germans
100 stack up right under the Dutch. American men and women, meanwhile, measure just 5'9" and 5'4", respectively, barely edging out the Southern Europeans. John Komlos, an economic historian who has
105 studied height extensively, thinks we Americans lost our height advantage because of poorer overall healthcare and nutrition compared to Europe. Our social

shortcomings, he believes, are literally
110 making us come up short.

"American children might consume more meals prepared outside of the home, more fast food rich in fat, high in energy density, and low in essential
115 micronutrients," he and co-author Benjamin E. Lauderdale of Princeton University wrote in 2006. "Furthermore, the European welfare states provide a more comprehensive social safety net
120 including universal health care coverage."

*A "birth cohort" is the group of people born during a specified period of time.

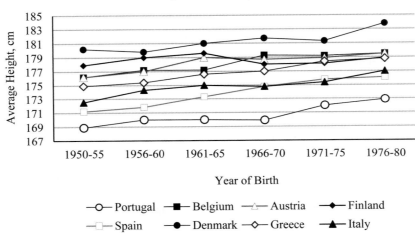

Evolution of Height
European Countries, Men

Country	Average Height of Birth Cohort, 1950-55 (cm)		Average Height of Birth Cohort, 1976-80 (cm)		Annual Growth Rate in Average Cohort Heights, %	
	Men	Women	Men	Women	Men	Women
Austria	176.3	165.6	179.6	167.1	0.07	0.04
Belgium	176.2	163.4	179.5	167.8	0.07	0.11
Denmark	180.3	167.2	183.7	168.6	0.07	0.03
Finland	177.8	164.3	178.7	165.9	0.02	0.04
Greece	174.7	163.3	178.6	165.9	0.09	0.06
Ireland	174.9	162.7	177.4	164.4	0.06	0.04
Italy	172.5	161.4	177.1	166.5	0.10	0.12
Portugal	168.8	158.9	172.9	162.5	0.10	0.09
Spain	171.3	160.4	176.1	165.5	0.11	0.12

Adapted from Jaume Garcia, Universitat Pompeu Fabra, "The Evolution of Adult Height in Europe: A Brief Note." ©2007 by Economics and Human Biology.

9

According to the table, graph, and passage, which of the following groups had the lowest average height?

A) Women born in Denmark in 1950-55

B) Women born in Austria in 1976-80

C) Men born in Portugal in 1966-70

D) Men born in Greece in 1950-55

10

It can reasonably be inferred from the passage and the graph that

A) all Greek men are taller than Italian men.

B) a man born in Finland in 1968 is taller than one born in 1964.

C) Danish people are the tallest people in the world.

D) conditions in Belgium are somewhat healthier than those in Portugal.

11

Based on the passage and the graph, in which pair of countries would you expect to find the most similar living conditions?

A) Austria in 1976-80 and Belgium during the same period

B) Belgium in 1976-80 and Spain during the same period

C) Italy in 1950-55 and Spain in 1976-80

D) Denmark in 1950-55 and Spain during the same period

12

Based on the passage and the table, which of the following statements is true?

A) Women in Ireland gained an average of .04 centimeters in height between 1950 and 1980.

B) Men in Spain got 11% taller between 1860 and 1980.

C) Women in Greece got 0.06% taller each year, on average, between 1950 and 1980.

D) Women born in Europe in 1960 were 1 cm taller than those born in 1950.

13

Based on information in the table, which of the following statements is true for every country included in the data presented?

A) The tallest individual man in any birth cohort was no taller than 183.7 cm.

B) The average height of the female birth cohort was lower but increased at a greater rate than the male birth cohort.

C) Male birth cohorts had a higher average height and higher average increase in height than female birth cohorts between 1950 and 1980.

D) Each male birth cohort had a higher average height than all female birth cohorts.

14

According to the graph, in which period's birth cohort did Belgian men first surpass Finnish men in height?

A) 1956-60

B) 1961-65

C) 1966-70

D) 1971-75

15

According to the table, which pair of groups saw the same annual increase in average height between 1950 and 1980?

A) Italian men and Italian women

B) Belgian women and Spanish men

C) Finnish women and Greek women

D) Greek men and Spanish men

Section 7
Vocabulary Building

The SAT's Reading and Writing Tests assess your ability to understand advanced reading material and vocabulary. In this section, we've provided a list of **roots, prefixes, and suffixes** to help you tackle this challenge. Learning these word parts is one of the fastest ways to quickly increase your ability to understand a wide variety of words, even if you haven't seen them before. Work through the lists to help build your vocabulary.

You can also access additional resources to further your study on our website. You'll find reading lists organized by grade level and subject, and a vocabulary list covering the difficulty level and content areas that are most likely to appear on the SAT.

 For additional resources, please visit **ivyglobal.com/study**.

Working through these materials will not only help you with your SAT score, but will also help you to become a better student in high school and college.

SAT Vocabulary
Part 1

The SAT's Reading and Writing Tests assess your knowledge of college-level vocabulary—the kinds of words that you will need to know in order to understand academic writing, as well as words that have different meanings in different contexts.

Building your vocabulary will help you not only on the SAT, but also in your future studies. In this part, we have included lists of common word parts to help you learn new vocabulary.

Word Roots, Prefixes, and Suffixes

Many words can be broken into basic parts. Roots carry the basic meaning of a word, prefixes come before roots and alter their meaning, and suffixes come after roots and alter either their meaning or their part of speech. Because English is related to French, German, Spanish, Latin, and Greek, many of these word parts will look familiar if you know one of those languages.

The lists below contain some of the most common English roots, prefixes, and suffixes. Start learning these basic parts to help you break down unfamiliar words and speed up your vocabulary-building process for the SAT.

Common Roots					
Root	Definition	Example	Root	Definition	Example
ag, act	do	action, activity, agent	*belli*	war	belligerent, rebellious, bellicose
ambul	walk, move	ambulance, ambulatory, amble	*ben, bene*	good	benefactor, beneficial, benevolence
ami, amo	love	amiable, amorous	*biblio*	book	bibliography, Bible
anim	mind, soul, spirit	animal, animate, unanimous	*bio*	life	biography, biology
anthro	human	anthropology, philanthropy	*carn*	flesh, meat	carnivore, carnal, incarnate
aud, audit	hear	audible, auditorium, audience	*chron*	time	chronic, chronology, synchronize
auto	self	automobile, autobiography, autograph	*cid, cis*	cut, kill	incision, homicide, insecticide

civi	citizen	civilization, civilian, civil	*omni*	all	omniscient, omnipotent, omnivorous
corp	body	corporation, corporeal, corpse	*pac, pas, pax*	peace	pacify, pacific, pacifist, passive
dem	people	democracy, demographic	*path, pass*	disease, feeling	pathology, sympathetic, apathy, antipathy
dic, dict	speak	dictate, contradict, prediction, verdict	*phil*	love	philanthropist, philosophy, philanderer
domin	master	dominant, domain, domineering	*port*	carry	portable, porter, transport, export
err	wander	error, erratic, errand	*poten*	able, powerful	potential, omnipotent, potentate, impotent
eu	good, beautiful	eulogize, euphoria, euphemism	*psych*	mind	psyche, psychology, psychosis, psychopath
fall, fals	deceive	fallacious, infallible, falsify	*reg, rect*	rule	regicide, regime, regent, insurrection
fid	faith	fidelity, confide, confidence	*sacr, secr*	holy	sacred, sacrilegious, sacrament, consecrate
graph, gram	writing	grammar, telegram, graphite	*scribe, script*	write	scribe, describe, script
loqu, locut	talk	soliloquy, loquacious, elocution	*somn*	sleep	insomnia, somnolent, somnambulist
luc	light	elucidate, lucid, translucent	*spec, spic*	see, look	spectators, spectacles, retrospect, conspicuous
magn	great	magnify, magnate, magnanimous	*tang, tact, ting*	touch	tactile, tangent, contact, contingent
mal	bad	malevolent, malediction, malicious	*terr*	land	terrain, terrestrial, subterranean
mori, mort	die	mortuary, immortal, moribund	*urb*	city	urban, urbane, suburban
morph	shape, form	amorphous, metamorphosis	*vac*	empty	vacation, vacuous, evacuate, vacant
nat	born	innate, natal, nativity	*ver*	truth	veracity, verify, veracious
nom	name	misnomer, nominal	*verb*	word	verbose, verbatim, proverb
nov	new	novice, innovate, renovate, novelty	*viv, vit*	alive	revival, vivacious, vitality

	Common Prefixes				
Prefix	Definition	Example	Prefix	Definition	Example
ambi, amphi	both	ambidextrous, ambiguous, ambivalent	*mis*	bad, hatred	misdemeanor, mischance, misanthrope
an, a	without	anarchy, anemia, amoral	*mono*	one	monarchy, monologue, monotheism
anti	against	antibody, antipathy, antisocial	*pan*	all, every	panacea, panorama, pandemic
circum	around	circumnavigate, circumspect, circumscribe	*peri*	around, near	perimeter, periphery, periscope
co, col, com, con	with, together	coauthor, collaborate, composition, concurrent	*poly*	many	polygon, polygamist, polyglot
contra, contro	against	contradict, contravene, controversy	*post*	after	postpone, posterity, postscript, posthumous
di, dif, dis	not, apart	digress, discord, differ, disparity	*pre*	before	preamble, prefix, premonition, prediction
dia	through, across	diagonal, diameter, dialogue	*pro*	forward, for, before	propulsive, proponent, prologue, prophet
dys	abnormal, bad	dysfunction, dyslexia, dystopia	*re, retro*	again, back	reiterate, reimburse, react, retrogress
e, ex, extra, extro	out, beyond	expel, excavate, eject, extrovert	*sub, suc, sup, sus*	under, less	subway, subjugate, suppress
in, il, im, ir (2)	in, upon	invite, incite, impression, illuminate	*syn, sym, syl, sys*	with, together	symmetry, synchronize, synthesize, sympathize
inter	between, among	intervene, international, interjection, intercept	*trans*	across	transfer, transport, transpose
intra	within	intramural, introvert, intravenous	*un*	not	unabridged, unkempt, unwitting

Common Suffixes					
Suffix	Definition	Example	Suffix	Definition	Example
able, ible	ADJ: capable of	edible, presentable, legible	*fy*	V: to make	magnify, petrify, beautify
ac, ic, ical	ADJ: like, related	cardiac, mythic, dramatic, musical	*ism*	N: doctrine, belief	monotheism, fanaticism, egotism
acious, icious	ADJ: full of	malicious, audacious	*ist*	N: dealer, doer	fascist, realist, artist
ant, ent	ADJ/N: full of	eloquent, verdant	*ize, ise*	V: make	victimize, rationalize, harmonize
ate	V: make, become	consecrate, enervate, eradicate	*logy*	N: study of	biology, geology, neurology
en	V: make, become	awaken, strengthen, soften	*oid*	ADJ: resembling	ovoid, anthropoid, spheroid
er (1)	ADJ: more	bigger, wiser, happier	*ose, ous*	ADJ: full of	verbose, lachrymose, nauseous, gaseous
er (2)	N: a person who does	teacher, baker, announcer	*osis*	N: condition	psychosis, neurosis, hypnosis
cy, ty, ity	N: state of being	democracy, accuracy, veracity	*tion, sion*	N: state of being	exasperation, irritation, transition, concession
ful	ADJ: full of	respectful, cheerful, wonderful	*tude*	N: state of	fortitude, beatitude, certitude

Writing
Chapter 3

Section 1
Introduction to the Writing Test

The Writing Test is not about *your* writing; it's about correcting the grammar, composition, and style of someone else's. On the Writing and Language Test, you will answer multiple choice questions that prompt you to revise and edit text on a variety of topics. Your job is to decide whether passages can be improved by making changes, and which changes best improve the passage.

First, let's go over some basic facts about the Writing Test.

The Basics

The SAT Writing Test is made up of four passages and 44 multiple choice questions. You will have 35 minutes to read the passages and answer the questions in this section.

The topics in the passages include Careers, Social Studies/History, Humanities, and Science. The passages will be 400-450 words in length, and broken up into sections across several pages. At least one passage will also contain an informational graphic. The graphic may be a table, graph, or chart that conveys information that is related to the passage topic.

Unlike on the Reading Test, the passages on the Writing and Language Test contain errors. The questions in this section challenge you to revise an underlined portion of the passage in order to make it better. Some questions may deal with one word in the passage, while other questions involve many words or many sentences within a paragraph. Some questions ask specifically about certain goals and how to achieve them. However, most questions on the Writing and Language Test don't actually "ask" a question; rather, a portion of the passage is underlined, and you will be asked to determine whether or not any of the answer options would improve the passage if they were to replace the underlined part. No matter what the question looks like, it should always be your goal to select the best option.

Scoring

The questions on the Writing Test contribute to several different scores on the SAT.

- **Writing Test Score**—this takes into account your answers to the questions on the Writing Test itself. Your Writing Test score will be reported as a number between 10 and 40.

- **Area Score for Evidence-Based Reading and Writing**—this combines your scores from the Reading and Writing Tests. Your Evidence-Based Reading and Writing Score will be reported as a number between 200 and 800, and will be half of your total Composite Score on your SAT.

- **Cross-Test Scores**—two cross-test scores combine scores from Reading, Writing, and Math to assess your skills in Analysis in History/Social Studies and Analysis in Science.

- **Subscores**—the Writing Test will also contribute to four subscores on the SAT: Command of Evidence, Words in Context, Expression of Ideas, and Standard English Conventions.

The Questions

Unlike the passages on the Reading Test, those on the Writing and Language Test contain errors. The questions in this section will ask you to choose the answer that corrects those errors or improves a passage.

Here is an example of what a single question might look like:

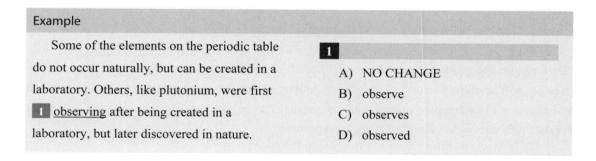

The first answer choice (NO CHANGE) indicates that the underlined portion of the passage shouldn't be changed. The second, third, and fourth answer choices provide different versions of the underlined portion of the passage. This question is asking you to select the best option for the underlined portion of the sentence, either by replacing it with one of the different versions provided, or by leaving it as it is. Here, the correct answer is (D).

Some questions may ask about one word in the passage, while other questions involve many words or many sentences within a paragraph. Sometimes, questions will ask more specific questions about what needs to be changed in the corresponding section. No matter what the question looks like, it should always be your goal to select the best option.

The Format

Below is an example of what the SAT Writing Test will look like. Notice that as you read through the passage, you will encounter numbers; when you reach a number, refer to the column on the right to find the question paired with the number. Many question numbers in the passage are followed by underlined portions of the passage. Usually, the answer options presented in the right-hand column are options for completely replacing the underlined portion. Sometimes, a question is asked about the underlined portion.

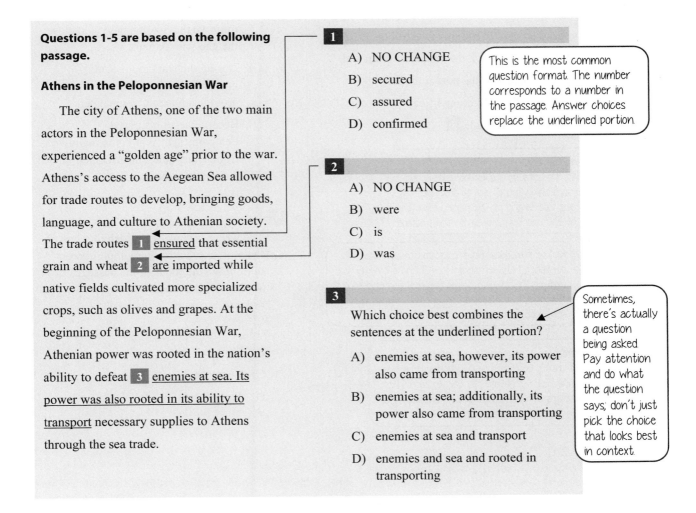

Questions 1-5 are based on the following passage.

Athens in the Peloponnesian War

The city of Athens, one of the two main actors in the Peloponnesian War, experienced a "golden age" prior to the war. Athens's access to the Aegean Sea allowed for trade routes to develop, bringing goods, language, and culture to Athenian society. The trade routes **1** ensured that essential grain and wheat **2** are imported while native fields cultivated more specialized crops, such as olives and grapes. At the beginning of the Peloponnesian War, Athenian power was rooted in the nation's ability to defeat **3** enemies at sea. Its power was also rooted in its ability to transport necessary supplies to Athens through the sea trade.

1
A) NO CHANGE
B) secured
C) assured
D) confirmed

This is the most common question format. The number corresponds to a number in the passage. Answer choices replace the underlined portion.

2
A) NO CHANGE
B) were
C) is
D) was

3
Which choice best combines the sentences at the underlined portion?

A) enemies at sea, however, its power also came from transporting

B) enemies at sea; additionally, its power also came from transporting

C) enemies at sea and transport

D) enemies and sea and rooted in transporting

Sometimes, there's actually a question being asked. Pay attention and do what the question says; don't just pick the choice that looks best in context.

[1] Athens's primary strategy was to avoid land battles and instead rely on this sea power. [2] This strategy served them well during the first half of the war. [3] However, this early advantage would not be enough to secure Athens's victory. **4** [4] Athens was struck by a plague, further weakening the Athenian effort. [5] Sparta was then able to use its naval resources to threaten and attack the supply of grain and silver going into the port at the city of Amphipolis, delivering a final blow to the Athenian war fund. **5**

When you see sentence numbers like this, it means that a question will appear later that refers to the numbered sentences. Don't count sentences; use these numbers.

There won't always be an underlined portion: sometimes, it's because a question asks about inserting something "here" or "at this point." That means inserting it at the place where the number of the question appears in the passage.

Notice how question 4 asks you to insert a sentence between sentences 3 and 4? After you answer that, which one is the real sentence 4? The one that's labeled sentence 4! Always use the sentence numbering.

Sometimes when there's no underlined portion, it's because the question is referring to numbered sentences in the passage. These questions can ask about whole paragraphs, or even the passage as a whole.

4

Which choice, inserted here, best develops the series of events described in the passage?

A) The Peloponnesian War would ultimately become the longest war in Greek history.

B) As the war continued, Sparta secured funds from Persia to improve the Spartan navy and close the gap with Athens.

C) During the war, soothsayers interpreted omens in order to provide advice to commanders.

D) Because accounts of the Peloponnesian War come mainly from Thucydides, an Athenian, there may be an Athenian bias.

5

The writer is considering deleting one of the sentences in this paragraph in order to improve the focus of the passage. Which sentence should be deleted in order to accomplish this goal?

A) Sentence 1

B) Sentence 2

C) Sentence 4

D) Sentence 5

Section 2
Approaching the Writing Test

In Section 1, you saw what the passages and questions on the Writing Test look like. Now we will discuss some strategies you can use to tackle these passages and questions.

In this section, you'll learn how to read the passages in the most efficient way. Then you'll learn how to work through the questions and choose the best answer. There are a few different kinds of questions on the Writing Test, so we will discuss how to deal with these using context clues and Process of Elimination. We'll also review general strategies for completing the Writing Test, including guessing and time management.

Reading the Passages
Part 1

Strategies

The first step in the Writing Test is to read the passages. Here are some strategies to help you read the passages effectively:

1. **Read the whole passage.** On the Writing Test, every sentence is important. Even if sentences don't have underlined portions, they may give you valuable information that you will use to answer the questions. Don't skip portions of the passage just because they don't include questions.

2. **Work on one passage at a time.** Make sure you attempt all questions for a passage before moving on. It is easiest to answer the questions while the passage is fresh in your mind. If you're not sure about a question, circle it in your test booklet and enter a guess on your answer sheet. That way, you can easily go back to the question if you have extra time to check your answers.

3. **Put your Pencil on Paper.** Mark up the passages in your test booklet as you read them to help keep track of important elements that will help you correctly answer questions.

4. **You're allowed to read passages out of order.** This is a helpful strategy if you feel rushed. Skim the first paragraph of each passage, and start with the passage that seems most interesting or least difficult. Taking the passages out of order can make it easy to make avoidable mistakes, so always be sure that you're bubbling in for the correct number on your answer sheet.

The practice tests at the back of this book will help you determine which strategies work best for you.

Pacing

No matter which strategies you choose to use, make sure to give yourself enough time to read the passage and answer the questions before moving on to the next passage. You have 35 minutes for the entire Writing Test. This is about 8.5 minutes per passage, but it's not a deadline: don't panic if you spend more than 8.5 minutes on a passage, but try not to spend more than 10 minutes on one. When you have spent 10 minutes on a passage, it's time to move on to the next passage. Skim the rest of the passage you're working on, take the time to answer easy questions, bubble in your best guesses for harder questions, and circle problems that you guessed on in your booklet so that you can come back to them later if you have time.

However, keep in mind that it's always better to answer a question than to leave it blank: try to answer every question carefully, but bubble in a guess for every question before time is up for that section.

Reading the Questions
Part 2

While you are reading the passages, you will come across underlined portions with question numbers next to them. As we saw in Section 1, these numbers signal that the question will ask you to revise the underlined section. You might need to revise words, phrases, or whole sentences in the passage. Depending on what part of the passage the question is asking about, you may want to pick certain questions or skip others.

Question Types Matter

There are two basic types of questions on the SAT Writing Test: questions of **Conventions**, and questions of **Expression**. Understanding which type of question you're looking at helps you to understand how to identify the correct answer.

Questions of Conventions are about the basic rules of English. There will be grammar or punctuation errors in the underlined portion, the answer choices, or both. Your task on a question of Conventions is simply to select the option that correctly follows the rules, or conventions, of standard written English. There will only ever be one choice on this type of question that is entirely free of errors, and that is always the correct choice.

If you learn all of the grammar rules in this book, you can always use Process of Elimination on this type of question by knocking out options that include errors.

Questions of Expression are about issues of logic, style, and tone. Neither the underlined portion nor any of the answer choices will contain errors of English. It's always important to pay attention to the type of question that you're answering: you don't want to come across a question of Expression and carelessly select "NO CHANGE" because the underlined portion is grammatically correct. The underlined portion may be grammatically correct, but not the best way of expressing the ideas in the passage. Your task on these questions is either to select the option that is the most clear, logical, and appropriate in the context of the passage, or to satisfy the requirements of a specific goal or question spelled out in the exam.

You can't necessarily use Process of Elimination to confidently eliminate every incorrect choice on this type of question. Instead, you have to compare your choices and select the best option. The best approach can often be to Plug In Options and consider how each choice sounds in context.

Decoding the Questions

A lot of students approach questions on the SAT Writing Test by thinking only about how each option sounds in context, and choosing the one that sounds best. We call that Plugging In Options: it's a quick way of approaching the questions, and can work for some types of errors. However, if you're not sure what type of problem you're supposed to be correcting, then it can be difficult to select the correct answer—and easy to make avoidable errors. If you identify the problem the test wants you to solve then you can confidently apply a rule to find the correct answer.

Some questions on the Writing and Language Test have prompts, and you should read them carefully to make sure that you know what the question is asking you to do. Most questions, however, don't clearly state exactly what you have to correct in the question. For these questions, you should look at the differences between answer options and the context of the question to work out what the question is asking about. Consider the following examples:

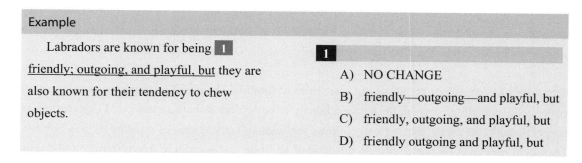

In this question, (A), (B), (C), and (D) all use the same words. The only difference is punctuation. Most of the punctuation comes between items in a list, so this is a question about how to punctuate lists. This is a question of Conventions.

Items in a list should be separated by commas (or sometimes semicolons). (A) incorrectly uses a semicolon, (B) unnecessarily separates "outgoing" from the rest of the list with em-dashes, and (D) doesn't separate the items in the list at all. Only (C) punctuates the list correctly.

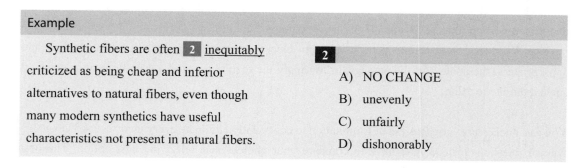

In this question, the difference between the underlined portion and the answer choices is the choice of a single word. All of these choices are adverbs, and any of them would be grammatically correct choices. The task here is to select the word that is most appropriate in context. This is a question of Expression.

To figure out which word is best in context, we need to think about the meaning, tone, and connotations of each word. All of the words have similar meanings. (A) means "in a biased way," (B) means "in an irregular or unbalanced way," (C) means "in a way that isn't fair," and (D) means "in a way that isn't honorable." Honor doesn't seem to be involved, so we can cross out (D). There's no mention of criticisms of other kinds of fabrics, or of why critics might be biased, but there is a suggestion that synthetic fibers have some virtues which make the criticisms untrue or unfair. The comparisons suggested by (A) and (B) don't make as much sense in context as (C).

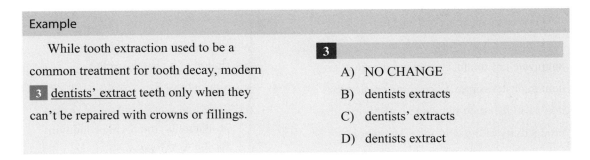

Example	
While tooth extraction used to be a common treatment for tooth decay, modern **3** <u>dentists' extract</u> teeth only when they can't be repaired with crowns or fillings.	**3** A) NO CHANGE B) dentists extracts C) dentists' extracts D) dentists extract

In this question, we're looking at both wording and punctuation differences. (A) and (C) both use apostrophes, making the noun possessive instead of plural, while (B) and (D) both use the non-possessive plural form. However, the verbs are also different. This question is asking about two concepts. That might seem to make it more complicated, but it actually helps you out: using Process of Elimination, you can take the rules one at a time and rule out answer options if they break even one rule.

Let's say you rule out the options that punctuate the noun incorrectly: after that, you only have to consider two options when you're figuring out which verb agrees with the subject. This is a question of Conventions.

We need to use the plural, non-possessive form of "dentist," so we can eliminate (A) and (C). We also need to use for the form of "extract" that agrees with the plural noun "dentists," and that is "extract." We can therefore rule out (B), and that leaves us with (D) as the correct answer.

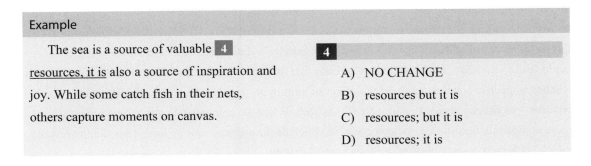

Example	
The sea is a source of valuable **4** <u>resources, it is</u> also a source of inspiration and joy. While some catch fish in their nets, others capture moments on canvas.	**4** A) NO CHANGE B) resources but it is C) resources; but it is D) resources; it is

Here's another question with punctuation and wording differences. (A) and (D) don't have a conjunction, but (B) and (C) do. In this case, the question is asking about how to correctly join two clauses. However, the same two clauses might be able to be joined with a conjunction or without one, depending on how punctuation is used. That means that you have to consider punctuation and wording together, not separately, to answer the question correctly. This is a question of Conventions.

The two parts of the sentence here are independent clauses. We can either join them with a semicolon, or with a comma and a conjunction. (A) uses a comma but no conjunction; (B) uses a conjunction but no comma; (C) uses a semicolon, but also incorrectly adds a conjunction. Only (D) correctly joins the two clauses.

Example

Poor labor relations can lead to a vicious cycle, in which two forces continuously aggravate one another—making the situation continuously worse. When some employees don't feel that they're being treated fairly, the productivity of the workforce as a whole tends to decline. Facing declining productivity, some employers may invest less in rewarding their workforce. Confronted with declining rewards, **5** more employees may feel that they're being treated unfairly, leading to additional declines in productivity.

5

Which example best completes the description of a vicious cycle?

A) NO CHANGE

B) some employees will increase their productivity, improving conditions for the workforce.

C) some employees might look for jobs elsewhere.

D) less productive employees will seek other jobs, increasing the overall efficiency of the workforce.

This question tells us about a specific goal, and asks how best to accomplish that goal. All of the choices provided create a grammatically complete and correct sentence. Questions with written prompts like this are always questions of Expression. We have a very specific task with these questions: satisfying the stated goal of the question. Usually, the answer that best satisfies that goal also sounds best. Sometimes, an incorrect choice might be tempting because it seems more concise or more interesting, but if it doesn't accomplish the stated goal then it isn't correct.

We're trying to complete the description of a vicious cycle. The passage has defined "vicious cycle," so we need to pick the situation that best matches the description. (B) describes a situation in which things improve, which isn't consistent with the passage's definition. (C) describes a situation which could lead to a vicious cycle, so let's hold onto that as a plausible option. (D) is similar to (C), but it reaches a specific conclusion about the effect of employees leaving. However, the effect described is positive—so we can probably eliminate (D) as well. When we compare (A) and (C), it's clear that (A) more completely describes a vicious cycle, in which declining productivity leads to declining rewards, which leads back to even further declines in productivity.

Part 2 Practice: Reading the Questions

It's time to practice some of the skills we've discussed in this section. In the following practice set, there are some questions that look just like the questions you'll see on the SAT. Since this section is about identifying some other information about the questions, we've added some special questions about the questions. The extra questions aren't like SAT questions, so we numbered them differently to help you tell the difference.

For the questions that have a little "a" in their number, you either need to pick the choice that "decodes" the question that came before it by describing what the question is really asking about or the choice that explains why the correct answer to the previous question is correct. Those will help you practice decoding the questions, because you have to identify the rule or goal that the question is about.

Questions 1-4 are based on the following passage.

Athens in the Peloponnesian War

The city of Athens, one of the two main actors in the Peloponnesian War, experienced a "golden age" prior to the war. Athens was located fairly centrally among the ancient Greek city states, with ready access to the Aegean sea. Access to the Aegean allowed for trade routes to develop, bringing goods, language, and culture to Athenian society. The trade routes **1** ensured that essential grain and wheat

1

A) NO CHANGE

B) secured

C) assured

D) established

1a

A) Conventions: Which choice corrects the sentence fragment by adding a verb?

B) Conventions: Which choice of verb uses the correct tense and agrees with its subject?

C) Expression: Which word choice most precisely expresses the main idea of the sentence?

D) Expression: Which word choice best maintains the pattern established in the previous sentence?

2 are imported, while native fields cultivated more specialized crops, such as olives and grapes.

At the beginning of the Peloponnesian War, Athenian power was rooted in the nation's ability to defeat **3** enemies at sea. Its power was also rooted in its ability to transport necessary supplies to Athens through the sea trade.

2

A) NO CHANGE

B) were

C) is

D) was

2a

A) Conventions: Which choice corrects the sentence fragment by adding a verb?

B) Conventions: Which choice of verb uses the correct tense and agrees with its subject?

C) Expression: Which word choice most precisely expresses the main idea of the sentence?

D) Expression: Which word choice best maintains the pattern established in the previous sentence?

3

Which choice best combines the sentences at the underlined portion?

A) enemies at sea, however, its power also came from transporting

B) enemies at sea; additionally, its power also came from transporting

C) enemies at sea and transport

D) enemies at sea, and rooted in transporting

3a

My choice is correct because it

A) uses the transitional word that best expresses the relationship between the two clauses in the sentence.

B) concisely combines the two sentences without any unnecessary words.

C) correctly combines the two sentences while making the fewest wording changes.

D) uses the transitional word that best emphasizes the most important part of the sentence.

[1] Athens's primary strategy was to avoid land battles and instead rely on this sea power. [2] This strategy served them well during the first half of the war. [3] However, this early advantage would not be enough to **4** secure Athen's victory. [4] As the war continued, Sparta secured funds from Persia to improve the Spartan navy and close the gap with Athens. [5] Athens was struck by a plague, further weakening the Athenian effort. [6] Sparta was then able to use its naval resources to attack the supply of grain and silver going into the port at the city of Amphipolis, delivering a final blow to the Athenian war fund. **5**

4

A) NO CHANGE
B) secured Athen's
C) secured Athens's
D) secure Athens's

4a

A) Conventions: Which choice uses the correct verb tense and possessive noun?
B) Conventions: Which choice uses the verb and object that agree with the subject?
C) Expression: Which choice best expresses the relationship between Athens and victory?
D) Expression: Which choice best helps the reader to understand when the events took place?

5

The writer is considering deleting one of the sentences in this paragraph in order to improve the focus of the passage. Which sentence should be deleted in order to accomplish this goal?

A) Sentence 1
B) Sentence 2
C) Sentence 4
D) Sentence 5

5a

My choice is correct because it

A) deletes a sentence that repeats an idea expressed in another sentence.
B) shortens the passage by removing the greatest number of words.
C) removes an idea that does not develop the main point of the paragraph.
D) deletes contradictory information.

Answering the Questions
Part 3

To get the most out of the passages and questions in the Writing Test, you should use the approaches we just discussed. Once you have read the passage and the questions, you will be ready to choose an answer. When choosing the best answer, you can also use the strategies presented below, including Plugging In Options, Process of Elimination, choosing (A) appropriately, and guessing wisely.

Use Context

Questions that require information from a whole paragraph or the whole passage are often more challenging and time-consuming to answer than those which require you to read only a single sentence. While it may seem tedious to read through many paragraphs to answer questions about one part of a sentence, the test writers have actually crafted the test in this way to help you! Full paragraphs give you access to examples of the author's style and clues to the meaning and usage of words.

In other words, full paragraphs allow you to use other sentences in the paragraph to help you answer questions. When you use other sentences in this way, you are relying on **context.** When you look at sentences in context, think about not only that sentence but also the ones before and after it. Context will help you to determine the author's tone and intention, the logical order of the passage, the style of writing and evidence, and the appropriate usage of words or phrases.

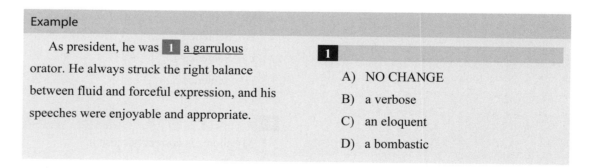

Example
As president, he was **1** a garrulous orator. He always struck the right balance between fluid and forceful expression, and his speeches were enjoyable and appropriate.

1

A) NO CHANGE
B) a verbose
C) an eloquent
D) a bombastic

To answer this question, you need to use context clues to help you. If you only read the first sentence, every answer choice could be correct! To get the context, you need to read the next sentence as well. The second sentence tells you that the president had "fluid and forceful expression," and his speeches were "enjoyable and appropriate."

Now you can tell that garrulous is not the right word because it means extremely talkative, and you want something that means fluid, forceful, enjoyable, and appropriate. Looking at the answer choices, you can see that "eloquent" is the best answer choice because its definition matches our context clues which describe the president as a talented speaker—not unnecessarily long-winded.

You will not only be asked if certain *words* are used correctly in context, but also if entire *sentences* make sense based on their place in the passage. You may be asked to move a sentence to another location or add new information to support an idea—things that you can only do if you have a good understanding of the passage as a whole!

Plugging In Options

Before bubbling in an answer, plug in your choice. Re-read the sentence, but substitute your answer choice for the underlined portion. The new sentence should make sense. Remember: the best version of a sentence or paragraph will correct any original errors and avoid any new errors. Furthermore, always consider options exactly as they are worded. If a choice seems like it might be the best option because all you would really need to do to make it perfectly correct is toss in a conjunction, then it's not correct. To avoid careless errors, plug in each of your answer choices before bubbling in—even when you're pretty confident.

Example

Amelia Earhart was a female aviation pioneer. **2** She set numerous aviation records, she disappeared somewhere over the Pacific Ocean and was never seen again.

2

A) NO CHANGE

B) Having set numerous aviation records, she and her plane

C) After setting numerous aviation records, she

D) She set numerous aviation records and then she

In the original passage, the second sentence is incorrect because it connects two independent clauses using only a comma. This is called a "comma splice." We will discuss this topic in detail in Section 3.

To revise the sentence, you will either need to change the underlined portion to include a dependent clause—a clause that could not stand by itself as a sentence—or use an appropriate method for connecting two independent clauses. Choice (B) corrects the problem by changing the beginning phrase to "Having set numerous aviation records," so you may be tempted to choose this answer. Remember to plug it back into the sentence! When you do so, it reads:

"Having set numerous aviation records, she and her plane disappeared somewhere over the Pacific Ocean and was never seen again."

You have now introduced a *new* error in the second half of the sentence. The phrase "she and her plane" is a plural subject, but "was never seen again" uses a verb that requires a singular subject. Therefore, choice (B) cannot be the answer.

Answer choice (D) uses a conjunction to connect the two clauses, but when connecting two independent clauses with a conjunction you also need to use a comma, so (D) isn't correct either.

The correct answer is choice (C), because it makes the appropriate revision and does not introduce any new errors. Remember, you should always check your answer by inserting it into the complete sentence to check that it is correct in context.

Choosing "NO CHANGE"

Much of this chapter will be focused on how to spot and correct errors in the passages on the Writing Test. However, some portions of the passages will need no correction. In these cases, the correct answer will be (A) NO CHANGE.

When questions have (A) NO CHANGE as a possible answer, you should not be afraid to pick it! Many students are hesitant to pick (A) because it seems "too easy." However, there *are* portions of the passage that are already in their best form. Remember to read the underlined portion using context and anticipation and go through the answer choices using Process of Elimination. If you do this and still think that the portion is best unchanged, then it probably is! Go ahead and bubble in (A) NO CHANGE as your answer.

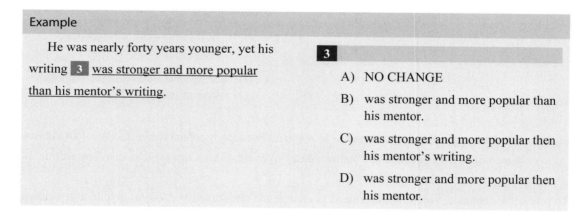

Example

He was nearly forty years younger, yet his writing [3] <u>was stronger and more popular than his mentor's writing.</u>

3

A) NO CHANGE
B) was stronger and more popular than his mentor.
C) was stronger and more popular then his mentor's writing.
D) was stronger and more popular then his mentor.

This sentence doesn't have any grammatical or stylistic errors, so the original version is correct. However, you also want to check the other answer choices to make sure that (A) is the best answer before you select it. Answer choice (B) compares unlike things ("his writing" and "his mentor"), (C) incorrectly uses "then" instead of "than," and (D) makes both errors, so none of those options are correct. Therefore, you would choose (A) NO CHANGE.

You may find that (A) is the answer for more than one question in a single passage. Again, don't second-guess your answer just because you think there isn't an error. Follow the strategies above and feel confident in your choice!

Guessing

In Chapter 1, you learned that there is no penalty to guessing on the new SAT, so you should always guess if you don't know the correct answer.

If you get to the end of a passage and are unsure about one or more questions, make a temporary guess on the answer sheet, and circle the question in your test booklet. Once you have completed all of the passages, you can use any remaining time to go back to your circled questions. See if you can eliminate any more answers and make a better guess. However, make sure you always bubble in your guesses on your answer sheet—you don't want to run out of time and leave a question blank!

Part 3 Practice: Answering the Questions

Read the passage below and answer the questions. For follow-up questions 1a, 3a, 4a, and 5a, select the option that best identifies the type of the preceding question and best poses the question. For question 2a, select the choice that best describes why your choice of answer is correct. Use the answer key at the end of this book to check your work.

Questions 1-5 are based on the following passage.

The Three Fates

According to Greek mythology, the Fates had the power to decide a person's destiny. They controlled each person's "thread of life." Clotho was the spinner of the thread, **1** she chose when people were born. Lachesis was

1

A) NO CHANGE
B) one choose
C) who chose
D) they chose

1a

A) Conventions. Which choice corrects the subject-verb disagreement by inserting both a subject and a verb that agree with one another?

B) Conventions. Which choice corrects the comma splice by changing the second clause into a dependent clause?

C) Expression. Which choice most nearly matches the pattern established in the preceding sentences?

D) Expression. Which word choice best emphasize Clotho's role as just one of the three Fates?

the measurer, who chose a person's "lot" in life. **2** <u>Lachesis had an iconic measuring rod. With her measuring rod, Lachesis</u> measured the thread of life. Atropos was responsible for cutting the thread of life, choosing the time of a person's death.

2

Which choice best combines the sentences at the underlined portion?

A) Lachesis had a measuring rod; it was iconic, and with it she

B) With her iconic measuring rod, Lachesis

C) Using her measuring rod, which was iconic, Lachesis

D) Lachesis both had and used an iconic measuring rod, with which she

2a

My choice is correct because it...

A) emphasizes the importance of Lachesis's measuring rod.

B) expresses the idea that Lachesis had to possess the rod in order to use it.

C) places all of the information about Lachesis's rod into a single, concise introductory clause.

D) eliminates unnecessary description in favor of a concise, factual expression.

The Fates [3] were independent by the other gods and goddesses, controlling mortal threads of life without [4] interference. The Fates are often described as stern and severe. They are usually depicted holding representative items, such as a spindle, staff, or cutting shears.

3

A) NO CHANGE
B) was independent of
C) was independent by
D) were independent of

3a

A) Conventions. Which choice uses both a verb that agrees with its subject and the correct preposition?
B) Conventions. Which choice corrects the subject-verb disagreement by inserting both a subject and a verb that agree?
C) Expression. Which transitional phrase best expresses the relationship between the Fates and other gods and goddesses?
D) Expression. Which word choice is most consistent with the style and tone of the passage as a whole?

4

A) NO CHANGE
B) static
C) distortion
D) invasion

4a

A) Conventions. Which choice of noun correctly agrees with the number of other nouns in this sentence?
B) Conventions. Which choice of noun best agrees with the verb that takes it as an object?
C) Expression. Which choice of transitional word best expresses the relationship between the Fates and the other gods and goddesses?
D) Expression. Which word choice most precisely expresses the main idea of this sentence?

The Fates are referenced in several ancient works, **5** including *The Iliad* and *The Odyssey,* which are works of Homer.

5

A) NO CHANGE

B) such as *The Iliad* and *The Odyssey,* which are two works of Homer.

C) including Homer's *The Iliad* and *The Odyssey.*

D) including two ancient works of Homer: *The Iliad* and *The Odyssey.*

5a

A) Conventions. Which choice corrects the comma splice by changing the final clause into a dependent clause?

B) Conventions. Which choice correctly punctuates the list of Homer's works?

C) Expression. Which choice arranges the information in the underlined portion in the clearest and most concise fashion?

D) Expression. Which choice best develops the ideas in the sentence by separating unique ideas and placing them in the most logical order?

Section 3
SAT Grammar

Before we can talk about the grammar questions you'll have to tackle on the SAT, we're going to go through a quick review of basic grammar concepts. Don't be scared by the technical names for these concepts—the SAT won't test you on any technical grammar terms. However, knowing these concepts will help you to understand and correct the grammar errors in SAT questions. In this section, you will review common grammar errors that you might see on the Writing and Language Test, and learn how to correct them.

In order to work with all of the materials in this chapter, you will need to have some foundational skills. Additional materials meant to build that foundation are available online at ivyglobal.com/study. If you need extra review of any of the following concepts, please refer to the supplemental materials online and work through the practice exercises.

- **Nouns and pronouns:** concrete and abstract nouns, proper and improper nouns, possessive nouns, pronouns and antecedents
- **Verbs:** verb number and tense, action verbs and linking verbs
- **Adjectives and adverbs:** identifying adjective and adverb forms of words and selecting appropriate word forms
- **Sentences:** subject and objects, direct and indirect objects, clauses, subordination and coordination, conjunctions
- **Punctuation:** using colons and semicolons, using commas

 For additional resources, please visit **ivyglobal.com/study**.

Common Grammar Errors
Part 1

Let's take a look at some of the specific kinds of errors the SAT will ask you to correct. We'll begin with some of the more straightforward error types that the SAT will include in its Writing and Language Test passages. Though the SAT will try to trick you by disguising these errors, most of them will be fairly easy to spot once you know what to look for. Many of them will sound wrong to your ear—or they would if you spoke them out loud.

Clauses, Phrases, and Fragments

Some of the errors you'll have to correct on the SAT will ask you to rearrange or combine **clauses** in order to fix a sentence that is incorrectly structured.

You may encounter sentence fragments on the SAT. A **fragment** is a set of words or clause that cannot stand on its own, but that a writer has tried to use as a complete sentence.

Example
X   Emma didn't show up <u>until 9 PM. Even though</u> she said she'd arrive at 7.

Although the second "sentence" has a subject and a verb, it is not complete. You can see that it is a dependent clause. To fix this problem, you can attach it to the first sentence with a comma.

✓   Emma didn't show up <u>until 9 PM, even though</u> she said she'd arrive at 7.

Sometimes phrases will occur as fragments as well. A **phrase** isn't even a clause—it doesn't have both a subject and a verb.

Example
X   She said she got stuck in traffic, but tried her <u>hardest to get there. Driving like a maniac and weaving</u> in and out of traffic.

You'll notice that the second "sentence" here doesn't have a subject. In general, if you see a "sentence" whose verbs are all in "-ing" form, chances are there is a problem with it. To fix the sentence in this example, you have a couple of options. Attaching it to the main sentence with a comma makes it clear that "she" was the one driving like a maniac and weaving in and out of traffic:

✓ She said she got stuck in traffic, but tried her <u>hardest to get there, driving like a maniac and weaving</u> in and out of traffic.

You can also resolve it by making the fragment into a stand-alone sentence:

✓ She said she got stuck in traffic, but tried her <u>hardest to get there. She drove like a maniac and weaved</u> in and out of traffic.

The second sentence now has a subject ("she") and two verbs that agree with it ("drove" and "weaved"). Both are appropriately in the past tense, since the narrator is describing a completed past event.

Some sentences you encounter on the SAT will have all the parts to make several complete sentences, but they will be missing the connectors that are required to put them all together in a single sentence. These include **run-on sentences**, which occur when two independent clauses are mashed together without proper conjunctions or punctuation.

Example

X <u>My cat is very mischievous she likes</u> to climb where she's not supposed to be.
X <u>My cat is very mischievous, she likes</u> to climb where she's not supposed to be.

These sentences are both wrong because they combine two independent clauses without the connectors required to put both clauses in the same sentence. With no punctuation, the sentence is a run-on. With just a comma, it is a **comma splice**. In either case, the SAT will ask you to correct the mistake. Look for multiple-choice options that accomplish the following changes.

You can break a run-on into two sentences:

✓ <u>My cat is very mischievous. She likes</u> to climb where she's not supposed to be.

You can also split it up with a semicolon:

✓ <u>My cat is very mischievous; she likes</u> to climb where she's not supposed to be.

You can also make one of the clauses into a dependent clause:

> ✓ <u>Because my cat is very mischievous, she likes</u> to climb where she's not supposed to be.

Be especially careful with **introductory** and **transitional** words. Most transitional words, like "however," "consequently," and "nevertheless," are adverbs. Sometimes, in informal conversation, they can sound like conjunctions—but they don't do the job of a conjunction in a formal English sentence.

Example
X   I needed to get a 97 on the exam to <u>pass the course, consequently, I studied</u> for weeks.

This is a comma splice. The word "consequently" is an adverb, which modifies the verb "studied." A new independent clause begins between the words "course" and "consequently," so you must split this sentence with a period or semicolon, or correctly join the clauses with a conjunction.

> ✓ I needed to get a 97 on the exam to <u>pass the course; consequently, I studied</u> for weeks.
> ✓ I needed to get a 97 on the exam to <u>pass the course, and, consequently, I studied</u> for weeks.

Verb and Pronoun Shifts

Some words in English change their form depending on certain factors. We will pay particular attention here to verbs and pronouns. When verbs or pronouns change their form because of other words in the sentence, this is called **agreement**. Some questions on the Writing and Language Test will test your ability to tell if verbs and pronouns correctly agree with other words in the sentence.

Subject-verb agreement is one of the forms of agreement the SAT will test. As the name implies, verbs must always agree with their subjects. Luckily, in English, this process is fairly simple. Verbs only have to agree with their subjects in number.

Most verbs do not change form in the present tense, except when the subject could be replaced with the pronouns "he," "she," or "it." For example, see these present-tense forms of the verb "to dance":

To Dance (Present Tense)			
Singular	I dance	You dance	He/she/it dances
Plural	We dance	You dance	They dance

The SAT will sometimes try to trick you by putting a lot of extra words between the subject and verb, making it unclear what the actual subject is. You must be a sleuth and find the verb's true subject!

Example

?   The artist in the studio by the warehouse full of robots <u>draw/draws</u> all day.

Reading this sentence quickly, you might see the noun "robots" next to the verb "draw(s)" and assume that "robots" is the subject, making the verb "draw." However, the correct verb is actually "draws." You can solve this question by asking yourself: "What noun is actually *doing* the verb here?" In this sentence, who was drawing? The *artist* was. Artist is singular, so the correct verb is "draws."

✓   The artist in the studio by the warehouse full of robots <u>draws</u> all day.

The SAT may also try to trick you with subjects that are ambiguously singular or plural. This can happen when parts of the subject are connected by "and" or "or."

Subjects with "and" are always plural.

✓   The bowl and the spoon <u>are</u> in the cabinet.

When the subject uses "or," the verb agrees with the *closer* word.

Example

?   Either Brian or his colleagues <u>is/are</u> bringing donuts.

Since the subject is "Brian or his colleagues," the verb has to agree with the closer part of the subject. In this case, that's "colleagues."

✓   Either Brian or his colleagues <u>are</u> bringing donuts.

Certain pronouns can also make it difficult to figure out whether the subject is singular or plural.

Example

?   Neither of my sisters <u>is/are</u> good at sports.
?   Each of the princes <u>has/have</u> a chance to take the throne.

In these cases, it may be tempting to use the plural verb form, especially if you think that the plural nouns ("sisters" or "princes") are the subjects. However, those plural nouns are both objects of the preposition "of," which means that they can't be the subjects. The true subjects here are the pronouns "neither" and "each," which are both singular.

✓ <u>Neither</u> of my sisters <u>is</u> good at sports.
✓ <u>Each</u> of the princes <u>has</u> a chance to take the throne.

Here are some other pronouns that are always singular:

Singular Pronouns	
Pronoun	Example
Either	<u>Either</u> of those gifts <u>is</u> a good choice.
Someone	I hope <u>someone brings</u> the cake!
Anyone	If <u>anyone speaks,</u> we will lose the game.
Somebody	<u>Somebody</u> always <u>forgets</u> to close the garage.
Nobody	By the time I got there, <u>nobody was</u> awake.
Everything	<u>Everything</u> in the kitchen <u>seems</u> clean.
Anybody	Let me know if <u>anybody finds</u> my keys.
Everyone	<u>Everyone</u> in my town <u>loves</u> football.

You will also need to watch out for **pronoun agreement**. Pronouns need to have the same number and gender as the nouns they are referring to (their antecedents). The SAT may try to trick you by changing a pronoun inappropriately or by making it unclear what noun it is referring to.

Avoid changing the pronoun you are using partway through the sentence:

Example
X If <u>one</u> changes pronouns midsentence, <u>you</u> are doing it wrong.

If you start a sentence with one pronoun, stick with it all the way through.

✓ If <u>you</u> change pronouns midsentence, <u>you</u> are doing it wrong.

Similarly, if you are using one pronoun to refer to something in one sentence, do not change to a different pronoun in the next sentence.

Instead, use the same pronoun in both sentences:

The SAT doesn't ask questions that require students to eliminate answers simply because the answers use "they" as a singular pronoun. However, in the example above, "they" is used in the second sentence to refer to the same antecedent that "he or she" refers to in the first sentence, creating an inconsistency.

If it is unclear what the pronoun is referring to, then you need to fix the sentence:

Who is "he?" That pronoun could refer to Carlos, Michael, or someone else who beat them both! Choose multiple-choice options that eliminate these kinds of unclear situations.

Last but not least, watch out for pronouns that are far away from the nouns they are referring to.

Reading this sentence quickly, you might see multiple cities mentioned ("New York or Los Angeles") and think the pronoun and verb should be plural ("they have"). However, try removing the part of the sentence that is set off between two commas. As we discussed in Part 2, material set off by commas in this way is often additional information that can be removed. You are left with:

The pronoun refers to the "urban center," which is singular. This means the pronoun and its verb should also be singular.

> ✓ The best part of living in a major urban center, like New York or Los Angeles, is that <u>it has</u> a lot of concerts, art exhibitions, and other cultural events to enjoy.

Tense, Voice, and Mood Shifts

In Part 2, we talked about verb tense and voice. Some of the questions on the SAT will ask you to find the correct version of a verb based on its place in the sentence. As you've seen, many sentences involve more than one clause. Clauses presented one after another form a **sequence**, and the verbs in these sequences have to be in the correct tense and voice.

Verb tenses reflect changes in time. Many tense mistakes involve the past tenses:

> **Example**
>
> X Patty <u>began</u> high school thirty years after her mother <u>graduates</u> from college.

If one of the events happened before the other one—it's farther in the past—then you can use the remote past tense to help make the order of events more clear. In this sentence, Patty's mother graduated college before Patty began high school, so you should use the past tense of "graduate:"

> ✓ Patty <u>began</u> high school thirty years after her mother <u>graduated</u> from college.

You should also watch out for verb tense in conditional sentences. **Conditional sentences** have a "condition" clause that starts with "if" or "when," connected to a "result" clause that gives the result of the condition. You use conditional sentences to talk about imaginary or possible situations.

If the result clause has "will," the condition clause should use the present tense of the verb.

> **Example**
>
> X If she <u>trains</u> rigorously, she <u>will be</u> able to run the marathon.

If the result clause has "would," the condition clause should use the past tense of the verb.

> ✓ If she <u>trained</u> rigorously, she <u>would be</u> able to run the marathon.

What if the imaginary part has already happened? If the result clause has "would have," use the remote past tense of the verb:

✓   If she <u>had trained</u> rigorously, she <u>would have been</u> able to run the marathon.

Let`s take a look at another example:

Example

X   If you <u>study</u> more, you <u>would get</u> better grades.
✓   If you <u>studied</u> more, you <u>would get</u> better grades.
✓   If you <u>had studied</u> more, you <u>would have gotten</u> better grades.

In Part 2, you also learned about the voice of a verb. You may remember that the active voice is usually preferable. However, the most important thing is to keep the voice of your verbs the same within a sentence—that is, use a **consistent voice**:

Example

X   The clown <u>makes balloon animals</u> for adults, and <u>children are entertained by him</u>.

This sentence uses both the active voice ("makes") and the passive voice ("are entertained"). Shifting voice in a sentence can be confusing. Be sure to keep the voice of verbs the same.

✓   The clown <u>makes balloon animals</u> for adults, and <u>he entertains the children</u>.

Another feature of verbs that can shift is the mood. The **mood** tells you if a sentence is a statement, question, command, suggestion, or desire. Just like voice, mood needs to be consistent within a sentence or group of sentences:

Example

X   Eric left some dogsitting directions for me: walk the dog twice a day, check his water after each walk, and <u>I must feed him</u> after the second walk.

The first two points in the directions are in the imperative mood, which is used for giving commands. There's no good reason to switch to the indicative mood, which is used for expressing facts. The third point should be changed to the imperative mood to make it consistent with the first two points.

✓   Eric left some dogsitting directions for me: walk the dog twice a day, check his water after each walk, and <u>feed him</u> after the second walk.

Part 1 Practice: Common Grammar Errors

1 Carolyn Doty has loved baking since she was a child. When she spent weekends and vacations at her grandparents' farm. "My grandmother cooked every meal we ate and she did all of her own baking," Doty explained. "I spent a lot of time in her kitchen, where she **2** teach me how make cookies, cakes, pies, and bread." Doty, inspired to take what **3** they had learned from her grandmother to the next **4** level, decided to make baking her career. She attended a culinary institute, graduating with a bachelor's degree in pastry arts. Now, she works as a pastry chef in one of America's best restaurants, a job **5** one loves.

1

A) NO CHANGE

B) When she spent weekends and vacations at her grandparents' farm; Carolyn Doty has loved baking since she was a child.

C) Carolyn Doty has loved baking since she was a child, and when she spent weekends and vacations at her grandparents' farm.

D) Carolyn Doty has loved baking since she was a child, when she spent weekends and vacations at her grandparents' farm.

2

A) NO CHANGE

B) is teaching

C) teaches

D) taught

3

A) NO CHANGE

B) them

C) she

D) those

4

A) NO CHANGE

B) level. Decided

C) level and decided

D) level, and decided

5

A) NO CHANGE

B) she loves

C) they love

D) she loved

Nevertheless, she has decided that she wants to use her expertise to become a food entrepreneur. She has permission to use the kitchen at her restaurant for her own projects, and the many pieces of large-scale cooking equipment in the restaurant's kitchen **6** makes it possible for her to cook large batches of cookies and pies, which **7** are sold by Doty at the local farmer's market. Now, she wants to make this her full-time job. Doty is taking courses in food entrepreneurship offered by her **8** alma mater, during which she is learning more about how to scale up her baking business, find financial backers, and market her products effectively.

6
A) NO CHANGE
B) make
C) has made
D) is making

7
A) NO CHANGE
B) has been sold by Doty
C) Doty sells
D) is sold by Doty

8
A) NO CHANGE
B) alma mater. During which
C) alma mater; during which,
D) alma mater and during which

Harder Grammar Errors
Part 2

The errors discussed in this part may be a little more difficult for you to spot. In fact, some of them may not sound wrong when you read through them in your head! Nevertheless, our tips will help you detect and correct these errors when you see them on the SAT.

Parallel Structure

Some sentences in the Writing and Language Test passages will be missing parallel structure. **Parallel structure** is a way of constructing a sentence so that different parts of the sentence all have the same grammatical structure. Parallel structure makes long sentences easy to read and gives them a natural flow. On SAT questions, you will sometimes be asked to change a part of a sentence to fix a broken parallel structure. Let's take a look at some examples.

Example

✓   After a long day, I like <u>listening to music, reading, and talking</u> with friends.

This sentence has three elements listed in a series: "listening to music," "reading," and "talking with friends." Each of these elements is an "-ing" form of a verb: "listening," "reading," and "talking." Because they are all in the same form, this sentence has parallel structure. Here is the same sentence with a broken parallel structure:

Example

X   After a long day, I like <u>listening to music, reading, and to talk</u> with friends.

Now the three elements in the list are in different forms. "Listening" and "reading" are in "-ing" forms, but "to talk" is not. To answer parallel structure questions, you will need to identify the odd one out and find the multiple choice option that puts all the elements in the same form. Let's look at another example:

Example

X   Whether you <u>fight</u> with Ron or <u>giving</u> him the silent treatment, you're going to have to resolve the argument eventually.

This example is a little less obvious than the last one we looked at. What elements are being listed here? If you're not sure, try looking for key words like "and" or "or" that suggest that things are being put together or compared. Here, we find that our options for how to deal with Ron are being contrasted: we can "fight" or "giving him the silent treatment." You may already see the problem: "fight" is a present-tense verb, while "giving" is an "-ing" form. To fix this sentence, let's bring them in line with each other.

✓ Whether you <u>fight</u> with Ron or <u>give</u> him the silent treatment, you're going to have to resolve the argument eventually.

This is better. Now both elements being compared are present-tense verbs. Let's try out one more example:

Example

X <u>Certification is required</u> for all applicants; <u>it is also mandatory to have prior experience.</u>

The parallelism issue in this kind of sentence might be a little less obvious. This sentence includes two independent clauses joined by a semicolon, and it's tempting to conclude that because the clauses are independent they don't need to be parallel. However, parallel structure is still an important part of good writing style in this kind of complex sentence. The first clause has the structure "[noun] is [adjective]." The second clause has the structure "It is [adjective] that [verb phrase]." This sentence will sound much better if we put both clauses in the same form:

✓ <u>Certification is required</u> for all applicants; <u>prior experience is also mandatory.</u>

Now both clauses are in the form "[noun phrase] is [adjective]." There are also other ways of improving this sentence—for example, combining the clauses into "Certification and prior experience are required for all applicants.

Finally, sentences must always have the same structure following each conjunction in a pair of **correlative conjunctions**. These are conjunctions that work together to connect two parallel parts of a sentence. These conjunctions include the following pairs:

Conjunction Pairs	
Both…and	Either…or
Neither…nor	Not only…but also
Not…but	Whether…or

Here is an example of a sentence that fails to use parallel structure around a pair of conjunctions:

> **Example**
>
> X   I not only enjoy <u>swimming</u>, but also <u>to read</u>.

Notice that this is incorrect because "swimming" is not in the same form as "to run." However, look at the following example:

> ?   I not only enjoy <u>swimming</u>, but also <u>reading</u>.

What do you think of this one?

It sounds a little better, and this is how we often use correlative conjunctions in casual conversation. However, this is technically incorrect. That's because we've got the verb "enjoy" sitting *after* the phrase "not only," and the word "reading" is not parallel with the phrase "enjoy swimming." To fix this, we need to put the verb "enjoy" in front of "not only."

> ✓   I enjoy not only <u>swimming</u>, but also <u>reading</u>.

We are allowed to have a verb after correlative conjunctions, but we have to make sure that there is a verb after each conjunction in the pair—and if it's the same verb, it's better just to put it in front of the first conjunction. Here are some correct examples:

> ✓   This weekend, I will either swim in the pool or read a book.
> ✓   A good workout stimulates both the body and the mind.

Misplaced Modifiers

The SAT will also ask you to move or revise misplaced modifiers. **Misplaced modifiers** are phrases or clauses that are separated from the words they are meant to describe, creating ambiguities or mistaken meanings. They're also the most likely errors to create accidental comedy. Let's take a look at an example:

> **Example**
>
> X   While biking to work this morning, <u>an odd thought struck Alanna</u>.

What this sentence *means* to say is that Alanna was the one biking to work, but the misplaced modifier "While biking to work this morning" creates the impression that the "odd thought" was actually biking. We know this can't be true, so it must be a misplaced modifier.

We have a couple of options for how to fix misplaced modifiers. The general rule is that we need to reorder the sentence so that the modifier is as close as possible to the word it's meant to modify.

> ✓ While biking to work this morning, <u>Alanna was struck by an odd thought</u>.
> ✓ <u>An odd thought struck Alanna</u> while <u>she was</u> biking to work this morning.

You'll notice that for these types of questions, you'll often need to change more than just a word or two. Often, entire clauses or the sentence as a whole will need to be reorganized or rewritten.

Usually, these modifying phrases will contain verbs in their "-ing" or "-ed" forms. Here's an example of a misplaced modifier sentence with an "-ed" form verb:

Example

> X   <u>Seasoned with many spices</u>, <u>Sam's mouth</u> burned when he ate a bite of <u>the curry</u>.

This sentence makes it sound like Sam's mouth was seasoned with many spices, which is not too likely. The modifier is meant to refer to the hot curry, so we'll need to rearrange the sentence to reflect that.

> ✓ <u>Sam's mouth</u> burned when he ate a bite of <u>the curry</u>, which was <u>seasoned with many spices</u>.
> ✓ <u>Seasoned with many spices</u>, <u>the curry</u> burned <u>Sam's mouth</u> when he ate a bite of it.

You have multiple options when fixing a misplaced modifier, depending on how much you want to change the sentence. Some multiple-choice options on the SAT will make relatively minor changes, whereas others will overhaul the sentence. Make sure that the answer you choose doesn't introduce any new mistakes.

Logical Comparison Errors

Errors in logical comparison can be some of the trickiest mistakes to spot on the SAT. **Logical comparison errors** occur when two unlike elements of a sentence are compared.

Example

> X   <u>Picasso's paintings</u> are even stranger than <u>Dalí</u>.

Though it seems like this sentence is just comparing two artists, it actually compares two unlike things: "Picasso's paintings" (the artworks) and "Dalí" (the person). While the artwork might indeed be stranger than the person, we need to compare paintings to paintings.

✓   <u>Picasso's paintings</u> are even stranger than <u>Dalí's paintings</u>.

We can also write this more concisely:

✓   <u>Picasso's paintings</u> are even stranger than <u>Dalí's</u>.

Let's take a look at another example:

Example

X   <u>France's poets</u> challenged artistic conventions, unlike <u>writing</u> anywhere else.

This sentence also compares two unlike things: "France's poets" (the people) and "writing" (the activity). This mistake can also be corrected with a minor change.

✓   <u>France's poets</u> challenged artistic conventions, unlike <u>those writing</u> anywhere else.

The pronoun "those" indicates that we are comparing France's poets to poets elsewhere. This makes the comparison logical.

Confused Words and Idioms

English is a difficult language to master. In fact, even native speakers confuse English words with each other. Sometimes this is because two words that sound or are spelled the same have different meanings. Other times, two similar sounding words are simply misused.

The table below shows some commonly misused words:

	Definition	Correct Usage
Accept vs. Except	**Accept** – to receive or take as payment **Except** – with the exclusion of	We **accept** credit cards for purchases **except** those under five dollars.
Affect vs. Effect	**Affect** (verb) – to influence or change; the object is the thing that is changed. **Affect** (noun) – emotion or feeling	The rain did not **affect** our crop yield. This was not the expected **effect.**

	Effect (noun) – a result **Effect** (verb) – to cause a change; the object is the change.	Bill sought to **effect** changes in environmental policy. Laura claimed indifference, but displayed an excited **affect**.
Precede vs. Proceed	**Precede** – to come before **Proceed** – to move forward	A loud noise **preceded** the fireworks. The officers told us to **proceed** with caution.
Than vs. Then	**Than** – a conjunction used to compare **Then** – next or soon after	I told her I liked peas more **than** candy. **Then** she really thought I was lying!
Too vs. To	**Too** – in addition, also, or excessively **To** – a preposition used to show direction toward a point	Please drive **to** the market this afternoon. Make sure you bring the coupons, **too**: you don't want to spend **too** much.
Wary vs. Weary	**Wary** – cautious; alert **Weary** – tired	The **weary** hikers were glad to make camp, and promptly retired to their sleeping bags; however, being **wary** of bears and other scavengers, they first tied their food safely out of reach on the limb of a tree.

There are also some words that are commonly confused but have specific grammatical rules that you can try to remember:

	Rule	Correct Usage
Among vs. Between	Use **between** only for relationships of two. Use **among** for relationships of more than two.	It was hard to choose **between** the red and pink scarves. **Among** the four gloves, the silk ones were best.
Less vs. Fewer	Use **fewer** for people or things you can count. Use **less** for things that can't be counted or don't have a plural.	**Fewer** people are opening their own businesses these days. Unfortunately, this means **less** money is being spent locally.
Its vs. It's	**Its** is the possessive form of "it." **It's** means "it is."	**It's** hard to tell when the baby will start crying. **Its** arched brows make it always appear upset!
Their vs. They're	**Their** is the possessive form of "they." **They're** means "they are."	The team practiced all year, and **their** hard work paid off. **They're** going to the championship.
Whose vs. Who's	**Whose** is the possessive form of "who." **Who's** means "who is."	**Who's** going to the store with me? Judy is. Now **whose** car should we take?
Your vs. You're	**Your** is the possessive form of "you." **You're** means "you are."	**You're** too talented to give up acting. Plus, **your** voice is incredible!
Who vs. Whom vs. Which	**Who** and **whom** both refer to people; who is used as subject pronoun, and whom is used as an object pronoun. **Which** refers to things or groups.	**Who** brought the salad? To **whom** should I return the bowl? The bowl, **which** has a beautiful pattern on the inside, looks like it might be expensive.

Part 2 Practice: Harder Grammar Errors

From 1812 to 1815 the United States and Great Britain fought the War of 1812. The War began because of American anger over trade issues, the taking—or "impressment"—of U.S. sailors to serve on British ships, and British support of Indian attacks on U.S. colonies on the western frontier. During the conflict, the U.S. invaded the British colony of Canada, British forces crossed the border to fight on U.S. soil, **1** and capital cities had been burned by both sides.

In April of 1813, U.S. forces invaded the capital city of York (better known today as Toronto). During the invasion, an explosion of ammunition in one of the city's magazines killed 300 Americans. Nevertheless, U.S. forces were successful in capturing York. Following the battle, the U.S. army **2** burned York's provincial parliament, looted homes, and destroyed the press at the Printing Office.

A series of other battles followed. Besieged by British and Native American forces, American forces successfully defended their position at Fort Meigs, in Ohio. American forces defeated British forces at the naval Battle of Lake Erie. British and Canadian forces defeated a larger American force at the Battle of Crysler's farm. **3** Chafing under wartime taxes, the war was becoming increasingly unpopular with the British public. Peace negotiations began in August, 1814.

1

A) NO CHANGE

B) and capital cities by both sides had been burned.

C) and, by both sides, capital cities had been burned.

D) and both sides burned capital cities.

2

A) NO CHANGE

B) burned, looted, and destroyed York's parliament, homes, and press at the Printing Office.

C) burned York's provincial parliament, had looted homes, and destroyed the press at the Printing Office.

D) burned York's provincial parliament, looted homes, and had destroyed the press at the Printing Office.

3

A) NO CHANGE

B) The war, chafing under wartime taxes, was becoming increasingly unpopular with the British public.

C) The war was, chafing under wartime taxes, becoming increasingly unpopular with the British public.

D) The war was becoming increasingly unpopular with the British public, who were chafing under wartime taxes.

The negotiations did not begin a cease-fire, however; people continued to suffer the terrible **4** effects on the war. Later that month, British troops captured Washington, D.C. Just as **5** American forces had done in York, Britain looted and burned numerous buildings in Washington.

In spite of the attack on the U.S. Capitol, the British and Americans continued treaty negotiations, and had a complete treaty by December, 1814. The final treaty **6** granted neither the main American demands, nor granted the main demands of the British, yet most of the causes of the war had been resolved by its end. Since the end of the War of 1812, Britain and America have enjoyed more than 200 years of peaceful relations.

4

A) NO CHANGE

B) affects on

C) effects of

D) affects of

5

A) NO CHANGE

B) American forces had done in York, British forces

C) American had done in York, British

D) America had done in York, British forces

6

A) NO CHANGE

B) granted neither the main demands of the Americans, nor the main demands of the British

C) neither granted the main American demands, nor the main demands of the British

D) neither the main American demands, nor the main British demands

Practice Set
Part 3

Patti Smith: Punk Poet Laureate

Patti Smith is a modern Renaissance woman. She wrote and recorded what many claim was the first true "punk" song in 1974, was a performance poet, starred in a play she co-wrote with Sam Shepard, wrote two memoirs and multiple volumes of **1** <u>poetry: and, she</u> is now turning her attention to fiction. However, Smith originally set out to become a high school art teacher, a goal she abandoned **2** <u>on principal</u> when school administrators objected to her focus on obscure and experimental artists.

After moving to New York City in 1967, Smith met the photographer Robert Mapplethorpe, with whom she had a short-lived romance that evolved into a deep friendship. Their relationship was the topic of her National Book Award-winning memoir, *Just Kids.* By 1974, Smith had become a well-known figure in the New York arts scene. **3** <u>After recording her famous "first punk rock song," a grassroots audience flocked to Smith.</u> Arista Records offered her a recording contract after Bob Dylan attended one of her concerts. Her debut album, *Horses,* **4** <u>meet</u> with huge critical and commercial success when it was released in 1975. That album, considered the definitive early punk rock album, frequently appears on lists of the best albums of all time.

1

A) NO CHANGE

B) poetry, and she

C) poetry and she,

D) poetry; and she

2

A) NO CHANGE

B) in principle

C) on principle

D) principally

3

A) NO CHANGE

B) A grassroots audience flocked to Smith after recording her famous "first punk rock song."

C) After recording her famous "first punk rock song," Smith was flocked by a grassroots audience.

D) A grassroots audience flocked to Smith after she recorded her famous "first punk rock song."

4

A) NO CHANGE

B) meets

C) met

D) is meeting

Smith had another megahit with "Because the Night," a song she co-wrote with Bruce Springsteen. It was a surprising collaboration because [5] Smith's music was always more alternative than Springsteen's. By 1980, Smith retreated from the music scene after marrying Fred Smith, the legendary guitarist in the band MC5; the couple moved to Detroit where they raised their two children. Following her husband's death in 1994, Patti Smith returned to the public arena where she is [6] writing, performing, and has recorded albums.

5

A) NO CHANGE

B) Smith's music was always more alternative than Springsteen

C) Smith was always more alternative than that of Springsteen

D) Smith's music was always more alternative than the music of Springsteen

6

A) NO CHANGE

B) writing, performing, and is recording albums

C) writing, performing, and recording albums

D) writes, performs, and records albums

Section 4
Expression of Ideas

On the SAT Writing Test, in addition to answering questions about the standard conventions of English, you will need to answer questions about how a writer can best and most logically express ideas. Expression of Ideas questions don't ask you to correct straightforward errors of English, and an answer choice isn't correct just because it doesn't include any such errors. While Standard English Conventions questions generally ask you to make only small changes to wording or punctuation, Expression of Ideas questions may ask you to add information to the passage, revise the presentation of information, or even delete some portions altogether.

These questions are concerned with three distinct categories: Development of Ideas, Organizing Ideas, and Effective Language Use. Every question requires you to select the choice that creates the best version of the passage, but different question types will require you to use slightly different skills to improve the passage. We'll review all of those skills in this section.

Development of Ideas
Part 1

The "development of ideas" in a passage refers to the way a writer explains, supports, and analyses the central ideas in a passage. Skillful writers make clear claims and compelling arguments by including relevant ideas that support their main thoughts or arguments while avoiding irrelevant additions. When writers include supporting elements like graphs and tables, it's also important for them to offer analysis that matches those supporting elements.

Because answering questions about effective development often depends on recognizing the style and purpose of a passage, it is important to be able to identify which style a writer is using. There are three passage styles that will appear on the SAT Writing Test:

- **Informative passages** will focus on presenting accurate information and may include summaries of data, research, or instructions. One or two passages will be written in this style.
- **Argumentative passages** will present the writer's position on an issue and use argument and evidence to support that position. One or two passages will be written in this style.
- **Nonfiction Narrative passages** tell a true story, but use many of the same techniques as fictional writing. One passage will be written in this style.

Informative and Argumentative passages are discussed in more detail in Chapter 2: Reading. Nonfiction Narrative passages are not specifically discussed in that chapter, but they may contain elements of both informative passages—like data, or quotes from experts—and literature passages—like metaphor.

	Passage Styles	
Style	Goal	Examples
Informative	Give accurate information	Research, summaries, instructions
Argumentative	Persuade the reader	Opinions, debates, editorials
Nonfiction narrative	Tell a true story	Biographies, anecdotes, narrative journalism

Proposition

A **proposition** is a central idea, claim, or counterclaim. The main proposition in a passage is sometimes expressed in a single sentence, or thesis statement, while the main points of individual paragraphs are often expressed as topic sentences.

Questions relating to propositions in a passage may take a number of forms. You may be asked to add a thesis statement, or revise sentences to introduce or explain the main idea of an entire passage. You may also be asked to add, delete, or revise topic sentences for individual paragraphs.

When answering questions about propositions, it's important to remember that propositions should:

- ✓ express the main idea of the passage as a whole or a portion of the passage.
- ✓ be expressed clearly and concisely.
- ✓ maintain the tone of the writer and style of the passage.
- ✓ agree with other information in the passage.

Look at the following example of a proposition question:

Example

1 <u>Traveling by train is more fun than driving.</u> All motorized travel has environmental impacts, but the amount of CO_2 emitted per passenger by a train is about half of the amount from car travel, and can be as little as a tenth of the amount from air travel. Furthermore, much of the impact of electric trains come from burning fuel for electricity—so if we move to cleaner power sources, electric trains will become cleaner even without changes to their design. Finally, trains are less disruptive to wildlife than is a highway.

1

Which choice best establishes the main point of the paragraph?

A) NO CHANGE

B) For passengers, trains are significantly safer than other forms of travel.

C) Until its environmental impacts are adequately addressed, train travel may not be a better option than the alternatives.

D) Train travel has significant environmental benefits over other modes of travel.

You need to read the entire paragraph in order to answer this question. The writer is providing information about train travel, and specifically about the environmental impact of train travel. Furthermore, the balance of the evidence offered suggests that the writer favors train travel. In this example, (A) and (C) each say something positive about train travel, but don't specifically address its environmental advantages. (B) does address the "environmental impacts" of trains, but it's not consistent with evidence that puts trains in a positive light. Only (D) best states the main point of this paragraph.

Support

In any passage, the main point is not enough to make a paragraph complete. Each paragraph will have **supporting information**—facts, statistics, examples, opinions, and anecdotes—that strengthens the main point. In some questions, you will be asked to support claims with additional evidence. Often, this means adding relevant information to strengthen a claim or clarify a point.

In questions about support, the key idea is whether the material strengthens a writer's claims through facts, details, examples, or explanations. Most of the questions related to support will ask you to revise sentences that provide supporting information; some answer choices will provide new facts, but the correct answer choice will always contain evidence that best supports the sentence or sentences before it.

Example

Humans only landed a spacecraft on an asteroid for the first time in 2014, and the prospect of capturing asteroids and mining them for resources is still a long way off. But while it's still a distant prospect, asteroid mining might someday bring real wealth back to Earth. **2** Considering its potential, perhaps it should be unsurprising that the U.S. Congress is already considering legislation to promote asteroid mining.

2

The writer wants to add evidence supporting the idea that asteroid mining could bring wealth to Earth. Which choice best accomplishes this goal?

A) Asteroids have collided with Earth in the past, with devastating consequences.

B) Astronauts could hollow out asteroids and ride inside of them for protection against cosmic rays.

C) A single large asteroid could contain more gold than has ever been mined.

D) The costs of asteroid mining are great, but its benefits could be even greater.

(A) discusses asteroids and Earth, but doesn't directly support the idea that asteroids could bring wealth to Earth; rather, it suggest that they could bring devastation. (B) discusses potential benefits from asteroids, but not in terms of wealth on Earth. (D) explicitly states that asteroids could have great benefits, but it doesn't actually provide evidence. Only (C) provides an additional fact as evidence in support of the claim that asteroids could bring wealth to Earth, in the form of gold.

Focus

Focus questions ask you to consider specific information in the context of the passage or paragraph as a whole. For example, a sentence may be included that provides irrelevant facts or evidence that goes against the main point or goal of the passage, taking away from the **focus** of the paragraph. Focus questions will either ask you to identify and delete irrelevant information or they will ask you to consider whether information is relevant enough to be added to a passage.

Example

It's generally agreed that design choices about color and decorations can have an effect on mood, but which choices are best probably depends on the setting. Warm colors, like red or orange, are stimulating, and might be a good choice when designing a high-energy office. Cool colors, like blue or green, are calming, and might be a good choice when designing a more mellow office. **3** <u>Noise levels also have an effect on mood and concentration.</u> Posters and artwork are generally reported to make the workplace more pleasant, but also to make work tasks seem more challenging. That suggests that artwork might be distracting, so it might not be the best choice for a setting in which high levels of focus are required.

3

The writer is considering deleting the underlined sentence. Should the writer make this change?

A) Yes, because it is not relevant to the main idea of the passage.

B) Yes, because it contradicts information elsewhere in the passage.

C) No, because it provides a specific detail that supports the main point of the paragraph.

D) No, because it provides important information about the main topic of the passage.

(A) is correct. The paragraph as a whole is about how color choices and decorations affect mood. Additional details about noise levels may be interesting, but are not relevant to that main idea.

(B) suggests deleting the underlined sentence, but the rationale that it provides for deleting the sentence is incorrect. The information in the underlined sentence doesn't contradict the rest of the passage because the topic of noise doesn't come up anywhere else. The sentence is simply not relevant.

(C) suggests keeping the sentence, on the grounds that it provides a specific detail supporting the main point of the paragraph. We can imagine what a specific, relevant detail might be. For example, "A study conducted at a large insurance agency showed that employees working in its offices with blue and green color schemes reported much lower levels of stress than those working in its white and grey offices." That provides a specific example supporting the general idea that blue and green are calming colors, and the main point that color choices can affect mood. A detail about noise levels doesn't accomplish that, because the main point of the passage is that color and decoration affect mood—not that noise does so.

(D) suggests keeping the sentence because it provides important information about the main topic. We also imagine important information about the main topic would look like. For example, "Studies suggest that red might have a negative impact on test performance, perhaps because it disrupts concentration, so it's probably not a great choice for a study area." That's relevant to the main topic of the effect of color and design choices on mood. Noise levels are not relevant to the main topic, though, so (D) is not the correct choice.

Quantitative Information

Some passages in the Writing test will include graphical representations of evidence, which may include graphs, charts, tables, or other types of graphics. **Quantitative Information** questions on the Writing Test don't test math skills; rather, the focus is on your understanding of both the text and the graphic. However, common graphics are discussed in detail in the Math chapter, in Section 6. Be sure to review that section carefully, because graphics will appear in every section of the SAT.

Sometimes, you might also run into unusual graphics that are not discussed in the Math chapter. Instead of using a common graphic type, the writer of a passage might devise a special kind of graphic to present supporting information. Consider the following example:

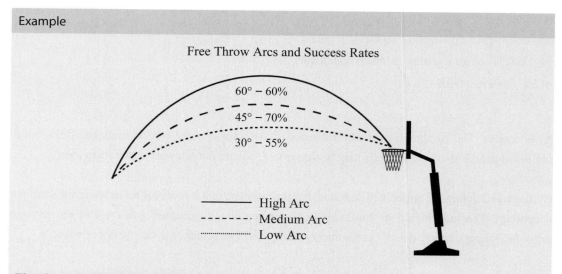

Example

Free Throw Arcs and Success Rates

60° – 60%
45° – 70%
30° – 55%

——————— High Arc
- - - - - - - Medium Arc
·············· Low Arc

The above graphic sorts free throws into low, medium, or high arc height categories, and presents the average angle of arc for each category and the average success rate of shots in that arc category for a high school basketball team.

When a graphic isn't a common type, look for common features to help you decipher it: data labels, a legend or key, units, and a caption that might explain the information in the graphic.

In the example above, we can figure out several pieces of important information from these features. The key tells us which line represents which arc category, that we have two different units (degrees and percentages), and the position of the labels in the graphic tells us which units go with which line. The caption explains what the units mean: degrees represent the "angle of arc" for shots in a category, and percentages represent the "success rate" for shots in a category. Even without a passage to accompany the graphic, from that information we can conclude that shots with a medium arc of 45 degrees had the highest success rate.

When passages contain a graphic, it will be your job to choose the answer that best translates the graphic into text. Look out for the following common mistakes when you're selecting the best choice.

- **Misreading Units:** Look out for answer choices that use a unit that's different from the unit used in the table, including units that use numbers. For example, a passage might discuss travel in miles and include a graphic that shows distances in "hundreds of miles." The graphic might have a value of 27.8 for the distance between New York and Los Angeles. An answer choice that indicated those two cities were 27.8 miles apart would be incorrect. So would one that gave a distance of 27.8 or even 2,780 kilometers. That's because the graphic says they are 27.8 *hundred* miles apart—that's 2,780 miles!

- **Misreading Axes:** Pay attention to what the axes measure. A chart that shows class attendance could have an axis labeled "total attendance" or one labeled "total absences." A line that moved up over time on the first graph would indicate *increasing* attendance. A line that moved up on the second graph would indicate *decreasing attendance*, because absence is the opposite of attendance.

- **Confusing Labels:** You might see a graphic that has numbers in a different place than data labels, and answer choices that use numbers that actually appear in the graphic but pair them with the wrong items. Pay close attention for a legend or key, and make sure that you're picking options that correctly pair numbers with the items they represent.

- **Picking Irrelevant Data:** Sometimes an answer choice is perfectly consistent with the graphic, but still incorrect. It expresses the right quantities in the right units for the right data points; it just doesn't have anything to do with the rest of the sentence or paragraph. Irrelevant data can be tempting if you're only looking for a correct reading of the graphic. Make sure that your answer choice not only agrees with the graphic, but also makes sense in the context of the passage.

- **Making Bad Inferences:** Some answers are wrong because they go beyond the scope of the passage and graphic. You can't necessarily make inferences about what causes trends shown in graphs or about data that's not shown in the graph. Don't pick an answer option that says that one thing in the graphic is caused by another unless there's supporting information in the passage. Don't pick an answer choice that makes inferences about data that's not presented in the graphic unless there's supporting information in the passage.

People are terrified of shark attacks, even though they are enormously unlikely. Comparing the odds of being attacked by a shark to other unlikely or even implausible fates has become a cliché. Shark attacks aren't just less common than many other accidents: with advances in emergency medicine, they've also been getting less deadly over time.

As more people live near coasts, the total number of shark attacks has increased—but the percentage of fatal attacks has decreased. As a result, **4** the number of fatal shark attacks has increased over time, even though the number of non-fatal shark attacks has not.

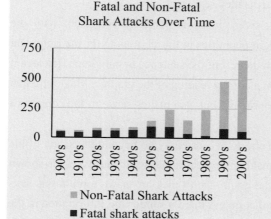

Fatal and Non-Fatal
Shark Attacks Over Time

4

Which choice offers an accurate interpretation of the data in the graph?

A) NO CHANGE

B) about the same percentage of attacks are fatal today, even though the rate of attacks increased over 600%.

C) more attacks occur today mainly because people are able to survive multiple attacks.

D) while the total number of shark attacks has greatly increased over time, the number of fatal shark attacks has not.

(A) is incorrect because it mixes up the data labels: it confuses fatal and non-fatal shark attacks. It also doesn't agree with information in the previous sentence, which is a strong clue that it's not the most accurate interpretation of the graph. (B) is wrong because it misreads the units, and misinterprets the numbers on the *y*-axis of the graphic as percentages. (C) is incorrect because it draws a conclusion which is beyond the scope of the information presented in the graphic. Sometimes, these sorts of speculative conclusions might seem plausible—but they don't accurately interpret information directly from the graphic. Only (D) offers an accurate interpretation of the data in the graph.

Part 1 Practice: Development of Ideas

Read the passage excerpt below and answer the questions that follow. Use the answer key at the end of this book to check your work.

Questions 1-4 are based on the following passage.

Have you ever heard that elephants never forget? Well, elephants aren't the only animals with exceptional memories. When compared with other bird species, the Clark's Nutcracker has been determined to have remarkable memory skills. Scientists have studied the Clark's Nutcracker and found that it performs better on memory tasks and have larger hippocampi, regions of the brain that are associated with memory. Why does the Clark's Nutcracker have such a good memory? [1] It seems that Clark's Nutcrackers have developed exceptional memory skills in order to survive in their environment.

The environment of Clark's Nutcrackers forces them to store seeds away for the winter months. Clark's Nutcrackers mainly live in mountains and rely on seeds of pines as their primary food source. [2] Nutcrackers typically nest in the early spring. Clark's Nutcrackers collect and store large amounts of seeds in the ground during the growing season. They then recover them with incredible accuracy when

1

Which choice most effectively establishes the main topic of the passage?

A) NO CHANGE

B) Not only do Clark's Nutcrackers have better memories, they also have larger brain structures that support memory.

C) Years of practice on experimental memory tasks have allowed the Clark's Nutcracker to develop their exceptional memories.

D) Scientists argue that the memory of the Clark's Nutcrackers affects their ability to reproduce.

2

The writer is considering deleting the underlined sentence. Should the writer do this?

A) Yes, because it contradicts information elsewhere in the passage.

B) Yes, because it provides an irrelevant detail that diminishes the focus of the passage.

C) No, because it explains why Clark's Nutcrackers are able to store seeds before winter.

D) No, because it establishes the sequence of events that is the main focus of the passage.

winter arrives. **3** In contrast, squirrels—also famous for storing food over winter—typically recover **4** between 30% and 100% of their caches.

Approximate Cache Recovery Rates: Squirrels Vs. Nutcrackers

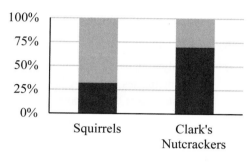

At this point, the writer is considering adding the following sentence.

> Typically, the Nutcrackers recover over 70% of their cached pine seeds.

Should the writer make this addition here?

A) Yes, because it supports the main claim of the passage and completes a contrast that follows.

B) Yes, because it introduces information which is necessary to determine whether the Nutcrackers recover enough seeds to survive the winter.

C) No, because the claim is an inaccurate interpretation of information from the graph.

D) No, because it undermines the passage's central claim about Nutcrackers' memory skills by suggesting that many of the seeds are not recovered.

4

A) NO CHANGE

B) Up to 100% of their caches

C) Only about 30% of their caches

D) Approximately 70% of their caches

Organizing Ideas
Part 2

The effective expression of ideas depends on solid organization. In other words, a writer must order and connect ideas in a logical way so that passages and paragraphs make sense to the reader. Questions related to the organization of ideas will focus on issues of the **Logical Sequence** of information and how the writer connects the ideas in the text with **Introductions**, **Transitions**, and **Conclusions**.

Signal Words

Some questions will ask you to choose the **signal word** or phrase that expresses the most logical relationship or transition between two or more pieces of information in a passage.

Signal words and phrases express the relationship between two or more pieces of information. The chart below provides a handy guide to some common signal words.

Common Signal Words		
Type of Signal Word	When to Use	Examples
Example	When introducing a specific piece of information to support a more general point	For example, much like, specifically, for instance
Continuation	When introducing additional information that supports the same point as earlier examples, or continuing a description of a series of events	Moreover, also, additionally, similarly, furthermore, next
Change	When introducing a contrasting piece of information, or to signal a shift in emphasis within a text	While, in spite of, yet, however, although
Conclusion	When introducing the last event or piece of information in a text, or concluding an argument	As a result, finally, therefore, consequently, hence

Consider the way that signal words are used in the following example:

> Many tenants have long complained about conditions in the building. <u>For example</u>, tenants are upset about the frequent lack of hot water. <u>Furthermore</u>, the building heat is often turned off during cold weather. <u>Finally</u>, some tenants' doors do not lock properly. <u>While</u> the building owners have often promised to address the problems, they have failed to actually make repairs. When pressed, the owners claim that they lack the funds for repairs. <u>However</u>, they have made significant investments in renovating vacant apartments. <u>As a result</u>, some of the tenants are now planning to sue the owners.

Now, try to pick the best signal word in the following example question:

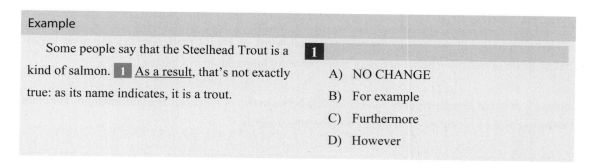

Example

Some people say that the Steelhead Trout is a kind of salmon. **1** <u>As a result</u>, that's not exactly true: as its name indicates, it is a trout.

1
A) NO CHANGE
B) For example
C) Furthermore
D) However

(A) is a conclusion word, but the fact that "some people say" doesn't *cause* it to be "not exactly true," so that's not the best choice. The fact that it's not exactly true that the Steelhead Trout is not a kind of salmon isn't an example of people saying that it is, so (B) isn't the best choice. (C) doesn't work very well, because saying that an idea isn't true isn't just a continuation of the idea—it's a contrasting idea. Only (D) correctly signals that "that's not exactly true" contrasts with the first sentence, and is therefore the correct choice.

Introductory, Transitional, and Concluding Sentences

An **introductory sentence** introduces some of the ideas that will be discussed. An introductory sentence doesn't necessarily spell out the whole main idea; it might just provide some basic facts that prepare the reader to understand the main idea. Sometimes a writer will phrase their introductory sentence in the form of a question and then answer that question in the rest of the passage.

As the writer moves through the passage, they will need to shift focus between different ideas. To accomplish that, they will use **transitional sentences**. A typical transitional sentence will bridge two ideas by explaining their relationship. Sometimes, instead of explaining the relationship between two ideas, a transitional sentence will simply explain why the focus of the passage is shifting from one idea to another.

Finally, writers usually end a passage on a strong **concluding sentence**. An effective concluding sentence ties together the ideas in the passage, usually by offering a summary of the key ideas and the conclusion of the writer's argument.

Consider the following example:

Example

Pigeons are often regarded as unusually dirty birds. Some city-dwellers even refer to them as "rats with wings." In reality, pigeons could hardly be more different than rats: rats directly transmit a wide array of diseases, while pigeons generally don't carry any diseases that are directly transmissible to humans. It's true that pigeon droppings can pose a small health risk, and it's true that people should generally avoid direct contact with any wild animal. **2** I wish people would just leave the birds alone!

2

Which choice most effectively concludes the paragraph?

A) NO CHANGE

B) However, pigeons are actually cleaner and safer than other urban wildlife; they certainly don't deserve their dirty reputation.

C) Pigeons have even been raised as gourmet poultry, while rats are generally not regarded as a delicacy.

D) That said, I'm still not planning to sit under a pigeon's perch.

This question is asking for an effective concluding sentence. An effective concluding sentence usually states the conclusion of the writer's argument, and summarizes key facts. Let's consider our choices: (A) is somewhat consistent with the writer's argument, but it doesn't effectively conclude it. We can tell that the writer disagrees with the idea that pigeons are dirty birds, and seems to be basically pro-pigeon; however, (A) doesn't summarize any key ideas or directly address the main point of the writer's argument that pigeons are not the dirty "rat with wings" that people say they are.

(C) introduces a new fact that supports the writer's argument, but introducing a new fact doesn't effectively conclude the argument.

(D) actually diminishes the strength of the writer's argument; if you're tempted by (D), then it might be because it's succinct and sort of entertaining, but remember: you shouldn't just pick the choice that sounds best to you. You need to pick the one that best answers the question being posed.

Only (B) summarizes and concludes the writer's main argument: pigeons don't deserve their dirty reputation, because they're actually not as dirty as the animals that people compare them to.

Logical Order

On the Writing Test, some questions will ask about moving a sentence from one place to another within a paragraph, ask where a new sentence should be added in a paragraph, or even ask about rearranging paragraphs within a passage as a whole.

In order to answer these questions, you should first identify what a sentence or paragraph is *doing*. Is it a main point, evidence, example, or conclusion? Once you've figured that out, you will be able to determine the best location for it within the paragraph or passage.

There are three important kinds of clues to help you order sentences correctly:

1. **Signal words**: if a sentence contains a signal word that expresses a specific type of relationship to another sentence, it should always be adjacent to—and should usually follow—the sentence to which it is related.

2. **References**: references within sentences to other information in a passage can be a big clue about where the sentence belongs. Sentences that refer to ideas that haven't been introduced yet should be moved so that they follow the sentences that introduce them; sentences that introduce ideas should be moved so that they come before sentences that refer to them.

3. **Purpose**: the purpose of a sentence isn't *always* clear when you're reading it out of context, but when the purpose is clear it's usually a very good clue about where the sentence belongs. Sentences that are designed to introduce the main idea of a paragraph usually come first, or near the beginning. Sentences that provide supporting information usually come in the middle. Sentences that provide a conclusion, or summarize the paragraph, usually come at the end.

Let's look at an example, to see how these clues can help us find the right spot for a sentence.

Example

[1] Workplace wellness initiatives include health screenings and health education, along with changes to the workplace environment to facilitate healthy behavior. [2] Some also offer discounted gym memberships and access to programs to assist those who want to quit smoking. [3] As a result, employees enjoy healthier lives, and employers enjoy a reduction in sick days and disability claims. [4] Many workplaces are now introducing workplace wellness initiatives, which provide benefits to both the employees and the company. [5] Those reductions translate to reduced costs. **3**

3

To make this paragraph most logical, sentence 4 should be

A) placed where it is now.

B) placed before sentence 1.

C) placed before sentence 2.

D) placed after sentence 5.

This question is asking about Sentence 4: "Many workplaces are now introducing workplace wellness initiatives, which provide benefits to both the employees and the company."

You may have noticed that Sentence 4 breaks up two sentences that should be linked (sentences 3 and 5). Sentence 5 refers to the reductions mentioned in Sentence 3, and Sentence 4 is disrupting the connection. If you see a sentence that breaks an important link, you should move that sentence to another location in the paragraph—so we can rule out (A).

Now, are there any relevant signal words or phrases? Yes: Sentence 2 includes the word "also," signaling that it continues an idea from the previous sentence. Sentence 1 discusses some of the specific benefits offered by workplace wellness initiatives, and so does Sentence 2—so that transition makes sense. Sentence 4 doesn't express exactly the same idea, so the signal word in Sentence 2 wouldn't make sense if we chose (C).

Finally, what's the purpose of the sentence? This sentence is a general statement that is supported by the facts and examples in the other sentences, and could serve to introduce the main idea of the paragraph. This type of sentence is a main point, and should be placed at or near the beginning of the paragraph. We can therefore eliminate (D), and select (B).

When you answer questions about logical order, make sure that you test your choice by placing it back in the paragraph. Before you bubble in your answer, re-read the paragraph with the sentence in its new location. Correct answers may involve keeping the sentence where it is, moving it to a new location, or deleting it altogether.

Part 2 Practice: Organizing Ideas

Read the passage excerpt below and answer the questions that follow. Use the answer key at the end of this book to check your work.

Questions 1-3 are based on the following passage.

[1] **1** While sign language is sometimes perceived as only an alternative to vocal speech, it's a complete language in its own right. [2] Some researchers have studied deaf children and compared those children who were exposed to sign language instruction and those who weren't. [3] They found that even without instruction, the children developed pointing and gestures that were very similar to those common to various sign languages. [4] Sometimes these gestures were even complex. [5] The children lacking instruction also shared other similarities with the children who had received instruction. [6] **2** Therefore, both groups of children relaxed their hands between "sentences," signaling an intuitive break in thought. **3**

1

Which choice best introduces the main idea of this paragraph?

A) NO CHANGE

B) Because sign language is used by only a fraction of the population, it is of special interest to researchers.

C) Researchers have found compelling evidence that some elements of sign language may emerge from a set of innate gestures.

D) Sign language is used by both children and adults, but children learn it more quickly than adults.

2

A) NO CHANGE

B) For example,

C) As a result,

D) Finally,

3

To make this paragraph most logical, sentence 4 should be

A) placed where it is now.

B) placed after sentence 1.

C) placed after sentence 5.

D) placed after sentence 6.

Effective Language Use
Part 3

Have you ever read something that was difficult to understand because it was too wordy or vague, or because the writer didn't seem to be using exactly the right words? These types of mistakes occur when writers use language ineffectively. Just as the order of sentences within a paragraph can help a writer express her ideas, so can the proper use of words and phrases.

On the Writing Test, you will be asked to revise a writer's language to more effectively convey her ideas. You can do this by making sentences **precise**, using exactly the right words, and **concise**, not using too many words, while matching the style and tone of the passage.

Precision

As Mark Twain once said, "The difference between the right word and the wrong word is the difference between lightning and a lightning bug." In other words, **precision** matters.

Some Writing Test questions concerned with precision will ask you to replace vague or unclear language that does not precisely express the writer's meaning. All of your options will be the same part of speech, and any of them would make a complete and grammatical sentence, but only one will clearly express the correct idea.

Consider the following example:

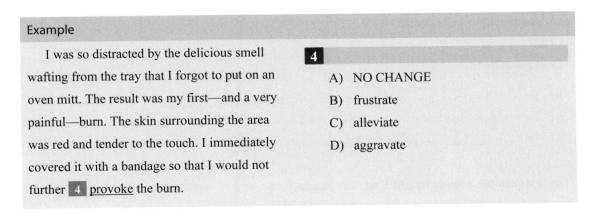

> **Example**
>
> I was so distracted by the delicious smell wafting from the tray that I forgot to put on an oven mitt. The result was my first—and a very painful—burn. The skin surrounding the area was red and tender to the touch. I immediately covered it with a bandage so that I would not further **4** provoke the burn.
>
> **4**
> A) NO CHANGE
> B) frustrate
> C) alleviate
> D) aggravate

Using the context of the paragraph, you can tell that the burn is painful, red, and tender. In the final sentence, the writer uses the word "further" to suggest that the bandage is being used to prevent more pain, redness, and tenderness. In order words, the bandage will prevent it from becoming more irritated. You want to choose an answer that means something like "irritate" or "make worse."

The correct answer is (D) aggravate, which means "to make worse or more serious." Answers (A), "provoke," and (B), "frustrate," are synonyms of aggravate, but don't fit in the sentence; "provoke" means to cause a response or to make angry, and "frustrate" means to prevent. The writer wouldn't "provoke" the burn, nor would she "frustrate" the burn. Answer (C), "alleviate," means "to ease or improve," so it is an antonym of aggravate.

To do your best on precision questions, you need to really flex your vocabulary. If you're having trouble with precision questions, then work on learning new words and learning more about words you already know. You can use the common word roots discussed in the Reading chapter, and go online for extra vocabulary lists.

 For additional resources, please visit **ivyglobal.com/study**.

Concision

The Writing Test will require you to consider whether a writer has expressed her ideas concisely. This means providing information without being redundant—using two or more words that each express the same idea—or wordy—using extra words and phrases where they aren't necessary.

Some **concision** questions will ask you to consider the passage as a whole and determine if the writer makes the same point more than once. Other questions will be concerned with single sentences that may include empty words, words that don't improve the sentence or add information. With concision questions, shorter is usually better, but not always: sometimes cutting out words also cuts out the main idea of the sentence, and that's not the correct way to make sentences more concise. You should pick the shortest option that effectively expresses the key idea.

Consider the following example:

Example
X   He is <u>a man who is always busy</u>. He often switches <u>in a hasty manner</u> from one task to the next.
X   He is <u>a man</u>. He often switches from one task to the next.
✓   He is <u>always busy</u>. He often switches <u>hastily</u> from one task to the next.

The first example is unnecessarily long. The phrase "a man who is" is redundant, because it only repeats the meaning of "he is," so we can cut that. "In a hasty manner" uses empty words; it can be more concisely written using the adverb "hastily." However, in the second example, we've cut too much. The main idea being expressed is that this man is so busy that he's always switching tasks; cutting out all of the descriptive words totally eliminates that meaning. We should just cut out empty or redundant words.

Always carefully consider the meaning of all of the words in a sentence, and keep an eye out for redundant phrases.

Consider the following example:

Example

X   Novice drivers <u>who don't have much experience driving</u> are more likely to be involved in car accidents.

✓   Novice drivers are more likely to be involved in car accidents.

In the first sentence, "who don't have much experience driving" is unnecessary because you already know they are "novice drivers." "Novice" means "lacking experience," so the writer does not need to repeat this using a phrase.

One final way you will be asked to make passages more concise is by combining sentences.

Example

?   Certain dog breeds have been bred as herding dogs. These breeds include sheepdogs and collies.

✓   Certain dog breeds, such as sheepdogs and collies, have been bred as herding dogs.

When you combine two short sentences using a phrase, you can keep the meaning the same but express an idea more concisely. Often, the correct answer will combine the two sentences by turning one sentence into a modifier or dependent phrase.

Style and Tone

Both style and tone are ways a writer develops her "voice" in a piece of writing. **Style** is the broad manner of a writer's writing: it involves the techniques she decides to use, the words she chooses, and even the way she structures and organizes her writing to accomplish a specific purpose. **Tone** relates to the way that a passage feels—or, at least, how it is supposed to feel.

To correctly answer questions about style and tone, you will need to consider what the writer is trying to accomplish in the passage and what techniques the writer uses to achieve her goal. A writer trying to express her own emotional experience might use the first-person voice ("I," "me"), very expressive language with strong positive or negative connotations ("ecstatic," "sorrowful"), expressive punctuation ("!"), and personal opinion. In contrast, a writer who is describing a recent experiment to inform readers might instead use the third-person voice ("he," "she," "they"), and avoid language with strong connotations, expressive punctuation, or personal opinions.

Many questions will focus on the differences between formal and informal style and tone. Formal writing is straightforward: it uses clear, concise wording. Formal writing usually favors words with neutral tone. Slang is never used in formal writing. Informal writing might use slang phrases like "that's really cool" or "she was like, 'what?'" Most passages on the Writing Test have a formal style and tone.

When you are asked to revise a section to better match the tone of the passage, choose the answer that continues the writer's style and tone, and uses techniques that match those used elsewhere in the passage. Ask yourself, does this fit in with the rest of the passage? Would the writer express this thought in this way? Is there a similar choice somewhere else in the passage?

Example

One of Jane Goodall's first observations about chimpanzees was that they possessed the ability to make and use tools. Previously, many scientists assumed only humans had this capability. Goodall observed chimpanzees creating rods out of grass; the chimpanzees would then use these rods to collect termites from a termite hole and lick the termites from the rod. **5** Chimpanzees are obviously as intelligent as humans.

5

Which choice is most consistent with the rest of the paragraph?

A) NO CHANGE

B) Those scientists who originally disagreed were totally not as observant as Goodall.

C) She determined that chimpanzees possess similar tool-making abilities to humans.

D) I will always admire Jane Goodall for her work in expanding our knowledge of chimpanzee abilities.

This paragraph is describing a discovery Jane Goodall made while living with chimpanzees. The paragraph primarily gives facts and uses descriptions to inform the reader.

The final sentence of the paragraph breaks the tone by introducing an opinion. The word "obviously" has strong connotations, and the use of an opinion is not consistent with the rest of the paragraph. (B) also introduces an opinion, and uses "totally" in an informal way, so it does not match the style or tone of the rest of the passage. (D) switches to first person, while the paragraph is written in third person. Only (C) continues the same tone by introducing a new fact about Goodall's conclusion from her discovery.

Syntax

Syntax refers to the arrangement of words and clauses within sentences. On the Writing Test, you will sometimes be asked to choose between different ways of ordering the parts of sentences in order to clearly express ideas.

Effective use of syntax means ordering the elements of a sentence in a clear and straightforward manner. Usually, it's best to place the subject before the verb, the object after the verb, and any modifiers directly next to the element that they modify.

Consider the following example:

Example	
?	Which choice best combines the underlined sentences?
X	<u>Colin and Zach were driving down the road. Colin and Zach saw a kangaroo.</u>
X	Driving down the road were Colin and Zach, who saw a kangaroo.
X	Colin and Zach were driving down the road, at which time they saw a kangaroo.
X	They saw a kangaroo, Colin and Zack did, while they were driving down the road.
✓	Colin and Zach saw a kangaroo while they were driving down the road.

The incorrect choices don't sound quite right, but they aren't grammatically incorrect. These sentences just order the parts of the sentence in ways that introduce a variety of problems. Some of them use the passive voice, while others use parenthetical elements to clarify ideas that could be expressed clearly without them.

Part 3 Practice: Effective Language Use

Read the passage below and answer the questions that follow. Use the answer key at the end of this book to check your work.

Questions 1-4 are based on the following passage.

Imagine you're doing your favorite activity. You might be playing baseball, piano, or chess. You might be painting, singing, or dancing. **1** <u>When you do this activity, is time lost track of by you? Do you feel energized?</u> If this happens to you, you are probably experiencing what is called "flow."

1

Which choice most effectively combines the underlined sentences?

A) Do you lose track of time when you do this activity, and also feel energized when you do it?

B) Do you, when you're doing this activity, feel energized, and lose track of time?

C) When you're doing this activity, do you feel energized and lose track of time?

D) Is time lost track of by you, and do you feel energized when you do this activity?

You experience flow when you are completely involved in an activity. **2** <u>An individual experiencing flow perceives the activity as both challenging and pleasant.</u> Flow involves intense and focused concentration on an activity. **3** <u>Due to the fact that</u> this activity is rewarding, you may feel as if time is flying or forget other worries. In order to continue to experience flow, you must **4** <u>unceasingly</u> seek new challenges. For example, if you achieve flow through sports, you should practice a few times every week and regularly establish new goals.

2

Which choice is most consistent with the style of the passage as a whole?

A) NO CHANGE

B) Flow is awesome: you're in the zone, challenged but happy.

C) Challenge and pleasure together is what makes for flow.

D) During flow, you are challenged but still have a pleasant experience.

3

A) NO CHANGE

B) Since you may feel like

C) Because of the fact that

D) Because

4

A) NO CHANGE

B) consistently

C) seldom

D) incessantly

Essay
Chapter 4

Section 1
Introduction to the SAT Essay

Unlike the other portions of the SAT discussed in this book, the Essay portion of the SAT is optional. If the schools you are applying to do not require the Essay, you can choose to not write it. There are, however, some compelling reasons to write the Essay even if the schools you want to attend don't require it.

Most important is that the Essay gives you a chance to demonstrate your skills in reading, analysis, and writing—all of which provide evidence of your readiness for college, and may help you decide if there are skills you still need to work on. Further, it is possible that you may later decide to apply to more schools than you originally anticipated, including schools that require the Essay. As you cannot take the Essay separately from the rest of the SAT, it makes the most sense to write the Essay the first time you write the test so your bases are covered.

Some things to bear in mind about the Essay portion include:

- **Order:** The Essay is administered at the end of the SAT, after the multiple-choice sections of the test.
- **Time**: You will have 50 minutes to complete the SAT Essay.
- **Prompt**: There is a single SAT Essay prompt that asks you to read and analyze one provided passage. The prompt itself is nearly the same on every exam—it is the passage that varies from test to test.
- **Task**: The SAT Essay asks you to analyze how the author of the passage builds an argument to persuade an audience. In other words, your task is to write a rhetorical analysis, focusing on how the author uses specific techniques and elements to create a specific effect. You will not be asked to take a stance on or form an opinion about an issue. Rather, the focus is on your ability to comprehend source material, analyze how the author presents her argument, and use textual evidence from the passage to support your position about how the author builds her argument.

Essay Scoring

The SAT Essay is evaluated based on three specific criteria: Reading, Analysis, and Writing. Each of these criteria will be scored on a scale of 1-4; because two raters will consider your essay, you will receive a score of 2-8 for each criterion for an overall score of 6-24. Your Essay score will not affect your score on other sections of the SAT. Below is a breakdown of what each of these scores means and what the College Board expects to see in your essay. They are explored in more detail in Section 4 of this chapter.

- **Reading:** The College Board wants to see evidence in your essay that you read and understood the passage. The best way to prove that you understood all the nuances of the passage is to use pieces of it effectively in your essay. We'll show you how to do this in Section 3.
- **Analysis:** The College Board wants to see that you can analyze the elements of someone else's argument and use this analysis to craft an argument of your own. You can achieve this by coming up with interesting, supportable claims and selecting strong, relevant evidence to support them. We will also be showing you how to do this in Section 3.
- **Writing:** The College Board wants to see evidence that you can not only come up with a good analysis, but that you can also effectively convey it to your reader. The scorers are evaluating your ability to organize your writing, use varied sentence structures, and make good word choices. You have likely learned many of these skills in school, but we'll still do some practice in the coming sections to reinforce them.

Sample Essay Prompt

Here is a sample essay prompt and passage. The prompt preceding the passage will always be the same; the instructions for your specific essay will appear after the passage.

This is the standard prompt.

As you read the next passage, consider how Yvon Chouinard uses
- evidence, such as facts or examples, to support claims.
- reasoning to develop ideas and to connect claims and evidence.
- stylistic or persuasive elements, such as word choice or appeals to emotion, to add power to the ideas expressed.

This is the passage you need to read and analyze in your essay.

Adapted from "Tear Down 'Deadbeat' Dams" by Yvon Chouinard. ©2014 by the New York Times Company. Originally published May 7, 2014.

1   Of the more than 80,000 dams listed by the federal government, more than 26,000 pose high or significant safety hazards. Many no longer serve any real purpose. All have limited life spans. Only about 1,750 produce hydropower, according to the National Hydropower Association.

2   In many cases, the benefits that dams have historically provided—for water use, flood control, and electricity—can now be met more effectively without continuing to choke entire watersheds.

3   Dams degrade water quality, block the movement of nutrients and sediment, destroy fish and wildlife habitats, damage coastal estuaries, and in some cases rob surrounding forests of nitrogen. Reservoirs can also be significant sources of greenhouse gas emissions.

4   Put simply, many dams have high environmental costs that outweigh their value. Removing them is the only sensible answer. And taking them down can often make economic sense as well. The River Alliance of Wisconsin estimates that removing dams in that state is three to five times less expensive than repairing them.

5   The message has been slowly spreading around the country. More and more communities and states have reclaimed rivers lost to jackhammers and concrete. Last year, 51 dams in 18 states were taken down, restoring more than 500 miles of streams, according to the group American Rivers. Nearly 850 have been removed in the last 20 years, and nearly 1,150 since 1912.

6   But the work is far from done. I was disappointed to see the Energy Department release a report last week on the potential to develop new "sustainable" hydroelectric dams on rivers and streams across the country. The report follows President Obama's signing of two laws last year to encourage small hydro projects and revive nonproducing dams.

7   New dams are a bad idea. We've glorified them for decades, but our pride in building these engineering marvels has often blinded us to the environmental damage they cause. The consequences run the length of the river and beyond. Our many complex attempts to work around these obstacles would make Rube Goldberg proud. Interventions like fish elevators and trap-and-haul programs that truck fish around impoundments don't lead to true recovery for wild fish populations or reverse the other environmental problems caused by blocking a river's flow.

8   But we do know that removing dams brings streams and rivers back to life and replenishes our degraded aquifers.

9   A case in point is the Elwha River on the Olympic Peninsula in Washington, where two hydroelectric dams built early in the last century exacted huge environmental costs but were no longer important as power generators. Salmon runs that once reached about 400,000 fish a year dropped to fewer than 3,000. A year after the Elwha Dam was removed, Chinook salmon returned to the river in numbers not seen in decades, with three-quarters of them observed spawning upstream of the former dam site. Today, the river runs free from its headwaters in Olympic National Park to the Strait of Juan de Fuca, and a terrible wrong imposed on the salmon-dependent Lower Elwha Klallam tribe has been righted.

10 President Obama should learn from that example. Most urgently, he should turn his attention to the Snake River in eastern Washington, where four dams along its lower reaches provide marginal (and replaceable) electricity generation that is outweighed by the opportunities for the revival of endangered salmon populations, plus the jobs and communities a healthy salmon fishery would support. Those deadbeat dams should be taken down and added to the list of dams in the process of being removed along the White Salmon River in Washington, the Penobscot in Maine, and the Klamath in southern Oregon.

11 I've been working to take down dams for most of my life. The idea, once considered crazy, is gaining momentum. We should seize it and push for the removal of the many dams with high costs and low or zero value. The environmental impacts are too enormous.

12 Time and again, I've witnessed the celebration that comes with the removal of an unnecessary dam. After a river is restored and the fish have returned you never hear a single person say, "Gee, I wish we had our dam back."

These are the specific instructions for what your essay should accomplish

Write an essay in which you explain how Yvon Chouinard builds an argument to persuade his audience that obsolete dams should be removed. In your essay, analyze how Chouinard uses one or more of the features listed in the box above (or features of your own choice) to strengthen the logic and persuasiveness of his argument. Be sure that your analysis focuses on the most relevant features of the passage.

Your essay should not explain whether you agree with Chouinard's claims, but rather explain how Chouinard builds an argument to persuade his audience.

Now that you've reviewed some basic information and a sample passage, we'll move on to more specific advice. We'll refer back to this example as we continue. In this chapter, we will cover:

- Some overall basics and tips to help you prepare for the Essay portion of the SAT
- What the College Board looks for in a good essay
- How to analyze someone else's argument
- How to use your time wisely
- How to put this all together to write a strong essay

Section 2
Approaching the Essay

Now that we've gone over the format of the SAT Essay, we're going to give you some tips for writing your essay. In this section, we're going to go over some basic strategies, and the broad picture of how you should plan and organize your essay.

SAT Essay Basics

Part 1

Because writing an SAT essay has a lot in common with writing assignments you may have received in school, some of the following guidance will be familiar. However, some of our tips will be quite specific to the SAT and what the College Board is looking for in an essay.

Use the Answer Sheet and Your Test Booklet

Write only in the designated section of the exam booklet. Use only the four lined pages provided for your essay. Remember, the only portion of your essay that the graders will see is what you write within the available lines; they won't see anything you write in the margins.

Write neatly. Unlike the other computer-graded sections of the SAT, the essay has to be read by another human being, which makes the legibility of your writing very important. Ensure that your grader sees the greatness of your essay by writing neatly and legibly. Don't use small handwriting to save space: bigger letters are easier to read.

Use your test booklet for outlining and notes. As you read, it's a good idea to underline or note the line number of quotes you'd like to use, and start outlining your essay in the margins.

Write as Much as Possible

Filling up as many of the answer pages as possible tells your graders that you have taken the time to write a thorough, well-argued essay. You have plenty of space to write; use as much of it as possible to develop your argument.

Write six full paragraphs. Fifty minutes is plenty of time to outline and write an introduction, four body paragraphs, and a conclusion. Writing six paragraphs will properly break up four pages of writing and make it easier for your graders to follow your argument; one long run-on paragraph or many short paragraphs can be difficult to follow.

Be Explicit

State your argument (which is, again, a claim about how the author built an argument, not an opinion about the subject of the author's essay) as clearly as possible. When you are writing it's easy to think that the main point of your argument is abundantly clear throughout your essay. However, your graders are going to need help following your argument. Make it easy for them by re-emphasizing your main point at the beginning and end of every paragraph.

Refer back to the provided text. One of the purposes of the SAT essay is to test your ability to read as well as write. There is no better way to demonstrate that you properly understood the passage than by quoting it throughout your analysis. Having the passage right in front of you provides you with abundant evidence to use in your essay—take advantage of it! Your test booklet notes will help you quickly and easily find quotes that support your argument.

Revise

Fifty minutes gives you plenty of time to go back and read over your essay after you've finished writing. Graders can penalize you for grammatical or spelling errors, particularly if they make your essay difficult to read. So once you've finished writing, take time to read over your essay and fix any spelling or grammatical mistakes or to make revisions.

Structuring an Essay
Part 2

The best way to showcase your argument is by using effective **external** and **internal structure**. External structure means properly arranging the introduction, body paragraphs, and conclusion; internal structure means properly structuring each paragraph. This section will show you the best ways to structure your SAT essay.

External Structure

The external structure of your essay should make it easy for your graders to follow your argument. The chart below illustrates the structure you should aim for and provides estimates of how much time you should spend on each section, including reading and analyzing the passage and proofreading your essay.

Analyze Passage (*10 minutes*)

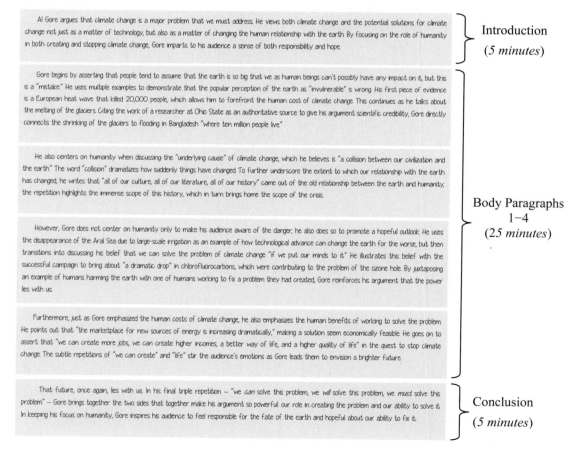

Introduction (*5 minutes*)

Body Paragraphs 1–4 (*25 minutes*)

Conclusion (*5 minutes*)

Proofread (*5 minutes*)

Internal Structure

The internal structure—how you build the individual paragraphs—is integral to writing an essay that expresses your argument in a clear and straightforward manner.

Introduction

Your introduction will set the tone for your essay and provide graders with their first impression of your writing. It's important that your introduction be clear because it's hard to structure a good, coherent essay if the introduction doesn't make any sense.

The best way to make your introduction clear is to keep it brief and straightforward. Your goal is to get to your point as quickly as possible so you can spend the bulk of your time focusing on your body paragraphs.

Start with a brief statement or two relevant to the prompt, demonstrating that you've read the passage and understood the author's claim. It's a good idea to refer to the title of the passage and introduce the author (by full name the first time; when you reference the author later, use her last name *only*), paraphrase the author's central claim, and describe the evidence the author uses to support that claim. Then move directly to your thesis, the sentence where you will lay out the main point of your essay and make a claim about the author's use of rhetorical devices that establishes a context for your analysis.

Body Paragraphs

In your body paragraphs, you will elaborate on the different points that you mentioned in your thesis statement and link them together to create your overall analysis.

Each body paragraph is like a mini-essay. Each paragraph should start with a **topic sentence**. A topic sentence is like a mini-thesis statement: it states what the rest of the paragraph is going to be about.

Following the topic sentence should be 3-4 **supporting sentences**. In these sentences, you should analyze evidence (including appropriate quotes) you have found in the passage and explain how it supports the argument you made in your topic sentence. Use effective transitions that link your ideas together. This helps your reader follow your argument. In the following sentences, the words in italics are examples of transitions:

- *However*, the author does not rely on personal experience alone.
- The author *also* builds her argument by using scientific evidence.
- *Furthermore*, the author uses vivid language to appeal to her readers' emotions as well as their intellect.

Finally, use a **concluding sentence** that summarizes the point you have made in your body paragraph so that you leave the reader with a solid foundation for going on to your next point.

Conclusion

Your conclusion sums up the argument you have been making throughout your entire essay so that your graders know exactly what your argument is. Therefore, it is very important that your conclusion be clear and, like your introduction, brief. Resist the urge to add new arguments in your conclusion; instead, just summarize the arguments you have already made.

The first sentence of your conclusion should rephrase the thesis statement you wrote in your introduction. Don't rewrite it word for word (your graders will notice), but generally restate the ideas present in the thesis. The purpose of this sentence is to show how you have proven the arguments of your thesis statement.

Following this restatement of purpose, you should say something about the importance or implications of your analysis. Does the passage make you think about the issue in a different way? Would the passage have been less effective if the author hadn't used the devices that you analyzed? Does your analysis reveal some flaws in the ways the author made and supported her argument?

Practice Set
Part 3

Read the sample introduction from a student essay below. Then, identify the different elements that make it effective at introducing the student's claims. Ask a trusted reader to check your work.

> In "Tear Down 'Deadbeat' Dams," Yvon Chouinard makes a compelling argument for why the United States government should remove ineffective, environmentally harmful dams. Four distinct features make Chouinard's argument so compelling: his use of impressively large statistics, his employment of specific examples, his telling of personal anecdotes, and the logical organization of his argument. These features in combination make Chouinard's essay very convincing.

1. How does the student demonstrate that he has read the passage and understood the author's claim?

2. What is the student's thesis statement?

3. How does the student describe the supporting arguments that he will be making in the essay?

Read the sample body paragraph below. Then, identify the components that make it effective at conveying its topic. Ask a trusted reader to check your work.

> One feature of Chouinard's essay that makes it convincing is the effective use of evidence, particularly undeniably large numbers. For example, in the very first paragraph, Chouinard cites that "[o]f the more than 80,000 dams listed by the federal government, more than 26,000 pose high or significant safety hazards." Safety hazards numbering in the tens of thousands are difficult to ignore. Chouinard utilizes large-number statistics later when describing the example of the Elwha River: "Salmon runs that once reached about 400,000 fish a year dropped to fewer than 3,000." Again, a 397,000 drop in salmon in a single river makes a fairly compelling case for dam removal. Chouinard's skillful employment of large, eye-grabbing statistics gives his obscure topic more force and makes his argument more powerful.

4. What is the student's topic sentence?

5. How does the student analyze evidence from the passage in order to support the argument in his topic sentence?

6. What is the student's concluding sentence?

Read the sample conclusion below. Then, identify the components that make it effective at summarizing the student's argument. Ask a trusted reader to check your work.

Chouinard utilizes many strategies to make his argument convincing, among them eye-grabbing statistics, specific examples, personal anecdotes, and logical organization. Together these strategies form a compelling claim for dam removal. Using these strategies is especially important in promoting a relatively low-profile environmental cause such as this.

7. How does the student re-state the ideas present in his thesis?

8. How does the student explain the importance or implications of his argument?

Section 3
Analyzing an Argument

The Essay is not just a test of your writing ability—it's also a test of your reading ability. The assignment doesn't ask you to write about the topic presented in the provided passage; instead, you need to write about how the author builds her argument in the passage. That means you can't write a great essay without first solidly understanding and analyzing the passage.

The first step to writing your essay is to read the prompt carefully. Use the Pencil on Paper strategy from Chapter 1 to be an active reader and mark up the provided passage. This way, you can easily refer back to the techniques the author uses to construct her argument. Those techniques are what the bulk of your essay should be about.

In this section, we're going to go over three different aspects of a passage you can examine when you're looking for ways to analyze the author's argument: language, organization, and evidence. We'll discuss how to write about these areas, as well as how to fully support your claims so that your essay is both insightful and thorough.

Language
Part 1

Authors choose every word carefully. The decision to use a certain word or phrase can tell you more than just the information the author is trying to get across. It can convey the author's opinion or add layers of emotion to what could have been just a statement of fact.

This might sound complicated, but you choose your words instinctively all the time. You use different vocabulary around your teachers than you do around your friends, or even around different groups of friends.

> **Example**
>
> After sleeping through his alarm, Carlos *ran* all the way to school.
> After sleeping through his alarm, Carlos *sprinted* all the way to school.

The information in these sentences is the same: Carlos slept through his alarm and headed to school quickly. The difference is in the language. By using "sprinted," the second sentence implies that Carlos was not only running, but was running as fast as he could, which conveys a greater sense of urgency.

The same principles will apply to the passage you'll be reading. When you see a word that sticks out to you, ask yourself how that word relates to the author's argument. What are the connotations of the words the author chooses? What rhetorical devices does he use to support his ideas?

Connotations

It can be useful to think about a word's **connotations**—ideas that might not be part of its dictionary definition, but are implied when people use that particular word. To identify the connotations of a word, think about how you usually hear people use it. A word that people generally use to describe something they don't like has a negative connotation; a word that people use for something they like has a positive connotation. If an author has chosen a word with a negative connotation, she is trying to paint what she's describing in a negative light.

Rhetorical Devices

A **rhetorical device** is a tool the author uses to persuade the reader to agree with his argument. Rhetorical devices aren't just about the literal meaning of the words; they're about how those words are used to make an argument more vivid or appeal to the reader's emotions.

For example, an author who is concerned about losses in the bee population could write, "Bees are dying in North America, South America, and Europe." However, she might also choose to write: "Bees are dying in North America. They're dying in South America. They're dying in Europe." That author would be using the rhetorical device of **repetition** to make her point more dramatic and persuade her reader to care.

Figurative language is another common rhetorical device for authors who want to spice up their arguments and make them more compelling. For example, let's say the author writes, "Bees are as important to the planet as bones are to the human body." This is an example of **figurative language**. In this case the author is using a **simile**, a comparison of two unlike things using the words "like" or "as." Comparing bees to human bones emphasizes how necessary bees are—without bones, the human body would collapse, so she's implying that without bees the planet would collapse. You can learn more about specific types of figurative language in Chapter 2 or online.

 For additional resources, please visit **ivyglobal.com/study**.

Remember that it is not enough just to identify tools the author uses. You must also pinpoint where the author uses these tools *and* state clearly how these tools contribute to the author's argument.

Example

Our nation's trees are crying out for relief from air pollution.

Trees don't cry; by giving a human characteristic to something that is not human, this sentence is using **personification**. However, your graders will not be impressed if you only write, "The author uses personification." You must be specific about where the author uses it, what it accomplishes, and, if possible, how it contributes to the overall argument: "The author states that our nation's trees are 'crying,' thus using personification to rouse the reader's sympathy. This gives emotional weight to her argument that we must work to end air pollution soon."

Suppose that in a passage arguing that it is important to preserve playgrounds, an author writes:

Example

Neglected playgrounds become dangerous playgrounds, and for most parents the risks posed by a dangerous playground are worse than no playground at all. Do we want future generations to grow up without memories of going down slides or playing on the swings?

The second sentence is a **rhetorical question**—not a question the author thinks needs to be answered, but a question used to make a point. Once again, it's not enough to write, "The author uses a rhetorical question," or even "The author uses a rhetorical question to support his point." A better claim to make about this would be: "By posing a rhetorical question about 'future generations,' the author invites the reader to imagine those generations growing up without safe playgrounds."

An author might also use a passing reference to a literary or artistic work, person, or event to illustrate a point.

Example

Regulatory agencies are often established to oversee potentially hazardous industries. But even if they are well-designed, well-intentioned, and staffed by competent employees, funding remains their Achilles heel. After high-profile regulatory legislation is passed, a budget can be quietly passed that strips funding from the regulatory agency.

In this example, the author refers to an "Achilles heel." This is a reference, or **allusion**, to the story of Achilles, a mythic Greek hero whose weakness was his heel. You might not always recognize allusions, but you should point them out when you do.

Part 1 Practice: Language

In the selection below, we've underlined writing choices you could address to analyze how the author uses language to add weight to his argument—that we should remove dams instead of building new ones. Choose four of these words or phrases and write a couple sentences explaining why the author has made these particular language choices. Remember to quote from the text and connect your examples to the author's purpose. Have a trusted reader check your work.

> **Example Essay Adapted from "Tear Down 'Deadbeat' Dams" by Yvon Chouinard. © 2014 by the New York Times Company. Originally published May 7, 2014.**
>
> 1   New dams are a bad idea. We've <u>glorified</u> them for decades, but our pride in building these engineering <u>marvels</u> has often <u>blinded</u> us to the environmental damage they cause. The consequences <u>run the length of the river and beyond</u>. Our many complex attempts to work around these obstacles would make <u>Rube Goldberg</u> proud. Interventions like fish elevators and trap-and-haul programs that truck fish around impoundments don't lead to true recovery for wild fish populations or reverse the other environmental problems caused by blocking a river's flow.
>
> 2   But we do know that removing dams brings streams and rivers <u>back to life</u> and replenishes our <u>degraded</u> aquifers.

1. The first word or phrase I am analyzing:

Why has the author chosen this word or phrase to use?

2. The second word or phrase I am analyzing:

   Why has the author chosen this word or phrase to use?

3. The third word or phrase I am analyzing:

   Why has the author chosen this word or phrase to use?

4. The fourth word or phrase I am analyzing:

   Why has the author chosen this word or phrase to use?

Evidence
Part 2

The author of the passage will use different kinds of evidence to support her point. In this part, we'll take a look at some of the evidence that an author might decide to use. The table below shows some common ways authors support their arguments.

Types of Evidence		
Type of Evidence	Definition	Example
Data or Quantitative Evidence	Uses statistics, percentages, or other kinds of numbers	We should be doing more to preserve wildlife habitats. Though it is common to lose one to five species each year, we are now losing species at an accelerated rate of 200 to 2000 a year.
Expert Opinion	Relies on the opinion or ideas of scholars, researchers, or other people with expert knowledge on the topic	The proposal to teach astronomy to young students is a good one. Dr. Yaskin, an astronomy researcher, believes it will drastically increase interest in the field.
Personal Example	Uses a personal experience or situation encountered by the author	Tourists are often unaware of local etiquette in the places they visit. I witnessed this first-hand on a recent trip to Guatemala.
Comparison	Compares an idea being discussed to something else to clarify or make a point	This engineering project is a poor idea. Building new bridges in small cities with few cars is like buying designer running shoes for toddlers; it is better to wait until they are big enough to need them.
Appeal to Emotion	Creates feelings in the reader to persuade them of an argument	This policy cannot be maintained if we are to consider ourselves a just nation. After all, how dispirited would you feel if your property, acquired through hard work over time, was taken from you without explanation?

Types of Sources

As demonstrated in the chart above, both personal and more expert sources can be used as effective evidence. However, these types of support may be used in different contexts and have different impacts.

Personal evidence often makes a topic more immediate for a reader. It can illustrate what a large issue looks like in someone's day-to-day life. Authors sometimes also use it to make themselves seem relatable and therefore trustworthy. For example, in the passage we've been using, Yvon Chouinard writes, "Time and again, I've witnessed the celebration that comes with the removal of an unnecessary dam." This enables the reader to attach a specific image to a larger situation.

On the other hand, authors can build credibility by drawing on an authoritative source, especially when using data. Governmental organizations ("the Bureau of Labor Statistics"), professional bodies ("the American Medical Association"), and international organizations ("the World Health Organization") are all examples of authoritative sources.

A source might also be authoritative because of where it was first presented, such as in a reputable publication like the *New England Journal of Medicine*. You can also look for the names of universities, which usually signal an authoritative source.

A source's expertise might also be established through other means. Someone might have written a book related to the subject ("Michelle Alexander, whose recently published *The New Jim Crow: Mass Incarceration in the Age of Colorblindness* deals with this topic…"). An expert might also have won a distinguished prize in his field ("Steven Chu, who received the 1997 Nobel Prize in Physics…"). Someone also might just have an extremely respected position that automatically lends her authority ("Supreme Court Justice Sonia Sotomayor has stated…").

Writing about Evidence

As we discussed above, identifying types of evidence is only the first step. It's crucial that when you bring up evidence in your essay, you spell out how the author uses it to support her broader argument. Let's look at an example:

Example

Recently, researchers at the University of Pennsylvania have found that sleep deprivation causes permanent brain damage in mice. This should give us pause as we contemplate the trade-offs of encouraging young people to achieve success at the expense of resting their bodies.

You could write, "The author uses an authoritative source to show that sleep deprivation causes brain damage in mice," and it would be accurate. However, it would not be sufficient, because the mice aren't central to the author's main point: the author is using this evidence to discuss the effects of sleep deprivation on people. A better way to discuss this would be, "The author cites research on mice from The University of Pennsylvania, an authoritative source which gives scientific credibility to her argument that we should be concerned about the physical dangers of sleep deprivation in people."

The key thing to notice is that we made the link between what the author did (use an authoritative source) and why the author did it (to support the passage's broader argument). Don't assume this connection is obvious to your reader; while it may be, you need to prove that *you* see that connection, too.

Part 2 Practice: Evidence

As you read the following selection, look for different ways the author uses evidence to support his argument that old dams should be torn down and new dams should not be built. Identify four pieces of evidence, along with their sources, and describe how this evidence supports the author's argument. Have a trusted reader check your work, and go online for some examples of possible answers.

 For additional resources, please visit **ivyglobal.com/study**.

Adapted from "Tear Down 'Deadbeat' Dams" by Yvon Chouinard. ©2014 by the New York Times Company. Originally published May 7, 2014.

1 Of the more than 80,000 dams listed by the federal government, more than 26,000 pose high or significant safety hazards. Many no longer serve any real purpose. All have limited life spans. Only about 1,750 produce hydropower, according to the National Hydropower Association.

2 Last year, 51 dams in 18 states were taken down, restoring more than 500 miles of streams, according to the group American Rivers. Nearly 850 have been removed in the last 20 years, and nearly 1,150 since 1912.

3 A case in point is the Elwha River on the Olympic Peninsula in Washington, where two hydroelectric dams built early in the last century exacted huge environmental costs but were no longer important as power generators. Salmon runs that once reached about 400,000 fish a year dropped to fewer than 3,000. A year after the Elwha Dam was removed, Chinook salmon returned to the river in numbers not seen in decades, with three-quarters of them observed spawning upstream of the former dam site.

4 Time and again, I've witnessed the celebration that comes with the removal of an unnecessary dam. After a river is restored and the fish have returned you never hear a single person say, "Gee, I wish we had our dam back."

---

 1. The first piece of evidence I am analyzing:

  Its source:

  How it supports the author's argument:

2.   The second piece of evidence I am analyzing:

     Its source:

     How it supports the author's argument:

3.   The third piece of evidence I am analyzing:

     Its source:

     How it supports the author's argument:

4.   The fourth piece of evidence I am analyzing:

     Its source:

     How it supports the author's argument:

Organization and Reasoning
Part 3

How authors choose to structure and reason through their arguments can be just as important as the language and facts they use to make them. We are now going to show you how to recognize the methods authors use to organize their arguments and how to write about them effectively.

Logical Structure

Picking out the logical structure of a piece of writing might sound difficult, but in fact our brains do it subconsciously all the time. We are geared to find patterns in everything around us in order to make sense of them.

Example

- Annie put a bandage on her scrapes.
- Annie fought with her mother about wearing knee pads while skating.
- Annie skated over some gravel and fell.
- Annie ignored her mother and went skating without knee pads.

On the first reading, these sentences don't make any sense at all, right? The events are out of order, and our brains pick up on that immediately. We might even try to start reorganizing the sentences without thinking about it (the correct order is 2, 4, 3, 1).

The SAT also tests this pattern-finding skill in the Writing Test, using multiple choice questions that ask you to select the best order for certain sentences. On the Essay, you'll be recognizing the organization on your own, rather than picking it up from a line-up of potential options, and you'll be writing about how that organization affects the author's argument.

Tracking the Author's Argument

The easiest way to think about organization and logical reasoning is to think about how the author moves from one point to another. As you read the following selection, let's track the different ways the author uses evidence to support his argument that we should remove obsolete dams.

Adapted from "Tear Down 'Deadbeat' Dams" by Yvon Chouinard, 2014, The New York Times Company.

1 Of the more than 80,000 dams listed by the federal government, more than 26,000 pose high or significant safety hazards. Many no longer serve any real purpose. All have limited life spans. Only about 1,750 produce hydropower, according to the National Hydropower Association.

The author begins his argument with several statements about the negative effects of dams. This establishes the harm posed by dams, setting up the author to propose a solution.

2 In many cases, the benefits that dams have historically provided—for water use, flood control, and electricity—can now be met more effectively without continuing to choke entire watersheds.

The author further establishes his argument by showing how dams are no longer useful.

"Now" is a word that can signal a logical contrast (ie. while something was like this then, now it is different).

3 Put simply, many dams have high environmental costs that outweigh their value. Removing them is the only sensible answer. And taking them down can often make economic sense as well. The River Alliance of Wisconsin estimates that removing dams in that state is three to five times less expensive than repairing them.

The author summarizes his prior points and shapes them into a coherent thesis statement. He also provides his solution: remove the deadbeat dams.

4 The message has been slowly spreading around the country. More and more communities and states have reclaimed rivers lost to jackhammers and concrete. Last year, 51 dams in 18 states were taken down, restoring more than 500 miles of streams, according to the group American Rivers. Nearly 850 have been removed in the last 20 years, and nearly 1,150 since 1912.

The author broadens his argument from a personal opinion to a national "message," giving his argument greater clout.

5 But the work is far from done. I was disappointed to see the Energy Department release a report last week on the potential to develop new "sustainable" hydroelectric dams on rivers and streams across the country. The report follows President Obama's signing of two laws last year to encourage small hydro projects and revive nonproducing dams.

"But" is another organizational signpost that signals a logical turn.

The author maintains the urgency of his argument by pointing out that there is still much work to be done in removing dams.

6 New dams are a bad idea. We've glorified them for decades, but our pride in building these engineering marvels has often blinded us to the environmental damage they cause. The consequences run the length of the river

The author moves to another point in his argument about dams: we shouldn't build any new ones. This both reinforces the points the author made earlier in the passage and allows him to introduce new evidence against dams.

and beyond. Our many complex attempts to work around these obstacles would make Rube Goldberg proud. Interventions like fish elevators and trap-and-haul programs that truck fish around impoundments don't lead to true recovery for wild fish populations or reverse the other environmental problems caused by blocking a river's flow.

7   But we do know that removing dams brings streams and rivers back to life and replenishes our degraded aquifers.

After showing how bad dams are, the author shows us the other side of his argument—the many benefits of dam removal.

8   A case in point is the Elwha River on the Olympic Peninsula in Washington, where two hydroelectric dams built early in the last century exacted huge environmental costs but were no longer important as power generators. Today, the river runs free from its headwaters in Olympic National Park to the Strait of Juan de Fuca, and a terrible wrong imposed on the salmon-dependent Lower Elwha Klallam tribe has been righted.

The author supports this logical turn with a specific example about the Elwha River. Again, the author uses a now/then contrast to illustrate the benefits of removing dams.

9   I've been working to take down dams for most of my life. The idea, once considered crazy, is gaining momentum. We should seize it and push for the removal of the many dams with high costs and low or zero value. The environmental impacts are too enormous.

The author brings the argument back to his personal perspective, using his authority as a life-long fighter of dams to make his argument even more credible.

The author summarizes his prior points and shapes them into a coherent thesis statement. He also provides his solution: remove the deadbeat dams.

10   Time and again, I've witnessed the celebration that comes with the removal of an unnecessary dam. After a river is restored and the fish have returned you never hear a single person say, "Gee, I wish we had our dam back."

The author concludes the passage with a statement that reinforces the apparent obviousness of his argument—who would ever want a dam back when its removal clearly provided so much good?

Following an author's argument is much like reading a roadmap: once you get used to the signs, it's easy to follow. But identifying the author's organizational and logical methods is only half of the job. You also need to be able to write about them effectively.

Writing about Structure

After you have tracked the author's main argument through the passage, you'll need to figure out how to write about that structure. The easiest way to do this is to ask the question "Why?" Why does the author move from a certain point to another? Why does she use a certain kind of logical reasoning to connect these points? Answering these "why" questions will enable you to write about how these organizational decisions on the author's part did or did not aid her argument.

Take the first organizational turn we noticed in our example passage.

We identified that the author places a turn in the middle of the sentence. The author acknowledges why we have built dams in the past, but then points out their current ineffectiveness. Why does the author do this? There are a few things we could write about to answer that question:

- First, acknowledging the past benefits of dams makes the author's argument seem more balanced and fair.
- Second, showing that these benefits can be provided by other more efficient mechanisms makes dams seem unnecessary.
- Third, showing that these other methods are more environmentally friendly makes dams seem unnecessary *and* bad.

And just like that, we have a paragraph's worth of writing about one small part of the passage's logical organization.

Part 3 Practice: Organization and Reasoning

Now it's your turn. Below are some more organizational and logical turns from the "'Deadbeat' Dams" passage. Explain why the author included these turns and how they help or hurt his argument. Have a trusted reader check your work, and go online for some examples of possible answers.

 For additional resources, please visit **ivyglobal.com/study**.

> 1   And taking them down can often make economic sense as well. The River Alliance of Wisconsin estimates that removing dams in that state is three to five times less expensive than repairing them.

1. Why did the author include this turn?

2. How does it help or hurt his argument?

1   New dams are a bad idea. We've glorified them for decades, but our pride in building these engineering marvels has often blinded us to the environmental damage they cause.

3.   Why did the author include this turn?

4.   How does it help or hurt his argument?

Putting It Together

Part 4

Now that we've gone over how to analyze an author's language, evidence, and organization, it's time to put them all together. In the sample passage below, we've marked up the full sample text we've been using with the kinds of observations you might use in your essay.

Sample Passage Analysis

As you read the passage below, consider how Yvon Chouinard uses

- evidence, such as facts or examples, to support claims.
- reasoning to develop ideas and to connect claims and evidence.
- stylistic or persuasive elements, such as word choice or appeals to emotion, to add power to the ideas expressed.

Adapted from "Tear Down 'Deadbeat' Dams" by Yvon Chouinard, 2014, The New York Times Company.

1   Of the more than 80,000 dams listed by the federal government, more than 26,000 pose high or significant safety hazards. Many no longer serve any real purpose. All have limited life spans. Only about 1,750 produce hydropower, according to the National Hydropower Association.

2   In many cases, the benefits that dams have historically provided—for water use, flood control, and electricity—can now be met more effectively without continuing to choke entire watersheds.

3   Dams degrade water quality, block the movement of nutrients and sediment, destroy fish and wildlife habitats, damage coastal estuaries and in some cases rob surrounding forests of nitrogen. Reservoirs can also be significant sources of greenhouse gas emissions.

(1) Yvon Chouinard uses evidence from an authoritative source (the federal government) to support his claim that dams pose serious dangers. Placing this statistic in the first sentence adds urgency to his pleas.

(2) The author uses evidence from another authoritative source (the National Hydropower Association) to show that many more dams pose serious hazards than produce hydropower, suggesting that the dangers outweigh the benefits.

(3) The author acknowledges that dams "originally provided" specific benefits and suggests that there are now better ways of meeting these needs without negative consequences. The author demonstrates that he is knowledgeable about several sides of the issue.

(4) Vivid word choices such as "degrade" and "destroy" dramatize the effect of dams on the environment. The word "rob" heightens their menace, implying that dams are stealing nitrogen that rightly belongs to forests.

4   Put simply, many dams have high environmental costs that outweigh their value. Removing them is the only sensible answer. And taking them down can often make economic sense as well. The River Alliance of Wisconsin estimates that removing dams in that state is three to five times less expensive than repairing them.

5   The message has been slowly spreading around the country. More and more communities and states have reclaimed rivers lost to jackhammers and concrete. Last year, 51 dams in 18 states were taken down, restoring more than 500 miles of streams, according to the group American Rivers. Nearly 850 have been removed in the last 20 years, and nearly 1,150 since 1912.

6   But the work is far from done. I was disappointed to see the Energy Department release a report last week on the potential to develop new "sustainable" hydroelectric dams on rivers and streams across the country. The report follows President Obama's signing of two laws last year to encourage small hydro projects and revive nonproducing dams.

7   New dams are a bad idea. We've glorified them for decades, but our pride in building these engineering marvels has often blinded us to the environmental damage they cause. The consequences run the length of the river and beyond. Our many complex attempts to work around these obstacles would make Rube Goldberg proud. Interventions like fish elevators and trap-and-haul programs that truck fish around impoundments don't lead to true recovery for wild fish populations or reverse the other environmental problems caused by blocking a river's flow.

8   But we do know that removing dams brings streams and rivers back to life and replenishes our degraded aquifers.

(5) After listing concrete examples of the damage caused by dams, the author summarizes his point that dams are harmful and not worth the environmental cost, and then concisely states his solution.

(6) The author uses statistics from another authoritative source (the River Alliance of Wisconsin) to support his claim that removing dams makes economic sense as well.

(7) By claiming that his solution is increasing in popularity, the author portrays his argument as viable, since communities and states have already adopted it.

(8) Careful word choice makes his cause seem righteous. Saying communities have "reclaimed" rivers that were "lost" positions dams as an injustice to the communities and environment.

(9) The author uses specific statistics as evidence to back up his claim that the removal of dams is already in process.

(10) The author clarifies that although his plan for dam removal is in some ways already in motion, the situation is still urgent.

(11) Referring to a specific event from as recently as a week ago makes the subject seem very timely.

(12) The author suggests that the appeal of new dams lies in our pride in building them rather than in anything they actually accomplish.

(13) Rube Goldberg was a cartoonist famous for drawings of gadgets that performed simple tasks in extremely complicated ways. By saying that our attempts to minimize the damage of dams would "make Rube Goldberg proud," the author is implying that we are doing many unnecessarily complicated things while overlooking the obvious solution.

(14) The author elaborates on the comparison he just made by naming some of those unnecessarily complicated interventions and stating that they are not effective.

(15) The author positions removing dams as the obvious solution being overlooked even though we already know that it is the one guaranteed solution.

9   A case in point is the Elwha River on the Olympic Peninsula in Washington, where two hydroelectric dams built early in the last century exacted huge environmental costs but were no longer important as power generators. Salmon runs that once reached about 400,000 fish a year dropped to fewer than 3,000. A year after the Elwha Dam was removed, Chinook salmon returned to the river in numbers not seen in decades, with three-quarters of them observed spawning upstream of the former dam site. Today, the river runs free from its headwaters in Olympic National Park to the Strait of Juan de Fuca, and a terrible wrong imposed on the salmon-dependent Lower Elwha Klallam tribe has been righted.

10   President Obama should learn from that example. Most urgently, he should turn his attention to the Snake River in eastern Washington, where four dams along its lower reaches provide marginal (and replaceable) electricity generation that is outweighed by the opportunities for the revival of endangered salmon populations, plus the jobs and communities a healthy salmon fisher would support. Those deadbeat dams should be taken down and added to the list of dams in the process of being removed along the White Salmon River in Washington, the Penobscot in Maine, and the Klamath in southern Oregon.

11   I've been working to take down dams for most of my life. The idea, once considered crazy, is gaining momentum. We should seize it and push for the removal of the many dams with high costs and low or zero value. The environmental impacts are too enormous.

12   Time and again, I've witnessed the celebration that comes with the removal of an unnecessary dam. After a river is restored and the fish have returned you never hear a single person say, "Gee, I wish we had our dam back."

(16) This specific example of the dams on the Elwha River underscores his points with vivid descriptions. The descriptions reinforce the idea of dams being obsolete, because these dams were no longer producing significant amounts of power. The descriptions also emphasize the harmfulness of dams, because of the large drop in salmon population. Finally, this case study also exemplifies the author's point that removing dams is an easy, obvious solution, since it only took a year after their removal to see dramatic positive results.

(17) The author portrays the dams as a terrible injustice to the environment—this time especially to a particular local tribe—and says the removal of these dams is necessary to restoring justice.

(18) Invoking the most powerful official in the country (President Obama) makes it clear that this is a national issue, lending the argument urgency and importance because of its national scope.

(19) The author makes clear that removing the dams in question would benefit both salmon (who would see their numbers replenished) and humans (who would see job creation opportunities).

(20) The author uses specific examples to restate his point that removing dams is something more and more communities are already choosing to do.

(21) By stating he has been active in this cause for a long time, the author grants himself the legitimacy of a firsthand witness to support his claim that the idea of taking down dams is gaining support.

(22) After several specific, concrete examples, the author summarizes his argument again for emphasis.

(23) The author ends the article by using his personal experience to position himself as a legitimate authority on the benefits of removing dams. A colloquial expression ("gee") gives it a personal feel.

We've annotated this text to illustrate the kinds of elements you should look out for when you read the passage. You can see that we don't focus on just one kind of tool. Instead, we look at different tools the author wields from a variety of angles. It's important to show that you can recognize a diverse set of strategies.

However, finding these strategies is only the first step. If you were to read our notes like an essay, it would be a mess: totally disorganized, hard to follow, and lacking a clear thesis. In order to turn your thoughts into an essay, you'll need to identify the passage's overarching themes. Then you'll use those themes to organize your essay.

Identify Themes

For the sample text that we've provided, you could pull out the following three themes. Pay attention to the way the author uses multiple strategies to develop each one.

Theme 1: Dams pose a problem that is both serious and urgent. This is the problem the author is trying to demonstrate.

- He uses authoritative sources to provide evidence that dams are harmful, including the federal government and the National Hydropower Association. Statistics support his claims that dams are dangerous. The example of the Snake River makes it easier for readers to visualize the damage dams cause. In addition, he highlights different *kinds* of harm that dams cause, including depleting the salmon population, destroying wildlife habitats, and hurting the Lower Elwha Klallam tribe.
- He chooses strong words to bring the tragedy to life. Dams don't just block watersheds, they *choke* them. The word "choke" suggests violence. The salmon population in the Elwha River didn't just decrease, it *dropped*. The word "dropped" makes it sound drastic and shocking.
- He emphasizes that this is a problem right *now*. The Energy Department report from the previous week shows that the fight is far from over. By naming President Obama, he implies this issue that must be dealt with immediately, not in the future.

Theme 2: Removing dams is the most logical solution. This is what the author is trying to persuade his audience to believe.

- He identifies several benefits of dam removal. He uses the Elwha River example to show how removing a dam can revive the local salmon population, which benefits the environment. He points out that more salmon would provide job opportunities for local residents, which benefits the community. He uses an authoritative source to show that removing harmful dams is cheaper than fixing them, which benefits the economy.
- He addresses counterarguments that others might make, suggesting that there are no downsides to his plan. He states that there are better ways to accomplish what dams provide. He points out that we could find a way to replace the electricity generated by the dams on Snake River. He also claims that he has never seen anyone regret that a dam has been taken down.

- He argues that removing dams is becoming more popular. This suggests that its effects are positive enough to win people over to his side. He admits that the idea was "once considered crazy," which implies it has become common for people to change their minds about it.

Theme 3: Unnecessary dams are an injustice that must be corrected. This theme is crucial for taking our analysis to the next level. The previous two themes lay out the facts of the author's argument: what is happening (dams pose a problem) and what we should do about it (tear them down). This theme is about why his argument matters—basically, why we should care. Here, he appeals to the reader's emotions and sense of justice.

- He uses language to frame the damage dams cause in moral terms. Dams "rob" forests of nitrogen, making them sound criminal. When communities take dams down, they "reclaim" rivers once "lost," suggesting that they have restored the natural order of things.
- He explicitly states that the loss of the salmon population of the Elwha River was a "terrible wrong" done to the Lower Elwha Klallam tribe, which was "righted" by removing the dam.
- He refers to dams which are deeply harmful and marginally beneficial as "deadbeat dams," using an adjective with a connotation that suggests a moral failing.

Notice that the author does not lay out these themes in order, detailing one in full and then abandoning it for the next. Instead, he weaves them together throughout the essay. By the time he gets to the example of the Elwha River, he can use it to make all of these ideas come together. This is important to watch out for as you plan your essay—remember that you might be drawing from different parts of the passage to fully support one of your points.

Part 4 Practice: Putting It Together

We've gone over how to structure your essay so that it's clear and easy to read. We've also given you the tools you need to analyze the different ways an author builds his argument, and write about it so that your own argument will be compelling. Now it's time to put these skills to work and write the essay we've been working on in this chapter. We've provided the prompt again below. Because we've already read and analyzed the passage and discussed how to identify the author's use of language and evidence, aim to complete this practice essay in under 50 minutes. There are additional prompts later in this chapter you should use for timed practice. Have a trusted reader check your work.

As you read the passage below, consider how Yvon Chouinard uses

- evidence, such as facts or examples, to support claims.
- reasoning to develop ideas and to connect claims and evidence.
- stylistic or persuasive elements, such as word choice or appeals to emotion, to add power to the ideas expressed.

Adapted from "Tear Down 'Deadbeat' Dams" by Yvon Chouinard, 2014, The New York Times Company

1   Of the more than 80,000 dams listed by the federal government, more than 26,000 pose high or significant safety hazards. Many no longer serve any real purpose. All have limited life spans. Only about 1,750 produce hydropower, according to the National Hydropower Association.

2   In many cases, the benefits that dams have historically provided — for water use, flood control, and electricity — can now be met more effectively without continuing to choke entire watersheds.

3   Dams degrade water quality, block the movement of nutrients and sediment, destroy fish and wildlife habitats, damage coastal estuaries, and in some cases rob surrounding forests of nitrogen. Reservoirs can also be significant sources of greenhouse gas emissions.

4   Put simply, many dams have high environmental costs that outweigh their value. Removing them is the only sensible answer. And taking them down can often make economic sense as well. The River Alliance of Wisconsin estimates that removing dams in that state is three to five times less expensive than repairing them.

5   The message has been slowly spreading around the country. More and more communities and states have reclaimed rivers lost to jackhammers and concrete. Last year, 51 dams in 18 states were taken down, restoring more than 500 miles of streams, according to the group American Rivers.

6   Nearly 850 have been removed in the last 20 years, and nearly 1,150 since 1912.

7   But the work is far from done. I was disappointed to see the Energy Department release a report last week on the potential to develop new "sustainable" hydroelectric dams on rivers and streams across the country.

8   The report follows President Obama's signing of two laws last year to encourage small hydro projects and revive nonproducing dams.

9   New dams are a bad idea. We've glorified them for decades, but our pride in building these engineering marvels has often blinded us to the environmental damage they cause. The consequences run the length of the river and beyond.

10   Our many complex attempts to work around these obstacles would make Rube Goldberg proud. Interventions like fish elevators and trap-and-haul programs that truck fish around impoundments don't lead to true recovery for wild fish populations or reverse the other environmental problems caused by blocking a river's flow.

11   But we do know that removing dams brings streams and rivers back to life and replenishes our degraded aquifers.

12   A case in point is the Elwha River on the Olympic Peninsula in Washington, where two hydroelectric dams built early in the last century exacted huge environmental costs but were no longer important as power generators. Salmon runs that once reached about 400,000 fish a year dropped to fewer than 3,000. A year after the Elwha Dam was removed, Chinook salmon returned to the river in numbers not seen in decades, with three-quarters of them observed spawning upstream of the former dam site. Today, the river runs free from its headwaters in Olympic National Park to the Strait of Juan de Fuca, and a terrible wrong imposed on the salmon-dependent Lower Elwha Klallam tribe has been righted.

13   President Obama should learn from that example. Most urgently, he should turn his attention to the Snake River in eastern Washington, where four dams along its lower reaches provide marginal (and replaceable) electricity generation that is outweighed by the opportunities for the revival of endangered salmon populations, plus the jobs and communities a healthy salmon fishery would support. Those

deadbeat dams should be taken down and added to the list of dams in the process of being removed along the White Salmon River in Washington, the Penobscot in Maine, and the Klamath in southern Oregon. I've been working to take down dams for most of my life. The idea, once considered crazy, is gaining momentum. We should seize it and push for the removal of the many dams with high costs and low or zero value. The environmental impacts are too enormous.

14 Time and again, I've witnessed the celebration that comes with the removal of an unnecessary dam. After a river is restored and the fish have returned you never hear a single person say, "Gee, I wish we had our dam back."

Write an essay in which you explain how Yvon Chouinard builds an argument to persuade his audience that obsolete dams should be removed. In your essay, analyze how Chouinard uses one or more of the features listed in the box above (or features of your own choice) to strengthen the logic and persuasiveness of his argument. Be sure that your analysis focuses on the most relevant features of the passage.

Your essay should not explain whether you agree with Chouinard's claims, but rather explain how Chouinard builds an argument to persuade his audience.

Section 4
Essay Rubric and Examples

Grading the Essay is more difficult than grading the rest of your practice exam. Unfortunately, there's no answer key for the Essay. Instead, you need carefully evaluate your own work or have a trusted reader evaluate your essay and provide honest feedback. In this section, we provide guidance about the College Board's grading rubric to help you understand how the College Board will evaluate your work, and how you can evaluate your own work or the work of others.

The College Board's Rubric
Part 1

In this section, we will look at the rubric for each grading criterion—Reading, Analysis, and Writing—used by the College Board graders in assessing your essay. We'll use examples from the annotated passage that we reviewed in Section 3, "Tear Down 'Deadbeat' Dams," by Yvon Chouinard.

Reading

In the reading category, your graders are evaluating how well you show that you understand the prompt passage, including its main argument, the important details, and how those details are related to the argument.. Here are some examples of what they'll be looking for.

What College Board Wants	Good Example	Bad Example
Get the main idea. Even though the prompt gives you a version of the main idea of the passage, the College Board wants to see evidence that you have accurately and comprehensively understood and interpreted the passage.	In this passage, Yvon Chouinard argues that dams have a negative impact on the environment and generally should be removed.	In this passage, Yvon Chouinard talks about his own personal agenda that has something to do with dams.
Use the evidence. The College Board is looking for references to the passage through quotes or paraphrasing that support your interpretation of the passage.	Chouinard supports his claim with statistics, such as the fact that "[o]f the more than 80,000 dams listed by the federal government, more than 26,000 pose high or significant safety hazards."	Chouinard talks about how lots of dams are doing bad things.
Use the evidence correctly. Use the evidence accurately, both by citing it correctly and by using it in the same spirit as the author.	Chouinard supports his claim with statistics, such as the fact that "[o]f the more than 80,000 dams listed by the federal government, more than 26,000 pose high or significant safety hazards."	Chouinard doesn't cite good facts to support his argument. For example, he states that only 20,000 of the more than 80,000 dams listed by the federal government pose significant safety hazards, which is not that many.

Analysis

In the Analysis category, your graders are evaluating how well you analyze an author's argument. They want you to evaluate the effectiveness of the author's use of evidence, reasoning, and rhetorical elements, not to give your own opinion. These are some things the graders will be looking at to determine your score.

What College Board Wants	Good Example	Bad Example
Analyze, don't respond to, the passage. Your job is to analyze the author's argument, *not* respond to it with your own opinions.	Chouinard utilizes a combination of statistical evidence, personal examples, and appeals to authority to make the argument that harmful dams should be removed.	Chouinard really doesn't know what he's talking about; in my opinion, dams are super helpful.
Pick good elements to write about. Read the passage, identify what tools the author uses to make her argument, and evaluate the effectiveness of the author's use of evidence, reasoning, and rhetorical elements.	Chouinard's use of strong numerical evidence shores up his argument and makes the issue seem more important and urgent.	Chouinard writes really well and thus makes a good argument.
Pick the right support for those elements. Pick the strongest, most relevant parts of the passage to support your claims.	For example, Chouinard uses statistics about the decreasing number of salmon in the Elwha River (400,000 down to fewer than 3,000) to demonstrate the negative effects dams have on wildlife.	Chouinard cites lots of statistics to support his argument. For example, he states once a dam is taken down, "you never hear a single person say, 'Gee, I wish we had our dam back.'" That's some strong statistical evidence.

Writing

In the Writing category, your graders are evaluating how well you structure your essay and how effectively you use language to express your ideas. Here are some things you should keep in mind.

What College Board Wants	Good Example	Bad Example
Make a precise claim. When you write an essay, you have to have some sort of claim or argument. This claim should be expressed as a clear, concise thesis statement.	Chouinard uses statistical evidence, personal examples, and appeals to authority to build his argument that removing harmful dams is necessary to restore justice.	This is an interesting article about dams.

Organize your argument. Write an effective introduction, develop your argument using body paragraphs that show a deliberate and clear progression of your ideas, and provide a clear conclusion.	See Section 2, Part 2 earlier in this chapter.	See Section 2, Part 2 earlier in this chapter.
Switch up your sentences. Don't just use simple sentences—mix it up!	Though some of Chouinard's evidence comes in the form of personal anecdotes, much of it comes from authoritative sources. This combination of evidence makes his argument more well-rounded as well as easier to read.	Chouinard is a good writer. He makes good points. He uses good evidence.
Choose precise words. Try to include higher caliber words in your sentences. However, never use words whose meanings you don't entirely understand. This can actually hurt your essay.	Chouinard appeals to the federal government when he directly addresses President Obama.	Chouinard pretends he's talking to President Obama to make a point.
Use an academic tone. For an academic essay, you should always use a formal and objective tone—avoid slang or informal language.	Although Chouinard can be didactic at times, overall he effectively argues for the removal of dams.	Even though this guy is pretty boring sometimes, you can really understand where he's coming from.
Use good grammar, spelling, and punctuation. Be sure to read over your essay at least once after you've finished writing to catch any mistakes.	Chouinard argues that there are many reasons to close down deadbeat dams.	Chouinard argues "there are many reasons closing down Deadbeat Dams"

Sample Essays
Part 2

In this section we apply the College Board's grading criteria to two student essays written in response to the prompt below. Recall that each criterion will be graded on a scale of 1-4. The sample essays demonstrate Reading, Analysis, and Writing scores of 2 and 4 respectively.

Your essays may merit different scores in each category. Additional sample essays are available online, including samples that demonstrate mixed scores and an example of how an incomplete essay would be scored.

 For additional resources, please visit **ivyglobal.com/study**.

Essay Prompt

> As you read the passage below, consider how Al Gore uses
>
> - evidence, such as facts or examples, to support claims.
> - reasoning to develop ideas and to connect claims and evidence.
> - stylistic or persuasive elements, such as word choice or appeals to emotion, to add power to the ideas expressed.

Adapted from former Vice President Al Gore's 2004 speech "The Climate Emergency," collected in Red, White, Blue, and Green: Politics and the Environment in the 2004 Election (2004), edited by members of Yale School of Forestry & Environmental Studies, James R. Lyons, Heather S. Kaplan, Fred Strebeigh, and Kathleen E. Campbell.

1 The environment is often felt to be relatively invulnerable because the earth is so big. People tend to assume that the earth is so big that we as human beings can't possibly have any impact on it. That is a mistake.

2 In Europe during the summer of 2003, we experienced an extreme heat wave that killed an estimated 20,000 people, and many predict such events will be much more commonplace as a result of increasing temperatures. The anomaly was extreme, particularly in France, with consequences that were well reported in the press. Year-to-year, decade-to-decade there's variation, but the overall upward trend worldwide since the American Civil War is really clear and really obvious, at least to me.

3 If you look at the glaciers around the world, you see that many are melting away. A friend of mine named Lonnie Thompson of Ohio State studies glaciers, and he reports that 15 to 20 years from now there will be no more snows of Kilimanjaro. This shrinking of glaciers is happening all

around the world, including Latin America, China, and the U.S. In our own Glacier National Park, all of the glaciers are predicted to be gone within 15 to 20 years.

4 An area of Bangladesh is due to be flooded where ten million people live. A large area of Florida is due to be flooded. The Florida Keys are very much at risk. The Everglades are at risk.

5 The trend is very clear. What's behind it all? I've come to believe that global warming, the disappearance of the ocean fisheries, the destruction of the rain forests, the stratospheric ozone depletion problem, the extinction crisis, all of these are really symptoms of an underlying cause. The underlying cause is a collision between our civilization and the earth. The relationship between the human species and our planet has been completely changed. All of our culture, all of our literature, all of our history, everything we've learned, was premised on one relationship between the earth and us, and now we have a different one.

6 Think about the subsistence that we have always drawn from the earth. The plow was a great advance, as was irrigation. But then we began to get more powerful with these tools. At the Aral Sea in Russia, something as simple as irrigation on a large scale led to the virtual disappearance of the fourth largest inland body of water in the world. We're changing the surface of the earth, and technology sometimes seems to dwarf our human scale. We now have to try to change this pattern.

7 There's another assumption that needs to be questioned. In contrast to the idea that the earth is so big that we can't have any impact on it, there are others who assume that the climate change problem is so big we can't solve it. I, however, believe that we can if we put our minds to it. We had a problem with the ozone hole, a big global problem that seemed too big to solve. In response, we had political leadership and the world passed a treaty outlawing chlorofluorocarbons, the chemicals that caused this problem. The United States led the way, and we brought about a dramatic drop in CFCs and are now in the process of solving that problem. We now have the ability to buy hybrid cars like the Toyota Prius and the marketplace for new sources of energy is increasing dramatically. We're also seeing new efficiencies with energy savings. If we have political leadership and the collective political will to say it is important to solve this problem, we can not only solve it, we can create more jobs, we can create higher incomes, a better way of life, and a higher quality of life by solving the problem.

8 Everything we have ever known—and Carl Sagan made a beautiful long statement about this—all the wars, all the heartbreak, all the romance, every triumph, every mistake, everything we've ever known is contained in this small planet. If we keep the right perspective and keep our eyes on the prize, we can solve this problem, we will solve this problem, we must solve this problem. It really is up to you.

Write an essay in which you explain how Al Gore builds an argument to persuade his audience that climate change is a serious problem we must address. In your essay, analyze how Gore uses one or more of the features listed in the box above (or features of your own choice) to strengthen the logic and persuasiveness of his argument. Be sure that your analysis focuses on the most relevant features of the passage.

Your essay should not explain whether you agree with Gore's claims, but rather explain how Gore builds an argument to persuade his audience.

Al Gore says that we need to take better care of the earth. If we don't, things will get worse, and things are already pretty bad. "In Europe during the summer of 2003, we experienced an extreme heat wave that killed an estimated 20,000 people, and many predict such events will be much more commonplace as a result of increasing temperatures." The earth is in bad shape, we need to fix it.

One example Al Gore uses is the glaciers. The glaciers is melting, according to his friend Lonnie, and that's a big problem. If there are no more glaciers, that will mean we no longer have Glacier National Park. This is a big problem. "The trend is very clear." Rain forests are being destroyed, fisheries are disappearing from the oceans. This situation could be deadly.

Things are basically different than they've ever been before. Humans used to be farmers, so they didn't need technology. Now we have made enormous technological advances, but their bad for the planet. All the machines that we use are causing global warming.

But don't worry, there is some hope. We can still stop this menace if we get to work right now. There is other new technology that is making things better. For example, the Toyota Prius is a hybrid car which is are better for the environment. The United States is striving to improve and lead the way. Right now. We need politicians to step up. "If we have political leadership and the collective political will to say it is important to solve this problem," we can get it done. Al Gore thinks that we can solve the problem and have "a higher quality of life by solving the problem." This means that things can only get better for us from hear on out, if we listen to what he says. We made this problem, but we can fix it.

Score Breakdown: Essay #1

Reading Score: 2. The writer demonstrates limited comprehension of the source text's central ideas.

The writer understands Gore's central argument—that we need to address a serious environmental problem—but she does not grasp the nuances of his argument about the relationship between humans and technology. Furthermore, she does not connect important details to how Gore uses them. For example, she highlights his example of glaciers melting, but does not link it to the mass flooding of areas where many people live, which is what makes this example significant in context.

Although the writer does not make any overt errors in referring to the passage, her discussion is not always precise. She does quote from the source text, but she does not provide context for the quotes, or explain why they are important. She also makes some unsupported claims.

Analysis Score: 2. The writer shows that she understands she is supposed to write about the passage, not the topic. However, her analysis lacks depth, and she often writes as if she is discussing her own opinion rather than Gore's argument.

The writer summarizes her perception of Gore's thesis, but she does not examine how he builds his argument. She discusses some of the most relevant features of Gore's argument (such as his example of the heat wave), but misses others (such as the changing relationship between humans and the planet). When she does refer to Gore's use of evidence, she does not always do so effectively and she does not provide any analysis of his reasoning or stylistic elements.

The writer does provide evidence for some of her claims, such as when she supports the statement that the earth is in bad shape by talking about the glaciers melting. However, other claims are both broad and not supported by the text.

Writing Score: 2. The writer demonstrates limited mastery of language and organization.

The tone in this essay is not conversational. However, the style is quite simple, and occasionally too casual for formal writing. Sentences vary in structure, but only slightly. There are also some errors in grammar and usage, including run-on sentences.

The writer does make a central claim—"The earth is in bad shape, and we need to fix it"— but it is not focused on the passage, which is what an essay's thesis should focus on. There is a clear series of ideas in the essay, but they are not well connected; the ideas do not build upon each other, and there is only one clear transition. Furthermore, although the essay is structured in distinct paragraphs that each has a clear topic, the sentences within those paragraphs are not clearly ordered to develop a point.

Sample Essay #2

Al Gore argues that climate change is a major problem that we must address. He views both climate change and the potential solutions for climate change not just as a matter of technology, but also as a matter of changing the human relationship with the earth. By focusing on the role of humanity in both creating and stopping climate change, Gore imparts to his audience a sense of both responsibility and hope.

Gore begins by asserting that "people tend to assume that the earth is so big that we as human beings can't possibly have any impact on it," but this is a "mistake." He uses multiple examples to demonstrate that the popular perception of the earth as "invulnerable" is wrong. His first piece of evidence is a European heat wave that killed 20,000 people, which allows him to foreground the human cost of climate change. This continues as he talks about the melting of the glaciers. Citing the work of a researcher at Ohio State as an authoritative source to give his argument scientific credibility, Gore directly connects the shrinking of the glaciers to flooding in Bangladesh "where ten million people live." Once more, he emphasizes the human cost of climate change as he is establishing the severity of the crisis.

He also centers on humanity when discussing the "underlying cause" of climate change, which he believes is "a collision between our civilization and the earth." The word "collision" dramatizes how suddenly things have changed. To further underscore the extent to which our relationship with the earth has changed, he writes that "all of our culture, all of our literature, all of our history" came out of the old relationship between the earth and humanity; the repetition highlights the immense scope of this history, which in turn brings home the scope of the crisis.

However, Gore does not center on humanity only to make his audience aware of the danger; he also does so to promote a hopeful outlook. He uses the disappearance of the Aral Sea due to large-scale irrigation as an example of how technological advance can change the earth for the worse, but then transitions into discussing his belief that we can solve the problem of climate change "if we put our minds to it." He illustrates this belief with the successful campaign to bring about "a dramatic drop" in chlorofluorocarbons, which were contributing to the problem of the ozone hole. By juxtaposing an example of humans harming the earth with one of humans working to fix a problem they had created, Gore reinforces his argument that the power lies with us.

Furthermore, just as Gore emphasized the human costs of climate change, he also emphasizes the human benefits of working to solve the problem. He points out that "the marketplace for new sources of energy is increasing dramatically," making a solution seem economically feasible. He goes on to assert that "we can create more jobs, we can create higher incomes, a better way of life, and a higher quality of life" in the quest to stop climate change. The subtle repetitions of "we can create" and "life" stir the audience's emotions as Gore leads them to envision a brighter future.

That future, once again, lies with us. In his final triple repetition—"we can solve this problem, we will solve this problem, we must solve this problem" —Gore brings together the two sides that together make his argument so powerful: our role in creating the problem and our ability to solve it. In keeping his focus on humanity, Gore inspires his audience to feel responsible for the fate of the earth and hopeful about our ability to fix it.

Score Breakdown: Essay #2

Reading Score: 4. The writer demonstrates a clear and nuanced understanding of different aspects of Gore's argument, and states them in her introduction.

The writer focuses on details relevant to the passage and highlights their importance to Gore's argument. She consistently uses evidence from the text to support her claims. She also provides both context and explanation for the quotes she uses.

Analysis Score: 4. The writer clearly understands the assignment, structuring her essay entirely around her own analysis of Gore's speech. Her thesis is both specific and clear.

The writer analyzes the role that evidence plays in Gore's argument in ways that are relevant to her own thesis about his speech. She also analyzes how both organizational choices and stylistic tools contribute to the aspect of Gore's argument she has chosen to focus on. She develops each of her claims using evidence from the text.

Writing Score: 4. The writer demonstrates exceptional mastery of language and strong organization.

The writer states her central claim clearly in her introduction, and develops it throughout the essay. Her essay is effectively organized, with focused paragraphs in a logical order so that each one builds on the point the previous one made. At the end of each paragraph, she makes its relationship to her main argument clear. She also uses transitions to make her argument easy to follow.

The tone is consistent and academic. The style is sophisticated, employing a variety of sentence structures and vocabulary that allows her to be specific and concise. She demonstrates full proficiency in grammar and usage.

Section 5
Sample SAT Essay Prompts

Here are five essay prompts to practice the strategies you learned in this chapter. Answer each prompt within a 50-minute time limit, and ask a trusted reader to check your work. In the chart below, we've also given you a checklist of questions you can ask yourself as you're reviewing your work.

Criteria	Checklist
Reading	✓ Did I show that I understand the passage's argument? (Remember that the prompt summarizes it for you!) ✓ Did I connect important details to the main idea? ✓ Did I use evidence from the text to support my claims?
Analysis	✓ Is my essay about the passage, *not* about the topic of the passage? ✓ Did I analyze the author's use of evidence, reasoning, and style, using specific examples from the text? ✓ Did I explain how my examples were relevant to my argument?
Writing	✓ Do I have a clear thesis statement? ✓ Do my paragraphs have topic sentences and transitions? ✓ Are my sentences grammatically correct?

Essay Prompt #1
Part 1

As you read the passage below, consider how Rodrigo A. Medellín, Don J. Melnick, and Mary C. Pearl use

- evidence, such as facts or examples, to support claims.

- reasoning to develop ideas and to connect claims and evidence.

- stylistic or persuasive elements, such as word choice or appeals to emotion, to add power to the ideas expressed.

Adapted from Rodrigo A. Medellín, Don J. Melnick, and Mary C. Pearl, "Protect Our Bats." © 2014 by the New York Times Company. Originally published May 11, 2014.

1 Disease and heedless management of wind turbines are killing North America's bats, with potentially devastating consequences for agriculture and human health.

2 We have yet to find a cure for the disease known as white-nose syndrome, which has decimated populations of hibernating, cave-dwelling bats in the Northeast. But we can reduce the turbine threat significantly without dismantling them or shutting them down.

3 White-nose syndrome (also known as W.N.S.) was first documented in February 2006 in upstate New York, where it may have been carried from Europe to a bat cave on an explorer's hiking boot. In Europe, bats appear to be immune. But in North America, bats are highly susceptible to the cold-loving fungus that appears in winter on the muzzle and other body parts during hibernation, irritating them awake at a time when there is no food. They end up burning precious stores of energy and starve to death.

4 The consequences have been catastrophic. A 2011 study of 42 sites across five Eastern states found that after 2006 the populations of tri-colored and Indiana bats declined by more than 70 percent, and little brown bats by more than 90 percent. The population of the northern long-eared bat, once common, has declined by an estimated 99 percent and prompted a proposal from the United States Fish and Wildlife Service to list it as an endangered species. Other species of hibernating cave-dwelling bats have declined precipitously as well.

5 Whether these bats will recover or go extinct is unclear. Meanwhile, W.N.S. continues to spread rapidly. On the back of this year's extremely cold winter, it moved into Michigan and Wisconsin. It is now confirmed in 23 states and five Canadian provinces.

6 Tree-dwelling bats don't seem to be affected by W.N.S., since they don't hibernate in caves. But wind farms are killing them. Wind turbines nationwide are estimated to kill between 600,000 and 900,000 bats a year, according to a recent study in the journal BioScience. About half of those lost to turbines are hoary bats, which migrate long distances seasonally throughout North America. Eastern red and silver-haired bats, commonly seen in Central Park in New York City hunting insects at night, are also being killed by turbines by the tens of thousands.

7   We can't afford to lose these creatures. In the Northeast, all of our native bat species eat insects. One little brown bat can eat 1,000 mosquitoes in an hour, reducing the potential for mosquito-borne diseases. A colony of 150 big brown bats can protect crops from up to 33 million rootworms over a growing season. The Mexican free-tailed bats of Bracken Cave in south-central Texas consume about 250 tons of insects every summer night. The natural pest control provided by that species across eight Texas counties has been valued at nearly $750,000 as it protects the $6 million summer cotton crop. Nationwide, the value of bats as pest controllers is estimated to be at least $3.7 billion and possibly much more.

8   Today, genetic engineering may seem to provide an effective way to protect crops from insects, but pests have already developed resistance to some of these products. Insects also readily evolve resistance to chemical insecticides, and increased use of these chemicals would come at a great cost to human health. But bats have shared the night skies with insects for at least 50 million years, and they know how to hunt and eat them.

9   Fortunately, we can reduce the mortality caused by wind farms, which are often located on windy routes favored by some migratory bats. Wind turbines usually switch on automatically at wind speeds of about 8 to 9 miles per hour, speeds at which insects and bats are active. But if, during times of peak bat activity, energy companies recalibrated their turbines to start at a wind speed of about 11 miles per hour, which is too windy for insects and bats to fly, turbine-related deaths could be reduced by 44 to 93 percent, according to a 2010 study published in the journal Frontiers in Ecology and the Environment. The effect on power output would be negligible—less than 1 percent annually.

10   Threats to bats also threaten us. We should step up research on the prevention and cure of white-nose syndrome. And we should require energy companies to take steps to protect bats from collisions with wind turbines. It is foolish to spend enormous sums to create pesticides and transgenic crops to fight insects, while investing little to protect bats, our most efficient insect fighters.

Write an essay in which you explain how Rodrigo A. Medellín, Don J. Melnick, and Mary C. Pearl build an argument to persuade their audience that we need to protect North America's bat population. In your essay, analyze how the authors use one or more of the features listed in the box above (or features of your own choice) to strengthen the logic and persuasiveness of their argument. Be sure that your analysis focuses on the most relevant features of the passage.

Your essay should not explain whether you agree with Medellín, Melnick, and Pearl's claims, but rather explain how the authors build an argument to persuade their audience.

Essay Prompt #2

Part 2

As you read the passage below, consider how Timothy D. Wilson uses

- evidence, such as facts or examples, to support claims.

- reasoning to develop ideas and to connect claims and evidence.

- stylistic or persuasive elements, such as word choice or appeals to emotion, to add power to the ideas expressed.

Adapted from Timothy D. Wilson, "Stop Bullying The 'Soft' Sciences." © 2012 by the Los Angeles Times. Originally published July 12, 2012.

1 Once, during a meeting at my university, a biologist mentioned that he was the only faculty member present from a science department. When I corrected him, noting that I was from the Department of Psychology, he waved his hand dismissively, as if I were a Little Leaguer telling a member of the New York Yankees that I too played baseball.

2 There has long been snobbery in the sciences, with the "hard" ones (physics, chemistry, biology) considering themselves to be more legitimate than the "soft" ones (psychology, sociology). It is thus no surprise that many members of the general public feel the same way. But of late, skepticism about the rigors of social science has reached absurd heights.

3 The U.S. House of Representatives recently voted to eliminate funding for political science research through the National Science Foundation. In the wake of that action, an opinion writer for the Washington Post suggested that the House didn't go far enough. The NSF should not fund any research in the social sciences, wrote Charles Lane, because "unlike hypotheses in the hard sciences, hypotheses about society usually can't be proven or disproven by experimentation."

4 This is news to me and the many other social scientists who have spent their careers doing carefully controlled experiments on human behavior, inside and outside the laboratory. What makes the criticism so galling is that those who voice it, or members of their families, have undoubtedly benefited from research in the disciplines they dismiss.

5 Most of us know someone who has suffered from depression and sought psychotherapy. He or she probably benefited from therapies such as cognitive behavioral therapy that have been shown to work in randomized clinical trials.

6 Ever hear of stereotype threat? It is the double jeopardy that people face when they are at risk of confirming a negative stereotype of their group. When African American students take a difficult test, for example, they are concerned not only about how well they will do but also about the possibility that performing poorly will reflect badly on their entire group. This added worry has been shown time and again, in carefully controlled experiments, to lower academic performance. But fortunately, experiments have also showed promising ways to reduce this threat. One intervention, for example, conducted in a middle school, reduced the achievement gap by 40%.

7   If you know someone who was unlucky enough to be arrested for a crime he didn't commit, he may have benefited from social psychological experiments that have resulted in fairer lineups and interrogations, making it less likely that innocent people are convicted.

8   An often-overlooked advantage of the experimental method is that it can demonstrate what doesn't work. Consider three popular programs that research psychologists have debunked: Critical Incident Stress Debriefing, used to prevent post-traumatic stress disorders in first responders and others who have witnessed horrific events; the D.A.R.E. anti-drug program, used in many schools throughout America; and Scared Straight programs designed to prevent at-risk teens from engaging in criminal behavior.

9   All three of these programs have been shown, with well-designed experimental studies, to be ineffective or, in some cases, to make matters worse. And as a result, the programs have become less popular or have changed their methods. By discovering what doesn't work, social scientists have saved the public billions of dollars.

10   To be fair to the critics, social scientists have not always taken advantage of the experimental method as much as they could. Too often, for example, educational programs have been implemented widely without being adequately tested. But increasingly, educational researchers are employing better methodologies. For example, in a recent study, researchers randomly assigned teachers to a program called My Teaching Partner, which is designed to improve teaching skills, or to a control group. Students taught by the teachers who participated in the program did significantly better on achievement tests than did students taught by teachers in the control group.

11   Are the social sciences perfect? Of course not. Human behavior is complex, and it is not possible to conduct experiments to test all aspects of what people do or why. There are entire disciplines devoted to the experimental study of human behavior, however, in tightly controlled, ethically acceptable ways. Many people benefit from the results, including those who, in their ignorance, believe that science is limited to the study of molecules.

Write an essay in which you explain how Timothy D. Wilson builds an argument to persuade his audience that the "soft" sciences are real sciences and should be funded. In your essay, analyze how Wilson uses one or more of the features listed in the box above (or features of your own choice) to strengthen the logic and persuasiveness of his argument. Be sure that your analysis focuses on the most relevant features of the passage.

Your essay should not explain whether you agree with Wilson's claims, but rather explain how Wilson builds an argument to persuade his audience.

Essay Prompt #3
Part 3

As you read the passage below, consider how Tom Vanderbilt uses

- evidence, such as facts or examples, to support claims.

- reasoning to develop ideas and to connect claims and evidence.

- stylistic or persuasive elements, such as word choice or appeals to emotion, to add power to the ideas expressed.

Adapted from Tom Vanderbilt, "When Pedestrians Get Mixed Signals." © 2014 by the New York Times Company. Originally published February 1, 2014.

1   Let's put aside the tired trope that no one walks in Los Angeles—Ray Bradbury nailed that one with his 1951 short story "The Pedestrian," about a man picked up by the police for the suspicious activity of walking. In fact, Los Angeles has many places that are quite pleasant for walking.

2   Take the Silver Lake neighborhood: It does not even rank among the city's top 20 "most walkable" areas, according to the website Walk Score, yet still wins 75 points ("most errands can be accomplished on foot")—a number that puts many American cities to shame. In 2012, the city hired its first "pedestrian coordinators."

3   But then came the surest indication of a walking resurgence in Los Angeles: It suddenly had a pedestrian problem. As The Los Angeles Times reported, the Police Department was targeting people for a variety of pedestrian violations in downtown Los Angeles. "We're heavily enforcing pedestrian violations because they're impeding traffic and causing too many accidents and deaths," said Lt. Lydia Leos of the Los Angeles Police Department.

4   Thus a familiar pattern reasserts itself: The best way to reduce pedestrian deaths is to issue tickets to pedestrians. A similar dynamic can be seen in recent weeks after a spate of pedestrian deaths in New York City, where Mayor Bill de Blasio has endorsed more aggressive enforcement by the New York Police Department against jaywalkers. Enforcement against jaywalking varies between states, but it is an infraction in most, even a misdemeanor in some.

5   But neither enforcement nor education has the effect we like to think it does on safety. Decades of graphic teenage driving safety films did not bring down teenage driving deaths; what did was limiting the age and conditions under which teenagers could begin to drive. Similarly, all the "awareness campaigns" on seatbelt usage have had a fraction of the impact of simply installing that annoying chime that impels drivers to buckle up.

6   If tough love will not make pedestrians safer, what will? The answer is: better walking infrastructure, slower car speeds and more pedestrians. But it's easier to write off the problem as one of jaywalkers.

7   Nowadays, the word connotes an amorphous urban nuisance. In fact, the term once referred to country bumpkins ("jays"), who came to the city and perambulated in a way that amused and exasperated savvy urban bipeds. As the historian Peter Norton has documented, the word was then overhauled in the early part of the 20th century. A coalition of pro-automobile interests Mr. Norton calls "motordom" succeeded in shifting the focus of street safety from curbing the actions of rogue drivers to curbing rogue walkers. The pedestrian pushback was shortlived: An attempt to popularize the term "jay driver" was left behind in a cloud of exhaust.

8   Sure, we may call an errant driver, per the comedian George Carlin, an "idiot" or a "maniac," but there is no word to tar an entire class of negligent motorists. This is because of the extent to which driving has been normalized for most Americans: We constantly see the world through what has been called the "windshield view."

9   Those humans in Los Angeles who began walking a second or two after the light was blinking were, after all, violating the "Vehicle Code." Note that cars, apparently, do not violate a "Human Code."

10   As for pedestrian safety, which is the typical stated purpose of jaywalking crackdowns, more pedestrians generally are killed in urban areas by cars violating their right of way than are rogue pedestrians violating vehicles' right of way. Then there are those people struck on sidewalks, even inside restaurants. What do we call that? Jay-living?

11   Pedestrians, who lack air bags and side-impact crash protection, are largely rational creatures. Studies have shown that when you shorten the wait to cross a street, fewer people will cross against the light. When you tell people how long they must wait to cross, fewer people will cross against the signal.

12   When you actually give people a signal, more will cross with it. As the field of behavioral economics has been discovering, rather than penalizing people for opting out of the system, a more effective approach is to make it easier to opt in.

13   The Los Angeles Police Department may be patrolling on foot in downtown Los Angeles, but it is still looking through the windshield.

Write an essay in which you explain how Tom Vanderbilt builds an argument to persuade his audience that penalizing jaywalking will not increase pedestrian safety. In your essay, analyze how Vanderbilt uses one or more of the features listed in the box above (or features of your own choice) to strengthen the logic and persuasiveness of his argument. Be sure that your analysis focuses on the most relevant features of the passage.

Your essay should not explain whether you agree with Vanderbilt's claims, but rather explain how Vanderbilt builds an argument to persuade his audience.

Essay Prompt #4
Part 4

As you read the passage below, consider how Alfie Kohn uses

- evidence, such as facts or examples, to support claims.

- reasoning to develop ideas and to connect claims and evidence.

- stylistic or persuasive elements, such as word choice or appeals to emotion, to add power to the ideas expressed.

Adapted from Alfie Kohn, "Do Our Kids Get Off Too Easy?" © 2014 by the New York Times Company. Originally published May 3, 2014.

1 The conventional wisdom these days is that kids come by everything too easily— stickers, praise, A's, trophies. It's outrageous, we're told, that all kids on the field may get a thanks-for-playing token, in contrast to the good old days, when recognition was reserved for the conquering heroes.

2 Most of all, it's assumed that the best way to get children ready for the miserable "real world" that awaits them is to make sure they have plenty of miserable experiences while they're young. Conversely, if they're spared any unhappiness, they'll be ill-prepared. This is precisely the logic employed not so long ago to frame bullying as a rite of passage that kids were expected to deal with on their own, without assistance from "overprotective" adults.

3 In any case, no one ever explains the mechanism by which the silence of a long drive home without a trophy is supposed to teach resilience. Nor are we told whether there's any support for this theory of inoculation by immersion. Have social scientists shown that those who are spared, say, the rigors of dodge ball (which turns children into human targets) or class rank (which pits students against one another) will wind up unprepared for adulthood?

4 Not that I can find. In fact, studies of those who attended the sort of nontraditional schools that afford an unusual amount of autonomy and nurturing suggest that the great majority seemed capable of navigating the transition to traditional colleges and workplaces.

5 But when you point out the absence of logic or evidence, it soon becomes clear that trophy rage is less about prediction— what will happen to kids later—than ideology —how they ought to be treated now. Fury over the possibility that kids will get off too easy or feel too good about themselves seems to rest on three underlying values.

6 The first is deprivation: Kids shouldn't be spared struggle and sacrifice, regardless of the effects. The second value is scarcity: the belief that excellence, by definition, is something that not everyone can attain. No matter how well a group of students performs, only a few should get A's. Otherwise we're sanctioning "grade inflation" and mediocrity. To have high standards, there must always be losers.

7 But it's the third conviction that really ties everything together: an endorsement of conditionality. Children ought never to receive something desirable—a sum of money, a trophy, a commendation— unless they've done enough to merit it. They shouldn't even be allowed to feel good about themselves

---

without being able to point to tangible accomplishments. In this view, we have a moral obligation to reward the deserving and, equally important, make sure the undeserving go conspicuously unrewarded. Hence the anger over participation trophies. The losers mustn't receive something that even looks like a reward.

8   A commitment to conditionality lives at the intersection of economics and theology. It's where lectures about the law of the marketplace meet sermons about what we must do to earn our way into heaven. Here, almost every human interaction, even among family members, is regarded as a kind of transaction.

9   Interestingly, no research that I know of has ever shown that unconditionality is harmful in terms of future achievement, psychological health or anything else. In fact, studies generally show exactly the opposite. One of the most destructive ways to raise a child is with "conditional regard."

10   Over the last decade or so, two Israeli researchers, Avi Assor and Guy Roth, and their colleagues in the United States and Belgium, have conducted a series of experiments whose consistent finding is that when children feel their parents' affection varies depending on the extent to which they are well behaved, self-controlled or impressive at school or sports, this promotes "the development of a fragile, contingent and unstable sense of self."

11   Other researchers, meanwhile, have shown that high self-esteem is beneficial, but that even more desirable is unconditional self-esteem: a solid core of belief in yourself, an abiding sense that you're competent and worthwhile—even when you screw up or fall short. In other words, the very unconditionality that seems to fuel attacks on participation trophies and the whole "self-esteem movement" turns out to be a defining feature of psychological health. It's precisely what we should be helping our children to acquire.

Write an essay in which you explain how Alfie Kohn builds an argument to persuade his audience that parents should show unconditional acceptance for their children. In your essay, analyze how Kohn uses one or more of the features listed in the box above (or features of your own choice) to strengthen the logic and persuasiveness of his argument. Be sure that your analysis focuses on the most relevant features of the passage.

Your essay should not explain whether you agree with Kohn's claims, but rather explain how Kohn builds an argument to persuade his audience.

Math

Chapter 5

Section 1
Introduction to the Math Test

The new SAT Math Test will test certain topics in math as well as your ability to use reasoning and critical thinking to solve real-world problems. These concepts and skills provide the foundations for the math you will learn in college and use in everyday life. The SAT groups these concepts into four major areas that you will see on the Math Test: Heart of Algebra, Problem Solving and Data Analysis, Passport to Advanced Math, and Additional Topics in Math.

In this chapter, we will review all of the topics that you may see on the Math Test. We will also practice strategies for solving different types of questions and for tackling difficult or unfamiliar problems. But first, let's look at the format of the Math Test.

The Basics

The SAT Math Test includes two sections and a total of 58 questions. You can use your calculator on only one of the sections:

Section	Number of Questions	Amount of Time
Calculator Section	38 questions	55 minutes
No-Calculator Section	20 questions	25 minutes

In the Calculator Section, you'll have about 1.5 minutes to answer each question. In the No-Calculator Section, you'll have 1.25 minutes to answer each question. This might not seem like a lot of time, but reviewing and practicing the concepts in this chapter will help you apply your knowledge quickly and efficiently on test day! We'll talk about time management and other test-taking strategies in Section 2 of this chapter.

Topics

There are four main content areas covered by the Math Test. Here is a breakdown of the topics and number of questions in each content area:

Content Area	Topics Covered	Number of Questions	
		Calculator	No-Calculator
Heart of Algebra	Fundamental concepts in algebra involving linear equations and inequalities	11	8
Problem Solving and Data Analysis	Interpreting qualitative and quantitative data, analyzing relationships	17	0
Passport to Advanced Math	More advanced concepts in algebra, including quadratic and higher-order equations	7	9
Additional Topics in Math	Geometry, trigonometry, complex numbers	3	3
Total		**38**	**20**

Sections 3-6 cover the topics in each of these content areas in depth. Fundamental math skills that apply to all of these topics are covered online.

 For a fundamental review, please visit **ivyglobal.com/study**.

Questions

Both sections on the Math Test will have two types of questions: multiple choice questions and student-produced response questions. In total, you will see 45 multiple choice questions and 13 student-produced response questions on the Math Test.

Each section will start with the multiple choice questions, then progress to the student-produced response questions.

Within each section, the multiple choice questions will be ordered by difficulty, and so will the student-produced response questions. For example, in the Calculator Section, you will see 30 multiple choice questions ordered from easy to difficult, then 8 student-produced response questions. The No-Calculator Section has 15 multiple choice questions and 5 student-produced response questions.

Some of the questions will include real-world contexts in areas such as science and social studies. These questions will require you to apply reasoning and critical thinking skills to analyze situations, create mathematical models, and find relevant solutions. You will also see graphs, charts, and diagrams in some of the problems and answer choices.

Scoring

Each question is worth one point. The number of points you receive on each section will contribute to your raw score, which will be scaled to give you your final math score from 200-800. The Calculator Section has nearly twice the weight of the No-Calculator Section in determining your score. Here is a chart that shows the scoring breakdown for each question type:

Section	Problem Type	Points	Percentage of Math Score	
Calculator	Multiple Choice	30	52%	66%
	Student-Produced Response Questions	8	14%	
No-Calculator	Multiple Choice	15	26%	34%
	Student-Produced Response Questions	5	8%	
Total		**58**	**100%**	**100%**

In the next section, we will discuss the different question types on the Math Test and learn strategies for approaching and solving each type of question. The rest of the chapter provides an in-depth review of the topics covered on the Math Test. To practice applying your knowledge, make sure to do the practice exercises for each section. Let's get started!

Section 2
Approaching the Math Test

To succeed on the SAT Math Test, you need to know specific math concepts and math skills. The good news is that the redesigned SAT Math Test evaluates math skills that you have learned in your high school classes. You just need to learn which skills the SAT tests, and what strategies you can use to apply your knowledge during the test.

In this section, you will learn about approaching problems, entering your answers, and using problem-solving strategies for the Math Test. You'll see how these techniques can be applied to sample math questions and practice using them.

Once you have mastered these strategies, you'll be ready to review the math concepts on the exam. All of these concepts are covered in Sections 3-6 of this chapter. If you feel comfortable with some or all of the material, you can complete the practice sets at the end of each section to determine which topics you should review.

Plan Your Approach
Part 1

When you take the SAT Math Test, you can reduce your stress by planning ahead. Know what the directions say, how you will approach each question, and how to pace yourself. We'll go through these steps with an example below.

Know the Directions

You will be given directions and reference information at the beginning of each math section of the SAT. The directions contain important information about the types of questions you will see and how much time you have to complete them. Make sure to read the directions before starting the problems so you know what to expect in each section.

The "Notes" section at the beginning of each math section will look similar to the one below. This section will tell you whether you can use a calculator on that section. It also gives you information about the figures and functions you will see and use on the test.

NOTES

1. You **may not** use a calculator.
2. Variables and expressions represent real numbers unless stated otherwise.
3. Figures are drawn to scale unless stated otherwise.
4. Figures lie in a plane unless stated otherwise.
5. The domain of a function f is defined as the set of all real numbers x for which $f(x)$ is also a real number, unless stated otherwise.

The Reference section contains important formulas and facts. To use this information to your advantage, be familiar with what formulas are provided. Use this reference information when practicing for the SAT. Remember that this information is only helpful if you know how to use it to solve problems.

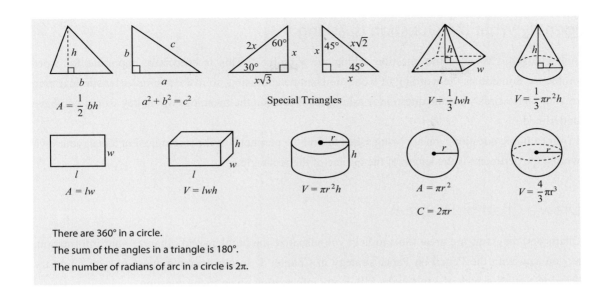

There are 360° in a circle.

The sum of the angles in a triangle is 180°.

The number of radians of arc in a circle is 2π.

Read the Question Carefully

Read through the whole question. Don't assume you understand the question just by reading the first few words! Reading the whole question will help you avoid making assumptions that can lead to careless errors.

If you see unfamiliar or difficult-looking material, stay calm and keep reading until the end of the question. There might be more information in the question that will help you figure out the solution. If you still think a question is too difficult after you have finished reading the whole thing, you should make your best guess, circle it in your question booklet, and come back to it if you have time.

Underline Key Words

Underline or circle any information given in the question that will help you solve it. Here's an example:

Example

The <u>width</u> of a <u>rectangular</u> field is <u>one-quarter its length</u>. If the <u>length is 16</u>, what is the <u>perimeter</u> of the field?

A) 4   B) 24   C) 36   D) 40

Identify What the Question is Asking

Ask yourself, "What is the question asking me to solve?" This is especially important for word problems. Sometimes the wording of a question can be confusing, so make it simpler by summarizing in your own words what the question is asking for. Focus on the meanings of the key words you have underlined.

In our example question, you are being asked to find the perimeter of the rectangle. Put this in your own words: the perimeter is the length of the outline of the rectangle.

Draw a Chart or Diagram

Charts and diagrams are great tools to help you visualize the problem and organize your information, as you saw with the Pencil on Paper strategy in Chapter 1. In our example question, you might try drawing a quick sketch of a rectangle. Fill in any information given in the question:

$$\text{width} = \frac{1}{4} \text{ length}$$

length = 16

Come up With a Strategy

Strategize the best way to solve the question. Think about all of the information provided in the question and how it is related. Think about where you have seen this type of question before, and what methods you have used to solve similar types of questions. If there is a formula you know that could help, write it down.

Here's a strategy we could use to solve our example question.

- We know: length = 16

$$\text{width} = \frac{1}{4} \text{ of length} = \frac{1}{4} \times 16 = \frac{16}{4} = 4$$

- We want: the perimeter of the whole rectangle
- Our strategy: we can use a formula that relates a rectangle's perimeter to its length and width

$$\text{perimeter} = (2 \times \text{length}) + (2 \times \text{width})$$

We can now plug in the values and solve:

$$\text{perimeter} = (2 \times 16) + (2 \times 4) = 32 + 8 = 40$$

Is our solution one of the answer choices? It is indeed! The answer is (D) 40.

Check Your Answer

Always check your work to make sure that you picked the best answer among all of the answer choices. Double-check your arithmetic to make sure that you didn't make any avoidable errors. Check that you solved for what the question was asking. For example, if the question asked you to solve for a perimeter, make sure you didn't solve for area.

Try to determine whether or not your answer seems reasonable based on context. For example, if the length of one side of the rectangle is 16, the perimeter of the whole rectangle has to be greater than twice the length, or 32. Answers (A) and (B) in the example are less than 32, so they are unreasonable.

Finally, check that you bubbled in the answer on your answer sheet correctly. It would be a shame to have solved the question correctly and not get credit! Take a look at Part 2 to learn how to enter your answers correctly.

Pace Yourself

Remember that you will be answering questions under a time limit, and you need to leave yourself enough time to attempt every question on the test. One way to save time during the test is to be familiar with the format and instructions before the test day. Be aware of the number and types of sections that you will see. Before starting a section, look at the number of questions you will be answering and the time you have to answer them.

Here is a chart showing how many minutes you should average per question on each section of the Math Test. The questions in the multiple choice section are ordered from easy to difficult. Plan to spend less time on the early questions so that you have enough time for the more challenging ones at the end of the section.

Pacing on the Math Test			
Section	Total Time	Total Questions	Time Per Question
Calculator Section	55 minutes	38 questions	1.4 minutes per question
No-Calculator Section	25 minutes	20 questions	1.25 minutes per question

Finally, remember that every question is worth the same number of points. If you get stuck on any problem, make a guess and return to that question if you have time at the end. You don't lose points for guessing, so you should never leave a question blank. In Part 3, we'll talk about some strategies for guessing efficiently on the SAT Math Test.

Entering Your Answers
Part 2

As we saw in Section 1, questions on the Math Test come in two types: regular multiple-choice questions and student-produced response questions. The **multiple-choice questions** ask you to choose an answer from four possible choices, but the **student-produced response questions** require you to come up with your own answer and enter it into a special grid.

For both question types, you'll need to bubble in your answer on your answer sheet. For a review of how to bubble in your answers to multiple-choice questions, see Chapter 1. Here, we'll discuss how to "grid in" your answers for the student-produced response questions. The gridding process can be confusing, so you should practice thoroughly before the test day. This will help you avoid mistakes, save time, and build confidence.

Gridding In

You will see directions for gridding answers immediately before the grid-in problems. Practice gridding answers before the test so you can skip the directions and have more time to work on the problems.

You will enter your answers to student-produced response questions in a grid like the one shown here. The grid has four columns, and in each column you can enter a digit from 0-9, a decimal point, or a fraction bar (/). This way, you can enter any whole number between 0 and 9,999. You can also enter fractions or decimal numbers.

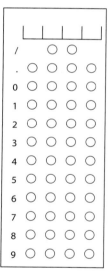

The machine will score the bubbles you fill in on the grid. Make sure to fill in bubbles completely and mark no more than one circle in any column. Completely erase any stray marks in the grid.

Answers written in the boxes above the grid are *not* scored. You can write your answer into those boxes as a guide when you bubble in your answers, and it is a good idea to use the boxes to avoid bubbling errors. However, remember that you always need to bubble your answers as well!

Placement

You can start your answer in any column as long as you can fit in the whole answer. You may leave columns blank if the answer is fewer than four characters. For example, 64 can be gridded in the three ways shown below; all are correct.

Signs

There is no negative sign in the grid, so all answers will be positive numbers or zero. If you get a negative number for an answer, either you have made a mistake or there are other possible answers. Check your work and rework the problem if necessary.

Fractions and Decimals

Grid-in responses may contain fractions or decimals. You can write these answers in either fraction or decimal form as long as you follow the rules below.

You can grid proper and improper fractions, but *not* mixed numbers. If the answer is a mixed number, you must convert it to an improper fraction or a decimal. For example, the answer $4\frac{1}{5}$ must be gridded as 21/5 or 4.2 as shown in the following grids.

If you grid the answer as the mixed number 4 1/5 like the example below, the machine will read it as $\frac{41}{5}$, which is incorrect.

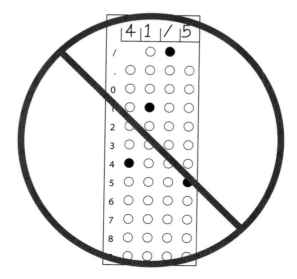

Some answers will not fit in the grid as a fraction and must be converted to a decimal. For example, $\frac{1}{100}$ must be gridded as .01 because 1/100 will not fit.

Decimals must be as accurate as possible. If a decimal is longer than four characters, grid the first four characters (including the decimal point) or it may be marked incorrect. For example, $\frac{4}{7}$ should be written as .571 with no zero before the decimal point. The response .57 may be scored as incorrect because it is less accurate than .571.

You do not have to follow rounding rules when shortening your answer. If you round, do so at the last digit that you can fit in the grid. 8.127 can be bubbled as 8.12 or 8.13, but not as 8.1, which is less accurate. Be sure to follow these guidelines, unless specific rounding instructions are given in the question.

Fractions may be left unreduced as long as they fit in the grid. If an answer was $\frac{3}{4}$, you could grid it as 3/4, 6/8, 9/12, or as a decimal.

Multiple Correct Answers

Some grid-in problems have more than one correct answer. In those cases, you may grid in any of the possible answers as long as it fits in the grid. There may also be multiple methods to arrive at a correct answer.

Math Strategies
Part 3

In Chapter 1, we reviewed general strategies that you can use on all parts of the SAT, such as Plugging in Options and Process of Elimination. In this section, we will review additional strategies that apply specifically to mathematics questions. These strategies will help you use your time and resources, like your calculator and the testing materials, to answer questions quickly, and will reduce your chance of making mistakes.

Use your Calculator

The Math Test is divided into a Calculator Section and a No-Calculator Section. Every math problem on the SAT can be solved without a calculator, but when you're allowed to use a calculator, it can help you save time and avoid errors.

You must provide your own calculator. A scientific or graphing calculator is recommended. You cannot use calculators with keypads, styluses, touchscreens, internet access, cellular access, or power cords. You also cannot use calculators that can play or record audio, video, or images. Your calculator can't make noise, and you can't use a laptop, tablet, or phone as a calculator. For a list of acceptable calculators, see ivyglobal.com/study/links/#calculator.

Make sure to practice using the calculator that you plan to bring to the SAT so you are familiar with it. Before the test, make sure your calculator is working properly and has fresh batteries. Consider bringing a spare set of batteries or a back-up calculator.

Don't rely too much on your calculator when you take the test. On some problems, using a calculator can slow you down. When starting a problem, think about how you will solve it and whether you need to use a calculator. Look for ways to simplify the problem that will make the calculation easier, such as factoring.

Write down calculations and scratch work in the test booklet. This will help you avoid calculator errors and makes it easier to check your work and find errors. Also, remember that every problem can be solved without a calculator. If you find yourself doing complicated or tedious calculations, there is likely a simpler method to find the answer.

Look for Shortcuts

None of the problems should require time-consuming calculations. If your solution strategy is long or complicated, look for a simpler method or a trick to solve the problem more quickly. Also double-check to make sure you are solving for the correct variable or value.

There are often multiple ways to solve a problem, so look for shortcuts or tricks that will save you time and unnecessary work. When possible, simplify equations and expressions.

Example
$$\frac{10x}{y} \times \frac{3}{4} \times \frac{2}{5} \times \frac{1}{6} =$$

A) $\dfrac{x}{3y}$ B) $\dfrac{x}{2y}$ C) $\dfrac{x}{y}$ D) $\dfrac{2x}{y}$

You could solve this problem by finding the product of all the terms. However, this is not the best approach. Instead, try to cancel as many factors as possible. The 3 × 2 in the numerator cancels the 6 in the denominator. You can rewrite the 4 × 5 in the denominator as 2 × 10 and cancel that 10 with the 10 in the numerator.

$$\frac{10x}{y} \times \frac{\cancel{3}}{\underbrace{\cancel{4}}_{2 \times 10}} \times \frac{\cancel{2}}{\cancel{5}} \times \frac{1}{\cancel{6}^{\,6}} = \frac{\cancel{10} \times \cancel{6} \times x}{2 \times \cancel{10} \times \cancel{6} \times y} = \frac{x}{2y}$$

Now you are left with $\dfrac{x}{2y}$, which gives you the correct answer, (B).

This approach reduces the chance of making an arithmetic or calculator error. In fact, it eliminates the need to use a calculator at all. If this question were on the no-calculator section, this approach is faster and safer than multiplying all the factors out by hand.

Use Figures

Any figure provided in the Math Test will be accurate unless noted otherwise. If an angle looks like a right angle, you can assume that it is one. It is safe to assume other features like parallel or perpendicular lines and relative angles or lengths. Charts, graphs, and gridded figures are always accurate.

Although you are not allowed to use a ruler, you can measure lengths by using the side of your answer sheet. Place the corner of the sheet at one point and mark the distance to another point. This strategy may help you eliminate answer choices or check your answer, although there will always be a way to solve these problems without measuring lengths.

Some figures may not show all of the lines that you need to solve the problem. You should add any necessary lines as accurately as possible.

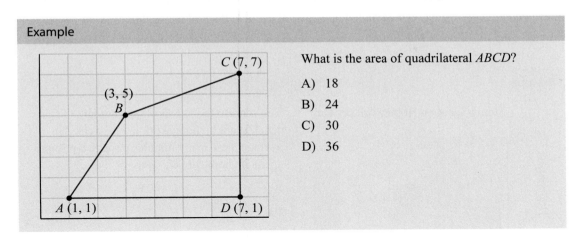

Example

What is the area of quadrilateral *ABCD*?

A) 18

B) 24

C) 30

D) 36

Since quadrilateral *ABCD* is irregular, you cannot easily find the area. However, if you draw a line between *B* and *D*, you will have two triangles whose areas you can calculate:

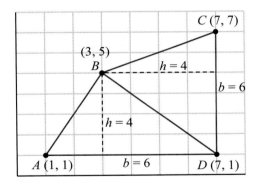

Define the base of triangle *ABD* to be $\overline{AD}$ and the base of triangle *BCD* to be $\overline{CD}$. The height of each triangle is the line segment from the base to the opposite vertex, perpendicular to the base. The bases and heights are labelled in the diagram.

We can use the formula $A = \frac{1}{2}bh$ to find the areas of each of these triangles. The area of triangle *ABD* is $\frac{1}{2}(6)(4) = 12$, and the area of triangle *BCD* is $\frac{1}{2}(6)(4) = 12$. Therefore, the area of quadrilateral *ABCD* is 24, which is answer choice (B).

Draw a diagram if a figure is not provided for a geometry problem, as you learned in Chapter 1. Figures may also be helpful for solving other types of problems. You might draw a number line, graph, or quick sketch of a situation. Keep your diagrams simple and accurate.

Pay Attention to Units and Variables

When choosing an answer, double check that it is in the correct units. The answer may have different units than the given data. Circle or underline any units given in the problem and the units of the answer. Problems involving units will almost always have answer choices that are correct for different units.

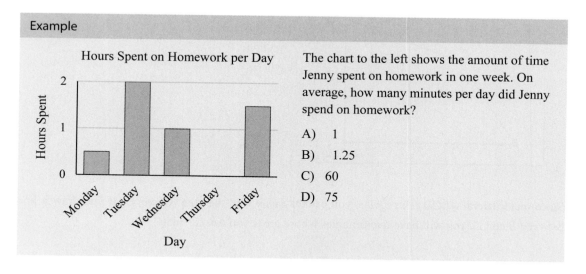

Example

Hours Spent on Homework per Day

The chart to the left shows the amount of time Jenny spent on homework in one week. On average, how many minutes per day did Jenny spend on homework?

A)   1

B)   1.25

C)   60

D)   75

Notice that the units of the graph are hours, but the answer must be in minutes. First, find the average number of hours Jenny spends on homework per day. We take the average by adding together her hours for each day and then dividing by the number of days:

$$\frac{.5 + 2 + 1 + 0 + 1.5}{5} = 1$$

Jenny spends an average of 1 hour per day, but you need to convert this into minutes. There are 60 minutes in 1 hour, so answer choice (C) is correct.

Check Your Answers

Before starting to work on a problem, make sure you know what the problem is asking. On problems that take multiple steps, double check that your final solution is the answer to the problem, not an intermediate step.

Watch out for answer choices that are factors, multiples, or other variations of your answer. You may have forgotten a final step or gone too far in your calculation.

Example

An isosceles triangle has a perimeter of 16. Two legs have length L and the other leg has a length of 6. What is the area of the triangle?

A) 4   B) 5   C) 6   D) 12

First, draw a diagram of the triangle:

Next, find the value of L using the equation for the perimeter:

$$2L + 6 = 16$$

$$2L = 10$$

$$L = 5$$

Notice that answer choice (B) is 5, but that is *not* the answer to the question, which asks for area, not L.

To find the area, we must find the height shown by the dashed line. Notice that if we divide the triangle into two halves at the dashed line, it becomes two right triangles. We know that L, the hypotenuse, is 5, and the base of each new triangle is $6 \div 2 = 3$.

We can use the Pythagorean Theorem to find the height, which we've labelled h:

$$3^2 + h^2 = 5^2$$

$$9 + h^2 = 25$$

$$h^2 = 16$$

$$h = 4$$

Be careful—this is another intermediate solution! Now we can find the area of the original triangle using our values for base and height:

$$A = \frac{1}{2}bh$$

$$A = \frac{1}{2}(6)(4) = 12$$

(D) 12 is the correct answer.

If you have extra time at the end of a section, double-check your answers, especially for grid-in problems. Try to use a different process to find the answer to avoid making the same mistake twice. Write out your calculations when solving problems to make it easier to find your mistakes. Remember to always guess on problems that you cannot solve.

Section 3
Heart of Algebra

The **Heart of Algebra** questions on the SAT test your fundamental algebra skills. Algebra is one of the most important "languages" of math, and is something you use every day—maybe even without knowing it. Using simple letters, numbers, and signs, you can represent a vast range of situations. Let's say, for example, you went out to dinner with six friends and wanted to split your $50 bill equally among you; how much should each person pay? Using algebra you can determine that each person should pay the total cost of the meal ÷ the number of people. This can be rewritten as the amount each person should pay $50 ÷ 6 people = $8.33 per person. The language of algebra allows you to create mathematical models for real world situations.

On the new SAT, a solid understanding of algebra is very important. Out of the 58 questions on the Math Test, 19 involve the Heart of Algebra topics. In this section you will learn how to use algebra to analyze, solve, and create linear equations, inequalities, and systems of equations. In addition to developing mathematical tools, you learn how to apply these principles to real world examples from science and social science.

The concepts covered in this section are:

- Algebraic Expressions
- Linear Equations
- Inequalities
- Absolute Value
- Systems of Equations and Inequalities
- Functions
- Interpreting Equations
- Graphing Equations and Inequalities

Algebraic Expressions
Part 1

An algebraic **expression** is a mathematical "phrase" containing numbers, variables, and operations. A **variable** stands for an unknown number, and is usually represented by a letter. Any letter—x, y, z, N, A—can be used to represent a number that is unknown. The opposite of a variable is a **constant**, which is an unchanging number in an expression.

An algebraic expression is made up of **terms**, which are variables or numbers multiplied together. When a number is right in front of a variable, it means the variable is being multiplied by that number. This number is called the **coefficient**.

Coefficient $\longleftarrow$ **9x** $\longrightarrow$ Variable

Term

When a variable does not have a written coefficient, it has a coefficient of one. For example, the term x is the same as $1x$.

Any expression with two or more terms is called a **polynomial**. An expression with one term only, like the one above, is called a **monomial**. The expression $4x + 6$ has two terms and is called a **binomial**.

Like Terms

You can simplify an algebraic expression by adding or subtracting like terms. **Like terms** have the same variable and are raised to the same power. For example, $4x$ and $6x$ are like terms. However, $3y$ and $3x$ are not like terms because they contain two different variables.

To add or subtract like terms, add or subtract their coefficients:

$$5x + 6x = 11x$$

If you have more than one term, add or subtract the like terms, and leave any remaining terms as they are.

Example

Add $(P + Q + 6)$ and $(2P - 4)$.

The two groups of like terms are P and $2P$, and 6 and -4. Add these like terms together, and leave Q as it is:

$$P + Q + 6 + 2P - 4$$
$$(P + 2P) + (6 - 4) + Q$$
$$3P + 2 + Q$$

Distributive Property

You can also simplify expressions by multiplying and dividing. To multiply or divide like terms, multiply or divide their coefficients:

$$\frac{4x}{2x} = 2$$

The distributive property can help you multiply and divide expressions with more than one term. Remember that according to the **distributive property**, multiplying a number by a sum of two other numbers in parentheses is the same as multiplying it by each number separately and then adding:

$$a(b + c) = ab + ac$$
$$6(x + 2y) = 6x + 12y$$

The distributive property also works for division. Dividing a sum of two numbers by another number is the same as dividing each number separately and then adding:

$$\frac{b + c}{a} = \frac{b}{a} + \frac{c}{a}$$
$$\frac{2x + 3y}{5} = \frac{2x}{5} + \frac{3y}{5}$$

Factoring

Factoring is the opposite of distributing. You can factor out numbers or variables from expressions. When **factoring** an expression, find the greatest common factor that all of your terms have in common. Then, work backwards to take this factor out of your expression.

Example

$$5x + 5y - 10$$

The greatest common factor is 5, so you can factor it out of each term in the expression. Factoring out 5 from $5x$ gives you x, 5 from $5y$ gives you y, and 5 from 10 gives you 2:

$$5x + 5y - 10 = 5(x + y - 2)$$

You can always check that you have factored correctly by distributing and checking that your answer matches the original expression.

Part 1 Practice: Algebraic Expressions

1

$$x + 3x$$

Which of the following correctly combines the like terms for the expression above?

A) $4x$

B) $3x$

C) $3x^2$

D) $x + 3x$

2

Which of the following expressions is equivalent to $17 - 6h - 23 + 2h$?

A) $40 - 4h$

B) $40 - 8h$

C) $-6 - 8h$

D) $-6 - 4h$

3

$$6x - 2y - x + 5y = P$$

Given the equation above, which of the following could be the value of P?

A) $5x + 3y$

B) $5x - 7y$

C) $7x + 3y$

D) $7x + 7y$

4

If twelve more than three times x equals y, which of the following is the expression for y?

A) $3x + 12$

B) $3x + 15$

C) $3x + 24$

D) $3x + 36$

5

Which of the following expressions is equal to $2\left(a - \dfrac{a}{2} + 3b\right)$?

A) $a + 3b$

B) $a + 6b$

C) $2a + 3b$

D) $2a + 6b$

Questions 6 and 7 refer to the following information.

$$4x + 16 - 2y$$

6

Which of the following is equivalent to the expression above?

A) $2(x + 4 - y)$

B) $2(2x + 4 - y)$

C) $2(2x + 8 - y)$

D) $4(x + 4 - y)$

7

If the expression is multiplied by 4, resulting in $ax + b - cy$, what is the value of $a + b - c$?

A) 64

B) 72

C) 80

D) 88

8

If $3g - 11 = 3y$, what is the value of y when g is 12?

9

$$3y - 15xy + 21x = a(y - 5xy + 7x)$$

What is the value of a in the equation above?

10

If $x = 2y$, what is the greatest common factor of $3x$ and $12y$ when $y = 1$?

Linear Equations
Part 2

An algebraic **equation** tells you that two expressions are equal to each other.

You can use an equation to say that $9x$ is equal to 36:

$$9x = 36$$

Often, you will be asked to solve an algebraic equation. If you are asked to "solve for x," you need to find a value for x that makes the equation true. For the equation above, you may know right away that $x = 4$ because $9 \times 4 = 36$.

Manipulating Equations

For more complicated algebraic equations, you may not be able to figure out the answer in your head. You will need to use a method to manipulate the equation and solve for the unknown variable. Your goal is always to **isolate** your variable—to get it by itself on one side of the equation. To do this, you can work backwards to "undo" all of the operations that are being performed on your variable until you can get it by itself.

There's one important rule to remember when working with equations: whatever you do to one side of the equation, you must also do to the other! If you violate this rule, the two sides of your equation will no longer be equal.

You know the equation $4 = 4$ is a true statement. However, if you add a number to one side of the equation but not to the other, the two sides are no longer equal:

$$4 + 2 \neq 4$$

You need to add the same number to both sides of the equation so they remain equal:

$$4 + 2 = 4 + 2$$

Let's see how this works with the following algebraic equation:

Example

$$3x - 2 = 13$$

On the left side of the equation, x is being multiplied by 3, and 2 is being subtracted from the product. You need to "undo" each of these operations by adding numbers to and dividing numbers from both sides of your equation. First, work with the operations that don't involve the variable. In this case, you can undo the subtraction by adding 2 to each side:

$$3x - 2 + 2 = 13 + 2$$

$$3x = 15$$

Then, undo the multiplication by dividing each side by 3:

$$\frac{3x}{3} = \frac{15}{3}$$

$$x = 5$$

What if the equation has variables on both sides? First, get all of the variables onto one side of the equation and combine like terms. Then, isolate the variable like you just did above.

Example

$$5a - 7 = 2a - 1$$

First, get all of your variables on one side of the equation by subtracting $2a$ from each side and combining like terms:

$$5a - 2a - 7 = 2a - 2a - 1$$

$$3a - 7 = -1$$

Then, undo the subtraction by adding 7 to each side:

$$3a - 7 + 7 = -1 + 7$$

$$3a = 6$$

And finally, undo the multiplication by dividing each side by 3:

$$\frac{3a}{3} = \frac{6}{3}$$

$$a = 2$$

To test if you got the right answer, you can plug this number back into the original equation:

$$5a - 7 = 2a - 1$$

$$5 \times 2 - 7 = 2 \times 2 - 1$$

$$10 - 7 = 4 - 1$$

$$3 = 3$$

More Complicated Equations

Some equations will look much more complicated than the ones above. Don't let this scare you! You will always use the same process for solving linear equations with one variable. Work carefully through each step. Get your variable on one side and then undo the operations.

Example
$$\dfrac{5(x + 7)}{4} = \dfrac{100 - 5x}{5}$$

You can see there are a lot of operations in this equation. You need to get the variable x on one side, but you'll have to do some other operations first. First, cross-multiply and use the distributive property:

$$(5 \times 5)(x + 7) = 4(100 - 5x)$$

$$25x + 175 = 400 - 20x$$

Then, undo the operations to get your variable on one side of the equation and your constant on the other side:

$$25x + 175 + 20x = 400 - 20x + 20x$$

$$45x + 175 = 400$$

$$45x + 175 - 175 = 400 - 175$$

$$45x = 225$$

Finally, divide by 45 on both sides to completely solve for x.

$$\frac{45x}{45} = \frac{225}{45}$$

$$x = 5$$

Equations with Two Variables

Sometimes you will see an equation that has two different variables in it, such as $y = 2x + 6$. You will not be able to find an exact number for x or y without more information, as we will see in Part 5. However, you can solve for one variable *in terms of* the other. This means that your answer will still contain a variable.

To solve for one variable in terms of the other, use the same steps as for single-variable equations and treat the second variable as if it were a number. For the equation above, let's solve for x in terms of y.

Because you're solving for x, you need to get x by itself. Start by subtracting 6 from both sides, and then divide by 2:

$$y = 2x + 6$$

$$y - 6 = 2x + 6 - 6$$

$$\frac{y-6}{2} = \frac{2x}{2}$$

$$\frac{y-6}{2} = x$$

$\frac{y-6}{2}$ is how you would represent x in terms of y.

You may also be asked to use an equation to solve for another algebraic expression.

Example

If $6x + 2y = 24$, what is the value of $3x + y$?

At first it might seem like you cannot find the answer without solving for x and y individually. Luckily, there is another way. We are looking for $3x + y$, not x or y alone. Look closely at the left side of the equation. You may notice that $6x + 2y$ divided by 2 gives you $3x + y$—the exact expression we are looking for! Therefore, divide both sides of the equation by 2:

$$\frac{6x}{2} + \frac{2y}{2} = \frac{24}{2}$$

$$3x + y = 12$$

$3x + y$ is equal to 12.

Part 2 Practice: Linear Equations

1

If $a + 20 = 5$, what is the value of a?

A) −25

B) −15

C) −4

D) 25

2

If $2x + 8 = 14$, what is the value of x?

A) −3

B) 1

C) 3

D) 6

3

$$2(x + 3) = y + 6$$

Given the expression above, which of the following expresses x in terms of y?

A) $\frac{y}{2}$

B) y

C) $2y$

D) $3y$

4

If 1 divided by $3x$ is equal to 4 divided by $7y$, which of the following expresses x in terms of y?

A) $\dfrac{7y}{12}$

B) $\dfrac{12y}{7}$

C) $7y$

D) $12y$

5

If $y = \dfrac{2(x + 10)}{3}$, which of the following represents $2x$ in terms of y?

A) $\dfrac{3y}{2} - 10$

B) $\dfrac{3y}{2} - 5$

C) $3y - 10$

D) $3y - 20$

Questions 6 and 7 refer to the following information.

The number of cows, c, and the number of ducks, d, a farmer has in his 4 acres of land is represented by the equation $\dfrac{2c}{3} + \dfrac{4d}{12} = 4$.

6

Given the equation above, what is $6c$ in terms of d?

A) $2d$

B) $36 - 3d$

C) $3d$

D) $48 - 4d$

7

If there are 6 ducks, how many cows does the farmer have?

A) 2

B) 3

C) 4

D) 5

8

If $3x - 5 = 7$, what is the value of x?

9

Charles' Law defines the relationship between the volume of a confined gas, V, and its temperature, T. When the temperature changes to a different temperature, D, the volume of the gas also changes to another volume, A. These relationships are defined as $\dfrac{V}{T} = \dfrac{A}{D}$. To start, V is 3 and the temperature is 2. If the temperature, T, is increased by 3, what will be the value of the new volume, A?

10

If $5j + z = 3$ and $2z = a - bj$, what is $a + b$?

Inequalities
Part 3

An **inequality** is a mathematical statement comparing two quantities that are not the same. Inequalities can be represented with these symbols:

Inequality Symbols	
Symbol	Meaning
>	greater than
<	less than
≥	greater than or equal to
≤	less than or equal to

An algebraic inequality states that a certain algebraic expression is greater than or less than another quantity. For example, $x < 3$ means "an unknown quantity, x, is less than 3." There are many possible solutions for this inequality. The variable x may equal 1, 2, 0.5, –4, –6, 0, or any other number that is less than three.

To solve a more complex inequality, treat it like an equation—manipulate the inequality to isolate your variable. You'll end up with a range of solutions that can satisfy the inequality.

Example
$4x \geq 24$

Isolate your variable by dividing both sides by 4:

$$\frac{4x}{4} \geq \frac{24}{4}$$
$$x \geq 6$$

If $4x$ is greater than or equal to 24, then x can be any value greater than or equal to 6.

Rules for Inequalities

Just as with an equation, you can add or subtract the same number from both sides of an inequality and the inequality will be **preserved** (the inequality symbol will stay the same).

Example
$x + 3 > 7$

To solve, subtract 3 from both sides of the inequality:

$$x + 3 - 3 > 7 - 3$$

$$x > 4$$

You have to be more careful when multiplying or dividing. Multiplying or dividing both sides of an inequality by a positive number preserves the inequality, but multiplying or dividing by a negative number *reverses* the inequality. When you multiply or divide by a negative number, you have to flip the sign. Consider the true inequality $7 > 2$. You can multiply both sides of this inequality by a positive number, and the inequality is still true:

$$7 \times 4 > 2 \times 4$$

$$28 > 8$$

However, if you multiply both sides by a negative number, you get a false result:

$$7 \times (-4) > 2 \times (-4)$$

$$-28 > -8$$

Wrong!

Therefore, you need to reverse the inequality when multiplying or dividing by a negative number:

$$7 \times (-4) < 2 \times (-4)$$

$$-28 < -8$$

Let's try a more complex example:

Example
$-4x + 1 > 3$

First, undo the addition by subtracting 1 from both sides:

$$-4x + 1 - 1 > 3 - 1$$

$$-4x > 2$$

Then, undo the multiplication by dividing both sides by –4. Remember to reverse the inequality sign because you are dividing by a negative number!

$$\frac{-4x}{-4} < \frac{2}{-4}$$

$$x < -\frac{1}{2}$$

Now you know x can be any number less than $-\frac{1}{2}$. You can check your solution by picking a possible value for x and plugging it back into the original inequality. Let's try –1:

$$-4x + 1 > 3$$

$$(-4 \times (-1)) + 1 > 3$$

$$4 + 1 > 3$$

$$5 > 3$$

Because 5 is greater than 3, you know your solution was correct.

Inequalities on a Number Line

Algebraic inequalities are sometimes shown using lines, line segments, and circles on a number line. A shaded line segment represents all of the possible solutions for the inequality. Circles show whether numbers at the end of a line segment are part of the solution set. If a circle is shaded in completely, it means the number is included in the solution set: it is a possible solution for the inequality. If a circle is unshaded, it means the number is excluded from the solution set: it is not a possible solution for the inequality.

For example, the number line below shows the possible solutions for $x > 1$:

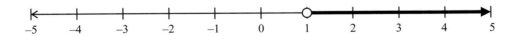

All numbers greater than 1 are possible solutions for this inequality, so a shaded line extends to the right of 1. The number 1 is not a possible solution for this inequality, so there is an unshaded circle over the number 1.

What inequality is represented by the number line below?

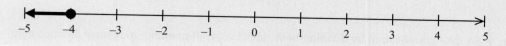

The shaded line segment to the left of –4 means that all numbers less than –4 are possible solutions for this inequality. The shaded circle over –4 means that –4 is a possible solution for this inequality. The inequality would therefore be written as:

$$x \leq -4$$

Inequalities with Two Variables

Sometimes you will see an inequality that has two different variables in it, such as $y < -4x - 5$. Just like you saw with equations in Part 2, you will not be able to find an exact number for x or y without more information. You can, however, solve for x in terms of y. Follow the same steps as you did for equations, but remember to be careful of the inequality sign.

For the inequality above, let's see how you would solve for x in terms of y. Start by adding 5 to both sides, then divide by –4 and reverse the inequality sign.

$$y < -4x - 5$$
$$y + 5 < -4x - 5 + 5$$
$$\frac{y + 5}{-4} > \frac{-4x}{-4}$$
$$\frac{y + 5}{-4} > x$$

Part 3 Practice: Inequalities

1

The inequality $-x > y$ is divided by negative one on both sides. Which of the following represents the correct result of this division?

A) There is no change in the original inequality.

B) $x > -y$

C) $-x < y$

D) $x < -y$

Questions 2 and 3 refer to the following information.

A geologist decides to use number line charts to determine whether a rock is the appropriate weight for his study, as shown below. He measures the rocks he excavates against a rock that has worked before in testing. The numbers on his line represent weight difference, in ounces, between his sample rock and his excavated rocks.

2

If the weight difference between the geologist's sample rock and an excavated rock is represented by w, which of the following represents his number line?

A) $w > -1$

B) $w \geq -1$

C) $w < -1$

D) $w \leq -1$

3

After further testing, the geologist determines that his initial number line is not correct. He sketches a number line, shown below, to reflect his new results.

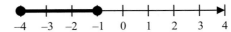

Which of the following expresses w in relation to this new inequality?

A) $-4 > w > -1$

B) $-4 \geq w \geq -1$

C) $-4 < w < -1$

D) $-4 \leq w \leq -1$

4

Jonas must score at least 79 on his next physics exam out of a maximum 100 points in order to pass his class. Which of the following inequalities models all the possible scores, x, that he could receive in order to pass the class?

A) $79 < x < 100$

B) $79 \leq x < 100$

C) $79 < x \leq 100$

D) $79 \leq x \leq 100$

5

If $23 \leq 7x + 2 \leq 37$, what is one possible value for x?

A) 2

B) 4

C) 6

D) 8

A sandwich shop sells all its subs, s, for $15 each and its drinks, d, for $3 each. The first customer of the day, Bonnie, has a budget of $45 to purchase drinks and subs at the shop.

6

Which of the following inequalities represents the number of drinks that Bonnie can purchase, in terms of the number of subs that she can purchase?

A) $d \geq 5s - 15$

B) $d \leq 5s + 15$

C) $d \geq -5s + 15$

D) $d \leq -5s + 15$

7

If she buys 2 subs, what is the maximum number of drinks she can purchase without spending more than $45?

A) 0

B) 3

C) 5

D) 9

8

If Larissa's GPA is somewhere between 3.8 and 3.9, what is one possible value for her GPA?

9

If $3x - 7 \geq x + 1$, what is one possible value of x?

10

$-2a + 10 > 4b$, and a is an integer. What is the maximum value of a if b is 1?

Absolute Value
Part 4

The **absolute value** of a number is its distance away from zero on a number line. To represent the absolute value of a quantity, you write two vertical bars around the quantity.

$|-5|$ represents the absolute value of -5, or the distance between -5 and zero on a number line. -5 is 5 units away from zero, so its absolute value is 5:

$$|-5| = 5$$

The absolute value of any number or expression will always be a positive number or zero.

Example

What is $|4-7|$?

This question is asking you to find the absolute value of the expression $4 - 7$. First, you need to solve for the quantity within the absolute value bars:

$$|4-7| = |-3|$$

Now, you need to find the absolute value of -3. -3 is 3 units away from zero, so its absolute value is 3:

$$|-3| = 3$$

Equations with Absolute Value

On the SAT, you may need to solve an absolute value equation using algebra. Here is an important rule to remember:

$$\text{If } |x| = a, \text{ then } x = a \text{ or } x = -a.$$

Example

If $|x| = 4$, then what values are possible for x?

This question is asking you to find any values of x that have an absolute value of 4. You know that 4 is a possible value. However, the value -4 is also possible. Think about it: both of these numbers are 4 units away from zero on the number line. Therefore, they both have an absolute value of 4.

$$\text{If } |x| = 4, \text{ then } x = 4 \text{ or } x = -4.$$

Heart of Algebra

If $|x-5|=4$, what are the possible values for x?

You know that both 4 and –4 have an absolute value of 4. Therefore, the quantity $x-5$ could either be equal to 4 or –4. You can set up two equations and solve each separately to find the two possible values of x:

$$x - 5 = 4 \qquad\qquad x - 5 = -4$$
$$x = 9 \qquad\qquad x = 1$$

You have two solutions: $x = 1$ or $x = 9$.

Absolute Value Inequalities

You may also need to solve an absolute value inequality on the SAT. Here are two rules for absolute value inequalities:

$$\text{If } |x| < a, \text{ then } -a < x < a.$$
$$\text{If } |x| > a, \text{ then } x < -a \text{ or } x > a.$$

If $|x| \le 3$, then what values are possible for x?

The inequality tells you that the distance between x and 0 is less than or equal to 3. All numbers between –3 and 3, including –3 and 3, have a distance from zero that is 3 units or less. If you were to graph the range of solutions for this inequality on a number line, it would look like this:

Therefore:

$$\text{If } |x| \le 3, \text{ then } -3 \le x \le 3.$$

You can always check your answer by making sure that a value from your solution set makes the original inequality true. For example, –2 is a value from your solution set. Is $|-2| \le 3$? The absolute value of –2 is 2, and 2 is certainly less than 3.

$$|-2| \le 3$$
$$2 \le 3$$

What values for x satisfy the inequality $|x-2|+1 > 3$?

First, you need to get the absolute value by itself. To do that, subtract 1 from each side:

$$|x-2|+1-1 > 3-1$$
$$|x-2| > 2$$

You know that all quantities less than -2 and greater than 2 have an absolute value greater than 2. Remember, when using the "greater than" sign to solve for an absolute value inequality, you need to set up two inequalities and solve:

$$x-2 > 2 \qquad\qquad\qquad\qquad x-2 < -2$$
$$x > 4 \qquad\qquad\qquad\qquad\qquad x < 0$$

The values of x that satisfy the inequality $|x-2| > 2$ are any values greater than 4 or less than 0. In other words, they are any values more than 2 units away from 2 on the number line.

Part 4 Practice: Absolute Value

1

Which of the following is equal to $|-3|$?

A) -9

B) -3

C) 3

D) 9

2

Which of the following is the absolute value of a number x that is 7 less than 2?

A) -9

B) -5

C) 5

D) 9

3

$$-|a-5| = -2$$

Based on the equation above, what is one possible value of a?

A) -3

B) -7

C) 3

D) There are no solutions.

4

$$\left|\frac{5a}{3}\right| = 10$$

Which of the following provides all possible values of a in the equation above?

A) 2

B) 6

C) 2 and -6

D) 6 and -6

5

If $-|b-3| < -5$, which of the following is true about b?

A) $b < -2, b > 8$

B) $-2 < b < 8$

C) $b < -8, b > 2$

D) $-8 < b < 2$

Questions 6 and 7 refer to the following information.

Camille's AP English class is scheduled to start at 10:00 A.M. Because there is another class directly before, the earliest she can enter is at 9:50 A.M.

6

If Camille's teacher marks all students who arrive after 10:10 A.M. as late, which of the following inequalities models the time in hours, t, that Camille can enter the class *and* be considered on time?

A) $|t-10| \le \dfrac{1}{6}$

B) $|t-10| \le \dfrac{1}{3}$

C) $|t-10| \le 10$

D) $|t-10| \le 20$

7

If Camille arrives at 10:15 A.M., by how many hours is she late?

A) $\dfrac{1}{12}$

B) $\dfrac{1}{6}$

C) 5

D) $\dfrac{5}{12}$

8

The average helicopter is 12.5 m long. If a Tyrannosaurus is thought to have been about 15.2 m long, what is the absolute value of the difference between the lengths of a helicopter and a Tyrannosaurus?

9

$$|b-9| \le 0.2$$

A construction company produces cold-drawn steel bars that must be 9 inches in length with a tolerance of 0.2 inches as shown above. What is one possible length for one of their steel bars, b, that conforms with the requirements?

10

$$\frac{|7a-2|}{3} + 5 = 9$$

In the equation above, what is the positive solution for the value of a?

Systems of Equations and Inequalities
Part 5

A **system of equations** is a group of equations that share like terms. On the SAT, you may see systems of two equations. Even though you now have to deal with two equations instead of one, systems of equations help simplify more complicated problems and are actually very useful! If you have two equations and two variables, you can use both equations to find the value of x and y.

Example

$$x + y = 3$$
$$2x - y = 12$$

You can use two methods to solve this system of equations: substitution and elimination.

Substitution

The **substitution method** allows you to solve for one variable at a time by substituting an equivalent equation for one variable. First, choose a variable to isolate in either equation. Let's try isolating y in the first equation. To isolate y, subtract x from both sides of the equation:

$$x + y - x = 3 - x$$
$$y = 3 - x$$

You now know that y is equal to the value of $3 - x$. Now, substitute this value into the second equation by writing $3 - x$ instead of y:

$$2x - y = 12$$
$$2x - (3 - x) = 12$$

Now you have a single equation with only one variable, so you can solve this equation for x:

$$2x - (3 - x) = 12$$
$$3x - 3 = 12$$
$$3x = 15$$
$$x = 5$$

Now that you know that $x = 5$, you can plug this value of x into either of the original two equations to solve for y. Let's plug this into the first equation:

$$x + y = 3$$
$$5 + y = 3$$
$$y = -2$$

You've found that $x = 5$ and $y = -2$. You can check that you've solved this system of equations correctly by plugging these values back into the original two equations and verifying that they are true:

$$5 + (-2) = 3$$
$$2 \times 5 - (-2) = 12$$

Elimination

You can also solve this system of equations using the elimination method. The **elimination method** allows you to cancel variables by adding or subtracting the two equations. In the example above, if you add the two equations together, the y's will cancel each other out:

$$\begin{array}{r} x + y = 3 \\ + \ 2x - y = 12 \\ \hline 3x \quad\ = 15 \end{array}$$

You now have one single equation in which you can solve for x:

$$3x = 15$$
$$x = 5$$

Then, you can plug this value for x back into one of the two original equations to solve for y, following the same steps you used above.

$$x + y = 3$$
$$5 + y = 3$$
$$y = -2$$

How do you know when to use substitution and when to use elimination? If one of the equations involves variables without coefficients (like $x + y = 3$) or could be easily simplified by dividing (like $2x + 2y = 8$), then substitution may be easier. However, some systems of equations are more effectively solved using elimination, even if they don't look like it at first. You may have to transform equations in order to use elimination.

Transforming Equations

Some systems of equations don't seem like they can be solved using elimination at first.

Example
$$6x + 3y = 18$$ $$2x + 5y = 14$$

You can transform one of the equations so that you can use elimination to solve the equations. To **transform** an equation, you multiply or divide both sides of the equation by the same number. Since you want to be able to eliminate one variable, you should choose a number that will change your equation so that it can be easily added to or subtracted from the other equation.

In the example above, you can transform the second equation by multiplying both sides by 3. Why? Because multiplying the equation by 3 gives you $6x + 15y = 42$. You can now use subtraction to eliminate the $6x$'s.

$$6x + 3y = 18$$
$$- \quad (6x + 15y = 42)$$
$$-12y = -24$$

$$\frac{-12y}{-12} = \frac{-24}{-12}$$

$$y = 2$$

Now plug y into one of the original equations to solve for x:

$$6x + 3(2) = 18$$
$$6x + 6 = 18$$
$$6x = 12$$
$$x = 2$$

Systems of Inequalities

On the SAT, you may also see **systems of inequalities**. You may be asked to solve for values of x that satisfy both inequalities.

Example
$$7x \geq 21$$ $$2x < 10$$

In order to find the values of x that would satisfy both inequalities, you need to solve each inequality, determine if there is any overlap, and create a range of possible values. For the example above, first solve each inequality individually:

$$\frac{7x}{7} \geq \frac{21}{7}$$

$$x \geq 3$$

$$\frac{2x}{2} < \frac{10}{2}$$

$$x < 5$$

In order for a value of x to satisfy both inequalities, x must be greater than or equal to 3, but also less than 5. Therefore, you can write a range of values that represents the possible solutions to both inequalities:

$$3 \leq x < 5$$

You can check your answer by plugging in a value of x from your solution set into both equations. Let's try 4:

$$7(4) \geq 21$$

$$28 \geq 21$$

$$2(4) < 10$$

$$8 < 10$$

Part 5 Practice: Systems of Equations and Inequalities

1

$$5x = 5$$
$$x + y = 5$$

In the system of equations above, what are the values of x and y?

A) $x = 1, y = -4$

B) $x = 1, y = 4$

C) $x = 1, y = 6$

D) $x = 1, y = -6$

2

$$2m = 3$$
$$4m + n = y$$

Given the system of equations above, which of the following is equal to y?

A) $3n$

B) $6n$

C) $6 + n$

D) $6 + 3n$

3

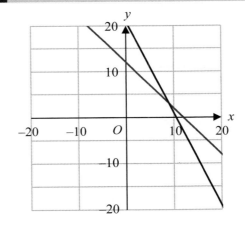

The graphs of $2x + y = 21$ and $3x + 3y = 36$ are shown above. Which of the following are the values for the point (x, y) where the two lines intersect?

A) $(-9, 3)$

B) $(-9, -3)$

C) $(9, 3)$

D) $(3, 9)$

4

Bullets travel at least ten times the speed of an average arrow. If the fastest bullet travels at 4,100 ft/s and the average arrow travels at 250 ft/s, which of the following systems of inequalities expresses all possible values of a bullet's speed, x?

A) $2500 \le x \le 4100$

B) $2500 < x \le 4100$

C) $2500 \le x < 4100$

D) $2500 < x < 4100$

5

$$x - 4 > 8$$
$$3x \le 39$$

In the system of inequalities above, which of the following models all the possible values of x?

A) $12 \le x \le 13$

B) $12 \le x < 13$

C) $12 < x \le 13$

D) $12 < x < 13$

Questions 6 and 7 refer to the following information.

Victoria is having a garage sale and prices all items at $15 each.

6

If her goal is to make at least $800, which of the following inequalities models the number of items x that she must sell?

A) $60 \le x$

B) $800 \le 15x$

C) $60 \le x \le 800$

D) $800 \le 15 + x$

7

What is the minimum number of items Victoria must sell in order to achieve her goal?

A) 52

B) 53

C) 54

D) 55

8

If $5p - 2q = 16$ and $4p + q = 5$, what is the value of $p - q$?

9

$$4x - 13 > 7$$
$$2x + 4 \ge 4x - 8$$

Given the system of inequalities above, what is one possible value of x that satisfies the relationship?

10

A pet store sells its puppies for $400 each and adult dogs for $300 each. If the store collected $5000 from a total of 15 puppies and adult dogs last month, how many adult dogs did the pet store sell?

Linear Functions
Part 6

A **function** is a relationship between inputs and outputs. A function shows how an "input" value is transformed into an "output" value. The input, x, will produce an output, $f(x)$, according to the rules of the function. The notation $f(x)$ is read as "f of x." Functions are most often referred to by f, but you may also see other letters such as g, h, or A. You can think about a function like a recipe for a cake: the inputs are your flour, egg, sugar, and butter, the "rules" of the function are your recipe, and your output, $f(x)$, is the cake itself.

Function Notation

The notation $f(x)$ is another way of representing the y-value in a function. For example, $f(x) = 2x - 3$ is the same thing as $y = 2x - 3$.

The function $f(x) = 2x - 3$ means that for any input x, the function assigns it the output $2x - 3$. Therefore:

$$f(2) = 2(2) - 3$$
$$f(2) = 1$$

This is how you **evaluate** a function—just replace the variable in the function with the given input value and solve. What if $x = a + b$?

$$f(a + b) = 2(a + b) - 3$$
$$f(a + b) = 2a + 2b - 3$$

The chart below represents the value of the input, x, and output, $f(x)$, for the function $f(x) = 2x - 3$. You can see how the function acts as a rule for what happens to the input to generate the output. You multiply each input by 2 and then subtract 3.

$f(x)$	−1	1	3	5
x	1	2	3	4

The following graph also represents $f(x) = 2x - 3$. Because the graph is a line, we call this a linear function. We will talk about how to graph linear functions in Part 8, but you can use this graph to visualize what the function means. You can see that when the input (x) is at 2, the output (y) is at 1— just like we found when we were evaluating the function.

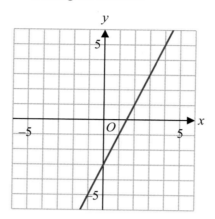

Domain and Range

Every linear function has a domain and range. The **domain** is the set of all values for which the function generates an output. The **range** is the set of all values that could be the output of the function.

Domain ⟶ Function ⟶ Range

Often, the domain of a linear function is "all real numbers." This is because most linear equations can use any input and still be defined. For example, in the function $f(x) = -2x - 3$, you'll get an output for any real number that you plug in for x. The exception is a function that produces a vertical line, which only has one possible x value.

The range of a linear function is also typically "all real numbers." Most lines can extend infinitely in both directions, so there are no limits to the range of y values that can be generated. The exception is a function that produces a horizontal line, which only has one possible y value.

Combining Functions

On the SAT, you might see functions combined through a notation like $f(g(x))$. This notation means that you need to take the output of $g(x)$, and use it as the input of $f(x)$. You would read this as "f of g of x."

Example

If $f(x) = 3x - 4$ and $g(x) = 8x$, what is the value of $f\left(g\left(\frac{1}{2}\right)\right)$?

Start by working from the inside out. First, find $g\left(\dfrac{1}{2}\right)$. Then, use that answer and plug it into $f(x)$:

$$g\left(\frac{1}{2}\right) = 8\left(\frac{1}{2}\right) = 4$$

$$f(4) = 3(4) - 4 = 8$$

There are many other things to learn about functions, such as how to graph and transform them. We will cover these topics in Part 8.

Part 6 Practice: Linear Functions

1

$f(x)$	x
3	1
5	2
9	4
13	6
?	34

The table above shows a linear function of $f(x)$. Which of the following is the value of $f(x)$ when x is 34?

A) 35

B) 47

C) 59

D) 69

2

If $h(x) = 5x + 3$, what is $h(x + 2)$?

A) $5x + 5$

B) $5x + 6$

C) $5x + 13$

D) 18

3

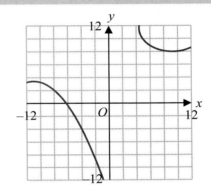

If the figure above shows the graph of $g(x)$, what is the value of $g(10)$?

A) 5

B) 8

C) −8

D) 10

4

$$f(x) = 3x - 2$$

Which of the following is the domain of $f(x)$ above?

A) All real numbers

B) All positive integers

C) All negative integers

D) No solution

5

$$m(v) = 3v$$

The momentum of a 3 kg object is provided by the function above, where v is the velocity in meters per second at which the object travels. If the object is traveling at a constant velocity of 5.5 m/s, which of the following is the value of the object's momentum?

A) 14.0 kg · m/s

B) 14.5 kg · m/s

C) 15.0 kg · m/s

D) 16.5 kg · m/s

Questions 6 and 7 refer to the following information.

An online movie streaming website charges a one-time $5 membership fee and $2 for every movie streamed.

6

If Leah rents x number of movies, which of the following functions models the total cost she will be charged?

A) $f(x) = 10x$

B) $f(x) = 2x$

C) $f(x) = 2x + 5$

D) $f(x) = 2x + 10$

7

If Leah joins the website in October and her budget for the month is $24, what is the maximum number of movies she can rent?

A) 9

B) 10

C) 11

D) 12

8

If $g(x) = | x - 3 | - 2$, what is $g(-2)$?

9

$$g(x) = 5x$$
$$h(x) = x - 5$$

Given $g(x)$ and $h(x)$ above, what is the value of $g(h(5))$?

10

A jeweler can cut x gems into $f(x) = \dfrac{x}{2} + 10$ usable pieces and creates $g(x) = \dfrac{2x}{5} + 4$ pieces of jewelry from those pieces. If the jeweler has 10 gems, how many pieces of jewelry can he make?

Interpreting Equations
Part 7

In the previous parts of this section, you learned how to work with the "vocabulary" of the language of algebra. For example, you learned how to solve linear equations and inequalities and perform operations on functions. Now, you need to learn how to interpret the vocabulary and create your own "sentences" with linear equations. In this part, we will discuss what the different parts of linear equations mean and how to use them in word problems.

Variables and Constants

In Part 1, you learned that both variables and constants represent values in algebraic expressions. The difference is that constants represent values that can't change, while variables represent values that can change.

Example

Jeannie's phone company charges her a flat rate of $40 per month plus $8 per 500 MB of data usage. If Jeannie uses 3.5 GB of data in January, how much will her phone company charge her for that month?

You can use an equation to solve this problem. Jeannie is charged $40 per month—this is a flat rate, so it is unchanging. She is also charged an unchanging rate of $8 per 500 MB of data. Therefore, $40 and $8 are constants. What will determine how much Jeannie's phone company charges her? How much data she uses. That is a variable, which you could decide to call d. You are looking for her total monthly charge, which you could call c. Using these variables, you could write the equation:

$$c = 8d + 40$$

This means that Jeannie's monthly phone bill is found by multiplying her total data usage by $8 and adding $40. Jeannie uses 3.5 GB, or 3500 MB, of data in January, so you can plug in $\frac{3500}{500} = 7$ for d:

$$c = 8 \times 7 + 40 = 96$$

Jeannie's phone company will charge her $96 for the month of January.

Translating from Words to Math

As you've seen in the examples above, to solve any word problem on the SAT, all you have to do is "translate" the words in the problem into letters and operations. Here is a chart you can use to translate between words and math:

Words	Meaning
Is, was, will be, has	Equals (=)
More, older, total, increased by, exceeds, gained, further, greater, sum	Addition (+)
Fewer, younger, less, decreased by, gave away, lost, difference	Subtraction (−)
Of, each, product	Multiplication (×)
For, per, out of, quotient	Division (÷)
At least	Greater than or equal to (≥)
At most	Less than or equal to (≤)
What, how many	Variable (x, y, etc.)

Example

The sum of Jake's and Amy's ages is 17. If A is Amy's current age, which expression represents Jake's age in 3 years, in terms of A?

The question tells you that A stands for Amy's current age. If you let J stand for Jake's current age, then you can use addition to represent the total of their ages right now:

$$J + A = 17$$

Then, you can isolate J to find an expression for Jake's age right now:

$$J + A = 17$$
$$J = 17 - A$$

However, the question isn't asking you for Jake's age right now—you need to find his age 3 years from now. Translating into math, you need to find the value of $J + 3$. To do this, add 3 to both sides of your equation:

$$J = 17 - A$$
$$J + 3 = 17 - A + 3$$
$$J + 3 = 20 - A$$

The expression $20 - A$ represents Jake's age three years from now.

Interpreting Absolute Value

You may also need to translate a word problem into an absolute value equation.

Example

A candle factory has machines that cut wax into candles. Each candle is supposed to be 6 inches long. If a candle differs from this length by more than 0.25 inches, it will be rejected. What absolute value inequality represents the lengths of the products that will be rejected?

Candles will be rejected if they are 0.25 inches greater or less than the target of 6 inches. This means any candles greater than 6.25 inches or less than 5.75 inches will be rejected. You can use an absolute value inequality to represent all values that are more than 0.25 units away from 6 on a number line:

$$|x - 6| > 0.25$$

The absolute value sign works here because it allows you to take into account candles that are greater than the target size and also those less than the target size. The amount that candles can differ from the target size is on the right side. The absolute value expression on the left represents the difference between the size of any candle and the target size.

To check that your inequality is correct, solve for x using the rules you learned in Part 5:

$$x - 6 > 0.25 \qquad\qquad x - 6 < -0.25$$
$$x > 6.25 \qquad\qquad x < 5.75$$

Your inequality generated all values greater than 6.25 and less than 5.75. You know that these are the lengths of candles that will be rejected, so your inequality is correct.

Creating a System of Equations

Some word problems will require you to create a system of equations.

Example

In a school cafeteria, students can either buy sandwiches or salads for lunch. Sandwiches cost $5.50 and salads cost $5.00. On one day, a total of 557 lunches were served for a total of $3036. Which set of equations could be used to solve for the number of sandwiches, x, and the number of salads, y, served that day?

The question tells you that the total number of lunches served was 557, so the sum of sandwiches, x, and salads, y, must be 557:

$$x + y = 557$$

You also know that the total cost was $3036. Sandwiches cost $5.50, so the cost of all the sandwiches would be $5.50 multiplied by the number of sandwiches purchased ($5.50x). Similarly, the cost of all the salads would be $5.00 multiplied by the number of salads purchased ($5.00y). The total cost is the sum of the sandwich cost and the salad cost:

$$5.50x + 5y = 3036$$

You have now found a system of equations that would allow you to solve for x and y:

$$x + y = 557$$

$$5.50x + 5y = 3036$$

Part 7 Practice: Interpreting Equations

1

Wendy has $10 and receives an additional $10 per week for her allowance. If she doesn't spend any of her money, which of the following equations expresses the total amount m she will have saved up at the end of w weeks?

A) $m = 10w$

B) $m = 10 + 10w$

C) $m = 100w$

D) $10m = 10w$

2

If Joy sells c number of cupcakes for $5 each, which of the following expresses the total revenue?

A) $5c$

B) $\dfrac{5}{c}$

C) $\dfrac{c}{5}$

D) $c + 5$

3

When 6 is subtracted from four times a number L, the result is 26. Which of the following equations represents the relationship?

A) $6 - 4L = 26$

B) $4L - 6 = 26$

C) $(4 - 6)L = 26$

D) $(6 - 4)L = 26$

4

The height of the players on High Ridge Elementary School's basketball team is shown below. Based on the table, which of the following inequalities represents all possible values for height h of the students?

Height (in meters)

1.65	1.69	1.58
1.48	1.40	1.63
1.78	1.73	1.8

A) $|1.6 - h| \le 0.2$

B) $|1.6 + h| \le 0.2$

C) $|1.6 - h| \ge 0.2$

D) $|1.6 + h| \ge 0.2$

5

If a certain medication is exposed to a temperature less than 55°F or greater than 85°F, it must be discarded. Which of the following inequalities models all temperatures x at which the medication does NOT need to be discarded?

A) $|70 - x| \leq 15$

B) $|70 + x| \leq 15$

C) $|70 - x| \geq 15$

D) $|70 + x| \geq 15$

Questions 6 and 7 refer to the following information.

Adult tickets for an event are $10 each and student tickets are $8 each. The ticket office has sold 77 tickets totaling $686.

6

Which of the following systems of equations can be used to find the number of adult tickets, a, and student tickets, s, sold?

A) $10a + 8s = 686$
    $a + s = 77$

B) $10a + 8s = 77$
    $a + s = 686$

C) $18as = 686$
    $as = 77$

D) $18as = 77$
    $as = 686$

7

Which of the following is the value of a?

A) 25

B) 32

C) 35

D) 42

8

If Irene runs two miles every morning, how many days would it take for her to run 26 miles?

9

If Jessica triples a number and divides the result by 2 to get 9, what is her original number?

10

There is a total of 15 cows and chickens on a farm. If the total number of legs for these animals equals 42, how many cows are on the farm?

Graphing Equations

Part 8

In the previous parts of this section, you learned how to solve equations, inequalities, absolute values, and systems of equations algebraically. While knowing how to solve these types of problems algebraically is essential, you also need to know how to solve them graphically on the SAT Math Test.

Graphing Linear Equations

Linear equations can be graphed as lines on a coordinate plane. Some equations represent horizontal or vertical lines.

- The equation of a **horizontal line** is $y = b$, where b represents the point where the line crosses the y-axis.

- The equation of a **vertical line** is $x = a$, where a represents the point where the line crosses the x-axis.

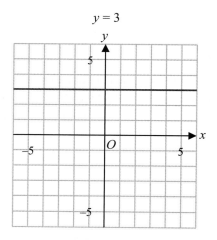

$y = 3$

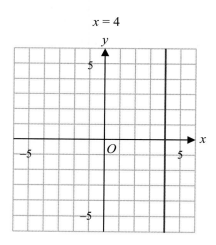

$x = 4$

You can also graph equations with two variables. The **standard equation** of a line can be represented as:

$$y = mx + b$$

Each part of this equation tells you something about how the line looks on the graph. The letter m represents the **slope**—how steep the line is. The letter b represents the **y-intercept**—the point where the line crosses the y-axis. Here is the graph of the line $y = 2x + 6$:

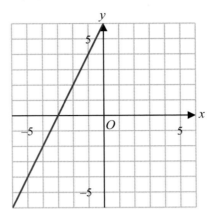

You can see that the line crosses the y-axis at 6. The equation also tells you that the slope of the line is 2. Let's see what that means.

Slope

The **slope** of a line tells you how steep it is—in other words, how quickly y is increasing for every unit that x increases. The equation of the line above tells us that the slope is 2. If you look at the graph, you can also see that y increases 2 units for every unit that x increases.

The SAT won't always give you the equation for a line. You might need to find the slope of a line using a graph. Choose any two points on the line and plug their coordinates into the slope formula. If the first point has the coordinates (x_1, y_1) and the second point has the coordinates (x_2, y_2), the slope formula tells you:

$$m = \frac{y_2 - y_1}{x_2 - x_1}$$

You might have also learned the slope formula as "rise over run." The "rise" between two points is the same thing as the vertical difference between their two y-coordinates, and the "run" is the horizontal difference between their two x-coordinates. Therefore, "rise over run" is the same as the formula above.

Let's test this formula by plugging in some points from the line graphed above. You can see that the line contains the points $(-3, 0)$ and $(0, 6)$. If you plug in these values for the formula for slope, you get:

$$m = \frac{y_2 - y_1}{x_2 - x_1} = \frac{6 - 0}{0 - (-3)} = \frac{6}{3} = 2$$

This formula tells us that the slope of the line is 2.

Here are a few important facts about slope:

- Vertical lines have undefined slopes.
- Horizontal lines have slopes of 0.
- A slope is positive if the line goes up from left to right.
- A slope is negative if the line goes down from left to right.
- Parallel lines have the same slope.
- The product of the slopes of two perpendicular lines is –1.

Let's talk a little bit more about that last point. The product of the slopes of two perpendicular lines is –1. To find the slope of a perpendicular line, flip the fraction to find the reciprocal, and then reverse the sign. For example, a line perpendicular to $y = -\frac{3}{4}x + 7$ will have a slope of $\frac{4}{3}$.

Graphing Inequalities

Graphing inequalities is similar to graphing equations. Start by graphing the inequality as if it were a linear equation. Use a solid line for $\leq$ or $\geq$, and a dashed line for $<$ or $>$. Then, shade in the solution area. For "greater than" inequalities, shade *above* the line. For "less than" inequalities, shade *below* the line.

Example

$$y \leq \frac{1}{2}x + 3$$

Start by graphing the line $y = \frac{1}{2}x + 3$. The line crosses the y-axis at 3. The slope of the line is $\frac{1}{2}$, so y increases 1 unit for every 2 units that x increases. Because the inequality uses the symbol $\leq$, you'll want to graph a solid line:

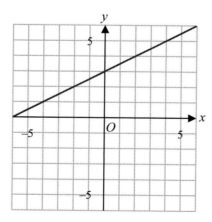

Next, shade in the solution area. Because this is a "less than" inequality, shade below the line.

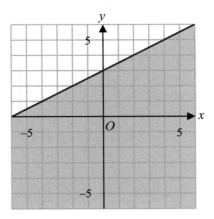

Graphing Absolute Values

In order to graph absolute values, you want to recall what the absolute value means. The absolute value of a number is its distance away from zero on a number line. Here is the graph of $y = 3x$.

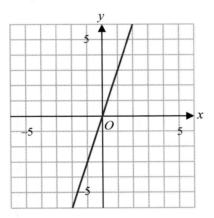

What about the graph of $y = |3x|$? For every positive value of x, the graph will stay the same. However, for negative values of x, the absolute value will be positive—so the left side of the graph needs to have positive values for y.

Absolute-value equations often give you a graph that looks like the "V" shape below. If you are given a graph like this on the SAT, the equation that it represents is probably an absolute value.

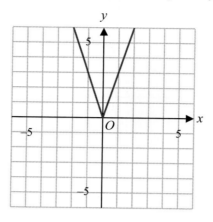

Graphing Systems of Equations

In Part 5, you learned how to solve for variables in a system of equations algebraically. You can also solve systems of equations graphically. To solve a system of two equations, graph the lines and find the point where they cross.

Start by rearranging each equation to get y by itself:

$$y = \frac{2}{3}x - 2$$

$$y = -x + 3$$

Now, graph each line using the slopes and y-intercepts:

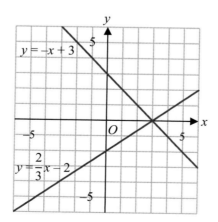

Math

The lines cross at the point (3, 0), so the solution for the system of equations is $x = 3$, $y = 0$. You can always check your answer by plugging the values into the original equations and confirming that they are both true.

Graphing Functions

Linear functions are graphed just like linear equations. You simply treat $f(x)$ as your y variable. Therefore, the graph of $f(x) = -2x - 3$ is the same as the graph of $y = -2x - 3$:

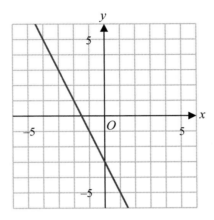

Some questions on the SAT will require you to create or recognize the transformation of a linear function. If you start with the function $f(x) = ax$, you can shift the function vertically b units by adding b to the right side of the function:

$$f(x) = ax + b$$

If b is positive, the function shifts b units up. If b is negative, the function shifts b units down.

The graphs below show the function $f(x) = 2x$ and the same function shifted 3 units up:

$$f(x) = 2x \qquad\qquad\qquad\qquad f(x) = 2x + 3$$

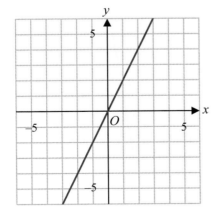 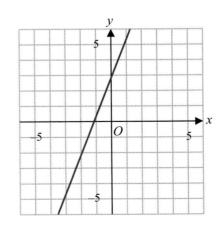

If you start with the function $f(x) = ax$, you can shift the function horizontally b units by taking the function of $x + b$:

$$f(x + b) = a(x + b)$$

If b is positive, the function shifts b units to the left. If b is negative, the function shifts b units to the right.

The graphs below show the function $f(x) = 2x$ and the same function shifted 1 unit to the left:

$f(x) = 2x$ $f(x + 1) = 2(x + 1)$

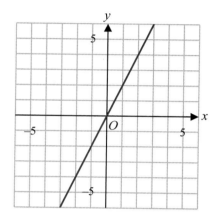 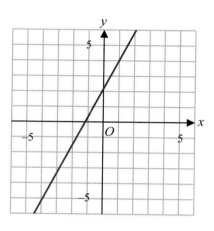

If you start with the function $f(x) = ax$, you can stretch the function by multiplying it by b:

$$b \times f(x) = b \times ax$$

For a linear function, this means the slope of the line is multiplied by b.

The graphs below show the function $f(x) = 2x$ and the same function stretched by a factor of 3:

$f(x) = 2x$ $3f(x) = 3 \times 2x$

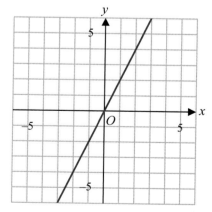 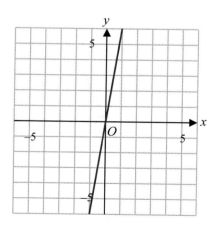

To reflect a function about the *x*-axis, multiply the whole function by −1.

The graphs below show the function $f(x) = \dfrac{1}{2}x + 1$ and the same function reflected about the *x*-axis:

$$f(x) = \frac{1}{2}x + 1$$

$$-f(x) = -\left(\frac{1}{2}x + 1\right)$$

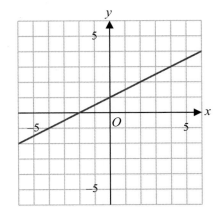

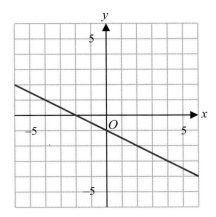

To reflect a function about the *y*-axis, take the function of −*x*.

The graphs below show the function $f(x) = \dfrac{1}{2}x + 1$ and the same function reflected about the *y*-axis:

$$f(x) = \frac{1}{2}x + 1$$

$$f(-x) = -\frac{1}{2}x + 1$$

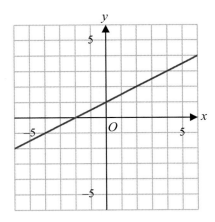

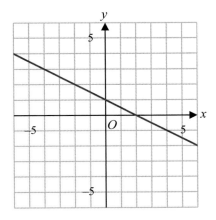

Part 8 Practice: Graphing Equations

1

Which of the following is the graph of $y = 3$?

A)

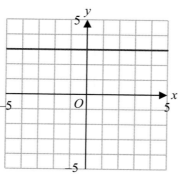

B)

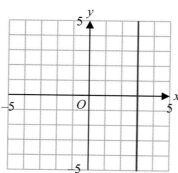

C)

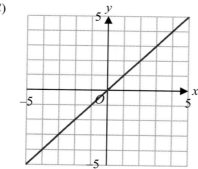

D)

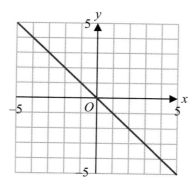

2

The function $y = x + 5$ is translated 5 units down and reflected across the y-axis. Which of the following is the graph of the resulting function?

A)

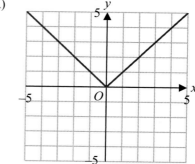

B)

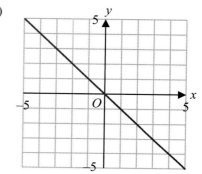

C)

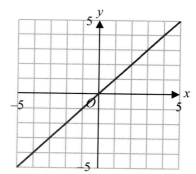

D)

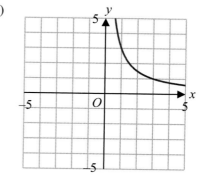

3

If $y = \dfrac{x}{2} - 3$, which of the following is the slope multiplied by the *y*-intercept?

A) $-\dfrac{3}{2}$

B) -3

C) $\dfrac{3}{2}$

D) 3

4

Which of the following is the graph of $y = |2x - 2|$?

A)

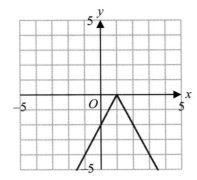

B)

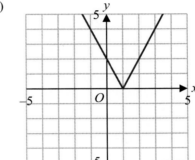

C)

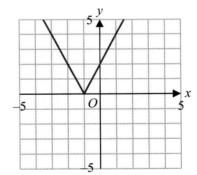

D)

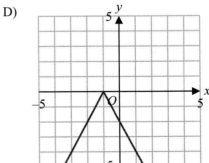

Which of the following is the graph of $y \geq |x+3| - 2$?

A)

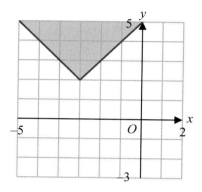

B)

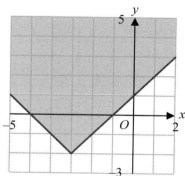

C)

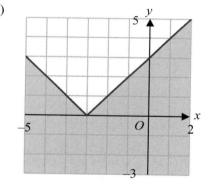

D)

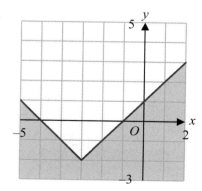

For questions 6-7, use the graph below.

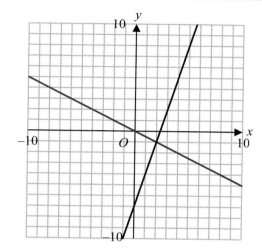

According to the graph above, which of the following represents the coordinates of the point where the two lines intersect.?

A) (–2, 1)

B) (–1, 2)

C) (1, –2)

D) (2, –1)

According to the graph, what is the product of the two x-intercepts?

A) 4

B) 2

C) 0

D) Cannot be determined from the information given.

8

Body Mass Index

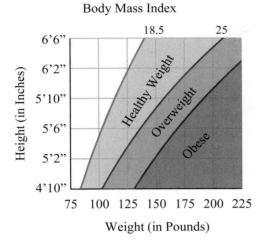

Weight (in Pounds)

The graph above shows an adult's BMI based on height and weight. If an individual who is 5' 8" is categorized as "overweight," what is one possible value for his weight?

9

Line L has an equation of $3 - 5x = 2y$. If Line M is drawn perpendicular to Line L, what is the slope of Line M?

10

If the graph below is reflected about the x-axis, what is the value of y-intercept in the new line?

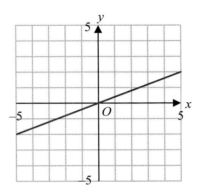

Section 4
Passport to Advanced Math

The **Passport to Advanced Math** questions cover important topics for college-level math, focusing on expressions, equations, and functions. You might think that this content seems similar to Heart of Algebra; it is in some ways, but with one major difference—every question uses higher order math. Whether calculating trajectories in astrophysics, the path of subatomic particles in quantum mechanics, or the chemical composition of fertilizer for high-yield crops, this math is the foundation for engineering, the social sciences, and the pure sciences. On the SAT, there will be sixteen Passport to Advanced Math questions: seven in the Calculator Section and nine in the No Calculator Section. In this section, we'll go over the following topics:

- Polynomial expressions
- Factoring polynomials
- Quadratic equations
- Quadratic functions and their graphs
- Advanced equations
- Applications of functions

Polynomial Expressions
Part 1

A **polynomial** is an expression that is a sum of one or more terms. Each **term** consists of one or more variables multiplied by a coefficient. Coefficients can be negative, so don't be surprised if you see a minus sign in a polynomial—that just means there's a term with a negative coefficient.

Here are some examples of polynomials:

$$5x^2$$

$$3x^3 + 2xy - y$$

$$-3x^2 + 6x - 7$$

Polynomials are classified by the number of terms they have when they are expressed in their simplest form. A **monomial** has one term, a **binomial** has two terms, and a **trinomial** has three. $3x + 2$ is a binomial, because it has two terms. $x^2 - 4x + 2$ is a trinomial, because it has three terms. It is important to notice that something like $3x + 2x$, while it looks like a binomial, is a monomial because it can be simplified to one term, $5x$.

Polynomials are also classified by their degree. The **degree** of a term is the sum of the exponents of its variables. The **degree of a polynomial** is the same as its highest degree term. For example, $x^2 + 3$ is a second-degree polynomial because its highest exponent is 2. The expression $x^3 + x^2 + 2x + 1$ is a third-degree polynomial because its highest exponent is 3.

Certain polynomials have special names determined by their degree:

Degree	0	1	2	3
Name	Constant	Linear	Quadratic	Cubic
Example	5	$x + 7$	$x^2 + 9$	$2x^3 + 19x^2 - 6x + 13$

Polynomials can be added, subtracted, and multiplied, just like regular numbers. Next up, we'll cover how to do this, and will also look at some basic techniques for polynomial division.

Adding Polynomials

To add two polynomials, you need to combine the like terms. **Like terms** have the same variables raised to the same powers. So $5x^3y^2z$ and $7x^3y^2z$ are like terms because each term has x cubed, y squared, and z. However, $5x^3y^2z$ and $7xyz$ are not like terms, because although they have the same variables, the variables are not raised to the same powers.

Let's say you want to find the sum of $3m^2 + 2m + 6$ and $m - 9$. You can join them with a plus sign:

Example

$$3m^2 + 2m + 6 + m - 9$$

Then, put like terms next to each other. Remember to pay attention to the signs!

$$3m^2 + 2m + m + 6 - 9$$

Finally, add and subtract the like terms, including the constants:

$$3m^2 + 3m - 3$$

Subtracting Polynomials

Subtracting polynomials is very similar to adding them: join the expressions and combine like terms. However, with subtraction, you first have to take care of the signs.

Example

What is the value of $4p^3 + 6p^2 - 8p + 11$ minus $3p^3 - 2p^2 + 12p - 3$?

Just like with addition, you'll need to join the like terms. With subtraction, however, you need to put the second term in parentheses:

$$4p^3 + 6p^2 - 8p + 11 - (3p^3 - 2p^2 + 12p - 3)$$

Then, distribute the negative sign across the parentheses:

$$4p^3 + 6p^2 - 8p + 11 - 3p^3 + 2p^2 - 12p + 3$$

Now you're ready to combine like terms for your result:

$$p^3 + 8p^2 - 20p + 14$$

Multiplying Polynomials

To multiply two monomials, use exponent rules.

$$\left(5x^3y^5z^2\right)\left(2x^6y^8z\right)$$

Remember that when you multiply two expressions with the same base, you can add their exponents. Don't forget to multiply the coefficients!

$$5x^3y^5z^2 \times 2x^6y^8z = 10x^{3+6}y^{5+8}z^{2+1}$$

Once you do the arithmetic, you're left with:

$$10x^9y^{13}z^3$$

When you multiply polynomials with more terms, you will need to use the Distributive Property, which we talked about in Section 4, Part 1. Take a moment to review the Distributive Property, and then look at this example:

$$2x(x+3)$$

Using the Distributive Property, you can rewrite the expression like this:

$$2x \times x + 2x \times 3$$

Then, simplify to get your solution:

$$2x^2 + 6x$$

When you're multiplying more than one polynomial with multiple terms, the idea is the same: use the Distributive Property and simplify. You just have to make sure you've multiplied every term in one polynomial by every term in the other. Luckily, for multiplying two binomials, there's an easy way to keep everything straight. The **FOIL method** tells you to multiply the **F**irst terms, the **O**uter terms, the **I**nner terms, and the **L**ast terms. Always remember to combine like terms when you've finished.

$$(x+3)(2x+5)$$

You need to multiply both terms in the first binomial by both terms in the second, like this:

$$(x + 3)(2x + 5)$$

The FOIL method makes this simple. Multiply together the *first* terms in the parentheses (x and $2x$), then the *outer* terms (x and 5), then the *inner* terms (3 and $2x$), and finally the *last* terms (3 and 5):

$$(x \times 2x) + (x \times 5) + (3 \times 2x) + (3 \times 5)$$

Then, simplify and combine like terms:

$$2x^2 + 5x + 6x + 15$$

$$2x^2 + 11x + 15$$

Dividing Polynomials

To divide polynomials, you can use the same techniques you learned for factoring expressions.

Example
$$\frac{2x^3 + 4x^2 - 6x}{2x}$$

This operation is asking you to divide each term of the polynomial by $2x$. Remember that dividing two expressions with the same base means you can divide the coefficients and subtract the exponents:

$$\frac{2}{2}x^{3-1} + \frac{4}{2}x^{2-1} - \frac{6}{2}x^{1-1}$$

Carry out that arithmetic, and simplify the coefficients where you can:

$$x^2 + 2x - 3$$

Don't worry if the number you're dividing the coefficients by isn't a common factor. It's fine to leave coefficients as fractions in lowest terms.

Let's look at something a little more complex:

Example
$$\frac{x^3 - x^2 + 3x - 10}{x - 2}$$

This operation is asking you to divide each term of the polynomial by the binomial $x - 2$. Because there are two terms in the denominator, we need to match these with the numerator through a process that looks a lot like long division. First we put the denominator on the left side and the numerator on the right side:

$$x - 2 \overline{) x^3 - x^2 + 3x - 10}$$

Next, create a match with the highest order term in the numerator, x^3, by multiplying the denominator, in this case by x^2:

$$(x - 2) \times x^2 = x^3 - 2x^2$$

Now subtract this result from your numerator:

$$
\begin{array}{r}
x^2 \\
x - 2 \overline{) x^3 - x^2 + 3x - 10} \\
- (x^3 - 2x^2) \\
\hline
x^2 + 3x - 10
\end{array}
$$

Now we match the next highest term, x^2, multiplying $x - 2$ by x:

$$(x - 2) \times x = x^2 - 2x$$

Now subtract this result from your numerator, like before:

$$
\begin{array}{r}
x^2 + x \\
x - 2 \overline{) x^3 - x^2 + 3x - 10} \\
- (x^3 - 2x^2) \\
\hline
x^2 + 3x - 10 \\
- (x^2 - 2x) \\
\hline
= 5x - 10
\end{array}
$$

Finally, we match the last variable term $5x$ to the denominator, by multiply the denominator by 5:

$$(x - 2) \times 5 = 5x - 10$$

Subtracting this result from the numerator:

$$
\begin{array}{r}
x^2 + x + 5 \\
x - 2 \overline{) x^3 - x^2 + 3x - 10} \\
- (x^3 - 2x^2) \\
\hline
x^2 + 3x - 10 \\
- (x^2 - 2x) \\
\hline
5x - 10 \\
- (5x - 10) \\
\hline
0
\end{array}
$$

Since we found a value of 0, the numerator is divisible by the denominator. Another way of looking at this is that the denominator is a factor of the numerator. If we had been left with a value different from zero, we would know that the denominator is not a factor of the numerator. The result of our long division, found above the numerator, is $x^2 + x + 5$:

$$
\begin{array}{r}
 \overbrace{x^2 + x + 5} \\
x - 2 \overline{)\, x^3 - x^2 + 3x - 10} \\
\underline{-(x^3 - 2x^2)} \\
x^2 + 3x - 10 \\
\underline{-(x^2 - 2x)} \\
5x - 10 \\
\underline{-(5x - 10)} \\
0
\end{array}
$$

You can double check your answer by multiplying this result by the denominator $(x^2 + x + 5)(x - 2)$. Since this is equal to $x^3 - x^2 + 3x - 10$, we can confirm that our calculations are correct:

$$
\frac{x^3 - x^2 + 3x - 10}{x - 2} = x^2 + x + 5
$$

Part 1 Practice: Polynomial Expressions

1

$$x^3 + 2x - 6 + 4x^3 - 5x + 9$$

What is the value of the expression above when $x = 3$?

A) 109

B) 129

C) 159

D) 171

2

If $m^4 + 4m^3 - m^2 + 17m - 2$ is added to $3m^4 - m^3 - 2m^2 + 3m - 8$, which of the following statements is true?

  I. The coefficient of its largest term is positive.

  II. It has no second-degree term.

  III. Its constant term is positive.

A) I only

B) II only

C) I and II

D) I, II, and III

3

Which of the following expressions is equal to $3x + 16 - 2y$ minus $x + 8 - y$?

A) $-2x - 16 + 2y$

B) $-2x - 8 - 3y$

C) $2x + 8 - 3y$

D) $2x + 8 - y$

4

The growth rate of a city's population can be modeled using the equation $p = 4x + 7$, where x represents the number of years since 1900, and p is the increase in the population of the city. If people leave the city at a rate of $2x - 10$ people per year, which of the following expressions accurately models the change in the city's total population in a given year?

A) $-2x - 17$

B) $2x - 3$

C) $2x + 17$

D) $6x - 3$

5

$$12m^2n^7 \times 5m^{10}n^3$$

Which of the following expressions is equivalent to the one shown above?

A) $17m^{12}n^{10}$

B) $17m^{20}n^{21}$

C) $60m^{12}n^{10}$

D) $60m^{20}n^{21}$

Questions 6 and 7 refer to the following information.

The equation below describes the path of a projectile thrown from an initial height of $\frac{9}{4}$ feet, where t is time in seconds and h is the height of the projectile.

$$\frac{-4t^2 + 16t + 9}{4} = h$$

6

What is the height of the projectile, in feet, at two seconds?

A) 2

B) $\frac{25}{2}$

C) 4

D) $\frac{25}{4}$

7

If the projectile is exactly 5.25 feet high in the air, how many seconds could it have elapsed since it was thrown?

A) 4 seconds

B) 2 seconds

C) 1.5 seconds

D) 1 second

8

$$(2x + 5)(11 - x)$$

If $2x + 5 = 11$, what is the value of the expression above?

9

What is the value of $100x^4 + 44x^2$ divided by $4x^2$ when $x = 2$?

10

$$\frac{3x^4 - 36x^3 - 12x^2}{-3x}$$

If $x = -2$, what is the value of the expression above?

Factoring Polynomials
Part 2

In the previous section you learned how to multiply polynomials. With multiplication, you start with two or more factors and find their product. Remember from Section 4 that factoring is the opposite of multiplication: you start with a product and find its factors. In this section, we'll build on what you learned in Section 4 and discuss how to factor quadratic and cubic polynomials. Here's what this relationship looks like:

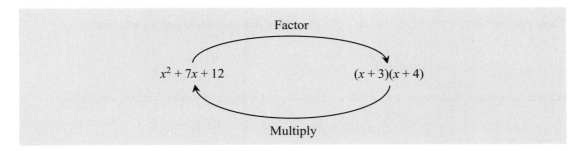

Factoring Quadratic Trinomials

Remember that a quadratic expression has a degree, or highest power, of two, and a trinomial is a polynomial with three terms. Therefore, a quadratic trinomial is a second-degree polynomial with three terms. You can write a general expression for quadratic trinomials like this:

$$ax^2 + bx + c$$

In this form, a is the coefficient of x^2, b is the coefficient of x, and c is the constant. So in the quadratic trinomial $x^2 + 2x - 8$, $a = 1$, $b = 2$, and $c = -8$. Quadratic trinomials where $a = 1$ are a little simpler to factor, so we'll take this one as our first example. To fully factor it, we want to write it as two binomials multiplied together, like this:

$$(x + m)(x + n)$$

How do we find m and n? Well, we can multiply these two binomials using FOIL, and then simplify:

$$x^2 + nx + mx + mn = x^2 + (n + m)x + mn$$

By comparing this to our general expression for quadratic trinomials above, we can see that two things must be true:

$$n + m = b$$

$$m \times n = c$$

In other words, to find m and n, we need to find two numbers that have a sum of b and a product of c. For the trinomial $x^2 + 2x - 8$, that means we're looking for two numbers that add up to 2 and multiply together to -8. First, let's see what numbers multiply to -8:

$$-1 \times 8 = -8$$
$$-8 \times 1 = -8$$
$$-2 \times 4 = -8$$
$$-4 \times 2 = -8$$

Which pair of numbers has a sum of 2? Only -2 and 4:

$$-2 + 4 = 2$$

Therefore, our two constants are -2 and 4. To plug them into our binomials, we add them to x:

$$\left(x + (-2)\right)(x + 4) = (x - 2)(x + 4)$$

We can then check that we have factored correctly by using FOIL to multiply the two binomials:

$$(x - 2)(x + 4) = x^2 + 4x - 2x - 8 = x^2 + 2x - 8$$

Because multiplying leads to the expression we started out with, we know we have factored correctly.

Factoring with Different Values

Now you know how to factor a quadratic trinomial when a—the coefficient of the quadratic term—is equal to 1. But what if a is equal to another number? First, check whether you can factor this number out of the entire expression.

Example

$$5x^2 + 15x + 10$$

Did you notice that every term has a common factor of 5? That means you can start by pulling 5 out of the entire expression:

$$5x^2 + 15x + 10 = 5(x^2 + 3x + 2)$$

Now you can use the method you've just learned to factor the quadratic expression in parentheses. You're looking for two numbers have a product of 2 and a sum of 3. The numbers 1 and 2 fit those requirements:

$$5(x^2 + 3x + 2) = 5(x + 1)(x + 2)$$

You can tell that you've factored correctly because when you multiply these binomials together using **FOIL**, you get the trinomial you were trying to factor:

$$5(x + 1)(x + 2) = 5(x^2 + 3x + 2) = 5x^2 + 15x + 10$$

However, what happens when you can't factor out a from the entire expression? This time, one or both of the x's in the binomials will have a coefficient, marked here by p and q:

$$ax^2 + bx + c = (px + m)(qx + n)$$

We need a few things to happen:

1. $p \times q = a$
2. $m \times n = c$
3. $p \times n + m \times q = b$

Example

$$3x^2 - 5x - 2$$

p and q will multiply to 3 so their values will be 1 and 3. (If a is negative, first factor -1 out of the equation.) Therefore, you know the two binomials will look something like this:

$$3x^2 - 5x - 2 = (3x + m)(x + n)$$

To find m and n, you need values that will multiply to -2. There are two sets of possible values: 1 and -2 or -1 and 2. Which of these values should you pick so that $3 \times n + m \times 1 = -5$? The only option is 1 and -2, because $3 \times -2 + 1 \times 1 = -5$. Therefore, the two binomials must be:

$$(3x + 1)(x - 2)$$

Factoring a Difference of Squares

Expressions that consist of subtracting one perfect square from another, such as $x^2 - 25$, are called a **difference of squares**. Recognizing when a polynomial is a difference of squares will come in handy because these expressions all factor according to a simple formula:

$$a^2 - b^2 = (a + b)(a - b)$$

Here are some examples:

$$x^2 - 4 = (x + 2)(x - 2)$$
$$x^2 - 64 = (x + 8)(x - 8)$$
$$x^2 - y^2 = (x + y)(x - y)$$
$$x^4 - y^4 = (x^2 + y^2)(x^2 - y^2)$$

But wait—notice that in our last example, the second factor is also a difference of squares! We can factor that, too:

$$x^4 - y^4 = (x^2 + y^2)(x + y)(x - y)$$

Factoring a Sum or Difference of Cubes

There are also special formulas for factoring a sum or difference of cubes:

$$a^3 + b^3 = (a + b)(a^2 - ab + b^2)$$
$$a^3 - b^3 = (a - b)(a^2 + ab + b^2)$$

These two formulas look very similar – in fact, the only differences are in the signs. To keep the signs straight, think **SOAP**: "same, opposite, always positive." The first sign is the same as the one in the original expression, the second sign is the opposite, and the last sign is always a plus sign.

Here are some examples:

$$x^3 + 8 = (x + 2)(x^2 - 2x + 4)$$
$$x^3 - 27 = (x - 3)(x^2 + 3x + 9)$$
$$x^6 - 64 = (x^2 - 4)(x^4 + 4x^2 + 16)$$

Did you catch that the first factor in our last example is a difference of squares? You can use the difference of squares formula to further simplify:

$$x^6 - 64 = (x + 2)(x - 2)(x^4 + 4x^2 + 16)$$

Using Factoring to Simplify Rational Equations

On the SAT, you won't have to do complicated division with polynomials. However, you may be asked to look at a rational expression involving polynomials and simplify. In Part 1, you learned about how to do some basic division with polynomials. Your new factoring skills will allow you to divide polynomials with multiple terms in the denominator.

Example

$$\frac{x^2 + 3x + 2}{x + 2}$$

The denominator is a linear expression and can't be factored. However, the numerator is a quadratic trinomial, which you can factor:

$$x^2 + 3x + 2 = (x + 1)(x + 2)$$

Substituting that into the original expression, you can quickly see that one of those factors is a common factor with the denominator:

$$\frac{(x+1)(x+2)}{x+2}$$

As with any rational expression, cancel common factors to simplify:

$$\frac{(x+1)(x+2)}{x+2} = x+1$$

Example

$$\frac{x^2 + 7x + 12}{x^2 - 9}$$

In this case, both polynomials can be factored (notice that the denominator is a difference of squares):

$$\frac{(x+3)(x+4)}{(x+3)(x-3)}$$

After cancelling out the common factor $(x+3)$, you're left with:

$$\frac{x+4}{x-3}$$

This can't be simplified any further, so you're all done!

Part 2 Practice: Factoring Polynomials

1

$$x^2 + 3x - 10$$

Which of the following expressions is a factor of the equation above?

A) $x + 5$

B) $x - 5$

C) $x + 2$

D) x

2

$$-9x^2 + 22x + 15$$

Which of the following expressions represents a complete factoring of the expression above?

A) $(-9x + 5)(x - 3)$

B) $(9x + 5)(x - 3)$

C) $-(9x - 5)(x + 3)$

D) $-(9x + 5)(x - 3)$

3

$$x^2 - 11x - 12$$

If a and b represent the two factors of the expression above, which of the following expressions represents $a + b$?

A) $2x - 13$

B) $2x - 11$

C) $2x + 11$

D) $2x + 13$

4

$$2x^3 + 3x^2 - 3x - 2$$

Which of the following expressions is a factor of the expression above?

A) $2x^2 + 2x + 2$

B) $2x^2 + 5x + 2$

C) $4x^2 - 6x + 2$

D) $8x^2 - 4x - 4$

Questions 5 and 6 refer to the following expression.

$$x^3 - 27$$

5

If the expression above is factored into its simplest form, which of the following statements about the factored form of the expression is true?

A) Both factors are of the first degree.

B) One factor is of the second degree, and one is of the first degree.

C) One factor has four terms, and the other has two.

D) Both factors have two terms.

6

What is the value of the product of all the coefficients of the expression's two factors?

A) 0

B) 1

C) 3

D) 4

7

The number of people with the INS gene, which is associated with diabetes, increases or decreases in a small town depending on the calendar year, according to the expression $4x^2 - 4x - 120$. If x is a positive integer representing the number of years since 2000, in what year was there no increase or decrease in the number of people with the INS gene in the small town?

A) 2004

B) 2005

C) 2006

D) 2007

8

$$-(x^2 - 100)$$

The number of used trucks sold by a car dealership decreases as the price increases according to the expression above, where x represents the price of the truck in thousands of dollars. At what price, in thousands of dollars, will the dealership sell no trucks?

9

$$x^3 - 125$$

If the expression above is represented by $(x - b)[(x + b)(x + b) - xb]$, what is the value for b?

10

$$x^2 - 9x + 18$$

The expression above is factored as $(x - a)(x - b)$. What is the value of ab?

Quadratic Equations
Part 3

Quadratic equations are equations with one variable raised to the second degree. Here's an example:

$$x^2 + 10x + 21 = 0$$

To solve quadratic equations, you can use what you've learned about factoring quadratic polynomials. How? Take a look at the quadratic equation above, and factor the left side:

$$x^2 + 10x + 21 = 0$$
$$(x + 3)(x + 7) = 0$$

On the left side, you now have two factors that have a product of zero. For two numbers to have a product of zero, at least one of them has to be equal to zero. In this equation, there are two ways for that to be true:

$$x + 3 = 0 \qquad\qquad\qquad x + 7 = 0$$
$$x = -3 \qquad\qquad\qquad\qquad x = -7$$

Therefore, this quadratic equation has two possible solutions: $x = -3$ or $x = -7$. These values are known as the **roots** of the equation.

Example

$$2x^2 + 21x + 40 = 13$$

Notice that unlike our first example, this equation is not set up so that one side is equal to zero. You have to gather all your terms on one side. In this case, subtract 13 from both sides to get zero on the right side of the equation:

$$2x^2 + 21x + 27 = 0$$

Now you are ready to factor the left side:

$$(2x + 3)(x + 9) = 0$$

Then, set each factor equal to zero in order to solve for x:

$$2x + 3 = 0 \qquad\qquad\qquad x + 9 = 0$$
$$x = -\frac{3}{2} \qquad\qquad\qquad\qquad x = -9$$

The two roots of the quadratic equation are $-\dfrac{3}{2}$ and -9.

Word Problems with Quadratic Equations

On the SAT, you may need to solve word problems using quadratic equations.

Example

Patricia throws a tennis ball out of her window. The height h of the ball at time t is given by $h = -t^2 - t + 20$. How many seconds does it take for the tennis ball to fall to the ground?

The height of something measures its distance from the ground. That means that when the tennis ball falls to the ground, its height (h) is zero. You can substitute 0 for h in the equation:

$$-t^2 - t + 20 = 0$$

Now that you have a quadratic equation, you can factor it to find the roots. Notice that right now, the coefficient of the quadratic term, t^2, is -1. Factoring would be simpler if that coefficient were 1. Since any number multiplied by zero equals zero, you can multiply both sides by -1 to get:

$$t^2 + t - 20 = 0$$

Now you have a quadratic polynomial that's easier to factor:

$$(t + 5)(t - 4) = 0$$

You've solved the equation: $t = -5$ or $t = 4$. However, remember that you're not just solving an equation this time; you're answering a word problem. The ball can't fall to the ground twice, so you need to figure out which one of your solutions makes sense for the problem.

This problem is asking you to find a particular time after Patricia throws the ball. Since you know that time is never negative, you can look at your solutions and realize that $t = -5$ doesn't make sense. This makes it an **extraneous solution**: a solution that works mathematically but doesn't make logical sense. This leaves you with only one solution: the tennis ball falls to the ground when $t = 4$.

The Quadratic Formula

Not all quadratic equations can be easily solved by factoring. For quadratic equations that can't be easily factored using the methods we've covered, you can use the Quadratic Formula. The **Quadratic Formula** states that if you have a quadratic equation in the form:

$$ax^2 + bx + c = 0$$

You can solve for x using this formula:

$$x = \frac{-b \pm \sqrt{b^2 - 4ac}}{2a}$$

Example

Solve for x in the equation:

$$x^2 + 17x + 72 = 0$$

In this equation, $a = 1$, $b = 17$, and $c = 72$. Putting these values into the Quadratic Formula gives you:

$$x = \frac{-17 \pm \sqrt{17^2 - 4(1)(72)}}{2(1)}$$

After this, it's just a matter of remembering your order of operations to simplify:

$$x = \frac{-17 \pm \sqrt{289 - 288}}{2}$$

$$x = \frac{-17 \pm \sqrt{1}}{2}$$

$$x = \frac{-17 \pm 1}{2}$$

That $\pm$ sign looks strange but just means "plus or minus." In other words, you need to both add those terms and subtract them. Doing so gives you:

$$x = \frac{-16}{2} \quad \text{or} \quad x = \frac{-18}{2}$$

Simplify those fractions for your final solutions:

$$x = -8 \quad \text{or} \quad x = -9$$

The two roots for the quadratic equation are -9 and -8. Take note that while we used the quadratic formula, this equation can also be solved by the factoring technique (try it!).

Irrational and Nonexistent Solutions

There are two types of quadratic equations that the Quadratic Formula is especially useful for. The first is quadratic equations with irrational solutions. Take this equation:

$$x^2 + 5x - 7 = 0$$

Applying the Quadratic Formula gives you:

$$x = \frac{-(5) \pm \sqrt{(5)^2 - 4(1)(-7)}}{2(1)}$$

$$x = \frac{-5 \pm \sqrt{25 + 28}}{2}$$

$$x = \frac{-5 \pm \sqrt{53}}{2}$$

This one couldn't be solved by factoring because its roots are irrational, so you needed to use the Quadratic Formula.

The other kind of quadratic equation, the Quadratic Formula, is especially useful for quadratic equations with *no* solutions.

Example

$$x^2 + x + 2 = 0$$

Look what happens when you try to apply the Quadratic Formula:

$$x = \frac{-1 \pm \sqrt{1^2 - 4(1)(2)}}{2(1)}$$

$$x = \frac{-1 \pm \sqrt{1 - 8}}{2}$$

$$x = \frac{-1 \pm \sqrt{-7}}{2}$$

Wait a minute! You can't take the square root of a negative number. That means there is **no solution**: the expression cannot be factored, and there are no values of x that will make the equation true. A quadratic equation will always have zero, one, or two roots, and you can use the Quadratic Formula to figure out how many it has.

Part 3 Practice: Quadratic Equations

1

$$x^2 - 4x - 21 = 0$$

If a and b are the two values of x that satisfy the equation above, what is the value of ab?

A) -21

B) -7

C) 0

D) 21

2

$$4x^2 - 12x + 8$$

Which of the following expressions is equal to the expression above?

A) $(x-2)(x-1)$

B) $(x+2)(x+1)$

C) $4(x-2)(x-1)$

D) $4(x+2)(x+1)$

3

$$(7,0), (5,0)$$

Which of the following equations contains both of the xy-coordinates of the set shown above?

A) $2x^2 - 70 = y$

B) $2x^2 - 24x + 70 = y$

C) $2x^2 + 24x - 70 = y$

D) $2x^2 + 24x + 70 = y$

4

$$3x^2 + 25x + 42 = 0$$

Which of the following equations is equivalent to the equation above?

A) $(x+6)(x+7) = 0$

B) $(3x+7)(x+6) = 0$

C) $3(x+6)(x+7) = 0$

D) $3(x+6)(3x+7) = 0$

5

$$3x^2 - 3x + 8 = 7x$$

Which of the following statements are true about the equation above?

    I.   Both of its solutions are integers.

    II. All of its solutions are positive.

    III. It has no real solutions.

A) Only I

B) Only II

C) Both I and II

D) I, II, and III

Questions 6 and 7 refer to the following information.

The number of votes a political candidate receives in a certain district can be predicted by the number of registered voters in that district using the equation $2x^2 + x + 13 = v$, where x represents 100 registered voters, and v represents the number of votes received.

6

If 1,000 voters register for the election, how many votes can this candidate expect to get?

A) 223

B) 200

C) 113

D) 100

7

If the candidate received 313 votes in her last election, how many voters were registered in the district?

A) 100

B) 120

C) 1200

D) 2489

8

$$x^2 - x = 6$$

What is the absolute value of the difference of the solutions for x in the equation above?

9

$$x^2 - 10x = 0$$

What is the sum of the values of x in the equation above?

10

$$3x^2 - 9x + 16 = s$$

The time it takes for a computer algorithm to calculate the average of a set of values is shown in the expression above, where x represents the number of values and s represents time in milliseconds. If the computer takes 10 milliseconds to calculate the average of a set of values, how many values could be in the set?

Quadratic Functions and Graphs
Part 4

So far you have learned about quadratic equations and now we turn our attention to quadratic functions. In Section 4, you learned that a **function** is a formula that turns every "input" value into an "output" value. **Quadratic functions** are simply functions with a variable raised to the second power. Since you are now quadratic experts, we will also take a look at graphs in this section. All of the principles for the graphs of functions will also apply to graphs of equations. Like linear functions, quadratic functions can either be written with the function notation $f(x)$, or with a second variable like y:

$$f(x) = ax^2 + bx + c$$
$$y = ax^2 + bx + c$$

Graphing Quadratic Functions

To graph quadratic functions, let's begin with the simplest quadratic function:

$$f(x) = x^2$$

To start graphing this quadratic function, you can create a chart with some input and output values:

x	-3	-2	-1	0	1	2	3
$f(x)$	9	4	1	0	1	4	9

Then, you can plot these points on a graph:

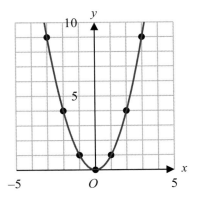

The type of curve created by graphing quadratic functions is called a **parabola**. Parabolas can move up or down, be wider or narrower, or flip upside down, but they will always retain this basic shape.

Notice that the parabola above is symmetric about the y-axis. All parabolas are symmetric about a vertical line drawn through their **vertex**, which is the highest or lowest point. To find the x-coordinate (h) of the vertex (h, k) of any parabola, you can use the following formula:

$$h = \frac{-b}{2a}$$

In the function above, b is equal to zero, so the vertex has the x-coordinate 0. If you plug $x = 0$ into the function, you can find the y-coordinate of the vertex: $f(x) = 0^2 = 0$. Therefore, the parabola's vertex is located at (0, 0)—which you can see on the graph.

What if we had the function $f(x) = x^2 + 4x$? In this case, $b = 4$, so the x-coordinate of the vertex would be $\frac{-b}{2a} = \frac{-4}{2 \times 1} = -2$. You can plug this x value into the function to find the y-coordinate: $f(x) = (-2)^2 + 4 \times (-2) = -4$. Therefore, the vertex is located at the point (–2, –4).

Transformations of Quadratic Functions

Like we saw in Section 4, manipulating a function will move or stretch the graph of the function on the coordinate plane.

If you add a constant to a quadratic function, this moves its vertex up or down. Adding a positive constant moves the vertex up, and adding a negative constant moves the vertex down. For example, if you add 5 to the function $f(x) = x^2$, you'll shift the vertex of the parabola up by 5 units. If you subtract 7, you'll shift the vertex of the parabola down by 7 units:

$$f(x) = x^2 + 5 \qquad\qquad\qquad f(x) = x^2 - 7$$

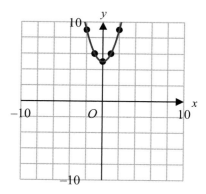
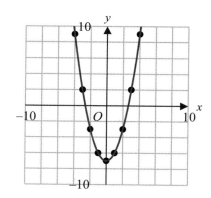

Instead of being located at (0, 0), the vertex of the function $f(x) = x^2 + 5$ is located at (0, 5). The vertex of the function $f(x) = x^2 - 7$ is located at (0, –7).

Just like with linear functions, you can shift a parabola left or right by taking the function of x plus a constant. Taking the function of x plus a constant for parabolas means replacing every x with x plus that constant. Adding a positive constant shifts the parabola's vertex to the left, and adding a negative constant shifts the parabola's vertex to the right. For example, if you take the function of $(x + 2)$, you'll shift the vertex of the parabola left by 2 units. If you take the function of $(x - 1)$, you'll shift the vertex of the parabola right by 1 unit:

$$f(x) = (x + 2)^2 \qquad\qquad\qquad f(x) = (x - 1)^2$$

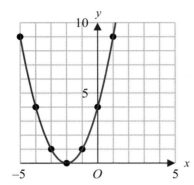 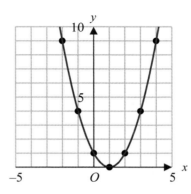

The vertex of the function $f(x) = (x + 2)^2$ is located at $(-2, 0)$. The vertex of the function $f(x) = (x - 1)^2$ is located at $(1, 0)$.

You can "stretch" a quadratic function by changing the value for a. If a is bigger than 1, you'll end up with a narrower parabola. If a is a fraction between 0 and 1, you'll end up with a wider parabola. For example, the function $f(x) = 2x^2$ is stretched so it is narrower, and the function $f(x) = \frac{1}{2}x^2$ is stretched so it is wider:

$$f(x) = 2x^2 \qquad\qquad\qquad f(x) = \frac{1}{2}x^2$$

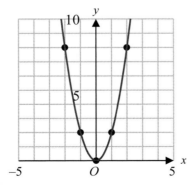 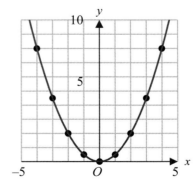

Finally, what about a negative constant? If a is equal to a negative number, the parabola flips upside down. In other words, it's reflected about the x-axis:

$$f(x) = -x^2$$

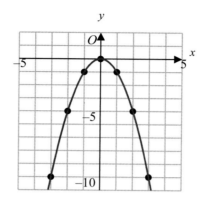

A parabola's **x-intercepts** are the points where the parabola meets the x-axis. A parabola can have zero, one, or two x-intercepts. The y-coordinate for any point on the x-axis is always zero, so the coordinates for the x-intercepts are x values of the quadratic function that will make y equal to 0.

You already know how to find the values of x that will make a quadratic function equal to 0—this is the same as finding the roots of any quadratic equation! Just set the quadratic function equal to zero, and then factor it into two binomials.

Example

$$f(x) = 6x^2 - 19x - 36$$

First, set this function equal to zero. Then, use the method you learned in Part 3 to factor and solve for x:

$$6x^2 - 19x - 36 = 0$$

$$(3x + 4)(2x - 9) = 0$$

$$3x + 4 = 0 \qquad\qquad 2x - 9 = 0$$

$$x = -\frac{4}{3} \qquad\qquad x = \frac{9}{2}$$

The x-intercepts of this parabola are $-\frac{4}{3}$ and $\frac{9}{2}$.

Systems of Equations

On the SAT, you might see systems of linear and quadratic equations. Since a linear equation represents a line and a quadratic equation represents a parabola, the solution to a system of a linear and a quadratic equation represents where that line and that parabola meet.

Systems of linear and quadratic equations can have zero, one, or two solutions. If there are no solutions, the line and the parabola do not intersect at all. If there is only one solution, the line is **tangent** to the parabola, touching it at exactly one point. If there are two solutions, the line intersects the parabola at two points.

To solve a system of equations consisting of one quadratic equation and one linear equation, you'll use substitution, just like with systems of linear equations.

Example

$$y + 30 = x^2 + 3x$$
$$y - 5x = 90$$

In order to substitute, you need to first solve for y in terms of x. Add $5x$ to both sides of the second equation:

$$y - 5x = 90$$
$$y = 5x + 90$$

Plug this value for y into the first equation:

$$y + 30 = x^2 + 3x$$
$$5x + 90 + 30 = x^2 + 3x$$

Then, solve this equation. Add and subtract like terms until one side is equal to zero:

$$5x + 90 + 30 = x^2 + 3x$$
$$x^2 - 2x - 120 = 0$$

Now you just need to use one of your strategies for solving quadratic equations. This one factors to:

$$(x + 10)(x - 12) = 0$$
$$x = -10 \quad \text{or} \quad x = 12$$

You're not done yet! You need to solve for both variables. Substitute these x values into either equation to find the corresponding y values. Both equations will give you the same values, so pick the easiest one to handle—usually the linear equation. Plug both x values into this equation:

$$y = 5 \, (-10) + 90 \qquad\qquad y = 5 \, (12) + 90$$

$$y = 40 \qquad\qquad\qquad\qquad y = 150$$

The parabola and the line intersect at two points: (–10, 40) and (12, 150).

Part 4 Practice: Quadratic Functions and Graphs

1

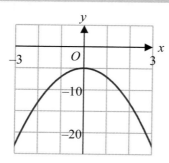

Which of the following functions could match the graph above?

A) $f(x) = -x^2 - 5$

B) $f(x) = x^2 - 5$

C) $f(x) = -2x^2 - 5$

D) $f(x) = 2x^2 - 5$

2

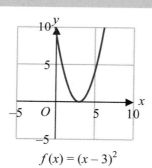

$$f(x) = (x - 3)^2$$

Which of the following statements is true about the graph of the function above?

A) It has a vertex at $x = -3$.

B) It has a vertex at $x = 3$.

C) It has no x-intercepts.

D) It has two x-intercepts.

3

Which of the following graphs could represent $f(x) = x^2 - 3$?

A)

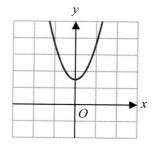

B)

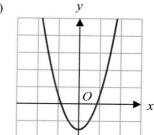

C)

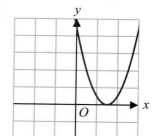

D)

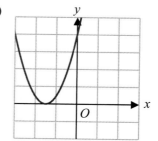

$$y = x^2 + 10x$$

$$y = 3x$$

At what value(s) of x do the two equations shown above intersect?

A) Only 0

B) Only -7

C) -7 and 0

D) 0 and 7

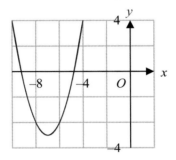

Which of the following functions models the graph above?

A) $f(x) = (x - 7)^2 - 3$

B) $f(x) = (x + 7)^2$

C) $f(x) = (x + 7)^2 - 3$

D) $f(x) = (x + 7)^2 + 3$

Questions 6 and 7 refer to the following information.

The Gross Domestic Product of a country (GDP) is the total goods and services produced by a country during a year. The GDP of Country A changes according to the equation $y = x^2 - 10x + 100$, where x represents the number of years since 2000, and y represents the country's GDP, in billions of dollars.

In what year does the equation predict that Country A's GDP will be 75 billion dollars?

A) 2005

B) 2006

C) 2007

D) 2008

The GDP of Country B changes according to the equation $y = 5x + 50$. In what year will Country A's GDP equal Country B's GDP?

A) 2007

B) 2008

C) 2009

D) 2010

8

$f(t)$

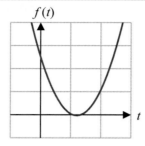

Alex throws a ball from the top of his house. The ball's motion can be modeled using the function $f(t) = t^2 - 14t + 49$, where t represents the number of milliseconds that have passed since Alex threw the ball. This function is shown above on the xy-axis. How many milliseconds will it take for the ball to hit the ground?

9

$$f(x) = x^2 - 8x + 16$$

What is the sum of the x-intercepts of the function above?

10

$$f(x) = x^2 - 6x + 8$$

What is the product of the x-intercepts in the function above?

Advanced Equations

Part 5

In this section, you'll learn about some more kinds of equations you might see on the SAT: exponential equations, rational equations, and radical equations.

Exponential Equations

In an **exponential equation**, the variable you are solving for is part of an exponent.

Example
$$2^x = 8$$

One way of putting this equation into words is, "2 raised to what power equals 8?" If you don't know off the top of your head, you can use trial and error:

$$2^1 = 2$$
$$2^2 = 4$$
$$2^3 = 8$$

Since $2^x = 8$ and $2^3 = 8$, you know that $x = 3$.

Sometimes the exponent will be a little more complicated:

Example
$$4^{2x-6} = 16$$

You know that $16 = 4^2$. Replacing 16 with 4^2 in the equation gives you:

$$4^{2x-6} = 4^2$$

Using exponent rules, since the bases are the same, you know that the exponents must also be the same. You can write an equation using only the exponents to solve for x:

$$2x - 6 = 2$$
$$x = 4$$

It's a good idea to check your work by plugging the value you found for x into the original equation:

$$4^{2(4)-6} = 4^{8-6} = 4^2 = 16$$

Since this gives you the same value, you know that x is equal to 4.

Rational Equations

A **rational equation** is one in which one or more terms are in the form of a fraction.

Example
$$\frac{x}{3} = \frac{1}{5}$$

You can cross-multiply to solve for x:

$$5 \times x = 1 \times 3$$

$$x = \frac{3}{5}$$

Now let's try something a little more complicated:

Example
$$\frac{1}{x+1} = \frac{2}{3x}$$

The idea is the same. You simply cross-multiply and divide to solve for x:

$$3x \times 1 = (x+1) \times 2$$

$$3x = 2x + 2$$

$$x = 2$$

You have solved for x, and determined that it is equal to 2. But you're not quite done. When dealing with rational equations, you have to check that the solution was allowed by the original equation, which had some restrictions.

Restrictions are rules that limit the values that your variable is allowed to take. In the original equation, x can't be equal to negative 1 or 0 because this would mean you are dividing by zero. However, it isn't an issue if x is equal to 2—this isn't one of the restrictions of the equation. Therefore, you can now confidently say that $x = 2$.

Radical Equations

A **radical equation** is an equation where the variable is inside a radical.

$$\sqrt{x} = 5$$

To solve this equation, you need to square both sides:

$$(\sqrt{x})^2 = 5^2$$
$$x = 25$$

You have determined that x is equal to 25.

What if the equation is a little more complicated?

$$2\sqrt{x + 8} - 4 = x + 1$$

Squaring both sides right away would lead to something very messy and unproductive. To save time and hassle, first isolate the radical by adding 4 to both sides:

$$2\sqrt{x + 8} = x + 5$$

Now you can square both sides:

$$\left(2\sqrt{x + 8}\right)^2 = (x + 5)^2$$
$$4(x + 8) = x^2 + 10x + 25$$
$$4x + 32 = x^2 + 10x + 25$$

Move everything to one side and combine like terms. Then, solve by factoring:

$$4x + 32 = x^2 + 10x + 25$$
$$x^2 + 6x - 7 = 0$$
$$(x + 7)(x - 1) = 0$$
$$x = -7 \quad \text{or} \quad x = 1$$

You have found that x is equal to -7 or 1, but you are not quite done. Squaring both sides of an equation can introduce extraneous solutions, so you need to check whether your values for x are real solutions of the equation. You can do this by plugging the solutions into both sides of the original equation and seeing if they match. Start with $x = -7$:

$$2\sqrt{-7 + 8} - 4 = -7 + 1$$
$$2 - 4 = -6$$
$$-2 = -6$$

Wrong!

Since the two sides are not equal, $x = -7$ is an extraneous solution. You have found that your solution for x doesn't include -7.

The fact that you ruled out one solution as extraneous doesn't necessarily mean the other solution is valid, so make sure to repeat the check with $x = 1$:

$$2\sqrt{1 + 8} - 4 = 1 + 1$$
$$2 \times 3 - 4 = 2$$
$$2 = 2$$

In this case, the two sides of the original equation match, so you can say that $x = 1$. This is the only solution for your equation.

Part 5 Practice: Advanced Equations

1

$$\frac{17}{2} = \frac{x}{5}$$

What is the value of x in the equation above?

A) $\dfrac{17}{5}$

B) $\dfrac{34}{5}$

C) $\dfrac{85}{4}$

D) $\dfrac{85}{2}$

2

$$\frac{x - 2}{6} = \frac{x}{12}$$

Given the equation above, what is the value of $\dfrac{x}{3}$?

A) $\dfrac{2}{3}$

B) $\dfrac{4}{3}$

C) 2

D) 4

3

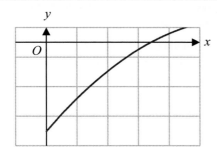

Which of the following equations could match the graph above?

A) $f(x) = \dfrac{1}{x} - 6$

B) $f(x) = 6x - 6$

C) $f(x) = \sqrt{x} - 6$

D) $f(x) = \sqrt{x} + 6$

4

$$y = \dfrac{4}{x - 1}$$

Which of the following statements is true about the equation above?

I. $x\text{ER}, x \neq 1$

II. $y\text{ER}, y \neq 1$

III. It has a y-intercept at $y = -4$

A) I only

B) II only

C) I and III

D) I, II, and III

5

$$f(x) = \sqrt{-x} - 9$$

Which of the following graphs could represent the equation above?

A)

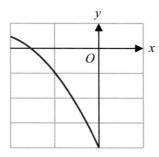

B)

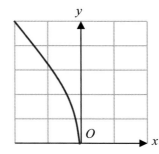

C)

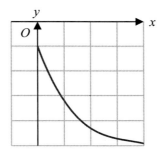

D)

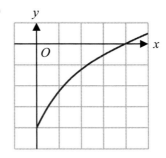

6

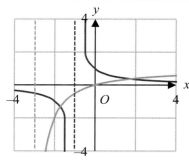

Which of the following pairs of functions could match the graph above?

A) $f(x) = \dfrac{1}{x+1}$ and $f(x) = \dfrac{x}{x+3}$

B) $f(x) = \dfrac{1}{x+1}$ and $f(x) = \dfrac{x}{x-3}$

C) $f(x) = \dfrac{1}{x-1}$ and $f(x) = \dfrac{1}{x-3}$

D) $f(x) = \dfrac{x}{x-1}$ and $f(x) = \dfrac{1}{x+3}$

7

$$\sqrt{2(x+15)} = 6$$

Based on the equation above, what is the value of $(4+x)^2$?

A) -4

B) 16

C) 36

D) 49

Questions 8 and 9 refer to the following information.

Salmonella bacteria are often the cause of food poisoning in humans. If more than 64 bacteria are present in a person's body at once, that person can begin to experience mild gastrointestinal problems. In Person A, the number of bacteria can be modeled by the equation $f(t) = 2^t$, where t represents the number of minutes since the first bacterium enters the person's body.

8

To the nearest minute, how many minutes will pass before this person begins to experience gastrointestinal issues?

9

In person B, whose body is less resistant to salmonella bacteria, the bacteria's growth can be modeled using the equation $f(t) = 16^{t-3}$. To the nearest minute, how many minutes earlier than person A will person B begin to experience gastrointestinal problems?

10

The median household income of Country A grows according to the equation $f(t) = \sqrt{3t-5}$, where t represents the number of years since 2010. The median household income of Country B grows according to the equation $f(t) = t - 3$. In what year will the two countries have the same median household income?

Applications of Functions
Part 6

The functions discussed in this chapter have several real-world applications. In this section you'll get a look at applications that you might see on the SAT.

Zeroes and Intercepts

Recall that the zeroes of a function are the places where its graph intersects the x-axis. This can also be used in real-world applications.

Example

Juana throws a paper airplane. Its height h meters above the ground at time t seconds is given by $h = -t^2 + 3t + 10$. At what time does it fall to the ground?

When the airplane falls to the ground, you know that its height above the ground is zero. Since you know that $h = 0$, you can write the function as:

$$0 = -t^2 + 3t + 10$$

Now you're back in familiar territory. Factoring out the negative sign will give you:

$$0 = t^2 - 3t - 10$$

From here we can find the factors of the equation:

$$0 = (t + 2)(t - 5)$$

As an equation, this has the solutions $t = -2$ or $t = 5$. However, you're looking for a specific time, and you know that a real quantity such as time can never be negative. This means that you know that the paper airplane hits the ground at $t = 5$ seconds.

Other Problems with Quadratics

The SAT may also ask you to find particular points in a function that show you understand its structure. Let's use the same paper airplane to solve a different problem:

Juana throws a paper airplane. Its height h above the ground at time t seconds is given by $h = -t^2 + 3t + 10$. At what time after it is thrown is its height the same as the height at which Juana threw it?

To solve this problem, you need to understand that when Juana threw the airplane, its time t was 0. You can find its height by plugging that value in for t:

$$h = -(0^2) + 3(0) + 10$$
$$h = 10$$

Now you want to find the other value of t that gives h a value of 10, which you can do by setting h equal to 10 and factoring.

$$10 = -t^2 + 3t + 10$$
$$0 = -t^2 + 3t + 10 - 10$$
$$0 = -t^2 + 3t$$
$$0 = (-t)(t - 3)$$

Factoring reveals that $t = 0$ or $t = 3$. In this case, you know that $t = 0$ when Juana threw the airplane, which means we want the other value. The airplane reaches the same height it was thrown from when $t = 3$.

Exponential Growth

One common use of exponential functions is to model the growth of particular populations. **Exponential growth** occurs when a quantity increases by the same factor over a particular period of time.

Example

A colony of bacteria that begins with 100 specimens doubles in size every hour. What function models the colony's rate of growth?

If the colony begins with 100 specimens, the equation after it has doubled in size can be given by:

$$y = 100 \times 2$$

That's the number that will double in the next hour, meaning that after two hours, the number of bacteria will be:

$$y = 100 \times 2 \times 2$$

Following this pattern, you can see that you are multiplying the original number by increasing powers of 2. You can create a general function for this that looks like this:

$$y = 100 \times 2^x$$

Where x stands for the number of hours the bacteria have been multiplying.

Exponential functions create graphs that look like this:

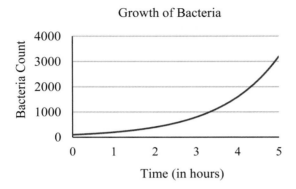

Growth of Bacteria

Exponential curves look similar to one half of a parabola. They're smooth curves that curve up slowly at first and become increasingly steep. They also don't reverse direction; one end is always going up and the other is always going down. If you see this shape on the SAT you'll know it represents exponential growth.

Equation Comparison

Linear, quadratic, and exponential functions can all be used to model situations. Here is a table and a graph comparing examples of the first few values of each of these types:

x	0	1	2	3	4	5
Linear: $y = 3x + 5$	5	8	11	14	17	20
Quadratic: $y = x^2 + 5$	5	6	9	14	21	30
Exponential: $y = 2^x + 4$	5	6	8	12	20	36

Notice that the linear function grows the fastest at the start, and the quadratic function catches up first. But, by the end, the exponential function is both the biggest and growing the fastest. The following graph shows the comparison of these three equation types:

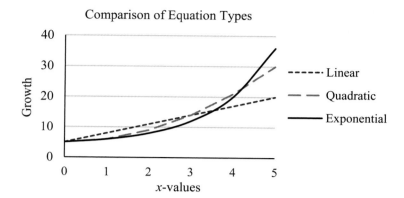

Comparison of Equation Types

Part 6 Practice: Applications of Functions

1

Rocks are falling and fill a large cavern according to the equation $c = 2^s + 2s$, where c is the volume of the rocks in cubic meters and s is the number of seconds that the rocks have been falling. What is the volume of rocks in the cavern, in cubic meters, after 4 seconds?

A)   4

B)   8

C)   24

D)   32

2

Bacteria are being cultured in a petri dish. The area covered by bacteria triples every hour. If the bacteria initially cover an area of 2 cm², which of the following functions could represent the growth of the area covered by the bacteria in square centimeters?

A) $b(t) = t^2 + 3$

B) $b(t) = \dfrac{t}{3} + 2$

C) $b(t) = 2(3^t)$

D) $b(t) = 3(2^t) + 2$

Questions 3 and 4 refer to the following information.

Paul throws a book straight up in the air. The height h of the book at time t is given by $h = -t^2 + 3t + 4$, where h is measured in meters.

3

There are approximately 3.281 feet in a meter. How many feet from the floor was Paul holding the book when he threw it?

A) 4.0 feet

B) 6.562 feet

C) 9.843 feet

D) 13.124 feet

4

Which of the following plots could show the trajectory of the book?

A)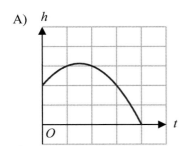

B)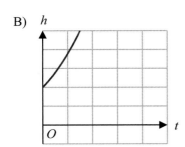

C)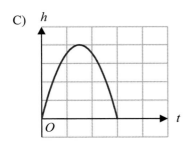

D)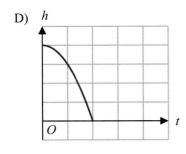

Questions 5 and 6 refer to the following information.

For the past 10 years since the opening of City X's subway system, annual ridership has been 1.2 times larger than it was the year before. The city develops a subway model where each rider represents one thousand people.

5

If there were originally 4000 subway riders in their model, what is the equation that expresses this pattern if t represents the number of years since the subway's opening?

A) $f(t) = 1.2^t + 4000$

B) $f(t) = 4000(1.2)^t$

C) $f(t) = 4000^t$

D) $f(t) = 4000^{1.2t}$

6

City Y's subway ridership grows according to the equation $f(t) = 60t + 1000$, and City Z's subway ridership grows according to the equation $f(t) = 10t^2 + 2000$. Which of the following options correctly orders their growth rates from smallest to largest?

A) City Y, City X, City Z

B) City X, City Z, City Y

C) City Z, City X, City Y

D) City Y, City Z, City X

7

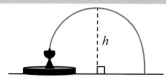

From its base, a fountain shoots water up to 25 feet into the air, as shown above. If the water takes 5 seconds to fall back to the ground from its highest point, which of the functions below models the water's height h at time t?

A) $h(t) = -t^2 + 25$

B) $h(t) = -t^2 + 10t + 25$

C) $h(t) = t^2 - 10t - 2$

D) $h(t) = 10t - t^2$

Questions 8 and 9 refer to the following information.

A watchmaker finds that the revenue in thousands of dollars, R, that she makes on watches is related to the price in dollars of the watches, p, according to the equation:

$$R = -p^2 + 9p - 20$$

8

If the watchmaker has no other costs, what is the lowest whole dollar amount she can charge without losing money?

9

If the watchmaker has no other costs, what is the highest whole dollar amount she can charge without losing money?

10

The volume V of a basin of water, in liters at time t, is given by the equation $V = t^2 - 24t + 144$. Time is measured in seconds. How many minutes will it take for the basin to be empty?

Section 5
Problem Solving and Data Analysis

What do music, football, and chemistry have in common with politics and the economy? Aside from improving college applications, all of these subjects can be analyzed in numbers, tables, and graphs. How many people who play football like to sing opera? Where do these people reside, and what kind of food do they eat—how is this food prepared, packaged and brought to their markets? In this section, we'll talk about how to measure and convert information, how to look at it in various forms, and what it all means. This section will show you how to analyze ideas and theories using numbers, text, tables, and different types of diagrams.

We will cover the following topics:

- Measurements and Units
- Properties of Data
- Ratios, Percentages, Rates, and Proportions
- Probability and Statistics
- Modeling Data
- Using Data as Evidence

Measurements and Units
Part 1

You use **units** in your life every day. The distance you travel to school, the time you spend studying, and the price of this book are all described in terms of units. Units like miles, feet, and meters are units of distance. Seconds, days, and years are units of time. Dollars and cents are units of currency. A dozen is a unit that refers to a group of 12 things.

There are two systems of units frequently used to measure mass, length, and volume. The **imperial system** is used frequently in the United States. While these units appear on the SAT regularly, they are always accompanied by their conversion values. The following table summarizes common units in imperial units of measurement:

Weight	Length	Volume
Ounce	Inch	Cup
Pound: 16 ounces	Foot: 12 inches	Pint: 2 cups
Ton: 2000 pounds	Yard: 3 feet	Quart: 2 pints (4 cups)
	Mile: 1760 yards (5280 feet)	Gallon: 4 quarts (16 cups)

The **metric system** is commonly used internationally and in the scientific community. This system also appears frequently on the SAT. However, their conversion values are not provided and must be memorized. In the metric system, mass is measured in grams (g), length is measured in meters (m), and volume is measured in liters (l).

The metric system uses prefixes, or different word beginnings, to indicate multiples of 10. These prefixes can be combined with any of the units (grams, meters, or liters). Each prefix has a short form that is combined with the unit abbreviation. The following table summarizes the metric system:

Factor	1,000	100	10	0.1	0.01	0.001
Prefix	Kilo	Hecto	Deca	Deci	Centi	Milli
Short Form	K	h	D	d	c	m

For example, a kilogram (kg) is 1,000 grams, a centimeter (cm) is 0.01 meters, and a milliliter (ml) is 0.001 liters.

Here's a quick way to remember the correct order of prefixes. If you write out the prefix abbreviations from biggest to smallest, you'll get:

$$k \quad h \quad D \quad d \quad c \quad m$$

A common phrase to remember this order is **K**ing **H**enry **D**ied **D**rinking **C**hocolate **M**ilk.

Conversions

Some problems on the SAT will require you to convert between different units. To do this, set up a ratio between the two units so that the numerator and the denominator are equal. For example, let's look at converting kilometers (km) to meters (m). Since 1 km = 1,000 m, the ratio of meters to kilometers is:

$$\frac{1,000 \text{ m}}{1 \text{ km}}$$

This can also be written as a ratio of kilometers to meters:

$$\frac{1,000 \text{ m}}{1 \text{ km}} = \frac{1 \text{ km}}{1,000 \text{ m}}$$

The ratio between two units is called a **conversion factor**. Conversion factors are always equal to 1 because the numerator is equal to the denominator.

To convert a measurement into a different value, multiply it by the conversion factor with the desired units on top and the current units on the bottom. When you multiply a measurement by a conversion factor, the old units cancel out in the numerator and denominator. You are left with the new units:

$$\frac{16 \cancel{\text{ km}}}{1} \times \frac{1,000 \text{ m}}{1 \cancel{\text{ km}}} = 16,000 \text{ m}$$

Always check that the units cancel out correctly. You should be able to cancel out all units in the conversion except for the units of the answer.

You may also have to convert between units in different systems on the SAT. The SAT problems will give you the necessary conversion factors.

Example

Approximately how many centimeters are in half a mile? (Assume that 1 mile is equal to 1.6 kilometers.)

This problem requires multiple conversions. First, convert 0.5 miles to kilometers:

$$0.5 \text{ miles} \times \frac{1.6 \text{ km}}{1 \text{ mile}} = 0.8 \text{ km}$$

Now convert 0.8 kilometers to centimeters. It may be easiest to convert first to meters, then centimeters like this:

$$0.8 \text{ km} \times \frac{1,000 \text{ m}}{1 \text{ km}} \times \frac{100 \text{ cm}}{1 \text{ m}} = 80,000 \text{ cm}$$

Half a mile is equal to 80,000 centimeters.

Compound Units

A car's speedometer measures its speed in miles per hour and kilometers per hour. Gas mileage is measured in miles per gallon. These quantities have **compound units**, or units that combine multiple measurements. Speed depends on measurements of both distance and time. Gas mileage depends on measurements of distance and volume of gas consumed.

When you use or convert compound measurements, pay extra attention to the units of quantities and answers. Convert one unit at a time. For example, speed is always distance divided by time. When you convert speed using different units, check that the new units are also distance over time.

Example
What is 15 m/s in km/hr?

You can solve this using the same conversion method you practiced earlier:

$$\frac{15 \text{ m}}{\text{s}} \times \frac{1 \text{ km}}{1,000 \text{ m}} \times \frac{60 \text{ s}}{1 \text{ min}} \times \frac{60 \text{ min}}{1 \text{ hr}} = \frac{54 \text{ km}}{\text{hr}}$$

15 m/s is equal to 54 km/hr. Both m/s and km/hr are correct units of speed because they are units of distance over time.

Word Problems

Units and measurements often appear in SAT word problems. Some of the problems will involve conversions and compound units. Most of the problems that you will solve will be either distance and rate problems, or geometry and measurement problems. Here is an example of a geometry and measurement problem:

Example
A wooden cube has a side length of 20 cm. Its density is 0.65 g/cm³. What is the mass of the block in kilograms? (Density is equal to mass divided by volume.)

Your first step is finding the volume of the block. The volume of a cube is equal to its side length cubed, so the volume of the block is equal to:

$$\text{volume} = (20 \text{ cm})^3 = 8,000 \text{ cm}^3$$

Now you can find the mass of the block through the density formula in the question. You can re-arrange that formula in order to solve for mass:

$$\text{density} = \frac{\text{mass}}{\text{volume}}$$

$$\text{mass} = \text{density} \times \text{volume}$$

Just plug in the values that you have for density and volume:

$$\text{mass} = \frac{0.65\text{g}}{\text{cm}^3} \times 8{,}000 \text{ cm}^3 = 5{,}200 \text{ g}$$

Now you have calculated that the mass of the block is 5,200 grams. The last step is converting the mass of the block from grams to kilograms:

$$5{,}200 \text{ g} \times \frac{1 \text{ kg}}{1{,}000 \text{ g}} = 5.2 \text{ kg}$$

The mass of the block is 5.2 kg.

Now let's take a look at a speed and distance problem:

Example

A train travels from Toronto to Hamilton, a distance of 72 km. The train travels at an average speed of 36 km/hr. How many hours did the trip take?

To solve this problem, all you need to use is the average speed as a conversion factor:

$$72 \text{ km} \times \frac{1 \text{ hr}}{36 \text{ km}} = 2 \text{ hours}$$

Since the kilometer units cancel, you are left with your answer of 2 hours.

Here is an important formula to remember when answering speed and distance questions:

$$\text{distance} = \text{rate} \times \text{time}$$

You could also solve the question above using this formula. Just plug in 72 km for distance and 36 km/hr for rate, and then solve for time:

$$72 \text{ km} = 36 \text{ km/hr} \times \text{time}$$

$$\text{time} = \frac{72 \text{ km}}{36 \text{ km/hr}} = 2 \text{ hours}$$

Using this formula, you get the same answer: the trip took 2 hours.

Part 1 Practice: Measurements and Units

1

How many milliliters are in 0.65 liters?

A)   650

B)   65

C)   6.5

D)   0.65

2

How many meters are there in 18,000 millimeters?

A)   1.8

B)   18

C)   180

D)   1,800

3

Lewis' car is 85 inches wide and he is trying to park in a space with a width of 2.4 yards. Which of the following most accurately states whether Lewis's car will fit in the parking space? (There are 12 inches in a foot and 3 feet in a yard.)

A)   The width of Lewis' car will fit in the parking space.

B)   Lewis' car is too wide for the parking space.

C)   Lewis' car precisely matches the width of the parking space.

D)   Lewis cannot compare the width of the car to the width of the parking space.

4

Seconds	$f(s) = sf(m)$
Minutes	$f(m) = mf(h)$
Hours	$f(h) = 0.8$

If s is the number of seconds in a minute and m is the number of minutes in an hour, what is the value of $f(s)$ in the table above?

A)   1.6

B)   2.9

C)   1,440

D)   2,880

5

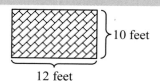

10 feet

12 feet

Mr. and Mrs. Liu are covering their living room floor with tiles, as shown in the diagram above. If the tiles cost $5 per square foot, how much will they spend on tiles?

A) $120

B) $240

C) $600

D) $2,400

6

Alex drove 6 miles from his house to the grocery store at an average speed of s mph. On the way back, Alex drove this same distance at an average speed of 33 mph. If Alex's average speed was 27.5 mph, what is the value for s?

A) 33

B) 22

C) 11

D) 10

7

Tyler went for a 20 km bike ride. If he rode for an hour and 20 minutes, what was his average speed, in kilometers per hour?

A) 30

B) 20

C) 16

D) 15

8

To train for an upcoming 10 km race, Mariam ran 5 km to the post office and back. If it took her 25 minutes to run there and 30 minutes to run back, what was her average pace over her whole run, in minutes per kilometer?

Questions 9 and 10 refer to the following information.

A factory produces silver and gold alloys for mass market jewelry stores. Its suppliers measure the silver and gold in grams, but the plant measures the two elements by volume.

9

If the density of silver is 10.5 g/cm³, what is the mass, in grams, of a rectangular block of silver with the dimensions 2 cm by 5 cm by 10 cm?

10

The density of gold is 19.3 g/cm³. What volume of gold, rounded to the nearest tenth of a cubic centimeter, has the same mass as 100 cm³ of silver?

Properties of Data
Part 2

Data sets are just collections of numbers. Without context, they are not very useful. In order to interpret what the numbers mean and to make conclusions based on the data, you need to be able to determine the data's properties.

Let's say that a small group gets scores of 20, 15, 13, 12, 20 and 18 on a test—are these good scores? If the test is out of 20, then perhaps they are, but what if the test is out of 25 or 30? Also, can we say that most of the group did well if the average score is fairly high? If another person, Michael, joins the group and gets a 17 on the same test, is this a good mark compared to the others? Further, how does the addition of Michael's individual score affect the group's overall score?

The properties of data, range, mean, median, mode, and standard deviation will help us to answer these questions. In addition to looking at numbers, you'll also need to be able to interpret data presented visually in a chart or a graph on the SAT. Let's look at these concepts and how to use them.

Range

The **range** of a set of data is the difference between its biggest and smallest values. All data in a set of data fall within the set's range. To find the range of any set of data, put the data in numerical order and subtract the smallest from the biggest value.

Example

Dmitri's History Quiz Scores				
Quiz 1	Quiz 2	Quiz 3	Quiz 4	Quiz 5
87	83	94	87	90

What is the range of Dmitri's quiz scores in the chart above?

To find the range of these scores, let's first put them in numerical order:

$$83, 87, 87, 90, 94$$

Dmitri's lowest score was 83 and his highest was 94, so his range is the difference between these two:

$$\text{Range} = 94 - 83 = 11$$

Dmitri's scores fall within a range of 11 points.

Mean

The **mean** (or arithmetic mean) of a set of data is the same as its **average**. To calculate the mean or average of a set of data, add up all of the data values and divide by the total number of data points:

$$\text{Mean} = \frac{\text{Sum of all values in the set}}{\text{Total number of terms in the set}}$$

Example

What is the mean of Dmitri's quiz scores from the previous chart?

First add up all his scores. Then divide by the number of quizzes:

$$\frac{87 + 83 + 94 + 87 + 90}{5} = \frac{441}{5} = 88.2$$

Dmitri's average score is 88.2.

Median

The **median** refers to the value that is exactly in the middle of a set of data. To find the median, put all of the data in numerical order and locate the middle number.

Example

What is the median of Dmitri's quiz scores?

Put the scores in numerical order:

$$83, 87, 87, 90, 94$$

The middle number in this data set is 87, so Dmitri's median history quiz score is 87.

What if your data set has an even number of values, so there is no middle number? In this case, the median is the average of the two numbers closest to the middle.

Example

Dmitri is able to score a 99 on his sixth history quiz. What is the median of his new set of scores?

The data set will now be:

$$83, 87, 87, 90, 94, 99$$

There is no number in the middle of this set of data, but the two numbers closest to the middle are 87 and 90. To find the median, take the average of these two numbers:

$$\frac{87 + 90}{2} = 88.5$$

The average of 87 and 90 is 88.5, so 88.5 is the median of Dmitri's six quiz scores.

Mode

The **mode** of a set of data refers to the value that occurs most frequently. A set of data can have one or more modes if there are one or more numbers that occur more frequently than any other number. A set of data may have no mode if all values occur the same number of times.

> **Example**
>
> Dmitri and his classmates received the following scores on their last history quiz: 91, 88, 94, 90, 82, 79, 84, 94, 85, 88, 93, 97, 92, 80, 96. Identify the mode or modes in this data set.

The answer to this question is easiest to find out if we put the data in numerical order:

$$79, 80, 82, 84, 85, 88, 88, 90, 91, 92, 93, 94, 94, 96, 97$$

Both 88 and 94 occur two times, and the rest of the values only occur once. Therefore, 88 and 94 are the two modes of these quiz scores.

Standard Deviation

Standard deviation measures how much the values in a set of data vary from its mean. The greater the standard deviation, the farther the data points are from the mean. For example, take a look at these two lists of data:

$$\text{List A: } 1, 2, 3, 10, 17, 18, 19$$
$$\text{List B: } 7, 8, 9, 10, 11, 12, 13$$

Although these two lists both have a mean of 10, List A has a higher standard deviation because the points are more spread out.

While you will most likely not need to calculate standard deviation on the SAT directly, standard deviation can be found with the following expression, where m is the mean of the data set, n is the number of data points, and each value of x represents an individual data point:

$$\sqrt{\frac{(x_1 - m)^2 + (x_2 - m)^2 + (x_3 - m)^2 + \ldots + (x_n - m)^2}{n}}$$

To use this formula, first square the difference between each data point and the mean. Then, add together these squares, divide by the number of data points, and take the square root of the result.

Example

What is the standard deviation of the data set $\{1, 3, 6, 8, 12\}$?

First, calculate the mean:

$$m = \frac{1 + 3 + 6 + 8 + 12}{5}$$

$$m = 6$$

For each data point, find its difference from the mean, square this difference, and add together the squares:

$$= (1 - 6)^2 + (3 - 6)^2 + (6 - 6)^2 + (8 - 6)^2 + (12 - 6)^2$$
$$= 25 + 9 + 0 + 4 + 36$$
$$= 74$$

Then, take the average of the differences by dividing the sum by the number of data points:

$$\frac{74}{5} = 14.8$$

And finally, take the square root:

$$\sqrt{14.8} \approx 3.85$$

The standard deviation of this data set is about 3.85.

You can also say that a data point is a certain number of standard deviations away from the mean. For example, let's look at the first number in the data set above—the number 1. The mean of the data set is 6, so 1 is 5 units away from the mean. In order to express this difference in terms of standard deviations, just divide by the standard deviation of the data set, which is 3.85:

$$\frac{5}{3.85} \approx 1.3$$

1 is approximately 1.3 standard deviations from the mean.

Charts

One way to make properties of data easy to see is to display them as a chart or graph. When you see a question with a chart or graph, examine it carefully to make sure you understand it. Ask yourself the following questions:

- What is the main purpose of this chart or graph?
- What is being measured?
- What is the **scale**, or what units are being used?

Let's use these questions to analyze the chart below:

Population (in thousands) by Town, 1960-2000			
Town	1960	1980	2000
Cedarville	72	83	104
Franklin	80	82	73
Pine Ridge	121	136	143

- What is the main purpose of this chart or graph? From the title, you can tell that the chart above shows the population of several towns from 1960 to 2000.
- What is being measured? The chart is comparing the population of these three different towns (Cedarville, Franklin, and Pine Ridge) at three different dates (1960, 1980, and 2000).
- What is the scale, or what units are being used? The numbers give the population of each town for each year. Notice that the data is represented in thousands.

Now that you are familiar with this data in chart format, let's take a look at how it might be represented in different types of graphs. The most common types of graphs on the SAT include pie charts, bar graphs, line graphs, and histograms.

Pie Charts

A **pie chart** compares different sections of data as fractions out of a whole. A circle represents the total amount, and differently sized sections of that circle represent parts out of the total amount. A legend or labels on the chart will explain what data each section represents.

Let's look again at the populations of Cedarville, Franklin, and Pine Ridge in 1960. Here is a representation of the data as a pie chart:

Population Breakdown
by Town in 1960

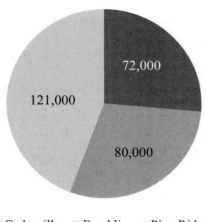

- Cedarville - Franklin - Pine Ridge

The title of this graph tells you that you are looking at the population of the three towns in 1960. The legend tells you that each of the slices in this pie chart represents a town, and the entire pie chart represents the total population of all three towns. The data labels for each slice also tell you exactly how many people lived in each town.

You can also estimate the relative proportion of residents by looking at the sizes of their slices in the pie chart. You can tell that slightly more than a quarter of the people lived in Cedarville, slightly less than a third lived in Franklin, and slightly less than half lived in Pine Ridge.

Bar Graphs

A **bar graph** uses bars of different lengths to compare different categories of data. Bar graphs represent data along two axes, using vertical or horizontal bars. If a bar graph uses differently colored or patterned bars, the legend will explain what other variables these colors or patterns represent.

The data from the chart we saw earlier can be represented in a bar graph:

Population by Town,
1960-2000

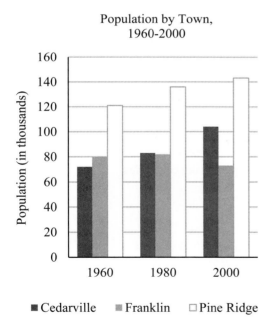

- Cedarville - Franklin □ Pine Ridge

In this graph, the legend tells you that the different-colored bars represent different towns. These are grouped together at each date along the horizontal axis. The vertical axis displays what is being measured: population. Again, you are told that the units are in thousands.

Because numbers are given in thousands, each tick mark along the vertical axis represents 20,000 people. With these tick marks, you can tell that the population of Pine Ridge in 1960 was about 120,000, and by 1980 it had grown by about 15,000. You can also tell that the populations of Cedarville and Franklin were relatively similar in 1960 and 1980, but they differed by about 30,000 people in 2000.

Line Graphs

A **line graph** uses a line or several lines to represent changes in amounts, usually over time. Like bar graphs, line graphs also represent data along two axes. The horizontal *x*-axis displays different dates or time periods, and the vertical *y*-axis displays the amounts being measured.

Here is the population data for Cedarville, Franklin, and Pine Ridge as a line graph:

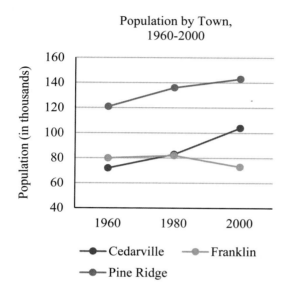

The legend tells you that each line on this graph represents the population of a different town. Just like our bar graph, the scale of the *y*-axis tells us that each tick mark represents 20,000 people.

Because this graph displays lines across the whole time period, you can use the graph to make estimates about population at specific years. For example, you don't know the exact population of Pine Ridge in 1970, but by looking at the middle of the line drawn from 1960 to 1980, you can estimate that the population was around 130,000. You can also use the slopes of line segments to determine the rate of change between two data points.

Histograms

A **histogram** is a graphical distribution of data, grouped together by values or ranges of values. By grouping the data together, a histogram displays the **frequency** of those groupings, which is the number of times those values or ranges occurred in the data set. A histogram is another tool that allows you to graphically calculate specific statistical information such as range, mean, median, and mode. Furthermore, the graphical representation of data often allows you to quickly find or estimate some of this information without calculation. Note that while they look similar, histograms will always display frequencies of one individual category, while bar graphs display many categories.

Here is an example of a histogram:

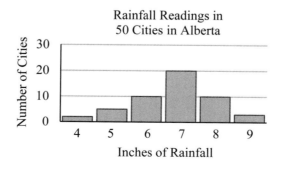

The *x*-axis displays the different rainfall readings (in inches) that were recorded. The *y*-axis displays the number of cities that recorded each reading. This information tells you the frequency with which each reading occurred. For example, the graph shows that 20 cities recorded 7" of rainfall, but only about 2 cities recorded 4" of rainfall.

It is easy to find the mode and the range of the data from the histogram. 7" was the most frequent value recorded, so 7 is the mode of this data. To find the range of this data, subtract the smallest rainfall reading (4") from the largest (9"): $9 - 4 = 5$. The range of the data is 5.

You can use the histogram to calculate the mean. First, you need to multiply each grouping by its frequency and add those products together:

$$(4 \times 2) + (5 \times 5) + (6 \times 10) + (7 \times 20) + (8 \times 10) + (9 \times 3) = 340$$

You can find the total number of readings in the graph by adding together all of the frequencies for each rainfall reading:

$$2 + 5 + 10 + 20 + 10 + 3 = 50$$

Finally, divide the sum of all of the data by the number of values:

$$\frac{340}{50} = 6.8$$

The mean rainfall reading in this data is 6.8 inches.

You can also find the median from the histogram. Because the median is the middle number in a data set, you need to find which rainfall reading would represent the middle number if all 50 readings were arranged in order from least to greatest. Because you have 50 readings, the middle number would be the average of the 25th and 26th readings.

Which group on the histogram would contain the 25th reading? To find this, start adding up the frequencies of each grouping, from left to right, and stop when you get above 25. There were 2 readings of 4", 5 readings of 5", and 10 readings of 6". This is 17 readings total, which is still less than 25. However, there were 20 readings of 7", which brings you to 37 readings total. Therefore, the 25th and 26th readings must both be in the 7" group. You can conclude that the median rainfall reading is 7".

Part 2 Practice: Properties of Data

1

A set of five numbers had an average of 14. When two of these numbers were removed, the remaining three numbers had an average of 13. What is the sum of the two numbers that were removed?

A)   1

B)   13.5

C)   15

D)   31

2

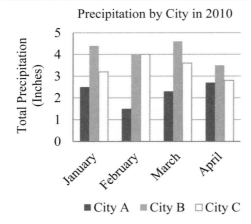

Precipitation by City in 2010

■ City A   ■ City B   □ City C

According to the graph above, during which month did City B experience about twice as much precipitation as City A?

A)   January

B)   February

C)   March

D)   April

3

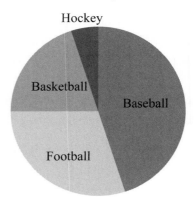

Survey of 200 Students' Favorite Sports

According to the diagram above, approximately how many surveyed students reported either hockey or basketball as their favorite sport?

A)   25

B)   50

C)   100

D)   200

Newspapers Delivered on Anthony's Paper Route

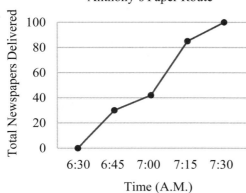

The histogram below shows the test scores of students in a writing class.

Test Scores in a Writing Class

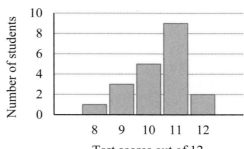

Test scores out of 12

4

Which of the following is the best estimate for the number of newspapers that Anthony delivered between 7:15 and 7:30 A.M.?

A) 15

B) 45

C) 75

D) 100

5

Over which 15-minute time period did Anthony deliver newspapers at the fastest rate?

A) 6:30 A.M.-6:45 A.M.

B) 6:45 A.M.-7:00 A.M.

C) 7:00 A.M.-7:15 A.M.

D) 7:15 A.M.-7:30 A.M.

6

What is the median test score?

A) 1.05

B) 10

C) 10.4

D) 11

7

What is the mode of this data set?

A) 1.05

B) 10

C) 10.4

D) 11

What is the mean of the data for the set {–4, 8, 2, 6}?

William measures the heights of his five friends in inches. His results, in inches, are 60, 62, 63, 66, and 69. What is the standard deviation of the heights of his friends, to the nearest hundredth of an inch?

Highway Repair Costs by County in 2011

County	Highway Repair Costs	Miles of Highway in County
Pinellas	$45,000	300
Hillsborough	$169,000	1,300
Glendale	$81,000	450

Pinellas County wants to reduce the amount of money it spends repairing each mile of highway. If Pinellas County had repaired its highways at the same repair cost per mile as Hillsborough County in the chart above, how much money, in dollars, would Pinellas County have saved in 2011? (Note: disregard the $ sign when gridding your answer.)

Ratios, Percentages, Proportions, and Rates
Part 3

Ratios, percentages, proportions, and rates compare two or more quantities, either by comparing parts to a whole or by representing a relationship between the quantities. In Section 3, we covered some basic properties of these topics. However, some of the problems involving these topics on the SAT will require more steps or more complex algebra than the examples in Section 3. Let's see what this looks like.

Fractions and Proportions

Word problems with fractions and proportions will often require you to multiply a number by a proportion or to find an equivalent proportion. To find a fraction of a number, multiply the number by the fraction:

$$\frac{3}{8} \text{ of } 24 = \frac{3}{8} \times 24 = 9$$

You can find equivalent proportions by setting them equal to each other. For example, if 12 is $\frac{3}{4}$ of x, you can find x by setting up the equivalent proportions:

$$\frac{12}{x} = \frac{3}{4}$$

Which you can solve by cross-multiplying:

$$3x = 4 \times 12$$

$$x = 16$$

Example

Four friends ate a whole pizza. Shelley had $\frac{1}{5}$ of the pizza, Ming had 4 slices, Lily had 3 slices, and Adam had 1 slice. How many slices did Shelley have?

To find the number of slices that Shelley had, you first need to find the total number of slices in the pizza. The four friends ate the whole pizza, and Shelley ate $\frac{1}{5}$, so Ming, Lily, and Adam must have eaten

$1 - \dfrac{1}{5} = \dfrac{4}{5}$ of the pizza. This means that $4 + 3 + 1 = 8$ slices make up $\dfrac{4}{5}$ of the pizza. You can write this as a proportion:

$$\dfrac{8 \text{ slices}}{\text{Total slices}} = \dfrac{4}{5}$$

Then, cross-multiply to find the total slices in the pizza:

$$40 \text{ slices} = 4 \times \text{Total slices}$$

$$\text{Total slices} = 10$$

Now, you can calculate the number of slices that Shelley ate by setting up a proportion and cross-multiplying:

$$\dfrac{\text{Shelley's slices}}{10 \text{ total slices}} = \dfrac{1}{5}$$

$$5 \times \text{Shelley's slices} = 10$$

$$\text{Shelley's slices} = 2$$

Shelley ate 2 slices of pizza.

Ratios

Ratio problems will involve applying ratios to quantities or finding ratios from quantities. It is important to remember that ratios are different than fractions or proportions: they compare a part to a part instead of a part to a whole. To find the whole, add all of the parts. For example, the ratio 2:5:3 has a whole of $2 + 5 + 3 = 10$.

Remember that you can convert ratios to fractions. Each part of the ratio becomes a numerator, and the denominator is the whole. If your ratio is 1:3:6, for example, the denominator will be $1 + 3 + 6 = 10$ and the fractions would be $\dfrac{1}{10}$, $\dfrac{3}{10}$, and $\dfrac{6}{10}$.

It may help to use variables when working with ratios. If you know the total quantity that the ratio describes, you can write it as the sum of each part multiplied by a variable.

Example

The measures of the two acute angles of a right triangle have the ratio 11:4. What is the difference between the two angle measures?

To solve this problem, you need to recall some geometric properties of triangles. First, the sum of the angle measures in a triangle is 180°. Since this is a right triangle, one of those angles is 90°, so the remaining acute angles must have a sum of $180° - 90° = 90°$.

You also know that one angle measure is equal to 11 times an integer, and the second angle measure is equal to 4 times the same integer. If you call the unknown integer x, you could represent the two angle measures as $11x$ and $4x$. Because you know that the two angles add to 90°, you can set up an equation to solve for x:

$$11x + 4x = 90°$$
$$15x = 90°$$
$$x = \frac{90°}{15}$$
$$x = 6°$$

Now, you can plug the value of x back into your expressions for each angle measure: $11x = 66°$ and $4x = 24°$. The question asks for the difference between these two angle measures:

$$66° - 24° = 42°$$

Your answer is 42 degrees.

Percentages

These word problems will give you a mix of percentages and quantities. If you have to find a percent of a whole number, like 12% of 4, multiply the percentage by the whole: $4 \times 0.12 = 0.48$.

If you are given a quantity that is a percent of a whole, divide the quantity by the percentage to get the whole. For example, if 3 is 5% of x, then $x = \dfrac{3}{0.05} = 60$.

Example

Two sweaters have the same original price. One sweater is then marked up 20% and the other is put on sale for 20% off. The difference between the new prices is $9.60. What was the original price of each sweater?

Let's say that p represents the original price of each sweater. The marked-up price of the first sweater is 20% greater, so you could represent this by $1.2p$. The sale price of the second sweater is 20% less, so you could present this by $0.8p$. You know that the difference between these prices is $9.60, so you can set up an equation to solve for p:

$$1.2p - 0.8p = 9.60$$

$$0.4p = 9.60$$

$$p = \frac{9.60}{0.4}$$

$$p = 24$$

The original price of each sweater was $24.

Rates

Rate problems appear frequently on the SAT. Remember that rates compare two related quantities, like distance and time. You can often set up rate problems as equivalent proportions. Be sure to write the proportions so that the two rates have the same units, and make sure that your answer is in the correct units as well.

Example

Paola is training for a 10 km race. She can run 5 miles in 36 minutes. If she keeps this pace, what will her race time be? (1 mile is equal to approximately 1.6 kilometers).

First you should find Paola's pace in minutes per mile:

$$\frac{36 \text{ min}}{5 \text{ miles}} = \frac{7.2 \text{ min}}{1 \text{ mile}}$$

Since the length of the race is in kilometers, you need to convert the pace to minutes per kilometer:

$$\frac{7.2 \text{ min}}{1 \text{ mile}} \times \frac{1 \text{ mile}}{1.6 \text{ km}} = \frac{4.5 \text{ min}}{1 \text{ km}}$$

Finally, to find the time it would take Paola to run 10 km, multiply her pace in minutes per km by the distance of the race:

$$10 \text{ km} \times \frac{4.5 \text{ min}}{1 \text{ km}} = 45 \text{ min}$$

Paola's race time will be 45 minutes.

For some rate problems, you will have to combine rates. To combine rates, first make sure that they have the same units. Then add them together in their fraction form with a common denominator. The units of the new rate will be the same as the units of each individual rate.

Rachel can grade 5 tests in 6 minutes and Sebastian can grade 2 tests in 3 minutes. Rachel and Sebastian have 21 tests to grade. If they work together, how long will it take them to grade the tests?

First, you need to find the rate at which Rachel and Sebastian can grade tests separately. Divide the number of tests by the number of minutes: Rachel's rate is $\frac{5}{6}$ tests/min and Sebastian's rate is $\frac{2}{3}$ tests/min.

Then, to find their combined rate, you need to add the two rates:

$$\frac{5}{6} + \frac{2}{3} = \frac{5}{6} + \frac{4}{6} = \frac{9}{6} = 1.5$$

Rachel and Sebastian have a combined rate of 1.5 tests per minute. Now you can use this rate to find the time it would take Rachel and Sebastian to grade the 21 tests. Remember to flip the rate so that the unit "tests" cancels:

$$21 \text{ tests} \times \frac{1 \text{ min}}{1.5 \text{ tests}} = 14 \text{ min}$$

It will take Rachel and Sebastian 14 minutes to grade the tests if they work together.

Part 3 Practice: Ratios, Percentages, Proportions, and Rates

1

When the width x is doubled and the height y is tripled, the rectangle above becomes a square. Which of the following expresses x in terms of y?

A) $\frac{2}{3}y$

B) $\frac{3}{2}y$

C) $2y$

D) $3y$

2

If $2x = 5y$ and $4y = 3z$, what is the ratio of x to z?

A) 8:15

B) 10:12

C) 12:10

D) 15:8

3

If Antony buys an $80 guitar on sale for 10% off and pays 8% sales tax on the reduced price, how much does he pay for the guitar?

A) $66.24

B) $72.00

C) $77.76

D) $86.40

4

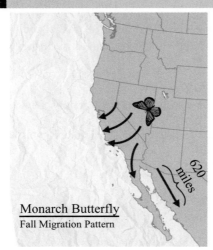

Monarch Butterfly
Fall Migration Pattern

The migratory routes of a population of Monarch butterflies on the west coast is shown in the graph above. If the butterflies travel an average of 5 miles per hour for 12 hours each day, how many days will it take for the Monarchs in the southern-most migratory route to reach their destination?

A)   8

B)   11

C)   12

D)   20

5

A store sells CDs at 20% off the displayed price. The store buys CDs for $12 each. If the store owner wants to make a 10% profit on the CDs, what price should she display for each CD?

A) $13.20

B) $15.60

C) $16.50

D) $17.80

6

Antja's Quizzes	Grade
Exam 1	85
Exam 2	93
Exam 3	91
Exam 4	97

The table above shows Antja's exam scores in her geometry class. The first exam had 20 questions and each additional exam had 20 more than the previous exam. What percent of the total number of questions did Antja get correct? (Note: Round your answer to the nearest percent.)

A)   84%

B)   86%

C)   88%

D)   93%

7

Factory Production Schedule

	Monday	Tuesday
Nails	30 tons	90 tons
Screws	18 tons	54 tons

A factory, producing nails and screws on Monday and Tuesday, discovers that 4% of the nails produced are defective, and 6% of the screws are defective. If nails and screws are produced in the ratio represented by its production schedule shown above, what percent of the total nails and screws produced are defective?

A)   3.8

B)   4.75

C)   5.25

D)   38

Mark's car has a gas mileage of 36 miles per gallon. If gas costs $2.40 per gallon and he drives 120 miles, how much gas money will Mark pay for his trip? (Note: Disregard the $ sign when gridding your answer.)

A jar of buttons contains purple, red and black buttons. The ratio of purple to black buttons is 12:7. If there are 5 red buttons for every 4 purple buttons that are in the jar, what fraction of the buttons is purple?

Person	Rate of Filing Papers
Lily	4 papers/16 seconds
Arjun	x papers/ 4 seconds
Emily	2 papers/ 8 seconds

Lily, Arjun, and Emily are filing papers at the rates represented by the chart above. Together, Lily, Arjun, and Emily can file 3 papers every 4 seconds. If Arjun works at the same rate, how many minutes would it take him, working alone, to file 60 papers?

Probability and Statistics
Part 4

If you've ever used a weather forecast or looked up the chance that your favorite sports team will win a game, you have used **probability**. Probability describes how likely something is to happen. On the SAT, you will use probability to solve word problems and problems involving data in charts or graphs. First, let's look at some important terms.

A **set** is a group of things, often numbers. Each number or thing in a set is called an **element**. Sets are often written inside brackets, like this: {−3, 0, 2, 6.6, 100}.

A useful tool for working with sets of numbers is the **Venn diagram**. A Venn diagram uses overlapping circles to demonstrate relationships between sets of numbers. Here is an example of a Venn diagram of two sets:

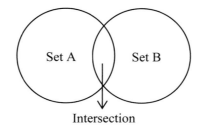

Each set is represented by a circle. If the sets share elements, those elements go in the portion of the Venn diagram where the circles overlap: this portion is called the **intersection** of the sets.

If you combine all the numbers in the Venn diagram, you will get the union of the sets. The **union** of two or more sets contains all the elements of all the sets.

Example

At Forestview High School, 60 students are taking math, science, or both. If 50 of these students are taking math and 30 students are taking science, how many are taking both?

You may have noticed that 50 + 30 is more than 60. This reminds us that some students are taking both math and science, so they are counted in both categories. These students represent the intersection of the two sets. Let's represent the intersection with the variable x. Our Venn Diagram then looks like this:

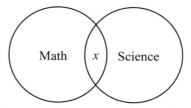

Since 50 students are taking math, you know that the total students in the "MATH" circle must be 50. Since there are x students overlapping both circles, the students only taking math is $50 - x$ because:

$$x + (50 - x) = 50$$

Notice that 50 are all the students in "MATH", and that this number also includes the students in both "MATH and SCIENCE" (your x variable).

In the same way, the number of students only taking science is $30 - x$. Our updated Venn diagram is:

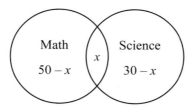

You know that the total number of students is 60. Since this number represents the union of the two sets, it equals the number of students in the three areas:

$$(50 - x) + x + (30 - x) = 60$$

Now you can solve for x:

$$80 - x = 60$$

$$x = 20$$

You have found that the number of students taking both math and science is 20.

Probability

Probability is the likelihood that something will happen. Scientists and mathematicians can make educated predictions about the future by analyzing data and using the principles of probability. For example, weather forecasters use probability to predict the chance of rain tomorrow, and medical researchers use probability to predict people's chance of developing heart or lung disease.

The formula to calculate probability is:

$$\text{Probability} = \frac{\text{Number of ways to get a certain outcome}}{\text{Number of possible outcomes}}$$

Let's take a look at a common SAT probability question:

Example

There is a group of six people who are each given a unique integer from 1 through 6. If one person is randomly selected from the group, what is the probability that they were given an even number?

Since one person is selected at random, there is an equal chance that they have any integer from 1 to 6. Therefore, there are six equal possible outcomes. To find the probability that they have an even number, you divide the number of even-number outcomes (3) by the number of possible outcomes (6):

$$\text{Probability of an even number} = \frac{3}{6} = \frac{1}{2}$$

The probability that the person has an even number is $\frac{1}{2}$. You can also state this as a decimal (0.5) or as a percent (50%).

Some problems will give you a probability and ask you to solve for numbers:

Example

A biologist is studying a pond of 40 frogs. If the probability of choosing a black frog is $\frac{1}{4}$, how many black frogs are in the pond?

The question tells us that there is a $\frac{1}{4}$ or 25% probability of choosing a black frog. You're told that the number of total frogs is 40. Let's write the probability of choosing a black frog using our formula:

$$\text{Probability of choosing a black frog} = \frac{\text{Number of black frogs}}{40} = \frac{1}{4}$$

Now all you need to do is solve by cross-multiplying your proportion:

$$\frac{x}{40} = \frac{1}{4}$$

$$40 = 4x$$

$$x = 10$$

The number of black frogs in the pond is equal to 10.

Understanding Probability

Probabilities are written as fractions or decimals between 0 and 1, or as percentages between 0% and 100%. The lower the probability, the less likely an event is to occur. The higher the probability, the more likely an event is to occur.

A probability of 0 means an event is impossible and will never occur.

Example

A group of six people are each given a unique integer from 1 through 6. If one person is randomly selected, what is the probability that they were given a 7?

There are six possible outcomes, but no one in the group was given the number 7. Therefore, there are zero ways that one person was given a 7. If you plug this into our formula, you get:

$$\text{Probability of a 7} = \frac{0}{6} = 0$$

The probability of selecting someone with a 7 is 0, so there is a no chance that the person will have a 7. This event is impossible.

On the other hand, a probability of 1 or 100% means that an event is absolutely certain to happen.

Example

A group of six people are each given a unique integer from 1 through 6. If one person is randomly selected, what is the probability that they were given a positive number?

There are six possible outcomes, and all six of these numbers are positive numbers. Therefore, there are also six ways to get a positive number outcome:

$$\text{Probability of a positive number} = \frac{6}{6} = 1$$

The probability of that the person has a positive number is 1, so this event is always going to happen.

Since a probability of 1 means an event will always happen, you will never get a probability greater than 1 or 100%.

If you know the probability of getting a certain outcome, you can also calculate the probability of *not* getting that outcome. These two possibilities are called **complementary events**. If you add the probabilities of complementary events, you will get 1. This means that every outcome will be one of the two complementary events.

A group of six people are each given a unique integer from 1 through 6. If one person is randomly selected, what is the probability that they do not have a 4?

Someone having a 4 and not having a 4 are complementary events. Since the probability of selecting someone with a 4 is $\frac{1}{6}$, the probability of not selecting someone with a 4 is:

$$1 - \frac{1}{6} = \frac{5}{6}$$

There is a $\frac{5}{6}$ chance of not selecting someone with a 4, but of selecting someone with any of the other possible numbers (1, 2, 3, 5, or 6).

Two events are **mutually exclusive** if it is impossible for both of them to happen at the same time. For example, if you select one person from a group of six people who are all given unique integers from 1 through 6, it is impossible that the person will have both the number 5 and the number 3. They will either have one number or the other. Complementary events are always mutually exclusive.

You can find the chance of one event *or* another event occurring by adding together their individual probabilities:

A group of six people are each given a unique integer from 1 through 6. If one person is randomly selected, what is the probability that they have a 5 or a 6?

The probability that they have 5 is $\frac{1}{6}$ and the probability that they have 3 is also $\frac{1}{6}$. To find your chances that they have a 5 or a 3, add their probabilities together:

$$\text{Probability of a 5 or 3} = \frac{1}{6} + \frac{1}{6} = \frac{1}{3}$$

If you add together the probabilities of all of the possible mutually-exclusive outcomes of an event, you will get the number 1. For example, there is a probability of 1 that your selected person will have a 1, 2, 3, 4, 5, or 6 if there are six people who are each given unique integers from 1 to 6.

Conditional Probability

Conditional probability is the probability that an event occurs given that another event has already occurred. Questions dealing with conditional probability are often phrased as, "If X is true, what is the probability of P?" This is the most important form of probability in the SAT. It pops up frequently in tables and in statistics. Since you are dealing with multiple events, you need to figure out what relationship the events have to each other.

If there are multiple events whose outcomes do *not* depend on each other, they are called **independent events**. The probability of multiple independent events is simply the product of their separate probabilities. If Event A has a probability of 0.7, and Event B has a probability of 0.2, the probability of both Event A and Event B occurring is:

$$0.7 \times 0.2 = 0.14$$

Events are **dependent** if one event affects the probability of the other event occurring. If two events are dependent, you need to figure out what happens to the probability of the second event after the first one has taken place:

Example

Janice, a geologist, is cataloguing the composition of a sample of 52 rocks. She selects her first rock and then sets it aside before selecting a second rock. If rocks with the same composition are always found in groups of four, what is the probability that both rocks are made of granite?

The probability for the first rock is easy: there are 52 rocks and 4 of them are granite, so Janice has a $\frac{4}{52}$ or $\frac{1}{13}$ chance of selecting a granite rock.

However, now that she has removed one rock, the number of rocks in the sample has changed. She now has only 51 rocks in her sample. If her first rock was made of granite, there are only 3 granite rocks left. Therefore, the probability that her second rock will also be made of granite is $\frac{3}{51}$. You've figured out the probability of the first event, and how the probability of the second event will be affected if the first event takes place. You can now multiply these probabilities together to find the probability of both events occurring:

$$\text{Probability of selecting two granite rocks} = \frac{1}{13} \times \frac{3}{51} = \frac{3}{663} = \frac{1}{221}$$

If Janice is selecting two rocks one at a time, the probability that she will pick two granite rocks is 1 out of 221.

Analyzing Two-Way Tables

Conditional probability may also be used to analyze two-way tables. This is by far the most frequent use of probability on the SAT exams.

	Classical	Rock	Pop	Total
9th grade	50	21	39	110
10th grade	63	22	20	105
11th grade	3	90	19	112
12th grade	47	12	44	103
Total	163	145	122	430

The table on the left summarizes students' preferences for music. If one student out of 430 students surveyed is randomly selected, what is the probability that the student is in the 9th grade?

This is a regular probability question. There are 110 9th graders out of 430 total students, so the probability that the student is in the 9th grade is $\frac{110}{430}$, or $\frac{11}{43}$, or approximately 26%.

A more complicated question for the same table is:

What is the probability that a student prefers rock music given that he is in the 11th grade?

This is a conditional probability question, since you are only looking at the students in 11th grade. There are 90 students who prefer rock music out of the 112 students in 11th grade, so the probability is $\frac{90}{112} = \frac{45}{56}$, or approximately 80%.

Making Predictions

You can use samples of data to make predictions about larger populations or groups. The accuracy of these estimates depends on properties of the sample data such as size and selection process. You will discuss how to evaluate sample data in Part 6.

In order to make an estimate for a population based on sample data, you treat the sample data as proportional to the entire population. This allows us to use proportions and percentages to make estimates for the whole population.

	For Mandatory Math	Against Mandatory Math	Total
Male	126	42	168
Female	81	69	150
Total	207	111	318

Jaetown surveyed residents about their opinion on mandatory math education. The results are summarized in the chart on the left. Jaetown has a population of 12,000 female residents and 13,000 male residents. Based on the survey results, how many female residents would the city predict to support the policy?

The question asks for the number of female residents who are "for" the policy. The survey found that $\frac{81}{150}$ = 54% of the women surveyed supported mandatory math education. Multiply the percent of women supporting the policy in the survey by the total number of female residents in the city:

$$12,000 \times 0.54 = 6,480$$

Our estimate is that around 6,480 of the female residents in Jaetown support mandatory math education.

Part 4 Practice: Probability and Statistics

1

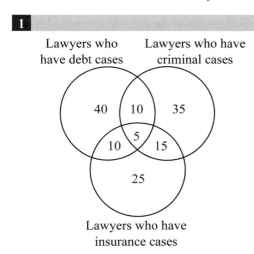

Lawyers who have debt cases   Lawyers who have criminal cases

Lawyers who have insurance cases

According to the Venn Diagram above, how many lawyers have both debt and criminal cases, but do not have insurance cases?

A) 10

B) 15

C) 25

D) 75

2

The Instruments that Students Play

Instrument	Number of Students
Piano	52
Violin	30
No Instrument	24

The results of a survey of students who play an instrument are shown above. If there were 100 students surveyed, how many students play both the piano and the violin?

A) 3

B) 6

C) 12

D) The answer cannot be determined from the information given.

Two cities compared how many hours their
population exercised over a one-month period.
The results, measured according to the age and
hours of exercise, are summarized in the table
below.

Monthly Average Number of Hours

Age of Population	Georgetown	Lakeview
18 years or younger	40	20
19 to 25 years	20	40
26 to 34 years	28	40
35 to 45 years	40	28
46 to 55 years	20	12
56 years or older	12	20

3

According to the data, if one Georgetown
resident from each age group were
compared with one Lakeview resident from
each age group, which of the following is
true?

A) The six Georgetown residents would
   most likely exercise more than the six
   Lakeview residents.

B) The six Georgetown residents would
   most likely exercise less than the six
   Lakeview residents.

C) Both the six Georgetown and six
   Lakeview residents would most likely
   exercise a similar amount.

D) There is not enough information to
   compare the residents from Georgetown
   and Lakeview.

4

Three 36-year-old residents are randomly
selected from Georgetown and from
Lakeview. If one 36-year-old person is
randomly picked from the group of 6 people,
how many hours would they most likely
exercise in a month?

A) 20

B) 28

C) 34

D) 40

5

The weatherman of Romley County predicts
that there will be no chance of rain on
Tuesday if the wind speeds are less than 15
mph and a 20% chance of rain if the
northern winds are over 15 mph. If satellite
imagery indicates that there is a 75% chance
that the northern winds will be over 15 mph,
what is the probability that rain will fall on
Tuesday in Romley County?

A) 26.66%

B) 21.33%

C) 20%

D) 15%

Repairs During the Year 2010 by Car Model

Car Model	Repaired	Not Repaired	Total
N-Model	397	305	702
K-Model	322	226	548
Total	719	531	1250

6

Based on the table above, what is the percent probability that a car is N-model given that it underwent a repair in 2010?

A) 31.8%

B) 55.2%

C) 56.2%

D) 56.6%

7

There were a total of 3000 K-model cars in 2010. Based on the table above, approximately how K-model cars would be expected to have been repaired in 2010?

A) 773

B) 1237

C) 1343

D) 1762

8

Two colonies of bacteria are grown in two separate petri dishes. There is a one in three chance that a colony of *E. coli* bacteria grows in either of the petri dishes. If a colony of *E. coli* bacteria grows in the first dish, what is the percent probability that it will grow in the second? (Note: Disregard the % sign when gridding your response.)

9

In the United States, about 40% of people will be diagnosed with cancer in their lifetime. If two people are randomly chosen from the United States, what is the percent probability that both of them will be diagnosed with cancer in their lifetime? (Note: Disregard the % sign when gridding your response.)

The male Satin Bowerbird builds a nest from twigs and blue objects to attract a mate. Males who build a larger nests area have a proportionately larger chance of attracting a mate. In the figure above, two nests are compared. The area of the smaller nest is the square root of the area of the larger nest. If a mate is nine times more likely to choose the male who built the larger nest than the male who built the smaller nest, what is the size of the smaller nest, in square units?

Modeling Data
Part 5

When scientists or researchers collect data, they look for relationships between different variables. For example, imagine Mario is running a lemonade stand. He wants to know if there is a relationship between the temperature and the amount of lemonade he sells. He collects the following information over a series of days:

Average Temperature (°F)	76	89	68	82	91	74	84
Cups Sold	19	54	12	25	61	23	41

One way to find trends in data is to create a scatterplot. A **scatterplot** is a graph of two variables compared against each other; these types of graphs are commonly found on the SAT. It is the most common means of analysis because you can visually see patterns, or **trends** of data. Here is a scatterplot of Mario's data:

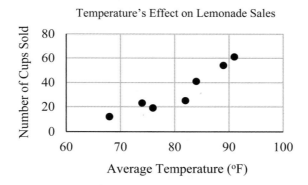

From this scatterplot, you can see that the number of cups of lemonade sold tended to be higher on days with a higher temperature. The trend is not a perfect line or curve, but you can estimate an equation that will approximate these data: this is called **modeling data**. Modeling data allows us to find an equation for the relationship between two pieces of information and to make estimates or predictions.

To model the data from Mario's lemonade stand, you first need to decide what type of curve best models the relationship between the temperature and the number of cups sold. This relationship could be linear, quadratic, polynomial, or exponential. The data in Mario's scatterplot appears to follow a linear trend.

Now you need to draw a trend line or a line of best fit. A **trend line** or **line of best fit** is a line that best approximates all the scatterplot data. It should be as close to *all* the points as possible, but it does not have to pass through all—or any—of the actual data points. The line of best fit of Mario's data is:

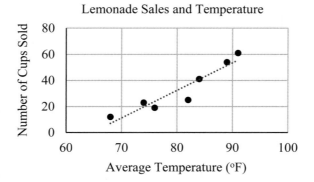

Lemonade Sales and Temperature

Estimating Using a Trend Line

You can estimate the equation of the trend line by using two points on the line. Make sure you do *not* use the experimental data points unless they fall exactly on the line!

Pick values that are easy to estimate from the graph. For example, you could use (70, 12) and (90, 54) from the trend line above. This would give us the equation:

$$y = 2.1x - 135$$

In this equation, y represents the number of cups sold and x is the temperature. If you wanted to predict how many cups of lemonade would be sold if the temperature were 80°F, for example, you would plug 80 into the formula:

$$\text{Cups Sold} = 2.1 \times 80 - 135 = 33$$

Based off of your line of best fit, you could estimate that 33 cups would be sold at an average temperature of 80°F. You can similarly predict all temperatures within the range of 68°F to 91°F this way.

The SAT may also include quadratic or exponential prediction models.

Example

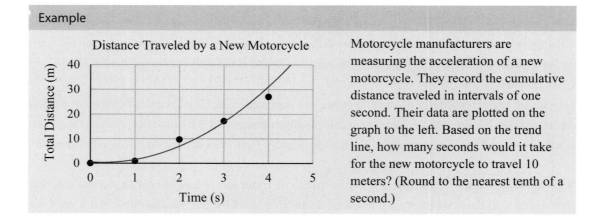

Distance Traveled by a New Motorcycle

Motorcycle manufacturers are measuring the acceleration of a new motorcycle. They record the cumulative distance traveled in intervals of one second. Their data are plotted on the graph to the left. Based on the trend line, how many seconds would it take for the new motorcycle to travel 10 meters? (Round to the nearest tenth of a second.)

Math

You need to find the point where the trend line reaches 10 meters. This occurs at the second tick mark after 2 seconds. Since there are 5 tick marks between each second, each tick mark represents 0.2 seconds. Therefore, the time it takes for the motorcycle to reach 10 meters is about 2.4 seconds.

Example

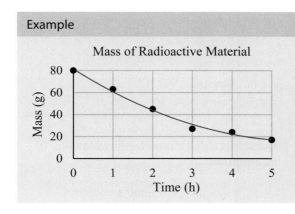

Mass of Radioactive Material

A researcher collects data on a mass of a radioactive material at different times and displays the results in the scatterplot on the right. Based on the graph, how long will it take the material to decrease to one quarter of its original mass? (Round to the nearest quarter of an hour.)

The original mass is 80 grams, so one quarter of the original mass is 20 grams. The trend line reaches 20 grams about half way between 4 and 5 hours, so our estimate is 4.5 hours.

Part 5 Practice: Modeling Data

1

Temperature (°C)	Reaction Time (s)
20	13.5
24	11
28	7.9
32	3.6
36	2.1
40	1.3

A chemist measures the reaction time of an experiment at different temperatures. The results are summarized in the chart above. If these data are displayed as a scatterplot, will the slope of the trend line be positive, negative, or zero?

A) Positive

B) Negative

C) Zero

D) The answer cannot be determined from the information given.

Questions 2 and 3 refer to the following information.

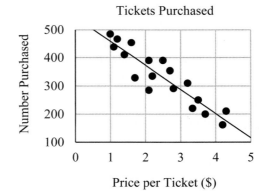

Tickets Purchased

2

According to the data above, how many tickets would you expect to be purchased if the price is $3.00?

A) 250

B) 290

C) 310

D) 350

3

If tickets are sold at $4.00 each, approximately how much is the total ticket revenue?

A) $400

B) $680

C) $740

D) $800

Questions 4 and 5 refer to the following information.

Fuel Economy at Different Speeds

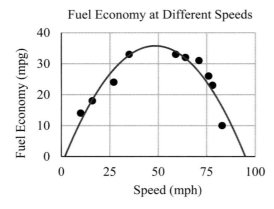

A group of researchers collects data on the fuel economy of a car at different speeds. The fuel economy is measured in miles per gallon (mpg) and speed is measured in miles per hour (mph). The data are displayed in the graph above.

4

Which of the following is the best estimate for the maximum fuel economy of this car?

A) 30 mpg

B) 32 mpg

C) 35 mpg

D) 82 mpg

5

The car has a fuel economy of 18 mpg at a speed of 18 mph. At which other speed should the car have the same fuel economy?

A) 70 mph

B) 75 mph

C) 80 mph

D) 90 mph

Questions 6 and 7 refer to the following information.

Employee Salaries

The graph above shows data collected on employees' salaries in relation to their experience. The data are modeled as a linear relationship where e is the employee's experience in years and S is their annual salary in thousands of dollars.

6

Which of the following best estimates the annual salary of an employee with 4 years of experience?

A) $55,000

B) $60,000

C) $65,000

D) $75,000

7

Which of the following best models the graph's trend line?

A) $S = 5e + 38$

B) $S = e + 38$

C) $S = \dfrac{1}{5}e + 38$

D) $S = -\dfrac{1}{5}e + 38$

8

Sea Level Rise 1990-2010

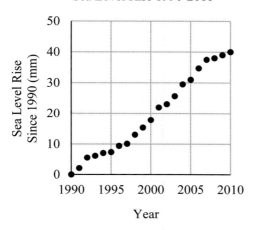

According to the graph above, by approximately how much did the sea level rise between 1990 and 2010? Round to the nearest millimeter.

Questions 9 and 10 refer to the following information.

Time (hours)	Number of Bacteria
0	20
1	43
2	71
3	100
4	144
5	230

A biologist is growing a culture of bacteria in his lab. He records the population at different times and displays the data in the chart above.

9

Based on the table above, to the nearest hour, what is the hour in which the population grows to seven times its original size?

10

The biologist determines that the equation for the trend line is modeled by $N = 46t - 8$, where t is time and N is the number of bacteria. According to the equation, approximately how many times greater is the number of bacteria after 11 hours than the number after 2 hours? Round your answer to the nearest whole number.

Using Data as Evidence
Part 6

In Section 5, we've covered many topics related to data analysis. In this part, you'll learn how these topics will appear on the SAT. Data analysis questions will test your ability to read different types of charts and graphs, interpret data and trends, make conclusions and predictions from data sets, and analyze data.

Reading Charts and Graphs

To solve any data analysis problem, you must first make sure that you understand the purpose of the graph. Ask yourself which quantities are being measured and compared, and know the scale and units of those quantities. Make sure that you are familiar with the types of charts and graphs introduced in Part 2.

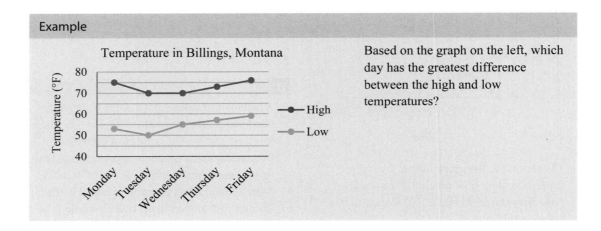

Example

Temperature in Billings, Montana

Based on the graph on the left, which day has the greatest difference between the high and low temperatures?

To solve the problem, you need to look at the graph and compare the high and low temperatures for each day. Monday and Tuesday have the widest gap between the high and low temperatures, so we should compare those more closely. There is a difference of about 22° between Monday's temperatures and only a 20° difference between Tuesday's temperatures, so the answer is Monday.

Interpreting Data

In some cases, you will need to use data in the chart or graph to find information that is not part of the data you are given. You will have to do calculations with the data you are given or make estimates and predictions based on data or trends.

Some of these questions might ask you to use data from a sample group to make predictions for a larger population. For these problems, you can use fractions or percentages to compare the sample group to the larger population.

GPA of Graduating Students	
GPA	Number of Students
3.5-4.0	25
3.0-3.4	37
2.5-2.9	24
2.0-2.4	14

The chart on the left shows a random sample of GPAs from a high school's graduating students. The entire graduating class contains 600 students. Based on the data, which is the best estimate for the number of students in the graduating class who had a GPA of 3 or higher?

A) 62   B) 150   C) 222   D) 372

We can use percentages to solve this problem. First, find the percentage of students in the sample who had a GPA of 3.0 or higher. This is 25 + 37 students out of 100 total students, so 62%. Now, multiply this percentage by the number of students in the graduating class:

$$600 \times 0.62 = 372 \text{ students}$$

The best estimate for the number of students in the graduating class who had a GPA of 3 or higher is 372 so (D) is the correct answer.

You may also be asked to model data or to use a model to make predictions. The scatterplot is often used in these types of questions; you could be asked, for example, to estimate the slope or to find the function that best models the data. These problems will look like the examples and practice exercises in Part 5.

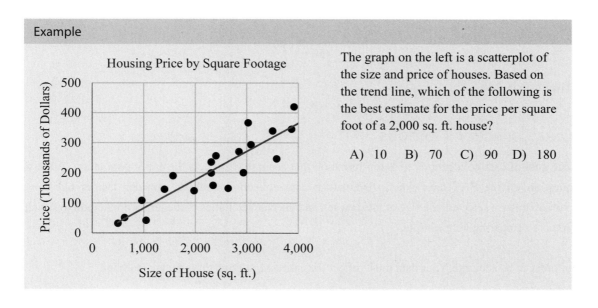

The graph on the left is a scatterplot of the size and price of houses. Based on the trend line, which of the following is the best estimate for the price per square foot of a 2,000 sq. ft. house?

A) 10   B) 70   C) 90   D) 180

Since the question asks us to use the trend line, find the price that corresponds to 2,000 sq. ft. on the trend line. This is approximately 180 thousand dollars. Make sure to check your units – $180 will give a much different answer than $180,000! To find price per sq. ft., divide $180,000 by 2,000 sq. ft. to get 90, which is choice (C).

Data analysis questions will ask you to find or compare the mean, median, mode, range, or standard deviation of data sets. These problems might include raw data sets, tables of values, or bar graphs, so you should be familiar with finding statistical quantities from these types of graphics.

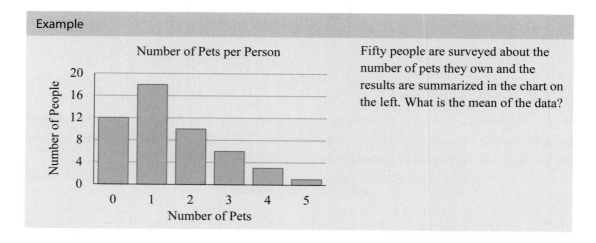

Example

Number of Pets per Person

Fifty people are surveyed about the number of pets they own and the results are summarized in the chart on the left. What is the mean of the data?

To find the mean from a bar graph, multiply each possible number of pets by the number of people who own that number, then add them together:

$$(0 \times 12) + (1 \times 18) + (2 \times 10) + (3 \times 6) + (4 \times 3) + (5 \times 1) = 73$$

This is the total number of pets owned by the 50 people. Now divide by the number of people, 50, to find the mean:

$$\frac{73}{50} = 1.46$$

The mean is 1.46.

Data Collection Methods

The goal of data collection is to get information that accurately reflects the entire population. When a question on the SAT asks you to evaluate a data collection method, consider factors like how participants are selected, the size of the data set, and the characteristics of the larger population to which you are comparing your sample.

In order to be accurate, your data must reflect the entire population that you are studying.

Consider the map below:

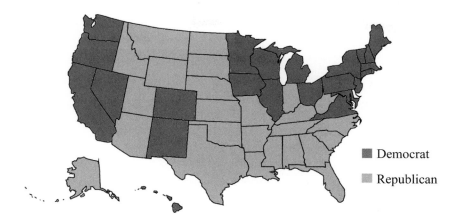

If you only surveyed people from the Northeast, you would get very different results than if you only surveyed people from southern states. Neither group would give you results that reflect the political preference of all U.S. residents.

The *type* of data that you are collecting also determines what makes a good sample. A sample group that includes only college students, for example, is a great sample group if you are studying college students. It is not, however, a good sample group to represent the entire population of the U.S.

When evaluating a sample selection, consider how well it represents the entire population and how that may affect results.

The *size* of the sample also affects the accuracy of data. If you only collect a few data points, they will not reflect the entire population as well as many data points.

Imagine you are rolling a six-sided number cube numbered 1 through 6 and recording the results. You would expect each number to be rolled about $\frac{1}{6}$ or 17% of the time. If you only rolled the cube 5 times, your data would look something like this:

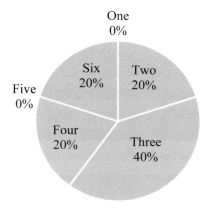

This data is not very accurate because the sample size is so small. If you rolled the number cube 50 or 100 times, you would get results that are much more accurate:

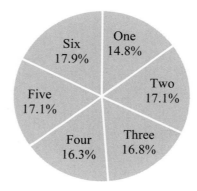

This principle is true for all kinds of data collection: the bigger the sample size, the better the chance it will give accurate results.

Measuring Error

Researchers can estimate the accuracy of their data with a margin of error or a confidence interval. You will not have to calculate margins of error or confidence intervals on the SAT, but you need to understand what these mean and know how to use them to analyze data.

A **margin of error** measures how well a sample group represents the entire population. Consider the chart below:

Pre-Election Survey			
Candidate	Jones	Liu	Albini
Percent of Votes (± 3%)	28%	37%	35%

The chart gives a margin of error of 3%. This means that the actual percentages may vary as much as 3% in either direction. Jones could have anywhere between 25% and 31% of the votes. Similarly, Liu's range is between 34% and 40%, and Albini's range is between 32% and 38%. These ranges are called confidence intervals.

The margin of error affects how we analyze the data. Notice that Liu has 2% more of the votes than Albini. However, the margin of error tells us that the percentages can vary up to 3%. This means that Liu could actually have 34% of the votes or Albini could have 38% of the votes, which would put Albini in the lead. A good rule is that if the difference between two numbers or percentages is smaller than the margin of error, you cannot conclude that one is greater or smaller than the other.

Margins of error and confidence intervals can also be represented visually on a graph. Confidence intervals are shown as vertical bars like the ones in the following graph.

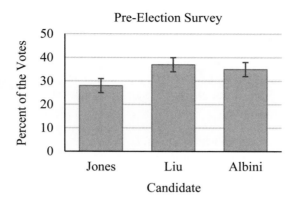

Pre-Election Survey

Since the margin of error is 3%, each confidence interval extends 3% above and below the measured percentage. You can see that the confidence intervals for Liu and Albini overlap, which tells you that you don't know for sure which candidate has a larger percentage of votes.

Part 6 Practice: Using Data as Evidence

Questions 1 and 2 refer to the following information.

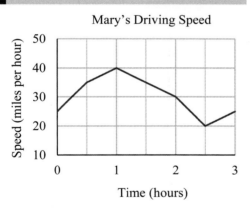

1

Mary's Driving Speed

Which of the following is the value of the difference between Mary's fastest and slowest speed over the three-hour period?

A) 15

B) 20

C) 25

D) 30

2

According to the graph, how many miles did Mary cover between hours 1 and 2?

A) 30

B) 33

C) 35

D) 40

3

Mass of Evaporating Substance

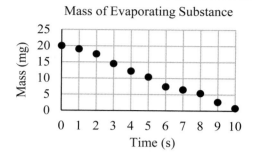

Susanne conducts an experiment in which she heats a solid to its boiling point so that it evaporates. She records the mass of the remaining solid every second. The plot above shows her resulting data.

If the data is modeled as the linear function $M = 20 + at$, where M is the mass of the substance in milligrams, t is time in seconds, and a is a constant, which of the following is the best estimate for a?

A) −2

B) −1

C) 1

D) 2

4

Product	Average Rating	Standard Deviation
A	4	0.43
B	3	0.76

Customers rate two products on a scale of 1-5. The chart above summarizes statistics from these reviews. Which of the following statements can you conclude from the information given?

A) More customers rated Product B than Product A.

B) All of the ratings for Product A were a 3, 4, or 5.

C) The ratings for Product B were more varied than for Product A.

D) The range of the ratings for Product B is larger than that for Product A.

5

College Expenses

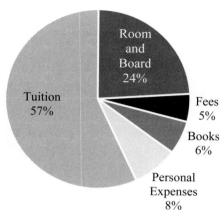

The chart above is a summary of Malik's expenditures for his first year in college. If Malik's total expenditure for the year is $30,000, how much more did Malik spend on tuition than on the other categories combined?

A) $2,100

B) $4,200

C) $12,900

D) $17,100

Questions 6 and 7 refer to the following information.

Labor Participation Rate

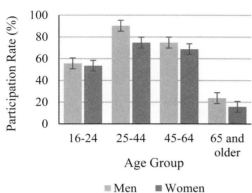

■ Men   ■ Women

6

Which of the following conclusions can you make from the graph above?

A) A higher percentage of men ages 16-24 work than the percentage of women ages 16-24.

B) Between 70% and 80% of women ages 25-44 work.

C) The margin of error is ±10%.

D) There are more men ages 65 or older than women ages 65 or older.

7

200 men ages 25-44 who took the original survey are selected for a second survey. Incorporating margin of error, what are the maximum and minimum number of men that you would expect to work in this age group?

A) 95 and 85

B) 115 and 105

C) 190 and 170

D) 200 and 180

8

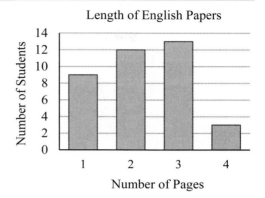

If the histogram above shows the length of 37 students' English papers, what is the median paper length?

Questions 9 and 10 refer to the following information.

November Sales Report

Store	Price of Product	Number Sold
A	$99	15
B	$85	21
C	$110	18

The chart above is a report on the sale of a product in three stores.

9

What is the value of the difference in sales between Store A and Store B?

10

If the product costs $80 for the stores to purchase, what is the combined total profit from the product's sales at all three stores?

Section 6
Additional Topics

The **Additional Topics** questions on the SAT test various advanced topics in geometry, trigonometry, and complex numbers. Although a variety of topics fall under this content area, Additional Topics questions make up the smallest portion of the Math Test. You'll only see a total of 6 questions on these topics: 2-4 in the Calculator Section and 2-4 in the No-Calculator Section. You'll want to ensure you understand the introductory concepts of lines, triangles, quadrilaterals, polygons, and circles. If you need to go over these concepts, you can find a thorough review online.

 For additional resources, please visit **ivyglobal.com/study**.

In this section, we will cover the following material tested in the Additional Topics questions:

- Angles and Volumes of Shapes
- Right Triangles
- Radians and The Unit Circle
- Circles
- Complex Numbers

Angles and Volumes of Shapes
Part 1

All geometric shapes have **dimensions**, or distances you can measure. Shapes with one dimension, like simple lines, can only be measured by length. Two dimensional shapes can be measured two ways, by length and width. Shapes in three dimensions can be measured three ways—by length, width, height or depth. Since lines and two-dimensional shapes are covered in our online review, we'll start by discussing angles, and then we'll talk about three-dimensional shapes.

Angles

An **angle** is formed when two lines or line segments intersect. Angles are measured in degrees from 0° to 360°, which represents the angle of a full circle. Angles are classified according to their degree measurements:

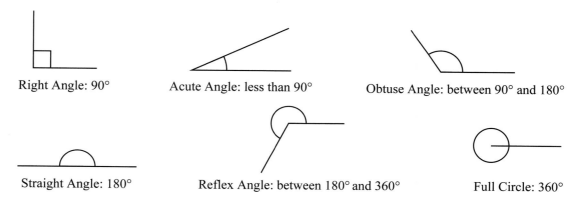

Right Angle: 90°   Acute Angle: less than 90°   Obtuse Angle: between 90° and 180°

Straight Angle: 180°   Reflex Angle: between 180° and 360°   Full Circle: 360°

Pairs of angles can also be classified by comparing their degree measurements. **Complementary** angles are a pair of angles that add up to 90°. **Supplementary** angles are a pair of angles that add up to 180°. **Congruent** angles are a pair of angles that have equal measures.

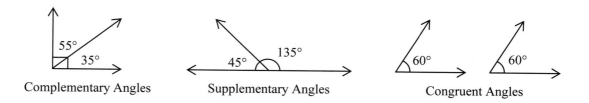

Complementary Angles   Supplementary Angles   Congruent Angles

A line that **bisects** an angle divides it into two equal parts. In the figure on the right, line $\overleftrightarrow{BD}$ bisects $\angle ABC$ and divides it into two congruent angles, $\angle ABD$ and $\angle DBC$:

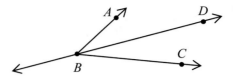

Intersecting Lines and Angles

Two lines are **perpendicular** if they intersect to form right angles. If two lines are **parallel**, then they will never intersect.

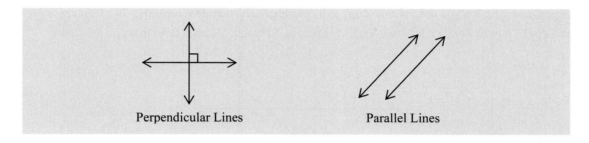

Perpendicular Lines   Parallel Lines

When one line intersects with another line, they form two sets of **vertical angles**. Vertical angles are congruent. In the figure below, $a = d$ and $b = c$.

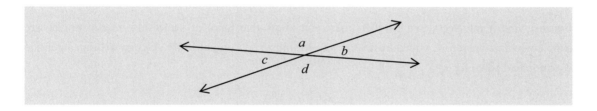

If a third line, or a **transversal**, intersects a pair of parallel lines, it forms eight angles:

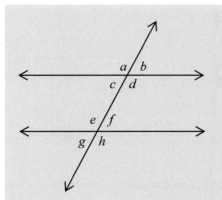

Here are some properties of transversals:

- The pairs of **corresponding angles** are congruent: $a = e$, $b = f$, $c = g$, and $d = h$.
- The pairs of **alternate interior angles** are congruent: $c = f$ and $d = e$.
- The pairs of **alternate exterior angles** are congruent: $a = h$ and $b = g$.
- The pairs of **same side interior angles** are supplementary: $c + e = 180°$ and $d + f = 180°$.

In the figure on the right, line *m* and line *n* are parallel, and line *p* bisects ∠*RST*. What is the value of *x*?

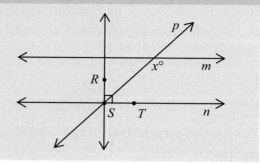

Based on the figure, you can see that ∠*RST* is a right angle and therefore measures 90°. If line *p* bisects this angle, it must divide it into two angles measuring 45° each. You can label these on the figure:

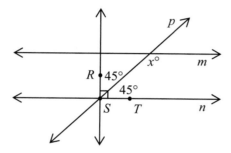

Because line *p* intersects two parallel lines, you know that pairs of same-side interior angles are supplementary. Therefore, you know that *x*° and 45° must add to equal 180°. You can write an algebraic equation and solve for *x*:

$$x + 45 = 180$$

$$x + 45 - 45 = 180 - 45$$

$$x = 135$$

Prisms

A **solid** is a three-dimensional shape. A **prism** is a solid with two congruent polygons, called **bases**, joined by perpendicular rectangles. Each exterior surface of a prism is called a **face**, the lines where these faces intersect are called **edges**, and the points where these edges intersect are called **vertices** (singular: vertex).

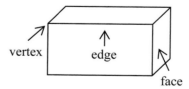

Prisms are named for the shape of their bases. The prism above is a **rectangular prism** because it has a rectangular base—in other words, it's a box.

The volume of a prism is the space contained within the prism. To find the volume of a rectangular prism, multiply its length by its width by its height. For example, the prism to the right has a volume of 40 units cubed:

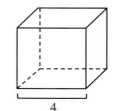

$$\text{Volume} = \text{length} \times \text{width} \times \text{height} = 5 \times 4 \times 2 = 40$$

A rectangular prism whose edges are all the same length is called a cube. The volume of a cube is equal to the length of one of its edges cubed. For example, the cube to the right has a volume of 64 units cubed:

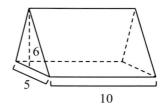

$$\text{Volume} = \text{edge}^3 = 4^3 = 64$$

The volume of any other type of prism can be found by multiplying the area of one of its bases by its length, or the edge perpendicular to its bases. For example, the triangular prism to the right has a volume of 150 cubed units:

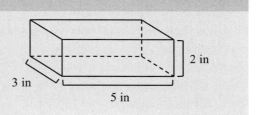

$$\text{Volume} = \text{base} \times \text{length} = \frac{6 \times 5}{2} \times 10 = 150$$

The surface area of any prism can be found by adding together the areas of its faces.

Example

The adjacent figure shows the dimensions of a cardboard box. If there are no overlapping sides, how many square inches of cardboard are needed to make this box?

This question is asking you to find the surface area of a rectangular prism with a height of 2 inches, a width of 3 inches, and a length of 5 inches. To find how many square inches of cardboard make up the exterior of the box, you need to find the area of each rectangular face and then add these areas together.

The top and bottom faces each have an area of $5 \text{ in} \times 3 \text{ in} = 15 \text{ in}^2$. The front and back faces each have an area of $5 \text{ in} \times 2 \text{ in} = 10 \text{ in}^2$. The left and right faces each have an area of $3 \text{ in} \times 2 \text{ in} = 6 \text{ in}^2$. To find the total surface area of the box, add together the areas of each of these faces:

$$(2 \times 15 \text{ in}^2) + (2 \times 10 \text{ in}^2) + (2 \times 6 \text{ in}^2) = 62 \text{ in}^2$$

If you wanted to build this box, you would need 62 in^2 of cardboard.

Cylinders

A **cylinder** is like a prism, but its base is a circle instead of a polygon. Two circular bases connected by a perpendicular curved surface form a cylinder:

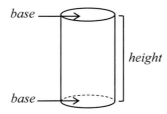

The volume of a cylinder is equal to the area of its base multiplied by its height. The area of the cylinder's base is equal to π times the radius of the cylinder squared, so you can use the formula below to find the volume of any cylinder:

$$\text{Volume} = \pi \times \text{radius}^2 \times \text{height}$$

Example

What is the volume of the cylinder?

12 cm

4 cm

First, find the area of the cylinder's base, and then multiply by its height:

$$\text{Volume} = \pi \times \text{radius}^2 \times \text{height}$$

$$= \pi \times 4^2 \times 12$$

$$= \pi \times 16 \times 12$$

$$= 192\pi$$

The volume of the cylinder is 192π cubic centimeters.

To find the surface area of a cylinder, imagine that the cylinder was sliced along its height and "unfolded" on a flat surface. You would then have two circular bases and one rectangle that wraps around the bases. To find the surface area of the cylinder, you need to add up the areas of the bases and the area of this rectangle.

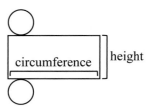

This rectangle has a length that is equal to the circumference of one of the bases, and a width that is equal to the height of the cylinder. Therefore, to find the area of this rectangle, you would multiply the cylinder's circumference by its height. You would then add this number to the area of the two bases to find the total surface area of the cylinder:

$$\text{surface area} = (\text{area of bases}) + (\text{circumference} \times \text{height})$$

Example

Find the surface area of the cylinder.

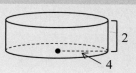

First, find the area of the bases:

$$\text{Area of each base} = \pi \times 4^2 = 16\pi$$

Then, find the circumference:

$$\text{Circumference} = 2 \times \pi \times 4 = 8\pi$$

Finally, add the area of the bases to the product of the circumference and the height:

$$\text{Surface area} = (\text{area of bases}) + (\text{circumference} \times \text{height})$$

$$= (2 \times 16\pi) + (8\pi \times 2)$$
$$= 32\pi + 16\pi$$

$$= 48\pi$$

The total surface area of the cylinder is 48π square units.

Spheres

A **sphere** is like a three-dimensional circle: the surface of the sphere is a collection of points that are all the same distance away from the center. As in a circle, the line segment drawn from the center to a point on the sphere's surface is called the sphere's radius, and all radii of a sphere are equal lengths.

The volume of a sphere is equal to $\frac{4}{3}\pi$ times its radius cubed. For example, the sphere to the right has a volume of $\frac{32}{3}\pi$ units cubed:

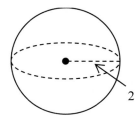

$$\text{volume} = \frac{4}{3}\pi r^3 = \frac{4}{3}\pi \times 2^3 = \frac{4}{3}\pi \times 8 = \frac{32}{3}\pi$$

You don't need to memorize this formula because it's included in the reference section of the SAT Math Test. You should, however, be familiar with how to use it; the less you have to flip back and forth from the reference section to your question, the more time you will be able to spend on the question!

In this part, we reviewed some properties of lines, angles, quadrilaterals, triangles, and circles. We also reviewed some properties of solids, such as prisms, cylinders, and spheres. During the rest of the section, we'll build on these simple concepts in order to solve some of the more complex Additional Topics questions on the SAT.

Part 1 Practice: Angles and Volumes of Shapes

1

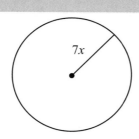

What is the area of the circle above, in terms of x?

A) $7\pi x^2$

B) $49\pi x$

C) $49\pi^2 x$

D) $49\pi x^2$

2

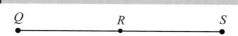

In the figure above, R is the midpoint of $\overline{QS}$. If $\overline{QR} = \dfrac{3}{4}$, which of the following statements must be true?

A) $\overline{QR}$ is longer than $\overline{RS}$.

B) $\overline{QR}$ and $\overline{QS}$ are both of length $\dfrac{3}{4}$.

C) $\overline{QS}$ is of length $\dfrac{3}{2}$.

D) $\overline{QS}$ and $\overline{RS}$ have the same length.

3

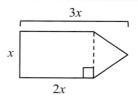

What is the area of the polygon shown above, in terms of x?

A) $\dfrac{3x^2}{2}$

B) $2x^2$

C) $\dfrac{5x^2}{2}$

D) $3x^2$

4

The surface area of the rectangular prism above, in squared units, is equal to its volume, in cubed units. Which of the following equations is true for the prism?

A) $a = 3$

B) $a = 6$

C) $a^2 = 6$

D) $a^3 = 6$

5

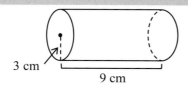

3 cm

9 cm

A food company wants to sell tomato sauce in a can whose shape is shown above. It costs the company two cents per cm^3 to produce and package the tomato sauce, and it sells the cans for $7.00. How much profit does it make per can, rounded to the nearest cent?

A) $0.63

B) $1.91

C) $2.76

D) $5.30

Questions 6 and 7 refer to the following information.

The volume of a sphere is 36π centimeters cubed. Its volume with a radius r and volume v is calculated according to the equation $v = \dfrac{4}{3}\pi r^3$.

6

What is the sphere's radius?

A) 3 cm

B) 6 cm

C) 9 cm

D) 24 cm

7

If the sphere has a density of $\dfrac{4\text{ g}}{\pi \text{ cm}^3}$, what is its mass, in grams?

A) 9

B) 72

C) 144

D) 388

8

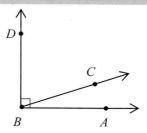

In the figure above, angles ABC and CBD are complementary. If $\angle CBD$ measures $70°$, what is the measure of $\angle ABC$? (Ignore the degree symbol when gridding your response.)

9

If the area of a square is 81 m^2, what is the length of one of the square's sides, in meters?

10

If the area of a circle is 64π, what is its diameter?

Right Triangles
Part 2

The basic properties of triangles, their side lengths, perimeters, and areas, are covered in our online material. The SAT will ask questions about these properties, but in the context of a more complex situation. Specific rules that the SAT lists in their reference section include the Pythagorean theorem $c^2 = a^2 + b^2$, and the special right triangles with angles of 30-60-90 and 45-45-90 degrees. In this section we will cover this reference material as we look at right triangles and see how you can use their special properties to find angles and lengths.

Angles of Right Triangles

In a **right triangle**, one of the angles is always 90°. As discussed in the online review, the interior angles of any triangle add to 180°. Therefore, the sum of the two acute angles of a right triangle is always equal to $180 - 90 = 90°$. You can use this information to find unknown angles in a right triangle.

Example

Find the value of the angle x.

Because this is a right triangle, you know that the sum of the two acute angles is 90°. You can write an equation to solve for x:

$$20° + x = 90°$$
$$x = 90° - 20°$$
$$x = 70°$$

The angle x is 70°.

Pythagorean Theorem

We've seen how to find a missing angle of a right triangle. Now we are going to look at how to find a missing side length of a right triangle.

The sides of a right triangle have special names. The **hypotenuse** of a right triangle is the side opposite the right angle, and the other two sides of a right triangle are called its **legs**. The Pythagorean theorem gives us a formula to solve for the side lengths of a right triangle. According to the **Pythagorean theorem**, if a and b are the lengths of the triangle's legs and c is the length of its hypotenuse, then a squared plus b squared equals c squared.

This is the Pythagorean theorem:

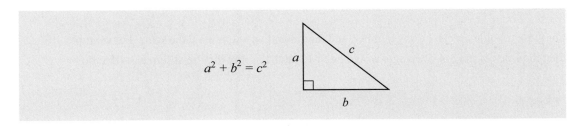

$$a^2 + b^2 = c^2$$

Example

What is the value of x in the adjacent figure?

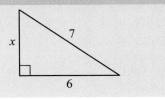

To find the length of the missing side, plug the lengths of the two sides given into the Pythagorean theorem and solve for x. The sum of the lengths of our two sides squared ($x^2 + 6^2$) is equal to the length of the hypotenuse squared (7^2):

$$x^2 + 6^2 = 7^2$$
$$x^2 + 36 = 49$$
$$x^2 = 13$$
$$x = \sqrt{13}$$

13 isn't a perfect square, so you can't simplify this expression further. For calculator grid-in questions on the SAT, you may occasionally be asked to calculate this as $x = 3.61$. Most often, however, you will find a multiple-choice answer in the form of $x = \sqrt{13}$.

Special Triangles

While the Pythagorean theorem can help you find the sides of a right triangle, many triangles don't need so much calculation. The SAT is full of **special triangles**—triangles whose three side lengths have fixed ratios. These include 3-4-5 triangles, 5-12-13 triangles, 30-60-90 triangles, and 45-45-90 triangles. Recognizing a special triangle reduces the time you need to calculate the missing sides.

3-4-5 and 5-12-13 triangles are named for the ratios of their side lengths. **3-4-5 triangles** have side lengths in the ratio of 3:4:5, and **5-12-13 triangles** have side lengths in the ratio of 5:12:13.

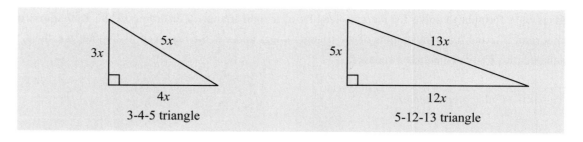

For these triangles, x can be any number, and the side ratios will remain the same. For example, if $x = 3$, then the sides of the 3-4-5 triangle would be 9, 12, and 15—but they're still in a 3:4:5 ratio.

Example

Find the missing side of the triangle.

This is a right triangle whose sides have a common factor of 2. You can re-write the side lengths as multiples of 2:

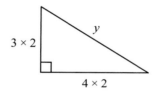

Now you see that these sides are in the ratio of 3:4, and you can use your knowledge of the 3-4-5 special triangle to calculate the missing side. If the lengths of the two legs are 3×2 and 4×2, then the length of the hypotenuse must be 5×2:

$$y = 5 \times 2 = 10$$

The missing side is equal to 10.

30-60-90 triangles and 45-45-90 triangles are named for their angles. **30-60-90 triangles** have angles measured 30°, 60°, and 90°, and side lengths in a ratio of $1:\sqrt{3}:2$. **45-45-90 triangles** have angles measured 45°, 45°, and 90°, and side lengths in a ratio of $1:1:\sqrt{2}$.

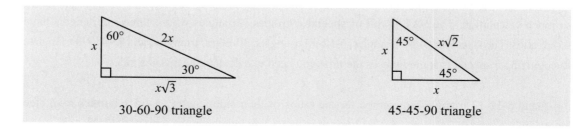

What are the values of *x* and *y* in the triangle?

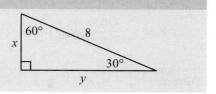

Using what you know about 30-60-90 triangles, you can easily find *x* and *y*. You know that *x* is half of the value of the hypotenuse because it is located opposite the 30 degree angle:

$$x = 8 \div 2 = 4$$

Now that you have the value of *x*, you can find *y* by multiplying *x* by $\sqrt{3}$:

$$y = 4 \times \sqrt{3} = 4\sqrt{3}$$

An easy way to remember the side lengths of these triangles is by thinking about their angles. The triangle with two different angles has a side length of the square root of two, and the triangle with three different angles has a side length of the square root of three. Knowing the value of just one side and one angle (other than the right angle) of a 30-60-90 triangle allows you to find the values for all three sides!

Trigonometry

Trigonometry is a more specialized type of math that deals with relationships between sides and angles in right triangles. In addition to using the Pythagorean theorem and special triangle ratios, you can use trigonometry to calculate the length of sides in right triangles.

In trigonometry, the relationships between sides and angles of right triangles can be written as ratios with specific names. The three ratios you will find on the SAT are sine (abbreviated sin), cosine (abbreviated cos), and tangent (abbreviated tan). These ratios need to be memorized, and are not provided in the SAT's reference material. We will now take a look at what these ratios mean and review an easy way to remember them.

You can find the **sine** of an angle by dividing the length of the side opposite to the angle by the length of the triangle's hypotenuse. You can find the **cosine** by dividing the length of the side adjacent to the angle by the length of the hypotenuse. You can find the **tangent** by dividing the length of the opposite side by the length of the adjacent side. These ratios are summarized in the following formulas, where *x* stands for the measure of any angle in the triangle:

$$\sin(x) = \frac{\text{opposite}}{\text{hypotenuse}} \qquad \cos(x) = \frac{\text{adjacent}}{\text{hypotenuse}} \qquad \tan(x) = \frac{\text{opposite}}{\text{adjacent}}$$

In order to help you remember these ratios, we recommend you memorize the acronym **SOHCAHTOA**:

$$\text{Sine} = \frac{\textbf{Opposite}}{\textbf{Hypotenuse}} \qquad \text{Cosine} = \frac{\textbf{Adjacent}}{\textbf{Hypotenuse}} \qquad \text{Tangent} = \frac{\textbf{Opposite}}{\textbf{Adjacent}}$$

Example

What is the sine of $x°$?

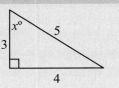

In order to calculate the sine for angle x in this triangle, first locate the side opposite to $x°$. The opposite side has a length of 4. Then, plug this value into the formula for sine:

$$\sin(x°) = \frac{\text{opposite}}{\text{hypotenuse}} = \frac{4}{5}$$

The sine of $x°$ is $\frac{4}{5}$.

You can use your knowledge of sine, cosine, and tangent to solve for the length of one of the sides of a triangle. For example, let's look at the following question:

Example

In the adjacent triangle, what is the value of B?

In this triangle, you know the measure of an angle and the length of the hypotenuse. You need to find the length of the side adjacent to the angle. "**SOHCAHTOA**" reminds us that the cosine of an angle compares the adjacent side with the hypotenuse. You can plug the values from the triangle into the cosine ratio formula:

$$\cos(x) = \frac{\text{adjacent}}{\text{hypotenuse}}$$

$$\cos(30°) = \frac{B}{3}$$

Then, you can solve for B:

$$B = \cos(30°) \times 3$$

Using trigonometry, you have determined that the length of B is equal to $\cos(30°) \times 3$. On the SAT, the answer will normally remain in this format. You will not be required to memorize trigonometric values such as $\cos(30°)$.

Before you leave this chapter, make sure that you understand how to find the missing angles and sides of right triangles using the Pythagorean theorem and trigonometry. Also remember that many questions on the SAT use special right triangles. By memorizing just a few of their ratios and angles, you will save a lot of time and avoid many complex calculations!

Part 2 Practice: Right Triangles

1

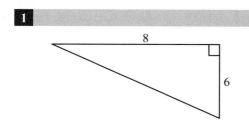

Which of the following triangles is similar to the one above?

A)
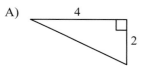

B)
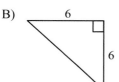

C)
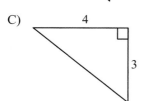

D)
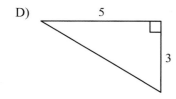

2

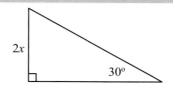

Which of the following expressions correctly represents the length of the hypotenuse of the triangle above?

A) $x\sqrt{3}$

B) $x\sqrt{5}$

C) $4x$

D) $5x$

3

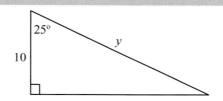

What is the value of y in the triangle above?

A) $\dfrac{10}{\cos(25°)}$

B) $\dfrac{10}{\sin(25°)}$

C) $10\sin(25°)$

D) $\sin(25°)$

4

If you know two side lengths of a right triangle, what other information can you calculate?

    I.   The length of the third side
    II. The sine of every angle in the triangle
    III. The cosine of every angle in the triangle

A) I only

B) II only

C) I, II, and III

D) None of the above

5

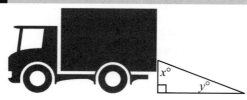

Felicia owns a furniture company and wants to build a ramp to push furniture from her warehouse into a truck, as shown above. Her contractor tells her that he will charge her $10 for every degree of the angle between the floor and the ramp (y). If $\sin(x) = \dfrac{\sqrt{3}}{2}$, how much money will she have to pay to build the ramp?

A) $150

B) $300

C) $600

D) $900

Questions 6 and 7 use the following information.

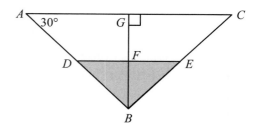

The area that is viewable by an astronomer from a telescope is diagrammed above. The larger triangle represents the area that is viewable from the telescope less clearly, and the smaller shaded triangle represents the area that the telescope can show the most clearly. In the figure above, $\overline{AB} = \overline{BC} = 10$ light years, $\overline{DB} = 4$ light years, and $\overline{DE}$ is parallel to $\overline{AC}$.

6

What is the length of $\overline{BG}$?

A) 2.5 light years

B) 5 light years

C) 10 light years

D) 20 light years

7

What is the length of $\overline{FG}$?

A) 0.25 light years

B) 0.5 light years

C) 2 light years

D) 3 light years

8

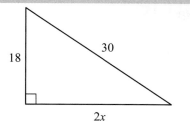

What is the value of *x* in the triangle above?

9

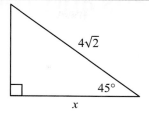

What is the value of *x* in the triangle above?

10

Tim draws an isosceles right triangle with a hypotenuse of $\sqrt{8}$ in. How many inches long are each of the triangle's legs?

Radians and The Unit Circle
Part 3

So far, we have been measuring angles using lines and polygons by using degrees. Angles can also be measured in another unit called radians. A **radian** is a unit that measures an angle as a part of a circle. Radians are expressed in the unit π. They are used when measuring sectors of the unit circle, a useful tool for looking at the relationship between sine and cosine. The Math test may require you to make a direct conversion of degrees to radians or vice-versa. Knowing how to do this conversion will also help you with figuring out chords and arc lengths, which are covered in part 4.

Measuring Angles

There are 2π radians in a circle, or full rotation. Since both 2π radians and $360°$ are equal to a full rotation, $360° = 2\pi$ radians. You can divide both sides by 2 to get the following equation:

$$180° = \pi \text{ radians}$$

You can use this equation to convert between degrees and radians.

Example
What is $270°$ in radians?

You know that there are π radians in $180°$, so you can convert from degrees to radians by multiplying by the conversion factor $\dfrac{\pi}{180°}$:

$$270° \times \frac{\pi \text{ radians}}{180°} = \frac{3\pi}{2} \text{ radians}$$

Here is a table of common angles in degrees and radians:

Degrees	30°	45°	60°	90°	180°	270°	360°
Radians	$\dfrac{\pi}{6}$	$\dfrac{\pi}{4}$	$\dfrac{\pi}{3}$	$\dfrac{\pi}{2}$	π	$\dfrac{3\pi}{2}$	2π

The Unit Circle

On the SAT, you'll often see questions involving radians and trigonometry. You can solve these questions using a special circle called the unit circle. The **unit circle** is a circle drawn on the *xy*-plane, centered at (0, 0), with a radius of 1 unit:

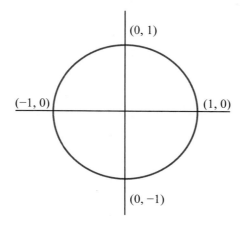

In the unit circle, angles and radians are calculated counterclockwise from the point (1, 0). For example, the angle formed between point (1, 0) and (0, 1) is 90° or $\frac{\pi}{2}$ radians. The angle formed between point (1, 0) and (0, −1) is 270° or $\frac{3\pi}{2}$ radians.

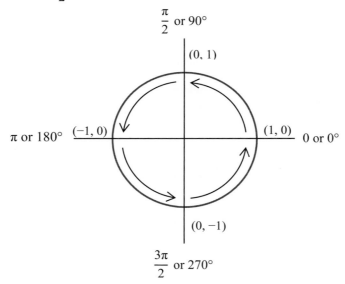

As you move counterclockwise around the unit circle, you can divide it into four quadrants. A **quadrant** is one quarter of the circle. In the diagram below, the labels I, II, III, and IV show you the first, second, third, and fourth quadrants.

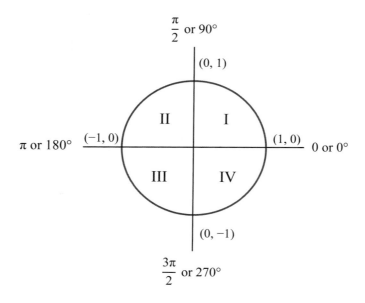

Trigonometry and the Unit Circle

Using the unit circle, you can figure out the sine and cosine of any angle in radians. So far, we've determined where 90°, 180°, and 270° are located on the unit circle. But what if you wanted to draw a different angle, like 60°? 60° is the same as $\frac{\pi}{3}$ radians. Moving counterclockwise from the point (1, 0), you'd draw a line segment that forms a 60° angle with the x-axis. You can make a right triangle with this angle by drawing a line segment down to the x-axis:

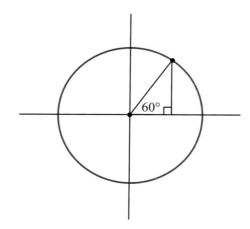

Because you know that the unit circle has a radius of 1, the hypotenuse of the right triangle must be equal to 1. From Part 2, you also know that a right triangle with a 60° angle is a type of special right triangle—a 30-60-90 triangle. Using the formula for the side lengths of 30-60-90 triangles, you can figure out that the lengths of the two sides must be equal to $\frac{1}{2}$ and $\frac{\sqrt{3}}{2}$.

You can then figure out the point where the right triangle intersects the unit circle. It is $\frac{\sqrt{3}}{2}$ units above the x-axis and $\frac{1}{2}$ units to the right of the y-axis, so it must be the point $\left(\frac{1}{2}, \frac{\sqrt{3}}{2}\right)$:

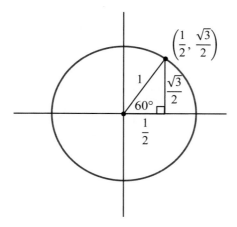

Even though you can calculate the coordinates of this point using 30-60-90 triangles, you actually won't have to do this on the SAT. If you're asked a question about a point on the unit circle, you'll be given its coordinates.

Now that you have all of the side lengths for your right triangle, you can calculate the sine and cosine of $60°$, or $\frac{\pi}{3}$ radians. Remember that $\sin(x) = \dfrac{\text{opposite}}{\text{hypotenuse}}$ and that $\cos(x) = \dfrac{\text{adjacent}}{\text{hypotenuse}}$. The hypotenuse of the triangle has a length of 1, the side opposite to the $60°$ angle has a length of $\frac{\sqrt{3}}{2}$, and the side adjacent to the $60°$ angle has a length of $\frac{1}{2}$. You just have to plug these values into the trigonometric ratios:

$$\sin(60) = \frac{\text{opposite}}{1} = \frac{\sqrt{3}}{2}$$

$$\cos(60) = \frac{\text{adjacent}}{1} = \frac{1}{2}$$

Remember that the point formed by $60°$ on the unit circle has the coordinates $\left(\frac{1}{2}, \frac{\sqrt{3}}{2}\right)$. The sine of $60°$ is $\frac{\sqrt{3}}{2}$, which is the y-coordinate of that point. The cosine of $60°$ is $\frac{1}{2}$, which is the x-coordinate of that point.

Therefore, when you're given a point that corresponds to an angle on the unit circle, you know that:

- The sine of the angle is equal to the *y*-coordinate.
- The cosine of the angle is equal to the *x*-coordinate.

Trigonometry and Quadrants

Remember that the unit circle is divided into four quadrants. What if we wanted to find the sine and cosine of an angle in a different quadrant? Let's take a look at the angle 120°, or $\frac{2\pi}{3}$ radians:

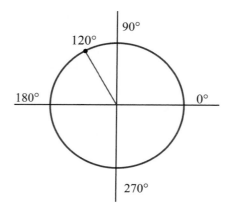

If you draw a line from this point to the *x*-axis, you'll form another 30-60-90 triangle with side lengths $\frac{1}{2}$ and $\frac{\sqrt{3}}{2}$. The point where this angle intersects the unit circle is $\frac{\sqrt{3}}{2}$ units above the *x*-axis and $\frac{1}{2}$ units to the left of the *y*-axis, so it must have the coordinates $\left(-\frac{1}{2}, \frac{\sqrt{3}}{2}\right)$:

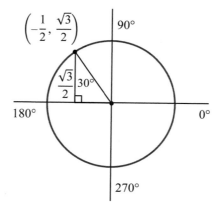

Remember that, for any point corresponding to an angle on the unit circle, the sine of the angle is equal to the *y*-coordinate and the cosine of the angle is equal to the *x*-coordinate. Because 120° has the coordinates $\left(-\frac{1}{2}, \frac{\sqrt{3}}{2}\right)$ on the unit circle, you know that:

$$\sin(120°) \text{ equals the } y\text{-coordinate: } \frac{\sqrt{3}}{2}$$

$$\cos(120°) \text{ equals the } x\text{-coordinate: } -\frac{1}{2}$$

In the first quadrant, you saw that both the sine and cosine were positive. Now that you've drawn an angle in the second quadrant, the sine is still positive but the cosine is negative. This is because all of the points in the second quadrant have positive y-coordinates but negative x-coordinates.

While the SAT will not ask you to calculate the coordinates of points on the unit circle, you need to know the signs of both sine and cosine as you move counterclockwise along the unit circle. An easy way of remembering these signs is by thinking of **CAST**. Starting in the fourth quadrant $\cos(x)$ is always positive, in the first quadrant all of the functions are positive, in the second quadrant $\sin(x)$ is positive, and in the third quadrant $\tan(x)$ is positive. All other functions in the quadrants are negative. The diagram below illustrates this acronym:

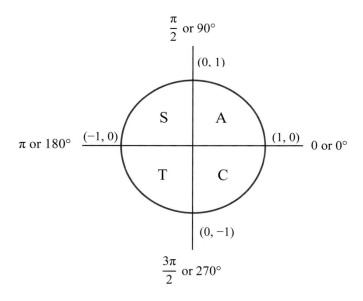

Here is a table to help you remember:

Signs of Sine and Cosine around the Unit Circle			
	Quadrant I	Quadrant II	Quadrant III	Quadrant IV
sine	+	+	−	−
cosine	+	−	−	+

$$\cos(x) = \frac{\sqrt{2}}{2}$$

Which of the following could be a value for x, in radians?

A) $\dfrac{\pi}{4}$ B) $\dfrac{3\pi}{4}$ C) $\dfrac{6\pi}{5}$ D) $\dfrac{5\pi}{4}$

First, notice that the cosine of the angle is a positive number. Using the unit circle, you know that cosines are only positive for angles in the first or fourth quadrant, where all points have positive x-coordinates. Next, take a look at the answer options, and draw these angles on the unit circle:

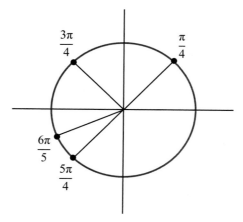

You can see that $\dfrac{3\pi}{4}$ is located in the second quadrant, and $\dfrac{5\pi}{4}$ and $\dfrac{6\pi}{5}$ are located in the third quadrant. You know that cosine is negative in the second and third quadrants, so these angles can't possibly have a cosine equal to $\dfrac{\sqrt{2}}{2}$. Therefore, you can eliminate answer choices (B), (C), and (D).

Since $\dfrac{\pi}{4}$ is located in the first quadrant, we know that its cosine is positive. Therefore, (A) is the only possible answer choice that could have a cosine equal to $\dfrac{\sqrt{2}}{2}$. The correct answer is (A).

Part 3 Practice: Radians and The Unit Circle

1

A woodworker determines that he must drill a hole by spinning a power drill for 3π radians. If one turn of the drill is equal to 360°, how many complete turns must he use to drill the hole?

A) 1

B) 1.5

C) 2

D) 2.5

2

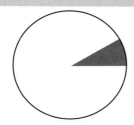

A shaded sector of a circle, with an arc length of $\frac{\pi}{6}$ radians is shown above. What is the arc length, in degrees, of this sector?

A) 20

B) 30

C) 45

D) 60

4

When evaluating the unit circle on the *xy*-plane, which quadrant does $\frac{\pi}{4}$ fall into?

A) Quadrant I

B) Quadrant II

C) Quadrant III

D) Quadrant IV

3

Xiao is playing a game of tether ball with his friend Mei, as shown above. If Xiao needs to hit the ball so that it moves 300° to get to Mei, how many radians must the ball travel?

A) $\frac{5\pi}{3}$

B) $\frac{4\pi}{3}$

C) π

D) $\frac{2\pi}{3}$

5

Cos (32°) is used in a calculation and is multiplied by 13. Which of the following statements is true?

A) Cos(32°) × 13 is negative.

B) Cos(32°) × 13 is positive.

C) Cos(32°) × 13 is equal to sin(32°) × 13.

D) Cos(32°) × 13 cannot be calculated.

6

If cos(317°) is multiplied by 2, which of the following statements is true?

A) Since cos(317°) is negative, the result would be negative.

B) Since cos(317°) is equal to 1, the result would be 2.

C) Since cos(317°) is equal to 0, the result would be 0.

D) There is not enough information to determine the result of this equation.

7

Which of the following is FALSE when considering the value of $\sin\left(\frac{\pi}{2}\right)$?

A) $\sin\left(\frac{\pi}{2}\right)$ is positive.

B) $\sin\left(\frac{\pi}{2}\right) \times \pi = \pi$.

C) $\sin\left(\frac{\pi}{2}\right) \times \cos\left(\frac{\pi}{2}\right)$ is negative.

D) $\sin\left(\frac{\pi}{2}\right) = \sin\left(\frac{5\pi}{2}\right)$.

8

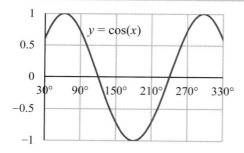

If $\cos\left(\frac{\pi}{6}\right)$ is approximated by $-0.89 \times a$, what is the approximate value of the coefficient of a for $\cos\left(\frac{7\pi}{6}\right)$?

Questions 9 and 10 refer to the following information.

A metal pipe is being cut for use in the manufacturing of sculptural elements for the garden courtyard of a new condominium complex. The engineer has drawn up the transverse of the pipe on an *xy*-graph, as shown below, in order to calculate where it needs to be cut.

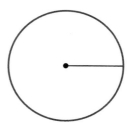

9

One straight horizontal line is drawn from a circle's midpoint to the circle's edge, as shown above. If another line is drawn at an angle of 228° with respect to the first line, which quadrant does this line fall into?

10

The engineer then decides that the pipe should instead be cut at an angle of 179°. Assuming that the first cut is made at an angle of 0°, in which quadrant should the second cut be made?

Circles
Part 4

In Part 1, we discussed how to find the area and circumference of a circle using the circle's radius and diameter. In this part, we'll talk about different parts of circles, and we'll discuss how to find the perimeters and areas of sections within a circle, subjects that frequently appear on the Additional Topics content of the Math test.

Chords

A **chord** is a line segment that connects two different points on the circumference of a circle.

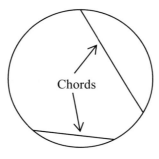

In order to find the length of a chord, you will need to know the circle's radius (r) and the distance from the middle of the chord to the center of the circle (t). You can plug these values into the following formula for chord length:

$$\text{Chord length} = 2\sqrt{r^2 - t^2}$$

You might notice that this formula looks very similar to the Pythagorean theorem. This is because you can derive this formula by using a right triangle. Half of the chord is one leg of the triangle, so in order to find the whole chord, you multiply the leg by two. Can you figure out how to get the rest of the formula from the Pythagorean theorem? Hint: the radius of the circle is the hypotenuse of the right triangle.

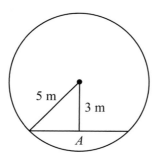

The circle has a radius of 5 m, and chord A is 3 m from the center of the circle. To find the length of chord A, plug these values into the formula for chord length:

$$2\sqrt{(5)^2 - (3)^2} = 2\sqrt{16} = 8$$

The length of the chord is 8 m.

Arcs

An **arc** is a portion of the circumference of a circle. You can think of the arc as being "enclosed" by two radii:

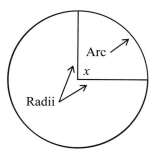

Each arc corresponds to the angle formed between the two radii. The arc in the diagram above corresponds to the angle x.

Arc length is the measure of distance along an arc. The ratio of the arc length to the circumference of the circle is equal to the ratio of the arc angle to the angle of the entire circle, which is 2π radians or $360°$.

To calculate the arc length for an arc angle x, use the following proportions:

$$\frac{\text{Arc Length}}{\text{Circumference}} = \frac{x°}{360°}$$

$$\frac{\text{Arc Length}}{\text{Circumference}} = \frac{x \text{ radians}}{2\pi \text{ radians}}$$

Example

What is the arc length for a circle with a radius of 3 and an arc angle of $120°$?

First, calculate the circumference of the circle:

$$\text{Circumference} = 2\pi r = 2\pi \times 3 = 6\pi$$

Then, set up the proportion to solve for arc length:

$$\frac{\text{Arc Length}}{\text{Circumference}} = \frac{x°}{360°}$$

$$\frac{\text{Arc Length}}{6\pi} = \frac{120°}{360°}$$

$$\text{Arc Length} = 6\pi \times \frac{120°}{360°}$$

$$\text{Arc Length} = 2\pi$$

The arc length is 2π.

If the arc angle x is in radians, you can manipulate the arc length proportion above to create a very simple formula for arc length. Here's the proportion again:

$$\frac{\text{Arc Length}}{\text{Circumference}} = \frac{x}{2\pi}$$

First, plug in $2\pi r$ for the circumference, and then simplify:

$$\frac{\text{Arc Length}}{2\pi r} = \frac{x}{2\pi}$$

$$\text{Arc Length} = 2\pi r \times \frac{x}{2\pi}$$

$$\text{Arc Length} = r \times x$$

The length of an arc is equal to the radius of the circle multiplied by the arc angle in radians. To solve the example question above, you could also convert $120°$ into radians and multiply by the radius. $120°$ is equal to $\frac{2\pi}{3}$ radians, and the radius is 3, so the arc length is equal to:

$$r \times x = 3 \times \frac{2\pi}{3} = 2\pi$$

Sectors

A **sector** is the area enclosed by two radii and the arc that they create. Think of a sector as a slice from a circular pizza.

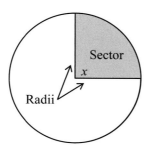

The area of a sector is also determined by the angle x between the two radii. The ratio of the sector area to the area of the circle is equal to the ratio of the sector angle to the angle of the entire circle. To calculate the sector area for a sector angle x, use the following proportions:

$$\frac{\text{Sector Area}}{\text{Circle Area}} = \frac{x°}{360°} \qquad \frac{\text{Sector Area}}{\text{Circle Area}} = \frac{x \text{ radians}}{2\pi \text{ radians}}$$

Example

What is the area of a sector with an angle of 120° and a radius of 3?

First, calculate the area of the circle:

$$\text{Circle Area} = \pi r^2 = \pi \times 3^2 = 9\pi$$

Then, set up the proportion to solve for sector area:

$$\frac{\text{Sector Area}}{\text{Circle Area}} = \frac{x°}{360°}$$

$$\frac{\text{Sector Area}}{9\pi} = \frac{120°}{360°}$$

$$\text{Sector Area} = 9\pi \times \frac{120°}{360°}$$

$$\text{Sector Area} = 3\pi$$

The area of the sector is 3π.

Graphing Circles

Circles can be graphed on the xy-plane. On the SAT, you will need to know the equation of a circle on the xy-plane. You will also need to know how to find the circle's center and radius from its equation or its graph. If you know the central point of the circle and another point on the circumference, you can find the radius of the circle.

The figure below shows a circle with a center at point (h, k). The point (x, y) is found on the circumference of the circle. You can connect these two points with a radius of the circle, and draw a right triangle:

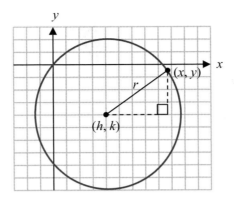

The hypotenuse of this right triangle is the radius of the circle, r. The base of the triangle is equal to the difference between the two x-coordinates of the points: $x - h$. The height of the triangle is equal to the difference between the two y-coordinates: $y - k$.

To set up an equation that describes the relationship between the radius and the two points, you can plug in the lengths for the sides of the triangle into the Pythagorean theorem:

$$(x - h)^2 + (y - k)^2 = r^2$$

This is the standard form for the equation of a circle. This equation tells you that the circle has its center at point (h, k) and a radius with length r.

Example

The equation of a circle is defined by the equation $(x - 2)^2 + (y + 1)^2 = 144$. What are the center and radius of this circle?

In order to find the center and radius of this circle, you'll need to rewrite its equation so it looks like the formula above:

$$(x - 2)^2 + (y - (-1))^2 = 12^2$$

Now that the equation is in standard form, you can see that $h = 2$, $k = -1$, and $r = 12$. Therefore, the circle's center is located at $(2, -1)$, and the circle's radius is 12.

1

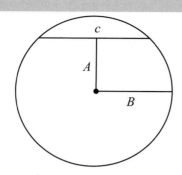

In the figure above, chord c is perpendicular to A and parallel to the radius B. If the length of A is 2 and B is 3, which of the following is the length of chord c?

A) $\sqrt{5}$

B) $2\sqrt{5}$

C) $\sqrt{13}$

D) $2\sqrt{13}$

2

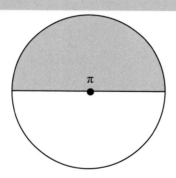

In the figure above the circle's diameter is 20. If the angle of the shaded area is π radians, which of the following is the length of the corresponding arc?

A) π

B)   10

C) 10π

D)   30

3

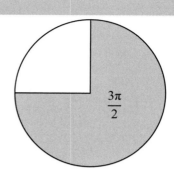

In the circle above, the radius is 4 and the angle of the shaded area is $\dfrac{3\pi}{2}$ radians. Which of the following is the length of the corresponding arc?

A) 6π

B) 16π

C) 25π

D) 32π

4

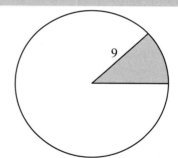

Susan orders a pizza pie that is divided into 8 equally sized slices. If she takes one slice out of the pie as shown above, which of the following is the arc length of the slice?

A) 2π

B) 2.25π

C) 2.5π

D) 4π

Questions 5 and 6 refer to the following information.

The circle below has a radius of 4. Its shaded sector represents $\frac{1}{16}$ of the total area of the circle.

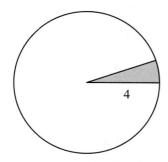

5

According to the figure, which of the following is the value for the area that is twice the shaded sector?

A) π

B) 2π

C) $\frac{3\pi}{2}$

D) 4π

6

Which of the following is the value of the angle, in radians, that corresponds to the shaded sector?

A) $\frac{\pi}{4}$

B) $\frac{3\pi}{8}$

C) $\frac{\pi}{8}$

D) $\frac{\pi}{16}$

7

Revenue for O'Chicken

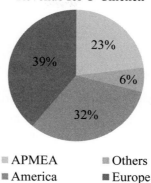

- APMEA
- America
- Others
- Europe

The figure above shows worldwide income distribution for O'Chicken Corporation in 2012. What is the value of the sector angle, in degrees, that corresponds to America?

A) 32

B) 82.8

C) 115.2

D) 140.4

8

If Sector Z of a circle with a diameter of 1 m has an area of 0.5 m^2, what is the value of the sector angle that corresponds to Sector Z to the nearest degree?

9

If a 10 foot long chord is located 12 feet from the center of a circle, what is the value of the circle's radius?

10

$$(x-1)^2 + (y-1)^2 = 9$$

The circle provided by the equation above has radius a, and its center is located at the point (b, c). What is the value of abc?

Complex Numbers

Part 5

So far, we have discussed the properties of real numbers, or any number that can be found on a number line. In this part, we'll see what numbers lie beyond the real numbers. These include imaginary and complex numbers, which use the symbol i and follow special rules. These numbers are often tested in the SAT as a part of simple- or medium-difficulty algebraic expressions or equations.

Imaginary Numbers

Normally, it is impossible to take the square root of a negative number. Even when you square a negative number, you end up with a positive result. Therefore, there isn't a way to work backwards and find a real number that is the square root of a negative number.

However, sometimes it is helpful to "imagine" that we can take the square root of a negative number and use this in our calculations. We can do this by introducing the unit i, which is equal to the square root of -1:

$$i^2 = -1$$

$$i = \sqrt{-1}$$

Because a number like i does not exist in the set of real numbers, we call it an **imaginary number**. In equations and calculations that involve imaginary numbers, we can use i as a placeholder for $\sqrt{-1}$. In questions using imaginary numbers, the SAT Math Test will always provide the equation for i, as shown above.

Simplifying Expressions With i

In an expression that involves imaginary numbers, you can simplify the square root of any negative number by using i.

Example
Simplify $\dfrac{\sqrt{-16}}{2}$ in terms of i.

First, re-write the square root as the product of two square roots:

$$\frac{\sqrt{-16}}{2} = \frac{\sqrt{-1} \times \sqrt{16}}{2}$$

Then, plug in i for $\sqrt{-1}$ and simplify:

$$\frac{\sqrt{-1} \times \sqrt{16}}{2} = \frac{i \times \sqrt{16}}{2} = \frac{4i}{2} = 2i$$

Your final answer is $2i$.

We know that the square of i is -1, but now let's look at what happens when we raise i to another exponent. For example, what happens when you take the cube of i? You can substitute $\sqrt{-1}$ for i in order to work out the equation:

$$i^3 = \left(\sqrt{-1}\right)^3$$
$$i^3 = \sqrt{-1} \times \sqrt{-1} \times \sqrt{-1}$$
$$i^3 = -1 \times \sqrt{-1}$$
$$i^3 = -1 \times i$$
$$i^3 = -i$$

The square of i is -1, but the cube of i is $-i$.

Using the same method, values of i raised to other common exponents are summarized below:

$i^0 = 1$	$i^1 = i$	$i^2 = -1$	$i^3 = -i$	$i^4 = 1$

You will notice that the values of i^0 and i^4 are the same. This is also true for the values of i^1 and i^5. In fact, there are only four values possible for i raised to an exponent: 1, i, -1, and $-i$; these values always repeat in a pattern of four. Using this table, you can determine the value of i raised to any other power.

Let's see how to figure out the value of i^5.

You know that $i^4 = 1$ and $i^5 = i^4 \times i$. Plugging in these values, you can write:

$$i^5 = 1 \times i = i$$

Therefore, i^5 is the same thing as i, or $\sqrt{-1}$.

Complex Numbers

A **complex number** is the sum of a real number and an imaginary number. Complex numbers are normally written in the form $a + bi$, where a is the real component and bi is the imaginary component. For example, $4 + 2i$ is a complex number with a real component, 4, and an imaginary component, $2i$.

On the SAT, you'll need to know how to simplify expressions with complex numbers by adding, subtracting, and multiplying. These operations are simple if you treat the imaginary variable i like any other variable in an algebraic expression.

To add or subtract expressions with complex numbers, first group together like terms—that is, group real numbers together and group imaginary numbers together. Then, add or subtract the real numbers, and add or subtract the imaginary numbers.

Example
$(3 + 5i) + (2 + 3i)$

First, group together the real numbers and the imaginary numbers:

$$3 + 5i + 2 + 3i = (3 + 2) + (5i + 3i)$$

Then, add the like terms:

$$(3 + 2) + (5i + 3i) = 5 + 8i$$

The final answer is $5 + 8i$.

Multiplying complex numbers is similar to multiplying binomials: use the FOIL method to multiply all of the components in the complex numbers. The only difference is that you'll need to simplify i raised to any power greater than 1. See Section 5 for a review of the FOIL method.

Example
$(3 - 4i)(6 + 2i)$

Use the FOIL method to multiply out the two binomials:

$$(3 - 4i)(6 + 2i) = 18 + 6i - 24i - 8i^2$$

Then, combine like terms:

$$18 + 6i - 24i - 8i^2 = -8i^2 - 18i + 18$$

Notice that you have i^2 in the answer. Because $i^2 = -1$, you can plug -1 into the answer in place of i^2:

$$-8(-1) - 18i + 18 = 8 - 18i + 18$$

Finally, combine like terms again:

$$26 - 18i$$

The final simplified answer is $26 - 18i$.

Part 5 Practice: Complex Numbers

1

For $i = \sqrt{-1}$, which of the following expresses $\sqrt{-64}$ in terms of i?

A) $-\sqrt{8}i$

B) $\sqrt{-8}i$

C) $8i$

D) $64i$

2

Which of the following expressions is NOT equal to $8\sqrt{-49}$? $\left(\text{Note: } i = \sqrt{-1}\right)$

A) $\sqrt{3136}i$

B) $7\sqrt{64}i$

C) $\sqrt{56}i$

D) $56i$

3

Which of the following is equal to $(8 + 2i) + (2 + 8i)$? $\left(\text{Note: } i = \sqrt{-1}\right)$

A) 0

B) $10 + 10i$

C) $10 + 16i$

D) -6

4

If $\dfrac{5\sqrt{-4}}{2i} = 3w$, what is the value of w? $\left(\text{Note: } i = \sqrt{-1}\right)$

A) $\dfrac{3}{5}$

B) $\dfrac{5}{3}$

C) $\dfrac{10}{3}$

D) 5

Questions 5 and 6 use the following information.

Measure of impedance in an electrical circuit is commonly calculated in electrical engineering. It is represented, in a simple form, by the equation $Z = C + jL$, where Z is the circuit's impedance, C and L are constants, and j is a function of i. $\left(\text{Note: } i = \sqrt{-1}\right)$

5

If C is 2, $j = i^3$, and L is 5, which of the following is equal to the circuit's impedance?

A) 7

B) $5i + 2$

C) -7

D) $-5i + 2$

6

If C is 0, $j = i^{10}$, and L is 1, which of the following is NOT equal to the circuit's impedance?

A) i

B) i^2

C) i^6

D) i^{14}

7

If $(1 + i) \times (7 + i) = 2r$ and $i = \sqrt{-1}$, what is the value of r?

A) $4i + 3$

B) $8i + 6$

C) $9i$

D) 7

8

If $(49 - 2i) - (48 - i) = \dfrac{x - 4i}{4}$, what is the value of x? (Note: $i = \sqrt{-1}$)

9

If $(1 + i) \times (1 - i) = 2x$, what is the value of x? (Note: $i = \sqrt{-1}$)

10

If $i = \sqrt{-1}$, what is the value of $(3 + 3i) \times (4 - 4i)$?

Practice Tests

Chapter 6

Practice Test 1

SAT

Directions

- Work on just one section at a time.

- If you complete a section before the end of your allotted time, use the extra minutes to check your work on that section only. Do NOT use the time to work on another section.

Using Your Test Booklet

- No credit will be given for anything written in the test booklet. You may use the test booklet for scratch paper.

- You are not allowed to continue answering questions in a section after the allotted time has run out. This includes marking answers on your answer sheet that you previously noted in your test booklet.

- You are not allowed to fold pages, take pages out of the test booklet, or take any pages home.

Answering Questions

- Each answer must be marked in the corresponding row on the answer sheet.

- Each bubble must be filled in completely and darkly within the lines.

Correct ●   Incorrect

- Be careful to bubble in the correct part of the answer sheet.

- Extra marks on your answer sheet may be marked as incorrect answers and lower your score.

- Make sure you use a No. 2 pencil.

Scoring

- You will receive one point for each correct answer.

- Incorrect answers will NOT result in points deducted. Even if you are unsure about an answer, you should make a guess.

DO NOT BEGIN THIS TEST

UNTIL YOUR PROCTOR TELLS YOU TO DO SO

For printable answer sheets, please visit **ivyglobal.com/study**.

Section 1

	A	B	C	D			A	B	C	D			A	B	C	D			A	B	C	D			A	B	C	D
1	○	○	○	○		12	○	○	○	○		23	○	○	○	○		34	○	○	○	○		45	○	○	○	○
2	○	○	○	○		13	○	○	○	○		24	○	○	○	○		35	○	○	○	○		46	○	○	○	○
3	○	○	○	○		14	○	○	○	○		25	○	○	○	○		36	○	○	○	○		47	○	○	○	○
4	○	○	○	○		15	○	○	○	○		26	○	○	○	○		37	○	○	○	○		48	○	○	○	○
5	○	○	○	○		16	○	○	○	○		27	○	○	○	○		38	○	○	○	○		49	○	○	○	○
6	○	○	○	○		17	○	○	○	○		28	○	○	○	○		39	○	○	○	○		50	○	○	○	○
7	○	○	○	○		18	○	○	○	○		29	○	○	○	○		40	○	○	○	○		51	○	○	○	○
8	○	○	○	○		19	○	○	○	○		30	○	○	○	○		41	○	○	○	○		52	○	○	○	○
9	○	○	○	○		20	○	○	○	○		31	○	○	○	○		42	○	○	○	○						
10	○	○	○	○		21	○	○	○	○		32	○	○	○	○		43	○	○	○	○						
11	○	○	○	○		22	○	○	○	○		33	○	○	○	○		44	○	○	○	○						

Section 2

	A	B	C	D			A	B	C	D			A	B	C	D			A	B	C	D			A	B	C	D
1	○	○	○	○		10	○	○	○	○		19	○	○	○	○		28	○	○	○	○		37	○	○	○	○
2	○	○	○	○		11	○	○	○	○		20	○	○	○	○		29	○	○	○	○		38	○	○	○	○
3	○	○	○	○		12	○	○	○	○		21	○	○	○	○		30	○	○	○	○		39	○	○	○	○
4	○	○	○	○		13	○	○	○	○		22	○	○	○	○		31	○	○	○	○		40	○	○	○	○
5	○	○	○	○		14	○	○	○	○		23	○	○	○	○		32	○	○	○	○		41	○	○	○	○
6	○	○	○	○		15	○	○	○	○		24	○	○	○	○		33	○	○	○	○		42	○	○	○	○
7	○	○	○	○		16	○	○	○	○		25	○	○	○	○		34	○	○	○	○		43	○	○	○	○
8	○	○	○	○		17	○	○	○	○		26	○	○	○	○		35	○	○	○	○		44	○	○	○	○
9	○	○	○	○		18	○	○	○	○		27	○	○	○	○		36	○	○	○	○						

Section 3 (No-Calculator)

	A	B	C	D		A	B	C	D		A	B	C	D		A	B	C	D		A	B	C	D
1	○	○	○	○	4	○	○	○	○	7	○	○	○	○	10	○	○	○	○	13	○	○	○	○
2	○	○	○	○	5	○	○	○	○	8	○	○	○	○	11	○	○	○	○	14	○	○	○	○
3	○	○	○	○	6	○	○	○	○	9	○	○	○	○	12	○	○	○	○	15	○	○	○	○

Only answers that are gridded will be scored. You will not receive credit for anything written in the boxes.

16 17 18 19 20

(grid-in answer bubbles for questions 16–20, with digits 0–9, decimal point, and fraction slash)

Section 4 (Calculator)

	A	B	C	D		A	B	C	D		A	B	C	D		A	B	C	D		A	B	C	D
1	○	○	○	○	7	○	○	○	○	13	○	○	○	○	19	○	○	○	○	25	○	○	○	○
2	○	○	○	○	8	○	○	○	○	14	○	○	○	○	20	○	○	○	○	26	○	○	○	○
3	○	○	○	○	9	○	○	○	○	15	○	○	○	○	21	○	○	○	○	27	○	○	○	○
4	○	○	○	○	10	○	○	○	○	16	○	○	○	○	22	○	○	○	○	28	○	○	○	○
5	○	○	○	○	11	○	○	○	○	17	○	○	○	○	23	○	○	○	○	29	○	○	○	○
6	○	○	○	○	12	○	○	○	○	18	○	○	○	○	24	○	○	○	○	30	○	○	○	○

Only answers that are gridded will be scored. You will not receive credit for anything written in the boxes.

31 | **32** | **33** | **34** | **35**

(grid-in answer bubbles for questions 31–35, each with fraction bar, decimal point, and digits 0–9)

Only answers that are gridded will be scored. You will not receive credit for anything written in the boxes.

36 | **37** | **38**

(grid-in answer bubbles for questions 36–38, each with fraction bar, decimal point, and digits 0–9)

Important: Use a No. 2 pencil. Write inside the borders.

You may use the space below to plan your essay, but be sure to write your essay on the lined pages. Work on this page will not be scored.

Use this space to plan your essay.

START YOUR ESSAY HERE.

_____

_____

_____

_____

_____

_____

_____

_____

_____

_____

_____

_____

_____

_____

_____

_____

_____

_____

_____

_____

_____

_____

_____

_____

Continue on the next page.

Continue on the next page.

Practice Tests

_____

_____

_____

_____

_____

_____

_____

_____

_____

_____

_____

_____

_____

_____

_____

_____

_____

_____

_____

_____

_____

_____

_____

_____

_____

_____

_____

_____

_____

Continue on the next page.

STOP.

Practice Tests

Reading Test

65 MINUTES, 52 QUESTIONS

Turn to Section 1 of your answer sheet to answer the questions in this section.

DIRECTIONS

Every passage or paired set of passages is accompanied by a number of questions. Read the passage or paired set of passages, then use what is said or implied in what you read and in any given graphics to choose the best answer to each question.

Questions 1-11 are based on the following passage and supplementary material.

This passage is adapted from The Economist, "The U-Bend of Life." © 2014 by The Economist.

Ask people how they feel about getting older, and they will probably reply in the same vein as Maurice Chevalier: "Old age isn't so bad when you consider
Line the alternative." Stiffening joints, weakening muscles,
5 fading eyesight and the clouding of memory, coupled with the modern world's careless contempt for the old, seem a fearful prospect—better than death, perhaps, but not much. Yet mankind is wrong to dread aging. Life is not a long slow decline from
10 sunlit uplands towards the valley of death. It is, rather, a U-bend.

When people start out on adult life, they are, on average, pretty cheerful. Things go downhill from youth to middle age until they reach a nadir
15 commonly known as the mid-life crisis. So far, so familiar. The surprising part happens after that. Although as people move towards old age they lose things they treasure—vitality, mental sharpness and looks—they also gain what people spend their lives
20 pursuing: happiness.

This curious finding has emerged from a new branch of economics that seeks a more satisfactory measure than money of human well-being.

Conventional economics uses money as a proxy
25 for utility—the dismal way in which the discipline

talks about happiness. But some economists, unconvinced that there is a direct relationship between money and well-being, have decided to go to the nub of the matter and measure happiness itself.
30 Ask a bunch of 30-year-olds and another of 70-year-olds (as Peter Ubel, of the Sanford School of Public Policy at Duke University, did with two colleagues, Heather Lacey and Dylan Smith, in 2006) which group they think is likely to be happier, and
35 both lots point to the 30-year-olds. Ask them to rate their own well-being, and the 70-year-olds are the happier bunch. The academics quoted lyrics written by Pete Townshend of The Who when he was 20: "Things they do look awful cold / Hope I die before I
40 get old". They pointed out that Mr. Townshend, having passed his 60th birthday, was writing a blog that glowed with good humor.

Mr. Townshend may have thought of himself as a youthful radical, but this view is ancient and
45 conventional. The "seven ages of man"—the dominant image of the life-course in the 16th and 17th centuries—was almost invariably conceived as a rise in stature and contentedness to middle age, followed by a sharp decline towards the grave.
50 Inverting the rise and fall is a recent idea. "A few of us noticed the U-bend in the early 1990s," says Andrew Oswald, professor of economics at Warwick Business School. "We ran a conference about it, but nobody came."

CONTINUE

55   Since then, interest in the U-bend has been growing. Its effect on happiness is significant. It appears all over the world. David Blanchflower, professor of economics at Dartmouth College, and Mr. Oswald looked at the figures for 72 countries.

60   The nadir varies among countries—Ukrainians, at the top of the range, are at their most miserable at 62, and Swiss, at the bottom, at 35—but in the great majority of countries people are at their unhappiest in their 40s and early 50s. The global average is 46.

Approximate Age of Minimum
Happiness Across Countries

Country Name	Age of Minimum Happiness
All countries	46
Australia	40
Brazil	37
Canada	54
France	62
Mexico	41
Puerto Rico	36
Ukraine	62
United States	40

1

The primary purpose of the passage is to

A) interpret a phenomenon observed by economists.

B) discuss the findings of a group of economists.

C) explore competing measures of happiness.

D) relate an interesting anecdote about happiness and aging.

2

The passage most strongly implies that

A) conventional economic measures of happiness are unsatisfactory.

B) the "seven ages of man" can still describe the lives of some seniors.

C) conventional economists have not previously been interested in happiness.

D) the trend of happiness increasing in old age means people will no longer fear aging.

3

Which choice provides the best evidence for the answer to the previous question?

A) Lines 9-11 ("Life is … death")

B) Lines 17-20 ("Although as … happiness")

C) Lines 24-26 ("Conventional economics … happiness")

D) Lines 30-37 ("Ask … happier bunch")

4

The passage suggests that the conventional view of aging as a "slow decline" (line 10) from joyful youth to unhappy old age is

A) the opposite of most adults' real experience.

B) basically correct about life through middle age, but not old age.

C) usually correct but with a few notable exceptions.

D) accurate with respect to the elderly but not the young.

CONTINUE

5

As used in line 2, "vein" most nearly means

A) style.

B) humor.

C) strain.

D) streak.

6

The Duke University academics most likely quoted Pete Townshend in their study (lines 39-40) in order to

A) support the idea that most 70-year-olds underestimate their happiness.

B) exemplify a typical contrast between expectations and experiences of aging.

C) suggest that most seniors are happier than they expected to be as they aged.

D) explain why a conventional view has often been perceived as radical.

7

Which choice provides the best evidence for the answer to the previous question?

A) Lines 1-4 ("Ask … the alternative")

B) Lines 26-29 ("But some … itself")

C) Lines 40-42 ("They … good humor")

D) Lines 50-53 ("Inverting the … School")

8

The author refers to the "seven ages of man" (line 45) primarily in order to

A) highlight how the definition of happiness has changed over time.

B) suggest that some attitudes about aging have a basis in history.

C) contrast an earlier view of happiness and aging with the one introduced in the passage.

D) emphasize that numerous models exist for predicting happiness during various life stages.

9

As used in line 60, "nadir" most nearly means

A) abyss.

B) low point.

C) zero.

D) bedrock.

10

The passage and table most strongly support which of the following conclusions?

A) Most Ukrainians are happier at 70 than at 62.

B) Most Ukrainians are at their happiest in their 70s.

C) Few Ukrainians are as happy as the Swiss.

D) Ukrainian 35-year-olds are happier than Swiss 35-year-olds.

11

It can reasonably be inferred from the passage and table that

A) the countries with the happiest citizens also tend to have the earliest ages of minimum happiness.

B) Brazilians tend to be happiest around the age of 36.6, while Mexicans are not at their happiest until 41.4.

C) Australians and Americans experience roughly the same levels of unhappiness during adulthood.

D) after the age of 54, Canadians tend to become happier, while the French tend to become less happy.

CONTINUE

Questions 12-21 are based on the following passage.

This passage is adapted from "Address Before the General Assembly of the United Nations on Peaceful Uses of Atomic Energy," a speech given by President Dwight D. Eisenhower to the General Assembly of the United Nations in 1953.

I feel impelled to speak today in a language that in a sense is new—one which I, who have spent so much of my life in the military profession, would
Line have preferred never to use. That new language is the
5 language of atomic warfare.

The atomic age has moved forward at such a pace that every citizen of the world should have some comprehension, at least in comparative terms, of the extent of this development of the utmost significance
10 to every one of us. Clearly, if the peoples of the world are to conduct an intelligent search for peace, they must be armed with the significant facts of today's existence. Atomic bombs today are more than 25 times as powerful as the weapons with which the
15 atomic age dawned, while hydrogen weapons are in the ranges of millions of tons of TNT equivalent. Today, the United States' stockpile of atomic weapons, which, of course, increases daily, exceeds by many times the explosive equivalent of the total
20 of all bombs and all shells that came from every plane and every gun in every theatre of war in all of the years of World War II.

But the dread secret, and the fearful engines of atomic might, are not ours alone. In the first place,
25 the secret is possessed by our friends and allies, Great Britain and Canada, whose scientific genius made a tremendous contribution to our original discoveries, and the designs of atomic bombs. The secret is also known by the Soviet Union. The Soviet
30 Union has informed us that, over recent years, it has devoted extensive resources to atomic weapons. During this period, the Soviet Union has exploded a series of atomic devices, including at least one involving thermo-nuclear reactions.
35 If at one time the United States possessed what might have been called a monopoly of atomic power, that monopoly ceased to exist several years ago.

Therefore, although our earlier start has permitted us to accumulate what is today a great quantitative
40 advantage, the atomic realities of today comprehend two facts of even greater significance.

First, the knowledge now possessed by several nations will eventually be shared by others—possibly all others. Second, even a vast superiority in numbers
45 of weapons, and a consequent capability of devastating retaliation, is no preventive, of itself, against the fearful material damage and toll of human lives that would be inflicted by surprise aggression.

The free world, at least dimly aware of these
50 facts, has naturally embarked on a large program of warning and defense systems. That program will be accelerated and expanded. But let no one think that the expenditure of vast sums for weapons and systems of defense can guarantee absolute safety for
55 the cities and citizens of any nation. The awful arithmetic of the atomic bomb does not permit of any such easy solution. Even against the most powerful defense, an aggressor in possession of the effective minimum number of atomic bombs for a surprise
60 attack could probably place a sufficient number of his bombs on the chosen targets to cause hideous damage.

Surely no sane member of the human race could discover victory in such desolation. Could anyone
65 wish his name to be coupled by history with such human degradation and destruction? Occasional pages of history do record the faces of the "Great Destroyers" but the whole book of history reveals mankind's never-ending quest for peace. It is with
70 the book of history, and not with isolated pages, that the United States will ever wish to be identified. My country wants to be constructive, not destructive. It wants agreements, not wars, among nations. It wants itself to live in freedom, and in the confidence that
75 the people of every other nation enjoy equally the right of choosing their own way of life.

So my country's purpose is to help us move out of the dark chamber of horrors into the light, to find a way by which the minds of men, the hopes of men,
80 the souls of men everywhere, can move forward toward peace and happiness and well being.

CONTINUE

12

The passage primarily focuses on which of the following characteristics of atomic warfare?

A) The serious threat it poses to the future of humanity

B) Its application to new situations in warfare

C) How recently it became available to Western nations

D) Its advantages over other types of warfare

13

Which choice provides the best evidence for the answer to the previous question?

A) Lines 13-16 ("Atomic … TNT equivalent")

B) Lines 35-37 ("If at … years ago")

C) Lines 57-62 ("Even against … hideous damage")

D) Lines 73-76 ("It wants … of life")

14

Eisenhower's tone is best described as

A) apologetic.

B) exhilarated.

C) concerned.

D) cynical.

15

The passage most strongly suggests that Eisenhower would wish to pursue which of the following?

A) Expansion of the United States' nuclear weapons production

B) Development of a peaceful nuclear energy program for the United States and other countries

C) Agreements between the United States and other countries to limit nuclear weapons usage

D) The sharing of United States nuclear weapons expertise with other countries

16

Which choice provides the best evidence for the answer to the previous question?

A) Lines 42-44 ("First … all others")

B) Lines 49-51 ("The … defense systems")

C) Lines 52-55 ("But let … nation")

D) Lines 72-73 ("It wants … among nations")

17

The main rhetorical effect of lines 17-22 is to

A) emphasize the unprecedented power of atomic weapons.

B) explain how numerous the weapons of World War II were.

C) provide background information on other types of weaponry.

D) suggest that atomic weapons function in similar ways to older types of arms.

CONTINUE

18

As used in line 47, "material" most nearly means

A) physical.

B) essential.

C) relevant.

D) worldly.

19

As used in line 65, "coupled" most nearly means

A) compounded.

B) fused.

C) married.

D) associated.

20

Eisenhower refers to "the book of history" (line 70) in order to suggest that the United States

A) wishes to be associated with seeking peace rather than destruction.

B) is able to shape history through the choices it makes.

C) has sought compromises with other nations to avoid atomic warfare.

D) identifies strongly with the history of warfare.

21

The final paragraph primarily serves to

A) contradict Eisenhower's earlier statements about peace.

B) offer a concrete strategy for avoiding warfare.

C) suggest how Eisenhower wishes the United States to proceed.

D) encourage other countries to cooperate with the United States.

CONTINUE

Questions 22-32 are based on the following passage and supplementary material.

This passage is adapted from Carl Zimmer, "This Is Your Brain on Writing." © 2014 by The New York Times Company.

A novelist scrawling away in a notebook in seclusion may not seem to have much in common with an NBA player doing a reverse layup on a basketball court before a screaming crowd. But if
5 you could peer inside their heads, you might see some striking similarities in how their brains were churning.

That's one of the implications of new research on the neuroscience of creative writing. For the first
10 time, neuroscientists have used fMRI scanners to track the brain activity of both experienced and novice writers as they sat down—or, in this case, lay down—to turn out a piece of fiction. The researchers, led by Martin Lotze of the University of
15 Greifswald in Germany, observed a broad network of regions in the brain working together as people produced their stories. But there were notable differences between the two groups of subjects. The inner workings of the professionally trained writers in
20 the bunch, the scientists argue, showed some similarities to people who are skilled at other complex actions, like music or sports.

To begin, Dr. Lotze asked 28 volunteers to simply copy some text, giving him a baseline
25 reading of their brain activity during writing. Next, he showed his volunteers a few lines from a short story and asked them to continue it in their own words. The volunteers could brainstorm for a minute, and then write creatively for a little over two minutes.
30 Some regions of the brain became active only during the creative process, but not while copying, the researchers found. During the brainstorming sessions, some vision-processing regions of volunteers became active. It's possible that they were, in effect,
35 seeing the scenes they wanted to write.

Other regions became active when the volunteers started jotting down their stories. Dr. Lotze suspects that one of them, the hippocampus, was retrieving factual information that the volunteers could use. One
40 region near the front of the brain, known to be crucial for holding several pieces of information in mind at once, became active as well. Juggling several characters and plot lines may put special demands on it.

But Dr. Lotze also recognized a big limit of the
45 study: his subjects had no previous experience in creative writing. Would the brains of full-time writers respond differently? To find out, he and his colleagues went to another German university, the University of Hildesheim, which runs a highly competitive creative
50 writing program. The scientists recruited 20 writers there (their average age was 25). Dr. Lotze and his colleagues had them take the same tests and then compared their performance with the novices'.

As the scientists report in a new study in the journal
55 *NeuroImage*, the brains of expert writers appeared to work differently, even before they set pen to paper. During brainstorming, the novice writers activated their visual centers. By contrast, the brains of expert writers showed more activity in regions involved in speech. "I
60 think both groups are using different strategies," Dr. Lotze said. It's possible that the novices are watching their stories like a film inside their heads, while the writers are narrating them with an inner voice.

When the two groups started to write, another set of
65 differences emerged. Deep inside the brains of expert writers, a region called the caudate nucleus became active. In the novices, the caudate nucleus was quiet. The caudate nucleus is a familiar part of the brain for scientists like Dr. Lotze who study expertise. It plays an
70 essential role in the skill that comes with practice, including activities like board games.

When we first start learning a skill—be it playing a piano or playing basketball—we use a lot of conscious effort. With practice, those actions become more
75 automatic. The caudate nucleus and nearby regions start to coordinate the brain's activity as this shift happens. "I was really happy to see this," said Ronald T. Kellogg, a psychologist who studies writing at Saint Louis University. "You don't want to see this as an analog to what James
80 Joyce was doing in Dublin. But to see that they were able to get clean results with this, I think that's a major step right there." But Steven Pinker, a Harvard psychologist, was skeptical that the experiments could provide a clear picture of creativity. "It's a messy comparison," he said.

CONTINUE

Brain Activity in Expert Writers

Area*	Level of Activity
Brainstorming	
Inf. occipital gyrus le	7.51
Inf. occipital gyrus ri	7.47
Inf. frontal gyrus le	6.20
Inf. frontal gyrus ri	5.47
Creative writing	
Inf. occipital le	9.41
Inf. occipital ri	9.15
Inf. frontal gyrus le	9.07
Inf. frontal gyrus ri	6.95
Thalamus le	5.40

*Anatomical description; ri: right; le: left; inf.: inferior.

22

The stance the author takes in the passage is best described as that of

A) an interested observer.

B) an excited colleague.

C) a skeptical rival scientist.

D) a concerned creative writer.

23

The passage most strongly suggests that

A) writers draw on their own knowledge during creative writing.

B) most people may not realize that creative writing is a learnable skill.

C) it is important for all neuroscience studies to include both experts and novices.

D) all expert writers employ the same approach to writing.

24

Which choice provides the best evidence for the answer to the previous question?

A) Lines 37-39 ("Dr. Lotze … use")

B) Lines 61-63 ("It's possible … voice")

C) Lines 65-67 ("Deep inside … active")

D) Lines 75-76 ("The caudate … happens")

25

It can reasonably be inferred from the passage that

A) the hippocampus plays a role in memory.

B) the caudate nucleus grows larger as people learn more skills.

C) experts in any field are less likely to rely on their visual centers when writing creatively.

D) most skills activate only a single area of the brain.

26

As used in line 7, "churning" most nearly means

A) producing.

B) working.

C) proceeding.

D) spinning.

27

The first paragraph primarily serves to

A) make a surprising comparison that the rest of the passage will explain.

B) lay out a hypothesis that the passage will prove to be false.

C) describe a question that has long puzzled researchers.

D) prove that a surprising comparison is indeed true.

CONTINUE

28

Based on the passage, which choice best describes the relationship between novice and expert writers?

A) Novices' brains are less active than experts' brains during writing.

B) Novices' brains are more active than experts' brains during writing.

C) Novices' behavior is less automatic than experts' behavior during writing.

D) Novices' behavior is less intense than experts' behavior during writing.

29

Which choice provides the best evidence for the answer to the previous question?

A) Lines 4-7 ("But if … churning")

B) Lines 13-17 ("The researchers … their stories")

C) Lines 30-32 ("Some … researchers found")

D) Lines 72-74 ("When we … effort")

30

As used in line 76, "coordinate" most nearly means

A) match.

B) organize.

C) correlate.

D) negotiate.

31

The passage most strongly suggests that Steven Pinker would agree with which of the following statements?

A) It is impossible for neuroscientists to truly study creativity.

B) Dr. Lotze's results may not support the broad conclusions discussed in the passage.

C) The caudate nucleus does not become more active in the brains of expert writers.

D) Writing is not a skill that can be easily improved.

32

Which of the following statements is supported by the graphic at the end of the passage?

A) Non-expert writers relied mainly on their occipital and frontal lobes when brainstorming.

B) Non-expert writers saw no significant activation in brain regions that were activated in expert writers.

C) Expert writers used more neural energy in creative writing than in brainstorming.

D) Expert writers showed activity in areas including the left inferior frontal gyrus and left thalamus during creative writing.

CONTINUE

Questions 33-42 are based on the following passage.

This passage is adapted from Jerome K. Jerome, *Three Men in a Boat*, originally published in 1889.

It is a most extraordinary thing, but I never read a patent medicine advertisement without being impelled to the conclusion that I am suffering from
Line the particular disease therein dealt with in its most
5 virulent form. The diagnosis seems in every case to correspond exactly with all the sensations that I have ever felt.

I remember going to the British Museum one day to read up on the treatment for some slight ailment of
10 which I had a touch—hay fever, I fancy it was. I got down the book, and read all I came to read; and then, in an unthinking moment, I idly turned the leaves, and began to indolently study diseases, generally. I forget which was the first distemper I plunged into—
15 some fearful, devastating scourge, I know—and, before I had glanced half down the list of "premonitory symptoms," it was borne in upon me that I had fairly got it.

I sat for awhile, frozen with horror; and then, in
20 the listlessness of despair, I again turned over the pages. I came to typhoid fever—read the symptoms—discovered that I had typhoid fever, must have had it for months without knowing it— wondered what else I had got; turned up St. Vitus's
25 Dance—found, as I expected, that I had that too,— began to get interested in my case, and determined to sift it to the bottom, and so started alphabetically — read up ague, and learnt that I was sickening for it, and that the acute stage would commence in about
30 another fortnight. Bright's disease, I was relieved to find, I had only in a modified form, and, so far as that was concerned, I might live for years. Cholera I had, with severe complications; and diphtheria I seemed to have been born with. I plodded
35 conscientiously through the twenty-six letters, and the only malady I could conclude I had not got was housemaid's knee.

I felt rather hurt about this at first; it seemed somehow to be a sort of slight. Why hadn't I got
40 housemaid's knee? Why this invidious reservation? After a while, however, less grasping feelings prevailed. I reflected that I had every other known malady in the pharmacology, and I grew less selfish, and determined to do without housemaid's knee.
45 Gout, in its most malignant stage, it would appear, had seized me without my being aware of it; and zymosis I had evidently been suffering with from boyhood. There were no more diseases after zymosis, so I concluded there was nothing else the
50 matter with me.

I sat and pondered. I thought what an interesting case I must be from a medical point of view, what an acquisition I should be to a class! Students would have no need to "walk the hospitals," if they had me.
55 I was a hospital in myself. All they need do would be to walk round me, and, after that, take their diploma.

Then I wondered how long I had to live. I tried to examine myself. I felt my pulse. I could not at first feel any pulse at all. Then, all of a sudden, it seemed
60 to start off. I pulled out my watch and timed it. I made it a hundred and forty-seven to the minute. I tried to feel my heart. I could not feel my heart. It had stopped beating. I have since been induced to come to the opinion that it must have been there all
65 the time, and must have been beating, but I cannot account for it. I patted myself all over my front, from what I call my waist up to my head, and I went a bit round each side, and a little way up the back. But I could not feel or hear anything. I tried to look at my
70 tongue. I stuck it out as far as ever it would go, and I shut one eye, and tried to examine it with the other. I could only see the tip, and the only thing that I could gain from that was to feel more certain than before that I had scarlet fever.
75 I had walked into that reading-room a happy, healthy man. I crawled out a decrepit wreck.

CONTINUE

33

Which of the following best describes the passage?

A) An argument about the state of diagnostics in medicine

B) A chilling and cautionary anecdote

C) An entertaining story about false beliefs

D) A description of the symptoms of several common diseases

34

The passage most strongly suggests that the narrator's self-diagnoses of disease are based on

A) his tendency to be swayed by what he reads.

B) changes to his health that he had observed.

C) careful examination by medical professionals.

D) his rigorous study of medicine.

35

Which choice provides the best evidence for the answer to the previous question?

A) Lines 1-5 ("It is ... virulent form")

B) Lines 51-53 ("I thought ... a class")

C) Lines 67-69 ("I patted ... the back")

D) Lines 73-75 ("I could ... fever")

36

The author's approach to retelling this story is best described as

A) reflective.

B) panicked.

C) apologetic.

D) humorous.

37

It can reasonably be inferred from the passage that the narrator

A) somewhat enjoys believing he has many illnesses.

B) is likely to seek medical treatment for his many ailments.

C) has a great respect for the practice of medicine.

D) frequently visits the British Museum.

38

Which choice provides the best evidence for the answer to the previous question?

A) Lines 8-10 ("I remember ... it was")

B) Lines 32-34 ("Cholera ... born with")

C) Lines 42-44 ("I reflected ... housemaid's knee")

D) Lines 71-73 ("I stuck ... the other")

39

As used in line 34, "plodded" most nearly means

A) stumbled.

B) blundered.

C) worked.

D) strived.

40

As used in line 39, "slight" most nearly means

A) indignity.

B) criticism.

C) outrage.

D) shame.

CONTINUE

41

The statement "I was a hospital in myself" (line 55) suggests that the narrator

A) suffered from nearly as many diseases as can be found in an entire hospital.

B) had knowledge of so many illnesses that he could run a hospital.

C) was cured of many illnesses, just like patients in a hospital.

D) was typical of patients found in hospitals of the time.

42

The last two lines (76-77) primarily serve to

A) summarize the transformation that the narrator recounts during the passage.

B) suggest that the narrator was permanently changed by his visit to the British Museum.

C) emphasize the severity of the author's many illnesses.

D) demonstrate that the narrator's experience in the British Museum was unusual for him.

Questions 43-52 are based on the following passages.

Passage 1 is adapted from Erik Olsen, "Protected Reef Offers Model for Conservation." © 2010 by The New York Times Company. Passage 2 is adapted from The New York Times Editorial Board, "To Save Fish and Birds." © 2014 by The New York Times Company.

Passage 1

Glover's Reef, about 28 miles from the coast of Belize, is one of the only true atolls in the Atlantic Ocean. It is also the site of Belize's largest "no-take"
Line marine reserve, a 17,500-acre zone where all types of
5 fishing are prohibited. The no-take zone makes up about 20 percent of the wider 87,000-acre Marine Protected Area here. Within 75 percent of the reserve, some types of fishing are allowed, although there are restrictions on the type of gear that can be
10 used.

According to scientists here, the marine reserve at Glover's Reef offers a test case for the viability of similar reserves around the world. They are now hoping to apply some of the conservation strategies
15 here to make other places succeed. "I think Glover's Reef is a model of hope," says Ellen K. Pikitch, a marine biologist at the Stony Brook University School of Marine and Atmospheric Sciences. Dr. Pikitch runs the Institute for Ocean Conservation
20 Science, an organization seeking wider protection for sharks worldwide. She said that the effort at Glover's "shows that marine reserves, even small marine reserves, can work. I think it's very transportable, this concept."

25 Dr. Pikitch, a self-professed "shark fanatic," has other reasons to be hopeful. She leads the largest shark population study in the Caribbean here at Glover's Reef, now in its 10th year. Shark populations here have remained stable, while others
30 around the world are in severe decline.

The sharks are an integral part of a healthy reef. Along with other top predators they help keep barracuda populations in check, which is important because barracuda consume algae grazers like
35 parrotfish that prevent runaway algae growth from choking the corals.

CONTINUE →

There are still significant challenges. Enforcement remains a problem. The Wildlife Conservation Society shares its home on Middle
40 Caye with an outpost of the Belize Fisheries Department. The department employs four rangers here whose job is to patrol the reef and catch fishermen who violate the fishing ban or who poach undersized conch and spiny lobster outside the no-
45 take zone.

Dr. Pikitch acknowledges that the problems facing reefs here are significant, but she remains optimistic that new information, including data from her shark study, will increase awareness and prompt
50 action to protect reefs. "We are losing coral reefs at an astounding rate," she said. "It's like death by a thousand cuts. So when you have a success like this in a coral ecosystem you say, 'Wow this is great.'"

Passage 2

One of the few bright spots in the struggle to
55 protect the world's fragile oceans has been the rapidly increasing number of "marine protected areas," places where fishing is limited or banned and where, presumably, depleted species can recover by simply being left to themselves. The benefits of
60 hands-off environmental protection may seem self-evident. But creating a preserve and rebuilding a healthy ecosystem are not necessarily the same thing. A recent study published in Nature found that, more often than not, marine protected areas don't work as
65 well as they could.

Researchers with the University of Tasmania studied 87 marine protected areas in 40 countries worldwide, and found that 59 percent of the areas were no better off than areas where fishing was
70 allowed. The reasons for failure varied, but they boiled down to this: not all marine protected areas are alike. Some allow fishing; others forbid it. Some are managed well; others are managed badly. Some are relatively intact; others have been left barren by
75 generations of overfishing.

The researchers identified five essential characteristics of the most successful marine protected areas: These areas were designated "no take" (allowing no fishing whatsoever), their rules
80 were well enforced, they were more than 10 years old, they were bigger than 100 square kilometers, and they were isolated by deep water or sand. Compared with regular fished areas, the areas that had four or five of those attributes had a far richer
85 variety of species, five times the biomass of large fish and 14 times the biomass of sharks, which are indicators of ecological health.

Most underachieving marine sanctuaries had only one or two of these magic factors, and thus
90 "were not ecologically distinguishable from fished sites." The four sanctuaries lucky enough to have all five characteristics were isolated areas in the oceans off Costa Rica, Colombia, New Zealand, and Australia. The "coral triangle" of Southeast Asia also
95 got high marks, but it did not have as great an array of large species as its more isolated counterparts.

43

As used in line 23, "transportable" most nearly means

A) addressable.

B) transmittable.

C) easily moved.

D) transferable.

44

Which of the following situations is most analogous to the role of sharks presented in lines 31-36?

A) Bears contribute to healthy ecosystems by consuming unwanted human trash, which benefits other species.

B) Bears contribute to healthy ecosystems only when their populations are kept low so they do not excessively hunt other animals.

C) Bears contribute to healthy ecosystems by keeping salmon populations under control, which ensures that smaller fish can survive.

D) Bears damage healthy ecosystems by over-fishing salmon populations, which prevents salmon from controlling smaller fish populations.

CONTINUE

45

Information from Passage 2 most strongly suggests that designating a reef as a marine protected area

A) is the only way to safeguard the variety of fish species inhabiting the reef.

B) has no effect unless the marine protected area covers more than 100 square kilometers.

C) is less effective than other methods of protecting marine ecosystems.

D) can be an effective method of protecting fish populations if certain standards are met.

46

Which choice provides the best evidence for the correct answer to the previous question?

A) Lines 54-59 ("One of ... to themselves")

B) Lines 70-72 ("The reasons ... are alike")

C) Lines 83-87 ("Compared with ... health")

D) Lines 91-93 ("The four ... Australia")

47

The author of Passage 2 would most likely agree with which of the following?

A) Marine protected areas are a poor approach to marine conservation and not worth pursuing.

B) Unsuccessful marine protected areas are often undistinguishable from areas that permit fishing.

C) Even when they meet rigorous standards, marine protected areas are not the best method for protecting marine species.

D) Ocean health cannot be improved by a hands-off approach, so marine protected areas are ineffective.

48

Which choice provides the best evidence for the answer to the previous question?

A) Lines 63-65 ("A recent ... could")

B) Lines 66-70 ("Researchers with ... allowed")

C) Lines 78-82 ("These areas ... sand")

D) Lines 94-96 ("The ... isolated counterparts")

49

As used in line 74, "intact" most nearly means

A) solid.

B) faultless.

C) unspoiled.

D) complete.

50

Both Passage 1 and Passage 2 include

A) statistical information about fish populations.

B) data on the ecological health of various protected sites.

C) information about marine predator populations.

D) a summary of recently published scientific research.

CONTINUE

51

Compared to Passage 2, Passage 1 is

A) narrower in its focus.

B) more persuasive in tone.

C) less adamant about its conclusion.

D) more complex in its reasoning.

52

Passage 1 discusses the difficulty of ensuring which of the essential characteristics of marine protected areas discussed in Passage 2?

A) Having areas designated "no-take"

B) Proper enforcement of the rules

C) Being isolated by deep water

D) Placing restrictions on what fishing gear can be used

STOP

If you complete this section before the end of your allotted time, check your work on this section only. Do NOT use the time to work on another section.

Writing and Language Test

35 MINUTES, 44 QUESTIONS

Turn to Section 2 of your answer sheet to answer the questions in this section.

DIRECTIONS

Every passage comes with a set of questions. Some questions will ask you to consider how the writer might revise the passage to improve the expression of ideas. Other questions will ask you to consider correcting potential errors in sentence structure, usage, or punctuation. There may be one or more graphics that you will need to consult as you revise and edit the passage.

Some questions will refer to a portion of the passage that has been underlined. Other questions will refer to a particular spot in a passage or ask that you consider the passage in full.

After you read the passage, select the answers to questions that most effectively improve the passage's writing quality or that adjust the passage to follow the conventions of standard written English. Many questions give you the option to select "NO CHANGE." Select that option in cases where you think the relevant part of the passage should remain as it currently is.

Questions 1-11 are based on the following passage.

Decoding Honey Bee Dance Language

If you look inside a bustling honey bee hive, you may see a single bee dancing wildly among a crowd. On the honey bee "dance floor," other bees gather around to watch and **1** imitate the dancing bee. After a few minutes of matching the movements, the bees leave the hive and all take flight in the same direction.

Scientists have studied the dances of **2** honey bees and the scientists then determined that honey bees readily communicate reliable food sources to each other by dancing. How does this process work? First, honey bees called "scouts" go out to find flowers rich with the bees'

1

A) NO CHANGE
B) impersonate
C) mock
D) duplicate

2

A) NO CHANGE
B) honey bees; then determined
C) honey bees and have determined
D) honey bees then determining

CONTINUE

main source of energy—nectar. **3** <u>At the end of the scout's long day, it returns to the hive to rest and recover for its next trip</u>. The scout dances in quick and deliberate circuits. Forager bees dance behind the scout, "practicing" the scout's dance. The foragers then leave to seek out the nectar and bring it back to the hive.

[1] Researchers have begun to decode the dances by noting what sort of dances scouts perform under varying circumstances. [2] When a nectar source is closer than fifty meters from the hive, scouts perform a "round dance." [3] When the food is farther than seventy-five meters from the hive, scouts perform a "waggle dance." [4] The waggle dance consists of elaborate "figure eight" circuits. [5] The number of dance circuits per fifteen seconds signals how far the nectar source is **4** <u>from the hive, and the angle of the dance</u> tells the forager bees the direction they should fly. [6] For instance, if the nectar source is in the opposite direction from the sun, the bee **5** <u>will perform at least 180 circuits</u>. [7] The circuits signal important information about the location of food to the rest of the hive. **6**

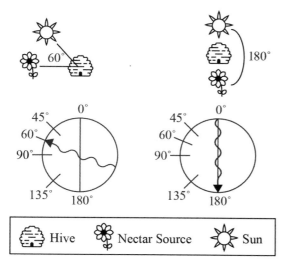

The figure above illustrates the waggle dances performed based on the location of the nectar source (flowers) in relation to the hive and the sun.

3

Which choice most effectively sets up the information that follows?

A) NO CHANGE

B) Bees share the nectar by passing it from one worker to another, and eventually storing it as honey.

C) If the flowers are in bloom, the scout should find plenty of nectar.

D) When a scout finds a promising location of nectar, it returns to the hive and "performs" for the other bees.

4

A) NO CHANGE

B) from the hive and the angle of the dance

C) from the hive: and the angle of the dance

D) from the hive; and the angle of the dance

5

Which choice offers an accurate interpretation of the data in the graph?

A) NO CHANGE

B) will perform the dance at a 180° angle.

C) will perform the dance at a 60° angle.

D) will perform no circuits.

6

To make this paragraph most logical, sentence 7 should be placed

A) where it is now.

B) before sentence 2.

C) before sentence 4.

D) before sentence 5.

CONTINUE

Both the forager bees and the scout **7** <u>plays</u> important roles in the process of collecting nectar. Scouts must find the best locations for nectar. Scouts must also be cautious of sites with damaged flowers or deceased bees, as these may be signs of predators. **8** <u>The foragers watch and imitate the dance. Then the foragers use the cues from the scouts to locate the nectar site.</u>

7

A) NO CHANGE
B) play
C) is playing
D) am playing

8

Which choice most effectively combines the underlined sentences?

A) The foragers watch and imitate the dance, then the foragers use cues from the scouts to locate the nectar site.

B) The foragers watch and imitate the dance, and they also use cues from the scouts to locate the nectar site.

C) The foragers both watch and imitate the dance of the scouts, and then they use cues to locate the nectar site.

D) After watching and imitating the dance, the foragers use the cues from the scouts to locate the nectar site.

CONTINUE

9 Because bees have small brains relative to humans, they can convey complex and vital information to each other through **10** they're dances. Scientists suggest that the bees "understand" the dance because it elicits a uniform response from the viewers; most forager bees fly to the location encoded in the dance. In this way, honey bees use these dances as **11** tools to both navigate and for communication.

9

A) NO CHANGE
B) Although bees have small brains
C) Without their small brains
D) Insofar as bees have small brains

10

A) NO CHANGE
B) their dances
C) they're: dances
D) their: dances

11

A) NO CHANGE
B) tools for both navigation and to communicate
C) tools for both navigation and communication
D) tools for navigation and for communicating

CONTINUE

Questions 12-22 are based on the following passage.

Maya Angelou: A Voice for Caged Birds

At President Bill Clinton's inauguration, Maya Angelou stands at the podium to recite a poem just as she did when she was a young girl in church. As a child, **12** too nervous to complete her reading in front of her congregation. Now on stage in front of the world, **13** however, Angelou does not resemble that frightened girl at all. She reads "On the Pulse of Morning," a poem she composed that proposes inclusion, change, and progress as America's goals. It is easy to see how her life and journey **14** have not only influenced her work but also embodied the change and progress for which she calls. Passion and courage are evident in her performance, not fear or anxiety. She speaks with a strong voice—a voice that has long touched generations of listeners.

Angelou faced a difficult childhood. She and her brother, Bailey, were raised for a period of time with their grandmother **15** in Arkansas. It was here that Angelou experienced the devastating effects of racism firsthand.

12

A) NO CHANGE

B) she was too nervous. Too nervous to complete her reading

C) she was too nervous, she could not complete her reading

D) she was too nervous to complete her reading

13

A) NO CHANGE

B) for instance

C) therefore

D) moreover

14

A) NO CHANGE

B) have influenced not only her work but also embodied the change

C) have not influenced only her work but embodied also the change

D) not only have influenced her work but also embodied the change

15

Which choice most effectively combines the sentences at the underlined portion?

A) in Arkansas, and she experienced

B) and Angelou experienced, in Arkansas,

C) in Arkansas, where Angelou experienced

D) in Arkansas, but experienced

CONTINUE

16 Angelou also struggled with her own insecurities; in her autobiographical work, *I Know Why the Caged Bird Sings*, she notes that her awkward looks brought on ridicule, and she felt she did not fit in with her peers.

17 Angelou first tried her hand at singing and dancing, touring Europe and releasing a musical album. During this time, she gained a sense of confidence and a set of valuable mentors and collaborators. With the help of these connections, she wrote and produced a documentary series and began work on *I Know Why the Caged Bird Sings*. Finally able to shake the insecurities of her youth, Maya Angelou **18** had found her voice.

16

At this point, the writer is considering adding the following sentence.

> For example, the white dentist in the town refused to treat Angelou because of her skin color.

Should the writer make this addition here?

A) Yes, because it supports the claim that Angelou experienced the effects of racism with a specific example.

B) Yes, because it explains why Angelou decided to live with her grandmother in Arkansas.

C) No, because the dentist is not a central figure in Angelou's story, and detracts from the focus of the paragraph.

D) No, because the paragraph already states that Angelou experienced the effects of racism.

17

Which sentence, inserted here, would most effectively establish the main topic of the paragraph?

A) Angelou was a pioneer for African American women in film.

B) Angelou was the recipient of many honors and awards for her work in the arts.

C) *I Know Why the Caged Bird Sings* was the first work in Angelou's autobiographical series.

D) Angelou's life changed when she began discovering her creativity.

18

A) NO CHANGE

B) had found, her voice.

C) had found; her voice.

D) had: found her voice.

CONTINUE

Angelou put her voice to use throughout the rest of her life **19** by composing and producing; acting and writing. Her poetry and prose were widely **20** lionized, and her script for the film *Georgia, Georgia* was nominated for a Pulitzer Prize. Much of Angelou's success has been attributed to her ability to connect with her audience through vivid imagery, **21** instigating powerful emotions from her listeners.

In "On the Pulse of Morning," Angelou encourages Americans to have courage to live each day with hope. She invites **22** them to move forward with her into the light of the morning. On stage at the inauguration, she is not a caged bird or a shy little girl; she is a songbird whose melodies echo through television cables and touch hearts across the nation.

19

A) NO CHANGE

B) by composing; producing; acting and writing.

C) by composing, producing, acting, and writing.

D) by composing and producing; and acting and writing.

20

A) NO CHANGE

B) acclaimed

C) prized

D) championed

21

A) NO CHANGE

B) infuriating

C) agitating

D) evoking

22

A) NO CHANGE

B) themselves

C) him or her

D) oneself

CONTINUE

Questions 23-33 are based on the following passage.

Living the Wild Life

Many branches of science are devoted to ▇23▇ preserving, protecting, and studying animals, and their habitats. For example, biologists and environmentalists may make observations and collect data to determine the ▇24▇ effect's of temperature increase on rainforest wildlife. However, these scientists cannot do their work alone. ▇25▇ To help them carry out their projects, scientists often employ assistants. These are called "wildlife technicians." By assisting scientists who study animals and their relationships to the Earth, wildlife technicians enjoy a rewarding career working with both humans and animals.

23

A) NO CHANGE

B) preserving; protecting; and studying animals, and their habitats.

C) preserving, protecting, and studying animals and their habitats.

D) preserving protecting and studying animals, and their habitats.

24

A) NO CHANGE

B) affect's

C) affects

D) effects

25

Which choice most effectively combines the underlined sentences?

A) To help them carry out their projects, scientists often employ assistants; furthermore, these are called "wildlife technicians."

B) To help them carry out their projects, scientists often employ assistants, but they call them "wildlife technicians."

C) To help them carry out their projects, scientists often employ assistants, called "wildlife technicians."

D) To help them carry out their projects, scientists often employ assistants, while the assistants are called "wildlife technicians."

CONTINUE

Wildlife technicians have a variety of responsibilities. Most often, they work directly with animals or natural resources. Wildlife technicians are responsible for collecting data for use in research. Sometimes they collect data [26] by tagging and observing animals; other times, they collect samples or follow trails to determine patterns. Some wildlife technicians are able to perform hands-on work, such as caring for injured animals or restoring areas that have been disturbed or destroyed. Technicians may also use or create maps to help scientists understand patterns of weather or animal migration.

Once they collect data, wildlife technicians then input the data into computer databases to be used as inventories for further research. They may also create reports, develop hypotheses, and make suggestions based on [27] his or her observations. [28] Thus, some wildlife technicians are able to utilize their knowledge of science, math, and statistics to uncover valuable information about environments and the animals that live on earth.

26

A) NO CHANGE

B) by tagging and observing animals, other times, they collect

C) through the use of tagging and observation of animals and other times they collect

D) to tag and observe animals, other times they collect

27

A) NO CHANGE

B) their

C) one's

D) its

28

A) NO CHANGE

B) However,

C) Unfortunately,

D) Conversely,

CONTINUE

29 Many wildlife technicians work in nature parks or nature centers, but others work in harsh and **30** <u>reserved</u> environments, such as the isolated lands of the tundra. In some of these environments, wildlife technicians may encounter uncomfortable weather or dangerous conditions.

Which choice, inserted here, would most effectively establish the main topic of the paragraph?

A) Wildlife technicians need several skills to perform their difficult tasks.

B) Some wildlife technicians need to drive large trucks in order to travel.

C) The life of a wildlife technician is not always easy.

D) Wildlife technicians are able to work with a variety of animal species.

A) NO CHANGE

B) improbable

C) diffident

D) remote

CONTINUE

Wildlife technicians need a two-year degree to get started, but many **31** chose to pursue a bachelor's degree to obtain the benefits of a more advanced degree. Wildlife technicians study in numerous areas, including biology, ecology, forestry, and zoology. Wildlife technicians need to be skilled in science, math, and computer technology and be comfortable working with animals. Some students develop a focus area in a particular topic, such as aquatic life or resource conservation. **32** Many aspiring wildlife technicians also get involved in relevant extracurricular activities. They might join nature or outdoors clubs or volunteer at local zoos or arboretums.

For nature lovers, the work of a wildlife technician could be an exciting and satisfying job. Wildlife technicians **33** allocate their lives to helping animals and the Earth, and often find fulfillment through their careers.

31

A) NO CHANGE

B) choose

C) will have chosen

D) DELETE the underlined portion

32

The writer is considering deleting the underlined sentence. Should the writer make this change?

A) Yes, because information about extracurricular activities are not pertinent to this passage.

B) Yes, because it does not logically follow from the previous sentence.

C) No, because it does logically follow from the previous sentence.

D) No, because it provides information that sets up the examples that follow.

33

A) NO CHANGE

B) consign

C) dedicate

D) designate

CONTINUE

Questions 34-44 are based on the following passage.

Children of the Industrial Revolution

Imagine this is your daily routine: You wake up at 5:00 A.M. and walk to your job at a coal mine. There you spend fourteen hours in a mine shaft, breaking and collecting rock. At the end of the day, you receive ten cents and return home. Before going to sleep, [34] they put the money in a jar set aside for family expenses.

This was the routine of many children during the Industrial Revolution. The Industrial Revolution marked a dramatic change in the way goods were produced and manufactured, making the processes quicker and easier. Although the gains of the Industrial Revolution were great, the extreme use of child labor casts a shadow of disgrace over the period.

[35] Before the Industrial Revolution, many children did work. Some children completed tasks at home or assisted with a family farm or business. [36] But during the Industrial Revolution, the role of the child in the labor force changed dramatically.

34

Which choice best maintains the pattern already established in the passage?

A) NO CHANGE

B) children were asked to put the money in the jar for family expenses.

C) the money is put in a jar for family expenses.

D) you put the money in a jar set aside for family expenses.

35

At this point, the writer is considering adding the following sentence.

> Of course, I'm not totally opposed to child labor in all circumstances.

Should the writer make this addition here?

A) Yes, because it serves as an effective introduction for the main idea of the paragraph.

B) Yes, because it clarifies the writer's opinion.

C) No, because child labor is unacceptable in all circumstances.

D) No, because it is inconsistent with the style of the passage as a whole.

36

Which choice, inserted here, would be the most relevant addition to the paragraph?

A) Others still do chores at home in modern times.

B) Some people might consider mandatory school attendance to be a form of labor.

C) The children of affluent families were less likely to perform that sort of work.

D) Other children became apprentices, assistants to workers who would teach them a trade in exchange for labor.

CONTINUE

Young children were allowed to work in many industries, including coal mines, textile mills, tobacco factories, and sweatshops. In fact, children were often the preferred type of employee. Children's pay was much less than **37** adults, even when they produced the same amount of work. They could also perform some tasks that adults could not, like reaching into small compartments under running machines **38** for replace moving parts.

Many accounts of child labor investigations describe horrific and deplorable working conditions. In mills and factories, children were forced to use dangerous equipment. After working more than twelve hours per day, **39** many fatigued children were injured by the machinery. Many child laborers also faced cruel treatment by their supervisors. Children had always received discipline at home, but employers took extreme measures **40** to ensure that the work of the children was happening efficiently.

37

A) NO CHANGE

B) the adults

C) an adult

D) adults' pay

38

A) NO CHANGE

B) while

C) to

D) into

39

A) NO CHANGE

B) many children were fatigued and injured by the machinery.

C) the machinery injured many fatigued children.

D) the machinery injured many of the children who were fatigued.

40

A) NO CHANGE

B) to ensure that the work of the children was efficiently being done.

C) to ensure that the children were working efficiently.

D) in order to ensure that the children's work was being done efficiently.

CONTINUE

One of the most dangerous jobs for **41** children were coal mining. Not only did they face the immediate danger of working underground with heavy machinery, but they also risked chronic health problems. **42** Because mining was so dangerous, boys had to be at least fourteen years old to work underground. However, some parents would create fake birth certificates to allow their young boys to work in the mines.

Overall, the conditions for children during the Industrial Revolution were atrocious. Children were missing out on education and **43** worked in dangerous situations. The increase in productivity did not **44** validate the harms caused to child laborers.

41

A) NO CHANGE
B) children being
C) children was
D) children are

42

Which choice, inserted here, would best support the statement in the previous sentence?

A) During the mining process, coal dust and poisonous gases were released.
B) Mineworkers could develop "black lung," a condition in which coal dust builds up in the lungs causing permanent damage.
C) The emergency medicine of the time was less sophisticated than modern medicine, and injuries were more likely to be fatal.
D) Mining is even considered a dangerous job for adults today.

43

A) NO CHANGE
B) had worked
C) working
D) had been working

44

A) NO CHANGE
B) justify
C) rate
D) corroborate

STOP

If you complete this section before the end of your allotted time, check your work on this section only. Do NOT use the time to work on another section.

Math Test – No Calculator

25 MINUTES, 20 QUESTIONS

Turn to Section 3 of your answer sheet to answer the questions in this section.

DIRECTIONS

Questions **1-15** ask you to solve a problem, select the best answer among four choices, and fill in the corresponding circle on your answer sheet. Questions **16-20** ask you to solve a problem and enter your answer in the grid provided on your answer sheet. There are detailed instructions on entering answers into the grid before question 16. You may use your test booklet for scratch work.

NOTES

1. You **may not** use a calculator.
2. Variables and expressions represent real numbers unless stated otherwise.
3. Figures are drawn to scale unless stated otherwise.
4. Figures lie in a plane unless stated otherwise.
5. The domain of a function f is defined as the set of all real numbers x for which $f(x)$ is also a real number, unless stated otherwise.

REFERENCE

$$A = \frac{1}{2}bh$$

$$a^2 + b^2 = c^2$$

Special Triangles

$$V = \frac{1}{3}lwh$$

$$V = \frac{1}{3}\pi r^2 h$$

$$A = lw$$

$$V = lwh$$

$$V = \pi r^2 h$$

$$A = \pi r^2$$

$$C = 2\pi r$$

$$V = \frac{4}{3}\pi r^3$$

There are 360° in a circle.

The sum of the angles in a triangle is 180°.

The number of radians of arc in a circle is 2π.

CONTINUE

1

What is the difference when $-3 + 3x$ is subtracted from $4 - x$?

A) $7 + 2x$

B) $1 + 2x$

C) $7 - 4x$

D) $1 - 4x$

2

A car lease costs a flat fee of $1000 plus a monthly charge of $100. A 5% tax is applied to the monthly rate. Which of the following expressions represents the total cost, in dollars, if the car is leased for m months?

A) $1.05(100m) + 1000$

B) $1.05(100m + 1000)$

C) $(100 + 0.05m) + 1000$

D) $1.05(100 + 1000)m$

3

If k is a positive integer greater than 2, which of the following could be a graph of $y = \dfrac{kx}{2}$?

A)

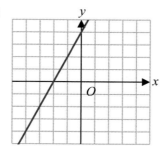

B)

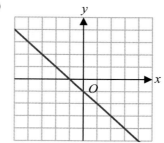

C)

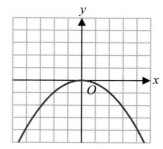

D)

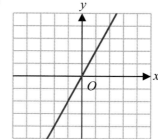

CONTINUE

4

If $-\dfrac{5}{3} < -2x - 1 < \dfrac{1}{5}$, what is one possible value of $4x + 2$?

A) −1

B) 0

C) 4

D) 5

5

$$x^2 + y^2 = 25$$
$$y = -2x$$

In the system of equations above, what is the value of x^2?

A) 25

B) $\sqrt{5}$

C) 5

D) 20

6

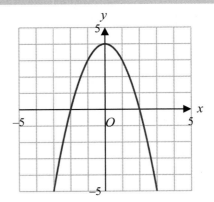

If p represents the product of the x-intercepts in the graph above, what is the value of $\dfrac{p}{6}$?

A) 2

B) $\dfrac{2}{3}$

C) $-\dfrac{1}{3}$

D) $-\dfrac{2}{3}$

CONTINUE

Practice Tests

7

$$m = \frac{1}{x} + \frac{3}{x}$$

A chemist is measuring the corrosive properties of a certain acid on two metals. She submerges identical cubes of each metal in the acid for one hour, then measures the mass of the corroded metal from each sample. She finds that corroded mass of Metal A is three times the corroded mass of Metal B. She writes the equation above for m, the combined mass of corroded metal from both

samples. What does the expression $\frac{3}{x}$ represent?

A) The time, in hours, that it will take the acid to corrode all of Metal A.

B) The mass of Metal A that the acid corroded in one hour.

C) The mass of Metal B that the acid corroded in one hour.

D) The rate at which the acid corrodes Metal B.

8

If $n^{2+x} = 125$ and $n^0 = x$, what is the value of n?

A) 1

B) 2

C) 3

D) 5

9

$$\frac{L}{W} = 1 + \frac{1}{4}S$$

Mathematical models can be used to predict characteristics of wildfires. Fires tend to take an elliptical shape whose length and width depend on the wind speed. The equation above gives the ratio of the length, L, and width, W, of the predicted ellipse based on the wind speed, S, measured in feet per second. What is the predicted length of a fire with a width of 3,000 ft at a wind speed of 12 ft/s?

A) 12,000 ft

B) 9,000 ft

C) 4,000 ft

D) 1,000 ft

10

$$\frac{1}{4}x - \frac{y}{2} = 4$$
$$ax - 2y = 16$$

If the system of equations above has an infinite number of solutions, what is the value of a?

A) 1

B) $\frac{3}{2}$

C) $\frac{1}{4}$

D) 3

CONTINUE

11

$$y = -(ax + c)(ax - c)$$

Which of the following values of c results in the largest range of positive integers for the equation above?

A) −11

B)   0

C)   10

D) It cannot be determined from the information given.

13

If $\dfrac{2x^2}{x-1} = \dfrac{2}{x-1} + M$, what is M in terms of x?

A) $2x - 2$

B) $2x + 2$

C) $2x^2$

D) $2x^2 - 2$

12

$$PV = \dfrac{\dfrac{C}{1+r}}{1 - \dfrac{1+g}{1+r}}$$

The equation above can be used to determine the value of investment returns, PV, on an annual payment, C, which has a rate of return of r and a growth rate of g. Which of the following is an equivalent expression for PV?

A) $\dfrac{Cr}{r-g}$

B) $\dfrac{C}{r+g}$

C) $\dfrac{C}{r-g}$

D) $\dfrac{C(1+r)}{r+g}$

CONTINUE

14

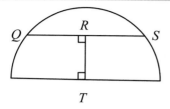

The semicircle above has a diameter of 2. If the length of $\overline{RT}$ is $\dfrac{1}{2}$, what is the length of the chord $\overline{QS}$?

A) $\dfrac{\sqrt{2}}{2}$

B) $\dfrac{\sqrt{3}}{2}$

C) $\sqrt{3}$

D) 2

15

If $0 < x < \dfrac{\pi}{2}$, what is the value of $\cos(x + \pi)$?

A) $-\dfrac{\cos x}{2}$

B) $-\cos x$

C) $\dfrac{\cos x}{2}$

D) $\cos x$

CONTINUE

DIRECTIONS

Questions **16-20** ask you to solve a problem and enter your answer in the grid provided on your answer sheet. When completing grid-in questions:

1. You are required to bubble in the circles for your answers. It is recommended, but not required, that you also write your answer in the boxes above the columns of circles. Points will be awarded based only on whether the circles are filled in correctly.

2. Fill in only one circle in a column.

3. You can start your answer in any column as long as you can fit in the whole answer.

4. For questions 16-20, no answers will be negative numbers.

5. **Mixed numbers,** such as $4\frac{2}{5}$, must be gridded as decimals or improper fractions, such as 4.4 or as 22/5. "42/5" will be read as "forty-two over five," not as "four and two-fifths."

6. If your answer is a **decimal** with more digits than will fit on the grid, you may round it or cut it off, but you must fill the entire grid.

7. If there are **multiple correct solutions** to a problem, all of them will be considered correct. Enter only **one** on the grid.

CONTINUE

16

$$10 = |x - 4|$$

What is the greatest possible integer value for x that satisfies the equation above?

17

If the product of three different positive integers is 48 and the sum of these integers is less than 13, what is the largest of these numbers?

18

If $\frac{1}{4}x + \frac{1}{5}y = 6$, what is the value of $5x + 4y$?

19

$$E = (0.5)4^{\left(\frac{h}{16}\right)}$$

A hospital is studying the effect of the length of resident physicians' work shifts on the physicians' error rate. Researchers collect data and model the physicians' error rate, E, as a function of the length of the shift in hours, h, with the equation above. Based on this model, the physicians' error rate doubles every x hours. What is the value of x?

20

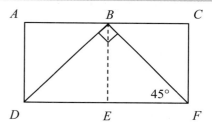

In the diagram above, $2 \times BE = DF$, and $BF = \sqrt{2}$. What is the perimeter of rectangle $ACFD$?

STOP

If you complete this section before the end of your allotted time, check your work on this section only. Do NOT use the time to work on another section.

Math Test – Calculator

55 MINUTES, 38 QUESTIONS

Turn to Section 4 of your answer sheet to answer the questions in this section.

DIRECTIONS

Questions **1-30** ask you to solve a problem, select the best answer among four choices, and fill in the corresponding circle on your answer sheet. Questions **31-38** ask you to solve a problem and enter your answer in a grid provided on your answer sheet. There are detailed instructions on entering answers into the grid before question 31. You may use your test booklet for scratch work.

NOTES

1. You **may** use a calculator.
2. Variables and expressions represent real numbers unless stated otherwise.
3. Figures are drawn to scale unless stated otherwise.
4. Figures lie in a plane unless stated otherwise.
5. The domain of a function f is defined as the set of all real numbers x for which $f(x)$ is also a real number, unless stated otherwise.

REFERENCE

$A = \frac{1}{2}bh$ $a^2 + b^2 = c^2$ Special Triangles $V = \frac{1}{3}lwh$ $V = \frac{1}{3}\pi r^2 h$

$A = lw$ $V = lwh$ $V = \pi r^2 h$ $A = \pi r^2$ $V = \frac{4}{3}\pi r^3$

$C = 2\pi r$

There are 360° in a circle.

The sum of the angles in a triangle is 180°.

The number of radians of arc in a circle is 2π.

CONTINUE

1

How much smaller is $p - 3$ than $p + 4$?

A) 1

B) 3

C) 6

D) 7

2

The sum of three consecutive integers is 900. What is the value of the largest of these three integers?

A) 300

B) 301

C) 303

D) 900

3

Peter	Rita	Juan	Isabella	Ming
19	8	9	7	2

The table above shows the number of CDs purchased by a group of students during the month of July. What was the average number of CDs purchased per student?

A) 9

B) 13

C) 17

D) 45

4

The population of Manchester increased by 12.0% between 1990 and 1999, and then decreased by 5.0% between 1999 and 2009. What was the percentage change in Manchester's population between 1990 and 2009?

A) 6.4%

B) 7.1%

C) 16.1%

D) 17.7%

5

The U.S. Department of Health and Human Services determined that the optimal level of fluoride in drinking water is 0.7 mg per liter of water. A county water district requires that the fluoride level should remain within 0.3 mg per liter of the optimal level. If x is the fluoride level per liter of water, which of the following inequalities expresses the range of fluoride levels, in mg per liter, that meet the city's requirements?

A) $|x - 0.3| \geq 0.7$

B) $|x - 0.7| \geq 0.3$

C) $|x - 0.3| \leq 0.7$

D) $|x - 0.7| \leq 0.3$

CONTINUE

6

Populations of Lions and Zebras

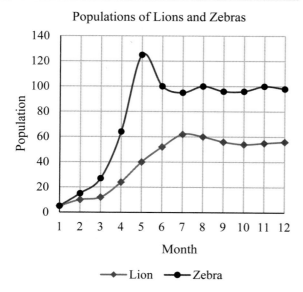

Researchers measured the populations of lions and zebras every month during a one-year period. The population data is fit to a curve, as shown above. Which of the following is a correct interpretation of the data?

A) At the 1ˢᵗ month, the population of lions and zebras is zero.

B) At the 2ⁿᵈ month, the population of lions and zebras is the same.

C) At the 4ᵗʰ month, there are about 3 times more zebras than lions.

D) At the 7ᵗʰ month, the populations of lions and zebras is the closest.

7

What is the slope of the line that connects the points $(2, 5)$ and $\left(-\dfrac{10}{3}, 1\right)$?

A) $-\dfrac{2}{9}$

B) $\dfrac{2}{9}$

C) $\dfrac{3}{4}$

D) $\dfrac{4}{3}$

8

$$\frac{2x - 1}{3} = 7x - 1$$

What is the value of x in the equation above?

A) $\dfrac{1}{21}$

B) $\dfrac{1}{19}$

C) $\dfrac{2}{19}$

D) $\dfrac{5}{19}$

CONTINUE

9

If $4^{2y} = 256$, what is the value of y?

A) 1

B) 2

C) 3

D) 4

10

Speed of light in a vacuum	3.0×10^8 m/s
Distance between Earth and Sun	1.5×10^{11} m

A common unit of length used in astronomy is a light year, which is defined as the distance light travels in a vacuum in one year. For smaller distances, astronomers can use units like the light minute, which is the distance light travels in a vacuum in one minute. Based on the table above, what is the approximate distance between the Earth and the Sun, in light minutes?

A)　　0.12

B)　　8.33

C)　500

D)　30,000

11

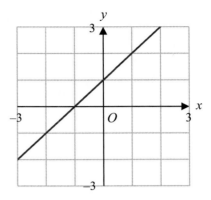

The figure above shows the graph of $y = mx + b$. If the slope of this line were doubled, what would be the value for y at $x = 2$?

A) 5

B) 6

C) 7

D) 8

CONTINUE

12

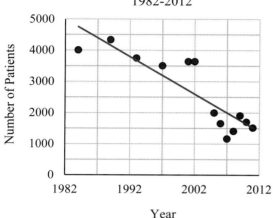

Patients Treated for Chicken Pox, 1982-2012

The scatterplot above shows the number of patients treated for chicken pox in a hospital from 1982 to 2012. The line of best fit shown has the equation $y = -120x + 5000$, where x is the number of years since 1982. Which of the following best describes the meaning of the number -120 in the equation of the line of best fit?

A) The average annual change in the number of patients treated for chicken pox between 1982 and 2012

B) The average number of patients treated for chicken pox each year between 1982 and 2012

C) The difference between the number of patients that received treatment for chicken pox in 1982 and 2012

D) The percent decrease in patients treated for chicken pox each year between 1982 and 2012

13

If $x = -2$, what is the value of $\left| x^3 \right| - x^2 - x$?

A) -14

B) -10

C) 2

D) 6

14

If $f(x) = x^2 + 7$ and $g(x) = -f(x) + 3$, what is $g(4)$?

A) 26

B) 19

C) -1

D) -20

CONTINUE

15

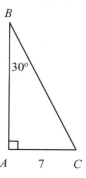

In the figure above, what is the length of $\overline{BC}$?

A) 7

B) 10

C) 11

D) 14

16

Carlos walks at a constant pace of 13 miles per x minutes. How many miles does he walk in 35 minutes, in terms of x?

A) $455x$

B) $\dfrac{13}{35x}$

C) $\dfrac{35}{13x}$

D) $\dfrac{455}{x}$

17

Rating	Number of Customers
1	0
2	1
3	3
4	3
5	2

An online store allows customers to give products a rating of 1, 2, 3, 4, or 5. The table above shows customers' ratings for a certain product. How many more customers would have to give a rating of 5 in order for the product to have an average rating of 4?

A) 3

B) 5

C) 7

D) 9

18

The genetic code in RNA is stored in strings of 3 base nucleotides, called codons. There are 4 base nucleotides, which are represented by U, C, A, and G. Some examples of possible codon sequences are: ACG, CGU, and UCA. How many codon sequences do NOT have any repeated base nucleotides?

A)   4

B) 24

C) 44

D) 64

CONTINUE

Questions 19 and 20 refer to the following information.

A survey on cereal preference was conducted among a random sample of United States citizens in 2010. The table below displays a summary of the survey results.

Favorite Cereal Grain				
	Corn	Oats	Other	Total
18 years or younger	3,401	2,305	2,532	8,238
19- to 44-year-olds	7,325	5,321	8,432	21,078
45- to 64-year-olds	5,643	3,423	9,647	18,713
Total	16,369	11,049	20,611	48,029

19

According to the table, which age group has the greatest percentage of people who prefer corn cereal?

A) 18 years or younger

B) 19- to 44-year-olds

C) 45- to 64-year-olds

D) All the groups' percentages are equal

20

In 2010, there were 81 million 45- to 64-year-olds in the United States. If the sample in the survey accurately reflects the rest of the population, which of the following is the best estimate of the number of 45- to 64-year-olds in the United States who preferred oat cereal?

A) 13 million

B) 15 million

C) 32 million

D) 42 million

CONTINUE

21

List 1	List 2
$-a, a, b, 118$	$a, b, 76$

Two lists of variables and numbers are written in ascending order in the table above. If $a > 42$, which of the following expressions represents the difference between the ranges of List 1 and List 2?

A) 42

B) $a - 42$

C) $a + 42$

D) $2a + 42$

22

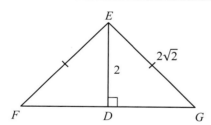

What is the area of the triangle EFG above?

A) $\sqrt{2}$

B) 4

C) $4\sqrt{2}$

D) 8

23

There is a 33% chance of rain in Boston and a 62% chance of rain in London. If weather conditions in London are independent of weather conditions in Boston, what is the approximate percent probability that it rains in both Boston and London?

A) 20%

B) 48%

C) 71%

D) 95%

24

$$12x + 15y = 106$$
$$36x + 45y = 6z$$

In the system of equations above, which value of z would result in infinitely many solutions?

A) 318

B) 106

C) 53

D) 18

CONTINUE

25

$$f(x) = \frac{2}{5}x + 1$$

If $g(x) = -2f(x)$, which of the following is the graph of $g(x)$?

A)

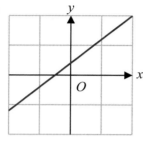

B)

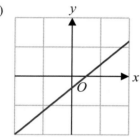

C)

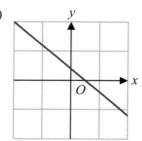

D)

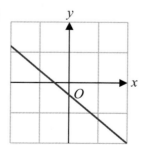

26

The data in List A has a standard deviation of 10, and the data in List B has a standard deviation of 7. Which of the following statements must be true?

A) The mean for List A is different than the mean for List B

B) The data for List A vary less than the data for List B

C) The data for List A vary more than the data for List B

D) List A has more accurate data than List B

27

Which of the following expressions is equivalent to $x^3y^3 - 64$?

A) $(xy - 4)(x^2y^2 + 2xy + 12)$

B) $(xy - 4)(x^2y^2 + 4xy + 16)$

C) $(xy - 4)(2x^2y^2 + 4xy + 16)$

D) $(xy - 6)(x^2y^2 + 2xy + 12)$

CONTINUE

28

Drag Coefficient at
Different Wind Speeds

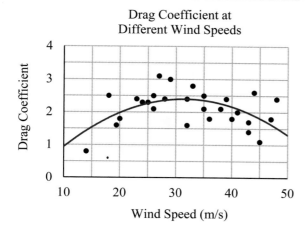

The scatterplot above shows wind speed and drag coefficient data collected in hurricane conditions by meteorologists. The scientists modeled the relationship between wind speed, w, and the drag coefficient, D, using the equation $D = aw^2 + bw + c$, where a, b, and c are constants. The model predicts that the drag coefficient will be equivalent for wind speeds of 24 m/s and 38 m/s. According to the model, what wind speed will give the maximum drag coefficient?

A) 24 m/s

B) 28 m/s

C) 31 m/s

D) 33 m/s

29

The rate of a chemical reaction depends on the concentrations of the reacting substances. The concentration of a substance A is given by $[A]$. The rate of a reaction is $r = k\,[NO]^3[H_2]$, where k is a constant. Based on the equation, which of the following is true?

I.   If the concentration of NO is doubled, the reaction rate will be six times its original value.
II. The reaction rate is directly proportional to the concentration of H_2.
III. An increase in the concentration of NO and H_2 will increase the reaction rate.

A) I and II only

B) I and III only

C) II and III only

D) I, II, and III

30

$$f(x) = x^2 - 16$$

The graph of the function above intersects the x-axis at the points $(b, 0)$, and $(c, 0)$. What is the value of $b + c$?

A) −4

B)   0

C)   4

D)   8

CONTINUE

DIRECTIONS

Questions **31-38** ask you to solve a problem and enter your answer in the grid provided on your answer sheet. When completing grid-in questions:

1. You are required to bubble in the circles for your answers. It is recommended, but not required, that you also write your answer in the boxes above the columns of circles. Points will be awarded based only on whether the circles are filled in correctly.

2. Fill in only one circle in a column.

3. You can start your answer in any column as long as you can fit in the whole answer.

4. For questions 31-38, no answers will be negative numbers.

5. **Mixed numbers,** such as $4\frac{2}{5}$, must be gridded as decimals or improper fractions, such as 4.4 or as 22/5. "42/5" will be read as "forty-two over five," not as "four and two-fifths."

6. If your answer is a **decimal** with more digits than will fit on the grid, you may round it or cut it off, but you must fill the entire grid.

7. If there are **multiple correct solutions** to a problem, all of them will be considered correct. Enter only **one** on the grid.

CONTINUE

31

When three times a number is divided by 4, the result is 6. What is the number?

32

The density of lead is 11.3 g per cm^3. A lead pipe weighs 50 kg. What is the volume of the pipe, rounded to the nearest cubic centimeter? (Density is equal to mass/volume.)

33

If $-3 < -4x + 6 < -\dfrac{2}{3}$, what is one possible value of x?

34

Results of Circuit Voltage Experiment						
Test	1	2	3	4	5	6
Voltage Differential	0.52	0.54	0.56	0.52	0.52	0.55

Students in a physics course are studying electricity. An experiment requires them to find the voltage differential between two points in a circuit. They take multiple measurements to ensure the accuracy of their reading and record the results in the table above. What is the median voltage reading of the students' measurements?

CONTINUE

35

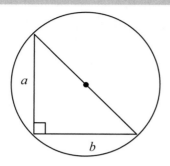

The circumference of the circle above is 20π. What is the value of $a^2 + b^2$?

36

If $x = 2^{2t} + 5$ and $y = t - 1$, what is the value of $x + y$ when $t = 1.5$?

CONTINUE

Questions 37 and 38 refer to the following information.

Monique is a student who frequently uses her American debit card to make purchases when traveling abroad. When she makes a purchase, the bank converts the purchase price at the daily foreign exchange rate and then charges a 3% fee on the converted cost.

Monique also converts cash from one currency to another at her bank. To convert cash into a different currency, her bank uses the daily foreign exchange rate and charges a 2.5% fee on the converted cost.

37

In Mexico, Monique used her debit card for a purchase that cost 235 pesos. The bank charged her card 18.62 U.S. dollars, including the 3% conversion fee. What foreign exchange rate, in Mexican pesos per U.S. dollar, did the bank use for Monique's purchase? Round your answer to the nearest whole number.

38

Before her trip, Monique asked her bank to convert 100 U.S. dollars into Mexican pesos. Monique did not spend any of these pesos during her trip, and she asked her bank to convert them back into U.S. dollars when she returned. If the daily foreign exchange rate stayed the same, how many U.S. dollars did Monique lose after these two conversions? Round your answer to the nearest whole number.

STOP

If you complete this section before the end of your allotted time, check your work on this section only. Do NOT use the time to work on another section.

Essay (Optional)

50 MINUTES

Turn to the lined pages of your answer sheet to write your essay.

DIRECTIONS

This essay is optional. It is a chance for you to demonstrate how well you can understand and analyze a written passage. Your essay should show that you have carefully read the passage and should be a concisely written analysis that is both logical and clear.

You must write your entire essay on the lines in your answer booklet. No additional paper will be provided aside from the Planning Page inside your answer booklet. You will be able to write your entire essay in the space provided if you make use of every line, keep tight margins, and write at a suitable size. Don't forget to keep your handwriting legible for the readers evaluating your essay.

You will have 50 minutes to read the passage in this booklet and to write an essay in response to the prompt provided at the end of the passage.

REMINDERS

- What you write in this booklet will not be evaluated. Write your essay in the answer booklet only.

- Essays that are off-topic will not be evaluated.

As you read the passage below, consider how Theresa Brown uses

- evidence, such as facts or examples, to support claims.
- reasoning to develop ideas and to connect claims and evidence.
- stylistic or persuasive elements, such as word choice or appeals to emotion, to add power to the ideas expressed.

Adapted from Theresa Brown, "When No One Is on Call." © 2013 by the New York Times Company. Originally published August 17, 2013.

1   We nurses all have stories—if we're lucky, it's just one—about the time we failed a patient. It's usually a problem of being too busy: too many cases, too many procedures to keep track of until one critical step, just one, slips through our frenetic fingers and someone gets hurt.

2   I saw it happen the first time while in nursing school. A patient needed an escalating dose of pain medicine. Her pain eased, but her breathing slowed and her oxygen level dropped. I told her nurse that the patient might need narcan, a reversing agent for opioids.

3   "Narcan?" The nurse didn't have time for that. Caring for eight patients on a busy medical-surgery floor meant that getting through the day's tasks took up all her time. Half an hour later, though, the patient needed an emergency team to revive her.

4   Bedside nurses are the hospital's front line, but we can't do the first-alert part of our jobs if there aren't enough of us on the floor. More demands for paperwork, along with increasing complexity of care, means the amount of time any one nurse has for all her patients is diminishing. And as hospitals face increasing financial pressure, nurse staffing often takes a hit, because nurses make up the biggest portion of any hospital's labor costs.

5   For patients, though, the moral calculus of the nurses-for-money exchange doesn't add up. Pioneering work done by Linda H. Aiken at the University of Pennsylvania in 2002 showed that each extra patient a nurse had above an established nurse-patient ratio made it 7 percent more likely that one of the patients would die. She found that 20,000 people died a year because they were in hospitals with overworked nurses.

6   Research also shows that when floors are adequately staffed with bedside nurses, the number of patients injured by falls declines. Staff increases lead to decreases in hospital-acquired infections, which kill 100,000 patients every year.

7   The importance of sufficient nurse staffing is becoming irrefutable, so much so that the Registered Nurse Safe-Staffing Act of 2013 was recently introduced by Representatives Lois Capps, a Democrat from California and a nurse, and David Joyce, a Republican from Ohio. Concerns over money will determine whether this bill has even a chance at passing.

8   It's hard to do a definitive cost-benefit analysis of a variable as complicated as nurse staffing because health care accounting systems are often byzantine. But data suggest that sufficient staffing can significantly reduce hospital costs.

9   Medicare penalizes hospitals for readmitting too many patients within 30 days of discharge, and a full nursing staff is one way to reduce readmissions. Having enough nurses increases patient-satisfaction scores, which also helps maintain Medicare reimbursement levels. Understaffing leads to burnout and nurses' quitting their jobs, both of which cost money in terms of absenteeism and training new staff. Finally, falls and infections have associated costs.

10   What this discussion of finances misses, though, is that having enough nurses is not just about dollars and cents. It's about limiting the suffering of human beings. When hospitals have insufficient nursing staffs, patients who would have gotten better can get hurt, or worse.

11   Several months ago I started a new job and a few weeks in, I heard my name being called. A patient getting a drug that can cause dangerous reactions was struggling to breathe. I hurried to her room, only to discover that I wasn't needed. The other nurses from the floor were already there, stopping the infusion, checking the patient's oxygen and drawing up the rescue medication. The patient was rattled, but there were enough nurses to respond, and in the end she was completely fine.

12   Now picture the same events in a different hospital, one that doesn't adequately staff, and this time the patient is you. As the drug drips in, you feel a malaise. You breathe deeply but can't quite get enough air. Your thinking becomes confused, your heart races. Terrified, you press the call light, you yell for help, but the too few nurses on the floor are spread thin and no one comes to help in time. A routine infusion ends with a call to a rapid-response team, a stay in intensive care, intubation, ventilation, death.

13   This kind of breakdown is not the nurses' fault, but the system's. We are not an elastic resource. We can be where we are needed, but only if there are enough of us.

Write an essay in which you explain how Theresa Brown builds an argument to persuade her audience that hospitals must have sufficiently large nursing staffs. In your essay, analyze how Brown uses one or more of the features listed in the box above (or features of your own choice) to strengthen the logic and persuasiveness of her argument. Be sure that your analysis focuses on the most relevant features of the passage.

Your essay should not explain whether you agree with Brown's claims, but rather explain how Brown builds an argument to persuade her audience.

Practice Test 2

SAT

Directions

- Work on just one section at a time.

- If you complete a section before the end of your allotted time, use the extra minutes to check your work on that section only. Do NOT use the time to work on another section.

Using Your Test Booklet

- No credit will be given for anything written in the test booklet. You may use the test booklet for scratch paper.

- You are not allowed to continue answering questions in a section after the allotted time has run out. This includes marking answers on your answer sheet that you previously noted in your test booklet.

- You are not allowed to fold pages, take pages out of the test booklet, or take any pages home.

Answering Questions

- Each answer must be marked in the corresponding row on the answer sheet.

- Each bubble must be filled in completely and darkly within the lines.

Correct   Incorrect
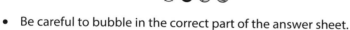

- Be careful to bubble in the correct part of the answer sheet.

- Extra marks on your answer sheet may be marked as incorrect answers and lower your score.

- Make sure you use a No. 2 pencil.

Scoring

- You will receive one point for each correct answer.

- Incorrect answers will NOT result in points deducted. Even if you are unsure about an answer, you should make a guess.

DO NOT BEGIN THIS TEST

UNTIL YOUR PROCTOR TELLS YOU TO DO SO

For printable answer sheets, please visit **ivyglobal.com/study**.

Section 1

	A B C D		A B C D		A B C D		A B C D		A B C D
1	○ ○ ○ ○	12	○ ○ ○ ○	23	○ ○ ○ ○	34	○ ○ ○ ○	45	○ ○ ○ ○
2	○ ○ ○ ○	13	○ ○ ○ ○	24	○ ○ ○ ○	35	○ ○ ○ ○	46	○ ○ ○ ○
3	○ ○ ○ ○	14	○ ○ ○ ○	25	○ ○ ○ ○	36	○ ○ ○ ○	47	○ ○ ○ ○
4	○ ○ ○ ○	15	○ ○ ○ ○	26	○ ○ ○ ○	37	○ ○ ○ ○	48	○ ○ ○ ○
5	○ ○ ○ ○	16	○ ○ ○ ○	27	○ ○ ○ ○	38	○ ○ ○ ○	49	○ ○ ○ ○
6	○ ○ ○ ○	17	○ ○ ○ ○	28	○ ○ ○ ○	39	○ ○ ○ ○	50	○ ○ ○ ○
7	○ ○ ○ ○	18	○ ○ ○ ○	29	○ ○ ○ ○	40	○ ○ ○ ○	51	○ ○ ○ ○
8	○ ○ ○ ○	19	○ ○ ○ ○	30	○ ○ ○ ○	41	○ ○ ○ ○	52	○ ○ ○ ○
9	○ ○ ○ ○	20	○ ○ ○ ○	31	○ ○ ○ ○	42	○ ○ ○ ○		
10	○ ○ ○ ○	21	○ ○ ○ ○	32	○ ○ ○ ○	43	○ ○ ○ ○		
11	○ ○ ○ ○	22	○ ○ ○ ○	33	○ ○ ○ ○	44	○ ○ ○ ○		

Section 2

	A B C D		A B C D		A B C D		A B C D		A B C D
1	○ ○ ○ ○	10	○ ○ ○ ○	19	○ ○ ○ ○	28	○ ○ ○ ○	37	○ ○ ○ ○
2	○ ○ ○ ○	11	○ ○ ○ ○	20	○ ○ ○ ○	29	○ ○ ○ ○	38	○ ○ ○ ○
3	○ ○ ○ ○	12	○ ○ ○ ○	21	○ ○ ○ ○	30	○ ○ ○ ○	39	○ ○ ○ ○
4	○ ○ ○ ○	13	○ ○ ○ ○	22	○ ○ ○ ○	31	○ ○ ○ ○	40	○ ○ ○ ○
5	○ ○ ○ ○	14	○ ○ ○ ○	23	○ ○ ○ ○	32	○ ○ ○ ○	41	○ ○ ○ ○
6	○ ○ ○ ○	15	○ ○ ○ ○	24	○ ○ ○ ○	33	○ ○ ○ ○	42	○ ○ ○ ○
7	○ ○ ○ ○	16	○ ○ ○ ○	25	○ ○ ○ ○	34	○ ○ ○ ○	43	○ ○ ○ ○
8	○ ○ ○ ○	17	○ ○ ○ ○	26	○ ○ ○ ○	35	○ ○ ○ ○	44	○ ○ ○ ○
9	○ ○ ○ ○	18	○ ○ ○ ○	27	○ ○ ○ ○	36	○ ○ ○ ○		

Section 3 (No-Calculator)

	A	B	C	D			A	B	C	D			A	B	C	D			A	B	C	D			A	B	C	D
1	○	○	○	○		4	○	○	○	○		7	○	○	○	○		10	○	○	○	○		13	○	○	○	○
2	○	○	○	○		5	○	○	○	○		8	○	○	○	○		11	○	○	○	○		14	○	○	○	○
3	○	○	○	○		6	○	○	○	○		9	○	○	○	○		12	○	○	○	○		15	○	○	○	○

Only answers that are gridded will be scored. You will not receive credit for anything written in the boxes.

16   17   18   19   20

(gridded response grids for 16–20, digits 0–9 with decimal point and fraction bar)

Section 4 (Calculator)

	A	B	C	D			A	B	C	D			A	B	C	D			A	B	C	D			A	B	C	D
1	○	○	○	○		7	○	○	○	○		13	○	○	○	○		19	○	○	○	○		25	○	○	○	○
2	○	○	○	○		8	○	○	○	○		14	○	○	○	○		20	○	○	○	○		26	○	○	○	○
3	○	○	○	○		9	○	○	○	○		15	○	○	○	○		21	○	○	○	○		27	○	○	○	○
4	○	○	○	○		10	○	○	○	○		16	○	○	○	○		22	○	○	○	○		28	○	○	○	○
5	○	○	○	○		11	○	○	○	○		17	○	○	○	○		23	○	○	○	○		29	○	○	○	○
6	○	○	○	○		12	○	○	○	○		18	○	○	○	○		24	○	○	○	○		30	○	○	○	○

Only answers that are gridded will be scored. You will not receive credit for anything written in the boxes.

31   32   33   34   35

Only answers that are gridded will be scored. You will not receive credit for anything written in the boxes.

36   37   38

■ Section 5 (Optional)

Important: Use a No. 2 pencil. Write inside the borders.

You may use the space below to plan your essay, but be sure to write your essay on the lined pages. Work on this page will not be scored.

Use this space to plan your essay.

START YOUR ESSAY HERE.

_____

_____

_____

_____

_____

_____

_____

_____

_____

_____

_____

_____

_____

_____

_____

_____

_____

_____

_____

_____

_____

_____

_____

_____

Continue on the next page.

Continue on the next page.

_____

_____

_____

_____

_____

_____

_____

_____

_____

_____

_____

_____

_____

_____

_____

_____

_____

_____

_____

_____

_____

_____

_____

_____

_____

_____

_____

Continue on the next page.

STOP.

Reading Test

65 MINUTES, 52 QUESTIONS

Turn to Section 1 of your answer sheet to answer the questions in this section.

DIRECTIONS

Every passage or paired set of passages is accompanied by a number of questions. Read the passage or paired set of passages, then use what is said or implied in what you read and in any given graphics to choose the best answer to each question.

Questions 1-11 are based on the following passage and supplementary material.

This passage is adapted from Adam Minter, "Plastic Arts: What Really Happens to Human Junk." © 2014 by The Economist.

Recycling bins overflow after the holidays, stuffed with gift wrapping and tangled Christmas-tree lights. Rarely does this junk earn a second thought.
Line But where does it all go? Probably Asia, and
5 particularly China, the largest importer of recycling from the rich world. Those broken lights, for example, may turn up in Guangdong province where factories salvage the copper wire and melt the stripped plastic into new slipper soles. China's thriving economy is
10 desperate for stuff that consumers in America and elsewhere carelessly throw away.

The multibillion-dollar recycling trade stands as "one of globalization's great, green successes," writes Adam Minter, an American journalist, in
15 *Junkyard Planet*. It is also a largely unsung one, as under-appreciated as a rusty bike. The industry turns over as much as $500 billion annually, and employs a huge number of people. After years spent traveling the junk heaps of the world, and a decade living in
20 China, Mr. Minter is keen to give the scrap-dealers their due. Son of an American scrap-yard owner, he approaches the industry with affectionate curiosity, marveling at the "groan and crunch" of machines that turn rubbish into usable goods.

25 When Mr. Minter first moved to Shanghai in 2002, the city had three subway lines; ten years later it boasts one of the world's largest systems, with 11 lines and 270 miles of track. Building booms in the developing world, particularly in China, have caused
30 an explosion of demand for steel, copper, and other resources. Yet China lacks the raw materials it needs, so it imports the metal, often as scrap. This has pushed up prices; a pound of copper has risen from 60 cents in the late 1990s to nearly $3.40 today.
35 Americans, meanwhile, have more scrap than they can handle. Known among scrap traders as the "Saudi Arabia of Scrap," the country lacks real demand for manufacturing materials. American labor costs are too high—and environmental regulations too
40 onerous—for it to be cost-effective to salvage most scrap anyway. For the savvy, fast-talking businessmen of the international scrap trade, this has created a profitable exchange. It has also driven the kind of innovation that diverts more junk from landfills.
45 For example, people now worry more about the afterlife of their mobile phones than their cars because of the invention of the motor shredder, which turns old vehicles into scrap metal. In 1970, at least 20 million rusting cars were abandoned across
50 America. In 2012, America recycled nearly 11.9 million cars. China, the world's biggest car buyer, has become the fastest growing market for shredders. America's trade deficit with China reinforces the two countries' relationship as recycling partners.

CONTINUE

Americans consume, and therefore dispose of,
more goods than their Chinese counterparts. And it is
also often cheaper for American scrap-yards to send
their goods to China than anywhere else in the world.
This is because shipping companies hauling goods to
60 America would rather not return to China empty, and
so they offer discounts on what they call their "back-
hauls."

Whether Mr. Minter is accompanying a Chinese
scrap buyer on a road trip through the American
65 Midwest or trying to sell his old mobile phones in
Guiyu, China's controversial electronic-waste
recycling zone, he is an authorial, engaging guide
through the global trash trade. Dirty, dangerous,
cheap to get into and not without romance, the junk
70 business extracts value from what others see as
worthless. Mr. Minter is not blind to the grim
realities of the industry. Wen'an County in China, a
place once known for its fertile soil, clear streams,
and peach trees, was the "most polluted place" he
75 ever visited because of its role in the plastics trade.

But any recrimination over these recycling
practices is best directed at the rich world and at the
increasingly wealthy Chinese who are beginning to
match their wasteful, spendthrift counterparts in the
80 West. The recycling industry squeezes value from
used goods, but nothing is 100% recyclable. The
special chemistry of many products, such as iPhone
touchscreens, means they cannot be recycled.
Consumers should be more aware of what is harmful,
85 and companies should be nudged to design products
that are easier to repair and recycle. In the meantime,
a bit more appreciation might be spared for
junkyards, without which "the world would be a
dirtier and less interesting place."

United States Scrap Exports to China

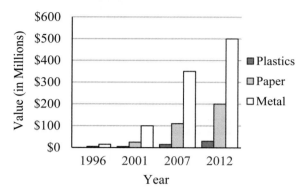

The above chart shows the amount of US scrap exports to
China by value over time. Data from the United States
International Trade Commission.

1

The main purpose of the passage is to

A) describe the economic relationship between two
countries.

B) criticize the environmental policies of a major
world power.

C) discuss the virtues of a valuable and growing
industry.

D) express an opinion about the rising cost of
certain metals.

2

It can be reasonably inferred from the passage that
the author would agree with which statement about
the global recycling industry?

A) Its economic importance has been over-
emphasized.

B) Its impact on other industries is largely
insignificant.

C) It disproportionately benefits already developed
economies.

D) Its benefits are often not fully appreciated.

CONTINUE

3

Which choice provides the best evidence for the answer to the previous question?

A) Lines 4-6 ("Probably … world")

B) Lines 15-16 ("It is … bike")

C) Lines 21-24 ("Son … goods")

D) Lines 28-31 ("Building … resources")

4

The author's attitude towards Adam Minter's book *Junkyard Planet* could best be described as

A) interested and approving.

B) perplexed and reserved.

C) enthusiastic and worshipful.

D) detached and unimpressed.

5

According to the passage, the rapid expansion of the global recycling trade in the past few decades has been caused mainly by

A) the depletion of natural resources in Asia through environmentally unsafe practices.

B) the increased demand for resources to sustain construction projects in the developing world.

C) the growing innovation in consumer goods that has caused products to become obsolete sooner.

D) the swiftly expanding Chinese population that has created a large new market for American goods.

6

According to the passage, which of the following claims is true about American scrap metal?

A) The price of scrap metal has increased more since the late 1990s than ever before.

B) Scrap metal has been used in the past to construct subway lines in major American cities.

C) It is usually not profitable to recycle scrap metal in America.

D) Safety regulations prevent scrap metal from being recycled for domestic construction projects.

7

Which choice provides the best evidence for the answer to the previous question?

A) Lines 25-28 ("When … track")

B) Lines 32-34 ("This has … today")

C) Lines 38-41 ("American … anyway")

D) Lines 43-44 ("It has … landfills")

8

As used in line 27, "boasts" most nearly means

A) gloats.

B) exaggerates.

C) brags.

D) features.

CONTINUE

9

The purpose of the fourth paragraph (lines 45-54) is to

A) provide evidence to support a claim made in an earlier paragraph.

B) define terms that were introduced in an earlier paragraph.

C) describe a scenario that demonstrates a general rule.

D) articulate the disadvantages of a position that was advocated for in an earlier paragraph.

10

As it is used in line 70, "extracts" most nearly means

A) removes.

B) derives.

C) selects.

D) exacts.

11

Which one of the following claims is supported by the graph?

A) Total United States plastic exports to China reached 200 million tons in 2012.

B) From 1996 to 2012, the value of United States scrap metal exported to China was greater than the value of paper and plastic exports combined.

C) In 2001, China imported less than $50 million worth of scrap paper from around the world.

D) The United States exported a total of $500 million worth of scrap metal in 2012, up from around $200 million in 2001.

Questions 12-22 are based on the following passages.

Passage 1 and Passage 2 are adapted from Robert S. Blumenthal and Rita Redberg, "Should Healthy People Take Cholesterol Drugs to Prevent Heart Disease?" © 2014 by Dow Jones & Company.

Passage 1

Heart disease is the leading cause of death in the U.S., and people with higher cholesterol are at higher risk for heart attacks. There's good evidence that
Line people who already have heart disease benefit from
5 cholesterol-lowering medications, or statins. Among those people, statin treatment reduces risk of heart attack and may prolong life.

But what about healthy people with high cholesterol? Many doctors have taken the evidence
10 from studies of people with heart disease and made a leap of logic: they've treated millions of healthy people with statins to prevent heart disease.

But there's a serious problem with that logic. For most healthy people, data show that statins do not
15 prevent heart disease, nor extend life or improve quality of life. And they come with considerable side effects. That's why I don't recommend giving statins to healthy people, even those with higher cholesterol.

Despite research that has included tens of
20 thousands of people, there is no evidence that taking statins prolongs life, although cholesterol levels do decrease. Using the most optimistic projections, for every 100 healthy people who take statins for five years, one or two will avoid a heart attack. One will
25 develop diabetes. But, on average, there is no evidence that the group taking statins will live any longer than those who don't.

Some argue that clinical trials of statin use among healthy people haven't demonstrated a reduced
30 mortality rate because each individual trial only follows patients for a few years—not long enough to show a reduction in mortality. Many doctors, including me, believe that we need clinical trials that actually follow healthy people treated with statins for
35 the long term to see if treatment really results in lower mortality. Statin proponents think such trials

CONTINUE

would be prohibitively expensive. That's a disappointing stance, considering the billions that have already been spent on statin prescriptions and
40 advertising.

Some statin supporters argue that even if the data don't support the benefits of statins in healthy people, they might help and can't hurt. But that's untenable, because statins undeniably harm some
45 people. Besides increasing the risk for developing diabetes, statins can cause memory loss, muscle weakness, stomach distress, and aches and pains. These aren't merely anecdotal results, as some critics assert; they're documented by recent studies.

Passage 2

50 We don't prescribe drugs to otherwise healthy people without rigorous scientific evidence. And, in this case, there is a mountain of high-quality scientific evidence.

Heart disease is an insidious process that takes
55 decades to manifest itself. Risk factors for developing heart disease often go unrecognized and undertreated until it's too late. So, the first manifestation of cardiovascular disease is often sudden cardiac death, heart attack, or stroke—which
60 may result in disability or death. A little late at that point to start prescribing statins.

Yet critics say we should wait until after a patient has gone through one of these life-shattering events before we prescribe a statin. It makes no sense that a
65 medication that slows the progression of hardening of the arteries would be harmful the day or week before a heart attack, but helpful the day or week after a heart attack.

The totality of the available biologic,
70 observational, and clinical-trial evidence strongly supports the selective use of statin therapy in adults demonstrated to be at high risk for heart disease. Studies have conclusively shown that statins prolong life and reduce the risk of heart attack, stroke, and
75 death in patients with known heart disease. Similarly, they have been shown to do the same in patients without heart disease, but who are at high risk of developing heart disease.

For instance, a study of 6,600 Scottish men who
80 hadn't had heart attacks showed a decrease in mortality rates after five years with statin therapy. Likewise, the recent world-wide Jupiter study of men and women without prior heart disease showed statins significantly decreased the risk of death after
85 two years in people with an average age of 66.

Critics raise a number of complaints about these studies—exaggerated, in my view—but many other large prevention trials of people with multiple risk factors have consistently shown reductions in total
90 cardiovascular events of 30% to 40% with the use of a statin.

12

It can be reasonably inferred from Passage 1 that the author would most likely recommend statins for a patient who

A) is male and between the ages of 65 and 74.

B) has an unusually high cholesterol level.

C) is at a higher than average risk of having a heart attack.

D) is already suffering from heart disease.

13

Which choice provides the best evidence for the answer to the previous question?

A) Lines 3-5 ("There's good … statins")

B) Lines 9-12 ("Many doctors … disease")

C) Lines 17-18 ("That's why … cholesterol")

D) Lines 32-36 ("Many … mortality")

CONTINUE

14

According to Passage 1, which of the following best describes the relationship between statins and diabetes?

A) People with diabetes are not allowed to take statins.

B) People are more likely to develop diabetes when using statins.

C) Statins are often prescribed for the treatment of diabetes.

D) People are less likely to develop diabetes when using statins.

15

As used in line 30, "individual" most nearly means

A) peculiar.

B) personal.

C) secluded.

D) particular.

16

Which of the following best summarizes the position held by the author of Passage 2?

A) Since it is unethical to treat people for a disease they don't have, statins should be considered preventative medication and prescribed to anyone who wants them.

B) Since many people with heart disease don't know they have it, doctors should prescribe statins to patients who might have or might develop heart disease.

C) Since statins are not known to prevent the development of heart disease, doctors should only prescribe them to patients at risk for diabetes.

D) Since doctors only prescribe medicines with well-documented records of success, patients should trust their doctors' recommendations.

17

The main rhetorical effect of lines 60-61 ("A little late… statins") is to

A) specify the correct moment for prescribing statins.

B) provide information about when the prescription of statins is most appropriate.

C) portray the opposing argument as nonsensical and dangerous.

D) convey a sense of regret about the preventable death of a patient.

CONTINUE

18

As used in line 71, "selective" most nearly means

A) exacting.

B) choosy.

C) judicious.

D) exclusive.

19

The authors of both passages would most likely agree with which of the following statements?

A) Drugs should never be prescribed to healthy patients.

B) Past studies measuring the effects of statin use have been flawed.

C) Statins are effective at treating patients with heart disease.

D) Statins should only be prescribed after a patient has experienced a cardiovascular incident.

20

Which one of the following pieces of evidence is included in Passage 2 but not Passage 1?

A) A discussion of the side effects of cholesterol-lowering medication

B) Statistics from specific scientific studies

C) Information about the prevalence of statin use

D) An analysis of the financial costs of statin use

21

How would the author of Passage 2 most likely respond to the claim made in lines 28-32 ("Some ... mortality") of Passage 1?

A) By asserting that certain studies have shown a reduction in mortality for healthy patients who use statins

B) By agreeing that more studies need to be conducted that follow patients for longer periods of time

C) By suggesting that scientists should examine the quality of life of statin users rather than just the risk of death

D) By arguing that following patients for only one year is enough to prove reduced mortality in healthy patients who use statins

22

Which choice provides the best evidence for the answer to the previous question?

A) Lines 55-57 ("Risk ... late")

B) Lines 64-68 ("It makes ... attack")

C) Lines 73-75 ("Studies ... disease")

D) Lines 79-81 ("For instance ... therapy")

CONTINUE

Questions 23-32 are based on the following passage.

This passage is adapted from John Jay, "Concerning Dangers From Foreign Force and Influence," originally published in 1787 in *The Federalist Papers: No. 3*. The Federalist Papers aimed to build support for ratification of the United States Constitution, which would unify the States under a national government.

The just causes of war, for the most part, arise either from violation of treaties or from direct violence. America has already formed treaties with
Line no less than six foreign nations. It is of high
5 importance to the peace of America that she observe the laws of nations towards all these powers, and to me it appears evident that this will be more perfectly and punctually done by one national government than it could be either by thirteen separate States or
10 by three or four distinct confederacies. For this opinion various reasons may be assigned.

The prospect of present loss or advantage may often tempt the governing party in one or two States to swerve from good faith and justice; but those
15 temptations, not reaching the other States, and consequently having little or no influence on the national government, the temptation will be fruitless, and good faith and justice be preserved. The case of the treaty of peace with Britain adds great weight to
20 this reasoning.

If even the governing party in a State should be disposed to resist such temptations, yet as such temptations may, and commonly do, result from circumstances peculiar to the State, and may affect a
25 great number of the inhabitants, the governing party may not always be able, if willing, to prevent the injustice meditated, or to punish the aggressors. But the national government, not being affected by those local circumstances, will neither be induced to commit
30 the wrong themselves, nor want power or inclination to prevent or punish its commission by others.

So far, therefore, as either designed or accidental violations of treaties and the laws of nations afford just causes of war, they are less to be apprehended
35 under one general government than under several lesser ones, and in that respect the former most favors the safety of the people.

As to those just causes of war which proceed from direct and unlawful violence, it appears equally clear
40 to me that one good national government affords vastly more security against dangers of that sort than can be derived from any other quarter.

Because such violences are more frequently caused by the passions and interests of a part than of
45 the whole; of one or two States than of the Union. Not a single Indian war has yet been occasioned by aggressions of the present federal government, feeble as it is; but there are several instances of Indian hostilities having been provoked by the improper
50 conduct of individual States, who, either unable or unwilling to restrain or punish offenses, have given occasion to the slaughter of many innocent inhabitants.

Besides, it is well known that acknowledgments,
55 explanations, and compensations are often accepted as satisfactory from a strong united nation, which would be rejected as unsatisfactory if offered by a State or confederacy of little consideration or power.

In the year 1685, the state of Genoa having
60 offended Louis XIV, endeavored to appease him. He demanded that they should send their Doge, or chief magistrate, accompanied by four of their senators, to France, to ask his pardon and receive his terms. They were obliged to submit to it for the sake of peace.
65 Would he on any occasion either have demanded or have received the like humiliation from Spain, or Britain, or any other powerful nation?

CONTINUE

23

The main purpose of the passage is to

A) illustrate how a united government should operate.

B) propose a new form of government.

C) explain some of the benefits of united government.

D) recount the recent history of the United States.

24

According to Jay, which of the following would most likely constitute a just cause of war?

A) A country seeks to expand its borders.

B) Treaty negotiations between two countries are stalled by one side's refusal to compromise.

C) One country discovers that its neighbor has been producing weapons and training troops.

D) A country repeatedly violates the terms of a treaty that it has signed.

25

Which of the following choices provides the best evidence for the answer to the previous question?

A) Lines 1-3 ("The just … violence")

B) Lines 4-10 ("It is … confederacies")

C) Lines 38-42 ("As to … quarter")

D) Lines 46-53 ("Not a … inhabitants")

26

As used in line 10, "distinct" most nearly means

A) separate.

B) prominent.

C) unmistakable.

D) precise.

27

As used in line 12, "prospect" most nearly means

A) hope.

B) candidate.

C) view.

D) possibility.

28

In lines 12-14, Jay raises the concern that individual states, if left to their own devices, might

A) behave improperly towards other nations for their own short-term gain.

B) allow their citizens to over-indulge in pleasurable activities.

C) start practicing a different religion from the rest of the union.

D) attack other nations without the consent of the national government.

CONTINUE

29

According to the passage, unlike state governments, a national government is

A) less likely to catch and punish foreign criminals.

B) less likely to be swayed by narrow public interests.

C) more likely to keep its people safe, happy, and obedient.

D) more likely to fund numerous foreign wars.

30

Which of the following choices provides the best evidence for the answer to the previous question?

A) Lines 12-18 ("The prospect … preserved")

B) Lines 18-20 ("The case ... reasoning")

C) Lines 54-58 ("Besides ... power")

D) Lines 63-67 ("They ... nation")

31

In the sixth paragraph (lines 43-53), Jay implies that the federal government has not provoked conflicts with American Indians because

A) it fears that the nation would suffer serious casualties in the case of war.

B) it is unwilling to punish its citizens for their inappropriate behavior.

C) such conflicts arise from local concerns that are not important to the nation as a whole.

D) such conflicts are best resolved on the local level without federal interference.

32

The final paragraph (lines 59-67) serves to

A) support the claim in the previous paragraph with a historical example.

B) direct the reader's attention to the United States' relationship with France.

C) predict what will happen to the United States if Jay's proposals are not acted upon.

D) illustrate how superior the United States is to Genoa.

CONTINUE

Questions 33-42 are based on the following passage and supplementary materials.

This passage is adapted from Gary Marcus and Christof Koch, "The Future of Brain Implants." © 2014 by Dow Jones & Company.

What would you give for a retinal chip that let you see in the dark or for a next-generation cochlear implant that let you hear any conversation in a noisy
Line restaurant, no matter how loud? Or for a memory
5 chip, wired directly into your brain's hippocampus, that gave you perfect recall of everything you read? Or for an implanted interface with the Internet that automatically translated a clearly articulated silent thought ("the French Sun King") into an online
10 search that digested the relevant Wikipedia page and projected a summary directly into your brain?

Science fiction? Perhaps not for very much longer. Brain implants today are where laser eye surgery was several decades ago. They are not risk-free and make
15 sense only for a narrowly defined set of patients—but they are a sign of things to come. Unlike pacemakers, dental crowns or implantable insulin pumps, neuroprosthetics—devices that restore or supplement the mind's capacities with electronics inserted
20 directly into the nervous system—change how we perceive the world and move through it. For better or worse, these devices become part of who we are.

Neuroprosthetics aren't new. They have been around commercially for three decades, in the form
25 of the cochlear implants used in the ears (the outer reaches of the nervous system) of more than 300,000 hearing-impaired people around the world. Last year, the Food and Drug Administration approved the first retinal implant, made by the company Second Sight.
30 Both technologies exploit the same principle: an external device, either a microphone or a video camera, captures sounds or images and processes them, using the results to drive a set of electrodes that stimulate either the auditory or the optic nerve,
35 approximating the naturally occurring output from the ear or the eye.

Another type of now-common implant, used by thousands of Parkinson's patients around the world, sends electrical pulses deep into the brain proper,

40 activating some of the pathways involved in motor control. A thin electrode is inserted into the brainthrough a small opening in the skull; it is connected by a wire that runs to a battery pack underneath the skin. The effect is to reduce or even
45 eliminate the tremors and rigid movement that are such prominent symptoms of Parkinson's (though, unfortunately, the device doesn't halt the progression of the disease itself). Experimental trials are now under way to test the efficacy of such "deep brain
50 stimulation" for treating other disorders as well.

Electrical stimulation can also improve some forms of memory, as the neurosurgeon Itzhak Fried and his colleagues at the University of California, Los Angeles, showed in a 2012 article in the *New*
55 *England Journal of Medicine*. Using a setup akin to a videogame, seven patients were taught to navigate a virtual city environment with a joystick, picking up passengers and delivering them to specific stores. Appropriate electrical stimulation to the brain during
60 the game increased their speed and accuracy in accomplishing the task.

But not all brain implants work by directly stimulating the brain. Some work instead by reading the brain's signals—to interpret, for example, the
65 intentions of a paralyzed user. Eventually, neuroprosthetic systems might try to do both, reading a user's desires, performing an action like a Web search, and then sending the results directly back to the brain.

Behavioral Performance on Spatial Learning Tasks

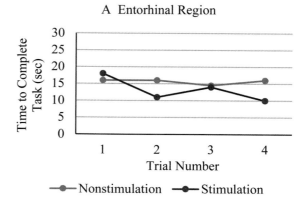

A Entorhinal Region

CONTINUE ➡

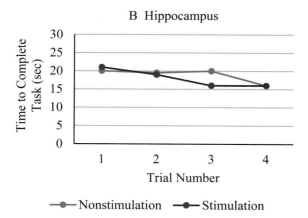

B Hippocampus

—●— Nonstimulation   —●— Stimulation

These two graphs show the time it took study participants to complete a memory task when certain brain regions were and were not stimulated with electrodes.

33

Which one of the following best describes the overall structure of the passage?

A) Disparate facts are joined by a central story.

B) A common misconception is explained and refuted.

C) Speculation about the future is supported with examples.

D) An experiment is discussed to support a prediction.

34

The series of questions in lines 1-11 ("What would … your brain") serves mainly to

A) demonstrate the incredible advances that have been achieved by a new technology.

B) prompt readers to consider the potential value of hypothetical technologies.

C) suggest that technologies that most people desire will soon be available.

D) challenge readers to consider the true costs of future advances in technology.

35

As used in line 15, "defined" most nearly means

A) explained.

B) interpreted.

C) expressed.

D) delineated.

36

The passage most strongly suggests that

A) neuroprosthetics are used exclusively to treat brain disorders.

B) retinal implants are currently used by nearly 300,000 people.

C) cochlear implants represent a significant improvement over pacemakers.

D) neuroprosthetics alter the way in which patients experience the world.

37

It can be reasonably inferred from the passage that cochlear and retinal implants

A) took a long time to become approved by the Food and Drug Administration.

B) attempt to recreate the sensations experienced by the average person.

C) allow the user to see or hear just as well as someone who does not need these implants.

D) are as safe and effective as laser eye surgery.

38

Which choice provides the best evidence for the answer to the previous question?

A) Lines 13-14 ("Brain … ago")

B) Lines 16-21 ("Unlike … through it")

C) Lines 23-27 ("They have … world")

D) Lines 30-36 ("an external … eye")

CONTINUE

39

As used in line 30, "exploit" most nearly means

A) harness.

B) abuse.

C) deceive.

D) contrive.

40

Information provided by the passage suggests that electrical stimulation of parts of the nervous system

A) is currently being used around the world to cure patients with Parkinson's disease and other disorders.

B) could soon become a part of commercially available video games.

C) may have the potential to alleviate the symptoms of patients living with a variety of medical conditions.

D) has been shown to improve memory in the vast majority of patients.

41

Which choice provides the best evidence for the answer to the previous question?

A) Lines 37-41 ("Another … control")

B) Lines 48-50 ("Experimental … well")

C) Lines 59-61 ("Appropriate … task")

D) Lines 63-65 ("Some work … user")

42

Which choice is supported by the passage and by the information in the graph?

A) Memory is stored mostly in the entorhinal region, and response time is governed by the hippocampus.

B) Memory is stored mostly in the hippocampus, and response time is governed by the entorhinal region.

C) Electrical stimulation to the entorhinal region and hippocampus leads to slower processing speeds in the brain.

D) Electrical stimulation to certain regions of the brain can increase the speed of task completion in a game.

CONTINUE

Questions 43-52 are based on the following passage.

This passage is adapted from Arthur Henry Howard Heming, *The Drama of the Forests*, originally published in 1921.

My traveling companion was a "Free Trader," whose name was Spear—a tall, stoop-shouldered man with heavy eyebrows and a shaggy, drooping
Line mustache. The way we met was amusing. It happened
5 in a certain frontier town. His first question was as to whether I was single. His second, as to whether my time was my own. Then he slowly looked me over from head to foot. He seemed to be measuring my stature and strength and to be noting the color of my
10 eyes and hair.

Narrowing his vision, he scrutinized me more carefully than before, for now he seemed to be reading my character—if not my soul. Then, smiling, he blurted out:
15 "Come, be my guest for a couple of weeks. Will you?"

I laughed.

He frowned. But on realizing that my mirth was caused only by surprise, he smiled again and
20 let flow a vivid description of a place he called Spearhead. It was the home of the northern fur trade. It was the center of a great timber region. It was the heart of a vast fertile belt that was rapidly becoming the greatest of all farming districts. It virtually stood
25 over the very vault that contained the richest veins of mineral to be found in the whole Dominion—at least that's what he said—and he also assured me that the Government had realized it too, for was it not going to hew a provincial highway clean through the forest to
30 Spearhead? Was it not going to build a fleet of steamers to ply upon the lakes and rivers in that section? And was it not going to build a line of railroad to the town itself? In fact, he also impressed upon me that Spearhead was a town created for young
35 men who were not averse to becoming wealthy in whatever line of business they might choose. It seemed that great riches were already there and had but to be lifted. Would I go?

But when I explained that although I was single,
40 and quite free, I was not a businessman, he became crestfallen, but presently revived enough to exclaim: "Well, what are you?"

"An artist," I replied.

"Oh, I see! Well … we need an artist very badly.
45 You'll have the field all to yourself in Spearhead. Besides, your pictures of the fur trade and of pioneer life would eventually become historical and bring you no end of wealth. You had better come. Better decide right away, or some other artist chap will get
50 ahead of you."

But when I further explained that I was going to spend the winter in the wilderness, that I had already written to the Hudson's Bay Factor at Fort Consolation and that he was expecting me, Spear gloated:
55 "Bully boy!" and slapping me on the shoulder, he chuckled: "Why, my town is just across the lake from Fort Consolation. A mere five-mile paddle, old chap, and remember, I extend to you the freedom of Spearhead in the name of its future mayor. And, man
60 alive, I'm leaving for there tomorrow morning in a big four-fathom birch bark. Be my guest. It won't cost you a farthing, and we'll make the trip together."

I gladly accepted. Free Trader Spear was a character, and I afterward learned that he was an
65 Oxford University man, who, having failed, left for Canada, entered the service of the Hudson's Bay Company, and had finally been moved to Fort Consolation where he served seven years, learned the fur-trade business, and resigned to become a "free
70 trader," as all fur traders are called who carry on business in opposition to "The Great Company." We were eight days upon the trip, but, strange to say, during each day's travel toward Spearhead, his conversation in reference to that thriving town made
75 it appear to grow smaller and smaller, until at last it actually dwindled down to such a point, that, about sunset on the day we were to arrive, he turned to me and casually remarked: "Presently you'll see Fort Consolation and the Ojibwa village beyond.
80 Spearhead is just across the lake, and by the bye, my boy, I forgot to tell you that Spearhead is just my log shack. But it's a nice little place, and you'll like it when you pay us a visit."

CONTINUE

43

Which of the following provides the most reasonable summary of the passage?

A) A businessman receives a rare financial opportunity that he finds impossible to pass up.

B) An explorer undertakes a journey that he later regrets.

C) A well-educated fur trader attempts to succeed independently.

D) A man is persuaded into undertaking a trip under false pretenses.

44

Spear's tone can best be described as

A) enthusiastic insistence.

B) reluctant acceptance.

C) zealous conviction.

D) restrained confidence.

45

The suggestion that Spear was reading the narrator's soul (line 13) serves to

A) highlight Spear's mystical inclinations.

B) emphasize the intensity of Spear's visual inspection.

C) imply that the narrator has something to hide.

D) illustrate Spear's ability to judge the character of a stranger.

46

As used in line 25, "richest" most nearly means

A) wealthiest.

B) most opulent.

C) most expensive.

D) most bountiful.

47

Which of the following does Spear assure the narrator that he will gain if he comes to Spearhead?

A) The opportunity to make a great deal of money

B) A life of independence and adventure

C) The reputation of one who opposes The Great Company

D) A tranquility which could not be found in other cities

48

Which choice provides the best evidence for the answer to the previous question?

A) Lines 22-24 ("It was … districts")

B) Lines 46-48 ("Besides … wealth")

C) Lines 57-59 ("A mere … mayor")

D) Lines 71-75 ("We … and smaller")

CONTINUE

49

As used in line 58, "extend" most nearly means

A) expand.

B) increase.

C) proffer.

D) exert.

50

Which of the following best describes the current relationship between Spear and the Hudson's Bay Company?

A) Spear trades in competition with the Hudson's Bay Company.

B) Spear lives in subservience to the Hudson's Bay Company.

C) The Hudson's Bay Company is pointedly disinterested in Spear's activities.

D) The Hudson's Bay Company appreciates the efforts of free traders like Spear.

51

Which choice provides the best evidence for the answer to the previous question?

A) Lines 1-4 ("My traveling … mustache")

B) Line 21 ("It was … fur trade")

C) Lines 39-42 ("But when … are you")

D) Lines 69-71 ("and resigned … Company")

52

The final paragraph of the passage (lines 80-83) serves mainly to

A) describe the town of Spearhead in detail.

B) expose the true intentions of the narrator's companion.

C) reveal how the narrator was misled by his companion.

D) indicate the precise location of the narrator's destination.

STOP

If you complete this section before the end of your allotted time, check your work on this section only. Do NOT use the time to work on another section.

Writing and Language Test

35 MINUTES, 44 QUESTIONS

Turn to Section 2 of your answer sheet to answer the questions in this section.

DIRECTIONS

Every passage comes with a set of questions. Some questions will ask you to consider how the writer might revise the passage to improve the expression of ideas. Other questions will ask you to consider correcting potential errors in sentence structure, usage, or punctuation. There may be one or more graphics that you will need to consult as you revise and edit the passage.

Some questions will refer to a portion of the passage that has been underlined. Other questions will refer to a particular spot in a passage or ask that you consider the passage in full.

After you read the passage, select the answers to questions that most effectively improve the passage's writing quality or that adjust the passage to follow the conventions of standard written English. Many questions give you the option to select "NO CHANGE." Select that option in cases where you think the relevant part of the passage should remain as it currently is.

Questions 1-11 are based on the following passage.

Good Work: Praising Effort over Intelligence

Our culture tends to place high value on natural ability as a measure of our potential. We often praise our children more for their talent than for their effort or ambition. We exalt musical or athletic prodigies, whose early successes seem to promise great things for the future, in the sincere belief that we are encouraging them to pursue their potential. **1**

Social science research has indicated that praising children for their talent instead of their effort can cause them to feel constrained by their own perceived limits. An influential study by Stanford psychologist Carol Dweck

1

Which choice most effectively sets up the information that follows?

A) Nevertheless, children should be shielded from criticism.

B) Therefore, children should be taught that they can overcome any obstacle through hard work and perseverance alone.

C) However, praising children for talent over effort may actually be stifling their development.

D) Accordingly, we should praise children for recognizing their own strengths and following them.

CONTINUE

2 identified the different effects of these two types of praise. Dweck and a colleague, Claudia Mueller, conducted a study with 128 children ranging in age from 10 to 12. Each child was given a set of moderately challenging puzzles. Regardless of **3** they performance on the puzzles, all the children were told that they had done well. Some children **4** were praised in that instance for their intelligence in particular, while others were praised for their effort.

Which choice best supports the statement made in the previous sentence?

A) NO CHANGE

B) identified how artistic and athletic prodigies perform in solving puzzles.

C) explored why some kids do well when they get praised for their effort while others don't.

D) identified ways parents can discover what natural talents their children possess.

3

A) NO CHANGE

B) his or her

C) their

D) him or her

4

A) NO CHANGE

B) were praised for their intelligence

C) were praised and complimented for their intelligence

D) were praised for their intellect and intelligence

CONTINUE

After receiving this praise, each child was asked whether he or she wanted to continue working on fairly easy problems or to move on to harder ones that would be [5] educational; but might not make the student "look smart." When presented with this choice, the students who had been praised for their intelligence [6] tend to ask for the easier puzzles. Furthermore, when these children were later presented with harder puzzles, they reported feeling very discouraged if they could not complete them. Dweck and her colleagues believe these children felt that if solving puzzles meant they were smart, [7] failure to solve them would then mean they were not smart. As a result, they avoided [8] risking failure. They were discouraged when they encountered it. The children who had been praised for effort, on the other hand, were more likely to seek out challenging but educational problems, and were less discouraged by failure.

5

A) NO CHANGE

B) educational but, might

C) educational but might

D) educational. But might

6

A) NO CHANGE

B) would have tended

C) will tend

D) tended

7

A) NO CHANGE

B) if they fail to solve them the that would

C) then failing to solve them would

D) failing would

8

Which choice most effectively combines the sentences at the underlined portion?

A) risking failure; they were also observed to be discouraged

B) risking failure; however, they were discouraged

C) risking failure and were discouraged

D) risking failure, but they were discouraged

CONTINUE

Practice Tests

Dweck's work has important implications for how parents and teachers should interact with children—even very intelligent ones. In Dweck's study, students who performed very well on the first set of puzzles responded to praise **9** <u>for they're</u> intelligence in the same way as students who performed less well. This means that even students who do **10** <u>manifest awesome promise</u> could be blocked from reaching their full potential by a fear of failure. **11** <u>Conversely, if children are criticized for not making an effort and then fail to make an effort in the future, that could be called a self-fulfilling prophecy.</u>

9

A) NO CHANGE

B) upon their

C) upon they're

D) for their

10

A) NO CHANGE

B) possess exceptional talents

C) develop smarts

D) show a knack for puzzles

11

The writer is considering deleting the underlined sentence. Should the writer do this?

A) Yes, because it contradicts information provided earlier in the passage.

B) Yes, because it needlessly introduces a new and distracting idea at the end of the passage.

C) No, because it suggests a tantalizing possibility for future investigation.

D) No, because it supports the idea that Dweck's research has implications for how parents and teachers should interact with children.

CONTINUE

Questions 12-22 are based on the following passage.

On Exhibit: Museum Professionals

The United States has 35,000 museums. If you visit one of these museums, **12** one can see pieces of art, historical documents, or scientific models. What you may not **13** see are the many people who work behind the scenes to collect, restore, and improve the collections of museums. The dedicated professionals that work for museums are **14** responsible for restoring, preserving, and promoting the treasures that museums hold.

Overseeing the museum's historical archives are its archivists. Archivists take care of records and documents, such as letters, diaries, maps, films, and **15** audio recordings and it is their job to preserve these records so that they can be accessed by both researchers and the general public. To properly preserve documents and records, archivists need to have an understanding of their unique physical properties. An archivist may need to **16** understand, for example, the conditions necessary to safely store papyrus, vellum, paper, or film media. Some archivists also create electronic versions of documents so that the information can be easily distributed. Perhaps most importantly, archivists maintain digital databases that keep track of the documents in a museum and those that are being borrowed. Without this information, it would be impossible to keep track of these valuable pieces of history.

12

A) NO CHANGE
B) one could see
C) you can see
D) someone could see

13

A) NO CHANGE
B) be seeing is
C) see is
D) seeing are

14

A) NO CHANGE
B) culpable
C) accountable
D) sensible

15

A) NO CHANGE
B) audio recordings, it is also their job to preserve
C) audio recordings: and it is their job to preserve
D) audio recordings; it is their job to preserve

16

A) NO CHANGE
B) understand; for example, the
C) understand, for example the
D) understand for example, the

CONTINUE

[17] While archivists care for documents in museums, conservators care for objects. The job of a conservator is to preserve and restore important objects. Depending on the museum that they work for, conservators may encounter many different kinds of objects. **[18]** Because they work with many different types of objects, conservators have to understand both history and chemistry. They have to understand how different materials will **[19]** decompress over time and what chemicals will best preserve them during this process. Conservators sometimes even use x-rays to determine the best way to protect or restore an aging object.

17

Which choice establishes the most effective transition between paragraphs?

A) NO CHANGE

B) While most people think documents are more important than objects,

C) Even though archivists care only for documents,

D) Since archivists have complete control of documents,

18

Which choice, inserted here, most effectively adds support for the previous sentence?

A) Conservators have to possess a broad range of skills and techniques to satisfy the requirements of their profession.

B) They also have to work with many different populations, including collectors and tourists.

C) A museum's collection might contain ivory carvings, bronze works, paintings, or even pieces of ancient buildings.

D) The objects that conservators work with are often expensive and precious.

19

A) NO CHANGE

B) decompose

C) denude

D) renege

CONTINUE

Conservators may also design replacements for missing parts of an object or create replicas for use in other museums. Some conservators become experts in a specific type of object or material. **20** However, some conservators specialize in restoring and preserving objects made of stone. Expert conservators may be asked to travel around the world in order to protect the world's supply of historical objects.

These are professions for people with a passion for learning and teaching. Most conservator and archivist positions require at least a Master's degree, and archivists and conservators continue to study and learn throughout **21** their life. **22** Many people, including archivists and conservators, enjoy reading books or visiting museums in their spare time.

20

A) NO CHANGE

B) On the other hand,

C) Therefore,

D) For instance,

21

A) NO CHANGE

B) each of their life

C) their lives

D) one's life

22

The writer wants to end the passage with a sentence that supports the central idea of this paragraph without repeating information. Which choice best accomplishes this goal?

A) NO CHANGE

B) Most will take graduate-level courses to enhance their knowledge.

C) Many of them study disciplines that will enable them to expand their opportunities for job growth.

D) They also have the satisfaction of knowing that their jobs help people of all ages learn about history, art, and science.

CONTINUE

Questions 23-33 are based on the following passage.

Flexing Your Brain

Individual practitioners of meditation have long touted its mental benefits, but **23** in recent decades it has now also been a subject of scientific interest—and the evidence suggests that the practice may actually promote brain health. Researchers have been conducting meditation studies since the 1950s, and it is now well-established that meditation can cause people to become more relaxed and that long-term practice can change the way that the brain works. In 2005, a group of scientists at Yale University conducted a study to investigate whether meditation might also **24** affecting the physical growth and development of certain parts of the brain.

[1] Previous studies had demonstrated that the physical structures of the brain **25** are changed by tasks that repeatedly activate specific areas of the brain. [2] In other words, just as muscles grow or shrink in response to use or disuse, different parts of the brain can physically change in response to how frequently they are used. [3] MRI scans reveal thickening of brain tissue in areas of the brain which have been **26** repeatedly activated over and over by stimulation. [4] These changes in brain structure are detectable through the use of magnetic resonance imaging, or MRI, which creates three-dimensional maps of the brain or other organs. [5] The Yale team hypothesized that regular meditation might cause similar thickening. **27**

23

A) NO CHANGE

B) in decades it has

C) in the most recent decades it has now also

D) in recent decades it has also

24

A) NO CHANGE

B) affect

C) effecting

D) effect

25

A) NO CHANGE

B) is changed by

C) was changed by

D) are changing by

26

A) NO CHANGE

B) activated again and again by repeated stimulation.

C) repeatedly activated by stimulation.

D) activated by stimulation.

27

To make this paragraph most logical, sentence 4 should be placed

A) where it is now.

B) before sentence 1.

C) before sentence 3.

D) after sentence 5.

CONTINUE

28 To confirm these findings, the Yale team designed a study to compare the brains of participants from two groups: a control group of non-meditators, and an experimental group of seasoned meditators. The researchers were most concerned with areas of the brain associated **29** with attention and sensory processing, which are activated during meditation. They designated these areas of the brain the "search area," used MRI scans to map out brain tissue thickness in certain search areas of the brain, and compared the brain scans of meditators with **30** the brains of non-meditators.

28

Which choice results in the most effective transition from the previous paragraph?

A) NO CHANGE

B) To verify this result,

C) To test this hypothesis,

D) To learn more about MRIs,

29

A) NO CHANGE

B) in

C) by

D) to

30

A) NO CHANGE

B) non-meditators.

C) the brain scans of non-meditators.

D) the search areas of non-meditators.

CONTINUE

The team's results indicated that tissue in the search area was indeed **31** much less thick overall in meditators' brains than in non-meditators'. Furthermore, while older subjects tended to have thinner brain tissue in the search area, age differences were much less pronounced within the group of meditators. While the study did not follow individuals over time, the differences between these groups do suggest that meditation may help to slow the thinning of brain tissue that takes place throughout the brain as people age.

The study did not determine whether the increased thickness was the result of larger **32** brain cells; new brain cells or the growth of blood vessels in the brain. However, any of these causes would likely be good for brain function. That gives researchers some reason to believe that meditation is likely to help **33** continuously improve brain function over time.

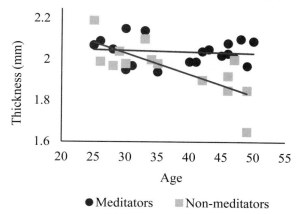

Thickness of Brain Tissue in the Search Areas of Meditators and Non-meditators

● Meditators   ▪ Non-meditators

31

Which choice is most consistent with the information provided in the graph?

A) NO CHANGE

B) healthier

C) somewhat thicker

D) somewhat younger

32

A) NO CHANGE

B) brain cells; new brain cells; or the growth

C) brain cells; new brain cells, or the growth

D) brain cells, new brain cells, or the growth

33

Which choice is most consistent with evidence presented earlier in the passage?

A) NO CHANGE

B) generate new brain cells to replace those that die.

C) preserve healthy brain function over time.

D) preserve the function of brain areas even as they become thinner over time.

CONTINUE

Questions 34-44 are based on the following passage.

The Great American Ballet

A lighted Christmas tree grows larger and larger until it fills half the stage. A pugnacious, many-headed mouse is defeated in battle by a living doll. Twenty-foot windows open onto a landscape awhirl with snow.

Every year since 1954, George Balanchine's *The Nutcracker* has delighted the thousands of families who come—some once, some a few times, some annually—to see this hallmark work of American ballet. [34] Performed around Christmas in theaters across the United States, *The Nutcracker* might not seem to be an obvious candidate for the title of "great American ballet." However, both its origins and [35] its reception have marked it as essentially American.

Balanchine choreographed *The Nutcracker* for New York City Ballet, [36] the company he had founded; with Lincoln Kirstein six years earlier. Balanchine was Russian by birth, but [37] Kirstein was an American. Kirstein longed to bring ballet, which was chiefly performed in Europe, to an American audience. Kirstein's love of ballet was kindled when, as a child, he saw the Russian ballerina Anna Pavlova perform on tour in Boston. But as much as he admired them, his hope was not merely to bring European artists to America: he wanted the art form itself to take root in his native soil.

34

Which choice would best support the second part of the sentence?

A) NO CHANGE

B) As the single most popular ballet in the United States

C) Choreographed by a Russian, to Russian music based on a German story

D) Introduced to the United States in San Francisco and made famous in New York

35

A) NO CHANGE

B) their reception have marked them

C) their reception has marked it

D) its reception have marked them

36

A) NO CHANGE

B) the company he had founded with Lincoln Kirstein six years earlier.

C) the company, he had founded with Lincoln Kirstein, six years earlier.

D) the company he had, founded with Lincoln Kirstein six years earlier.

37

Which choice most effectively combines the sentences at the underlined portion?

A) Kirstein, although he was an American, longed

B) Kirstein was an American, and also longed

C) Kirstein was an American who longed

D) American-born Kirstein longed

CONTINUE

[1] Kirstein first saw Balanchine's work in the late '20s in Paris, and he was impressed by **38** its physical vitality and modernism. [2] Balanchine's response, "but, first a school," suited Kirstein's ambitions perfectly. [3] In 1933, he invited the choreographer to move to the United States **39** and had founded an American ballet company. [4] Before staging his ballets with dancers unschooled in European techniques, **40** the dancers needed training. [5] In 1934, Kirstein and Balanchine founded the School of American Ballet, where Balanchine taught a technique that combined elements of the European tradition with **41** backwards notions of his own, many of them inspired by what he saw as the uniquely American qualities of his new ensemble. **42**

38

A) NO CHANGE

B) his

C) their

D) that

39

A) NO CHANGE

B) and found

C) and founding

D) and have founded

40

A) NO CHANGE

B) the dancers needed to train.

C) Balanchine needed to train them.

D) they needed training.

41

A) NO CHANGE

B) shocking thoughts

C) newfangled plans

D) fresh ideas

42

To make this paragraph most logical, sentence 2 should be placed

A) where it is now.

B) before sentence 1.

C) after sentence 3.

D) before sentence 5.

CONTINUE

The pair's attempts at founding a professional company were interrupted by World War II **43** but eventually reached their fruition with the event of the establishment of New York City Ballet in 1948. *The Nutcracker* was not the first ballet Balanchine staged for his new company, but it was his most ambitious project to date. **44** The dances for the children in Balanchine's production of *The Nutcracker* are choreographed to be easier than those of adults, but are still a joy to watch.

43

A) NO CHANGE

B) but reached fruition eventually when New York City Ballet was established at last in 1948.

C) but finally reached fruition with the establishment of New York City Ballet in 1948.

D) but reached their eventual fruition, finally, with New York City Ballet's establishment in 1948.

44

Which choice of conclusion best links the final sentences to the main point of the passage as a whole?

A) NO CHANGE

B) Balanchine would go on to choreograph dozens of other shows for American companies and companies around the world.

C) *The Nutcracker* is a major source of revenue for major American ballet companies today, generating up to 40% of all ticket sales.

D) *The Nutcracker* quickly became an American classic, performed annually not only by New York City Ballet but also by regional companies across the country.

STOP

If you complete this section before the end of your allotted time, check your work on this section only. Do NOT use the time to work on another section.

Math Test – No Calculator

25 MINUTES, 20 QUESTIONS

Turn to Section 3 of your answer sheet to answer the questions in this section.

DIRECTIONS

Questions **1-15** ask you to solve a problem, select the best answer among four choices, and fill in the corresponding circle on your answer sheet. Questions **16-20** ask you to solve a problem and enter your answer in the grid provided on your answer sheet. There are detailed instructions on entering answers into the grid before question 16. You may use your test booklet for scratch work.

NOTES

1. You **may not** use a calculator.
2. Variables and expressions represent real numbers unless stated otherwise.
3. Figures are drawn to scale unless stated otherwise.
4. Figures lie in a plane unless stated otherwise.
5. The domain of a function f is defined as the set of all real numbers x for which $f(x)$ is also a real number, unless stated otherwise.

REFERENCE

$A = \frac{1}{2}bh$

$a^2 + b^2 = c^2$

Special Triangles

$V = \frac{1}{3}lwh$

$V = \frac{1}{3}\pi r^2 h$

$A = lw$

$V = lwh$

$V = \pi r^2 h$

$A = \pi r^2$

$C = 2\pi r$

$V = \frac{4}{3}\pi r^3$

There are 360° in a circle.

The sum of the angles in a triangle is 180°.

The number of radians of arc in a circle is 2π.

CONTINUE

1

Which of the following represents the solution set to the inequality $1 \le -2x + 3$?

A)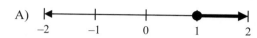
-2   -1   0   1   2

B)
-2   -1   0   1   2

C)
-2   -1   0   1   2

D)
-2   -1   0   1   2

3

$$3x \ge y - 1$$

Which of the following ordered pairs is NOT a solution to the inequality above?

A) $(-1, -4)$

B) $(0, 0)$

C) $(2, 7)$

D) $(3, 11)$

2

The chemical formula for water is H_2O, which indicates that each molecule of water contains two hydrogen atoms and one oxygen atom. A cup of water contains approximately 2.4×10^{25} hydrogen and oxygen atoms combined. How many of these atoms are hydrogen atoms?

A) 8×10^{24}

B) 1.6×10^{25}

C) 2.4×10^{25}

D) 4.8×10^{25}

CONTINUE

4

A gas station charges $3.39 per gallon of gas and a flat fee of $2 per transaction. Which of the following graphs represents the cost of a transaction as a function of the number of gallons of gas purchased?

A)

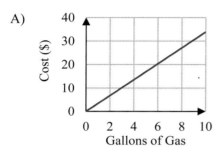

B)

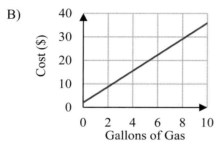

C)

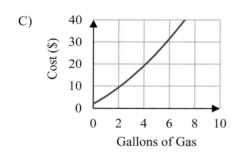

D)

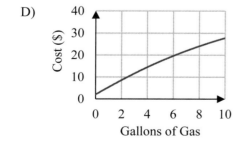

5

A lab produces 2 compounds in equal amounts from a single reaction, Compound A and Compound B. The lab sells 100mg of Compound A for $100 and 100mg of Compound B for $150. If the lab sells all of the products it creates in a single day for $2000, how many milligrams of each compound did the lab produce and sell?

A)   500

B)   600

C)   800

D) 1,000

6

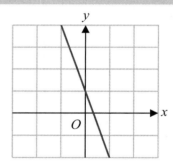

The graph above represents the function $y = mx + b$. Which of the following is the equation for x as a function of y?

A) $x = -my - b$

B) $x = -my + b$

C) $x = \dfrac{y - b}{m}$

D) $x = \dfrac{-y - b}{m}$

CONTINUE

7

	Membership Fee	Locker Rental	Day Fee
Membership	$100	Free	Free
No Membership	None	$10	$7

The table above shows possible rates at a gym. Without a membership, customers pay a fee of $10 per month for a locker and $7 per visit. A membership includes a locker and unlimited visits for $100 per month. How many times per month must a customer go to the gym in order to benefit from purchasing a membership?

A) 13

B) 12

C) 11

D) 2

8

Which of the following equations has exactly one real solution?

A) $x^2 + 6x + 3 = 0$

B) $2x^2 + 6x + 3 = 0$

C) $3x^2 + 6x + 3 = 0$

D) $4x^2 + 6x + 3 = 0$

9

Andre is planning a field trip to a museum for his class of s students. He has $200 to spend on tickets and meals, and each student gets one meal and one ticket. If tickets cost t dollars each, how much money can Andre spend on each meal?

A) $200 + ts$ dollars

B) $200 - ts$ dollars

C) $\dfrac{200 + ts}{s}$ dollars

D) $\dfrac{200 - ts}{s}$ dollars

10

Which of the following expressions is NOT equivalent to the others?

A) $2\sqrt{2x}$

B) $\sqrt{8x}$

C) $\sqrt[4]{16x^2}$

D) $\sqrt[4]{4^2 \times 4x^2}$

CONTINUE

11

For $i = \sqrt{-1}$, which of the following expressions is equivalent to $(5 - i)(2 + 6i)$?

A) $4 + 28i$

B) $11 - 28i$

C) $6 - 28i$

D) $16 + 28i$

12

If $f(x) = \dfrac{x + 1}{3x}$ and $g(x) = 2x^2$, what is the value of

$f(g(x))$?

A) $\dfrac{2x^2 + 1}{6x^2}$

B) $\dfrac{2y^2 + 1}{6y^2}$

C) $\dfrac{2x^2 + 1}{3x}$

D) $\dfrac{(x + 1)(2y^2)}{3x}$

13

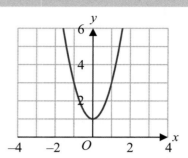

The graph above represents the function $f(x) = ax^2 + c$. This function includes the point $(2, 6)$. If $g(x) = 2f(x)$ and $g(x)$ includes the point $(2, b)$, what is the value of b?

A) 6

B) 12

C) 14

D) 16

CONTINUE

14

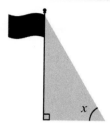

The diagram above shows a flag pole casting a shadow. The distance between the top of the flag pole and end of the shadow is 10. What is the difference between the height of the flag pole and the length of the shadow, in terms of x?

A) $\sin(x) \times 10 - \cos(x) \times 10$

B) $\dfrac{\sin(x)}{10} - \dfrac{\cos(x)}{10}$

C) $\dfrac{2\cos(x) \times 10 - \sin(x) \times 10x^2 + 1}{3x}$

D) $\dfrac{\cos(x)}{10} - \dfrac{\sin(x)}{10}$

15

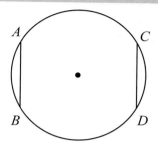

The circle above has a radius r and parallel chords $\overline{AB}$ and $\overline{CD}$. Each chord has a length of r. If a rectangle is formed by connecting the points A, B, C, and D, what is the area of the rectangle?

A) $r\sqrt{3}$

B) $r\sqrt{5}$

C) $r^2\sqrt{3}$

D) $r^2\sqrt{5}$

CONTINUE

DIRECTIONS

Questions **16-20** ask you to solve a problem and enter your answer in the grid provided on your answer sheet. When completing grid-in questions:

1. You are required to bubble in the circles for your answers. It is recommended, but not required, that you also write your answer in the boxes above the columns of circles. Points will be awarded based only on whether the circles are filled in correctly.

2. Fill in only one circle in a column.

3. You can start your answer in any column as long as you can fit in the whole answer.

4. For questions 16-20, no answers will be negative numbers.

5. **Mixed numbers,** such as $4\frac{2}{5}$, must be gridded as decimals or improper fractions, such as 4.4 or as 22/5. "42/5" will be read as "forty-two over five," not as "four and two-fifths."

6. If your answer is a **decimal** with more digits than will fit on the grid, you may round it or cut it off, but you must fill the entire grid.

7. If there are **multiple correct solutions** to a problem, all of them will be considered correct. Enter only **one** on the grid.

CONTINUE

Practice Tests

16

Josh has \$6.90 in quarters and nickels. If he has the same number of quarters and nickels, how many quarters does Josh have?

17

$$y + 3 = 2x^2 - 5x$$
$$y - 3 = 6x$$
$$x > 0$$

What is a value of x that satisfies the system of equations above?

18

Carlos runs directly towards Xiao at 15 miles per hour. Xiao walks directly toward Carlos at 3 miles per hour. If they meet after 20 minutes, how far apart were they, in miles, before they started moving?

19

$$\sqrt{5x - 4} = 2x - 4$$

What value of x satisfies the equation above?

20

$$2(a^3 + a^2 + 4a - 8) = 2a^3 + 4a^2 - 5a - 1$$

What is one possible value of a for the equation above?

STOP

If you complete this section before the end of your allotted time, check your work on this section only. Do NOT use the time to work on another section.

Math Test – Calculator

55 MINUTES, 38 QUESTIONS

Turn to Section 4 of your answer sheet to answer the questions in this section.

DIRECTIONS

Questions **1-30** ask you to solve a problem, select the best answer among four choices, and fill in the corresponding circle on your answer sheet. Questions **31-38** ask you to solve a problem and enter your answer in a grid provided on your answer sheet. There are detailed instructions on entering answers into the grid before question 31. You may use your test booklet for scratch work.

NOTES

1. You **may** use a calculator.
2. Variables and expressions represent real numbers unless stated otherwise.
3. Figures are drawn to scale unless stated otherwise.
4. Figures lie in a plane unless stated otherwise.
5. The domain of a function f is defined as the set of all real numbers x for which $f(x)$ is also a real number, unless stated otherwise.

REFERENCE

$$A = \frac{1}{2}bh$$　$$a^2 + b^2 = c^2$$　Special Triangles　$$V = \frac{1}{3}lwh$$　$$V = \frac{1}{3}\pi r^2 h$$

$$A = lw$$　$$V = lwh$$　$$V = \pi r^2 h$$　$$A = \pi r^2$$　$$V = \frac{4}{3}\pi r^3$$

$$C = 2\pi r$$

There are 360° in a circle.

The sum of the angles in a triangle is 180°.

The number of radians of arc in a circle is 2π.

CONTINUE

1

If $2x - 6 = 4x + 4$, what is the value of x?

A) -5

B) -1

C) 1

D) 5

2

If a and b are both even integers, which of the following must be an odd integer?

I. $(a + 1)(b + 1)$
II. $(a + 1)(b + 2)$
III. $(a - 1)(b + 1)$

A) I and II

B) I and III

C) II and III

D) I, II, and III

3

A tree is planted when it is 3 feet tall. If the tree's growth rate is linear, which of the following graphs could represent its height over time?

A)

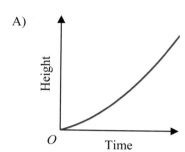

B)

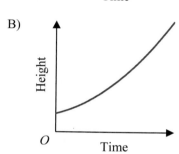

C)

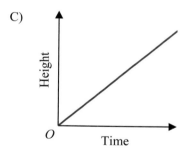

D)

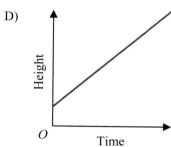

CONTINUE

4

$$3x + y < 8$$

How many pairs of positive integers (x, y) satisfy the inequality above?

A) 1

B) 3

C) 5

D) 7

5

Count of Monarch Butterflies

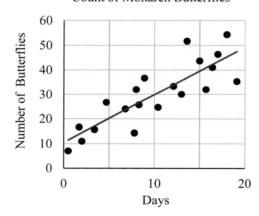

The scatterplot above shows the number of Monarch butterflies over a three-week period. Based on the line of best fit, which of the following values is closest to the average daily increase in the number of Monarch butterflies?

A) 0.5

B) 2

C) 10

D) 40

6

a is 8% of b and b is 150% greater than c. If c is 15, what is the value of a?

A) 4

B) 3

C) 2

D) 1

7

	Symptoms	No Symptoms
Vaccinated	216	1134
Not Vaccinated	584	336

A hospital collected data from patients who were exposed to a certain virus. The hospital recorded whether the patients had been vaccinated for the virus and whether they showed symptoms. The data is summarized in the chart above. What percentage of patients who showed symptoms had been vaccinated?

A) 16%

B) 27%

C) 37%

D) 73%

CONTINUE

8

If $3x = \frac{1}{2}y$, what is $\frac{y}{3}$ in terms of x?

A) $2x$

B) $\frac{3}{2}x$

C) x

D) $\frac{2}{3}x$

9

$$p(x) = |2x - 5|$$

$p(x)$ is defined above. What is the value of $p(2) + p(-2)$?

A) −10

B) −8

C)   8

D)   10

10

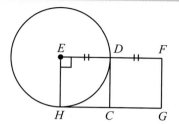

In the diagram above, the circumference of circle E is 6π. What is the area of rectangle $EFGH$?

A) 3π

B)   18

C)   24

D) 12π

11

What is the length of the line segment beginning at the point $(-2, 3)$ and ending at the point $(1, 7)$?

A) 0.75

B) 3

C) 4

D) 5

CONTINUE

Questions 12 and 13 refer to the following information.

A chemist is working with two groups of elements. He finds that each of the elements has either one, two, or three stable isotopes, which are forms of an element with different numbers of neutrons. He records the data in the charts below.

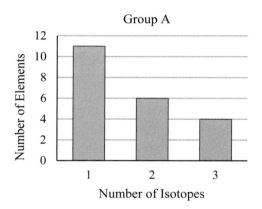

Group A

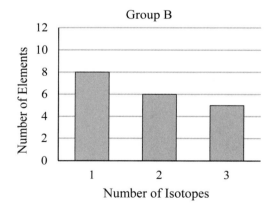

Group B

12

Approximately what percentage of elements in Group A have two stable isotopes?

A) 14%

B) 19%

C) 29%

D) 48%

13

Which of the following statements correctly compares the medians and modes of the data from the two groups of elements?

A) Group A's data have a smaller median than Group B's. Group A's data have the same mode as Group B's.

B) Group A's data have a larger median than Group B. Group A's data have the same mode as Group B's.

C) Group A's data have the same median as Group B's. Group A's data have a smaller mode than Group B.

D) Group A's data have the same median as Group B's. Group A's data have a larger mode than Group B's.

CONTINUE

14

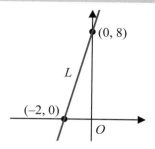

Which of the following equations describes a line that is perpendicular to line L above?

A) $y = 4x + 8$

B) $y = -4x + 8$

C) $y = \frac{1}{4}x + 8$

D) $y = -\frac{1}{4}x + 8$

15

A car dealer buys a car from a manufacturer. The dealer increases the price of the car by 20% to $36,000. The dealer then sells the car at a 5% discount. What is the dealer's total profit from the sale of the car?

A) $4,200

B) $6,000

C) $7,200

D) $9,000

16

$$\frac{4(x+1)-1}{3} = \frac{8-(5-x)}{5}$$

What is the value of x in the equation above?

A) $-\frac{24}{17}$

B) $-\frac{6}{17}$

C) $-\frac{24}{23}$

D) $-\frac{6}{23}$

17

Which of the following expressions is NOT equal to $3\sqrt{32x}$?

A) $12\sqrt{2x}$

B) $6\sqrt{8x}$

C) $4\sqrt{12x}$

D) $\sqrt{288x}$

CONTINUE

18

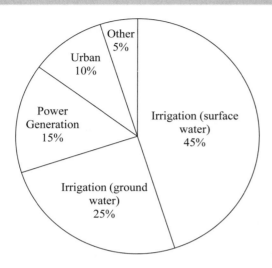

The chart above shows the distribution of water use in the South Platte River Basin. If the total water use is 4 billion gallons per day, how many gallons of water are used for irrigation every week?

A)   1.8 billion

B)   2.8 billion

C)   12.6 billion

D)   19.6 billion

19

Macey and Sam both have $100 in their bank accounts. Each year Macey's bank increases her balance by $10, and Sam's bank increases his balance by 10%. If Macey and Sam do not deposit or withdraw any money, what is the difference between Macey's balance and Sam's balance after 5 years?

A)   Macey's account will have $11.05 more than Sam's account.

B)   Macey's account will have the same balance as Sam's account.

C)   Macey's account will have $9.05 less than Sam's account.

D)   Macey's account will have $11.05 less than Sam's account.

20

For which of the following functions is $f(2) < f(-2)$?

A) $f(x) = \dfrac{3}{x}$

B) $f(x) = 3x^2 + 3$

C) $f(x) = 3 - x^3$

D) $f(x) = -3$

CONTINUE

Practice Tests

21

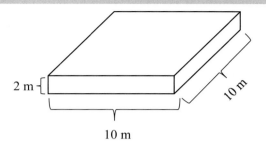

2 m

10 m

10 m

The width, depth, and length of a rectangular pool are shown above. If a pump fills the pool at a rate of 55 gallons per minute, how many hours will it take to fill half of the pool? (1 cubic meter equals approximately 264 gallons.)

A) 8

B) 16

C) 20

D) 30

22

$$y - x = -3x$$

Given the equation above, what is the value of $\dfrac{x}{y}$?

A) $-\dfrac{1}{4}$

B) $-\dfrac{1}{2}$

C) -2

D) -4

23

Wolf Population in a Protected Wilderness Area	
Year	Count of Wolves
0	20
6	27
12	36

A group of scientists have reintroduced a species of wolf into a protected wilderness area and are measuring the population growth, as summarized in the table above. The scientists modeled the population change as increasing at a rate of approximately 5% each year. Which of the following functions approximates the relationship between the wolf population, P, and time in years, t?

A) $P = 20 + 0.05t$

B) $P = 20 \times 1.05 \times t$

C) $P = 20(0.05)^t$

D) $P = 20(1.05)^t$

24

$$P = \dfrac{V^2}{R}$$

In an electrical circuit, the power, P, of the circuit is related to the voltage, V, and the resistance, R, as shown in the equation above. If both the voltage and the resistance are doubled, what happens to the value of P?

A) P is halved.

B) P is not changed.

C) P is doubled.

D) P is tripled.

CONTINUE

Questions 25 and 26 refer to the following information.

A survey was conducted to determine the types of vehicles owned by people in different age groups. The table below displays a summary of the survey results.

Car Type by Age

Age	SUV/ Minivan	Sedan/ Coupe	Truck	Electric/ Hybrid	None	Total
18-29	9,357	6,980	3,537	3,583	3,498	**26,955**
30-49	11,439	13,476	4,343	3,953	2,309	**35,520**
50-69	10,964	14,055	1,506	1,068	2,004	**29,597**
70+	7,033	15,610	680	792	5,377	**29,492**
Total	**38,793**	**50,121**	**10,066**	**9,396**	**13,188**	**121,564**

25

According to the table, which age group contained the smallest percentage of people who did not own a vehicle?

A) 18-29

B) 30-49

C) 50-69

D) 70+

26

According to the table, what is the approximate percent probability that the owner of a hybrid or electric car is 50 or more years old?

A) 3%

B) 11%

C) 20%

D) 24%

CONTINUE

27

Which of the following is NOT a solution to the equation $\sin(x) = \sin^2(x)$?

A) π

B) $\dfrac{\pi}{2}$

C) $-\dfrac{\pi}{2}$

D) $-\pi$

28

A construction worker uses a chain-link fence to completely enclose a rectangular area. The worker has 40 feet of fencing material. Which of the graphs below shows the total enclosed area as a function of the length of one side of the rectangle? (Note: Graphs are not drawn to scale.)

A)
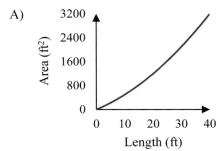

B)
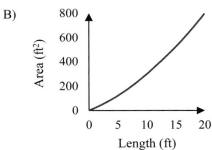

C)
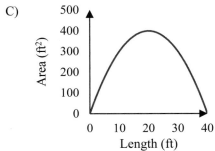

D)
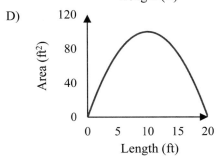

CONTINUE

29

Popularity of Social Media Site

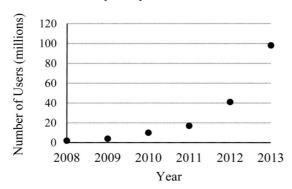

The scatter plot above shows the popularity of a social media site created in 2008. If y is the number of years since the site was founded and N is the number of people, in millions, using the site, which of the following functions best describes the relationship between y and N?

A) $N(y) = 20y$

B) $N(y) = 2.5^y$

C) $N(y) = -15y^2 + 100y$

D) $N(y) = 15y^2 - 100$

30

$\dfrac{9x^2}{3x + 1}$ is rewritten as $A + \dfrac{1}{3x + 1}$. What is A in terms of x?

A) $3x - 1$

B) $3x + 1$

C) $9x - 1$

D) $9x + 1$

CONTINUE

DIRECTIONS

Questions **31-38** ask you to solve a problem and enter your answer in the grid provided on your answer sheet. When completing grid-in questions:

1. You are required to bubble in the circles for your answers. It is recommended, but not required, that you also write your answer in the boxes above the columns of circles. Points will be awarded based only on whether the circles are filled in correctly.

2. Fill in only one circle in a column.

3. You can start your answer in any column as long as you can fit in the whole answer.

4. For questions 31-38, no answers will be negative numbers.

5. **Mixed numbers,** such as $4\frac{2}{5}$, must be gridded as decimals or improper fractions, such as 4.4 or as 22/5. "42/5" will be read as "forty-two over five," not as "four and two-fifths."

6. If your answer is a **decimal** with more digits than will fit on the grid, you may round it or cut it off, but you must fill the entire grid.

7. If there are **multiple correct solutions** to a problem, all of them will be considered correct. Enter only **one** on the grid.

CONTINUE

31

A train travels at an average speed of 30 miles per hour. How many minutes will it take the train to travel 75 miles?

32

If $\dfrac{2}{5}$ of n is 48, what is $\dfrac{2}{3}$ of n?

33

$$f(x) = x^3 + 3x^2 - 6x + 14$$

Give the equation above, what is the value of $f(-3)$?

34

Kavi takes two buses to get to work. Bus A has an average speed of 20 miles per hour, and Bus B has an average speed of 15 miles per hour. If Kavi takes Bus A for 3 miles and Bus B for 6 miles, how many minutes does Kavi spend on the two buses on his way to work?

35

$$\frac{12}{a-2} + \frac{5}{a+2} = 1$$

If a represents a positive value in the equation above, what is a possible value for a?

CONTINUE

36

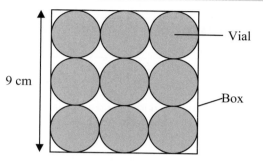

9 cm

Vial

Box

Top view of a box

A biotechnology company has built boxes with square bases that are 5 centimeters high; one side of the box is 9 cm long, as shown. Each box holds 9 cylindrical vials that contain bacteria colonies. The number of colonies initially in each vial is equal to the vial's total volume, in cubic centimeters. If the number of colonies decreases by one third for every hour that they are in storage, how many colonies remain in the box after it has been stored for two hours? (Use the approximation $\pi = 3.14$ and round to the nearest colony.)

Questions 37 and 38 refer to the following information.

Mia is graduating from college in four years. She took out a loan of $2,000 at the beginning of each year to pay for part of her tuition and expenses. The annual interest rate for her loan is 4%, calculated on her total debt at the end of each year. Interest is added to her total debt for that year.

37

What is Mia's total debt with interest at the end of the fourth year? Round to the nearest dollar.

38

Suppose Mia does not borrow more money or pay off any of her debt for two years after graduating. Her interest rate continues to accrue at the same 4% annual rate. At the beginning of her third year after graduating, Mia pays a lump sum of $8,000 toward her loan. After making that payment, how much debt does she still owe? Round to the nearest dollar.

STOP

If you complete this section before the end of your allotted time, check your work on this section only. Do NOT use the time to work on another section.

Essay (Optional)

50 MINUTES

Turn to the lined pages of your answer sheet to write your essay.

DIRECTIONS

This essay is optional. It is a chance for you to demonstrate how well you can understand and analyze a written passage. Your essay should show that you have carefully read the passage and should be a concisely written analysis that is both logical and clear.

You must write your entire essay on the lines in your answer booklet. No additional paper will be provided aside from the Planning Page inside your answer booklet. You will be able to write your entire essay in the space provided if you make use of every line, keep tight margins, and write at a suitable size. Don't forget to keep your handwriting legible for the readers evaluating your essay.

You will have 50 minutes to read the passage in this booklet and to write an essay in response to the prompt provided at the end of the passage.

REMINDERS

- What you write in this booklet will not be evaluated. Write your essay in the answer booklet only.

- Essays that are off-topic will not be evaluated.

As you read the passage below, consider how David Epstein uses

- evidence, such as facts or examples, to support claims.
- reasoning to develop ideas and to connect claims and evidence.
- stylistic or persuasive elements, such as word choice or appeals to emotion, to add power to the ideas expressed.

Adapted from David Epstein, "Sports Should Be Child's Play." © 2014 by the New York Times Company. Originally published June 10, 2014.

1   The national furor over concussions misses the primary scourge that is harming kids and damaging youth sports in America. The heightened pressure on child athletes to be, essentially, adult athletes has fostered an epidemic of hyperspecialization that is both dangerous and counterproductive.

2   Children are playing sports in too structured a manner too early in life on adult-size fields—i.e., too large for optimal skill development—and spending too much time in one sport. It can lead to serious injuries and, a growing body of sports science shows, a lesser ultimate level of athletic success. We should urge kids to avoid hyperspecialization and instead sample a variety of sports through at least age 12.

3   Nearly a third of youth athletes in a three-year longitudinal study led by Neeru Jayanthi, director of primary care sports medicine at Loyola University in Chicago, were highly specialized—they had quit multiple sports in order to focus on one for more than eight months a year — and another third weren't far behind. Even controlling for age and the total number of weekly hours in sports, kids in the study who were highly specialized had a 36 percent increased risk of suffering a serious overuse injury. Dr. Jayanthi saw kids with stress fractures in their backs, arms or legs; damage to elbow ligaments; and cracks in the cartilage in their joints.

4   Some young athletes now face surgeries befitting their grandparents. Young hockey goaltenders repeatedly practice butterfly style—which stresses the developing hip joint when the legs are splayed to block the bottom of the goal. The sports surgeon Marc Philippon, based in Vail, Colo., saw a 25-year-old goalie who already needed a hip replacement.

5   In the Loyola study, sport diversification had a protective effect. But in case health risks alone aren't reason enough for parents to ignore the siren call of specialization, diversification also provides performance benefits.

6   Kids who play multiple "attacking" sports, like basketball or field hockey, transfer learned motor and anticipatory skills—the unconscious ability to read bodies and game situations—to other sports. They take less time to master the sport they ultimately choose.

7   Several studies on skill acquisition now show that elite athletes generally practiced their sport less through their early teenage years and specialized only in the mid-to-late teenage years, while so-called sub-elites—those who never quite cracked the highest ranks—homed in on a single sport much sooner.

8   Data presented at the April meeting of the American Medical Society for Sports Medicine showed that varsity athletes at U.C.L.A.—many with full scholarships—specialized on average at age 15.4, whereas U.C.L.A. undergrads who played sports in high school, but did not make the intercollegiate level, specialized at 14.2.

9   We may prize the story of Tiger Woods, who demonstrated his swing at age 2 for Bob Hope. But the path of the two-time N.B.A. M.V.P. Steve Nash (who grew up playing soccer and didn't own a basketball until age 13) or the tennis star Roger Federer (whose parents encouraged him to play badminton, basketball and soccer) is actually the norm.

10   A Swedish study of sub-elite and elite tennis players—including five who ranked among the top 15 in the world—found that those who topped out as sub-elites dropped all other sports by age 11. Eventual elites developed in a "harmonious club environment without greater demands for success," and played multiple sports until age 14.

11   The sports science data support a "sampling period" through at least age 12. Mike Joyner, a Mayo Clinic physician and human performance expert, would add general physical literacy-building to the youth sports menu: perhaps using padded gymnastics gyms for parkour, which is essentially running, climbing, or vaulting on any obstacle one can find.

12   In addition to athletic diversity, kids' sports should be kid-size. In Brazil, host of this month's World Cup, kids are weaned on "futsal," a lightly structured and miniaturized form of soccer. Futsal is played on tiny patches of grass or concrete or on indoor courts and typically by teams of five players. Players touch the ball up to five times as frequently as they do in traditional soccer, and the tighter playing area forces children to develop foot and decision-making skills under pressure.

13   A futsalization of youth sports generally would serve engagement, skill development and health.

Write an essay in which you explain how David Epstein builds an argument to persuade his audience that kids should avoid specializing in a specific sport too early. In your essay, analyze how Epstein uses one or more of the features listed in the box above (or features of your own choice) to strengthen the logic and persuasiveness of his argument. Be sure that your analysis focuses on the most relevant features of the passage.

Your essay should not explain whether you agree with Epstein's claims, but rather explain how Epstein builds an argument to persuade his audience.

Practice Test 3

SAT

Directions

- Work on just one section at a time.

- If you complete a section before the end of your allotted time, use the extra minutes to check your work on that section only. Do NOT use the time to work on another section.

Using Your Test Booklet

- No credit will be given for anything written in the test booklet. You may use the test booklet for scratch paper.

- You are not allowed to continue answering questions in a section after the allotted time has run out. This includes marking answers on your answer sheet that you previously noted in your test booklet.

- You are not allowed to fold pages, take pages out of the test booklet, or take any pages home.

Answering Questions

- Each answer must be marked in the corresponding row on the answer sheet.

- Each bubble must be filled in completely and darkly within the lines.

Correct ●   Incorrect

- Be careful to bubble in the correct part of the answer sheet.

- Extra marks on your answer sheet may be marked as incorrect answers and lower your score.

- Make sure you use a No. 2 pencil.

Scoring

- You will receive one point for each correct answer.

- Incorrect answers will NOT result in points deducted. Even if you are unsure about an answer, you should make a guess.

DO NOT BEGIN THIS TEST

UNTIL YOUR PROCTOR TELLS YOU TO DO SO

For printable answer sheets, please visit **ivyglobal.com/study**.

Section 1

	A	B	C	D		A	B	C	D		A	B	C	D		A	B	C	D		A	B	C	D
1	○	○	○	○	12	○	○	○	○	23	○	○	○	○	34	○	○	○	○	45	○	○	○	○
2	○	○	○	○	13	○	○	○	○	24	○	○	○	○	35	○	○	○	○	46	○	○	○	○
3	○	○	○	○	14	○	○	○	○	25	○	○	○	○	36	○	○	○	○	47	○	○	○	○
4	○	○	○	○	15	○	○	○	○	26	○	○	○	○	37	○	○	○	○	48	○	○	○	○
5	○	○	○	○	16	○	○	○	○	27	○	○	○	○	38	○	○	○	○	49	○	○	○	○
6	○	○	○	○	17	○	○	○	○	28	○	○	○	○	39	○	○	○	○	50	○	○	○	○
7	○	○	○	○	18	○	○	○	○	29	○	○	○	○	40	○	○	○	○	51	○	○	○	○
8	○	○	○	○	19	○	○	○	○	30	○	○	○	○	41	○	○	○	○	52	○	○	○	○
9	○	○	○	○	20	○	○	○	○	31	○	○	○	○	42	○	○	○	○					
10	○	○	○	○	21	○	○	○	○	32	○	○	○	○	43	○	○	○	○					
11	○	○	○	○	22	○	○	○	○	33	○	○	○	○	44	○	○	○	○					

Section 2

	A	B	C	D		A	B	C	D		A	B	C	D		A	B	C	D		A	B	C	D
1	○	○	○	○	10	○	○	○	○	19	○	○	○	○	28	○	○	○	○	37	○	○	○	○
2	○	○	○	○	11	○	○	○	○	20	○	○	○	○	29	○	○	○	○	38	○	○	○	○
3	○	○	○	○	12	○	○	○	○	21	○	○	○	○	30	○	○	○	○	39	○	○	○	○
4	○	○	○	○	13	○	○	○	○	22	○	○	○	○	31	○	○	○	○	40	○	○	○	○
5	○	○	○	○	14	○	○	○	○	23	○	○	○	○	32	○	○	○	○	41	○	○	○	○
6	○	○	○	○	15	○	○	○	○	24	○	○	○	○	33	○	○	○	○	42	○	○	○	○
7	○	○	○	○	16	○	○	○	○	25	○	○	○	○	34	○	○	○	○	43	○	○	○	○
8	○	○	○	○	17	○	○	○	○	26	○	○	○	○	35	○	○	○	○	44	○	○	○	○
9	○	○	○	○	18	○	○	○	○	27	○	○	○	○	36	○	○	○	○					

Section 3 (No-Calculator)

	A	B	C	D			A	B	C	D			A	B	C	D			A	B	C	D			A	B	C	D
1	○	○	○	○		4	○	○	○	○		7	○	○	○	○		10	○	○	○	○		13	○	○	○	○
2	○	○	○	○		5	○	○	○	○		8	○	○	○	○		11	○	○	○	○		14	○	○	○	○
3	○	○	○	○		6	○	○	○	○		9	○	○	○	○		12	○	○	○	○		15	○	○	○	○

Only answers that are gridded will be scored. You will not receive credit for anything written in the boxes.

16   17   18   19   20

Section 4 (Calculator)

	A	B	C	D			A	B	C	D			A	B	C	D			A	B	C	D			A	B	C	D
1	○	○	○	○		7	○	○	○	○		13	○	○	○	○		19	○	○	○	○		25	○	○	○	○
2	○	○	○	○		8	○	○	○	○		14	○	○	○	○		20	○	○	○	○		26	○	○	○	○
3	○	○	○	○		9	○	○	○	○		15	○	○	○	○		21	○	○	○	○		27	○	○	○	○
4	○	○	○	○		10	○	○	○	○		16	○	○	○	○		22	○	○	○	○		28	○	○	○	○
5	○	○	○	○		11	○	○	○	○		17	○	○	○	○		23	○	○	○	○		29	○	○	○	○
6	○	○	○	○		12	○	○	○	○		18	○	○	○	○		24	○	○	○	○		30	○	○	○	○

Only answers that are gridded will be scored. You will not receive credit for anything written in the boxes.

31   32   33   34   35

Only answers that are gridded will be scored. You will not receive credit for anything written in the boxes.

36   37   38

Important: Use a No. 2 pencil. Write inside the borders.

You may use the space below to plan your essay, but be sure to write your essay on the lined pages. Work on this page will not be scored.

Use this space to plan your essay.

START YOUR ESSAY HERE.

_____

_____

_____

_____

_____

_____

_____

_____

_____

_____

_____

_____

_____

_____

_____

_____

_____

_____

_____

_____

Continue on the next page.

Continue on the next page.

Practice Tests

_____

_____

_____

_____

_____

_____

_____

_____

_____

_____

_____

_____

_____

_____

_____

_____

_____

_____

_____

_____

_____

_____

_____

Continue on the next page.

_____

_____

_____

_____

_____

_____

_____

_____

_____

_____

_____

_____

_____

_____

_____

_____

_____

_____

_____

_____

_____

_____

_____

_____

STOP.

Reading Test

65 MINUTES, 52 QUESTIONS

Turn to Section 1 of your answer sheet to answer the questions in this section.

DIRECTIONS

Every passage or paired set of passages is accompanied by a number of questions. Read the passage or paired set of passages, then use what is said or implied in what you read and in any given graphics to choose the best answer to each question.

Questions 1-10 are based on the following passage.

This passage is adapted from W.E.B. Du Bois, *A Negro Schoolmaster in the New South*, originally published in 1899. In this book, Du Bois describes his experience as a schoolmaster in a rural black community in Tennessee.

There came a day when all the teachers left the Institute, and began the hunt for schools. I learn from hearsay (for my mother was mortally afraid of
Line firearms) that the hunting of ducks and bears and
5 men is wonderfully interesting, but I am sure that the man who has never hunted a country school has something to learn of the pleasures of the chase. I see now the white, hot roads lazily rise and fall and wind before me under the burning July sun; I feel the deep
10 weariness of heart and limb, as ten, eight, six miles stretch relentlessly ahead; I feel my heart sink heavily as I hear again and again, "Got a teacher? Yes." So I walked on and on—horses were too expensive—until I had wandered beyond railways, beyond stage lines,
15 to a land of "varmints" and rattlesnakes, where the coming of a stranger was an event, and men lived and died in the shadow of one blue hill.

Sprinkled over hill and dale lay cabins and farmhouses, shut out from the world by the forests
20 and the rolling hills toward the east. There I found at last a little school. Josie told me of it; she was a thin, homely girl of twenty, with a dark brown face and thick, hard hair. I had crossed the stream at Watertown, and rested under the great willows; then I had gone to

25 the little cabin in the lot where Josie was resting on her way to town. The gaunt farmer made me welcome, and Josie, hearing my errand, told me anxiously that they wanted a school over the hill; that but once since the war had a teacher been there; that she
30 herself longed to learn,—and thus she ran on, talking fast and loud, with much earnestness and energy.

The schoolhouse was a log hut, where Colonel Wheeler used to shelter his corn. It sat in a lot behind a rail fence and thorn bushes. There was an entrance
35 where a door once was, and within, a massive rickety fireplace; great holes between the logs served as windows. Furniture was scarce. A pale blackboard crouched in the corner. My desk was made of three boards, reinforced at critical points, and my chair,
40 borrowed from the landlady, had to be returned every night. Seats for the children were rough plank benches without backs, and at times without legs. They had the one virtue of making naps dangerous— possibly fatal, for the floor was not to be trusted.

45 It was a hot morning late in July when the school opened. I trembled when I heard the patter of little feet down the dusty road, and saw the growing row of solemn faces and bright eager eyes facing me. There they sat, nearly thirty of them, on the rough
50 benches, their faces shading from a pale cream to a deep brown, the little feet bare and swinging, the eyes full of expectation, with here and there a twinkle of mischief, and the hands grasping Webster's blue- back spelling-book. I loved my school, and the fine

CONTINUE

55 faith the children had in my wisdom as their teacher
was truly marvelous. We read and spelled together,
wrote a little, picked flowers, sang, and listened to
stories of the world beyond the hill. At times the
school would dwindle away, and I would start out. I
60 would visit the Eddings, who lived in two very dirty
rooms, and ask why little Lugene, whose flaming
face seemed ever ablaze with the dark-red hair
uncombed, was absent all last week, or why the
unmistakable rags of Mack and Ed were so often
65 missing. Then their father would tell me how the
crops needed the boys, and their mother would assure
me that Lugene must mind the baby. "But we'll start
them again next week." When the Lawrences
stopped, I knew that the doubts of the old folks about
70 book-learning had conquered again, and so, toiling
up the hill, I put Cicero's "pro Archia Poeta" into the
simplest English, and usually convinced them—for a
week or so.

1

Which best describes Du Bois's attitude toward his
work as a teacher?

A) He was relieved to have work despite the poor
working conditions.

B) He was worried about living up to his students'
expectations.

C) He was indifferent toward the simple activities he
engaged in with his students.

D) He was proud of his school and felt respected by
his students.

2

Which choice provides the best evidence for the
answer to the previous question?

A) Lines 38-41 ("My … every night")

B) Lines 46-48 ("I trembled … me")

C) Lines 54-56 ("I loved … marvelous")

D) Lines 59-65 ("I would … missing")

3

Du Bois most likely discusses hunting (lines 2-7) in
order to

A) suggest that hunting for schools is more
dangerous than hunting game.

B) imply that he used similar techniques in finding a
school as hunters use in hunting animals.

C) argue that he enjoyed finding a school more than
he would have enjoyed hunting animals.

D) suggest that hunting for a school had its own
unique challenges.

4

The rhetorical effect of lines 13-18 is to suggest that
the places the narrator had reached

A) were small, isolated communities.

B) were very dangerous.

C) had abnormally high death rates.

A) had never been visited by outsiders before.

5

As used in line 43, "virtue" most nearly means

A) bravery.

B) character.

C) decency.

D) benefit.

6

Du Bois's reaction to the "patter of little feet" (lines
46-47) most strongly suggests that he felt a sense of

A) anxious anticipation.

B) unconstrained elation.

C) strong nostalgia.

D) unavoidable apathy.

CONTINUE

7

The passage most strongly suggests that when students stopped attending school Du Bois was

A) relieved that he would have fewer pupils.

B) compelled to ensure they returned.

C) indifferent about their absence.

D) angry that they did not value their education.

8

Which choice provides the best evidence for the answer to the previous question?

A) Lines 49-54 ("There they ... spelling-book)

B) Lines 56-58 ("We read ... hill")

C) Lines 58-59 ("At times ... start out")

D) Lines 65-67 ("Then ... the baby")

9

As used in line 70, "toiling" most nearly means

A) endeavoring.

B) sweating.

C) working.

D) plodding.

10

It can reasonably be inferred from the passage that Cicero's "pro Archia Poeta" (line 71) is

A) a Latin treatise about farming.

B) a short story about life in a small community.

C) a homework assignment that Du Bois's students had not completed.

D) a text that argues for the benefits of education.

CONTINUE

Questions 11-21 are based on the following passage.

This passage is adapted from "We Have Only Just Begun to Fight," a speech given by Franklin D. Roosevelt in Madison Square Garden in 1936. Roosevelt was campaigning for a second term as President after winning the previous election in 1932.

On the eve of a national election, it is well for us to stop for a moment and analyze calmly and without prejudice the effect on our Nation of a victory by
Line either of the major political parties. The problem of
5 the electorate is far deeper, far more than the continuance in the Presidency of any individual. For the greater issue goes beyond units of humanity—it goes to humanity itself.

In 1932 the issue was the *restoration* of American
10 democracy; and the American people were in a mood to win. They did win. In 1936 the issue is the preservation of their victory. Again they are in a mood to win. Again they will win.

More than four years ago in accepting the
15 Democratic nomination in Chicago, I said, "Give me your help not to win votes alone, but to win in this crusade to restore America to its own people." The banners of that crusade still fly in the van of a Nation that is on the march.

20 It is needless to repeat the details of the program which this Administration has been hammering out on the anvils of experience. No amount of misrepresentation or statistical contortion can conceal or blur or smear that record. Neither the attacks of
25 unscrupulous enemies nor the exaggerations of over-zealous friends will serve to mislead the American people.

What was our hope in 1932? Above all other things the American people wanted peace. They
30 wanted peace of mind instead of gnawing fear.

First, they sought escape from the personal terror which had stalked them for three years. They wanted the peace that comes from security in their homes: safety for their savings, permanence in their jobs, a
35 fair profit from their enterprise.

Next, they wanted peace in the community, the peace that springs from the ability to meet the needs of community life: schools, playgrounds, parks, sanitation, highways—those things which are expected
40 of solvent local government. They sought escape from disintegration and bankruptcy in local and state affairs. They also sought peace within the Nation: protection of their currency, fairer wages, the ending of long hours of toil, the abolition of child labor, the
45 elimination of wild-cat speculation, the safety of their children from kidnappers.

And, finally, they sought peace with other Nations—peace in a world of unrest. The Nation knows that I hate war, and I know that the Nation
50 hates war.

I submit to you a record of peace; and on that record a well-founded expectation for future peace—peace for the individual, peace for the community, peace for the Nation, and peace with the world.

55 Tonight I call the roll—the roll of honor of those who stood with us in 1932 and still stand with us today. Written on it are the names of millions who never had a chance—men at starvation wages, women in sweatshops, children at looms. Written on
60 it are the names of farmers whose acres yielded only bitterness, business men whose books were portents of disaster, homeowners who were faced with eviction, frugal citizens whose savings were insecure.

Written there in large letters are the names of
65 countless other Americans of all parties and all faiths, Americans who had eyes to see and hearts to understand, whose consciences were burdened because too many of their fellows were burdened, who looked on these things four years ago and said,
70 "This can be changed. We will change it."

We still lead that army in 1936. They stood with us then because in 1932 they believed. They stand with us today because in 1936 they know. And with them stand millions of new recruits who have come
75 to know. Their hopes have become our record.

We have not come this far without a struggle and I assure you we cannot go further without a struggle. For twelve years this Nation was afflicted with hear-nothing, see-nothing, do-nothing Government. The
80 Nation looked to Government but the Government looked away. Powerful influences strive today to

CONTINUE

restore that kind of Government with its doctrine that
that Government is best which is most indifferent.
For nearly four years you have had an Administration
85 which instead of twirling its thumbs has rolled up its
sleeves. We will keep our sleeves rolled up.

11

Based on the passage, which choice best describes
how Roosevelt feels about his previous term as
president?

A) His term was productive, and his record speaks
for itself.

B) His term was productive, but his friends have
overstated his success.

C) His term was a struggle that produced few good
results.

D) His term has resulted in a deeply divided
electorate.

12

Which choice provides the best evidence for the
answer to the previous question?

A) Lines 20-24 ("It is … record")

B) Lines 40-42 ("They sought … affairs")

C) Lines 56-57 ("Tonight … us today")

D) Lines 76-77 ("We have … struggle")

13

Based on the passage, which choice best describes the
relationship between Roosevelt's previous term and
his plans for his next term?

A) He will build upon his previous successes by
continuing to pursue the same goals.

B) He will learn from his failures and implement
very different policies.

C) He will learn from his failures and help the
struggling Americans he previously ignored.

D) He will alter his policies slightly based on the
criticisms of voters.

14

In this speech, Roosevelt does which of the following
to promote his administration?

A) Contrasts his administration's hard work with the
indifference of the previous administration

B) Lists the shortcomings of the opposition party

C) Compares his leadership style favorably to other
politicians

D) Offers statistics to demonstrate the effectiveness
of his policies

15

Which choice provides the best evidence for the
answer to the previous question?

A) Lines 4-6 ("The problem … individual")

B) Lines 24-27 ("Neither … American people")

C) Lines 32-35 ("They wanted … enterprise")

D) Lines 84-86 ("For nearly … sleeves")

CONTINUE

16

The main rhetorical effect of lines 9-13 is to

A) associate Roosevelt's past and future victory with victory for the whole American people.

B) highlight that America's mood has changed due to changing social and political factors.

C) imply that Americans' wishes have shifted from the desire to change society to the desire to preserve the status quo.

D) persuade listeners that the issues facing Americans are different than they were in 1932.

17

In line 28, what is the most likely reason that Roosevelt asks a question?

A) So he can answer it and demonstrate that he achieved what Americans hoped for

B) So he can answer it and argue that Americans' goals can only be accomplished if he is re-elected

C) To force the opposition to answer, and admit that they were ignorant of Americans' hopes

D) To encourage Americans to reflect on what they wanted in the past

18

As used in line 37, "springs" most nearly means

A) leaps.

B) vaults.

C) arises.

D) bounds.

19

It can reasonably be inferred from the passage that the phrase "farmers whose acres yielded only bitterness" (lines 60-61) most likely refers to farmers who

A) had crops that failed and therefore had nothing to harvest.

B) opposed the agriculture policies of the previous administration.

C) opposed Roosevelt's agriculture policies.

D) had crops that were too bitter to eat or sell.

20

Franklin D. Roosevelt uses words like "army" and "new recruits" in lines 71-74 in order to emphasize the

A) military nature of the coming challenges.

B) inner fortitude of his closest followers.

C) growing strength of his supporters.

D) deadly threats of international neighbors.

21

As used in line 83, "indifferent" most nearly means

A) impartial.

B) apathetic.

C) dispassionate.

D) objective

CONTINUE

Questions 22-31 are based on the following passages.

Passage 1 is adapted from Atul J. Butte, and Passage 2 is adapted from Robert Green, "Should Healthy People Have Their Genome Sequenced At This Time?" © 2013 by Dow Jones & Company.

Passage 1

We live in an amazing time. Very shortly, any individual will be able to know the sequence of his or her whole genome: the genetic recipe that guides the
Line creation and functioning of our bodies. It's just a
5 piece of what makes us unique individuals, but it's a critical piece.

What's to be gained from learning things about our bodies and our health that might scare us, but that we might not do anything about? There are four
10 important ways a healthy person can medically benefit from obtaining his or her whole genome sequence.

Thousands of DNA combinations have been identified as indicators of susceptibility to specific diseases. Some argue that you might go through life
15 worrying needlessly about a disease that never appears. On the other hand, spotting those DNA variants and recognizing whether you are at risk can lead directly to early diagnoses and preventive strategies.

Couples planning families can find out when they
20 carry genetic risks for severe disorders and so make more informed choices: to have a baby together and hope for the best, for example, or to adopt. Doctors can better determine what drugs will be most effective for a patient, at what dose, and what drugs
25 to avoid. Genome sequencing also can help in the diagnosis of illnesses yet to be identified.

Genome sequencing isn't perfect. There are mistakes. But not many. We can currently expect one misread bit of DNA among hundreds of thousands.
30 Other common preventive medical procedures aren't free from errors either: mammography and Pap smears have high overdiagnosis rates, and PSA testing (prostate specific antigen) is unreliable, yet we typically accept these problems. Moreover,
35 continuing research will certainly identify more of the inaccurate and "missing" bits, leading to better clinical interpretations.

There are limits. Despite the incredible science behind sequencing, we won't be able to predict every
40 possible condition in one's lifetime. Behaviors, environment, and other factors are involved. But there are already individuals who have had a whole genome sequenced, and who learned the pharmacological, environmental, medical, or
45 behavioral changes they could make to "compensate" for their genome.

There is no gene for compliance; it can require difficult changes to improve one's health. But for many people, that genome sequence may provide the
50 crucial first step to move from "knowing thyself" to "helping thyself."

Passage 2

Most of us agree that in a few years, affordable genomic and epigenomic analyses of healthy individuals will allow for more individually tailored
55 disease prevention and pharmaceutical treatment. But some serious challenges remain before this can be done safely.

One problem is that medically dangerous genetic mutations are quite rare in healthy individuals, but
60 finding them today would still be enormously expensive. This year an entire genome will cost somewhere around $5,000 to be sequenced, analyzed with bioinformatics, and interpreted. And while there is much to find in each genome that can reflect subtle
65 health risks or aid in reproductive planning, we currently estimate that less than 2% of healthy people will have a dangerous and well-recognized DNA mutation that might cause a doctor to initiate surveillance or treatment. That means spending
70 $250,000 to find even one such individual.

Finding well-recognized disease mutations in healthy people is just the tip of the genomic iceberg. We all have unique or novel mutations in disease-associated genes. I have 14 such mutations in my
75 own genome! But the smartest geneticists in the world cannot always agree as to whether a novel mutation is dangerous. If a healthy person without family history has a novel mutation in a cancer predisposition gene, should we take X-rays every

CONTINUE ➙

80 year for the cancer that might never appear? Should we do the same for their parents, brothers, sisters, and children that carry the same mutation?

Perhaps we all underestimated how complicated it would be to move genomic knowledge into the
85 practice of medicine and public health. Now is the time to make sure we get this right through rigorous basic and clinical studies that define which mutations are dangerous, and distinguish useful from unnecessary interventions. Soon, genomic insights
90 will give us early warnings about life-threatening illnesses that we may be able to prevent. Soon, standards will be available to guide doctors about which findings are meaningful and which are not. Soon, there may be evidence to support the benefits
95 of screening healthy individuals. But not today.

22

Both passages are primarily concerned with

A) creating new genome sequencing techniques.

B) reducing the existing risks of genome sequencing.

C) whether genome sequencing is ready for widespread use.

D) the costs currently associated with genome sequencing.

23

The author of Passage 1 can best be described as

A) an excited proponent of a new technology who still recognizes its potential limitations.

B) a skeptical critic of a new technology who is unconvinced by current supporting evidence.

C) a biased advocate of a new technology who ignores counterarguments from opponents.

D) a neutral scholar researching a debate over a new technology.

24

The author of Passage 1 supports his assertion that, despite some errors, genome sequencing is already accurate enough to be used by

A) noting that we accept errors in other common preventive tests.

B) discussing the impossibility of error-free tests.

C) disproving that genome sequencing will lead to overdiagnosis.

D) stating that less than 2% of healthy people will have a well-recognized DNA mutation.

25

Which choice provides the best evidence for the answer to the previous question?

A) Lines 31-34 ("Mammography … problems")

B) Lines 38-40 ("Despite the … lifetime")

C) Lines 41-46 ("But there … genome")

D) Lines 48-51 ("But for … thyself")

26

The author of Passage 1 would most likely agree with the author of Passage 2 about which of the following?

A) Healthy individuals should not have their genomes sequenced.

B) Genome sequencing will be more reliable in the future than it is now.

C) Genome sequencing is currently too expensive to be useful.

D) There is not enough consensus about which DNA mutations are dangerous.

CONTINUE

27

Which choice provides the best evidence for the answer to the previous question?

A) Lines 14-15 ("Some argue … appears")

B) Lines 27-28 ("Genome sequencing … mistakes")

C) Lines 34-37 ("Moreover … interpretations")

D) Lines 47-48 ("There is … health")

28

As used in line 64, "reflect" most nearly means

A) reconsider.

B) reveal.

C) mirror.

D) imitate.

29

The author of Passage 2 most likely mentions that his own genome has mutations (lines 74-75) in order to

A) emphasize how common mutations are.

B) prove that most genetic mutations are harmless.

C) give examples of well-recognized gene mutations.

D) urge readers to have their genome sequenced.

30

As used in line 78, "novel" most nearly means

A) innovative.

B) unconventional.

C) unfamiliar.

D) unique.

31

The main rhetorical effect of the repeated words in lines 89-95 is to

A) emphasize that the major benefits of genome sequencing have yet to be realized.

B) imply that further research needs to be undertaken as quickly as possible.

C) suggest that readers should sequence their genomes immediately.

D) indicate that the author is concerned about new developments in genome sequencing.

CONTINUE

Questions 32-41 are based on the following passage and supplementary material.

The following passage is adapted from Saab, A. Joan, "Without a humanistic inquiry, we will lose our creativity." © 2015 by A. Joan Saab.

Today it is hard to imagine that the national government would spend millions of dollars to put unemployed artists to work for the good of the
Line country. But that is precisely what happened in the
5 United States at the height of the Great Depression.

In the 1930s, Harry Hopkins, the head of the Works Progress Administration (WPA), oversaw the Federal Arts Project (FAP), one of the New Deal cultural programs. Hopkins repeatedly stressed "that
10 the objective of this whole project is … taking 3,500,000 off relief and putting them to work."

In the America of the 1930s, artists and their labor were considered to be important cultural assets. In its 8-year existence, the FAP created over 5,000
15 jobs and funded over 225,000 works of art. The artist George Biddle is credited with writing to his friend and former prep-schoolmate Franklin D. Roosevelt and encouraging him to emulate the Mexican mural program, which he called "the greatest national
20 school of mural painting since the Renaissance."

This type of engagement was crucial to the ideology of the WPA cultural projects. Biddle, Hopkins, and FDR all saw direct links between a strong democratic country and its artwork. They
25 believed that making art was a way of making strong citizens.

Indeed, Biddle advocated for including artists in the national relief program since, he argued, the artist was as valuable a worker to the health of the nation
30 as the "the farmer or the bricklayer." For New Dealers, the arts and the humanities—painting, sculpture,

music, theater, and literature—were not only a viable form of labor, they were key to America's past, present, and future success.

35 Many of the works created on the FAP directly addressed the relationship between manual and intellectual labor. For example, a two-panel series Inspired by the monumental Renaissance masterpieces by Michelangelo, Peters broke with his
40 exploring the Life of Action and its corollary, the Life of Contemplation, was painted in 1937 by the local Rochester artist Carl Peters. traditional, small-scale easel practice (he was primarily a landscape painter of local scenes) to depict a subject matter that
45 shows the need for balance between doing and thinking.

Peters imagined these classical themes within a visual vocabulary that stressed images of progress through learning and work. By explicitly linking the
50 past to the present, Peters transforms contemplation and its corollaries of education and imagination into an active process. Thus contemplation becomes a form of action akin to the work being performed in its partner panel.

55 Taken together these works provide an inventory of New Deal imagery: the teacher, the laborer, the architect, the student. They situate Peters, as the artist, as an important cultural laborer. They encapsulate in visual form the ideologies of the New
60 Deal and suggest that art and contemplative labor were valuable forms of work, as important to nation building as building bridges and skyscrapers.

In this way, Peters and other artists used media to help understand the world around them. Peters and
65 his peers on the WPA looked for a balance between action and contemplation, which they accomplished through humanistic inquiry and creative work.

Total FAP Employment as of November 1, 1936

Fine Arts 49%

Mural	Sculpture	Easel	Graphic Art

Practical Arts 29%

Poster & Applied Arts	Index of Design	Photography	Arts & Crafts	Stage Set & Diorama

Education 16%

Teaching	Art Centers	Research

Miscellaneous 6%

Technical & Coordinating

*Each figure represents 100 project workers.

32

Which one of the following best describes the organization of the passage?

A) The author discusses a historical government initiative and gives a specific example of what it produced.

B) The author argues in favor of governmental art programs and provides evidence of one's success.

C) The author explains the historical difficulties faced by the arts and suggests potential remedies.

D) The author explores different types of labor during the Depression, then considers one profession more in depth.

33

The passage indicates that, during the Great Depression, artists were considered

A) pitiable charity cases.

B) self-sacrificing heroes.

C) necessary and amusing distractions.

D) valuable community contributors.

34

Which choice provides the best evidence for the answer to the previous question?

A) Lines 6-9 ("In the … programs")

B) Lines 12-13 ("In the … assets")

C) Lines 14-15 ("In its … art")

D) Lines 21-22 ("This type … projects")

35

The passage most directly supports that Franklin D. Roosevelt believed art could

A) help comfort citizens weathering a difficult economic time.

B) inspire thousands of Americans to redouble their efforts in labor.

C) fortify the nation through its cultural products.

D) strengthen the ties between the U.S. and its neighboring countries.

36

Which choice provides the best evidence for the answer to the previous question?

A) Lines 1-4 ("Today … country")

B) Lines 15-20 ("The artist … Renaissance")

C) Lines 24-26 ("They believed … citizens")

D) Lines 27-30 ("Indeed … bricklayer")

CONTINUE ▶

37

As used in line 13, "assets" most nearly means

A) advantages.

B) belongings.

C) estates.

D) resources.

38

As used in line 32, "viable" most nearly means

A) worthwhile.

B) sustainable.

C) possible.

D) attainable.

39

Which of the following could serve as an additional example accomplishing Peters's goal for his mural, as stated in lines 44-45 ("to depict … thinking")?

A) The first panel depicting a teacher, and the second panel depicting a student

B) The first panel depicting a banker, and the second panel depicting a lawyer

C) The first panel depicting an architect, and the second panel depicting a building

D) The first panel depicting a railroad engineer, and the second panel depicting a physics researcher

40

In lines 58-62, what is the most likely reason that the author mentions bridges and skyscrapers?

A) To show that the artists' visions eventually were translated into reality

B) To demonstrate that artists had less selfish motives than some of their industrial counterparts

C) To illustrate a few of the themes that artists used in their imagery of the New Deal

D) To contrast the artists' work with more practical endeavors while arguing that both are essential

41

Which of the following choices is best supported by data in the graphic?

A) The majority of workers in the Great Depression had occupations in the fine arts.

B) More people in the FAP were employed in the creation of murals than in sculpture.

C) 16% of those employed by the FAP were teachers.

D) Over a quarter of workers in the arts program were involved in stage set & drama.

CONTINUE

Questions 42-52 are based on the following passage and supplementary material.

This passage is adapted from Justin Gillis, "A Warming Planet Struggles to Feed Itself." © 2014 by *The New York Times Company.*

For decades, scientists believed that the human dependence on fossil fuels, for all the problems it was expected to cause, would offer one enormous
Line benefit. Carbon dioxide, the main gas released by
5 combustion, is also the primary fuel for the growth of plants. They draw it out of the air and, using the energy from sunlight, convert the carbon into energy-dense compounds like glucose. All human and animal life runs on these compounds.

10 Humans have already raised the level of carbon dioxide in the atmosphere by 40 percent since the Industrial Revolution, and are on course to double or triple it over the coming century. Studies have long suggested that the extra gas would supercharge the
15 world's food crops, and might be especially helpful in years when the weather is difficult.

But many of those studies were done in artificial conditions, like greenhouses or special growth chambers. For the past decade, scientists at the
20 University of Illinois have been putting the "CO_2 fertilization effect" to a real-world test in the two most important crops grown in the United States.

They started by planting soybeans in a field, then sprayed extra carbon dioxide from a giant tank.
25 Based on the earlier research, they hoped the gas might bump yields as much as 30 percent under optimal growing conditions. But when they harvested their soybeans, they got a rude surprise: the bump was only half as large. "When we measured the
30 yields, it was like, 'wait a minute—this is not what we expected,'" said Elizabeth A. Ainsworth, a Department of Agriculture researcher who played a leading role in the work. When they grew the soybeans in the sort of conditions expected to prevail
35 in a future climate, with high temperatures or low water, the extra carbon dioxide could not fully offset the yield decline caused by those factors.

They also ran tests using corn, America's single most valuable crop and the basis for its meat
40 production and its biofuel industry. While that crop was already known to be less responsive to carbon dioxide, a yield bump was still expected—especially during droughts. The Illinois researchers got no bump.

45 Their work has contributed to a broader body of research suggesting that extra carbon dioxide does act as plant fertilizer, but that the benefits are less than previously believed—and probably less than needed to avert food shortages. "One of the things
50 that we're starting to believe is that the positives of CO_2 are unlikely to outweigh the negatives of the other factors," said Andrew D. B. Leakey, another of the Illinois researchers.

Other recent evidence suggests that longstanding
55 assumptions about food production on a warming planet may have been too optimistic. Two economists, Wolfram Schlenker of Columbia University and Michael J. Roberts of North Carolina State University, have pioneered ways to compare
60 crop yields and natural temperature variability at a fine scale. Their work shows that when crops are subjected to temperatures above a certain threshold— about 84 degrees for corn and 86 degrees for soybeans—yields fall sharply. This line of research
65 suggests that in the type of climate predicted for the United States by the end of the century, with more scorching days in the growing season, yields of today's crop varieties could fall by 30 percent or more.

CONTINUE

Corn

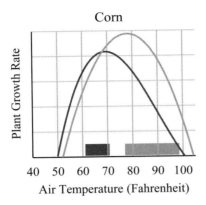

Plant Growth Rate

40 50 60 70 80 90 100
Air Temperature (Fahrenheit)

Soybean

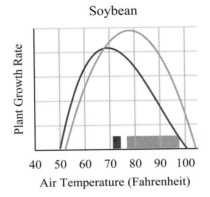

Plant Growth Rate

40 50 60 70 80 90 100
Air Temperature (Fahrenheit)

—— Reproductive Response Curve:
temperature range within which plants
can produce seed

▇ Optimum Range

—— Vegetative Response Curve: temperature
range within which plants can grow,
between germination and flowering

▇ Optimum Range

Corn Failure at 99°F, Soybean Failure at 102°F

Adapted from 2009 report of the US Global Change Research
Program, "Global Climate Change Impact in the United States."
Agricultural Research Service, USDA.

42

The primary purpose of the passage is to

A) convince readers to change their behavior in
response to new scientific evidence.

B) explain how new evidence challenges what
scientists previously believed.

C) describe the latest experiments being conducted
in a certain scientific field.

D) summarize the challenges facing farmers in the
future.

43

The passage most strongly suggests that scientists

A) previously ignored the potentially harmful
effects of fossil fuel consumption.

B) had expected to observe at least one benefit from
fossil fuel consumption.

C) underestimated the benefits of carbon dioxide
for crops.

D) only began studying the effect of carbon dioxide
on crops in the last decade.

44

Which choice provides the best evidence for the
answer to the previous question?

A) Lines 1-4 ("For decades ... benefit")

B) Lines 23-24 ("They started ... tank")

C) Lines 45-49 ("Their work ... shortages")

D) Lines 54-56 ("Other ... too optimistic")

CONTINUE

Based on the passage, which choice best describes the relationship between older studies about carbon dioxide's fertilizer effect and newer ones conducted by the Illinois researchers?

A) The newer studies completely confirm the findings of the older studies.

B) The newer studies support the basic findings of previous studies but show a more modest effect than expected.

C) The newer studies totally refute the findings of the older studies.

D) The newer studies partially refute the findings of the older studies by showing a much stronger effect than expected.

Which choice provides the best evidence for the answer to the previous question?

A) Lines 19-22 ("For ... United States")

B) Lines 27-29 ("But when ... as large")

C) Lines 40-43 ("While ... during droughts")

D) Lines 61-64 ("Their ... fall sharply")

As used in line 34, "prevail" most nearly means

A) win.

B) triumph.

C) impose.

D) predominate.

As used in line 48, "avert" most nearly means

A) prevent.

B) turn away.

C) frustrate.

D) help.

Lines 49-53 ("One of ... researchers") serve primarily to

A) summarize the techniques used by the Illinois researchers.

B) suggest that there is consensus about the future increase in extreme weather.

C) describe the Illinois researchers' predictions for the future based on their research.

D) provide reasons to support undertaking further crop research.

50

It can reasonably be inferred from the passage and graphic that

A) soybeans and corn grow best at very different temperatures, but reproduce in about the same range of temperatures.

B) constant temperatures above 100 degrees Fahrenheit could make it impossible to grow soybeans and corn.

C) soybean and corn yields could best be increased by temperatures below 55 degrees Fahrenheit.

D) soybean and corn yields could best be increased by temperatures above 95 degrees Fahrenheit.

CONTINUE

51

Based on data in the graphics, which of the following temperatures would be optimal for growing both soybeans and corn?

A) 40°F

B) 60°F

C) 80°F

D) 100°F

52

Which claim about crop growth and temperature is supported by the graphics?

A) Soybeans but not corn can grow at 50 degrees Fahrenheit.

B) Corn but not soybeans can grow at 70 degrees Fahrenheit.

C) Neither corn nor soybeans can grow at 50 degrees Fahrenheit.

D) Neither corn nor soybeans can grow at 70 degrees Fahrenheit.

STOP

If you complete this section before the end of your allotted time, check your work on this section only. Do NOT use the time to work on another section.

Writing and Language Test

35 MINUTES, 44 QUESTIONS

Turn to Section 2 of your answer sheet to answer the questions in this section.

DIRECTIONS

Every passage comes with a set of questions. Some questions will ask you to consider how the writer might revise the passage to improve the expression of ideas. Other questions will ask you to consider correcting potential errors in sentence structure, usage, or punctuation. There may be one or more graphics that you will need to consult as you revise and edit the passage.

Some questions will refer to a portion of the passage that has been underlined. Other questions will refer to a particular spot in a passage or ask that you consider the passage in full.

After you read the passage, select the answers to questions that most effectively improve the passage's writing quality or that adjust the passage to follow the conventions of standard written English. Many questions give you the option to select "NO CHANGE." Select that option in cases where you think the relevant part of the passage should remain as it currently is.

Questions 1-11 are based on the following passage and supplementary materials.

Conflict and Cooperation: The Robbers Cave

In the 1950s, social scientists were fascinated with group interactions. During this time, many psychologists studied belonging, cooperation, and **1** conflict. They hoped to better understand the sources of prejudice and war. Specifically, they wanted to know what circumstances bring about conflict or cooperation among groups and if it is possible to reproduce these effects in experiments. One such scientist was Muzafer Sherif, who became interested in group interactions after witnessing the violent invasion of his home country, Turkey. In 1954, Sherif published his landmark study on group relationships, "The Robbers Cave Experiment."

1

Which choice most effectively combines the sentences at the underlined portion?

A) conflict, and they also hoped to better understand

B) conflict, hoping thereby to reach a better understanding of

C) conflict to better understand

D) conflict, understanding

Sherif's experiment was original in a number of ways. Sherif used a real-world setting by placing twelve-year-old boys at a camp into two groups, the "Eagles" and the "Rattlers." The experiment had three stages. In stage one, the researchers separated the groups, and **2** they enjoyed the first days at the camp, each group unaware of the other. In stage two, the boys were asked to engage in an athletic **3** tournament, it consisted of activities like baseball and tug of war. This competition led to increased hostility and an **4** ascension in physical and emotional conflict. In stage three, the researchers introduced problems for the boys at the camp. **5** For example, the boys were told that the camp's water supply was blocked and that the boys needed to repair it together. The goal of this phase was to encourage cooperation **6** amidst the two groups to solve the problem. Throughout the experiment, the boys were asked questions about members of their own group, the "ingroup," and members of the other group, the "outgroup."

2

A) NO CHANGE
B) they all
C) the researchers
D) the boys

3

A) NO CHANGE
B) tournament consisting of activities
C) tournament; consisting of activities
D) tournament, it consisted of: activities

4

A) NO CHANGE
B) arising
C) expansion
D) increase

5

A) NO CHANGE
B) Successively,
C) Finally,
D) Yet,

6

A) NO CHANGE
B) concerning
C) between
D) through

CONTINUE

The researchers observed changes in the boys' feelings and behavior as the stages progressed. In stage two, the boys developed negative stereotypes of the outgroup and were unlikely to choose friends from among **7** it's members. During the competitions, the boys showed unfriendly and aggressive behavior. Yet after the cooperation in stage three, the boys rated outgroup members more positively and **8** are cooperating with each other more frequently. **9**

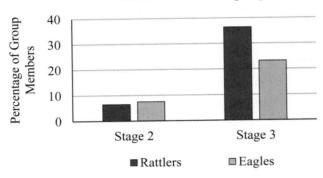

Have Friends in Outgroup

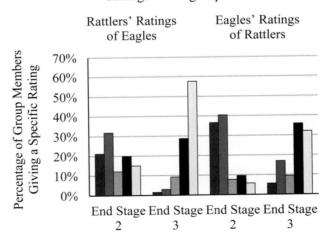

Ratings of Outgroup Members

Adapted from Sherif et al. "Intergroup Conflict and Cooperation: The Robbers Cave Experiment." 1954.

7

A) NO CHANGE

B) its members

C) their members

D) there members

8

A) NO CHANGE

B) cooperate with each other

C) will be cooperating with each other

D) cooperated with each other

9

At this point, the writer is considering adding the following sentence.

> The researchers also found that friendships with members of the outgroup increased for both groups between stages two and three.

Should the writer make this addition here?

A) Yes, because it explains how the information in the previous sentence is expressed in the graphs.

B) Yes, because it supplies accurate information from the graphs that supports the main idea of the paragraph.

C) No, because it contradicts the information presented in the graphs.

D) No, because it's excessively redundant to duplicate information from the graphs in the text of the passage.

CONTINUE

[1] From this experiment, Sherif was able to determine that competition tends to fuel conflict, and a **10** public goal tends to increase cooperation. [2] Shared goals also serve to reduce negative stereotypes and increase friendships between groups. [3] Other scientists used similar situations to bring out cooperation and conflict and witnessed the same effect. [4] From his experiment, Sherif concluded that while tension arises when groups form and compete, this tension can be relieved when a common goal is introduced. **11**

10

A) NO CHANGE

B) divided

C) popular

D) common

11

To best improve the focus and organization of this paragraph, sentence 3 should be

A) placed where it is now.

B) placed before sentence 1.

C) placed before sentence 2.

D) DELETED.

CONTINUE

Questions 12-22 are based on the following passage.

Jerome Robbins: Broadway and Beyond

Although Jerome Robbins began his career as a chorus dancer, today he is known as one of the most inventive choreographers in ballet and Broadway. **12** His Broadway shows are still performed around the world. They have remained some of the most beloved and acclaimed productions. Dancers and audiences alike **13** appreciates Robbins' works because of their engaging and dramatic style. During his career, Robbins created hundreds of theatrical masterpieces and captured the essence of American drama and dance in his work.

12

Which choice most effectively combines the sentences at the underlined portion?

A) His Broadway shows are still performed around the world, however, they remain

B) Although his Broadway shows are still performed around the world, they remain

C) His Broadway shows are still performed around the world, and they have also remained

D) His Broadway shows are still performed around the world, remaining

13

A) NO CHANGE

B) appreciate

C) to appreciate

D) appreciating

CONTINUE

In 1940, Robbins joined the American Ballet Theatre and performed there for four years. In 1944, he began choreographing ballets, which he continued to do throughout his career. Robbins was inspired by the American **14** way of life, many of his pieces, highlighted the vitality and diversity of American culture. His first work, *Fancy Free*, was a jazz-inspired ballet about American sailors **15** who enjoy an evening on the town. At its premiere, *Fancy Free* received twenty-two curtain calls. Later that year, Robbins turned his ballet sensation into a musical, *On the Town*. Seamlessly transitioning between ballet and Broadway, **16** storytelling in any form was Robbins's gift.

14

A) NO CHANGE

B) way of life, many of his pieces highlighted

C) way of life many of his pieces highlighted

D) way of life; many of his pieces highlighted

15

A) NO CHANGE

B) who enjoys

C) whom enjoy

D) whom enjoys

16

A) NO CHANGE

B) storytelling in any form was a gift of Robbins.

C) Robbins had a gift for storytelling in any form.

D) any form of storytelling was Robbins's gift.

CONTINUE

[1] In 1957, Robbins choreographed and directed *West Side Story*, which would become an iconic American musical. [2] Inspired by Shakespeare's *Romeo and Juliet*, *West Side Story* explores the conflicts between ethnic groups in New York City and the trials of young love. [3] However, some critics said the elements of dance **17** was even more compelling than the story itself. [4] The decade following the success of *West Side Story* was a prolific period in Robbins' Broadway career. **18** [5] During this time, Robbins received numerous honors for his work, including several Tony Awards. **19**

17

A) NO CHANGE

B) is

C) were

D) DELETE the underlined portion

18

Which choice best supports the claim made in the previous sentence?

A) NO CHANGE

B) Robbins experimented with the boundaries of dance and storytelling, and achieved wide recognition for his work.

C) With shows like *Moves*, a silent ballet, Robbins explored storytelling through pure movement.

D) Robbins worked on a dozen Broadway productions in this period, including such hits as *Gypsy* and *Fiddler on the Roof.*

19

The writer is considering inserting the following sentence.

> The show received praise for its endearing characters and gripping plot.

Where should the sentence be inserted in the paragraph?

A) Before sentence 1

B) Before sentence 2

C) Before sentence 3

D) Before sentence 4

CONTINUE

20 Conversely, Robbins also took some of his works from the stage to the screen. In 1956, he was asked to recreate his dances for the film *The King and I*. In 1961, he co-directed the film version of *West Side Story*, for which he won two Academy Awards. While Robbins's Broadway shows continued to be produced around the world, his expansion into film **21** condensed his artistic legacy.

Throughout a career lasting more than fifty years, Jerome Robbins created innovative and iconic works in ballet, theater, and film. **22**

20

A) NO CHANGE

B) In contrast,

C) Likewise,

D) DELETE the underlined portion.

21

A) NO CHANGE

B) settled

C) solidified

D) toughened

22

The writer wants to conclude the passage with a sentence that restates and affirms the main idea of the passage as a whole. Which choice best accomplishes this goal?

A) The stunning success of *West Side Story* on Broadway and on the big screen remains the greatest example of Jerome Robbins's work.

B) Looking back on his career, we are left with only one question: what masterpiece would Robbins make if he were still alive today?

C) Robbins continued working until the end of his life, staging *Les Noces*, his final project, just two months before his death.

D) Through the widespread success of his works on both stage and screen, Robbins shows himself to be a true master of the dramatic arts.

CONTINUE

Questions 23-33 are based on the following passage.

Physician Self-Referral

To combat the high costs of a medical education and increased reliance on technology, physicians sometimes establish themselves as investors in medical facilities to **23** whom they can refer patients. This arrangement is known as "physician self-referral." Traditionally, the American health care system has given physicians great professional freedom, trusting that they will act not in their narrow financial interests, but **24** thinking about their patients' most important interests. **25** However, health care costs are rising. Regulation aimed at cutting costs will become increasingly important.

23

A) NO CHANGE
B) which
C) who
D) that

24

A) NO CHANGE
B) with their patients' best interests in their minds
C) in their patients' best interests
D) in order to preserve their patients' interests

25

Which choice most effectively combines the sentences at the underlined portion?

A) However, as health care costs are rising, regulation aimed at
B) Although, even though health care costs are rising, regulation aimed at
C) But now we must consider that health care costs are rising, so regulation aimed at
D) Meanwhile, health care costs are rising, even though regulation aimed at

CONTINUE

26 The physician self-referral system creates incentives for doctors to provide unnecessary health care. In a self-referral arrangement, a physician invests money in another medical facility, such as an imaging center. The physician will make a profit when the imaging center **27** do well. This encourages the physician not only to increase the number of patients he or she refers but also **28** ordering more tests for each patient. For example, the physician may suggest an imaging procedure, such as an MRI, be conducted before completing a simpler, more cost effective test. This phenomenon has been documented in studies showing that self-referring physicians order more unnecessary tests. **29** Therefore, it is clear that the financial incentives created by self-referrals result in excessive use of expensive medical services.

26

Which sentence, inserted here, would most effectively establish the main argument of the passage?

A) Ethical concerns are equally important to financial concerns, and must also become a factor in many regulatory debates.

B) Medical school costs have more than doubled in the last fifty years, contributing to overcharging by physicians.

C) Such cost containment can be achieved in a variety of ways.

D) Regulation of self-referral arrangements has become necessary to reduce excessive service costs and maintain patient safety.

27

A) NO CHANGE

B) does

C) did

D) doing

28

A) NO CHANGE

B) to order more tests for each patient

C) the number of tests ordered for each patient

D) increase the number of tests per patient

29

A) NO CHANGE

B) Surprisingly

C) Nevertheless

D) However

CONTINUE

A physician's financial interest should never be placed above a patient's interest. Physicians typically know a great deal more about medicine **30** then their patients. Because of this, patients are inclined to trust the suggestions of their physician. In self-referral arrangements, physicians are able to take advantage **31** of this asymmetry, they may suggest unnecessary tests that are costly or painful. While many physicians who invest in medical facilities are likely able to uphold their **32** virtuous duty, regulation of physician self-referral is necessary as a protective measure for all patients.

[1] Some argue that self-referrals don't need to be placed under regulatory control. [2] After all, if we trust physicians with our health, why shouldn't we trust them with their own investments? [3] Further, physicians have specialized knowledge of medical services, so they might even seem like the "best" investors. **33** [4] But surely these benefits do not outweigh the risk of a corrupting influence on medical practice, and so it is clear that regulation of self-referral is essential for maintaining standards of practice.

30

A) NO CHANGE
B) than their patients know
C) than that of their patients
D) then their patients know

31

A) NO CHANGE
B) of this asymmetry, and they may suggest
C) of this asymmetry they may suggest
D) of this; asymmetry, they may suggest,

32

A) NO CHANGE
B) earnest
C) ethical
D) dispassionate

33

Which choice, inserted here, most effectively adds support for the statement in sentence 3?

A) Nurses also have specialized knowledge of medical services, but generally have less capital with which to invest.

B) Most physicians choose to save their income over time.

C) Many physicians are involved in charities outside of their practice.

D) First-hand knowledge of medical practices allows physicians to invest in the most needed facilities.

CONTINUE

Questions 34-44 are based on the following passage.

Submarine Volcanoes

Volcanic eruptions are remarkable and dangerous natural events. While most well-known eruptions have come from volcanoes on land, volcanoes are also common structures on the ocean floor. These underwater volcanoes, called submarine volcanoes, are often submerged beneath more than 8,500 feet of water but produce about three quarters of the total volcanic output on Earth. **34** Even though they are mostly hidden, submarine volcanoes are part of an interesting and productive system.

Before they were able to detect submarine volcanoes, oceanographers were aware that underwater eruptions were occurring. In the 1990s, scientists created a new system to measure the small earthquakes that accompany underwater eruptions. On land, scientists are able to measure vibrations of the earth's surface to gauge the power of an earthquake. When they need to gauge underwater earthquakes, **35** acoustic waves traveling through the water are measured. To see and explore the submarine volcanoes, oceanographers have utilized new aquatic technology that can handle the extreme heat and pressure around deep-sea volcanoes. **36** For example, scientists use remotely operated vehicles to capture images and video of volcanic structures, underwater eruptions, and the marine life dwelling in the volcanoes' surrounding areas.

34

Which choice most effectively establishes the main point of the passage?

A) NO CHANGE

B) Many varieties of marine life thrive around submarine volcanoes.

C) There are several major distinctions between land and submarine volcanoes.

D) Because submarine volcanoes are more productive than land volcanoes, scientists should conduct more research in this field.

35

A) NO CHANGE

B) the water conducts acoustic waves, which are measured.

C) acoustic waves in the water give the best clues.

D) scientists measure acoustic waves travelling through the water.

36

The writer is considering deleting the underlined sentence to improve the focus of this paragraph. Should the underlined sentence be deleted?

A) Yes, because information about additional techniques used by scientists detracts from the focus on measuring vibrations.

B) Yes, because details about how scientists use various pieces of equipment do not provide information about volcanoes.

C) No, because the use of new technologies has already been mentioned and supporting details are relevant.

D) No, because the sentence helps to establish a focus on the hazards of volcanic environments.

CONTINUE

[1] Using these techniques, scientists have observed the effects of submarine volcanic eruptions. [2] Over time, these eruptions have shaped the sea floor. [3] However, underwater lava behaves differently **37** than observations of terrestrial eruptions. [4] After an eruption, water rushes over **38** the lava, so that it then receives 250 times the pressure of the atmosphere. [5] Underwater, lava typically forms "pillows," whereas lava forms hard blocks on land. [6] Like land eruptions, underwater eruptions eject lava, a type of molten rock. [7] These pillows of lava **39** creates the edges of oceanic plates. [8] Because lava cools and solidifies quickly underwater, some lava turns into volcanic glass. [9] Lava from underwater eruptions also supplies heat and chemicals to unique volcanic ecosystems. **40**

Underwater volcanic ecosystems often form around thermal vents, openings in the Earth's surface that release water heated by volcanic activity. At these vents, water comes in and mixes with natural chemicals, minerals, and bacteria before **41** proceeding to exit the vents at high temperatures.

37

A) NO CHANGE

B) than does the behavior of terrestrial lava.

C) than does terrestrial lava.

D) than does the shaping of land.

38

A) NO CHANGE

B) the lava with

C) the lava, thereby applying

D) the lava, gushing over it with

39

A) NO CHANGE

B) create the edges

C) creating the edges

D) to create the edges

40

To make this paragraph most logical, sentence 6 should be

A) placed where it is now.

B) placed before sentence 3.

C) placed before sentence 5.

D) placed after sentence 7.

41

A) NO CHANGE

B) preceding to exit

C) proceeding exiting

D) preceding exiting

CONTINUE

These ecosystems are home to an abundance of marine life, 42 including mussels, giant clams, and other organisms, that thrive in warm conditions. The unique environment around thermal vents has allowed for an ecosystem of organisms that are able to live without energy from sunlight. 43

While the recent explorations of submarine volcanoes have given scientists insight into underwater eruptions, 44 it is imperative that more continues to be learned. New technologies may allow scientists to capture and measure eruptions of submarine volcanoes, as well as to study the marine life thriving in volcanic ecosystems.

42

A) NO CHANGE

B) including mussels, giant clams, and other organisms; that thrive in warm conditions.

C) including mussels, giant clams, and other organisms—that thrive in warm conditions.

D) including mussels, giant clams, and other organisms that thrive in warm conditions.

43

Which choice, inserted here, most effectively adds support for the statement in the previous sentence?

A) In fact, some companies are looking to collect the valuable minerals from the floor of the thermal vents.

B) Bacteria use the chemicals from the vents to produce organic material, supplying the necessary energy for other organisms to survive.

C) The chemicals present in the water at thermal vents usually come to the ocean through rain, rivers, or groundwater.

D) The water from the thermal vents range in temperature from 60 to 400°C.

44

A) NO CHANGE

B) I think we should still be learning more.

C) scientists still have more to learn.

D) scientists necessarily need to learn more.

STOP

If you complete this section before the end of your allotted time, check your work on this section only. Do NOT use the time to work on another section.

Math Test – No Calculator

25 MINUTES, 20 QUESTIONS

Turn to Section 3 of your answer sheet to answer the questions in this section.

DIRECTIONS

Questions **1-15** ask you to solve a problem, select the best answer among four choices, and fill in the corresponding circle on your answer sheet. Questions **16-20** ask you to solve a problem and enter your answer in the grid provided on your answer sheet. There are detailed instructions on entering answers into the grid before question 16. You may use your test booklet for scratch work.

NOTES

1. You **may not** use a calculator.
2. Variables and expressions represent real numbers unless stated otherwise.
3. Figures are drawn to scale unless stated otherwise.
4. Figures lie in a plane unless stated otherwise.
5. The domain of a function f is defined as the set of all real numbers x for which $f(x)$ is also a real number, unless stated otherwise.

REFERENCE

$$A = \frac{1}{2}bh$$

$$a^2 + b^2 = c^2$$

Special Triangles

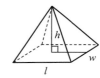
$$V = \frac{1}{3}lwh$$

$$V = \frac{1}{3}\pi r^2 h$$

$$A = lw$$

$$V = lwh$$

$$V = \pi r^2 h$$

$$A = \pi r^2$$
$$C = 2\pi r$$

$$V = \frac{4}{3}\pi r^3$$

There are 360° in a circle.

The sum of the angles in a triangle is 180°.

The number of radians of arc in a circle is 2π.

CONTINUE

1

If $f(x) = x^2 + 1$, what is the value of $f(3x)$?

A) $3x^2 + 1$

B) $3x^2 + 3$

C) $9x^2 + 1$

D) $9x^2 + 3$

3

If $|2x - 4| \le 6$, which of the following inequalities represents all possible values of x?

A) $-1 \le x \le 5$

B) $1 \le x \le 5$

C) $-5 \le x \le -1$

D) $-5 \le x \le 1$

2

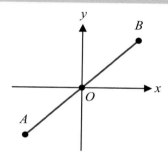

The coordinates of point B in the figure above are (c, d), where $c > d$. Which of the following could be the slope of $\overline{AB}$?

A) $-\dfrac{1}{2}$

B) 0

C) $\dfrac{3}{4}$

D) $\dfrac{4}{3}$

4

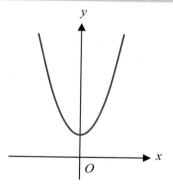

Which of the following equations could have the graph shown above?

A) $y = 2x + 2$

B) $y = x^2 + 2$

C) $y = x^2 - 2$

D) $y = (x + 2)(x - 2)$

CONTINUE

5

$$y = \frac{x^2 - 2x - 15}{x + 3}$$

Which of the following statements describes the domain of the equation above?

A) $x > 0$

B) $x < 0$

C) $x = -3$

D) $x \neq -3$

6

If $2^4 \times 8^x = 2^{16}$, what is the value of x?

A) 1

B) 2

C) 3

D) 4

7

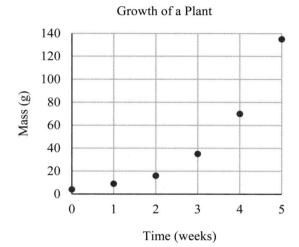

Growth of a Plant

A botanist is researching the growth of a type of plant. He measures the mass of the plant over five weeks. The scatterplot above shows his data. Which of the following best describes the plant's growth over time?

A) The plant's mass increases at a constant rate.

B) The plant's mass increases by approximately 50% each week.

C) The plant's mass approximately doubles every week.

D) The plant's mass is inversely related to time.

CONTINUE

8

If $x < 0$ and $y > -1$, which of the following must be true?

 I. $\dfrac{x}{y} > 0$
 II. $|x| + |y| > 0$
 III. $x < y$

A) I only

B) II only

C) III only

D) I and II only

9

Two cruise boats follow the same route up a river. Boat A is moving at 10 miles per hour, and Boat B is moving at 12 miles per hour in the same direction. If Boat A is 40 miles ahead of Boat B, how many hours will it take for Boat B to catch up to Boat A?

A) 5

B) 10

C) 15

D) 20

10

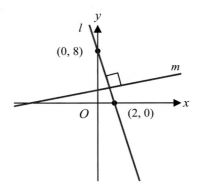

In the xy-coordinate plane above, line l is perpendicular to line m. What is the slope of line m?

A) $\dfrac{1}{4}$

B) 4

C) $-\dfrac{1}{4}$

D) -4

CONTINUE

11

If b and c are positive integers, which of the graphs below represents $y = -x^2 - 2cx + b^2$?

A)

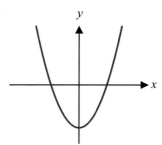

B)

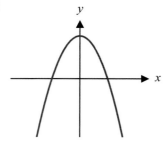

C)

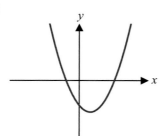

D)

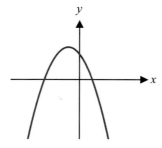

12

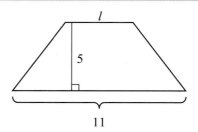

The trapezoid above has an area of 35. What is the value of l?

A) 1

B) 2

C) 3

D) 4

13

For $i = \sqrt{-1}$, which of the following expressions is equivalent to $\sqrt{-9}$?

A) $3i$

B) $3i^2$

C) $9i$

D) $9i^2$

CONTINUE

14

Hemoglobin is a protein molecule in red blood cells that transports oxygen from the lungs to the rest of the body. Doctors can use hemoglobin tests to diagnose or monitor certain medical conditions. Hemoglobin levels are measured in grams, g, per deciliter, dL. The normal range for hemoglobin levels in children is 11 to 13 g/dL. Which of the following inequalities can be used to determine if a child's hemoglobin level, l, is in the normal range?

A) $|l - 1| \leq 12$

B) $|l - 12| \leq 1$

C) $|l - 1| \geq 12$

D) $|l - 12| \geq 1$

15

If $\cos(x) = -\dfrac{3}{4}$, what is the value of $\cos(x + \pi)$?

A) $-\dfrac{3}{4}$

B) 0

C) $\dfrac{3}{4}$

D) $\dfrac{4}{3}$

CONTINUE

DIRECTIONS

Questions **16-20** ask you to solve a problem and enter your answer in the grid provided on your answer sheet. When completing grid-in questions:

1. You are required to bubble in the circles for your answers. It is recommended, but not required, that you also write your answer in the boxes above the columns of circles. Points will be awarded based only on whether the circles are filled in correctly.

2. Fill in only one circle in a column.

3. You can start your answer in any column as long as you can fit in the whole answer.

4. For questions 16-20, no answers will be negative numbers.

5. **Mixed numbers,** such as $4\frac{2}{5}$, must be gridded as decimals or improper fractions, such as 4.4 or as 22/5. "42/5" will be read as "forty-two over five," not as "four and two-fifths."

6. If your answer is a **decimal** with more digits than will fit on the grid, you may round it or cut it off, but you must fill the entire grid.

7. If there are **multiple correct solutions** to a problem, all of them will be considered correct. Enter only **one** on the grid.

| 5 | / | 1 | 1 | | | 8 | . | 4 | | | 3 | / | 7 |

| . | 4 | 2 | 2 | | | . | 3 | 2 | 6 | | | . | 1 | 2 | 5 |

CONTINUE →

16

If $3x - 4z = 0$, what is the value of $\dfrac{z}{x}$?

17

$$y = 2x - 2$$
$$z = 2x^2 - 2x$$

If $y = z$, what is the value of x in the system of equations above?

18

A company ordered $400 worth of promotional magnets and hats. Magnets cost $2 each, and hats cost $4 each. If the company ordered twice as many hats as magnets, how many total items did the company order?

19

What is the product of the solutions of x in the equation $(2x + 10)(x - 2) = -20$?

20

$$\frac{6}{x + 4} + 1 = \frac{6}{x + 1}$$

If $x > 0$, what is the value of x in the equation above

STOP

If you complete this section before the end of your allotted time, check your work on this section only. Do NOT use the time to work on another section.

Math Test – Calculator

55 MINUTES, 38 QUESTIONS

Turn to Section 4 of your answer sheet to answer the questions in this section.

DIRECTIONS

Questions **1-30** ask you to solve a problem, select the best answer among four choices, and fill in the corresponding circle on your answer sheet. Questions **31-38** ask you to solve a problem and enter your answer in a grid provided on your answer sheet. There are detailed instructions on entering answers into the grid before question 31. You may use your test booklet for scratch work.

NOTES

1. You **may** use a calculator.
2. Variables and expressions represent real numbers unless stated otherwise.
3. Figures are drawn to scale unless stated otherwise.
4. Figures lie in a plane unless stated otherwise.
5. The domain of a function f is defined as the set of all real numbers x for which $f(x)$ is also a real number, unless stated otherwise.

REFERENCE

    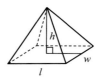

$$A = \frac{1}{2}bh \qquad a^2 + b^2 = c^2 \qquad \text{Special Triangles} \qquad V = \frac{1}{3}lwh \qquad V = \frac{1}{3}\pi r^2 h$$

$$A = lw \qquad V = lwh \qquad V = \pi r^2 h \qquad A = \pi r^2$$
$$C = 2\pi r \qquad V = \frac{4}{3}\pi r^3$$

There are 360° in a circle.

The sum of the angles in a triangle is 180°.

The number of radians of arc in a circle is 2π.

CONTINUE

1

If $m = \dfrac{5k}{3}$, what is k in terms of m?

A) $\dfrac{3m}{4}$

B) $\dfrac{4m}{3}$

C) $\dfrac{3m}{5}$

D) $\dfrac{5m}{4}$

2

A machine can cut 36 sheets of tin in 30 minutes. How many sheets of tin can it cut in two hours?

A) 18

B) 36

C) 72

D) 144

3

x	-2	0	2
$f(x)$	7	3	-1

Based on the table above, which of the following equations could represent $f(x)$?

A) $f(x) = -2x + 3$

B) $f(x) = -4x + 3$

C) $f(x) = 2x + 3$

D) $f(x) = 4x + 3$

4

The lines $y = 2x + 6$ and $y = -\dfrac{1}{2}x + 4$ intersect at point (j, k) in the xy-plane. What is the value of j?

A) $\dfrac{3}{2}$

B) $\dfrac{2}{3}$

C) $-\dfrac{4}{5}$

D) $-\dfrac{3}{2}$

CONTINUE

Questions 5 and 6 refer to the following information.

Akiko competes in the long jump for her track and field team. During her practice, she records the distance of each jump in the table below.

Jump Distances (m)			
5.21	4.85	5.34	4.76

5

What is the average of Akiko's distances for the practice?

A) 4.73 m

B) 4.98 m

C) 5.04 m

D) 5.34 m

6

What is the median distance for the practice?

A) 4.85 m

B) 5.03 m

C) 5.10 m

D) 5.21 m

7

If $f(x) = x^2 + 7$ and $g(x) = -f(x) + 3$, what is $g(4)$?

A) 26

B) 19

C) −1

D) −20

8

Monthly Budget	
Expenses	Percent of Budget
Rent	37.5
Entertainment	25
Food	25
Other	12.5

The chart above shows the breakdown of Diego's budget. If Diego spends $350 on food each month, which of the following is the best estimate for the amount Diego spends on rent each month?

A) $175

B) $400

C) $525

D) $700

CONTINUE

9

Which of the following is the equation of a line that is parallel to $5y = -6x + 10$?

A) $y = -\dfrac{5}{6}x - \dfrac{9}{10}$

B) $y = \dfrac{5}{6}x - \dfrac{5}{12}$

C) $y = -\dfrac{6}{5}x + \dfrac{1}{2}$

D) $y = -\dfrac{6}{5} + \dfrac{13}{10}$

10

The outermost layer of the Earth's surface is made up of tectonic plates that shift very slowly. Scientists determine that the plates move apart at an average rate of 8 mm per year. At the beginning of the study, two of the plates are 3 mm apart. Which of the following functions represents the distance, D, in millimeters, between the plates y years after the start of the study?

A) $D(y) = 3 + 8y$

B) $D(y) = 3 + 0.8y$

C) $D(y) = 3 + 0.08y$

D) $D(y) = 3 + 0.008y$

11

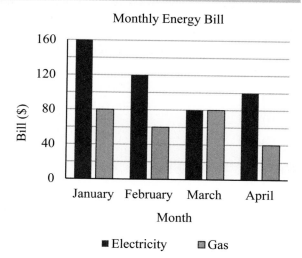

Monthly Energy Bill

The bar graph above shows a family's monthly energy bill for electricity and gas. For the four months shown, what is the ratio of the total electricity bill to the total gas bill?

A) 23:13

B) 21:12

C) 13:23

D) 12:21

12

A line passes through the points $(-3, 0)$ and $(0, 3)$. Which of the following points lies on the line?

A) $(-6, 0)$

B) $(-6, 3)$

C) $(3, 0)$

D) $(3, 6)$

CONTINUE

13

$$f(x) = 2x + 6$$

The function $f(x)$ is defined above. If $2f(k) = 24$, what is the value of $f(3k)$?

A) 12

B) 24

C) 36

D) 48

14

$$2k + 3n < 2k$$

Based on the inequality above, which of the following must be true?

A) $k > \dfrac{2}{3}n$

B) $k = 0$

C) $n < 0$

D) $k = 0$ and $n < 0$

15

$$h = -(t - 5)^2 + 3$$

The equation for the height h of a toy rocket above the top of its launch platform at time t is shown above. At what time will the rocket attain its maximum height?

A)   3

B)   5

C)   8

D) 10

16

Alex drove 20 km to work at an average speed of 80 km/hour. On the way back, he drove at an average speed of 60 km/hour along the same route. What was his average speed for the round trip?

A) 74.6 km/hour

B) 71.4 km/hour

C) 70.0 km/hour

D) 68.6 km/hour

CONTINUE

17

Which of the following graphs represents the equation $y = |x + 2| + 1$?

A)

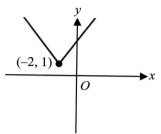

(−2, 1)

B)

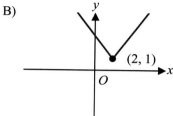

(2, 1)

C)

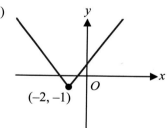

(−2, −1)

D)

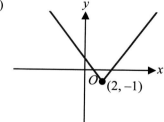

(2, −1)

18

A weather station measures the outdoor temperature, in degrees Fahrenheit, between 8:00 PM and 8:00 AM. Researchers use this data to create a model for overnight temperature patterns. They find the temperature T for one night's data was related to the number of hours after 8:00 PM, h, according to the equation $T = h^2 - 12h + 46$. Based on this model, at what time did the temperature reach its minimum?

A)   12:00 AM

B)   2:00 AM

C)   4:00 AM

D)   6:00 AM

19

If $\sin(x) = \dfrac{4}{5}$, what is $\cos(x)$?

A) $\dfrac{1}{5}$

B) $\dfrac{3}{5}$

C) $\dfrac{3}{4}$

D) $\dfrac{4}{3}$

CONTINUE

20

Popularity of New Songs		
	Number of Hits (thousands)	
Day	Song A	Song B
1	2.0	2.0
2	5.1	4.2
3	8.3	7.9
4	11.2	16.4

A band releases two songs on the same day. They record the number of hits each song receives at the end of each day after the release. The data is shown in the table above. Which of the following best describes the trends for the two songs?

A) Song A's hits show a linear increase while Song B's hits show an exponential increase.

B) Song A's hits show an exponential increase while Song B's hits show a linear increase.

C) Both Song A's hits and Song B's hits show a linear trend.

D) Both Song A's hits and Song B's hits show an exponential trend.

21

Turnout of Voting Age Population

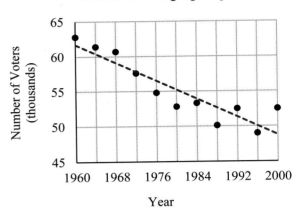

The scatterplot above shows the number of voters who participated in a municipal election from the year 1960 to 2000. Based on the line of best fit, which of the following is the best estimate for the annual decrease in voters between 1960 and 2000?

A) 250

B) 325

C) 2,500

D) 3,250

CONTINUE

Practice Tests

Questions 22 and 23 refer to the following information.

Artifacts at Site 1				
Material	Slate	Quartzite	Chert	**Total**
Bifaces	1	5	23	**29**
Knives	0	2	13	**15**
Wedges	0	3	5	**8**
Points	3	2	2	**7**
Total	**4**	**12**	**43**	**59**

Archaeologists studying a region in the arctic recorded the types of artifacts they found and the material of each artifact. The table above lists the artifacts found at one of the archaeological sites.

22

Which tool type had the highest percentage of quartzite artifacts?

A) Bifaces

B) Knives

C) Wedges

D) Points

23

The archaeologists expand the area of Site 1 by 40%. If the artifacts are distributed in the same ratio in the new area as in the original area, how many additional chert wedges should the archaeologists expect to find in the new area?

A) 2

B) 3

C) 6

D) 7

24

How many times do the graphs of $y = 4x^2 - 16x - 20$ and $y = 5x + 6$ intersect in the xy-plane?

A) 0

B) 1

C) 2

D) 3

CONTINUE

25

Mass of Radioactive Material

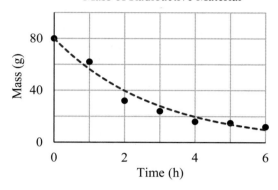

The half-life is the point at which radioactive material degrades to half its original mass. Based on the graph above, what is the approximate half-life of the radioactive material?

A) 2.0 hours

B) 2.5 hours

C) 4.0 hours

D) 6.0 hours

26

If the expression $\dfrac{x^2 + 2x - 3}{x^2 + 3}$ is equal to $\dfrac{C}{x^2 + 3} - 1$, what is C in terms of x?

A) $x + 4$

B) $x^2 + 3$

C) $2x^2 + x$

D) $2x^2 + 2x$

27

$$\text{Population density} = \frac{\text{Population}}{\text{Area}}$$

Coastal watershed areas, which account for about 500,000 square miles in the U.S., have three to four times the national average population density. In 2010, the population density in coastal watershed regions was approximately 320 people per square mile. Researchers estimate that the population in coastal watershed areas will grow by 20 million people between 2010 and 2020. Based on this estimate, which of the following is the best prediction for the population density in coastal watershed areas in 2020?

A) 330

B) 340

C) 350

D) 360

CONTINUE

28

A data set has a standard deviation equal to 4. If each number in the data set is multiplied by 6, which of the following statement is true?

A) The standard deviation of the data set increases.

B) The standard deviation of the data set doesn't change.

C) The standard deviation of the data set decreases.

D) It is impossible to determine with the information given.

29

A chemist needs to make a solution that is 8% acetic acid by volume. She does this by adding water to a solution that is 50% acetic acid and 50% water. Which of the following will give her 200 mL of the 8% acetic acid solution?

A) She adds 92 mL water to 8 mL of the stock solution.

B) She adds 84 mL water to 16 mL of the stock solution.

C) She adds 184 mL water to 16 mL of the stock solution.

D) She adds 168 mL water to 32 mL of the stock solution.

30

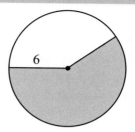

The circle above has a radius of 6. If the shaded region has an area of 24π, what is the arc length of the shaded region?

A) 4π

B) 8π

C) 9π

D) 12π

CONTINUE

DIRECTIONS

Questions **31-38** ask you to solve a problem and enter your answer in the grid provided on your answer sheet. When completing grid-in questions:

1. You are required to bubble in the circles for your answers. It is recommended, but not required, that you also write your answer in the boxes above the columns of circles. Points will be awarded based only on whether the circles are filled in correctly.
2. Fill in only one circle in a column.
3. You can start your answer in any column as long as you can fit in the whole answer.
4. For questions 31-38, no answers will be negative numbers.
5. **Mixed numbers,** such as $4\frac{2}{5}$, must be gridded as decimals or improper fractions, such as 4.4 or as 22/5. "42/5" will be read as "forty-two over five," not as "four and two-fifths."
6. If your answer is a **decimal** with more digits than will fit on the grid, you may round it or cut it off, but you must fill the entire grid.
7. If there are **multiple correct solutions** to a problem, all of them will be considered correct. Enter only **one** on the grid.

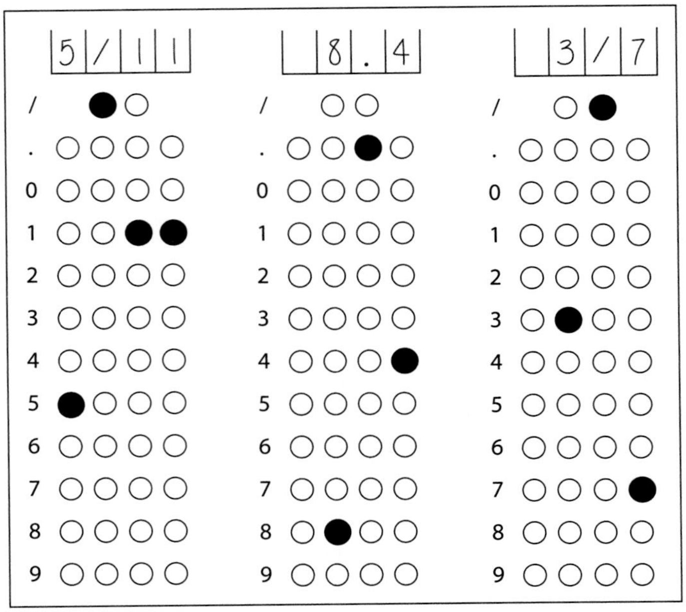
5/11
8.4
3/7

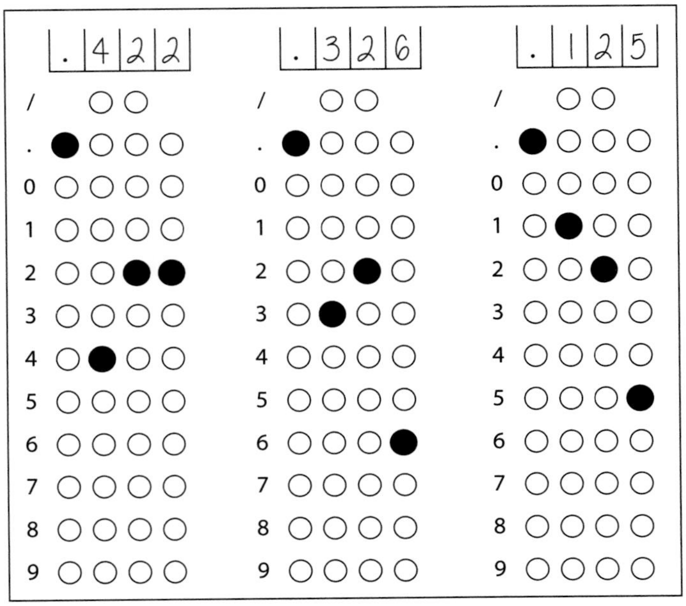
.422
.326
.125

CONTINUE

31

$$\sqrt{x+1} - 5 = x - c$$

If the solutions for x in the equation above are 0 or -1, what is the value of c?

32

Two miniature solar cars pass each other on a circular track with a circumference of 100 meters. Car 1 travels at a speed of 1 m/s along the track and Car 2 travels at a speed of 3 m/s in the opposite direction along the same track. If they both continue travelling at constant speeds, how many seconds will it take them to pass each other again?

33

$$\frac{y}{4} + \frac{x}{2} = 1$$

$$y - 2 = 2x$$

Based on the system of equations above, what is the value of $4x$?

34

On Monday the mean age of the employees of a bakery is 43 years. After hiring a new 19-year-old employee on Tuesday, the mean age of the bakery employees is now 41 years. How many employees did the bakery have on Monday?

CONTINUE

35

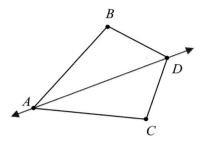

In the diagram above, $\overline{AD}$ bisects $\angle BAC$ and $\angle BDC$. $\angle BAC = 50°$ and $\angle BDC = 110°$. What is the measure, in degrees, of $\angle ABD$?

36

$$x^2 + px + q = 0$$

If the only solution for x in the equation above is 5, what is the value of $p + q$?

CONTINUE

Questions 37 and 38 refer to the following information.

A machine that shapes water bottles can be adjusted to produce bottles at different rates. A faster rate produces more water bottles per minute but, if the rate is too high, the machine produces defective bottles that cannot be sold. The manufacturer models the relationship between the machine's output efficiency, E, and its rate, r, as $E = -r\,(r - 20)$. The rate is measured in bottles produced per minute.

37

According to the manufacturer's model, the machine will produce no useable water bottles when it operates at a rate of b bottles per minute or higher. What is the value of b?

38

The machine is run at a rate of 8 bottles per minute for 8 hours. How many more water bottles would the machine produce in 8 hours if it were set to the rate with the maximum efficiency?

STOP

If you complete this section before the end of your allotted time, check your work on this section only. Do NOT use the time to work on another section.

Essay (Optional)

50 MINUTES

Turn to the lined pages of your answer sheet to write your essay.

DIRECTIONS

This essay is optional. It is a chance for you to demonstrate how well you can understand and analyze a written passage. Your essay should show that you have carefully read the passage and should be a concisely written analysis that is both logical and clear.

You must write your entire essay on the lines in your answer booklet. No additional paper will be provided aside from the Planning Page inside your answer booklet. You will be able to write your entire essay in the space provided if you make use of every line, keep tight margins, and write at a suitable size. Don't forget to keep your handwriting legible for the readers evaluating your essay.

You will have 50 minutes to read the passage in this booklet and to write an essay in response to the prompt provided at the end of the passage.

REMINDERS

- What you write in this booklet will not be evaluated. Write your essay in the answer booklet only.
- Essays that are off-topic will not be evaluated.

As you read the passage below, consider how Lindsey Lusher Shute and Benjamin Shute use

- evidence, such as facts or examples, to support claims.
- reasoning to develop ideas and to connect claims and evidence.
- stylistic or persuasive elements, such as word choice or appeals to emotion, to add power to the ideas expressed.

Adapted from Lindsey Lusher Shute and Benjamin Shute, "Keep Farmland for Farmers." © 2013 by the New York Times Company. Originally published September 20, 2013.

1   When we went looking in upstate New York for a home for our farm, we feared competition from deep-pocketed developers, a new subdivision or a big-box store. These turned out to be the least of our problems. Though the farms best suited for our vegetables were protected from development by conservation easements, we discovered that we couldn't compete, because conserved farmland is open to all buyers—millionaires included.

2   Few bankers farm; long days with little pay lack appeal. A new report by the National Young Farmers Coalition, a group we helped start, reveals that one-quarter of the land trusts that oversee these conservation easements have seen protected land go out of production. Why? A nonfarmer had bought it.

3   Still, tax incentives in New York encourage nonfarmers to rent their land to farmers, so you would think suitable land would be easy to find. Most landlords, however, offer only short-term leases. They want peace and quiet; they don't want vegetable or livestock operations that bring traffic, workers, noise and fences. But long-term land tenure is essential for vegetable and livestock growers, who need years to build soil fertility, improve pasture and add infrastructure. Only farms that grow low-value animal feed crops like hay, corn or beans are attracted to one-year leases.

4   Once well-off city residents who are looking for second homes buy the land, farmer ownership is over. After they've added an air-conditioned home, a heated pool and an asphalt drive, the value increases so much that no working farmer can afford it. The farm, and its capacity to feed a community, is lost.

5   Thankfully, there is a solution. The Vermont Land Trust and the State of Massachsuetts are keeping farmland in the hands of farmers through stricter conservation easements that limit who can own it, which keeps farms affordable and deters farm sales to nonfarmers.

6   In the next 20 years, 70 percent of the nation's farmland will change hands. Farmers do not live forever, and most farm kids do not choose to carry on the family business. An eager generation of young Americans is motivated to farm but, like us, they need land and few will be able to secure it without help.

7   The federal government and states spend hundreds of millions of dollars on farmland conservation each year, which can do much more than protect pastoral views for the wealthy. Those dollars must also be used to shore up rural economies and national food security with productive farms.

8   Eighty percent of us live in or near cities. It's critical that farms ring those cities, and that farmers in the ring be protected. The United States Department of Agriculture spends money to preserve farms, but matching funds are required, and there aren't enough.

9   Smart, self-interested cities would be wise to do their part. New York City needs to think about the land beyond the boroughs. The need is well documented: a recent study identified 614 vital unprotected farms in the Hudson Valley. New York City invested in the protection of its watershed in the Catskills; it needs to do the same with farmland to assure fresh food. It must come up with the money and leadership to help regional land trusts protect farms.

10   As water resources dwindle in the West, and as transportation and fuel costs climb and research shows that fresh, clean food is the key to a healthy life, isn't it the job of every city and town to secure the land and the farmers necessary to grow the food they need? Locking up land for farmers is the first step.

11   We started our Hearty Roots Community Farm nine years ago but quickly realized that we needed more stability than we were getting with the 20 acres we had rented in Dutchess County. After a grueling four-year search, a land trust came to our aid: with help from Scenic Hudson, we were able to buy a 70-acre farm in Clermont, a town of 2,000 people, just five miles north of where we'd been renting.

12   This land is protected only by a traditional conservation easement, but because it never made the transition to an estate and the previous landowner felt strongly that it be sold to a farmer, we got lucky. But what happens after us? We want to pass our stewardship of this land on to future farmers. We are now working with the land trust to tighten our easement and make sure that on our land, an American farm family will always have a chance to succeed.

Write an essay in which you explain how Lindsey Lusher Shute and Benjamin Shute build an argument to persuade their audience that the government should make it easier for farmland to stay with farmers. In your essay, analyze how Shute and Shute use one or more of the features listed in the box above (or features of your own choice) to strengthen the logic and persuasiveness of their argument. Be sure that your analysis focuses on the most relevant features of the passage.

Your essay should not explain whether you agree with Shute and Shute's claims, but rather explain how Shute and Shute build an argument to persuade their audience.

Answers
Chapter 7

Reading Chapter Answers
Part 1

Section 2: Approaching the Reading Test

Part 1: Marking Up a Passage (Pages 39-40)

Check how you did by comparing your marked-up passage to a fully marked-up version of the passage below. Don't worry if you did not underline your passage in exactly the same way. There can be more than one way to capture an idea. For example, in the fourth paragraph you may have underlined "shortly after 1285" rather than "late-medieval" to indicate when the Aracoeli fresco was painted. As long as you identified the same main ideas, you are on the right track.

This passage is adapted from Daniel Zalewski, "Under a Shroud of Kitsch May Lie a Master's Art." ©2001 by The New York Times Company.

Tommaso Strinati clambers to the top of the rickety scaffold and laughs. "It's a good thing that all this Baroque work is so
Line unimpressive," he says, pointing at the
5 clumsy trompe l'oeil painting covering the wall in front of him. "Otherwise, we might not have been allowed to scrape it off!"

A 28-year-old art historian, he is standing 16 feet above the marble floor of
10 San Pasquale Baylon chapel, a long-neglected nook of Santa Maria in Aracoeli, a Franciscan basilica in the center of Rome. Last year, Mr. Strinati, who is still a graduate student, began
15 studying the church's history. Records suggested that the Roman artist Pietro Cavallini—a painter and mosaicist whose greatest works have been destroyed—spent years decorating Aracoeli toward
20 the end of the 13th century. Yet only one small Cavallini fresco, in the church's left transept, remained visible. Mr. Strinati wondered: had other Cavallini frescoes been painted over with inferior work? And
25 if so, could modern restorers uncover them?

"The answer to both questions was yes," Mr. Strinati says. A close-up examination of the chapel's walls last
30 summer revealed ghostly images lying beneath the surface. The entire chapel, it seemed, was a painted palimpsest. And when a heavy altarpiece was removed from one wall, a remarkably tender
35 portrait of the Madonna and Child was found hidden behind it.

After months of careful paint-peeling, what has been uncovered are dazzling fragments of a late-medieval masterpiece
40 completed shortly after 1285. Although the Aracoeli fresco is not signed, the figures strongly resemble those in a surviving Cavallini work, the resplendent "Last Judgment" fresco at nearby Santa
45 Cecilia.

Mr. Strinati has grand ambitions for his discovery. He hopes that in a few years the fully restored fresco will not only rescue Cavallini's name from
50 obscurity, but also upend the widespread notion that the first flowers of the Renaissance budded in Florence, not Rome. For the fresco's lifelike figures—in particular, an impish Christ child with
55 charmingly flushed cheeks—suggest to Strinati that Cavallini may have

anticipated some of the extraordinary naturalistic innovations that have long been credited to the Florentine artist
60 Giotto.

Moreover, the Aracoeli fragments may provide a critical new clue in a decades-old battle concerning the "St. Francis Legend," the 1296 fresco cycle at Assisi,
65 universally recognized as one of the foundations of the Renaissance. For centuries, the 28-scene cycle—which recounts the life of the saint with a narrative zest and compositional depth
70 that leave the flat tableaus of the Byzantine era far behind—was attributed to Giotto. But since the 1930's, various scholars have questioned this judgment, claiming that the Assisi cycle doesn't

75 resemble Giotto's other work. Now, the Aracoeli discovery is ammunition for Italian art historians who believe that Cavallini might actually be the primary creative force behind the "St. Francis
80 Legend."

The growing debate about Cavallini's importance was the occasion for a symposium in Rome in November. *La Republicca*, an Italian daily, has cast the
85 debate as "War Between Rome and Florence." Mr. Strinati is enjoying the ruckus. "I had a hunch that there was more Cavallini lurking around here," he says of the Aracoeli basilica. "But I
90 didn't expect to find an exquisite work that could shake up the history of art."

Part 1: Summarizing (Pages 41–42)

- Paragraph 1: T.S. glad remove Baroque
- Paragraph 2: T.S. thinks hidden P.C. frescos
- Paragraph 3: Found P.C. frescoes
- Paragraph 4: Resemble other P.C. work
- Paragraph 5: P.C. maybe anticipated Giotto/Renaissance
- Paragraph 6: P.C. maybe painted "St. F"
- Paragraph 7: P.C. causing art history debates

Part 1: Reading a Passage (Page 43)

This passage is adapted from Glenn Hubbard, "The Unemployment Puzzle: Where Have All the Workers Gone?" ©2014 by Dow Jones & Company.

Unemployment down; labor force same

The unemployment rate, the figure that dominates reporting on the economy, is the fraction of the labor force (those
Line working or seeking work) that is
5 unemployed. This rate has declined slowly since the end of the Great Recession. What hasn't recovered over that same period is the labor force participation rate, which today stands roughly where it did in 1977.
10 Labor force participation rates increased from the mid-1960s through the 1990s, driven by more women entering the workforce, baby boomers entering prime working years in the 1970s and
15 1980s, and increasing pay for skilled laborers. But over the past decade, these trends have leveled off. At the same time, the participation rate has fallen, particularly in the aftermath of the
20 recession.

L.F. had increased, now stopped

In one view, this decline is just a temporary, cyclical result of the Great Recession. If so, we should expect workers to come back as the economy
25 continues to expand. Some research supports this view. A 2013 study by

Could be
recession
(temporary)

30 bigger declines in employment saw
bigger declines in labor-force
participation. It also found a positive
relationship between these variables in
past recessions and recoveries.

35   But structural changes are plainly at
work too, based in part on slower-moving

demographic factors. A 2012 study by
economists at the Federal Reserve Bank
of Chicago estimated that about one-
40 quarter of the decline in labor-force
participation since the start of the Great
Recession can be traced to retirements.
Other economists have attributed about
half of the drop to the aging of baby
45 boomers.

Could be
demographics
(structural)

Part 2: Reading the Questions (Page 46)

1. A   2. B   3. B   4. C

Part 3: Selecting Your Answers (Page 52)

1. C   2. D   3. A

Part 4: Practice Set (Pages 54-59)

1. C	6. C	11. D	16. D	21. A
2. A	7. A	12. A	17. A	
3. A	8. D	13. A	18. B	
4. C	9. A	14. A	19. B	
5. D	10. A	15. C	20. B	

Section 3: SAT Passage Types

Part 1: Literature Passages (Pages 66-67)

1. B   2. D   3. C

Part 2: Science Passages (Pages 72-73)

1. B   2. D   3. C

Part 3: Social Studies and History Passages (Pages 76-77)

1. C   2. B   3. D

Section 4: Understanding the Facts

Part 1: Words in Context (Pages 81-83)

1. C   3. A   5. A
2. C   4. C   6. A

Part 2: Explicit and Implicit Meaning (Page 87-88)

1. D   2. A   3. B   4. B

Part 3: Summarizing, Central Ideas, and Relationships (Pages 93-94)

   1. A   2. A   3. C

Part 4: Command of Evidence (Pages 98-99)

   1. B   2. A   3. C   4. C

Part 5: Analogical Reasoning (Pages 102-103)

   1. C   2. B   3. A

Part 6: Practice Set (Pages 104-109)

1.	C	5.	D	9.	C	13.	B	17.	C
2.	B	6.	C	10.	A	14.	B	18.	A
3.	B	7.	C	11.	B	15.	A	19.	A
4.	B	8.	D	12.	A	16.	C		

Section 5: Persuasive Language

Part 1: Analyzing Word Choice (Page 115)

   1. C   2. D

Part 2: Analyzing Text Structure (Pages 119-120)

   1. B   2. D   3. A

Part 3: Point of View and Analyzing Purpose (Page 124)

   1. A   2. B

Part 4: Analyzing Arguments (Pages 129-130)

   1. B   2. D   3. B

Part 5: Practice Set (Pages 131-136)

1.	C	5.	D	9.	D	13.	C	17.	D
2.	A	6.	B	10.	A	14.	B		
3.	C	7.	D	11.	B	15.	C		
4.	A	8.	C	12.	C	16.	D		

Section 6: Combining Ideas

Part 1: Paired Passages (Pages 142-143)

   1. B   2. D   3. A

Part 2: Passages with Graphics (Pages 147-150)

   1. C   2. B   3. D   4. A   5. B

Part 3: Practice Set (Pages 151-157)

   1. C   4. C   7. B   10. D   13. D

   2. A   5. B   8. D   11. A   14. C

   3. D   6. A   9. B   12. C   15. B

Writing Chapter Answers
Part 2

Section 2: Approaching the Writing Test

Part 2: Reading the Questions (Pages 177-179)

1. A	2. B	3. C	4. D	5. D
1a. C	2a. B	3a. B	4a. A	5a. C

Part 3: Answering the Questions (Pages 183-186)

1. C	2. B	3. D	4. A	5. C
1a. B	2a. C	3a. A	4a. D	5a. C

Section 3: SAT Grammar

Part 1: Common Grammar Errors (Pages 196-197)

1. D	3. C	5. B	7. C
2. D	4. A	6. B	8. A

Part 2: Harder Grammar Errors (Pages 204-205)

1. D	3. D	5. B
2. A	4. C	6. B

Part 3: Practice Set (Pages 206-207)

1. B	3. D	5. A
2. C	4. C	6. C

Section 4: Expression of Ideas

Part 1: Development of Ideas (Pages 217-218)

1. A	2. B	3. A	4. C

Part 2: Organizing Ideas (Page 224)

1. C	2. B	3. A

Part 3: Effective Language Use (Pages 229-230)

1. C	2. D	3. D	4. B

Math Chapter Answers
Part 3

Section 3: Heart of Algebra

Part 1: Algebraic Expressions (Pages 312-313)

1. A	3. A	5. B	7. B	9. 3
2. D	4. A	6. C	8. 25/3	10. 6

Part 2: Linear Equations (Pages 317-318)

1. B	3. A	5. D	7. B	9. 15/2 or 7.5
2. C	4. A	6. B	8. 4	10. 16

Part 3: Inequalities (Pages 323-324)

1. D	3. D	5. B	7. C	9. $x \geq 4$
2. A	4. D	6. D	8. $3.8 < \text{GPA} < 3.9$	10. 2

Part 4: Absolute Value (Pages 327-329)

1. C	3. C	5. A	7. A	9. $8.8 \leq b \leq 9.2$
2. C	4. D	6. A	8. 2.7	10. 2

Part 5: Systems of Equations and Inequalities (Pages 333-334)

1. B	3. C	5. C	7. C	9. $5 < x \leq 6$
2. C	4. A	6. B	8. 5	10. 10

Part 6: Linear Functions (Pages 337-338)

1. D	3. B	5. D	7. A	9. 0
2. C	4. A	6. C	8. 3	10. 10

Part 7: Interpreting Equations (Pages 342-343)

1. B	3. B	5. A	7. C	9. 6
2. A	4. A	6. A	8. 13	10. 6

Part 8: Graphing Equations (Pages 352-355)

1. A	3. A	5. B	7. C	9. 2/5 or 0.4
2. D	4. B	6. D	8. $145 < x < 185$	10. 0

Section 4: Passport to Advanced Math

Part 1: Polynomial Expressions (Pages 363-364)

1. B	3. D	5. C	7. D	9. 111
2. A	4. C	6. D	8. 88	10. 48

Part 2: Factoring Polynomials (Pages 369-370)

1. A	3. B	5. B	7. C	9. 5
2. D	4. B	6. C	8. 10	10. 18

Part 3: Quadratic Equations (Pages 375-376)

1. A	3. B	5. B	7. C	9. 10
2. C	4. B	6. A	8. 5	10. 1 or 2

Part 4: Quadratic Functions and Graphs (Pages 382-383)

1. C	3. B	5. C	7. D	9. 4
2. B	4. C	6. A	8. 7	10. 8

Part 5: Advanced Equations (Pages 388-390)

1. D	3. C	5. A	7. D	9. 1.5
2. B	4. D	6. A	8. 6	10. 2012 or 2017

Part 6: Applications of Functions (Pages 394-396)

1. C	3. D	5. B	7. D	9. 5
2. C	4. A	6. D	8. 4	10. 0.2 or 1/5

Section 5: Problem Solving and Data Analysis

Part 1: Measurement and Units (Pages 402-403)

1. A	3. A	5. C	7. D	9. 1050
2. B	4. D	6. B	8. 5.5	10. 54.4

Part 2: Properties of Data (Pages 412-414)

1. D	3. B	5. C	7. D	9. 3.16
2. C	4. A	6. D	8. 3	10. 6000

Part 3: Ratios, Percentages, Proportions, and Rates (Pages 419-421)

1. B	3. C	5. C	7. B	9. 6/17
2. D	4. B	6. D	8. 8	10. 4

Part 4: Probability and Statistics (Pages 429-432)

| 1. A | 3. C | 5. D | 7. D | 9. 16 |
| 2. B | 4. C | 6. B | 8. 33 or 33.3 | 10. 9 |

Part 5: Modeling Data (Pages 435-437)

| 1. B | 3. D | 5. C | 7. A | 9. 4 |
| 2. B | 4. C | 6. A | 8. 2 | 10. 6 |

Part 6: Using Data as Evidence (Pages 435-437)

| 1. B | 3. A | 5. B | 7. C | 9. 300 |
| 2. C | 4. C | 6. B | 8. 2 | 10. 930 |

Section 6: Additional Topics

Part 1: Angles and Volumes of Shapes (Pages 454-455)

| 1. D | 3. C | 5. B | 7. C | 9. 9 |
| 2. C | 4. B | 6. A | 8. 20 | 10. 16 |

Part 2: Right Triangles (Pages 461-463)

| 1. C | 3. A | 5. B | 7. D | 9. 4 |
| 2. C | 4. C | 6. B | 8. 12 | 10. 2 |

Part 3: Radians and the Unit Circle (Pages 471-472)

| 1. B | 3. A | 5. B | 7. C | 9. 3 |
| 2. B | 4. A | 6. A | 8. 0.89 | 10. 2 |

Part 4: Circles (Pages 478-479)

| 1. B | 3. A | 5. B | 7. C | 9. 13 |
| 2. C | 4. B | 6. C | 8. 229 | 10. 3 |

Part 5: Complex Numbers (Pages 483-484)

| 1. C | 3. B | 5. D | 7. A | 9. 1 |
| 2. C | 4. B | 6. A | 8. 4 | 10. 24 |

Practice Test Chapter Answers

Part 4

 For live scoring and scaling, please visit **ivyglobal.com/study**.

Practice Test 1

Reading (Pages 499-513)

1. B	12. A	23. A	34. A	45. D
2. A	13. C	24. A	35. A	46. C
3. C	14. C	25. A	36. D	47. B
4. B	15. C	26. B	37. A	48. B
5. A	16. D	27. A	38. C	49. C
6. B	17. A	28. C	39. C	50. C
7. C	18. A	29. D	40. A	51. A
8. C	19. D	30. B	41. A	52. B
9. B	20. A	31. B	42. A	
10. A	21. C	32. D	43. D	
11. D	22. A	33. C	44. C	

Writing (Pages 514-527)

1. A	10. B	19. C	28. A	37. D
2. C	11. C	20. B	29. C	38. C
3. D	12. D	21. D	30. D	39. A
4. A	13. A	22. A	31. B	40. C
5. B	14. A	23. C	32. D	41. C
6. D	15. C	24. D	33. C	42. B
7. B	16. A	25. C	34. D	43. C
8. D	17. D	26. A	35. D	44. B
9. B	18. A	27. B	36. D	

Math: No-Calculator (Pages 528-535)

1.	C	5.	C	9.	A	13.	B	17.	6
2.	A	6.	D	10.	A	14.	C	18.	120
3.	D	7.	B	11.	A	15.	B	19.	8
4.	B	8.	D	12.	C	16.	14	20.	6

Math: Calculator (Pages 536-549)

1.	D	9.	B	17.	A	25.	D	33.	$5/3 < x < 9/4$
2.	B	10.	B	18.	B	26.	C		
3.	A	11.	A	19.	A	27.	B	34.	.53
4.	A	12.	A	20.	B	28.	C	35.	400
5.	D	13.	D	21.	D	29.	C	36.	13.5
6.	C	14.	D	22.	B	30.	B	37.	13
7.	C	15.	D	23.	A	31.	8	38.	5
8.	C	16.	D	24.	C	32.	4425		

Practice Test 2

Reading (Pages 565-580)

1.	C	12.	D	23.	C	34.	B	45.	B
2.	D	13.	A	24.	D	35.	D	46.	D
3.	B	14.	B	25.	A	36.	D	47.	A
4.	A	15.	D	26.	A	37.	B	48.	B
5.	B	16.	B	27.	D	38.	D	49.	C
6.	C	17.	C	28.	A	39.	A	50.	A
7.	C	18.	C	29.	B	40.	C	51.	D
8.	D	19.	C	30.	A	41.	B	52.	C
9.	A	20.	B	31.	C	42.	D		
10.	B	21.	A	32.	A	43.	D		
11.	B	22.	D	33.	C	44.	A		

Writing (Pages 582-594)

1.	C	10.	B	19.	B	28.	C	37.	C
2.	A	11.	B	20.	D	29.	A	38.	A
3.	C	12.	C	21.	C	30.	C	39.	B
4.	B	13.	A	22.	D	31.	C	40.	C
5.	C	14.	A	23.	D	32.	D	41.	D
6.	D	15.	D	24.	B	33.	C	42.	C
7.	C	16.	A	25.	A	34.	C	43.	C
8.	C	17.	A	26.	C	35.	A	44.	D
9.	D	18.	C	27.	C	36.	B		

Math: No-Calculator (Pages 596-603)

1. B	5. C	9. D	13. B	17. 6
2. B	6. C	10. C	14. A	18. 6
3. D	7. A	11. D	15. C	19. 4 or 5/4
4. B	8. C	12. A	16. 23	20. 5 or 1.5 or 3/2

Math: Calculator (Pages 604-617)

1. A	9. D	17. C	25. B	33. 32
2. B	10. B	18. D	26. C	34. 33
3. D	11. D	19. D	27. C	35. 18
4. C	12. C	20. C	28. D	36. 141
5. B	13. A	21. A	29. B	37. 8833
6. B	14. D	22. B	30. A	38. 1553 or 1554
7. B	15. A	23. D	31. 150	
8. A	16. B	24. C	32. 80	

Practice Test 3

Reading (Pages 633-648)

1. D	12. A	23. A	34. B	45. B
2. C	13. A	24. A	35. C	46. B
3. D	14. A	25. A	36. C	47. D
4. A	15. D	26. B	37. D	48. A
5. D	16. A	27. C	38. A	49. C
6. A	17. A	28. B	39. D	50. B
7. B	18. C	29. A	40. D	51. C
8. C	19. A	30. C	41. B	52. C
9. D	20. C	31. A	42. B	
10. D	21. B	32. A	43. B	
11. A	22. C	33. D	44. A	

Writing (Pages 650-663)

1. C	10. D	19. C	28. B	37. C
2. D	11. D	20. D	29. A	38. B
3. B	12. D	21. C	30. B	39. B
4. D	13. B	22. D	31. B	40. B
5. A	14. D	23. B	32. C	41. A
6. C	15. A	24. C	33. D	42. D
7. B	16. C	25. A	34. A	43. B
8. D	17. C	26. D	35. D	44. C
9. B	18. D	27. B	36. C	

Math: No-Calculator (Pages 664-671)

1. C	5. D	9. D	13. A	17. 1
2. C	6. D	10. A	14. B	18. 120
3. A	7. C	11. D	15. C	19. 0
4. B	8. B	12. C	16. 3/4	20. 2

Math: Calculator (Pages 672-685)

1. C	9. C	17. A	25. A	33. 2
2. D	10. A	18. B	26. D	34. 11
3. A	11. A	19. B	27. D	35. 100
4. C	12. D	20. A	28. A	36. 15
5. C	13. B	21. B	29. D	37. 20
6. B	14. C	22. C	30. B	38. 960
7. D	15. B	23. A	31. 4	
8. C	16. D	24. C	32. 25	

College Application Help

Craft the strongest possible college application. We embrace the individuality of each student and understand the difficulty of conveying that personality in a stressful application process. Working together, we ensure that students stand out among a sea of candidates.

What is it?

✓ **Application assistance** and **review**
✓ **Expert essay support**
✓ **Resume review**
✓ **Interview preparation**
✓ **Assessment** of academics & extracurriculars
✓ **School recommendations**
✓ **Early decision/action** application strategies

Why Ivy Global Consulting?

⊘ *Proven Results.* We've helped over 500 students in the last 10 years.
⊘ *Leaders in the Field.* Our consultants know the admissions process inside and out.
⊘ *Genuine Interest.* We want you to reach your potential.
⊘ *A Diverse Clientele.* We've helped students locally and overseas.
⊘ *Holistic Approach.* We advise students on academic, mental, and emotional growth.

Our Results

Below is a partial list of schools to which Ivy Global students have been admitted.

Harvard University	Princeton University	Yale University
Stanford University	MIT	University of Pennsylvania
Caltech	Columbia University	Cornell University
Duke University	Dartmouth College	Brown University
Northwestern University	University of Chicago	Emory University
UCLA	Johns Hopkins University	University of Chicago
UC Berkeley	Northwestern University	Tufts University
USC	Georgetown University	Carnegie Mellon University
University of Notre Dame	Rice University	Boston College
New York University	Washington University	Vanderbilt University

To set up a free initial consultation, contact us at **1-888-588-7955** or **info@ivyglobal.com**.
Visit **www.ivyglobal.com** for more information.

Ivy Global

SAT Tutoring

Ivy Global's SAT Tutoring Program is a premium test prep resource for students looking to increase their test scores and confidence.

This program brings students together with experienced tutors for one-on-one instruction. Each student is provided a custom curriculum, which seamlessly interweaves test strategies and assignments to address their individual strengths and weaknesses.

Why Ivy Global?

Top Tutors
Trust their 99th percentile scores and extensive experience

Mentorship
Discover an academic mentor in your tutor

Long-Term Skills
Master concepts and develop effective study habits

Expert Understanding
Work with prep materials created by SAT experts

How does it work?

1 Student is paired with a tutor based on their needs

2 Sessions are scheduled in-office, online, or, if available, in-home

3 Student meets tutor weekly, writes diagnostic tests, and improves scores

Learn more

For pricing and other inquiries, visit our website at www.ivyglobal.com.

About Ivy Global

Since 2007, Ivy Global has provided premium consulting services for prospective students applying to top private schools and US colleges. With offices in New York, Silicon Valley and Toronto, we have helped thousands of students maximize their educational opportunities in North America and abroad.

To set up a free initial consultation, contact us at 1-888-588-7955 or info@ivyglobal.com, or visit www.ivyglobal.com for more information.

Notes

Notes

Notes

Notes